THE SEXUAL OFFENCES REFERENCER

A Practitioner's Guide to Indictments and Sentencing

SECOND EDITION

HHJ Patricia Lees

Eleanor Laws QC

OXFORD
UNIVERSITY PRESS

OXFORD
UNIVERSITY PRESS

Great Clarendon Street, Oxford, OX2 6DP,
United Kingdom

Oxford University Press is a department of the University of Oxford.
It furthers the University's objective of excellence in research, scholarship,
and education by publishing worldwide. Oxford is a registered trade mark of
Oxford University Press in the UK and in certain other countries

First Edition published in 2007
Second Edition published in 2014

Impression: 1

Published in the United States of America by Oxford University Press
198 Madison Avenue, New York, NY 10016, United States of America

British Library Cataloguing in Publication Data
Data available

Library of Congress Control Number: 2014947266

ISBN 978–0–19–968576–9

Printed and bound by
CPI Group (UK) Ltd, Croydon, CR0 4YY

This book is dedicated to all those who nagged, begged and cajoled us…
…you know who you are.
We trust the wait has not been in vain.

FOREWORD TO THE FIRST EDITION

This excellent book is a welcome and timely addition to the literature covering sexual offences. Nowadays there is a much greater public awareness of the nature and effect of sexual assaults, combined with an increase in reporting sexual crimes. During the last decade or so the issue has steadily climbed the political agenda. It became increasingly apparent that the 1956 Sexual Offences Act (itself a consolidating Act) failed to reflect the morality and prevalent sexual practices of the present day. As a result the Government responded by enacting the Sexual Offences Act 2003, which came into force on 1 May 2004, creating over 50 offences in contrast to the French and German Criminal Codes which cover all sexual offences in less than ten offences. Inevitably, this has made the law in this area increasingly complex. For instance, sometimes the maximum sentences vary according to the factual ingredients proved. There are still some areas of sexual offending not covered in the Sexual Offences Act 2003 such as indecent photographs and some of the prostitution offences.

Whilst the new Act overhauled the legislation governing sexual offences redefining offences as well as introducing many new offences, and abolishing many of the earlier offences, the old offences still apply to offences committed before 1 May 2004. In any event, some of those old offences had been amended or the maximum sentences had been increased over the years when there were incremental changes responding to particular political imperatives. The availability of ancillary orders to sentencers has also changed over the years.

For many years to come, the courts will have to deal with offences committed before the new Act came into force or defendants will face indictments which actually straddle the periods of the new and old offences. Now, thanks to the industry of Patricia Lees and Eleanor Laws, when dealing with a historic sex case, practitioners and judges will no longer have to locate old editions of textbooks in dusty cupboards to discover appropriate sentencing powers.

Quite apart from its coverage of the old law, it is very useful to have an up to date and comprehensive summary of sentencing powers in respect of the offences created by the Sexual Offences Act 2003. The authors are to be congratulated for their clear presentation of all this complex material. All those who work in this area will be grateful for its easy accessibility.

HH Judge Peter Rook QC
Central Criminal Court
May 2007

ACKNOWLEDGEMENTS TO THE FIRST EDITION

In preparing this book we were greatly assisted by a number of individuals, and we would like to take this opportunity to thank some of them.

We are grateful to a number of people whose own achievements mark them as leaders in this field and who have been kind enough to give us the benefit of their knowledge and support us in this venture. Firstly, our thanks go to both HHJ Peter Rook QC and to David Ormerod, Professor of Criminal Justice, for their generous assistance throughout, with too many areas touched on in this referencer to mention individually. Thank you also to Robin Johnson for frequently acting as a sounding board and for his input into more than one area. Our sincere thanks for her generosity with her own research into and work on the increasingly knotty area of sentencing go to HHJ Beatrice Bolton, as well as to HHJ Richard McGregor Johnson for being kind enough to allow us to steal his excellent flow charts on dangerous offenders for the same chapter.

A big thank you to Lucy Luttman, Alex Mills, Iestyn Morgan, and Darren Weir for their hard work in completing the unenviable task of checking each chapter. In addition, our thanks to Alex Mills for compiling all the tables and much of the text in all the Appendices, apart from 6 and 8, and to Lucy Luttman who compiled both the Index to Indictments and the table of relevant legislative changes to be found in Chapter One.

We acknowledge also the work of Amanda Bowring, Policy, and Nigel Gibbs, both of CPS Headquarters; Appendix 6, CPS charging guidance on the SOA 2003, is the product of their joint efforts. We also thank Amanda for her support and patience in dealing with all our queries.

Our sincere thanks also go to Jane Kavanagh, Marjorie Francois, Kathryn Grant, and Jodi Towler of Oxford University Press for all their help, good humour, and unfailing patience in dealing with two busy criminal practitioners!

Last, but by no means least, we would like to acknowledge the input of His Honour Judge Andrew Patience QC, whose suggestion it was that someone ought to write a 'pamphlet' to assist with historic sex cases and especially the changes in sentences. Eleanor Laws was not only in front of him at the time but also listening... and the rest, as they say, is history.

ACKNOWLEDGEMENTS TO THE SECOND EDITION

We owe thanks in particular to the following people:

Lucy Luttman, for her meticulous work throughout this update in reviewing chapters, updating her original Indictments Table (see end Chapter 1) and devising a comprehensive new Sentencing Table (see end Chapter 12).

Alex Mills, for his research and updating parts of the appendices.

Micky Singh, for his research and cross-referencing.

Eammon Hurley-Flynn, for his cross-referencing.

CONTENTS

CONTENTS

TABLE OF CASES

TABLE OF STATUTES AND STATUTORY INSTRUMENTS

STATUTES

STATUTORY INSTRUMENTS

LIST OF ABBREVIATIONS

AA 1976	Adoption Act 1976
AMA 1929	Age of Marriage Act 1929
CA 1989	Children Act 1989
CAA 1981	Criminal Attempts Act 1981
CAA 1985	Criminal Attempts Act 1985
CAJA 2009	Coroners and Justice Act 2009
CDA 1988	Crime and Disorder Act 1988
CJA 1948	Criminal Justice Act 1948
CJA 1988	Criminal Justice Act 1988
CJA 1991	Criminal Justice Act 1991
CJA 2003	Criminal Justice Act 2003
CJCSA 2000	Criminal Justice and Courts Services Act 2000
CJPOA 1994	Criminal Justice and Public Order Act 1994
CJS	Criminal Justice System
CLA 1967	Criminal Law Act 1967
CLA 1977	Criminal Law Act 1977
CLAA 1885	Criminal Law Amendment Act 1885
CLAA 1922	Criminal Law Amendment Act 1922
CO	Confiscation Order
CPA 1851	Criminal Procedure Act 1851
CPIA 1996	Criminal Procedure and Investigations Act 1996
CPR 2013	Criminal Procedure Rules 2013
CPS	Crown Prosecution Service
C(S)A 1997	Crime (Sentences) Act 1997
CYPA 1933	Children and Young Persons Act 1933
DBS	Disclosure and Barring Service
DPP	Director of Public Prosecutions
DVCVA 2004	Domestic Violence, Crime and Victims Act 2004
ECHR	European Convention on Human Rights
FP	Forensic Physician
FRO	Financial Reporting Order
IPP	Imprisonment for the Protection of the Public
ISA	Independent Safeguarding Authority
ISVA	Independent Sexual Violence Advisor
IwCA 1960	Indecency with Children Act 1960
LASPO 2012	Legal Aid and Punishment of Offenders Act 2012
MA 1949	Marriage Act 1949
MCA 1980	Magistrates' Courts Act 1980
MDA 1913	Mental Deficiency Act 1913
MHA 1959	Mental Health Act 1959
OAPA 1861	Offences Against the Person Act 1861
OPA 1959	Obscene Publications Act 1959
OPA 1964	Obscene Publications Act 1964
PCA 1978	Protection of Children Act 1978
PCA 2002	Protection of Children Act 2002

PCC(S)A 2000	Powers of Criminal Courts (Sentencing) Act 2000
PCMH	Plea and Case Management Hearing
PFA 2012	Protection of Freedoms Act 2012
PIA 1908	Punishment of Incest Act 1908
PII	public interest immunity
POA 1986	Public Order Act 1986
POCA 2002	Proceeds of Crime Act 2002
SARC	Sexual Assault Referral Centre
SC	Sentencing Council
SGC	Sentencing Guidance Council
SI	Statutory Instrument
SOA 1956	Sexual Offences Act 1956
SOA 1967	Sexual Offences Act 1967
SO(A)A 1976	Sexual Offences (Amendment) Act 1976
SOA 1985	Sexual Offences Act 1985
SOA 1993	Sexual Offences Act 1993
SOA 2000	Sexual Offences Act 2000
SOA 2003	Sexual Offences Act 2003
SOCPA 2005	Serious Organised Crime and Police Act 2005
SOPO	Sexual Offences Prevention Order
SOTP	Sex Offender Treatment Programme
StOA 1959	Street Offences Act 1959
SVGA 2006	Safeguarding and Vulnerable Groups Act 2006
TA 1968	Theft Act 1968
USI	unlawful sexual intercourse
VA 1824	Vagrancy Act 1824
VA 1898	Vagrancy Act 1898
VCRA 2006	Violent Crime Reduction Act 2006
YJCEA 1999	Youth Justice and Criminal Evidence Act 1999
YOI	Young Offender Institution
YOT	Youth Offending Team

INDEX TO INDICTMENTS

Chapter 2 Rape

Offence	Period	Provision	Maximum Penalty	Para Reference
RAPE 'Unlawful carnal knowledge of a woman without her consent by force, fear or fraud'	1.11.1861–31.12.1956	Contrary to common law	LIFE	2.06
RAPE 'Sexual intercourse with a woman without consent'	1.1.1957–21.12.1976	SOA 1956, s 1(1)	LIFE	2.19
RAPE 'Sexual intercourse with a woman without consent or recklessness as to consent'	22.12.1976–30.4.2004	SOA 1956, s 1(2)	LIFE	2.29
RAPE 'Intentional penetration of the vagina/anus/mouth of another who did not consent to the penetration without reasonable belief as to consent'	1.5.2004 to date	SOA 2003, s 1(1)	LIFE	2.50

Chapter 3 Sexual Assaults

Offence	Period	Provision	Maximum Penalty	Para Reference
Indecent assault	1.11.1861–31.12.1956	OAPA 1861, s 52	2 years	3.06
Indecent assault on a woman	1.1.1957–30.4.2004	SOA 1956, s 14	2 years or 5 years after 1.1.1961 if complainant under 13. 10 years if after 16.9.1985	3.17
Indecent assault on a man	1.1.1957–30.4.2004	SOA 1956, s 15(1)	10 years	3.27
Assault by penetration	1.5.2004 to date	SOA 2003, s 2(1)	LIFE	3.40

Offence	Period	Provision	Maximum Penalty	Para Reference
Sexual assault	1.5.2004 to date	SOA 2003, s 3(1)	10 years	3.48
Causing a person to engage in sexual activity	1.5.2004	SOA 2003, s 4(1)	10 years	3.58
Causing a person to engage in penetrative sexual activity	1.5.2004	SOA 2003, s 4(1)(4)	LIFE	3.59

Chapter 4 Offences Involving Children

Offence	Period	Provision	Maximum Penalty	Para Reference
Indecency with a child [D commits act with/towards C]	1.1.1961–30.4.2004	IwCA 1960, s 1	2 years until 1.10.1997, thereafter 10 years	4.11
Indecency with a child [D incites C to commit act]	1.1.1961–30.4.2004	IwCA 1960, s 1	2 years until 1.10.1997, thereafter 10 years	4.12
Causing/inciting a child to engage in sexual activity [non-penetrative, D over 18]	1.5.2004 to date	SOA 2003, s 10	14 years	4.24
Causing/inciting a child to engage in sexual activity [Penetrative, D over 18]	1.5.2004 to date	SOA 2003, s 10	14 years	4.25
Causing/inciting a child to engage in sexual activity [Non-penetrative, D under 18]	1.5.2004 to date	SOA 2003, s 10 and s 13	5 years	4.26
Causing/inciting a child to engage in sexual activity [Penetrative, D under 18]	1.5.2004 to date	SOA 2003, s 10 and s 13	5 years	4.27
Causing/inciting a child under 13 to engage in sexual activity [Non-penetrative]	1.5.2004 to date	SOA 2003, s 8	14 years	4.38
Causing/inciting a child under 13 to engage in sexual activity [Penetrative]	1.5.2004 to date	SOA 2003, s 8	LIFE	4.39
Carnal knowledge of a girl under 13	1.1.1886–31.12.1956	CLAA 1885, s 4	LIFE (D over 16) Not less than 3 years (D under 16)	4.49

Offence	Period	Provision	Maximum Penalty	Para Reference
Carnal knowledge of a girl [13–16]	1.1.1886–31.12.1956	CLAA 1885, s 5	2 years	4.59
Sexual intercourse with a girl under 13	1.1.1957–30.4.2004	SOA 1956, s 5	LIFE	4.68
Sexual intercourse with a girl under 16	1.1.1957–30.4.2004	SOA 1956, s 6	2 years	4.79
Rape of a child under 13	1.5.2004 to date	SOA 2003, s 5	LIFE	4.92
Assault by penetration of a child under 13	1.5.2004 to date	SOA 2003, s 6	LIFE	4.100
Penetrative sexual activity with a child [D over 18]	1.5.2004 to date	SOA 2003, s 9	14 years	4.110
Penetrative sexual activity with a child [D under 18]	1.5.2004 to date	SOA 2003, s 9 and s 13	5 years	4.111
Sexual assault of a child under 13	1.5.2004 to date	SOA 2003, s 7	14 years	4.122
Sexual activity with a child [Non-penetrative]	1.5.2004 to date	SOA 2003, s 9(1)	14 years where D over 18, otherwise 5 years	4.132
Sexual activity with a child [Penetrative]	1.5.2004 to date	SOA 2003, s 9(1) and (2)	14 years where D over 18, otherwise 5 years	4.134
Abuse of position of trust	8.1.2001–30.4.2004	SO(A)A 2000, s 3	5 years	4.146
Sexual activity with a child by a person in a position of trust	1.5.2004 to date	SOA 2003, s 16	5 years	4.156
Causing a child to engage in sexual activity by a person in a position of trust	1.5.2004 to date	SOA 2003, s 17	5 years	4.165
Engaging in sexual activity in the presence of a child	1.5.2004 to date	SOA 2003, s 18	5 years	4.174
Causing a child to watch a sexual act by a person in a position of trust	1.5.2004 to date	SOA 2003, s 19	5 years	4.183
Engaging in sexual activity in the presence of a child [D over 18]	1.5.2004 to date	SOA 2003, s 11	10 years	4.194
Engaging in sexual activity in the presence of a child [D under 18]	1.5.2004 to date	SOA 2003, s 11 and s 13	5 years	4.195

Offence	Period	Provision	Maximum Penalty	Para Reference
Causing a child to watch a sexual act [D over 18]	1.5.2004 to date	SOA 2003, s 12	10 years	4.205
Causing a child to watch a sexual act [D under 18]	1.5.2004 to date	SOA 2003, s 12 and s 13	5 years	4.206
Arranging or facilitating the commission of a child sex offence	1.5.2004 to date	SOA 2003, s 14	14 years	4.215
Meeting a child following sexual grooming	1.5.2004 to date	SOA 2003, s 15	10 years	4.226

Chapter 5 Buggery and Offences of Indecency

Offence	Period	Provision	Maximum Penalty	Para Reference
Buggery	1.11.1861–31.12.1956	OAPA, s 61	LIFE (dependent on facts)	5.13
Assault with intent to commit buggery	1.11.1861–31.12.1956	OAPA 1861, s 62	10 years	5.28
Indecent assault upon a male person	1.11.1861–31.12.1956	OAPA 1861, s 62	10 years	5.36
Gross indecency	1.1.1885–31.12.1956	CLAA 1885, s 11	2-5 years (dependent on facts)	5.44
Buggery	1.1.1957–2.11.1994	SOA 1956, s 12(1)	LIFE	5.51
Buggery	3.11.1994–30.4.2004	SOA 1956, s 12(1)	LIFE	5.64
Assault with intent to commit buggery	1.1.1957–3.11.1994	SOA 1956, s 16(1)	10 years	5.78
Indecent assault upon a male person	1.1.1957–30.4.2004	SOA 1956, s 15(1)	10 years	5.87
Gross indecency	1.1.1957–30.4.2004	SOA 1956, s 13	5 years (dependent on facts)	5.96
Procuring an act of buggery	27.7.1967–30.4.2004	SOA 1967, s 4(1)	2 years	5.110

Chapter 6 Familial Offences

Offence	Period	Provision	Maximum Penalty	Para Reference
Incest by a male person	1.1.1909–31.12.1956	PIA 1908, s 1(1)	3–7 years 3 years– LIFE where Complainant under 13 years	6.10
Incest by a female person	1.1.1909–31.12.1956	PIA 1908, s 2	3–7 years or 2 years with hard labour	6.18
Incest by a male person	1.1.1957–30.4.2004	SOA 1956, s 10(1)	LIFE where Complainant under 13, otherwise 7 years	6.26
Incest by a female person	1.1.1957–30.4.2004	SOA 1956, s 11(1)	7 years	6.35
Incitement of a girl under 16 to commit incest	8.9.1977–30.4.2004	CLA 1977, s 54	2 years	6.44
Penetrative sexual activity with an adult relative	1.5.2004 to date	SOA 2003, s 64(1)	2 years	6.51
Consenting to penetrative sex with an adult relative	1.5.2004 to date	SOA 2003, s 65(1	2 years	6.59
Penetrative sexual activity with a child family member	1.5.2004 to date	SOA 2003, s 25(1) and (6)	14 years where Defendant is 18 or over, otherwise 5 years	6.68
Non-penetrative sexual activity with a child family member	1.5.2004 to date	SOA 2003, s 25(1)	5 years	6.69
Inciting a child family member to engage in penetrative sexual activity	1.5.2004 to date	SOA 2003, s 26(1) and (6)	14 years where Defendant is 18 or over, otherwise 5 years	6.77
Inciting a child family member to engage in non-penetrative sexual activity	1.5.2004 to date	SOA 2003, s 26(1)	5 years	6.78

Chapter 7 Offences Involving the Mentally Disordered

Offence	Period	Provision	Maximum Penalty	Para Reference
Carnal knowledge of an idiot/ imbecile	14.8.1885–31.12.1956	CLAA 1885, s 5(2)	2 years	7.07
Intercourse with an idiot/imbecile	1.1.1957–31.10.1960	SOA 1956, s 7	2 years	7.14
Sexual activity with person mentally disordered impeding choice	1.5.2004 to date	SOA 2003, s 30(1)	LIFE (if penetration) otherwise 14 years	7.26
Causing/inciting a person with a mental disorder impeding choice to engage in sexual activity	1.5.2004 to date	SOA 2003, s 31(1)	LIFE (if penetration) otherwise 14 years	7.33
Engaging in sexual activity in the presence of a person with a mental disorder impeding choice	1.5.2004 to date	SOA 2003, s 32	10 years	7.40
Causing a person with a mental disorder impeding choice to watch a sexual act	1.5.2004 to date	SOA 2003, s 33	10 years	7.47
Intercourse with a mentally defective patient	1.1.1957–1.11.1960	SOA 1956, s 8	2 years	7.60
Intercourse with a mentally disordered patient	1.11.1960–30.4.2004	MHA 1959, s 128(a)	2 years	7.68
Sexual activity by a care worker with a person with a mental disorder	1.5.2004 to date	SOA 2003, s 38(1)	14 years if penetration, otherwise 10 years	7.76
Causing or inciting sexual activity with a person with a mental disorder by a care worker	1.5.2004 to date	SOA 2003, s 39(3)	10 years	7.83
Sexual activity in the presence of a person with a mental disorder	1.5.2004 to date	SOA 2003, s 40	7 years	7.90
Causing a person with a mental disorder to watch a sexual act by a care worker	1.5.2004 to date	SOA 2003, s 41(1)	7 years	7.97
Procurement of a defective	1.1.1957–30.4.2004	SOA 1956, s 9(1)	2 years	7.109
Inducement, threat or deception to procure sexual activity with a person with a mental disorder	1.5.2004 to date	SOA 2003, s 34(1)	LIFE if penetration, otherwise 14 years	7.117

Offence	Period	Provision	Maximum Penalty	Para Reference
Causing a person with a mental disorder to engage in sexual activity	1.5.2004 to date	SOA 2003, s 35(2)	LIFE if penetration, otherwise 14 years	7.124
Engaging in sexual activity in the presence, procured by inducement, threat or deception, of a person with a mental disorder	1.5.2004 to date	SOA 2003, s 36(1)	10 years	7.131
Causing a person with a mental disorder to watch a sexual act by inducement, threat or deception	1.5.2004 to date	SOA 2003, s 37(1)	10 years	7.138
Causing/encouraging prostitution of a defective	1.1.1957–30.4.2004	SOA 1956, s 29	2 years	7.157
Permitting a defective to use premises for intercourse	1.1.1957–30.4.2004	SOA 1956, s 27	2 years	7.163
Causing or inciting prostitution for gain	1.5.2004 to date	SOA 2003, s 52(1)	7 years	7.170
Controlling prostitution for gain	1.5.2004 to date	SOA 2003, s 53(1)	7 years	7.177

Chapter 8 Prostitution and Trafficking

Offence	Period	Provision	Maximum Penalty	Para Reference
Procuring a woman under 21 to become a common prostitute	1.1.1950–31.12.1956	CLAA 1885, s 2(1)	2 years	8.10
Causing or encouraging prostitution of a girl under 16	1.1.1957–30.4.2004	SOA 1956, s 28(1)	2 years	8.17
Procuring a girl under 21 to have unlawful sexual intercourse	1.1.1957–30.4.2004	SOA 1956, s 23(1)	2 years	8.24
Paying for sexual services of a child	1.5.2004 to date	SOA 2003, s 47(1)	LIFE	8.32
Causing or inciting child prostitution or pornography	1.5.2004 to date	SOA 2003, s 48(1)	14 years	8.39
Controlling child prostitution/pornography	1.5.2004 to date	SOA 2003, s 49(1)	14 years	8.46
Arranging/facilitating child prostitution or pornography	1.5.2004 to date	SOA 2003, s 50(1)	14 years	8.53

Offence	Period	Provision	Maximum Penalty	Para Reference
Procuring prostitution of women	1.1.1957–30.4.2004	SOA 1956, s 22(1)	2 years	8.61
Causing/inciting prostitution for gain	1.5.2004 to date	SOA 2003, s 52(1)	7 years	8.69
Male living on earnings of prostitution	1.1.1957–30.4.2004	SOA 1956, s 30(1)	7 years	8.78
Women exercising control/direction/influence over a prostitute	1.1.1957–30.4.2004	SOA 1956, s 31	7 years	8.86
Detention of a women in a brothel or other premises	1.1.1957–30.4.2004	SOA 1956, s 24(1)	2 years	8.92
Solicitation for immoral purposes	1.1.1957–30.4.2004	SOA 1956, s 32	2 years	8.99
Living on the earnings of male prostitution	22.7.1967–30.4.2004	SOA 1967, s 5	7 years	8.106
Keeping a brothel used for prostitution	1.5.2004 to date	SOA 2003, s 33A	7 years	8.113
Controlling prostitution for gain	1.5.2004 to date	SOA 2003, s 53(1)	7 years	8.120
Trafficking into the UK for sexual exploitation	1.5.2004 to 5.4.2013	SOA 2003, s 57(1)(a)	14 years	8.130
Trafficking within the UK for sexual exploitation	1.5.2004 to 5.4.2013	SOA 2003, s 58(1)(a)	14 years	8.137
Trafficking out of the UK for sexual exploitation	1.5.2004 to 5.4.2013	SOA 2003, s 59(1)(a)	14 years	8.144
Trafficking people for sexual exploitation	6.4.2013 to date	SOA 2003, s 59A(1)(a)	14 years	8.153

Chapter 9 Obscene Publications

Offence	Period	Provision	Maximum Penalty	Para Reference
Taking indecent photographs of a child	20.8.1978 to date	PCA 1978, s 1(1)(a)	3 years increased to 10 years on 11.1.2001	9.08
Possession of indecent photograph of a child	11.1.1988 to date	CJA 1988, s 160(1)	6 months, summary only offence. Amended with maximum of 5 years on 11.1.2001	9.22
Possession of prohibited images of children	6.4.2010 to date	CAJA 2009, ss 62(1) and 6(a)	3 years	9.31

Offence	Period	Provision	Maximum Penalty	Para Reference
Publishing an obscene article	29.8.1959 to date	OPA 1959, s 2(1)	3 years	9.47
Having an obscene article for publication for gain	31.8.1964 to date	OPA 1959, s 2(1)	3 years	9.48

Chapter 10 Offences Against Public Decency

Offence	Period	Provision	Maximum Penalty	Para Reference
Outraging public decency	1.1.1950 to date	Contrary to Common Law	No maximum	10.09
Indecent exposure	1.5.2004 to date	SOA 2003, s 66(1)	2 years	10.24
Voyeurism	1.5.2004 to date	SOA 2003, s 67(1)	2 years	10.30

Chapter 11 Preparatory Offences

Offence	Period	Provision	Maximum Penalty	Para Reference
Procurement of a woman by threats	1.1.1957–30.4.2004	SOA 1956, s 2(1)	2 years	11.07
Procurement of a woman by false pretences or representations	1.1.1957–30.4.2004	SOA 1956, s 3(1)	2 years	11.14
Administering drugs to obtain or facilitate intercourse	1.1.1957–30.4.2004	SOA 1956, s 4(1)	2 years	11.22
Burglary with intent to commit rape	1.1.1969–30.4.2004	TA 1968, s 9(1)(a)	14 years if building a dwelling, otherwise 10 years	11.30
Administering a substance with intent	1.5.2004 to date	SOA 2003, s 61(1)	10 years	11.38
Committing an offence with intent to commit a sexual offence	1.5.2004 to date	SOA 2003, s 62(1)	LIFE if kidnapping or false imprisonment, otherwise 10 years	11.45

1

INDICTMENTS

Introduction

This chapter is intended to provide some helpful tips on drafting indictments in sex cases, although some of the advice will apply generally. As long as the Indictment Rules are not offended, the contents of an indictment are largely a matter of style; this obviously will apply more to the Particulars. The law in relation to indictments is primarily set out in the Indictments Act 1915, which Act is expanded upon by Part 14, Criminal Procedure Rules (CPR) 2013.[1] Part 14 itself is supplemented by the new Criminal Practice Directions.[2] The Criminal Procedure Rules 2013 and the new Criminal Practice Directions should be read together. **1.01**

It remains the ultimate responsibility of prosecution counsel, once instructed, to ensure that the indictment is in a proper form; *R v Moss*.[3] In cases involving many counts, perhaps over several years, which are frequently seen in cases involving sexual offences, the style adopted should be carefully considered in order to assist those using it as a working document. A carefully drawn indictment in such a case will take time to draft but be invaluable for all involved in a trial. It should provide the starting point for preparation of the prosecution opening and clarity of the prosecution case for defence lawyers, judge and jury. **1.02**

It is important that an indictment covering multiple allegations over a period of time is carefully balanced to ensure that whilst it properly reflects the criminality alleged, it is not overloaded. **1.03**

[1] In force from 7.10.2013. The Indictment Rules 1971 have been revoked.

[2] In force from 7.10.2013. These replace the 2002 Consolidated Criminal Practice Direction (as amended), specifically para IV.34).

[3] [1995].

Particularizing Counts

1.04 Although there is no requirement to aver for example the place of an offence, when indicting in a case involving numerous allegations over a period of time it is necessary to be as precise as possible in particularizing counts so that the act alleged is clear to all on the face of the document. CPR 2013, rule 14.2(b) requires 'such particulars of the conduct constituting the commission of the offence as to make clear what the prosecutor alleges against the defendant'.

1.05 In *Rackham*[4] the Court of Appeal, quashing the convictions, ruled that the trial judge should have acceded to a defence request for better identification by the prosecution of the specific incidents upon which the different counts were based. The court held that the indictment should be drawn with as much particularity as the circumstances of the case would permit and that a difficulty in being precise in every respect is not a reason for not being precise when it is possible to be so.

1.06 It is therefore suggested that a prudent prosecutor will include details which are apparent from the statements over and above simply the time frame; for example, the details of the assault, the place where the act occurred (if that will help to identify it), the day of the week, and so on. This should be possible within the Particulars but if it is felt to be too cumbersome by the drafter, sometimes (where there is no objection taken) a short summary is added below a count, for example in italics.

1.07 It is essential to aver a child's age when that is a material particular affecting sentence. Failure to do so will result in the lower maximum sentence being applied.[5] See individual chapters for relevant offences.

Duplicity and Multiple Incident Counts

1.08 The Criminal Procedure (Amendment) Rules 2007[6] brought about an important change to the rule against particularizing a series of like offences within a single count, meaning that it is no longer essential for a count to relate to a single act. Of all the amendments introduced on 2.4.2007, this is likely to have the greatest impact upon indicting cases involving allegations of repeated sexual abuse.

1.09 Rule 14.2(2) of the Criminal Procedure Rules 2005 was a revision of what is often called the 'rule against duplicity'.[7] Rule 14.2(2) allows a prosecutor in certain circumstances to bring a single charge against a defendant even though that includes more than one incident of the offence alleged. An example of when this will apply is given by the Criminal Procedure Rules Committee in its guidance note to the Rules, and is typical of many sex cases; when, for example, a defendant is alleged to have repeatedly assaulted the same victim in the same way over a period of time. The intention of the Committee in creating this new rule was to take account, among other things, of the potential under the old rules for a perceived unfairness to a victim of multiple offending where, out of many alleged offences, only a few are prosecuted as examples, giving the impression that the victim's distress has been underestimated, or that he or she has not been believed.[8]

---

4 [1997] 2 Cr App R 222.

5 *R v SG and DG* [2009] EWCA Crim 2241; *R v R (Paul Brian)* [1993] Crim LR 541.

6 SI 2007/699.

7 Rule 14.2(2) remains unamended within the current Criminal Procedure Rules.

8 Reprinted with kind permission of the Department for Constitutional Affairs; taken from the note prepared by the Secretariat to the Committee, 27.3.2007, published with the Guide to the Rules.

Part 14 of the Criminal Procedure Rules permits more than one incident of the same offence to be charged in one count. This means that an indictment may be drafted in order to reflect a continuing course of conduct rather than single incidents. Therefore, instead of drafting a series of specimen/sample counts, it is now proper to draft a single count covering a series of similar allegations. **1.10**

Consideration will still need to be given as to whether this is the correct approach in each particular case. It is most likely to be appropriate when a complainant cannot differentiate between many occasions over a period of time, making a broad allegation without more detail of, for example, several years of regular and repeated acts; but where, for example, there are differences within the evidence creating the possibility of different verdicts dependent upon dates or other factors, it is less likely to be. An indictment can of course contain specific counts reflecting specific incidents as well as multiple incident counts reflecting a course of conduct over a period of time; in many cases this will be the best approach. **1.11**

A multiple incident count has the advantage of enabling the sentencing judge to reflect the true criminality in a case involving a series of similar offences which sample counts do not provide.[9] **1.12**

Drafting a Multiple Incident Count: the Practicalities

It will still be necessary to draft separate counts to reflect each type of assault both in order for the jury to differentiate between types of assault alleged and for the sentencing judge to properly reflect the overall criminality revealed by the evidence in the total sentence. **1.13**

A multiple incident count is only appropriate when not only the precise allegation, but also the defendant's case in respect of it, are the same. If the evidence reveals these to be different, separate counts should be left to the jury. **1.14**

Unlike a sample count, which can be left to a jury on the basis that they are sure the alleged offence occurred at least once, a multiple incident count should only be left on the basis that the jury are sure the alleged offence occurred at least twice ('On occasions between...', etc.). For this reason, as well as to ensure clarity for the sentence, it is wise for any indictment containing a multiple incident count to also have a single incident count to reflect the same alleged offence occurring on one occasion within the same time frame ('On an occasion between...', etc.). **1.15**

The new Criminal Practice Directions[10] give guidance as to when a 'multiple incident' count under rule 14.2(2) may be appropriate. This provides the framework for drafting such a count: **1.16**

Multiple offending: count charging more than one incident

(IV.34.8) Rule 14.2(2) of the Criminal Procedure Rules allows a single count to allege more than one incident of the commission of an offence in certain circumstances. Each incident must be of the same offence. The circumstances in which such a count may be appropriate include, but are not limited to, the following:

(a) the victim on each occasion was the same, or there was no identifiable individual victim as, for example, in a case of the unlawful importation of controlled drugs or of money laundering;
(b) the alleged incidents involved a marked degree of repetition in the method employed or in their location, or both;
(c) the alleged incidents took place over a clearly defined period, typically (but not necessarily) no more than about a year;

[9] *R v Canavan, Kidd and Shaw* [1998] 1 Cr App R 79; a defendant can only be sentenced for that of which he has been convicted. Also, *R v Hartley* [2011] EWCA Crim 1299.

[10] In force from 7.10.2013, replacing and simply restating the guidance provided by the Consolidated Criminal Practice Directions 2002, Amendment No 15.

(d) in any event, the defence case in relation to every alleged incident is the same. Where the matter(s) in issue differ between different incidents, a single 'multiple incidents' count will not be appropriate, though it may be appropriate to use two or more such counts according to the circumstances and to the issues raised by the defence.

(IV.34.09) Not reproduced, lacking relevance to sexual offences.

(IV.34.10) For some offences, particularly sexual offences, the penalty for the offence may have changed during the period over which the alleged incidents took place. In such a case, additional 'multiple incidents' counts should be used so that each count only alleges incidents to which the same maximum penalty applies.

(IV.34.11) In some cases, usually those involving money laundering or theft, there will be documented evidence of individual incidents but the sheer number of these will make it desirable to cover them in a single count. Where the indictment contains a count alleging multiple incidents of the commission of such offences and during the course of the trial it becomes clear that the jury may bring in a verdict in relation to a lesser amount than that alleged by the prosecution, it will normally be desirable to direct the jury that they should return a partial verdict with reference to that lesser amount.

It is suggested by the authors that for multiple sexual offences this possibility is usually better catered for by a separate count alleging a single but otherwise identical offence, as per para 1.15 above, in addition to any other identifiable single offence as suggested below in IV.34.12.

(IV.34.12) In other cases, such as sexual or physical abuse, a complainant may be in a position only to give evidence of a series of similar incidents without being able to specify when or the precise circumstances in which they occurred. In these cases, a 'multiple incidents' count may be desirable. If, on the other hand, the complainant is able to identify particular incidents of the offence by reference to a date or other specific event, but alleges that in addition there were other incidents which the complainant is unable to specify, then it may be desirable to include separate counts for the identified incidents and a 'multiple incidents' count or counts alleging that incidents of the same offence occurred 'many' times. Using a 'multiple incidents' count may be an appropriate alternative to using 'specimen' counts in some cases where repeated sexual or physical abuse is alleged. The choice of count will depend on the particular circumstances of the case and should be determined bearing in mind the implications for sentencing set out in *R v Canavan; R v Kidd; R v Shaw.*[11]

1.17 Note also the guidance provided in *R v Hartley*[12] in drafting indictments containing multiple incident count(s).

Proving Counts without a Jury

1.18 Sections 17–21 of the Domestic Violence, Crime and Victims Act 2004 provides that where a defendant is convicted by the jury on a sample of other counts to be tried in the proceedings, those other counts can then be tried by a judge alone. In practice, this is rarely used.

1.19 If such an application is made and the judge is satisfied that the following three conditions are fulfilled, he may make an order for the trial to take place on the basis that the trial of some, but not all, of the counts included in the indictment may be conducted without a jury.

1.20 The three conditions to be satisfied are set out in s 17:

- The number of counts included in the indictment is likely to mean that a trial by jury involving all of those counts would be impracticable.

---

[11] *R v Canavan, Kidd and Shaw* [1998] 1 Cr App R 79.

[12] [2011] EWCA Crim 1299.

- If an order under subsection (2) were made, each count or group of counts which would accordingly be tried with a jury can be regarded as a sample of counts which could accordingly be tried without a jury.
- It is in the interests of justice for an order under s 17(2) to be made.

Section 17 further provides: **1.21**

- In deciding whether or not to make an order under s 17(2), the judge must have regard to any steps which might reasonably be taken to facilitate a trial by jury.
- Step is not to be regarded as reasonable if it could lead to the possibility of a defendant in the trial receiving a lesser sentence than would be the case if that step were not taken.
- An order under s 17(2) must specify the counts which may be tried without a jury.

Form of Indictment for use where an order is made under s 17(2) of the Domestic Violence, Crime and Victims Act 2004: **1.22**

(Criminal Procedure Rules, Part 14)

Indictment

IN THE CROWN COURT AT ....

THE QUEEN v. ....

.... is charged as follows: -

PART 1

Count 1

STATEMENT OF OFFENCE

PARTICULARS

Count 2

STATEMENT OF OFFENCE

PARTICULARS

etc.

PART 2

Section 1: counts associated with Count 1 in Part 1 of this indictment.

Count 1.1

STATEMENT OF OFFENCE

PARTICULARS

Count 1.2

STATEMENT OF OFFENCE

PARTICULARS

etc.

Section 2: counts associated with Count 2 in Part 1 of this indictment.

Count 2.1

STATEMENT OF OFFENCE

PARTICULARS

Count 2.2

STATEMENT OF OFFENCE

PARTICULARS

etc.

Date............................

.... Officer of the Crown Court

Offences Straddling Implementation Dates of Different Acts

1.23 It is essential that indictments reflecting allegations which potentially or actually straddle two different statutes are carefully drawn to avoid the problems which may arise if a count runs through a commencement date. Those problems were identified by the then Lord Chief Justice Lord Judge in *R v Harries.*[13]

1.24 A lacuna was created by the failure to enact transitional provisions, despite the provision for such power created by s 141 of the Sexual Offences Act (SOA) 2003. This meant that if there was doubt as to whether a sexual offence occurred before or after the implementation of the SOA 2003, the prosecution failed only because it could not prove under which SOA the offence was committed. That lacuna was addressed by the implementation of s 55 of the Violent Crime Reduction Act 2006 on 12.2.2007.

Section 55 provides:

(1) This section applies where, in any proceedings—
   (a) person ('the defendant') is charged in respect of the same conduct both with an offence under the Sexual Offences Act 2003 ('the 2003 Act offence') and with an offence specified in subsection (2) ('the pre-commencement offence');
   (b) the only thing preventing the defendant from being found guilty of the 2003 Act offence is the fact that it has not been proved beyond a reasonable doubt that the time when the conduct took place was after the coming into force of the enactment providing for the offence; and
   (c) the only thing preventing the defendant from being found guilty of the pre-commencement offence is the fact that it has not been proved beyond a reasonable doubt that that time was before the coming into force of the repeal of the enactment providing for the offence.
(2) The offences referred to in subsection (1)(a) are—
   (a) any offence under the Sexual Offences Act 1956 (c. 69);
   (b) an offence under section 4 of the Vagrancy Act 1824 (c. 83) (obscene exposure);
   (c) an offence under section 28 of the Town Police Clauses Act 1847 (c. 89) (indecent exposure);

[13] *R v Michael Harries and Others* [2007] EWCA Crim 1622.

(d) an offence under section 61 or 62 of the Offences against the Person Act 1861 (c. 100) (buggery etc.);
(e) an offence under section 128 of the Mental Health Act 1959 (c. 72) (sexual intercourse with patients);
(f) an offence under section 1 of the Indecency with Children Act 1960 (c. 33) (indecency with children);
(g) an offence under section 4 or 5 of the Sexual Offences Act 1967 (procuring an man to commit buggery and living on the earnings of male prostitution);
(h) an offence under section 9 of the Theft Act 1968 (c. 60) (burglary, including entering premises with intent to commit rape);
(i) an offence under section 54 of the Criminal Law Act 1977 (c. 45) (incitement of girl under 16 to commit incest);
(j) an offence under section 1 of the Protection of Children Act 1978 (c. 37) (indecent photographs of children);
(k) an offence under section 3 of the Sexual Offences (Amendment) Act 2000 (c. 44) (abuse of position of trust);
(l) an offence under section 145 of the Nationality, Immigration and Asylum Act 2002 (c. 41) (traffic in prostitution).

Note: offences of incitement, conspiracy and attempt to commit any of the above offences including those under the SOA 2003 are included (s 55(5)).

In such circumstances it will be conclusively presumed, for the purpose of determining guilt, that the time when the conduct occurred was under the old law if the maximum penalty for it was lower then; if it is not lower, then it will be presumed that the conduct occurred under the new law; s 55(3). **1.25**

Drafting Counts where an Allegation Straddles Legislation: the Practicalities

Where an allegation straddles the implementation dates of two different Acts, typically but not exclusively the 1956 and 2003 Sexual Offences Acts, the trial indictment should contain two counts to reflect that one allegation; one under each Act alleging the offence either side of the implementation date of the new Act. That is, one count covering the period up to the day before the commencement date and the other starting on the commencement date. For s 55 to have effect, both the SOA 2003 and the earlier legislation must be pleaded in the alternative: *Chaney* [2009].[14] The practice amongst some prosecutors in sex cases, especially in a case where the indictment is already necessarily lengthy, to draft a single count by adopting the device of putting the Particulars of Offence under both the old and new law in the same count has been disapproved by the Court of Appeal: *Marshall* (2.12.2009).[15] Such a count would be duplicitous and would impede the proper working of s 55; directions to the jury would be difficult, if not impossible. **1.26**

This will apply equally to a single incident count where the date is in dispute (as in *Cairns*[16]) as to multiple incidents or sample counts where an alleged course of conduct straddles the relevant legislation. **1.27**

If, by the time the evidence has closed, there is still no clarity as to which time frame the allegation occurred in, then the count which should be left to the jury for its consideration is that **1.28**

[14] *R v Chaney* [2009] EWCA Crim 52.
[15] Unreported, Woolwich CC.
[16] *R v Cairns* [1998] Crim LR 141.

which attracts the lowest maximum sentence for the offence alleged; this will usually be under the earlier Act. The second, alternative count should be withdrawn from the jury.

1.29 Care must be taken even if a guilty plea is known to be intended upon arraignment; *where the dates of an allegation straddle the commencement date of new legislation* this will affect the sentencing powers for the offence. There should therefore never be a single count which runs through the commencement date; otherwise, the sentencer is faced with a single count for which two different sentences are possible.[17]

1.30 Failure to consider this is likely to result in the sentencing tribunal being restricted to the lower sentencing maxima of the two sets of legislation (unless the evidence unequivocally reveals that the offence occurred after the implementation of the new Act) *R v R (Paul Brian)*.[18]

1.31 See para 12.36 for sentencing under the dangerousness provisions where counts span the provisions.

Defective Counts: the Effect of Drafting a Count under the Wrong Act

1.32 Where an indictment straddles periods covered for example by the SOA 1956 and the SOA 2003, it is important to check that each count is drafted under the correct Act.

1.33 In *Stocker* [2013][19] the appellant was convicted of rape, contrary to s 1(1) of the SOA 1956. The offence was committed in 2008 and so the relevant statutory provision had been wrongly identified: it should have been s 1(1) of the SOA 2003. The question for the Court of Appeal was whether this was a purely technical defect or whether the count was fundamentally flawed because it breached rule 14(2) of the Criminal Procedure Rules by failing to identify accurately the legislation contravened. From the beginning to the end of the process the charge was, in substance, one of rape under the 2003 Act. The error could have been cured easily by an amendment at any time. The Court of Appeal did not accept that an error in the date of the statute on these facts was so fundamental as to render the proceedings a nullity, or that the draftsman of rule 14(2) would have intended such an outcome for a breach of this kind. Nothing had occurred during the trial to render the indictment a nullity or the conviction unsafe.

1.34 *Stocker* was 'clearly distinguishable' from *MC* [2012]:[20] in *R v MC*, there was not simply a technicality which had caused no prejudice to the appellant. In *Stocker*, the court observed that there is a clear judicial and legislative steer away from quashing an indictment and allowing appeals on the basis of a purely technical defect. The position in *MC* was different; the appellant was charged with sexual offences against his natural daughter. The matters were alleged to have occurred some time ago and an additional count under s 14(1) of the SOA 1956 was added by a late amendment to the indictment. The particulars alleged that the offence had taken place at a time when the 1956 Act had long since been repealed and replaced by the 2003 Act. On appeal it was submitted that it was open to the court to substitute a conviction under s 9 of the SOA 2003. The Court of Appeal rejected this argument because it did not pay sufficient attention to the requirement in s 3 of the Criminal Appeal Act 1968 that the jury could on the indictment have found the appellant guilty of some other offence. The offence which the respondents sought to argue could be substituted under s 3 was not a known offence. The words 'on the indictment' were important because in order to find a person guilty of an alternative offence, the

---

[17] *R v Cairns* [1998] Crim LR 141.

[18] *R v R (Paul Brian)* [1993] Crim LR 541. See also para 12.18.

[19] [2013] EWCA Crim 1993.

[20] [2012] EWCA Crim 213.

allegations in the indictment had to amount to or include an allegation of that other offence: *R v Graham and Others.*[21]

It follows that the court concluded that s 3 of the Criminal Appeal Act did not allow the court to substitute a verdict under s 9 of the 2003 Act in respect of the jury's verdict on the defective count. The allegation did not expressly or impliedly amount to or include an allegation under s 9.In addition and more fundamentally, the allegation of an offence under the SOA 1956 could not sensibly be said to amount to an offence under the 2003 Act, which superseded and repealed the 1956 Act. **1.35**

Alternative Verdicts

Rather than relying on alternatives included within the legislation, prosecutors would be well advised to draft alternatives expressly on the indictment where appropriate or to apply to add counts where the evidence given at trial reveals an alternative offence. **1.36**

Under the SOA 2003 a number of offences contain essential ingredients which are identical to but less in number than other, more serious offences. There will therefore often be occasions on which if the offence charged is not proved in one or more of its elements, the defendant will be guilty of a lesser offence. An obvious example of this would be those offences of penetrative assault where the evidence at trial falls short on the issue of penetration. In addition, some offences under the SOA 2003 carry different sentences depending upon the precise factual ingredients proved, for example whether penetration has occurred; following the principle in *Courtie,*[22] these are separate offences, meaning yet more offences are created. It will therefore be particularly important for charges and indictments to be carefully drafted in order to accurately reflect the prosecution case. **1.37**

The Principle in *Courtie*[23]

In *Courtie,* the House of Lords was dealing with an offence under the SOA 1967 which, like the SOA 2003, created a number of specific offences for which the maximum punishment prescribed varied upon a descending scale, according to the existence or absence of particular factual ingredients. **1.38**

The House of Lords held that where a statute provides for different maximum sentences dependent upon the prosecution's ability to successfully prove a particular factual ingredient, two distinct offences are created by the Act. It was further held that where a not guilty plea is entered, it is the jury's function to determine the facts upon which a person is guilty; it is therefore essential that the indictment correctly sets out those facts, if necessary in separate counts, so that in the event that the difference in a finding of fact will affect the maximum sentence available, the verdict(s) reflect that difference. It is also simpler for the judge to sum the case up to the jury and for the jury to immediately see what alternatives are open to them. **1.39**

The SOA 2003 creates over 50 offences, some carrying different maximum sentences depending upon the facts proved. Under the principle in *Courtie* this means yet more offences[24] are created. An illustration of this would be one of the number of offences where if the sexual activity alleges penetration, the charge is both indictable only and carries a higher maximum sentence than a non-penetrative allegation under the same section; as such, they are separate offences. **1.40**

21 [1997] 1 Cr App R(S) 302.
22 [1984] AC 463.
23 [1984] AC 463.
24 Over 70 when the subcategories of offences are included.

The indictment should therefore be properly particularized, to set out the facts upon which the elements of the offence relied upon by the prosecution are based.

1.41 Careful thought must be given to how many offences are in fact revealed by the evidence: see *R v Grout*,[25] a case involving offences under s 8 of the SOA 2003. Section 8 creates four separate offences applying *Courtie*. The Court of Appeal quashed the conviction, ruling that the indictment should have included more than one count to clearly set out the different offences alleged. This is of course necessary to both ensure clarity for the jury and, upon conviction, provide the correct maximum sentence(s).

Offences of Attempt

1.42 The premise that alternative counts should be added rather than read into an indictment will also apply when an attempt to commit the full offence is an obvious alternative from the outset; indeed, it is thought preferable to have a count added in the event that an alternative of attempt to commit the full offence is to be left to the jury after evidence has been heard.

1.43 Where a count of attempt is to be drafted,[26] it should be indicted under the common law until 27.8.1981[27] and thereafter under the Criminal Attempts Act 1985. It is helpful to aver the relevant section of the SOA as well, so that all parties can immediately refer to the appropriate elements, sentence(s), etc. The attempt should be averred in both the Statement and Particulars of Offence.

Familial Offences under the Sexual Offences Act 2003

1.44 In drafting indictments generally for a familial offence it is important to remember the following:

(i) The maximum penalties such offences attract are usually significantly lower than the equivalent offence drafted outside the familial bracket because they are intended to reflect circumstances where there is consent. Where the complainant is under 13, however, it is suggested that it will be appropriate to indict a non-familial offence or to simply draft, for example, a count of rape of a child under 13 (life) rather than sexual activity with a child family member (5 years where the defendant is under 18 even when the child is under 13). This is the clear intention of Parliament and underpins the current Crown Prosecution Service guidance for indicting such offences.[28]

(ii) Where possible, counts should relate to a specific incident. Where that is impossible because of, for example, several years of regular and repeated acts, it is now appropriate to draft a single multiple-incident count relating to repeated similar offences against the same complainant, preferably using 12 month periods as breaks in the overall timespan (provided the defence is the same to all allegations reflected by the single count). See paras 1.08–1.17 in this chapter.

(iii) If both parties to the sexual act are charged, it is possible for a guilty verdict against one only to stand; one party might be unaware of the relationship or there might not be true consent by the party alleged to have consented to the act.[29]

---

[25] [2011] EWCA Crim 299.

[26] It is not strictly necessary to add a count where a full offence is charged; the jury may convict of attempt having acquitted of the full offence, Criminal Law Act (CLA) 1967, s 693(4).

[27] CAA 1981 implementation date.

[28] See App B.

[29] *R v Gordon* (1925) 19 Cr App R 20 CA; brother and sister both charged in same indictment but tried separately. She was acquitted; that did not make his conviction bad.

Offences under the Sexual Offences Act 2003, s 13

1.45 When indicting offences under s 13, that is those offences under ss 9–12 for which a defendant under 18 can be charged, it is suggested that it will be good practice to indict both sections, so that the offence to which the indictment relates is obvious. It is suggested that s 13 be indicted first, followed by the relevant section and that the particulars make the act alleged clear. See paras 4.26, 4.27, 4.111, 4.195 and 4.206 for sample indictments.

Procedure when Summary Only Offences Remain on an Indictment

1.46 Circumstances may arise where an indictment is amended or otherwise altered to remove indictable only matters which leave only matters triable either way before the Crown Court; for example, either on a successful application for severance or dismissal of the indictable only charges following the sending of a case to the Crown Court under the Crime and Disorder Act (CDA) 1988, s 51. In such an event, the correct course is for the Crown Court to adopt a procedure akin to that used in the magistrates' court to determine mode of trial. The CDA 1988, ss 7–13, sets out the procedure to be followed. However, failure to do so will no longer necessarily render the proceedings a nullity; the Court of Appeal in *R v Thwaites* [2006],[30] upholding *R v Ashton* [2006][31] ruled:

> Where a court was confronted by failure to take a required step, properly or at all, before a power was exercised it should first ask itself whether the intention of the legislature was that any act done following that procedural failure should be invalid. If the answer was no, then the court should go on to consider the interests of justice generally, and in particular whether there was a real possibility that either the prosecution or the defence might suffer prejudice on account of the procedural failure.

R v Haye[32] and *R v Gayle*[33] were doubted.

Note a Crown Court Judge's power to sit as a District Judge during the course of Crown Court proceedings in order to deal with summary matters.

Quashing Indictments

1.47 It is proper for two indictments to exist at the same time as long as both are not proceeded with.[34] In the event that an indictment is heavily amended and so preferred as a new indictment, it will be prudent not to apply to quash the existing indictment until after trial. This is in order to ensure that if, for example, the new indictment were invalid for some reason, the only valid indictment is not quashed, leaving the proceedings a nullity.

1.48 Equally, a prudent prosecutor when accepting a guilty plea to lesser alternative counts will not proceed to 'offer no evidence' until after sentence has been passed in order to ensure that no application to vacate the plea is made in the interim; counts not intended to be proceeded with should lie on the court file until then.

Delay

1.49 The question of delay in an historic sex case is likely to be considered, at least by the prosecutor, prior to the drafting of an indictment. This is, however, a convenient point at which to draw the reader's attention to the current authorities on this subject. *R v F* [2011][35] provides guidance on abuse of process applications from a five-Judge Court of Appeal led by the then Lord Chief

[30] *R v Thwaites* [2006] EWCA Crim 3235.
[31] *R v Ashton (John)* [2006] EWCA Crim 794, [2007] 1 WLR 181.
[32] *R v Haye (Conrad)* [2002] EWCA Crim 2476, [2003] Crim LR 287.
[33] *R v Gayle (Kelvin)* [2004] EWCA Crim 2937.
[34] *R v Poole* [1961] AC 223.
[35] EWCA Crim 1844.

Justice, Lord Judge. Since then, appeals following conviction based on significant periods of delay have been considered and rejected on their facts: *R v PS* [2013][36] (delay of 34 years; provides guidance as to directing the jury on delay); *R v RD* [2013][37] (delays of between 39 and 63 years). For the effects of delay on a sentence, see para 12.13 et seq.

1.50 Table of Changes in Sexual Offences Legislation

Table 1.1 Table of Changes in Sexual Offences Legislation

Act	Commencement Date	Cessation Date	Explanatory Note
CAJA 2009, s 62	6.4.2010	In force	Section enacted by SI 2010 No 816
CAA 1981	27.8.1981	In force	
CJA 1988, s 160	29.9.1988	In force	
Criminal Justice and Immigration Act 2008, s 63	26.1.2009	In force	Section enacted by SI 2008 No 2993
CLA 1977, s 54	8.9.1977	1.5.2004	Section enacted by SI 1977 No 1365 Section repealed by SOA 2003
CLAA 1885	14.8.1885	1.1.1957	Act repealed by SOA 1956
IwCA 1960	2.7.1960	1.5.2004	Act repealed by SOA 2003
MDA 1913	1.4.1914	1.11.1960	Act repealed by SI 1960 No 1698
MHA 1959, s 128	1.11.1960	1.5.2004	Section enacted by SI 1960 No 1698 Section repealed by SOA 2003
OPA 1959, s 2	29.8.1959	In force	
OAPA 1861, s 52 s 61 s 62	1.11.1861 1.11.1861 1.11.1861	1.1.1957 1.1.1957 1.1.1957	Sections repealed by SOA 1956
PCA 1978, s 1	20.8.1978	In force	
PIA 1908	1.1.1909	1.1.1957	Act repealed by SOA 1956
SOA 1956	1.1.1957	1.5.2004	Act repealed by SOA 2003
SOA 1967	27.7.1967	1.5.2004	Act repealed by SOA 2003
SOA 2003	1.5.2004	Largely in force	Sections 57, 58 and 59 repealed and replaced by s 59A as of 6.4.2013

[36] [2013] EWCA Crim 1592.

[37] *RD* [2013] EWCA Crim 1592.

Act	Commencement Date	Cessation Date	Explanatory Note
SO(A)A 2000, s 3	8.1.2001	1.5.2004	Section enacted by SI 2000 No 452 Act repealed by SOA 2003
TA 1968, s 9(1)(a)	1.1.1969	1.5.2004	Sexual element of offence repealed by SOA 2003

Note: the authors wish to thank Lucy Luttman, Barrister, for researching, creating and updating this table.

2

RAPE

Introduction

The offence of rape, originally a common law offence, became a statutory offence in 1957,[1] and was later defined by statute in 1976.[2] The offence was extended in 1992 so that a husband could be convicted of raping his wife.[3] In 1994 the definition of rape was extended to include non-consensual anal intercourse upon a male or female.[4] The SOA 2003 extends the definition further. Most notably, non-consensual penile penetration of the mouth is now defined by s 1 as rape. **2.01**

Offences committed pre-1.1.1957

Rape was originally an offence at common law. **2.02**

Definition

Unlawful carnal knowledge of a woman without her consent by force, fear or fraud.[5] **2.03**

Proof

(i) Carnal knowledge: penile penetration of the vagina, even the slightest penetration was sufficient (proof of hymenal damage is not required). Proof of ejaculation is not necessary.[6] **2.04**

(ii) Lack of consent: even if the girl was under 16[7] her submission is not to be classified as consent.[8] The lack of consent may have been brought about by drink, drugs, sleep, age or mental handicap, so as to render the complainant incapable of giving consent.[9]

(iii) *Mens rea*; proof of intention or recklessness as to consent is required (see para 2.17).

---

1 SOA 1956, s 1, commencement date 1.1.1957.

2 SO(A)A 1976, s 1(1).

3 *R v R* [1992] 1 AC 599.

4 Criminal Justice and Public Order Act (CJPOA) 1994, s 142.

5 East PC 434.

6 *R v Marsden* 2 QB 149 and later OAPA 1861, s 63.

7 *R v Harling* 26 Cr App R 127 CA.

8 *R v Olugboja* 73 Cr App R 344 CA.

9 *R v Malone* (1998) 2 Cr App R 447 CA.

Notes

2.05 (i) Triable only on indictment.

(ii) A boy under 14 was presumed by law to be incapable of committing rape as principal[10] (that is until 1993), but may be guilty of indecent assault[11] (see para 3.03.)

(iii) A boy under 14 could not be convicted of an assault with intent to rape.[12]

(iv) Only a male may be convicted as a principal,[13] but a female may be convicted as an aider and abettor.[14]

(v) If a woman consents to sexual intercourse then changes her mind during intercourse, the male may be convicted if he has the requisite *mens rea*.[15]

Indictment

2.06 RAPE Pre-1.1.1957

Statement of Offence

RAPE.

Particulars of Offence

D on the... day of... had carnal knowledge of C without her consent.

Alternative Offences

Criminal Law Amendment Act 1885

2.07 The following offences constituted alternatives to rape:

(i) CLAA 1885, s 3: procuring defilement of a woman or girl by threats, fraud or under the influence of drugs: **2 YEARS**.

(ii) CLAA 1885, s 4: carnal knowledge of a girl aged under 13: **LIFE** (see paras 4.46–4.53).

(iii) for an attempt to commit this offence: **2 YEARS**.

(iv) CLAA 1885, s 5: defilement of a girl aged between 13 and 16 years of age, or an attempt to do the same: **2 YEARS** (see paras 4.54–4.63).

Offences Against the Person Act 1861

2.08 OAPA 1861, s 52: indecent assault:[16] **2 YEARS** (see paras 3.03–3.09).

Punishment of Incest Act 1908

2.09 PIA 1908, s 4(3): incest: **LIFE** (see paras 6.12 and 6.20).

(i) As defined by common law.

(ii) Attempted rape: fine and/or **LIFE**.

(iii) Up until 1948 maximum sentence available is **LIFE**, thereafter it was lowered to **7 YEARS** until 1985 when maximum was again increased to **LIFE**.[17]

Indictment

2.10 ATTEMPTED RAPE Pre-26.8.1981

---

10 Hale, *The History of Pleas of the Crown*, vol I.

11 *R v Williams* (1893)1 QB 320; CLAA 1885, s 9.

12 *R v Williams*.

13 SOA 1956, s 1.

14 *R v Ram* (1893) 17 Cox 609 (in 1893 referred to as principal in second degree).

15 *R v Kaitamaki* (1985) AC 147 PC.

16 OAPA 1861, s 52.

17 SOA 1985, s 3(2), commencement date 16.9.1985.

Statement of Offence

ATTEMPTED RAPE.

Particulars of Offence

D on the . . . day of . . . attempted to have carnal knowledge of C without her consent.

Sentence

(i) For the full offence: **LIFE.**[18] **2.11**
(ii) Attempted rape: **LIFE.**
- This was reduced to 7 **YEARS**[19] in 1948 but increased again to **LIFE** imprisonment in 1985.[20]

Sentencing Guidance

See paras 12.13–12.26. **2.12**

Upon Conviction/Sentence

(i) Notification: not applicable.[21] **2.13**
(ii) Disqualification/barring from working with children/vulnerable adults. See paras 12.135 and 16.33.
(iii) Sexual Offences Prevention Order (SOPO), not applicable.[22]

Offences committed between 1.1.1957 and 21.12.1976

Sexual Offences Act 1956

(i) This Act consolidated the law with regard to sexual offences in general and to rape—by s 1 and Sch 1. **2.14**
(ii) Rape was still a common law offence.

Definition

Sexual Offences Act 1956, s 1(1) and (2)

> (1) It is a felony for a man to rape a woman. **2.15**
> (2) A man who induces a married woman to have sexual intercourse with him by impersonating her husband commits rape.

The common law definition remained unchanged 'unlawful sexual intercourse with a woman without her consent by force, fear or fraud'.[23] **2.16**

Proof

(i) Any penile penetration of the vagina was sufficient, even the slightest, not necessarily proof of ejaculation.[24] **2.17**
(ii) Lack of consent (as at para 2.04).

---

18 CJA 1948, s 1.
19 Attempted Rape Act 1948, s 1.
20 SOA 1985, s 3(2).
21 SOA 2003, s 80(1) (not listed in Sch 3). See Chapter 14.
22 SOA 2003, s 104 (not listed in Sch 3). See Chapter 16.
23 Hale, *The History of Pleas of the Crown*, vol I.
24 *R v M'Rue* (1838) 8 C&P 641.

Note

2.18 The offence is indictable only.[25]

Indictment

2.19 RAPE 1.1.1957 to 21.12.1976

Statement of Offence
RAPE, contrary to section 1(1) of the Sexual Offences Act 1956.
Particulars of Offence
D on the . . . day of . . . had sexual intercourse with C, without her consent.

Alternative Offences

Sexual Offences Act 1956, s 37, Sch II

2.20 (i) s 2 procurement of a woman by threats: **2 YEARS** (see paras 11.04–11.10).
(ii) s 3 procurement of a woman by false pretences: **2 YEARS** (see paras 11.11–11.18).
(iii) s 4 administering drugs to obtain or facilitate intercourse: **2 YEARS** (see paras 11.19–11.26).
(iv) s 14 indecent assault (on a woman): **2 YEARS** (see paras 3.03–3.09).

However if the *only* issue is consent, then indecent assault cannot be an alternative,[26] unless the victim is under 16.

2.21 The following were available alternatives to an offence of rape from 1956 to 1967[27] (but not after 1967):
(i) s 5 intercourse with a girl under 13: **LIFE** (see paras 4.64–4.74).
(ii) s 6 intercourse with a girl between 13 and 16: **2 YEARS** (see paras 4.75–4.86).
(iii) s 7 intercourse with an idiot or imbecile: **2 YEARS** (see paras 7.11–7.21).
(iv) s 8 intercourse with a defective: **2 YEARS** (see paras 7.57–7.64).
(v) s 10 incest: **LIFE** if child under 13: **7 YEARS** otherwise (see paras 6.23–6.31).

Sentence

2.22 (i) For the full offence: **LIFE.**[28]
(ii) Attempted rape: 7 **YEARS**[29] (increases to life in 1985).[30]

Sentencing Guidance

2.23 See the SGC guidelines at App C, pages 316–319.

Upon Conviction/Sentence

2.24 (i) Notification: if criteria apply.[31]
(ii) Disqualification/barring from working with children/vulnerable adults. See paras 12.135 and 16.33.
(iii) SOPO applies, if criteria met.[32]

None of the above applies to an offence of attempted rape.

---

[25] SOA 1956, s 37.
[26] *R v Touhey* (1961) 45 Cr App R 23.
[27] CLA 1967, s 10.
[28] SOA 1956, s 37.
[29] SOA 1956, s 37, Sch II(1)(b).
[30] SOA 1985, s 3(2), commencement date 16.9.1985.
[31] SOA 2003, s 80(1), Sch 3. See Chapter 14.
[32] SOA 2003, s 104, Sch 3. See Chapter 16.

Offences committed between 22.12.1976 and 2.11.1993

Sexual Offences (Amendment) Act 1976

The definition of rape remains (as at para 2.15). Following the decision in *DPP v Morgan*[33] the House of Lords emphasized the requirement of the mental element: the defendant must be at least reckless as to whether consent was given. A genuine belief in consent, however unreasonable, provided a defence to the charge. **2.25**

Following on from this decision, the SO(A)A 1976 was passed,[34] which included a declaration confirming that the jury, in deciding whether the defendant believed in consent, could consider whether reasonable grounds existed for such.[35] **2.26**

Definition

Section 1(1) provides that a rape offence consists of: **2.27**

(i) unlawful sexual intercourse with a woman who at the time of the intercourse does not consent to it;
(ii) at that time he knows that she does not consent to the intercourse or he is reckless as to whether she consents to it.

Proof

As per Definition. **2.28**

Indictment

RAPE 22.12.1976 to 30.4.2004 **2.29**

Statement of Offence

RAPE, contrary to section 1(1) of the Sexual Offences Act 1956.

Particulars of Offence

D on the... day of... 19/20.., had unlawful sexual intercourse with C who at the time of the said intercourse did not consent to it, said D knowing that the said C did not so consent or being reckless as to whether she so consented.

or

D on the... day of... raped C.

Alternative Offences

Sexual Offences Act 1956, s 37, Sch II

(i) s 2 'procurement of a woman by threats': **2 YEARS** (see paras 11.04–11.10). **2.30**
(ii) s 3 'procurement of a woman by false pretences': **2 YEARS** (see paras 11.11–11.18).
(iii) s 4 'administering drugs to obtain or facilitate intercourse': **2 YEARS** (see paras 11.19–11.26).
(iv) s 14 'indecent assault' (on a woman): **2 YEARS** (see paras 3.12–3.22).

However if the *only* issue is consent, then indecent assault cannot be an alternative,[36] unless the victim is under 16.

Attempted rape: **7 YEARS** until 15.9.1985. **LIFE** from 16.9.1985.[37]

---

33 [1976] AC 182, 61 Cr App R 136.
34 Commencement date 22.12.1976.
35 SO(A)A 1976, s 1(2).
36 *R v Touhey* (1961) 45 Cr App R 23.
37 As of 16.9.1985; SOA 1985, s 3.

2.31 Before 27.8.1981 when indicting attempted rape follows the model indictment set out at para 2.10. In 1981 the Criminal Attempts Act was passed. Section 1(1) defines a criminal attempt as: 'If with intent to commit an offence to which this section applies, a person does an act which is more than merely preparatory to the commission of the offence, he is guilty of attempting to commit the offence'.

From 27.8.1981 an indictment for attempted rape should be drafted as follows.

Indictment

2.32 ATTEMPTED RAPE 27.8.1981 to 30.4.2004

Statement of Offence
ATTEMPTED RAPE, contrary to section 1(1) of the Criminal Attempts Act 1981
Particulars of Offence
D on the... day of... attempted to rape C.

Sentence

2.33 See paras 2.22 and 12.13–12.26.

20.9.1993

2.34 As of 20.9.1993 SOA 1993, s 1 abolishes the presumption[38] that a boy under 14 was incapable of sexual intercourse. Any male aged 10 or over may be convicted of any sexual offence involving his penetration of the vagina or anus of a female.

Offences committed between 3.11.1994 and 30.4.2004

Introduction

2.35 Rape was redefined to include non-consensual anal intercourse with a male or female as of 3.11.1994.[39] In addition, the requirement upon the prosecution to prove that sexual intercourse was unlawful (outside the bonds of legal marriage) is abandoned. Thereafter a man may be convicted of raping his wife.[40]

Definition

Sexual Offences Act 1956, s 1

2.36
(1) It is an offence for a man to rape a woman or another man.
(2) A man commits rape if:
  (a) he has sexual intercourse with a person (whether vaginal or anal) who at the time of the intercourse does not consent to it; and
  (b) at the time he knows that the person does not consent to the intercourse or is reckless as to whether that person consents to it.

Section 1(1) of the SO(A)A 1976 only was repealed.[41] Section 1(2) of the SO(A)A 1976 was not repealed (reasonable belief in consent) (see para 2.26).

---

38 Children and Young Persons Act 1933, s 50.
39 CJPOA 1994, s 142.
40 *R v R* [1992] AC 599.
41 CJPOA 1994, s 168.

Proof

As per Definition. 2.37

Notes

(i) It should be remembered that this change in the law did not have a retrospective effect. Non-consensual anal intercourse pre–3.11.1994 should be charged as 'buggery' and not rape (see paras 5.04–5.06). This is a mistake often made. Indeed, made by all involved in the case of *R v Fowler*,[42] including the Court of Appeal. 2.38

(ii) In certain cases it may clarify issues if the particulars aver 'per vaginam' or 'per anum' after the word 'intercourse'.

(iii) Recklessness/knowledge does not have to be separately averred.

Indictment

See para 2.29. If anal rape is alleged then the Particulars should include 'per anum' after the words 'unlawful sexual intercourse'. 2.39

Alternative Offences

See para 2.30. 2.40

Sentence

See para 2.22. 2.41

Sentencing Guidance

The Court of Appeal issued guidelines for sentencing rape offences in *R v Billam*[43] that have been modified in *Millberry, Morgan and Lackenby.*[44] 2.42

Rape and attempted rape, post-30.9.97, are classified as 'serious'[45] offences for the purposes of the Powers of Criminal Courts (Sentencing) Act (PCC(S)A) 2000, s 109; that is a qualifying offence for mandatory life sentences for the second such offence committed after 30.9.97 where the defendant is over 18. 2.43

Both rape and attempted rape qualify for the imposition of an extended sentence,[46] provided that the court considers that the ordinary licence period would not be adequate to prevent further offending and securing rehabilitation. 2.44

Offences committed from 1.5.2004 to date

Sexual Offences Act 2003

As of 1.5.2004 the SOA 2003 came into force. This Act modernizes the law in relation to sexual offences and represents a complete overhaul of the law. 2.45

Section 1 extends the definition of rape to include non-consensual penile penetration of the mouth of a male or female. The Act further seeks to define consent as 'free agreement'.[47] Free agreement has been clarified as covering drunken consent given by a complainant who has consumed even substantial quantities of alcohol, provided that the complainant has not lost the 2.46

[42] [2002] EWCA Crim 620, [2002] Crim LR 521.

[43] 82 Cr App R 347 CA.

[44] [2002] EWCA Crim 2891, [2003] 1 Cr App R 25.

[45] PCC(S)A 2000, s 109, repealed by CJA 2003 as of 4.4.2005.

[46] PCC(S)A 2000, ss 85 and 86. Section 85 is still in force, it applies to sex offences committed before 30.9.1998. Section 86 was repealed by CJA 2003 as of 4.4.2003.

[47] SOA 2003, s 74.

capacity to choose whether to have intercourse.[48] If a complainant had not agreed to intercourse if ejaculation were to take place,[49] or intercourse without the use of a condom,[50] then consent was not given. Note that a failure by a party to communicate that he/she has a sexually transmitted disease does not have any bearing on consent, notwithstanding the fact that the complainant would not consent if he/she had known this fact.[51] Further, the Act introduces a presumption of lack of consent by the complainant in certain specified circumstances.[52] In addition, the defence of honest belief in consent, however unreasonable, has been eradicated by s 1(1)(c), which requires the prosecution to prove an absence of a reasonable belief in consent. An objectively judged unreasonably held belief in consent which arises from conditions such as delusional psychotic illness or personality disorders, is caught by s 1(1)(c),[53] and so does not afford a defence. See para 3.37.

Definition

Sexual Offences Act 2003, s 1

2.47 (1) A person (A) commits an offence if—
(a) he intentionally penetrates the vagina, anus or mouth of another person (B) with the penis,
(b) B does not consent to the penetration and
(c) A does not reasonably believe B consents.
(2) Whether a belief is reasonable is to be determined having regard to all the circumstances, including any steps A has taken to ascertain whether B consents.

Note: mistaken identity is no defence.[54]

Proof

2.48 As per Definition.

Notes

2.49 (i) The offence is indictable only.
(ii) Following the judgment in *R v Heard*,[55] it seems that all the sexual offences in the 2003 Act (certainly those in ss 1–4 and 5–15) will be regarded as offences for which a plea of voluntary intoxication is no defence.[56]

Indictment

2.50 RAPE 1.5.2004 to date

Statement of Offence

RAPE, contrary to section 1(1) of the Sexual Offences Act 2003

Particulars of Offence

D on the...day of 20..., intentionally penetrated with his penis the [vagina] *or* [anus][57] *or* [mouth] of C who did not consent to the penetration, D not reasonably believing that C consented.

---

48 *R v Bree* [2007] EWCA Crim 804.
49 *R (F) v DPP* [2013] EWHC 945 (Admin). [2013] Cr App R 21.
50 *Julian Assange v Swedish Prosecution Authority* [2011] EWHC 2849 (Admin).
51 *R v B* [2006] EWCA Crim 2945, [2007] 1 WLR 1567.
52 SOA 2003, ss 75 and 76.
53 *R v B (MA)* [2013] EWCA Crim 3.
54 *R v Whitta* [2006] EWCA Crim 2626.
55 [2007] EWCA Crim 125.
56 Professor David Ormerod, March 2007.
57 Where the evidence is unclear it is permissible to allege penetration of the vagina or anus. The jury must be sure that there was non-consensual penetration of one or the other. *R v K (Robert)* [2009] 1 Cr App R 24 CA.

Alternative Offences

(i) Attempted rape: **LIFE.** 2.51
(ii) s 3 sexual assault:[58] **10 YEARS** (see paras 3.45–3.52).
(iii) s 2 sexual assault (footnote 58: s 2 SOA 2003) **LIFE** (see paras 3.35–3.44).
(iv) s 4 causing a person to engage in sexual activity without consent:[59] **LIFE** (see paras 3.53–3.64).

Sentence

(i) For the full offence: **LIFE.**[60] 2.52
(ii) For an attempt: **LIFE.**

Sentencing Guidance

See the SGC guidelines at App C, pages 316–319. 2.53

Upon Conviction/Sentence

(i) Notification requirements apply if criteria met.[61] 2.54
(ii) Disqualification/barring from working with children/vulnerable adults. See paras 12.135 and 16.33.
(iii) SOPO.[62]

---

58 SOA 2003, s 3.
59 SOA 2003, s 1(4).
60 SOA 2003, s 4.
61 SOA 2003, s 80(1) and Sch 3. See Chapter 14.
62 SOA 2003, s 104 and Sch 3. See Chapter 16.

3

SEXUAL ASSAULTS

Introduction

Prior to 31.12.1956, the law did not differentiate as between the gender of the person assaulted. The first section of this chapter therefore applies equally to assaults upon males and females. **3.01**

Thereafter, for allegations falling within the period 1.1.1957 to 30.4.2004, the chapter deals first with assaults upon women/girls and then with assaults upon men/boys under the 1956 Act, followed by assaults upon adults of both genders under the 2003 Act (commencement date 1.5.2004), which reverted to there being no differentiation between genders but does categorize offender and complainant. **3.02**

Offences committed pre-31.12.1956

1. Indecent Assault

Offences Against the Person Act 1861, s 52

Definition

An assault, accompanied with circumstances of indecency on the part of the prisoner[1] (towards the person assaulted).[2] **3.03**

Proof

(i) An assault (any unlawful touching). **3.04**
(ii) The assault must be either obviously sexual itself or take place in circumstances which make the touching indecent.
(iii) The assault must be directed towards the person assaulted.

---

1 *Lord Goddard CJ Beal v Kelley* (1951) 35 Cr App R 128, 130.

2 Words in parentheses added by editors of Archbold, 33rd edn, 1954–1959.

Notes

3.05 (i) Triable either way.

(ii) Where the assault is on a girl under 16 that fact should be stated in the indictment,[3] but an indictment is not defective without it.[4]

(iii) Belief that the girl upon whom the assault is committed was 16 years of age or more at the time the offence was committed affords no defence to the person accused.[5]

(iv) A woman may be guilty of an offence under this section.[6]

(v) Consent cannot be a defence where the indecent assault consists of the infliction of blows intended or likely to cause bodily harm,[7] although standards current at the time of the offence must apply. It is likely that current attitudes towards consensual sexual relations are different to those of the 1930s and therefore the view of injuries which are 'transient or trifling… calculated to interfere with health or comfort',[8] will reflect those attitudes.[9]

(vi) The Divisional Court held[10] in the case of a man (the respondent) exposing himself to a 9-year-old girl and inviting her to touch his exposed penis, which she did: an invitation to another to touch the invitor could not amount to an assault on the invitee, and therefore there had been no assault and consequently no indecent assault. This lacuna was remedied by the implementation of s 1(1) of the Indecency with Children Act (IwCA) 1960[11] (see paras 4.05–4.17).

(vii) However, where a man asked a boy to handle his (the defendant's) penis and, when the boy refused, pulled the boy towards him before letting him go, it was held to be an indecent act (having the requisite ingredients of an assault in circumstances of indecency even although the act itself was not indecent).[12]

(viii) Indecent assault is an alternative to:
- Rape (see para 2.06).
- Having carnal knowledge of/unlawful sexual intercourse with a girl under 13[13] (see para 4.64).
- Having carnal knowledge of/unlawful sexual intercourse with a girl under 16[14] (see para 4.54).

Indictment

3.06 INDECENT ASSAULT 1.11.1861 to 31.12.1956

Statement of Offence

INDECENT ASSAULT, contrary to section 52 of the Offences Against the Person Act 1861.

Particulars of Offence

D, on the… day of… 19.., indecently assaulted C.

---

[3] CLAA 1922, s 1.
[4] *R v Stephenson* [1912] 3 KB 341 and Indictments Act 1915.
[5] *R v Maughan* (1934) 24 Cr App R 130.
[6] *R v Hare* [1934] 1 KB 354.
[7] *R v Donovan* [1934] 2 KB 498.
[8] *R v Donovan* [1934] 2 KB 498, 509 per Swift J.
[9] *R v Boyea* [1992] Crim LR 574 CA.
[10] *Fairclough v Whipp* (1951) 35 Cr App R 138 DC.
[11] Commencement date 2.7.1960.
[12] *Beal v Kelley* (1951) 35 Cr App R 128.
[13] CLAA 1885, s 4.
[14] CLAA 1885, s 5.

Alternative Offences

Attempt to commit the full offence. When indicting offences of attempted indecent assault before 27.8.1981,[15] do so under common law. Aver the attempt in both the Statement and Particulars of Offence. See Indictments, para 1.24. **3.07**

Sentence

(i) On indictment: 2 YEARS.[16] **3.08**
(ii) Summarily: **6 months.**

Upon Conviction/Sentence

(i) Notification; not applicable.[17] **3.09**
(ii) Disqualification/barring from working with children/vulnerable adults. See paras 12.135 and 16.33.
(iii) SOPO; not applicable.[18]

Offences committed between 1.1.1957 and 30.4.2004

The SOA 1956 consolidated the law with regard to sexual offences. It introduced the specific offence of indecent assault on a man as well as a woman. **3.10**

> The use in any provision of this Act of the word 'man' without the addition of the word 'boy', or *vice versa*, shall not prevent the provision applying to any person to whom it would have applied if both words had been used, and similarly with the words 'woman' and 'girl'.[19]

This applies equally for the purposes of the provisions of the SOA 1967[20] and has effect as if the reference to the SOA 1956 included a reference to the SO(A)A 1976.[21]

As of 31.12.1956 s 52 of the OAPA 1861 is repealed. From 1.1.1957, s 14 of the SOA 1956 replaces this offence as against a woman or girl. For indecent assault upon a man or boy, see para 3.23. **3.11**

2. Indecent Assault on a Woman

Sexual Offences Act 1956, s 14

Definition

> An assault, accompanied with circumstances of indecency on the part of the person assaulting towards the person alleged to have been assaulted.[22] **3.12**

Proof

(i) An intentional assault (any unlawful touching) by D of C; **3.13**
(ii) the assault, or the assault and the circumstances accompanying it, are capable of being considered by right-minded persons as indecent, and
(iii) that D intended not just an assault, but an indecent assault.

15 CAA 1981; implementation date 27.8.1981.
16 OAPA 1861, s 52.
17 SOA 2003, s 80(1) (not listed in Sch 3); see Chapter 14.
18 SOA 2003, s 104 (not listed in Sch 3); see Chapter 16.
19 SOA 1956, s 46.
20 SOA 1967, s 11(3).
21 SO(A)A 1976, s 7(2).
22 *R v Court* [1989] AC 28 HL; defines and sets out the elements of the offence.

Notes

3.14 (i) Triable either way.

(ii) Where indecency is clear from the facts of the case there is no difficulty; however, where the circumstances of the assault could be innocent, the jury might be assisted by looking at surrounding factors, such as the relationship if any between D and C and how the assault/touching came about.[23]

(iii) Age must be averred when it will affect the maximum sentence available.[24] For offences which occurred between 2.7.1960 and 15.9.1985 inclusive, it is therefore essential to aver the girl's age if she is/was under 13 for the higher maximum sentence to be available.[25] See also para 1.07.

3.15 Indecent assault on a woman is itself an alternative to the following: rape;[26] unlawful sexual intercourse with a girl under 13; unlawful sexual intercourse with a girl under 16.[27] However, an historic prosecution charging indecent assault as an alternative to unlawful sexual intercourse with a girl under 16 is not possible following the majority opinions of the House of Lords in *J*,[28] as it would circumvent the time-bar then in place for the primary offence. The SOA 2003 abolished any time-bar but it is not retrospective.

3.16 It is important that indictments based upon allegations which either potentially or actually straddle any implementation date are carefully drawn so that they do not run through a commencement date and so that a sentencing judge is mindful of the change in the maximum sentence(s) available to him/her.[29] Counts in an indictment which do straddle an implementation date will limit the sentencer to the lower maximum of the two Acts, unless it is obvious from the way in which the case has been conducted that the offences took place after the later Act came into force.[30] See also para 1.23.

(i) A girl under the age of 16 cannot in law give any consent which would prevent an act being an assault for the purposes of this section.[31]

(ii) A defence is provided by D's reasonable belief that C is his wife; the fact that the marriage is in fact invalid by virtue of C's age (being under 16)[32] does not make D guilty.[33]

(iii) A woman who is classed as a 'defective' cannot in law give any consent which would prevent an act being an assault for the purposes of this section. However, a person is only to be treated as guilty of an indecent assault on a mentally disordered woman by reason of that incapacity to consent, if that person knew or had reason to suspect her to be a 'defective'.[34]

See Chapter 7 for assaults upon 'defectives'.

Indictment

3.17 **INDECENT ASSAULT ON A WOMAN** 1.1.1957 to 30.4.2004

Statement of Offence
INDECENT ASSAULT, contrary to section 14 of the Sexual Offences Act 1956.
Particulars of Offence
D, on the... day of... 19.., indecently assaulted C (add C's age if under 13).

[23] *R v Court* [1989] AC 28 HL.

[24] *R v Hodgson* [1973] QB 565 CA, (1973) 57 Cr App R 502.

[25] IwCA 1960, s 2(1); SOA 1985, s 3(3). Implementation date 16.9.1985.

[26] SOA 1956, s 37 and Sch II(1)(a)(ix).

[27] SOA 1956, s 37 and Sch II(2)(a).

[28] *R v J* [2004] UKHL 42, Baroness Hale dissenting.

[29] *R v R (Paul Brian)* [1993] Crim LR 541; no distinction had been drawn when drafting the indictment between the Acts, nor was there any proper citation of age leading to the higher maximum. This gave rise to the sentencing judge passing all sentences under the lower maximum provision and under one Act.

[30] *R v R* [1993] Crim LR 541.

[31] SOA 1956, s 14(2).

[32] Age of Marriage Act (AMA) 1929, ss 1 and 2.

[33] SOA 1956, s 14(3).

[34] SOA 1956, s 14(4).

Alternative Offences

(i) Attempt to commit the full offence. When indicting offences of attempt, do so under the common law until 27.8.1981;[35] thereafter, under the Criminal Attempts Act 1985. See Indictments, para 1.42. **3.18**

(ii) Common assault; **6 months, fine, or both**[36] although this must now be included in the indictment.[37]

Sentence

(i) On indictment: **2 YEARS**, or **5 YEARS** after 1.1.1961[38] if the complainant is a girl under 13 and that fact is averred.[39] **3.19**

- Note: maximum increased to **10 YEARS** after 16.9.1985;[40] therefore no need to aver age (for this reason alone) after that date.

(ii) Summarily: **6 months.**

Sentencing Guidance

(i) Sentencing a charge of indecent assault laid because of the time-bar to unlawful sexual intercourse with a girl under 16 will no longer arise and so the sentencing guidance which existed prior to the decision in *J*[41] is obsolete. However, where the facts of a case include a separate indecent assault (or any other separate offence) common sense dictates—and the House of Lords concurs[42]—that it is perfectly proper to charge that without the unlawful sexual intercourse. **3.20**

(ii) Sentence must be passed in accordance with the factual basis reflected by a jury's verdict(s).[43]

(iii) The fact that a young person who is indecently assaulted has been sexually abused before may well increase the gravity of the offence and is certainly no mitigation.[44]

(iv) Cases decided before the implementation of an Act which alters the maximum sentences are not to be regarded as authoritative when considering the tariff after the increase.[45]

Upon Conviction/Sentence

(i) Notification applies if complainant/other party was under 18 or defendant is/was sentenced to 30 months or more or to a hospital order subject to a restriction.[46] **3.21**

(ii) Disqualification/barring from working with children/vulnerable adults. See paras 12.135 and 16.33.

(iii) SOPO applies if complainant was under 18 or defendant is/was sentenced to 30 months or more or to a hospital order subject to a restriction.[47]

The SOA 2003 repealed this section in full on 30.4.2004. See paras 3.40 and 3.47 for the offences which now cover indecent assault. **3.22**

---

35 CAA 1981; implementation date 27.8.1981.

36 *R v Bostock* (1893) 17 Cox 700.

37 *R v Mearns* (1990) 91 Cr App R 312.

38 SOA 1956, s 37 and Sch 2(17).

39 2.7.1960; IwCA 1960 was implemented, impacting on sentence for indecent assault, in that by s 2 it amended the SOA 1956, s 37 and Sch 2(17) to increase the sentence to 5 years if the indecent assault was on a girl under 13 years and that fact was stated in the indictment. (Otherwise, the maximum is still 2 years.)

40 SOA 1985, s 3(3). Implementation date 16.9.1985.

41 *R v J* [2004] UKHL 42; the House of Lords, overruling the Court of Appeal ruled that substituting indecent assault to circumvent the time-bar was not lawful.

42 *R v J* [2004] UKHL 42.

43 *R v Gillespie* [1998] Crim LR 139; *R v Isles* [1998] Crim LR 140.

44 *A-G's Reference (No 2 of 1995)* [1996] 1 Cr App R(S) 274.

45 *R v L* [1999] 1 Cr App R 117 CA.

46 SOA 2003, s 80(1) and Sch 3(7). See Chapter 14.

47 SOA 2003, s 80(1) and Sch 3(7). See Chapter 16.

3. Indecent Assault on a Man

Sexual Offences Act 1956, s 15

Introduction

3.23 The SOA 1956 consolidated the law with regard to sexual offences. It introduced the specific offence of indecent assault on a man as well as a woman.

> The use in any provision of this Act of the word 'man' without the addition of the word 'boy', or *vice versa*, shall not prevent the provision applying to any person to whom it would have applied if both words had been used, and similarly with the words 'woman' and 'girl'.[48]

This applies equally for the purposes of the provisions of the SOA 1967[49] and has effect as if the reference to the SOA 1956 included a reference to the SO(A)A 1976.[50]

Definition

3.24 An assault, accompanied with circumstances of indecency on the part of the person assaulting towards the person alleged to have been assaulted.[51]

Proof

3.25
- (i) An intentional assault (any unlawful touching) by D of C;
- (ii) the assault, or the assault and the circumstances accompanying it, are capable of being considered by right-minded persons as indecent; and
- (iii) that D intended not just an assault, but an indecent assault.

Notes

3.26
- (i) Triable either way.
- (ii) A woman may be guilty of this offence;[52] the sexual touching by a woman of a boy under 16, even as part of or preliminary to an act of sexual intercourse and with his consent, is an offence.[53]
- (iii) A boy under the age of 16 cannot in law give any consent which would prevent an act being an assault for the purposes of this section.[54]
- (iv) A man who is a 'defective'[55] cannot in law give any consent which would prevent an act being an assault for the purposes of this section, but a person is only to be treated as guilty of an indecent assault on a mentally disordered man by reason of that incapacity to consent, if that person knew or had reason to suspect him to be mentally disordered.
- (v) Section 39 of this Act (which makes the spouse of the defendant not competent as a witness) does not apply in the case of this section, except on a charge of indecent assault on a boy under the age of 17.[56]
- (vi) Indecent assault on a man is itself an alternative to: buggery; attempt to commit buggery; assault with intent to commit buggery. See paras 5.48 to 5.91.

Indictment

3.27 INDECENT ASSAULT ON A MALE 1.1.1957 to 30.4.2004

48 SOA 1956, s 46.
49 SOA 1967, s 11(3).
50 SO(A)A 1976, s 7(2).
51 *R v Court* [1989] AC 28 HL; defines and sets out the elements of the offence.
52 *R v Hare* [1934] 1 KB 354.
53 *R v Faulkner v Talbot* (1982) 74 Cr App R 1.
54 SOA 1956, s 15(2).
55 '[D]efective' is the term used within the SOA 2003 for a mentally disordered person, as it was within the 1956 Act.
56 See n 57.

Statement of Offence

INDECENT ASSAULT, contrary to section 15(1) of the Sexual Offences Act 1956.

Particulars of Offence

D, on the . . . day of . . . 19/20.., indecently assaulted C, a man/boy (where the person is under 16 years add the age).

Alternative Offences

(i) Attempt to commit the full offence. When indicting offences of attempt, do so under the common law until 27.8.1981;[57] thereafter, under the CAA 1985. See para 1.43. Aver the attempt in both the Statement and Particulars of Offence. **3.28**

(ii) Common assault,[58] **6 months, fine, or both** although this must now be included in the indictment.[59]

Sentence

(i) On indictment: **10 YEARS.**[60] **3.29**

(ii) Summarily: **6 months.**[61]

Upon Conviction/Sentence

(i) Notification applies if complainant/other party was under 18 or defendant is/was sentenced to 30 months or more or to a hospital order subject to a restriction.[62] **3.30**

(ii) Disqualification/barring from working with children/vulnerable adults. See paras 12.135 and 16.33.

(iii) SOPO applies if complainant/other party was under 18 or defendant is/was sentenced to 30 months or more or to a hospital order subject to a restriction.[63]

4. Assault with Intent to Commit Buggery

Sexual Offences Act 1956, s 16

See para 5.75 where this offence is set out. **3.31**

Offences Committed from 1.5.2004 to date

Introduction

On 30.4.2004 ss 14 and 15 were repealed. With the implementation of the SOA 2003 on 1.5.2004 came the introduction of a number of new offences and the re-wording of others. Sentences and the notification provisions were also amended. **3.32**

The umbrella of 'indecent assault' was replaced by a number of potential alternative offences, breaking down the types of assault and the categories of complainant. The SOA 2003 creates offences based on 'touching' as defined in s 79(8) and further explained in *R v H*.[64] Section 3 sexual assault is an example of this. The shift from 'assault' in 'indecent assault' under the old law **3.33**

[57] CAA 1981; implementation date 27.8.1981.
[58] *R v Bostock* (1893) 17 Cox 700.
[59] *R v Mearns* (1990) 91 Cr App R 312.
[60] SOA 1956, s 37(3) and Sch 2(18).
[61] 12 months if CJA 2003, s 282(4) implemented.
[62] SOA 2003, s 80(1) and Sch 3(8); Chapter 14.
[63] SOA 2003, s 104 and Sch 3(8); see Chapter 16.
[64] *R v H* [2005] EWCA Crim 732.

as opposed to 'touching' under the new law in 'sexual assault' is significant, and, in some respects, narrows the scope of the offence. See para 3.37.

3.34 The following section deals only with adult complainants; for sexual assaults upon children see Chapter 4, Part I.

5. Assault by Penetration

Sexual Offences Act 2003, s 2

Definition

3.35 As per Proof.

Proof

3.36 D assaults C by sexual penetration of either the vagina or anus with a part of D's body or anything else when at the time C does not consent and D does not reasonably believe that C consents.

Notes

3.37 (i) Indictable only.

(ii) 'Sexual' is defined by SOA 2003, s 78:

> 'Sexual' touching is sexual if a reasonable person would consider that—(a) whatever its circumstances or any person's purpose in relation to it, it is because of its nature sexual, or (b) because of its nature it may be sexual and because of its circumstances or the purpose of any person in relation to it (or both) it is sexual.

(iii) *R v H*[65] is the leading authority: where s 78(b) applied because the nature of the touching concerned was not inevitably sexual, it would be desirable for a judge to identify two distinct questions for the jury:

- whether they, as 12 reasonable people, considered that, because of its nature, the touching might be sexual;
- and, if so,
- whether, in view of the circumstances and/or the purpose of any person in relation to it, the touching was in fact sexual. It was clear from the use of the words 'because of its nature may be sexual', which would otherwise be surplus, that there were two requirements to s 78(b).

(iv) Consent is defined by the 2003 Act, s 74, to the extent that it provides: 'a person consents if he agrees by choice, and has the freedom and capacity to make that choice.' This definition plainly relates to mental capacity and is important to have in mind when dealing with the often problematic issue of the complainant's lack of capacity through intoxication. The level of intoxication will obviously affect the capability to make a free choice. The government's intention in creating a set of evidential presumptions, was that these would not cover voluntary intoxication leading to incapacity falling short of sleep or a lack of consciousness:

> I have rejected the suggestion that someone who is inebriated could claim they were unable to give consent—as opposed to someone who is unconscious for whatever reason, including because of alcohol—on the ground that we do not want mischievous accusations.[66]

---

[65] [2005] EWCA Crim 732, [2005] Crim LR 735.

[66] Home Office (2002), *Protecting the Public; Strengthening Protection Against Sex Offenders and Reforming the Law on Sexual offences,* Home Office Consultation Paper, Cmnd 5668, November.

However, following the case of *R v Dougal*,[67] the government was considering new legislation on this issue: 'Does the law on capacity need to be changed. Should there be a statutory definition of capacity?'[68]

There has been no further legislation and Court of Appeal has since addressed the question in *R v Bree* [2007].[69] The following extracts are taken from the judgment of the court, delivered by the President of the Queen's Bench Division, Sir Igor Judge:

> This appeal required us to address the effect of voluntary heavy alcohol consumption as it applies to the law of rape.
>
> ...at the start of the trial the prosecution alleged that the appellant raped M when her level of intoxication was so great that she was effectively unconscious. She lacked the capacity to consent, and therefore did not consent. However, by the end of the evidence, the prosecution case against the appellant had changed. The jury were no longer invited to conclude that M had been unable to consent to intercourse because she was unconscious, rather, the prosecution accepted that the gaps in her recollection were probably the result of intoxication, and lack of memory, rather than unconsciousness. The prosecution case, therefore, was not that the complainant lacked the capacity to consent, but that she did not in fact consent to intercourse. Her ability to resist was hampered by the effects of alcohol, but her capacity to consent remained. She knew what was happening. She knew that she did not want to have sexual intercourse, and so far as she could, made that clear. The appellant's case, as we have indicated, was unchanged from start to finish, that notwithstanding, and perhaps because of drink, M was consenting. He reasonably believed that she was.
>
> ...it is clear that for the purposes of the 2003 Act 'capacity' is integral to the concept of 'choice', and therefore to 'consent'.
>
> ...Some of the hugely critical discussion arising after *Dougal* missed the essential point. Neither counsel for the Crown, nor for that matter the judge, was saying or coming anywhere near saying, either that a complainant who through drink is incapable of consenting to intercourse must nevertheless be deemed to have consented to it, or that a man is at liberty to have sexual intercourse with a woman who happens to be drunk, on the basis that her drunkenness deprives her of her right to choose whether to have intercourse or not. Such ideas are wrong in law, and indeed, offensive. All that was being said in *Dougal* was that when someone who has had a lot to drink is in fact consenting to intercourse, then that is what she is doing, consenting: equally, if after taking drink, she is not consenting, then by definition intercourse is taking place without her consent. This is unexceptionable.
>
> ...In our judgment, the proper construction of section 74 of the 2003 Act, as applied to the problem now under discussion, leads to clear conclusions. If, through drink (or for any other reason) the complainant has temporarily lost her capacity to choose whether to have intercourse on the relevant occasion, she is not consenting, and subject to questions about the defendant's state of mind, if intercourse takes place, this would be rape. However, where the complainant has voluntarily consumed even substantial quantities of alcohol, but nevertheless remains capable of choosing whether or not to have intercourse, and in drink agrees to do so, this would not be rape. We should perhaps underline that, as a matter of practical reality, capacity to consent may evaporate well before a complainant becomes unconscious. Whether this is so or not, however, is fact specific, or more accurately, depends on the actual state of mind of the individuals involved on the particular occasion.
>
> ...Considerations like these underline the fact that it would be unrealistic to endeavour to create some kind of grid system which would enable the answer to these questions to be related to some prescribed level of alcohol consumption. Experience shows that different individuals have a greater or lesser capacity to cope with alcohol than others, and indeed the ability of a single individual to do so may vary from day to day. The practical reality is that there are some areas of human behaviour which are inapt for detailed legislative structures. In this context, provisions intended to protect women from sexual assaults might very well be conflated into a system which would provide patronising interference with the right of autonomous adults to make personal decisions for themselves.

---

[67] [2005] Swansea Crown Court; jury directed to return a verdict of 'not guilty' after prosecution counsel informed him that the Crown did not propose to proceed further because they were unable to prove that the complainant had not given consent because of her level of intoxication.

[68] Government Paper after *R v Dougal; Convicting Rapists and Protecting Victims.*

[69] [2007] EWCA Crim 804.

> ... For these reasons, notwithstanding criticisms of the statutory provisions, in our view the 2003 Act provides a clear definition of 'consent' for the purposes of the law of rape, and by defining it with reference to 'capacity to make that choice', sufficiently addresses the issue of consent in the context of voluntary consumption of alcohol by the complainant. The problems do not arise from the legal principles. They lie with infinite circumstances of human behaviour, usually taking place in private without independent evidence, and the consequent difficulties of proving this very serious offence.

(v) Specific intention and defendant's voluntary intoxication: *R v Heard*:[70]

> It is not open to a defendant charged with sexual assault to contend that his voluntary intoxication prevented him from intending to touch. The Judge was accordingly correct, not only to direct the jury that the touching must be deliberate, but also to direct it that the defence that voluntary drunkenness rendered him unable to form the intent to touch was not open to him.[71]

3.38 Following the judgment in *Heard*, it seems that all the sexual offences in the 2003 Act (certainly those in ss 1–4 and 5–15) will be regarded as offences for which a plea of voluntary intoxication is no defence.[72]

3.39 Note also the judgment of the Court of Appeal in *R v H*,[73] an expedited prosecution appeal during trial, during which both *Bree* and *Dougal* were considered. Per Hallett LJ, delivering the judgment of the full court in allowing the appeal:

> Issues of consent and capacity to consent to intercourse in cases of rape should normally be left to a jury to determine. It would be a rare case indeed where it would be appropriate for a judge to stop a case in which, on one view, a 16 year old girl, alone at night and vulnerable through drink, is picked up by a stranger who has sex with her within minutes of meeting her and she says repeatedly she would not have consented to sex in these circumstances.

Indictment

3.40 ASSAULT BY PENETRATION 1.5.2004 to date

Statement of Offence

ASSAULT BY PENETRATION, contrary to section 2(1) of the Sexual Offences Act 2003.

Particulars of Offence

D, on the... day of... 20.., intentionally and sexually penetrated the [vagina] *or* [anus] of C with [his finger] *or* [a part of his body, namely his... or with a...], C did not consent to the penetration, and D did not reasonably believe that C was consenting.

Alternative Offences

3.41 Attempt to commit the full offence. When indicting offences of attempt, do so under the Criminal Attempts Act 1981. Aver the attempt in both the statement and particulars of offence. See para 1.43.

Sentence

3.42 On indictment: **LIFE**.

Sentencing Guidance

3.43 See the Sentencing Guidance Council (SGC) guidelines at App C, pages 320–323.

Upon Conviction/Sentence

3.44 (i) Notification applies.[74]

[70] [2007] EWCA Crim 125.
[71] Per Hughes LJ at para 25.
[72] David Ormerod QC.
[73] [2007] EWCA Crim 2056.
[74] SOA 2003, s 80(1) and Sch 3. See Chapter 2.

(ii) Disqualification/barring from working with children/vulnerable adults. See paras 12.135 and 16.33.
(iii) SOPO applies.[75]

6. Sexual Assault

Sexual Offences Act 2003, s 3

Definition

As per Proof. **3.45**

Proof

D intentionally and sexually touches C who does not consent to it and D does not reasonably believe that C is consenting. **3.46**

Notes

(i) Triable either way. **3.47**
(ii) 'Sexual' is defined by the SOA 2003, s 78.
(iii) The SOA 2003 creates offences based on 'touching' as defined in s 79(8) and further explained in *R v H.*[76] Section 3 sexual assault is an example of this. The shift from 'assault' in 'indecent assault' under the old law as opposed to 'touching' under the new law in 'sexual assault' is significant, and, in some respects, narrows the scope of the offence. Examples which might have been an indecent assault, but would not be a sexual assault under the SOA, s 3 as the offence is based on touching include:
- Sexual words alone without touching.
- Defendant walking towards someone with his penis exposed.[77]
- Soaking the complainant's T-shirt without physical contact.[78]
- Touching the complainant's clothing without touching the person.[79]

(iv) Consent; see notes at para 3.37.
(v) Defendant's intoxication; see notes at para 3.37.

Indictment

SEXUAL ASSAULT 1.5.2004 to date **3.48**

> **Statement of Offence**
> SEXUAL ASSAULT, contrary to section 3(1) of the Sexual Offences Act 2003.
> **Particulars of Offence**
> D, on the... day of... 20.., intentionally and sexually touched C, C did not consent to the touching, and D did not reasonably believe that C consented.
> *OR*:
> D, on the... day of... 20.., intentionally touched C, the circumstances being that the touching was sexual, C did not consent to the touching, and D did not reasonably believe that C consented.

---

[75] SOA 2003, s 104 and Sch 3. See Chapter 16.
[76] *R v H* [2005] EWCA Crim 732.
[77] *R v Rolfe* (1952) 36 Cr App R 4.
[78] J.C. Smith and Brian Hogan, *Criminal Law*, 3rd edn (London: Butterworths, 1973), p 614.
[79] *R v H* [2005] EWCA Crim 732 (note para 26) even though V is not being touched through the clothing.

Alternative Offences

3.49 Attempt to commit the full offence. When indicting offences of attempt, do so under the Criminal Attempts Act 1981. Aver the attempt in both the statement and particulars of offence. See para 1.43.

Sentence

3.50 (i) On indictment: **10 YEARS.**
(ii) Summarily: **6 months.**[80]

Sentencing Guidance

3.51 See the SGC guidelines at App C, pages 323–327.

Upon Conviction/Sentence

3.52 (i) Notification applies if criteria met: see paras 14.02–14.03.[81]
(ii) Disqualification/barring from working with children/vulnerable adults. See paras 12.135 and 16.33.
(iii) SOPO applies.[82]

7. Causing a Person to Engage in Sexual Activity Without Consent

Sexual Offences Act 2003, s 4

Introduction

3.53 This is an offence created by the SOA 2003 covering sexual behaviour which has no direct precedent in law. It is included in this chapter for convenience, although it plainly covers activity which does not necessarily involve an assault by D, such as engaging in a conversation or web chat of a sexual nature.[83] There are a number of similar offences without precedent, for example those relating to child complainants, dealt with at Chapter 4 from para 4.189.

Definition

3.54 As per Proof.

Proof

3.55 Section 4(1): D intentionally causes another person (C) to engage in a sexual activity when C is not consenting and D does not reasonably believe that C is consenting.

3.56 **Penetration**; also indict under s 4(4) where the sexual activity involves or includes:
(a) penetration of C's anus or vagina;
(b) penetration of C's mouth with a person's (X or Y) penis;
(c) penetration of a person's (X or Y's) anus or vagina with part of C's body or by C with anything else;
(d) penetration of a person's (X or Y's) mouth with C's penis.

Notes

3.57 (i) Triable either way if non-penetrative; triable on indictment only if penetration is alleged.

---

[80] 12 months if CJA 2003, s 282(4) implemented.
[81] SOA 2003, s 80(1) and Sch 3; see Chapter 14.
[82] SOA 2003, s 104 and Sch 3; see Chapter 16.
[83] *R v Grout* [2011] EWCA Crim 299, para 29.

(ii) Whether a belief in consent is reasonable is to be determined having regard to all the circumstances, including any steps D has taken to ascertain whether C consents.[84]
(iii) A belief induced by a defendant's mental illness (short of insanity) or personality disorder must be judged by objective standards of reasonableness and not by taking into account the defendant's disorder: *R v B (MA)* at paras 40 and 41.[85] See also para 2.46.
(iv) The evidential and conclusive presumptions (SOA 2003, ss 75 and 76) apply to this section.[86]
(v) This offence is an alternative to rape.
(vi) The parties to the offence can be of either gender and there is no age restriction but note: if C is under 13 the offence should be charged under s 8 (see para 4.33).
If C is a child aged 13, 14 or 15 the offence should be charged under s 10 (see para 4.18).
If D is aged 18 or over and in a position of trust towards C and C is aged 16 or 17, the offence should be charged under s 17 (see para 4.162).
(vi) The extended jurisdiction provisions[87] apply to this section. See Chapter 17.

Indictment

Non-penetrative activity

CAUSING A PERSON TO ENGAGE IN SEXUAL ACTIVITY WITHOUT CONSENT **3.58**
1.5.2004 to date

Statement of Offence

CAUSING A PERSON TO ENGAGE IN SEXUAL ACTIVITY WITHOUT CONSENT, contrary to section 4(1) of the Sexual Offences Act 2003.

Particulars of Offence

D, on the... day of... 20.., intentionally caused C to engage in a sexual activity, namely..., when C did not consent to engage in the said activity and D did not reasonably believe that C was consenting.

Penetrative activity

CAUSING A PERSON TO ENGAGE IN SEXUAL ACTIVITY WITHOUT CONSENT **3.59**
1.5.2004 to date

Statement of Offence

CAUSING A PERSON TO ENGAGE IN PENETRATIVE SEXUAL ACTIVITY, contrary to sections 4(1) and (4) of the Sexual Offences Act 2003.

Particulars of Offence

D, on the... day of... 20.., intentionally caused C to engage in a sexual activity, [namely...,] involving the penetration of... with... when C did not consent to engaging in the said activity and D did not reasonably believe that C was consenting.

Alternative Offences

Attempt to commit the full offence. Indict under the Criminal Attempts Act 1981.[88] Aver the attempt in both the Statement and Particulars of Offence. **3.60**

[84] SOA 2003, s 4(2).
[85] [2013] EWCA Crim 3.
[86] SOA 2003, s 4(3).
[87] SOA 2003, s 72; provides for the prosecution within the jurisdiction of a sexual offence committed outside it. See Chapter 17.
[88] Implementation date 27.8.1981.

Sentence[89]

3.61 On indictment:

(i) Without penetration **10 YEARS.**
(ii) With penetration **LIFE.**

Summarily: **6 months.**[90]

Sentencing Guidance

3.62 See the SGC guidelines at App C, pages 327–331.

Upon Conviction/Sentence

3.63 (i) Notification requirements apply (see Chapter 14).
(ii) Disqualification/barring from working with children/vulnerable adults. See paras 12.135 and 16.33.
(iii) SOPO applicable (see Chapter 16).

Child Complainants

3.64 These are dealt with in Chapter 4, Part 1 and Chapter 6. The following are the direct alternative offences under the SOA 2003 to indecent assault (of a child):

(i) Child not related to Defendant and Defendant not in position of trust:
Sexual Activity with a Child; s 9 SOA 2003; see para 4.106.
(ii) Child Complainant related to the Defendant:
Sexual Activity with a Child Family Member; s 25, SOA 2003; see para 6.64.
(iii) Where D is in a position of trust in respect of C:
Abuse of Position of Trust: Sexual Activity with a Child; s 16, SOA 2003; see para 4.153.

[89] SOA 2003, s 8(3).

[90] 12 months if CJA 2003, s 282(4) implemented.

4

OFFENCES INVOLVING CHILDREN

Introduction

This chapter includes offences committed both against and by children or young persons. Offences committed by those under 18 appear in this chapter together with the offence as set out for an adult defendant, with amended particulars for indictments and information on maximum sentences available. The notification requirements for a child/young person convicted of a sexual offence also differ from those for adults; these are set out in Chapter 14. **4.01**

Where offences cover the same behaviour, notwithstanding that they are called something different, they appear together as a type of offence from 1950 to date; for example, carnal knowledge of a girl, unlawful sexual intercourse with a girl (under 13 and under 16), sexual assault of a child by penetration under 13, and sexual activity with a child involving penetration. Some offences involving children appear in separate chapters, for example where a child is related to the defendant the offence will appear within Chapter 6. **4.02**

The SOA 2003 introduced eight offences in respect of which according to current interpretation of the statute neither consent nor belief in consent are defences (although see footnote 1). Four (ss 5–8 inclusive) relate to victims under 13 and four to offences where the child victim is aged between 13 and 16 (ss 9–13). **4.03**

There will be situations where a decision has to be taken as to which is the correct section to charge on the facts or whether to charge alternative sections. The case of *R v G*[1] reinforces the **4.04**

---

[1] *R v G* [2008] UKHL 37; and the HL decision rejecting a challenge to the decision: *G v UK* [2012] CLR 46.

point that s 5 is a strict liability offence. The CPS Guidance,[2] in cases where a defendant admits sexual activity with a child under 13 but states that the victim consented, is that the proper course is to charge a s 5 offence (rape of a child under 13) and invite the court to hold a Newton hearing. It is stated that on no account should a s 1 rape count be added as an alternative. That Guidance also reflects the clear intention of Parliament that judges should decide the issue of consent when it arises in this way. Notwithstanding that, it could be argued that in appropriate circumstances the fundamental issue of consent ought to be tried by a jury, and a s 1 offence added to the indictment for that sole purpose. It is suggested that an example of such circumstances might be a 12-year-old girl who alleges wholly non-consensual intercourse whereas the defendant in his mid-teens asserts consensual intercourse, albeit with a girl who is in law unable to give consent.

See also para 4.88 *et seq*.

I. Offences Against Children

A. SEXUAL BEHAVIOUR WITH OR TOWARDS A CHILD

Offences committed between 1.7.1960 and 30.4.2004

1. Gross Indecency with a Child

Indecency with Children Act 1960, s 1

4.05 Until the implementation of the IwCA 1960, there was no offence covering a situation where a defendant caused a child to touch him (D) or another in a sexual manner or committed a sexual act in the presence of a child for his (D's) own sexual gratification.

4.06 The IwCA 1960 provides for the offence of gross indecency with/towards a child or incitement of a child to commit an act of gross indecency with D or another (X).

Definition

4.07 For offences committed up until 11.1.2001: D committed an act of gross indecency with or towards a child *under 14* or incited a child *under 14* to commit such an act with D or another (X).

4.08 For offences committed from 11.1.2001:[3] D committed an act of gross indecency with or towards a child *under 16* or incited a child *under 16* to commit such an act with D or another (X).

Proof

4.09 As per Definition; note that the age of the child is an essential ingredient about which the jury must be satisfied and unless it is admitted between the parties as a fact, requires a judicial direction.[4]

Notes

4.10 (i) Triable either way.
(ii) Consent of DPP not required, despite being offence involving 'gross indecency'.[5]

---

[2] App B.
[3] Crime (Sentences) Act 1997 (C(S)A) (Commencement No 2 and Transitional Provisions) Order 1997 (SI 1997 No 2200); not retrospective. Criminal Justice and Courts Services Act 2000 (Commencement Order No 1) 2000.
[4] *R v Goss and Goss* (1990) 90 Cr App R 400 CA.
[5] CJA 1972, s 48.

(iii) A genuine belief that C was 16 or over will afford D with a defence.[6]
(iv) It is necessary to specify the exact age of the child; it is an essential ingredient of the offence[7] and unless admitted requires a judicial direction.[8]
(v) 'With or towards' is to be read as a phrase, not separately.[9]
(vi) The act must be directed towards C, with D at least deriving sexual satisfaction from knowing C is watching him.[10]
(vii) Allowing a young child's hand to remain on D's penis for 5 minutes without more, amounts to an 'invitation' to continue the indecent activity;[11] this invitation is therefore sufficient to be an 'act'.

Indictment

Where D commits an act with or towards C

INDECENCY WITH A CHILD 2.7.1960 to 30.4.2004 **4.11**

Statement of Offence

INDECENCY WITH A CHILD, contrary to section 1(1) of the Indecency with Children Act 1960.

Particulars of Offence

D, on the... day of..., ..., committed an act of gross indecency with or towards C, a child of the age of... years (in that he/by...).

Where D incites C to commit an act

INDECENCY WITH A CHILD 2.7.1960 to 30.4.2004 **4.12**

Statement of Offence

INDECENCY WITH A CHILD, contrary to section 1(1) of the Indecency with Children Act 1960.

Particulars of Offence

D, on the... day of..., ..., incited C, a child of the age of... years, to commit an act of gross indecency with him, the said D/with D (by...).

It may be desirable to specify the act alleged, particularly where there are a number of counts on the indictment, hence the option in brackets '(by...)'. Aver the child's precise age (see Notes at para 4.10). **4.13**

Alternative Offences

(i) Attempt to commit the full offence. When indicting offences of attempted indecent assault before 27.8.1981,[12] do so under common law. Aver the attempt in both the Statement and Particulars of Offence. See para 1.42. **4.14**
(ii) Outraging public decency; indict under common law: sentence at large, see para 10.03.

Sentence

(i) On indictment: **4.15**
- Until 1.10.1997: **2 YEARS.**[13]

[6] *B (A Minor) v DPP* [2000] 2 AC 428 HL.
[7] *R v Goss and Goss* (1990) 90 Cr App R 400 CA.
[8] *R v Radcliffe* [1990] Crim LR 524 CA.
[9] *DPP v Burgess* [1971] QB 432.
[10] *R v Francis* (1989) 88 Cr App R 127 CA.
[11] *R v Speck* (1977) 65 Cr App R 161 CA; *R v B* [1999] Crim LR 594 CA.
[12] CAA 1981; implementation date 27.8.1981.
[13] IwCA 1960, s 1(1).

- From 1.10.1997:[14] **10 YEARS.**[15]

(ii) Summarily: **6 months.**[16]

Upon Conviction/Sentence

4.16 (i) Notification applies[17] (mandatory; see Chapter 14).
(ii) Disqualification/barring from working with children/vulnerable adults. See paras 12.135 and 16.33.
(iii) SOPO applies[18] (see Chapter 16).

4.17 As of 30.4.2004 s 1 of the IwCA 1960 is repealed. From 1.5.2004 s 10 of the SOA 2003 covers this offence.

Offences committed from 30.4.2004 to date

2. Causing/Inciting a Child to Engage in Sexual Activity

Sexual Offences Act 2003, s 10

Introduction

4.18 This is intended to cover situations where the defendant (D) is using a child either alone or together with a third party (X) for D's sexual gratification. It will include circumstances where D is obtaining sexual gratification from merely observing C and X (and others) rather than taking an active role in the sexual activity (as long as he has caused or incited its happening).

4.19 See notes at para 4.23 in respect of the duplication of s 10 and the effects of charging under this section where C is under 13 (covered under s 8 at para 4.33 *et seq*).

4.20 Note: although s 10 relates to defendants over 18, this is one of the four offences for which a defendant under 18 can be prosecuted by virtue of s 13[19] and so that option is set out here as well.

Definition

4.21 As per Proof. The definition of 'sexual' as set out in s 78 applies (see para 3.37).

Proof

4.22 (i) D, aged 18 or over, intentionally cause/incites C to engage in a sexual activity when C is either under 16 (and D does not reasonably believe that C is 16 or over) or C is under 13.
(ii) Penetration; also indict under s 10(2) where the sexual activity involves or includes:
- penetration of C's anus or vagina;
- penetration of C's mouth with another person's (X or Y's) penis;
- penetration of a person's (X or Y's) anus or vagina with a part of C's body or by C with anything else;
- penetration of a person's (X or Y's) mouth with C's penis.

(iii) Where D is under 18 and so liable by virtue of s 13:
- Identical, except in respect of D's age.

---

14 C(S)A (Commencement No 2 and Transitional Provisions) Order 1997 (SI 1997 No 2200).
15 IwCA 1960, s 1(1) as amended by C(S)A 1997, s 52.
16 12 months if CJA 2003, s 282(4) implemented.
17 SOA 2003, s 80(1) and Sch 3; see Chapter 14.
18 SOA 2003, s 104 and Sch 3; see Chapter 16.
19 SOA 2003, s 13 provides for the prosecution of anything which would be an offence under ss 9–12 inclusive if the defendant were aged 18; the maximum sentence is 5 years on indictment under s 13.

Notes

(i) Triable either way if non-penetrative; triable on indictment only if penetration is alleged. **4.23**
(ii) The type of activity is not specified, save that it must be 'sexual' as per the SOA 2003, s 78.
(iii) This offence is an alternative to rape (SOA 2003, s 1; see para 2.47).
(iv) Neither consent nor belief in consent is a defence to this offence.
(v) A belief on the defendant's part that the child is aged 16 or over will afford him a defence, provided that the belief is reasonable.
(vi) Following the judgment in *R v Heard*,[20] it seems that all the sexual offences in the 2003 Act (certainly those in ss 1–4 and 5–15) will be regarded as offences for which a plea of voluntary intoxication is no defence.[21]
(vii) This section duplicates s 8 (causing/inciting a child under 13 to engage in sexual activity) where C is under 13. Where the defendant is 18 or over, it will be appropriate when charging/indicting in such a case to use s 8; s 8 is simpler to indict and explain to a jury, is indictable only reflecting the seriousness of the offence, and has a higher maximum sentence. (Note: s 8 is not available under s 13 when D is under 18.)
(viii) The extended jurisdiction provisions apply to this section.[22] See Chapter 17.

Indictment

Non-penetrative activity where D is over 18

CAUSING (OR INCITING) A CHILD TO ENGAGE IN SEXUAL ACTIVITY 1.5.2004 to date **4.24**

Statement of Offence

CAUSING (OR INCITING) A CHILD TO ENGAGE IN SEXUAL ACTIVITY, contrary to section 10(1) of the Sexual Offences Act 2003.

Particulars of Offence

D, a person of or over the age of 18 years, on the...day of...20.., intentionally caused or incited C to engage in an activity, namely...the circumstances being such that the activity was sexual [C was aged under 16 years (namely..., years) and D did not reasonably believe that C was of or over the age of 16 years] *or* [C was under 13 years].

Penetrative activity where D is over 18

CAUSING (OR INCITING) A CHILD TO ENGAGE IN SEXUAL ACTIVITY 1.5.2004 to date **4.25**

Statement of Offence

CAUSING (OR INCITING) A CHILD TO ENGAGE IN SEXUAL ACTIVITY, contrary to sections 10(1) and (2) of the Sexual Offences Act 2003.

Particulars of Offence

D, a person of or over the age of 18 years, on the...day of...20.., intentionally caused or incited C to engage in an activity, namely...involving the penetration of...with..., the circumstances being such that the activity was sexual [C was aged under 16 years (namely...years) and D did not reasonably believe that C was of or over the age of 16] *or* [C was under 13 years].

---

20 [2007] EWCA Crim 125.
21 Professor David Ormerod, March 2007.
22 SOA 2003, s 72; provides for the prosecution within the jurisdiction of a sexual offence committed outside it. See Chapter 17.

Non-penetrative where D is under 18

4.26 CAUSING (OR INCITING) A CHILD TO ENGAGE IN SEXUAL ACTIVITY 1.5.2004 to date

Statement of Offence

CAUSING (OR INCITING) A CHILD TO ENGAGE IN SEXUAL ACTIVITY, contrary to sections 13(1) and 10(1) of the Sexual Offences Act 2003.

Particulars of Offence

D, a person under the age of 18 years, on the... day of... 20.., intentionally caused or incited C to engage in an activity, namely..., the circumstances being such that the activity was sexual [C was aged under 16 or 13 years (namely... years) and D did not reasonably believe that C was of or over the age of 16 years] *or* [C was under 13 years].

Penetrative where D is under 18

4.27 CAUSING (OR INCITING) A CHILD TO ENGAGE IN SEXUAL ACTIVITY 1.5.2004 to date

Statement of Offence

CAUSING (OR INCITING) A CHILD TO ENGAGE IN SEXUAL ACTIVITY, contrary to sections 13(1), 10(1) and 10(2) of the Sexual Offences Act 2003.

Particulars of Offence

D, a person under the age of 18 years, on the... day of... 20.., intentionally caused or incited C to engage in a sexual activity, (namely...), involving the penetration of... with..., when [C was aged under 16/13 years (namely... years) and D did not reasonably believe that C was of or over the age of 16 years] *or* [C was under 13 years].

Alternative Offences

4.28 Attempt to commit the full offence. When indicting offences of attempt, do so under the CAA 1981.[23] Aver the attempt in both the Statement and Particulars of Offence.

4.29 The SOA 2003 has created a number of possible alternatives which are self-evident; where to prove a particular offence requires elements which are identical to but fewer than another, usually more serious, offence. This will include those offences of assault which do not include penetration as possible alternatives to penetrative offences, if that is evidentially an appropriate course. There will therefore often be occasions on which if the offence charged is not proved in one or more of its elements, the defendant will be guilty of a lesser offence. An obvious example of this would be those offences of penetrative assault where the evidence at trial falls short on the issue of penetration. Prosecutors would be well advised to draft alternatives on the indictment where appropriate, or to apply to add counts where the evidence given at trial reveals an alternative offence, rather than rely on included offences.

Sentence

4.30 (i) Where D is 18 or over (s 10):
- On indictment: **14 YEARS.**
- Summarily: **6 months.**[24]

[23] Implementation date 27.8.1981.

[24] 12 months if CJA 2003, s 282(4) implemented.

(ii) Where D is under 18 (s 13):
- On indictment: **5 YEARS.**
- Summarily: **6 months.**[25]

Sentencing Guidance

4.31 See the Sentencing Guidance Council (SGC) guidelines at App C, pages 345–348. See also paras 12.90–12.106 and 12.133.

Upon Conviction/Sentence

4.32 (i) Notification requirements apply (mandatory but duration halved when D under 18; see Chapter 14).
(ii) Disqualification/barring from working with children/vulnerable adults. See paras 12.135 and 16.33.
(iii) SOPO applies; see Chapter 16.

3. Causing or Inciting a Child under 13 to Engage in Sexual Activity

Sexual Offences Act 2003, s 8

Introduction

4.33 It is suggested that this is the appropriate section under which to charge/indict a defendant where he (D) is using a child under 13, either alone or together with a third party for D's sexual gratification; see notes at para 4.37 for its duplication and the effects of charging under the correct section where C is under 13. It is interesting to note that under s 8, D can be under 18 but will be liable to a maximum of life imprisonment, higher than the identical offence under s 10 and far higher than the 5-year maximum penalty for young offenders convicted of offences under ss 9–12 by virtue of s 13.

4.34 In *Grout*[26] the Court of Appeal held that s 8 creates four offences, each of which must be carried out intentionally. The first is causing penetrative sexual activity; the second is inciting such activity; the third is causing non-penetrative sexual activity and the fourth is inciting such activity. It is therefore important that the charge or indictment specifies which of these offences is being alleged (para 27).

> [T]he offences created by section 8 are directed towards a defendant who intentionally causes or incites *the child*, that is (B) himself or herself, to engage in 'sexual activity'. The offence is not concerned with whether the defendant engages in sexual activity (para 28).

In *Jones*[27] it was made clear that the offence was concerned with incitement of a child and not the effect upon the child.

Definition

4.35 As per Proof.

Proof

4.36 (i) Section 8(1): D intentionally causes or incites another person (C) to engage in a sexual activity and C is under 13.
(ii) Penetration; also indict under s 8(2) where the sexual activity involves or includes:
- penetration of C's anus or vagina;
- penetration of C's mouth with a person's (X or Y's) penis;

[25] 12 months if CJA 2003, s 282(4) implemented.
[26] *R v Grout* [2011] EWCA Crim 299.
[27] *R v Jones* [2007] EWCA Crim 1118, para 16.

- penetration of a person's (X or Y's) anus or vagina with part of C's body by C with anything else;
- penetration of a person's (X or Y's) mouth with C's penis.

Notes

4.37 (i) Triable either way if non-penetrative; triable on indictment only if penetration is alleged.
(ii) This section duplicates s 10 (causing/inciting a child to engage in sexual activity) where C is either under 16 or 13. It will be appropriate when charging/indicting in such a case to use s 8; s 8 is simpler to indict and explain to a jury, is indictable only reflecting the seriousness of the offence, and has a higher maximum sentence.
(iii) Neither consent nor belief in consent is a defence to this offence.
(iv) Following the judgment in *R v Heard*,[28] it seems that all the sexual offences in the 2003 Act (certainly those in ss 1–4 and 5–15) will be regarded as offences for which a plea of voluntary intoxication is no defence.[29]
(v) This offence is an alternative to rape.
(vi) The extended jurisdiction provisions[30] apply to this section. See Chapter 17.

Indictment

Non-penetrative

4.38 CAUSING (OR INCITING) A CHILD UNDER 13 TO ENGAGE IN SEXUAL ACTIVITY 1.5.2004 to date

Statement of Offence

CAUSING (OR INCITING) A CHILD UNDER 13 TO ENGAGE IN SEXUAL ACTIVITY, contrary to section 8(1) of the Sexual Offences Act 2003.

Particulars of Offence

D, on the...day of...20.., intentionally caused or incited C to engage in a sexual activity, namely..., when C was aged under 13 years (namely...years).

Penetrative

4.39 CAUSING (OR INCITING) A CHILD UNDER 13 TO ENGAGE IN SEXUAL ACTIVITY 1.5.2004 to date

Statement of Offence

CAUSING (OR INCITING) A CHILD UNDER 13 TO ENGAGE IN SEXUAL ACTIVITY, contrary to sections 8(1) and (2) of the Sexual Offences Act 2003.

Particulars of Offence

D, on the...day of...20.., intentionally caused or incited C to engage in a sexual activity, (namely...,) involving the penetration of...with...when C was aged under 13 years (namely...years).

---

28 [2007] EWCA Crim 125.
29 Professor David Ormerod, March 2007.
30 SOA 2003, s 72; provides for the prosecution within the jurisdiction of a sexual offence committed outside it. See Chapter 17.

Alternative Offences

Attempt to commit the full offence. When indicting offences of attempt, do so under the CAA 1981.[31] Aver the attempt in both the Statement and Particulars of Offence. **4.40**

The SOA 2003 has created a number of possible alternatives which are self-evident; where to prove a particular offence requires elements which are identical to but less than another, usually more serious, offence. This will include those offences of assault which do not include penetration as possible alternatives to penetrative offences if that is evidentially an appropriate course. There will therefore often be occasions on which if the offence charged is not proved in one or more of its elements, the defendant will be guilty of a lesser offence. An obvious example of this would be those offences of penetrative assault where the evidence at trial falls short on the issue of penetration. **4.41**

Prosecutors would be well advised to draft alternatives on the indictment where appropriate, or to apply to add counts where the evidence given at trial reveals an alternative offence, rather than rely on included offences. **4.42**

Sentence

(i) On indictment: **4.43**
- With penetration: **LIFE.**[32]
- Without penetration: **14 YEARS.**[33]

(ii) Summarily: **6 months.**[34]

Sentencing Guidance

See Sentencing Guidance Council (SGC) guidelines at pages 341–345, also paras 12.90–12.106 and 12.133. **4.44**

Upon Conviction/Sentence

(i) Notification requirements apply; see Chapter 14. **4.45**
(ii) Disqualification/barring from working with children/vulnerable adults. See paras 12.135 and 16.33.
(iii) SOPO (see App B).

B. INTERCOURSE WITH A PERSON UNDER THE AGE OF CONSENT

Offences committed pre-31.12.1956

1. Carnal Knowledge of Girls Aged Under 13

Criminal Law Amendment Act 1885, s 4

Definition

> Any person who unlawfully and carnally knows any girl under the age of 13 years...[35] **4.46**

[31] Implementation date 27.8.1981.
[32] SOA 2003, s 8(2).
[33] SOA 2003, s 8(3).
[34] 12 months if CJA 2003, s 282(4) implemented.
[35] CLAA 1885, s 4.

Proof

4.47 (i) Unlawful sexual intercourse. For 'sexual intercourse', any degree of penetration is sufficient[36] and ejaculation is not required.[37]
(ii) With a girl aged under 13 at the time of the offence.
(iii) Consent is immaterial.

Notes

4.48 (i) Triable only on indictment.
(ii) The irrebuttable presumption[38] at the time that a boy under 14 was incapable of sexual intercourse applies to this offence; he could, however, be convicted of indecent assault.[39]
(iii) It is no defence to a charge under s 4 that the defendant made a mistake as to the girl's age, even if that is based on reasonable grounds.[40]
(iv) There is no limitation of time in respect of prosecuting a s 4 offence.
(v) Consent is immaterial,[41] although where a girl under 13 does not consent a count of rape should be preferred.[42]
(vi) This offence is an alternative to rape.

Indictment

4.49 CARNAL KNOWLEDGE OF A GIRL UNDER 13 Pre-31.12.1956

Statement of Offence

CARNAL KNOWLEDGE OF A GIRL UNDER 13, contrary to section 4 of the Criminal Law Amendment Act 1885.

Particulars of Offence

D, on the... day of... 19.., had carnal knowledge of or sexual intercourse with C, a girl of the age of... (specify age under 13).

Alternative Offences

4.50 (i) Attempt to commit the full offence.[43]
(ii) Indecent assault;[44] **2 YEARS**[45] (see para 3.03).
(iii) Carnal knowledge of 'idiot or imbecile'[46] **2 YEARS** (see paras 7.04–7.10).

Sentence

4.51 On indictment:[47]
- Defendant over 16: **LIFE.**
- Defendant under 16: **Not less than 3 YEARS.**[48]
- Attempt at any age: **2 YEARS.**

Upon Conviction/Sentence

4.52 (i) Notification; not applicable.[49]
(ii) Disqualification/barring from working with children/vulnerable adults. See paras 12.135 and 16.33.

---

[36] *R v Russen* 1 East PC.
[37] *R v Jennings* 4 C&P 249.
[38] *R v Phillips* 8 C&P 736.
[39] *R v Williams* [1893] 1 QB 320.
[40] *R v Prince* [1875] LR 2 CCR 154.
[41] *R v Beale* 10 Cox 157.
[42] *R v Dicken* 14 Cox 8.
[43] Criminal Procedure Act (CPA) 1851, s 9; CLAA 1885, s 4.
[44] By virtue of CLAA 1885, s 9.
[45] OAPA 1861, s 52.
[46] The words used in drafting the Act.
[47] CLAA 1885, s 4.
[48] *R v Cawthron* [1913] 3 KB 168.
[49] SOA 2003, s 80(1) (not listed in Sch 3); see Chapter 14.

(iii) SOPO; not applicable.[50]

As of 31.12.1956, s 4 of the CLAA 1885 is repealed. From 1.1.1957 s 5 (see paras 4.64–4.74) of the SOA 1956 replaces this offence. **4.53**

2. Carnal Knowledge of Girls Aged 13 to 16

Criminal Law Amendment Act 1885, s 5

Definition

> Any person who unlawfully and carnally knows or attempts to have unlawful carnal knowledge of a girl over the age of 13 years[51] and under the age of 16 years... **4.54**

Proof

(i) Unlawful sexual intercourse; for 'sexual intercourse' any degree of penetration is sufficient[52] and ejaculation is not required;[53] **4.55**
(ii) with a girl aged over 13 and under 16[54] at the time of the offence.
(iii) Consent is immaterial.

Notes

A prosecution under s 5(1) (for the full offence or an attempt) cannot be brought more than 12 months after the offence has been committed.[55] In practice, therefore, the offence under this section will no longer appear on an indictment. **4.56**

It is no longer permissible to charge indecent assault as a substitute when the time-bar for an offence under s 5 makes it impossible to charge.[56] A defence is provided to s 5(1) if D is 23 or under, believed C was over 16 and there was reasonable cause[57] to believe that C was over 16 at the time, and it is the first occasion on which he is charged with a s 5 offence.[58] A defence is provided to s 5(1) to prove that at the time when the offence was allegedly committed D had reasonable cause to believe that C was his wife (notwithstanding that a marriage where either party is under 16 shall be void).[59] **4.57**

The presumption at the time that a boy under 14 was incapable of sexual intercourse applies to this offence; he could, however, be convicted of indecent assault.[60] **4.58**

Indictment

CARNAL KNOWLEDGE OF A GIRL Pre-31.12.1956 **4.59**

Statement of Offence

CARNAL KNOWLEDGE OF A GIRL, contrary to section 5(1) of the Criminal Law Amendment Act 1885.

Particulars of Offence

D on the...day of...19.., had carnal knowledge of C, a girl of the age of...(specify age between 13–16).

---

50 SOA 2003, s 104 (not listed in Sch 3); see Chapter 16.
51 CLAA 1885, s 5.
52 *R v Russen* 1 East PC.
53 *R v Jennings* 4 C&P 249.
54 *R v Shott* 3 C&K 206; when the girl is under 13 there cannot be a conviction.
55 CLAA 1928, s 1 and SOA 1956, s 37 Sch II(10)(a) and (b).
56 *R v Jones (Michael)* [2003] 2 Cr App R 8 CA.
57 *R v Banks* [1916] 2 KB 621.
58 CLAA 1922, s 2.
59 AMA 1929, s 1(1) and Marriage Act (MA) 1949, s 2.
60 *R v Williams* [1893] 1 QB 320; 20.9.1993; presumption abolished by SOA 1993, s 1.

Alternative Offences

4.60 (i) Attempt to commit the full offence.[61]
(ii) Indecent assault:[62] 2 YEARS[63] (should be added to the indictment as an alternative).
(iii) Common assault: at common law, sentence at large, unless C consented.[64]

Sentence

4.61 On indictment: full offence and attempt: 2 YEARS.

Upon Conviction/Sentence

4.62 (i) Notification; not applicable.[65]
(ii) Disqualification/barring from working with children/vulnerable adults. See paras 12.135 and 16.33.
(iii) SOPO; not applicable.[66]

4.63 As of 31.12.1956 s 5 of the CLAA 1885 is repealed. From 1.1.1957 s 6 (see para 4.75) of the SOA 1956 replaces this offence.

Offences committed between 1.1.1957 and 30.4.2004

3. Sexual Intercourse with a Girl under 13

Sexual Offences Act 1956, s 5

Introduction

4.64 Also known as unlawful sexual intercourse (or USI) with a girl under 13.

The offence remains essentially the same as under the CLAA 1885: that D had unlawful sexual intercourse with C, she being a girl under 13 at the time of the offence. Sexual intercourse remains as defined at para 4.47 (penetration is sufficient, ejaculation unnecessary).

Definition

4.65 It is an offence for a man[67] to have unlawful sexual intercourse with a girl under the age of 13.[68]

Proof

4.66 (i) Unlawful sexual intercourse. For 'sexual intercourse' any degree of penetration is sufficient and ejaculation is not required.[69]
(ii) With a girl aged under 13 at the time of the offence.
(iii) Consent is immaterial.

Notes

4.67 (i) Triable only on indictment.
(ii) Neither consent nor belief in consent is a defence to this offence.
(iii) It is no defence to a charge under s 5 that D made a mistake as to C's age, even if that is based on reasonable grounds.[70]

---

61 CLAA 1885, s 5.
62 CLAA 1885, s 9.
63 OAPA 1861, s 52.
64 *R v Bostock* 17 Cox 700.
65 SOA 2003, s 80(1) (not listed in Sch 3); see Chapter 14.
66 SOA 2003, s 104 (not listed in Sch 3); see Chapter 16.
67 SOA 1956, s 46; 'man' and 'boy' are interchangeable—no need to aver both.
68 SOA 1956, s 5.
69 SOA 1956, s 44.
70 *R v Prince* [1875] LR 2 CCR 154.

(iv) There is no limitation of time in respect of prosecuting a s 5 offence.
(v) The irrebuttable presumption at the time that a boy under 14 was incapable of sexual intercourse applies to this offence;[71] he could, however, be convicted of indecent assault.[72]
(vi) The full offence of USI with a girl under 13 (SOA 1956, s 5) is a 'serious offence' for the purposes of the PCC(S)A 2000, s 109;[73] that is, a qualifying offence for mandatory life sentences for the second such offence committed after 30.9.1997 where the defendant is over 18.

Indictment

SEXUAL INTERCOURSE WITH A GIRL UNDER 13 1.1.1957 to 30.4.2004 **4.68**

Statement of Offence

SEXUAL INTERCOURSE WITH A GIRL UNDER 13, contrary to section 5 of the Sexual Offences Act 1956.

Particulars of Offence

D, on the... day of... 20.., had sexual intercourse with C, a girl under the age of 13 years (namely... years).

Alternative Offences

(i) Attempt to commit the full offence. **4.69**
(ii) Indecent assault:[74] **5 YEARS** to 16.9.1985[75] if fact of age stated in the indictment (otherwise **2 YEARS** for a female over 13), thereafter **10 YEARS** (see para 3.19).[76]
(iii) The offence is itself an alternative to rape: **LIFE** (see para 2.22).

Sentence

On indictment: **4.70**
- For the full offence: **LIFE.**[77]
- For an an attempt: **7 YEARS.**[78]

Sentencing Guidance

The full offence of USI with a girl under 13 (SOA 1956, s 5) is a 'serious offence' for the purposes of the PCC(S)A 2000, s 109;[79] that is, a qualifying offence for mandatory life sentences for the second such offence committed after 30.9.1997 where D is over 18. It is also a specified offence under the CJA 2003, Sch 15 (dangerousness). See App A. **4.71**

Custodial sentences are usually to be imposed where C is under 13, except where D is of limited intelligence or suffers from a psychological abnormality.[80] **4.72**

Upon Conviction/Sentence

(i) Notification applies.[81] **4.73**
(ii) Disqualification/barring from working with children/vulnerable adults. (See paras 12.135 and 16.33.)

---

71 SOA 1993, s 1 abolished the presumption for acts on or after 20.9.1993.
72 *R v Williams* [1893] 1 QB 320.
73 *R v Offen* [2001] 1 Cr App R 24 (NB: report begins at p 372 despite citation).
74 By virtue of CLAA 1885, s 9.
75 SOA 1956, s 37 and Sch 37, as amended by SOA 1985, s 3(3).
76 See para 3.17. *R v Hodgson* (1973) 57 Cr App R 502.
77 SOA 1956, s 37(3) and Sch 2(2)(a).
78 SOA 1956, s 37(3) and Sch 2(2)(b).
79 *R v Offen* [2001] 1 Cr App R 24 (NB: report begins at p 372 despite citation). Although this case was actually decided at a time when the previous legislation, C(S)A 1997, s 2 applied, the point still stands.
80 *A-G's Reference (No 20 of 1994)*, 16 Cr App R(S) 578.
81 SOA 2003, s 80(1) and Sch 3; see Chapter 14.

(iii) SOPO applies.[82]

4.74 The SOA 2003 repealed this section in full. Two new offences in this area are created; rape of a child under 13 (SOA 2003, s 5) (see para 4.88), assault of a child under 13 by penetration.

4. Sexual Intercourse with a Girl under 16

Sexual Offences Act 1956, s 6

Introduction

4.75 Also known as unlawful sexual intercourse (or USI) with a girl under 16.

The offence remains essentially the same as under the CLAA 1885: that D had unlawful sexual intercourse with C, she being a girl aged between 13 and 16 at the time of the offence. Sexual intercourse remains as defined at para 4.47 (penetration is sufficient, ejaculation unnecessary). Consent is immaterial but if she was not consenting a count of rape should be preferred; unlawful sexual intercourse is a proper alternative to rape and so both can be put before the jury in appropriate circumstances. The only difference between proving this offence and rape is that consent is immaterial here.

Definition

4.76 It is an offence for a man[83] to have unlawful sexual intercourse with a girl... under the age of 16.[84]

Proof

4.77 (i) Unlawful sexual intercourse. For 'sexual intercourse' any degree of penetration is sufficient and ejaculation is not required.[85]
(ii) With a girl aged under 16 at the time of the offence.
(iii) Consent is immaterial.

Notes

4.78 (i) Triable either way.
(ii) A prosecution under s 6 (for either the full offence or an attempt) cannot be brought more than 12 months after the offence has been committed.[86] In practice, therefore, the offence under this section will no longer appear on an indictment or be the subject of a charge.
(iii) It will depend on the facts of the case as to whether it would be an abuse of process to charge indecent assault when the time-bar for an offence under s 5 makes it impossible to charge.[87] Where that is done, however, the court should bear in mind the two-year maximum s 6 USI would have attracted and the sentencing guidelines for s 6 USI.
(iv) A defence is afforded to D if he is under 24, believed C was over 16[88] and there was reasonable cause to believe that C was over 16 at the time, and it is the first occasion on which he is charged with a like offence. Here, a 'like offence' means one under the same section/an attempt, or one under the CLAA 1885, s 5(1) (which s 6 replaced).[89]

---

[82] SOA 2003, s 104 and Sch 3; see Chapter 14.
[83] SOA 1956, s 46; 'man' and 'boy' are interchangeable—no need to aver both.
[84] SOA 1956, s 6(1).
[85] SOA 1956, s 44.
[86] CLAA 1928, s 1 and SOA 1956, s 37 and Sch II(10)(a) and (b); *R v West* [1898] 1 QB 174.
[87] *R v Jones (Michael)* [2003] 2 Cr App R 8 CA.
[88] SOA 1956, s 6(3) and *R v Banks* [1916] 2 KB 621, 12 Cr App R 74.
[89] SOA 1956, s 6(3).

(v) A defence[90] is also provided to s 5(1) by proof that at the time when the offence was allegedly committed D had reasonable cause to believe that C was his wife (notwithstanding that a marriage where either party is under 16 shall be void).[91]
(vi) This offence is an alternative to rape.

Indictment

SEXUAL INTERCOURSE WITH A GIRL UNDER 16 1.1.1957 to 30.4.2004 **4.79**

Statement of Offence

SEXUAL INTERCOURSE WITH A GIRL UNDER 16, contrary to section 6 of the Sexual Offences Act 1956.

Particulars of Offence

D on the...day of...20.., had sexual intercourse with C, a girl under the age of 16 years (namely...years).

It is not necessary to aver the specific age of the girl over and above being under 16, but, depending upon the complexity of the prosecution case, it is good practice to particularize the counts as fully as possible,[92] hence the option contained within brackets. **4.80**

Alternative Offences

(i) Attempt to commit the full offence. When indicting offences of attempt after 27.8.1981, do so under the CAA 1981;[93] prior to that, under common law. Aver the attempt in both the Statement and Particulars of Offence. **4.81**
(ii) Indecent assault:[94] **2 YEARS** to 16.9.1985[95] thereafter **10 YEARS** (see para 3.19).
(iii) The offence is an alternative to rape: **LIFE** (see para 2.35).

Sentence

(i) On indictment:[96] **4.82**
  - For the full offence: **2 YEARS.**
  - For an attempt: **2 YEARS.**

(ii) Summarily:
  - **6 months.**[97]

Sentencing Guidance

Cases where 'virtuous friendship' between teenagers of a similar age culminates in sexual intercourse were distinguished from those where a man in a position of authority sets out to seduce a girl under 16 in his charge; the latter should attract sentences of imprisonment close to the two-year maximum.[98] **4.83**

The SOA 2003 has created specific offences in relation to those who take advantage of the position of trust they are in over those under 18, raising the maximum sentences available. Sentencing guidelines delivered under the previous statutory regime must therefore be considered with some caution. **4.84**

---

[90] SOA 1956, s 6(2).
[91] AMA 1929, s 1(1) and MA 1949, s 2.
[92] See Indictments, para 1.09.
[93] Implementation date 27.8.1981.
[94] CLAA 1885, s 9.
[95] SOA 1956, s 37 and Sch 37, as amended by SOA 1985, s 3(3).
[96] SOA 1956, s 37(3) and Sch 2, (10)(a) and (b).
[97] 12 months if CJA 2003, s 282(4) implemented.
[98] *Practice Statement (Crime: Sentencing)* [1992] 1 WLR 948.

Upon Conviction/Sentence

4.85 (i) Notification applies[99] (mandatory but with an exception for a defendant under 20; see Chapter 14).
(ii) Disqualification/barring from working with children/vulnerable adults. See paras 12.135 and 16.33.
(iii) SOPO applies.[100] See Chapter 16.

4.86 The SOA 2003 repealed the SOA 1956, s 6. Within the umbrella offence of the SOA 2003, s 9, s 9(2)(a) (see para 4.224) specifically replaces the old offence of USI with a girl under 16. In addition, the SOA 2003, s 9(2) expands the ambit of sexual activity with a girl under 16 to include penetrative sexual activity beyond vaginal or anal penetration. In keeping with the rest of the Act, s 9 includes both genders rather than only female children as potential complainants.

Offences committed from 1.5.2004 to date

4.87 The SOA 2003 (implementation date 1.5.2004) substituted the following two offences under s 5 (rape of a child under 13) and s 6 (assault of a child under 13 by penetration) (see para 4.64 for the old offence of USI with a girl under 13 under the SOA 1956).

5. Rape of a Child under 13

Sexual Offences Act 2003, s 5

Introduction

4.88 This offence is arguably one of the replacement offences for the old offence of s 5 USI because consent is not an ingredient of it; a child under 13 is presumed to be unable to give consent. The purpose of the 2003 legislation is to protect children under 13 from themselves as well as from others. However, where the child did in fact consent it is likely to affect sentence, especially where the defendant is also young.[101]

See para 4.04.

Definition

4.89 As per Proof.

Proof

4.90 (i) D intentionally penetrated;
(ii) C's vagina/anus/mouth with his penis and
(iii) at the time C was under 13.
(iv) Consent is no defence.

Notes

4.91 (i) The offence is triable only on indictment.

---

[99] SOA 2003, s 80(1) and Sch 3; see Chapter 14.
[100] SOA 2003, s 104 and Sch 3; see Chapter 16.
[101] *A-G's Ref (Nos 11 and 12 of 2012)* [2012] EWCA Crim 1119; *Cleverley* [2010] EWCA Crim 1842; *A-G's Ref (Nos 74 and 83 of 2007)* [2007] EWCA 2550.

(ii) This offence is an alternative to rape (see para 4.04 for commentary in respect of charging these as alternatives). See para 2.46 for s 1 rape. It is also an alternative to attempted rape (para 2.51), assault by penetration (para 3.35), s 7 sexual assault of a child under 13 (para 4.119), and s 9(2) penetrative sexual activity with a child (para 4.107).

(iii) Neither consent nor belief in consent are defences to this offence. Mistake as to the age of the victim is not a defence to a charge under s 5, making this element one of strict liability.[102] Where it is a defence, the SOA 2003 sets that fact out specifically. Following the judgment in *R v Heard*,[103] it seems that all the sexual offences in the 2003 Act (certainly those in ss 1–4 and 5–15) will be regarded as offences for which a plea of voluntary intoxication is no defence.[104]

Indictment

RAPE OF A CHILD UNDER 13 1.5.2004 to date **4.92**

Statement of Offence

RAPE OF A CHILD UNDER 13, contrary to section 5(1) of the Sexual Offences Act 2003.

Particulars of Offence

D, on the... day of... 20.., intentionally penetrated the [vagina] *or* [anus] *or* [mouth] of C, a person under the age of 13 years (namely... years), with his penis.

Alternative Offences

(i) Attempt to commit the full offence. When indicting offences of attempt do so under the CAA 1981.[105] Aver the attempt in both the statement and particulars of offence. **4.93**

(ii) Sexual assault of a child under 13 (s 7) (see para 4.119).

(iii) Penetrative sexual activity with a child (s 9(2)) (see para 4.107). Note if the elements of a s 5 offence are made out, the prosecution should not charge a s 9 offence instead.[106]

Sentence

On indictment: **LIFE**.[107] **4.94**

Sentencing Guidance

(i) Where the child consented this is likely to affect sentence, especially where the defendant is also young. See *R v Corran; R v Cutler; R v Heard; R v Williams*.[108] See para 12.133. **4.95**

(ii) Where a defendant under 18 is charged under this section rather than under a s 13[109] offence, the court cannot offend Article 8 if it passes an appropriate sentence.[110]

Upon Conviction/Sentence

(i) Notification applies.[111] **4.96**

(ii) Disqualification/barring from working with children/vulnerable adults. See paras 12.135 and 16.33.

(iii) SOPO applies.[112]

---

[102] *R v G* [2006] EWCA Crim 821.

[103] [2007] EWCA Crim 125.

[104] Professor David Ormerod, March 2007.

[105] Implementation date 27.8.1981.

[106] *Tollhurst v DPP* [2008] EWHC 2976 (Admin).

[107] SOA 2003, s 5(2).

[108] [2005] Crim LR 404.

[109] Section 13 governs the prosecution of defendants under 18 who but for their age would commit an offence under ss 9–12; it provides a maximum sentence of 5 years.

[110] *R v G* [2006] EWCA Crim 821.

[111] SOA 2003, s 80(1) and Sch 3; see Chapter 14.

[112] SOA 2003, s 104 and Sch 3; see Chapter 16.

6. Assault of a Child under 13 by Penetration

Sexual Offences Act 2003, s 6

Definition

4.97 Intentional sexual penetration by a person (D) of another's (C's) vagina or anus with either a part of his body or anything else when that other person (C) was under 13.

Proof

4.98 (i) Intentional sexual penetration by a person (D) of another's (C's) vagina or anus;
(ii) with either a part of his body or anything else; and
(iii) at the time C was under 13.

Notes

4.99 (i) Triable only on indictment.
(ii) Although the umbrella offence under s 9 (Sexual Activity with a Child) also covers the elements of this offence, it is suggested that s 6 is the appropriate charge/count where the allegation is sexual intercourse with a girl under 13; s 6 is simpler to indict and explain to a jury, is indictable only, reflecting the seriousness of the offence, and has a higher maximum sentence.
(iii) Neither consent nor belief in consent is a defence to this offence.
(iv) Following the judgment in *R v Heard*,[113] it seems that all the sexual offences in the 2003 Act (certainly those in ss 1–4 and 5–15) will be regarded as offences for which a plea of voluntary intoxication is no defence.[114]
(v) The offence is itself an alternative to rape (specifically, rape of a child under 13); see para 4.88.
(vi) The extended jurisdiction provisions[115] apply to this section. See Chapter 17.

Indictment

4.100 ASSAULT BY PENETRATION OF A CHILD UNDER 13 1.5.2004 to date

Statement of Offence

ASSAULT BY PENETRATION OF A CHILD UNDER 13, contrary to section 6(1) of the Sexual Offences Act 2003.

Particulars of Offence

D, on the...day of...20.., intentionally penetrated the [vagina] *or* [anus] of C, a person under the age of 13 years (namely...years).

4.101 It is not strictly necessary to aver the specific age of the complainant over and above being under 13 but, depending upon the complexity of the prosecution case, its inclusion would help to clarify it in particularizing several counts on an indictment; hence the option contained within brackets.[116]

Alternative Offences

4.102 (i) Attempt to commit the full offence. When indicting offences of attempt, do so under the CAA 1981.[117] Aver the attempt in both the Statement and Particulars of Offence.
(ii) Sexual assault of a child under 13; **14 YEARS**; see para 4.119.

113 [2007] EWCA Crim 125.
114 Professor David Ormerod, March 2007.
115 SOA 2003, s 72; provides for the prosecution within the jurisdiction of a sexual offence committed outside it. See Chapter 17.
116 *R v Rackham* [1997] 2 Cr App R 222.
117 Implementation date 27.8.1981.

Sentence

On indictment: LIFE.[118] **4.103**

Sentencing Guidance

(i) See *R v Corran; R v Cutler; R v Heard; R v Williams.*[119] See para 12.133. **4.104**
(ii) Guidelines which pre-date the Act will still be appropriate to have in mind, particularly given that the maximum sentence remains the same.

Upon Conviction/Sentence

(i) Notification applies.[120] **4.105**
(ii) Disqualification/barring from working with children/vulnerable adults. See paras 12.135 and 16.33.
(iii) SOPO applies.[121]

7. Penetrative Sexual Activity with a Child

Sexual Offences Act 2003, s 9(1) and (2)

Introduction

A defendant under 18 may be prosecuted for this offence under s 13. Within the umbrella offence of s 9 (see para 4.129 for non-penetrative assaults under s 9), s 9(2)(a) covers the old offence of USI with a girl under 16. Section 9(2) in general expands the ambit of such offences beyond sexual intercourse to include other penetrative sexual activity. **4.106**

Definition

As per Proof. **4.107**

Proof

(i) Intentional sexual touching by D of C; **4.108**
(ii) when C is either under 16 (and D does not reasonably believe that C is 16 or over) or C is under 13;
(iii) which involves any of the following:
- penetration of C's anus or vagina with part of D's body or anything else;
- penetration of C's mouth with D's penis;
- penetration of D's anus or vagina with part of C's body;
- penetration of C's mouth with D's penis.

Notes

(i) A penetrative offence under s 9(2) is indictable only. **4.109**
(ii) The offence under s 9(2) is itself an alternative to rape (of a child under 13 where appropriate).
(iii) Neither consent nor belief in consent is a defence to this offence.
(iv) Following the judgment in *R v Heard*,[122] it seems that all the sexual offences in the 2003 Act (certainly those in ss 1–4 and 5–15) will be regarded as offences for which a plea of voluntary intoxication is no defence.[123]

---

[118] SOA 2003, s 6(2).
[119] [2005] Crim LR 404.
[120] SOA 2003, s 80(1) and Sch 3; see Chapter 14.
[121] SOA 2003, s 104 and Sch 3; see Chapter 16.
[122] [2007] EWCA Crim 125.
[123] Professor David Ormerod, March 2007.

(v) The extended jurisdiction provisions[124] apply to this section. See Chapter 17.

Indictment

Defendant is over 18

4.110 PENETRATIVE SEXUAL ACTIVITY WITH A CHILD 1.5.2004 to date

Statement of Offence

PENETRATIVE SEXUAL ACTIVITY WITH A CHILD, contrary to ss 9(1) and (2) of the Sexual Offences Act 2003.

Particulars of Offence

D, a person of at least 18 years, on the... day of... 20.., intentionally and sexually touched C and that touching involved penetration of C's [mouth] *or* [vagina] *or* [anus] with D's penis, (in that he/she...), when C was aged under 16 years (namely... years) and [D did not reasonably believe that C was of or over the age of 16 years] *or* [C was under 13 years].

Defendant is under 18

4.111 PENETRATIVE SEXUAL ACTIVITY WITH A CHILD 1.5.2004 to date

Statement of Offence

PENETRATIVE SEXUAL ACTIVITY WITH A CHILD, contrary to sections 13, 9(1) and (2) of the Sexual Offences Act 2003.

Particulars of Offence

D, a person under the age of 18 years *or* (of... years), on the... day of... 20.., intentionally and sexually touched C and the touching involved penetration of C's [mouth] *or* [vagina] *or* [anus] with D's penis, (in that he/she...), when C was aged under 16 years (namely... years) and [D did not reasonably believe that C was of or over the age of 16 years] *or* [C was under 13 years].

4.112 Where the offence is a penetrative offence under s 9(2), it is necessary to aver the age of the complainant and it may be useful to aver the exact age. Also, depending upon the complexity of the prosecution case, it is good practice where possible to particularize the count(s) as fully as possible, hence the options contained within brackets 'in that he/she...'.[125]

Alternative Offences

4.113 (i) Attempt to commit the full offence. When indicting offences of attempt, do so under the CAA 1981.[126] Aver the attempt in both the Statement and Particulars of Offence.

(ii) Sexual assault of a child under **13 YEARS**; see para 4.119.

Sentence

4.114 On indictment:

- where defendant is 18 or over: **14 YEARS.**[127]
- where defendant is under 18: **5 YEARS.**[128]

[124] SOA 2003, s 72; provides for the prosecution within the jurisdiction of a sexual offence committed outside it. See Chapter 17.

[125] *R v Rackham* [1997] 2 Crim App R 222.

[126] Implementation date 27.8.1981.

[127] SOA 2003, s 9(2).

[128] SOA 2003, s 13(2).

Sentencing Guidance

(i) See *R v Corran; R v Cutler; R v Heard; R v Williams*[129] for recent guidelines. See paras 12.133–12.134. **4.115**
(ii) Guidelines which pre-date the Act should be regarded with caution, bearing in mind that the maximum sentence has been increased dramatically.
(iii) This offence is not a serious specified offence under the dangerous offender provisions of the CJA 2003.[130]

Upon Conviction/Sentence

(i) Notification applies[131] (duration halved when D under 18). **4.116**
(ii) Disqualification/barring from working with children/vulnerable adults. See paras 12.135 and 16.33.
(iii) SOPO applies.[132]

C. SEXUAL ASSAULT UPON A CHILD

Offences committed pre-31.12.1956

1. Indecent Assault Upon a Child

Offences Against the Person Act 1861, s 52

Definition

See paras 3.01–3.09. **4.117**

Offences committed between 1.1.1957 and 30.4.2004

Sexual Offences Act 1956

Definition

See paras 3.10–3.30. **4.118**

2. Sexual Assault of a Child under 13

Sexual Offences Act 2003, s 7

Definition

As per Proof. **4.119**

Proof

(i) D intentionally touches C. **4.120**
(ii) The touching is sexual.
(iii) C is under 13.

[129] [2005] Crim LR 404 and see paras 12.133–12.134.
[130] *R v B* [2009] 1 Cr App R(S) b6 CA.
[131] SOA 2003, s 80(1) and Sch 3; see Chapter 14.
[132] SOA 2003, s 104 and Sch 3; see Chapter 16.

Notes

4.121 (i) Triable either way.
(ii) This offence is an alternative to a number of offences, including: s 5 rape of a child under 13 (para 4.88), s 6 assault of a child under 13 by penetration (para 4.97), s 9 sexual activity with a child (paras 4.107 and 4.129).
(iii) Neither consent nor belief in consent is a defence to this offence.
(iv) Following the judgment in *R v Heard*,[133] it seems that all the sexual offences in the 2003 Act (certainly those in ss 1–4 and 5–15) will be regarded as offences for which a plea of voluntary intoxication is no defence.[134]
(v) The extended jurisdiction provisions[135] apply to this section. See Chapter 17.

Indictment

4.122 SEXUAL ASSAULT OF A CHILD UNDER 13 1.5.2004 to date

Statement of Offence

SEXUAL ASSAULT OF A CHILD UNDER 13, contrary to section 7(1) of the Sexual Offences Act 2003.

Particulars of Offence

D, on the...day of...20.., intentionally touched C, a girl/boy under 13 (namely.. years), in that he/she...eg masturbated C, the circumstances being that the touching was sexual.

4.123 It is not necessary to aver the particular act alleged or to specify the age of the complainant over and above being under 13, but depending upon the nature and complexity of the prosecution case it is good practice, and sometimes essential, to particularize the counts as fully as possible, hence the options contained within brackets.[136]

Alternative Offences

4.124 (i) Attempt to commit the full offence. Indict offences under the CAA 1981.[137] Aver the attempt in both the Statement and Particulars of Offence.
(ii) Section 3 Sexual Assault: **10 YEARS** (see para 3.42).

Sentence

4.125 (i) On indictment: **14 YEARS.**[138]
(ii) Summarily: **6 months.**[139]

Sentencing Guidance

4.126 See the SGC guidelines at App C, pages 338–341. See also paras 12.90–12.106 and 12.133.

Upon Conviction/Sentence

4.127 (i) Notification applies.[140]

133 [2007] EWCA Crim 125.
134 Professor David Ormerod, March 2007.
135 SOA 2003, s 72; provides for the prosecution within the jurisdiction of a sexual offence committed outside it. See Chapter 17.
136 *R v Rackham* [1997] 2 Cr App R 222; see also Indictments, para 1.09.
137 Implementation date 27.8.1981.
138 SOA 2003, s 7(2).
139 SOA 2003, s 7(2). CJA 2003, s 282(2), s 7(3); to be applied for offences committed after 1.5.2004.
140 SOA 2003, s 80(1) and Sch 3; see Chapter 14.

(ii) Disqualification/barring from working with children/vulnerable adults. See paras 12.135 and 16.33.
(iii) SOPO applies.[141]

3. Sexual Activity with a Child

Sexual Offences Act 2003, s 9

A defendant under 18 may be charged with this offence under s 13. **4.128**

Definition

As per Proof. **4.129**

Proof

(i) D intentionally touches C sexually when: **4.130**
(ii) either:
- C is under 16 and D does not reasonably believe C is 16 or over; or
- C is under 13.

(iii) Penetration; also indict under s 9(2) where any of the following are alleged:
- penetration of C's anus or vagina with a part of D's body or anything else;
- penetration of C's mouth with D's penis;
- penetration of D's anus or vagina with a part of C's body or anything else;
- penetration of D's mouth with C's penis.

Notes

(i) Triable only on indictment where penetration averred; otherwise either way. **4.131**
(ii) Neither consent nor belief in consent are defences to this offence.
(iii) Following the judgment in *R v Heard*,[142] it seems that all the sexual offences in the 2003 Act (certainly those in ss 1–4 and 5–15) will be regarded as offences for which a plea of voluntary intoxication is no defence.[143]
(iv) The extended jurisdiction provisions[144] apply to this section. See Chapter 17.

Indictment

Where the activity is non-penetrative

SEXUAL ACTIVITY WITH A CHILD 1.5.2004 to date **4.132**

Statement of Offence

SEXUAL ACTIVITY WITH A CHILD, contrary to section 9(1) of the Sexual Offences Act 2003.

Particulars of Offence

D, under the age of 18/of 18 years/over 18 years/aged…, on the…day of…20.., intentionally touched C sexually in that he/she…eg masturbated C, at a time when C was under 16 (namely… years) and [D did not reasonably believe that C was 16 or over] *or* [C was under 13 years].

If the defendant is under 18 years indict contrary to both ss 13 and 9(1).[145] **4.133**

141 SOA 2003, s 104 and Sch 3; see Chapter 16.
142 [2007] EWCA Crim 125.
143 Professor David Ormerod, March 2007.
144 SOA 2003, s 72 provides for the prosecution within the jurisdiction of a sexual offence committed outside it. See Chapter 17.
145 See Indictment, para 1.45.

Where the activity is penetrative

4.134 SEXUAL ACTIVITY WITH A CHILD 1.5.2004 to date

Statement of Offence

SEXUAL ACTIVITY WITH A CHILD, contrary to section 9(1) and (2) of the Sexual Offences Act 2003.

Particulars of Offence

D, under the age of 18/of 18 years/over 18 years/aged…, on the…day of…20.., intentionally touched C sexually in that he/she…eg masturbated C/ digitally penetrated C's vagina, at a time when C was under 16 (namely…years) and [D did not reasonably believe that C was 16 or over] *or* [C was under 13 years].

4.135 If the defendant is under 18 years indict contrary to ss 13, 9(1) and (2).[146]

Alternative Offences

4.136 (i) Attempt to commit the full offence. Indict offences under the CAA 1981.[147] Aver the attempt in both the Statement and Particulars of Offence.

(ii) Section 3 Sexual Assault: **10 YEARS** see para 3.51; other offences under the SOA 2003 may also be alternatives depending on the factual elements such as age of the child and whether there was penetration or not.

Sentence

4.137 Defendant **18 or over:**[148]

(i) On indictment: **14 YEARS.**

(ii) Summarily: **6**[149] **months.**[150]

4.138 Defendant under **18:**[151]

(i) On indictment: 5 **YEARS.**

(ii) Summarily: **6**[152] **months.**[153]

Sentencing Guidance

4.139 See the SGC guidelines at App C, pages 345–348. See also paras 12.135 and 16.33.

Upon Conviction/Sentence

4.140 (i) Notification applies.[154]

(ii) Disqualification/barring from working with children/vulnerable adults. See paras 12.135 and 16.33.

(iii) SOPO applies.[155]

---

146 See Indictments, para 1.46.

147 Implementation date 27.8.1981.

148 SOA 2003, s 9(2).

149 CJA 2003, s 282(2), s 9(3); to be applied for offences committed after 1.5.2004.

150 SOA 2003, s 9(3).

151 SOA 2003, s 13(2).

152 CJA 2003, s 282(2), s 7(3); to be applied for offences committed after 1.5.2004.

153 SOA 2003, s 9(3).

154 SOA 2003, s 80(1) and Sch 3; see Chapter 14.

155 SOA 2003, s 104 and Sch 3; see Chapter 16.

D. OFFENCES INVOLVING ABUSE OF A POSITION OF TRUST

Offences committed between 8.1.2001 and 30.4.2004

The SO(A)A 2000 created an offence of Abuse of Trust (ss 3 and 4 govern it). This covers sexual relationships between teacher and pupil as well as others in a caring/supervisory position in relation to under 18s. **4.141**

'Position of Trust' is defined[156] thus; briefly, it covers where D is 18 or over and looks after people under 18, and C is such a person in D's care being either: **4.142**

(i) cared for in a hospital/children's/care/nursing home or other similar residential accommodation, or
(ii) in receipt of full-time education at an educational institution.

D 'looks after' if he is regularly involved in caring for, training, supervising, or being in sole charge.

Note, spouses and civil partners are exempt from these offences.[157] In addition sexual relationships that pre-date the position of trust are also not encompassed within these offences.[158]

1. Abuse of Position of Trust

Sexual Offences (Amendment) Act 2000, s 3

Definition

As per Proof. **4.143**

Proof

(i) D, aged 18 or over; **4.144**
(ii) was in a position of trust[159] in respect of C;
(iii) when he had sexual intercourse (vaginal/anal) with C or engaged in any other sexual activity with or directed towards C; and
(iv) C was under 18 at the time.

Notes

(i) Triable either way. **4.145**
(ii) Note: statutory defences:
- actual and reasonable lack of knowledge in respect of either C's age[160] or the position of trust;[161]
- and C were lawfully married at the time.[162]
- If the position of trust and sexual relationship between D and C already existed before the commencement of the SO(A)A 2000.[163]

Indictment

ABUSE OF POSITION OF TRUST 8.1.2001 to 30.4.2004 **4.146**

---

156 SOA(A) 2000, s 4.
157 SOA 2003, s 23.
158 SOA 2003, s 24. It is for the defendant to prove that such a relationship existed before 8.1.2001.
159 See Introductory note at para 4.142; see SO(A)A 2000, s 4 for full definition.
160 SOA 2000, s 3(2)(a).
161 SO(A)A 2000, s 3(2)(b).
162 SO(A)A 2000, s 3(2)(c).
163 SO(A)A 2000, s 3(3).

Statement of Offence

ABUSE OF A POSITION OF TRUST, contrary to section 3(1) of the Sexual Offences (Amendment) Act 2000.

Particulars of Offence

D, on the...day of...20.., being a person of at least 18 years, had sexual intercourse with C, s/he being a person under the age of 18 years, and being at the time in a position of trust in relation to C, in that he looked after persons under the age of 18 years who...

For example:

were resident on the children's ward at...hospital and C was at the time a residential/ in-patient receiving such care at...hospital

or

were in receipt of full-time education at...school and C was at the time receiving such education at...school (D being her English teacher).

Alternative Offences

4.147 Attempt to commit the full offence. When indicting offences of attempt, do so under the CAA 1981.[164] Aver the attempt in both the Statement and Particulars of Offence.

Sentence

4.148 (i) On indictment: **5 YEARS.**
(ii) Summarily: **6 months.**[165]

Upon Conviction/Sentence

4.149 (i) Notification applies.[166]
(ii) Disqualification/barring from working with children/vulnerable adults. See paras 12.135 and 16.33.
(iii) SOPO applies.[167]

Offences committed from 1.5.2004 to date

Introduction

4.150 The SOA 2003 repealed ss 3 and 4 of the SO(A)A 2000. Section 16 of the SOA 2003 replaces this offence but widens its ambit beyond intercourse to include any intentional sexual touching. In addition, three new offences by persons in a position of trust are created; Causing/Inciting Child to Engage in Sexual Activity (s 17; see para 4.162), Sexual Activity in Presence of Child (s 18; see para 4.171) and Causing a Child to Watch a Sexual Act (s 19; see para 4.180).

4.151 These four offences under the 2003 Act essentially mirror the child sex offences under ss 9–12 in terms of elements to be proved, except that the age of the child afforded protection is under 18 rather than under 16 and there is the additional factor of the position of trust the defendant is said to be in. Interestingly, the maximum sentence each of the abuse of trust offences attracts is 5 years, rather than the 14-year maximum attracted by ss 9–12. No doubt those behind the drafting of the 2003 Act intended these offences to reflect situations where consent is not an issue but where young people need to be protected from those taking advantage of them and indeed from themselves in not being able to form a fully mature perspective on such a relationship, hence

164 Implementation date 27.8.1981.
165 12 months if CJA 2003, s 282(4) implemented.
166 SOA 2003, s 80(1) and Sch 3; see Chapter 14.
167 SOA 2003, s 104 and Sch 3; see Chapter 16.

the lower maximum sentences;[168] it has, however, provided an odd anomaly as between similar sections of the Act.

Section 21 of the 2003 Act defines those in a position of trust; s 22 interprets those definitions. Section 23 exempts spouses and civil partners from these offences. Section 24 exempts a defendant where the sexual relationship pre-dated the position of trust. **4.152**

2. Abuse of Position of Trust: Sexual Activity with a Child

Sexual Offences Act 2003, s 16

Definition

As per Proof. **4.153**

Proof

(i) D, aged 18 or over; **4.154**
(ii) intentionally touches another person (C) sexually;
(iii) when D is in a position of trust in relation to C, who is either under 18 (and D does not reasonably believe that C is 18 or over), or under 13.

Notes

(i) Triable either way. **4.155**
(ii) Statutory defences exist in relation to D's knowledge of both C's age and the position of trust but there is in relation to all these latest sexual offences of abuse of trust an evidential burden on D to raise 'sufficient evidence' to show that he either did not know that C was under 18[169] or did not know of the relationship of trust between them[170] (or both, if that is his case). Once D has raised the issue(s) through sufficient evidence, it will be for the prosecution to disprove to the criminal standard.
(iii) The extended jurisdiction provisions[171] apply to this section where C is under 16 at the time. See Chapter 17.

Indictment

SEXUAL ACTIVITY WITH A CHILD BY A PERSON IN A POSITION OF TRUST 1.5.2004 to date **4.156**

Statement of Offence

SEXUAL ACTIVITY WITH A CHILD BY A PERSON IN A POSITION OF TRUST, contrary to section 16(1) and 21(5) of the Sexual Offences Act 2003.

Particulars of Offence

D, a person of at least 18 years, on the... day of... 20.., intentionally touched C sexually (in that he...), when [C was under 18 years and D did not reasonably believe that s/he was of or over the age of 18] *or* [C was under 13] and when D was in a position of trust in relation to C, in that whilst D looked after persons receiving education at... school, C was a pupil receiving education there and D could reasonably be expected to know of the circumstances by virtue of which s/he was in a position of trust in relation to C (in that s/he was C's physical education teacher).

---

168 See CPS charging guidance at App B.
169 SOA 2003, s 16(3).
170 SOA 2003, s 16 (4).
171 SOA 2003, s 72; provides for the prosecution within the jurisdiction of a sexual offence committed outside it. See Chapter 17.

4.157 Note: subsection (5) provides for circumstances where C is receiving education at an institution where D is in a position of trust towards C, hence its addition to the facts of this sample indictment.

Alternative Offences

4.158 (i) Attempt to commit the full offence. Indict under the CAA 1981.[172] Aver the attempt in both the Statement and Particulars of Offence.

(ii) Attempt to commit the corresponding offence under s 9 if there is concern over the proof of D's position of trust, although the higher sentence under s 9 makes that a more attractive primary count to a prosecutor.[173]

Sentence

4.159 (i) On indictment: **5 YEARS.**[174]

(ii) Summarily: **6 months.**[175]

Sentencing Guidance

4.160 See the SGC guidelines at App C, pages 359–363.

Upon Conviction/Sentence

4.161 (i) Notification applies.[176]

(ii) Disqualification/barring from working with children/vulnerable adults.

See paras 12.135 and 16.33.

(iii) SOPO applies.[177]

3. Abuse of Position of Trust: Causing/Inciting a Child to Engage in Sexual Activity

Sexual Offences Act 2003, s 17

Definition

4.162 As per Proof.

Proof

4.163 (i) D, aged 18 or over;

(ii) intentionally causes/incites C to engage in a sexual activity; and

(iii) when D is in a position of trust in relation to C, who is either under 18 (and D does not reasonably believe that C is 18 or over), or under 13; and

(iv) where subsection (2) applies, D knows or could reasonably be expected to know of the circumstances by virtue of which he is in a position of trust in relation to C.

Notes

4.164 (i) Triable either way.

(ii) Statutory defences exist in relation to D's knowledge of both C's age and the position of trust but there is in relation to all these latest sexual offences of abuse of trust an evidential burden on D to raise 'sufficient evidence' to show that he either did not know that C was under 18[178]

---

[172] Implementation date 27.8.1981.

[173] Note, however, that any 'excessive sentence' could offend Article 8.

[174] SOA 2003, s 16(5).

[175] SOA 2003, s 16(5). 12 months if CJA 2003, s 282(4) implemented.

[176] SOA 2003, s 80(1) and Sch 3; see Chapter 14.

[177] SOA 2003, s 104 and Sch 3; see Chapter 16.

[178] SOA 2003, s 17(3).

or did not know of the relationship of trust between them[179] (or both, if that is his case). Once D has raised the issue(s) through sufficient evidence, it will be for the prosecution to disprove to the criminal standard.

(iii) The extended jurisdiction provisions[180] apply to this section where C is under 16 at the time. See Chapter 17.

Indictment

CAUSING A CHILD TO ENGAGE IN SEXUAL ACTIVITY BY A PERSON IN A POSITION OF TRUST 1.5.2004 to date **4.165**

Statement of Offence

CAUSING A CHILD TO ENGAGE IN SEXUAL ACTIVITY BY A PERSON IN A POSITION OF TRUST, contrary to section 17(1) and 21 (4)(a) of the Sexual Offences Act 2003.

Particulars of Offence

D, a person of at least 18 years, on the... day of... 20.., intentionally caused/incited C to engage in a sexual activity, namely..., when [C was under 18 years and D did not reasonably believe that s/he was of or over the age of 18] *or* [C was under 13] and when D was in a position of trust in relation to C, in that whilst D looked after persons receiving treatment at... hospital, C was an in-patient staying and receiving treatment there and D could reasonably be expected to know of the circumstances by virtue of which s/he was in a position of trust in relation to C (in that s/he was C's ward sister).

Note: subsection (4) provides for circumstances where C is being cared for and accommodated at an institution such as a hospital (subsection 4(a)) or care home where D is in a position of trust towards C, hence its addition to the facts of this sample indictment. **4.166**

Alternative Offences

(i) Attempt to commit the full offence. Indict under the CAA 1981.[181] Aver the attempt in both the Statement and Particulars of Offence. **4.167**

(ii) Attempt to commit the corresponding offence under s 10 if there is concern over the proof of D's position of trust, although the higher sentence under s 10 makes that a more attractive primary count to a prosecutor.[182] See para 4.18.

Sentence

(i) On indictment: **5 YEARS.**[183] **4.168**

(ii) Summarily: **6 months.**[184]

Sentencing Guidance

See the SGC guidelines at App C, pages 359–363. **4.169**

Upon Conviction/Sentence

(i) Notification applies.[185] **4.170**

---

179 SOA 2003, s 17(4).

180 SOA 2003, s 72; provides for the prosecution within the jurisdiction of a sexual offence committed outside it. See Chapter 17.

181 Implementation date 27.8.1981.

182 Note, however, that any 'excessive sentence' could offend Article 8.

183 SOA 2003, s 17(5).

184 SOA 2003, s 17(5). 12 months if CJA 2003, s 282(4) implemented.

185 SOA 2003, s 80(1) and Sch 3; see Chapter 14.

(ii) Disqualification/barring from working with children/vulnerable adults. See paras 12.135 and 16.33.
(iii) SOPO applies.[186]

4. Abuse of Position of Trust: Engaging in Sexual Activity in the Presence of a Child

Sexual Offences Act 2003, s 18

Definition

4.171 As per Proof.

Proof

4.172 (i) D, aged 18 or over;
(ii) intentionally engages in a sexual activity for the purpose of obtaining sexual gratification;
(iii) when C is either present or in a place from which D can be observed; and
(iv) knowing or believing that C is aware, or intending that C should be aware, that he is engaging in it;
(v) when D is in a position of trust in relation to C, who is either under 18 (and D does not reasonably believe that C is 18 or over), or under 13; and
(vi) where subsection (2) applies, D knows or could reasonably be expected to know of the circumstances by virtue of which he is in a position of trust in relation to C.

Notes

4.173 (i) Triable either way.
(ii) Statutory defences exist in relation to D's knowledge of both C's age and the position of trust but there is in relation to all these latest sexual offences of abuse of trust an evidential burden on D to raise 'sufficient evidence' to show that he either did not know that C was under 18[187] or did not know of the relationship of trust between them[188] (or both, if that is his case). Once D has raised the issue(s) through sufficient evidence, it will be for the prosecution to disprove to the criminal standard.
(iii) The extended jurisdiction provisions[189] apply to this section where C is under 16 at the time. See Chapter 17.

Indictment

4.174 ENGAGING IN SEXUAL ACTIVITY IN THE PRESENCE OF A CHILD 1.5.2004 to date

Statement of Offence

ENGAGING IN SEXUAL ACTIVITY IN THE PRESENCE OF A CHILD, contrary to section 18(1) and 21(4)(d) of the Sexual Offences Act 2003.

Particulars of Offence

D, a person of at least 18 years, on the... day of... 20.., for the purpose of obtaining sexual gratification, intentionally engaged in sexual activity when C was present/in a place from which D could be observed, when [C was under 18 years and D did not reasonably believe

[186] SOA 2003, s 104 and Sch 3; see Chapter 16.
[187] SOA 2003, s 18(3).
[188] SOA 2003, s 18(4).
[189] SOA 2003, s 72; provides for the prosecution within the jurisdiction of a sexual offence committed outside it. See Chapter 17.

that s/he was of or over the age of 18] *or* [C was under 13] and when D was in a position of trust in relation to C, in that whilst D looked after persons living in a children's home, namely...when C was a child cared for and accommodated there and D could reasonably be expected to know of the circumstances by virtue of which s/he was in a position of trust in relation to C (in that s/he was the home's matron).

Note: subsection (4) provides for circumstances where C is being cared for and accommodated at an institution such as a children's home (subsection 4(d)), hospital, or care home where D is in a position of trust towards C, hence its addition to the facts of this sample indictment. **4.175**

Alternative Offences

(i) Attempt to commit the full offence. Indict under the CAA 1981.[190] Aver the attempt in both the Statement and Particulars of Offence. **4.176**
(ii) The corresponding offence under s 11 if there is concern over the proof of D's position of trust, although the higher sentence under s 11 makes that a more attractive primary count to a prosecutor.[191] See para 4.191.

Sentence

(i) On indictment: **5 YEARS.**[192] **4.177**
(ii) Summarily: **6 months.**[193]

Sentencing Guidance

See the SGC guidelines at App C, pages 363–366. **4.178**

Upon Conviction/Sentence

(i) Notification applies.[194] **4.179**
(ii) Disqualification/barring from working with children/vulnerable adults. See paras 12.135 and 16.33.
(iii) SOPO applies.[195]

5. Abuse of Position of Trust: Causing a Child to Watch a Sexual Act

Sexual Offences Act 2003, s 19

Definition

As per Proof. **4.180**

Proof

(i) D, aged 18 or over; **4.181**
(ii) intentionally causes (C) to either watch a third person (X) engaging in a sexual activity, or to look at an image of any person engaging in a sexual activity;
(iii) when D is in a position of trust in relation to C, who is either under 18 (and D does not reasonably believe that C is 18 or over), or under 13; and

---

[190] Implementation date 27.8.1981.
[191] Note, however, that any 'excessive sentence' could offend Article 8.
[192] SOA 2003, s 18(5).
[193] SOA 2003, s 18(5). 12 months if CJA 2003, s 282(4) implemented.
[194] SOA 2003, s 80(1) and Sch 3; see App Chapter 14.
[195] SOA 2003, s 104 and Sch 3; see Chapter 16.

(iv) where subsection (2) applies, D knows or could reasonably be expected to know of the circumstances by virtue of which he is in a position of trust in relation to C.

Notes

4.182 (i) Triable either way.

(ii) Statutory defences exist in relation to D's knowledge of both C's age and the position of trust but there is in relation to all these latest sexual offences of abuse of trust an evidential burden on D to raise 'sufficient evidence' to show that he either did not know that C was under 18[196] or did not know of the relationship of trust between them[197] (or both, if that is his case). Once D has raised the issue(s) through sufficient evidence, it will be for the prosecution to disprove to the criminal standard.

(iii) The extended jurisdiction provisions[198] apply to this section where C is under 16 at the time. See Chapter 17.

Indictment

4.183 **CAUSING A CHILD TO WATCH A SEXUAL ACT BY A PERSON IN A POSITION OF TRUST** 1.5.2004 to date

Statement of Offence

CAUSING A CHILD TO WATCH A SEXUAL ACT BY A PERSON IN A POSITION OF TRUST, contrary to section 19(1) and 21 (5) of the Sexual Offences Act 2003.

Particulars of Offence

D, a person of at least 18 years, on the... day of... 20.., for the purpose of obtaining sexual gratification, intentionally caused C to watch X engaging in a sexual activity/look at an image of a person engaging in a sexual activity, C was under 18 years at the time and the said D did not reasonably believe that s/he was of or over the age of 18, or C was under 13 and the said D was in a position of trust in relation to C in that whilst D looked after persons receiving education at... school, C was a pupil receiving education there and the said D could reasonably be expected to know of the circumstances by virtue of which s/he was in a position of trust in relation to C (in that s/he was the head teacher).

4.184 Note: subsection (5) provides for circumstances where C is being cared for and taught at an institution such as a school where D is not receiving education and so is in a position of trust towards C, hence its addition to the facts of this sample indictment.

Alternative Offences

4.185 (i) Attempt to commit the full offence. Indict under the CAA 1981.[199] Aver the attempt in both the Statement and Particulars of Offence.

(ii) The corresponding offence under s 12 if there is concern over the proof of D's position of trust, although the higher sentence under s 12 makes that a more attractive primary count to a prosecutor.[200] See para 4.202.

Sentence

4.186 (i) On indictment: **5 YEARS.**[201]

(ii) Summarily: **6 months.**[202]

---

196 SOA 2003, s 19(3).
197 SOA 2003, s 19 (4).
198 SOA 2003, s 72; provides for the prosecution within the jurisdiction of a sexual offence committed outside it. See Chapter 17.
199 Implementation date 27.8.1981.
200 Note, however, that any 'excessive sentence' could offend Art 8.
201 SOA 2003, s 19(5).
202 SOA 2003, s 19(5). 12 months if CJA 2003, s 282(4) implemented.

Sentencing Guidance

See the SGC guidelines at App C. **4.187**

Upon Conviction/Sentence

(i) Notification applies.[203] **4.188**
(ii) Disqualification/barring from working with children/vulnerable adults. See paras 12.135 and 16.33.
(iii) SOPO applies.[204]

E. OFFENCES WITHOUT PRECEDENT

The SOA 2003 has created a number of offences covering sexual behaviour in relation to children either not previously the subject of criminal charges or duplicated at least in part by other offences. **4.189**

1. Engaging in Sexual Activity in the Presence of a Child

Sexual Offences Act 2003, s 11

A defendant under 18 may be prosecuted for this offence under s 13. **4.190**

Definition

As per Proof. **4.191**

Proof

(i) D intentionally engages in a sexual activity for the purpose of obtaining sexual gratification; and **4.192**
(ii) he engages in it when another person (C) is present or is in a place from which D can be observed; and
(iii) D knows or believes that C is aware, or intends that C should be aware, that he is engaging in it; and
(iv) either:
  - C is under 16 and D does not reasonably believe that C is 16 or over; or
  - C is under 13.
(v) Where D is under 18:
  - identical except for D's age.

Notes

(i) Triable either way. **4.193**
(ii) Neither consent nor belief in consent is a defence to this offence.
(iii) Following the judgment in *R v Heard*,[205] it seems that all the sexual offences in the 2003 Act (certainly those in ss 1–4 and 5–15) will be regarded as offences for which a plea of voluntary intoxication is no defence.[206]
(iv) The extended jurisdiction provisions[207] apply to this section. See Chapter 17.

---

203 SOA 2003, s 80(1) and Sch 3; see Chapter 14.
204 SOA 2003, s 104 and Sch 3; see Chapter 16.
205 [2007] EWCA Crim 125.
206 Professor David Ormerod, March 2007.
207 SOA 2003, s 72; provides for the prosecution within the jurisdiction of a sexual offence committed outside it. See Chapter 17.

Indictment

When D is 18 or over

4.194 ENGAGING IN SEXUAL ACTIVITY IN THE PRESENCE OF A CHILD 1.5.2004 to date

> **Statement of Offence**
> ENGAGING IN SEXUAL ACTIVITY IN THE PRESENCE OF A CHILD, contrary to section 11(1) of the Sexual Offences Act 2003.
>
> **Particulars of Offence**
> D, a person of or over the age of 18 years, on the..., day of...20.., for the purpose of obtaining sexual gratification, intentionally engaged in sexual activity when C, a person under the age of 16 years/under the age of 13 years, was present, in a place from which D could be observed, D [knowing] *or* [believing that C was aware] *or* [intending that C should be aware] that he was engaging in such activity, and not reasonably believing that C was aged 16 years or over.

When D is under18

4.195 ENGAGING IN SEXUAL ACTIVITY IN THE PRESENCE OF A CHILD 1.5.2004 to date

> **Statement of Offence**
> ENGAGING IN SEXUAL ACTIVITY IN THE PRESENCE OF A CHILD, contrary to sections 13 and 11(1) of the Sexual Offences Act 2003.
>
> **Particulars of Offence**
> D, a person aged under 18 years, on the...day of...20.., for the purpose of obtaining sexual gratification, intentionally engaged in sexual activity when C a person under the age of 16 years/under the age of 13 years, was present, in a place from which D could be observed, D [knowing] *or* [believing that C was aware], *or* [intending that C should be aware], that he was engaging in such activity, and not reasonably believing that C was aged 16 years or over.

Alternative Offences

4.196 Attempt to commit the full offence. Indict offences of attempt under the CAA 1981.[208] Aver the attempt in both the Statement and Particulars of Offence.

Sentence

4.197 (i) Where defendant is over 18:
- On indictment: **10 YEARS**; summarily: **6 months.**[209]

(ii) Where defendant is under 18:
- On indictment: **5 YEARS**; summarily: **6 months.**[210]

Sentencing Guidance

4.198 See the SGC guidelines at App C, pages 352–356. See also paras 12.90–12.106 and 12.133.

Upon Conviction/Sentence

4.199 (i) Notification applies.[211]
(ii) Disqualification/barring from working with children/vulnerable adults.

---

208 Implementation date 27.8.1981.
209 SOA 2003, s 11(2).
210 SOA 2003, s 11(2).
211 SOA 2003, s 80(1) and Sch 3; see Chapter 14.

See paras 12.135 and 16.33.
(iii) SOPO applies.[212]

2. Causing a Child to Watch a Sexual Act

Sexual Offences Act 2003, s 12

Introduction

In *R v Abdullahi*[213] the Court of Appeal (CA) held that this must be done 'for the purpose of obtaining sexual gratification' but the gratification need not be contemporaneous; so D is guilty if this is done in order to 'groom' a child with a view to sexual activity later. D caused the 13-year-old complainant, whom he plied with drink and drugs, to watch a pornographic film depicting heterosexual and homosexual sexual activity. Subsequently, in his room, he touched the complainant's penis. He was charged with offences under the SOA 2003, ss 12 and 14. It was sufficient that D showed the images for the purpose of obtaining sexual gratification, either by enjoying seeing the complainant looking at the images or with a view to putting him in the mood to provide sexual gratification to D later. **4.200**

A defendant under 18 may be prosecuted for this offence under s 13. **4.201**

Definition

As per Proof. **4.202**

Proof

(i) D, aged 18 or over; **4.203**
(ii) for the purpose of obtaining sexual gratification;[214]
(iii) intentionally causes C to watch a third person engaging in a sexual activity, or to look at an image of any person engaging in a sexual activity; and
(iv) either:
- C is under 16 and D does not reasonably believe that C is 16 or over; or
- C is under 13.

(v) Where D is under 18:
- identical except for D's age.

Notes

(i) Triable either way. **4.204**
(ii) Neither consent nor belief in consent is a defence to this offence.
(iii) *R v Abdullahi*;[215] the gratification which must be proved need not be contemporaneous. This could therefore be charged in respect of activity which is part of sexual 'grooming'.
(iv) The extended jurisdiction provisions[216] apply to this section. See Chapter 17.

Indictment

When D is 18 or over

CAUSING A CHILD TO WATCH A SEXUAL ACT 1.5.2004 to date **4.205**

---

212 SOA 2003, s 104 and Sch 3; see Chapter 16.
213 [2006] EWCA Crim 2060.
214 [2006] EWCA Crim 2060.
215 [2006] EWCA Crim 2060.
216 SOA 2003, s 72 provides for the prosecution within the jurisdiction of a sexual offence committed outside it. See Chapter 17.

> **Statement of Offence**
> CAUSING A CHILD TO WATCH A SEXUAL ACT, contrary to section 12(1) of the Sexual Offences Act 2003.
> **Particulars of Offence**
> D, a person of or over the age of 18 years, on the... day of... 20.., for the purpose of obtaining sexual gratification, intentionally caused C, a person under the age of 16 years/a person under 13 years (namely.. years), to watch X engaging in a sexual activity/look at an image of a person engaging in a sexual activity, D not reasonably believing that C was aged 16 years or over.

When D is under 18

4.206 **CAUSING A CHILD TO WATCH A SEXUAL ACT** 1.5.2004 to date

> **Statement of Offence**
> CAUSING A CHILD TO WATCH A SEXUAL ACT, contrary to sections 13 and 12(1) of the Sexual Offences Act 2003.
> **Particulars of Offence**
> D, a person under the age of 18 years, on the... day of... 20.., for the purpose of obtaining sexual gratification, intentionally caused C, a person under the age of 16 years/a person under 13 years (namely.. years), to watch X engaging in a sexual activity/look at an image of a person engaging in a sexual activity, D not reasonably believing that C was aged 16 years or over.

Alternative Offences

4.207 Attempt to commit the full offence. Indict offences of attempt under the CAA 1981.[217] Aver the attempt in both the Statement and Particulars of Offence.

Sentence

4.208 (i) On indictment:
- Where defendant is over 18: **10 YEARS.**
- Where defendant is under 18: **5 YEARS.**

(ii) Summarily:
- Where defendant is over 18: **6 months.**
- Where defendant is under 18: **6 months.**

Sentencing Guidance

4.209 (i) See most recent the SGC guidelines at App C, pages 352–356.

(ii) This offence usually attracts a lesser sentence than an offence of sexual activity with a child under s 5, 7, 8, 9, or 10; relevant factors include the defendant's age and character, the victim's age, the nature and duration of the act, number of occasions act watched or material observed, the impact on the victim and the degree of remorse shown, and the likelihood of repetition.[218] A victim impact statement should be obtained to assist with this; it may be appropriate for this to be from a parent/guardian. See also paras 12.90–12.106 and 12.133.

[217] Implementation date 27.8.1981.

[218] *R v Corran; R v Cutler; R v Heard; R v Williams* [2005] Crim LR 404.

Upon Conviction/Sentence

(i) Notification applies.[219] 4.210
(ii) Disqualification/barring from working with children/vulnerable adults. See paras 12.135 and 16.33.
(iii) SOPO applies.[220]

3. Arranging or Facilitating the Commission of a Child Sex Offence

Sexual Offences Act 2003, s 14

Introduction

This section makes it an offence for someone to arrange or facilitate the commission of the offences within ss 9–13 either within or outside the jurisdiction; the offence may be committed anywhere in the world. As s 13 provides for the prosecution of a defendant under 18 who has committed one of the ss 9–12 offences, this offence covers all age ranges. Note, however, that s 14 provides no difference in sentencing maxima for young defendants. 4.211

Definition

As per Proof. 4.212

Proof

(i) D intentionally arranges or facilitates something that he intends to do, intends another person to do, or believes that other person will do; 4.213
(ii) in any part of the world; and
(iii) doing it will involve the commission of an offence under any of ss 9–13.

Notes

(i) Triable either way. 4.214
(ii) Statutory defences as set out in s 14(2) and (3) protect those working, for example, in the field of sexual health who act for the protection of a child knowing that, for example, the person they are supplying contraceptives to is either under 16 themselves, or an adult in a sexual relationship with someone who is under 16.
(iii) The extended jurisdiction provisions[221] apply to this section. See Chapter 17.

Indictment

ARRANGING OR FACILITATING THE COMMISSION OF A CHILD SEX OFFENCE 1.5.2004 to date 4.215

Statement of Offence

ARRANGING OR FACILITATING THE COMMISSION OF A CHILD SEX OFFENCE, contrary to section 14(1) of the Sexual Offences Act 2003.

Particulars of Offence

D, on the... day of... 20.. (on or about the day of / between the... day of..., and the... day of...,...), intentionally arranged or facilitated the doing of an act, which he intended to

[219] SOA 2003, s 80(1) and Sch 3; see Chapter 14.
[220] SOA 2003, s 104 and Sch 3; see Chapter 16.
[221] SOA 2003, s 72 provides for the prosecution within the jurisdiction of a sexual offence committed outside it. See Chapter 17.

> do [or intended X to do/believed X would do], the doing of which act would involve the commission of an offence of sexual activity with a child, contrary to section... [9/10/11/12/ and 13] of the Sexual Offences Act 2003, in that he... (set out briefly the act of arrangement/facilitation; this could simply be done by setting out the particular offence under ss 9–12).

4.216 Add s 13 to the statement of offence if D is under 18 (see paras 4.112 and 4.206 for examples).

Alternative Offences

4.217 Attempt to commit the full offence. Indict offences of attempt under the CAA 1981.[222] Aver the attempt in both the Statement and Particulars of Offence.[223]

Sentence

4.218 (i) On indictment: **14 YEARS.**
(ii) Summarily: **6 months.**[224]

Sentencing Guidance

4.219 (i) See the SGC guidelines at App C, pages 356–359.
(ii) Although s 14 does not provide for a lesser sentence for a defendant under 18, arguably an 'excessive sentence' would offend Article 8.[225]

Upon Conviction/Sentence

4.220 (i) Notification applies.[226]
(ii) Disqualification/barring from working with children/vulnerable adults. See paras 12.135 and 16.33.
(iii) SOPO applies.[227]
(iv) A Financial Reporting Order may be made under s 76 of the Serious Organised Crime and Police Act (SOCPA) 2005. As this offence is a lifestyle offence within the PCA 2002.

4. Meeting a Child Following Sexual Grooming

Sexual Offences Act 2003, s 15

4.221 This offence may be committed anywhere in the world. It will be commonly used to deal with situations where a defendant sets up a meeting in order to commit sexual offences upon a child under 16 instigated by D after internet communication, for example in a 'chat room' where his age and identity are easily disguised. This is intended to protect children from themselves as well as from others.

Definition

4.222 As per Proof.

Proof

4.223 D, aged 18 or over, having met or communicated with C on at least two earlier occasions, intentionally meets C or travels with the intention of meeting C in any part of the world and, at the time, D intends to do anything to or in respect of C during or after meeting and in any part of the world, which if done will involve the commission by D of a 'relevant' offence. At the time C

[222] Implementation date 27.8.1981.
[223] *R* [2008] EWCA Crim 619.
[224] 12 months if CJA 2003, s 282(4) implemented.
[225] *R v G* [2006] EWCA Crim 821.
[226] SOA 2003, s 80(1) and Sch 3; see Chapter 14.
[227] SOA 2003, s 104 and Sch 3; see Chapter 16.

must be under 16, and D not reasonably believe that C was 16 or over. The two communications need not have been sexual in nature.[228]

Section 15(2)(a) states that the reference to D having met or communicated with C is a reference to D having met C in any part of the world or having communicated with C by any means from, to or in any part of the world. **4.224**

'Relevant offence'[229] means any of the following: **4.225**

- an offence under this Part (that is, an offence under SOA 2003, ss 1–79; this in fact covers all the offences within the Act);
- anything done outside England and Wales and Northern Ireland which is not an offence within subparagraph (i) or (ii) but would be an offence within subparagraph (i) if done in England and Wales. This is intended to cover offences abroad which are not named under the SOA 2003 but the elements of which constitute an offence within it.

Notes

(i) Triable either way.[230] **4.226**

(ii) Following the judgment in *R v Heard*,[231] it seems that all the sexual offences in the 2003 Act (certainly those in ss 1–4 and 5–15) will be regarded as offences for which a plea of voluntary intoxication is no defence.[232]

(iii) The extended jurisdiction provisions[233] apply to this section. See Chapter 17.

Indictment

MEETING A CHILD FOLLOWING SEXUAL GROOMING 1.5.2004 to date **4.227**

Statement of Offence

MEETING A CHILD FOLLOWING SEXUAL GROOMING, contrary to section 15(1) of the Sexual Offences Act 2003.

Particulars of Offence

D, a person of or over 18 years, having met or communicated with C on (at least) two previous occasions, on the...day of...20.., [intentionally met] *or* [travelled with the intention of meeting] C, a person under the age of 16 years (namely...years), D not reasonably believing that C was aged 16 years, and [intending to do anything to] *or* [in respect of C], [either during] *or* [after the meeting], which if done would involve the commission by D of a relevant offence (namely...).

It is not strictly necessary to aver C's specific age but it is a useful addition and may clarify matters, depending on the complexity of the case. Equally, if there is clear evidence of what the specific offence intended is you may wish to include it, as with the number of occasions on which D communicated with or met C prior to the intended meeting.

Alternative Offences

Attempt to commit the full offence. Indict offences of attempt under the CAA 1981.[234] Aver the attempt in both the Statement and Particulars of Offence. **4.228**

[228] *R v Gavrina* [2010] EWCA Crim 1693, para 16.
[229] SOA 2003, s 15(2)(b).
[230] SOA 2003. s 15(4).
[231] [2007] EWCA Crim 125.
[232] Professor David Ormerod, March 2007.
[233] SOA 2003, s 72 provides for the prosecution within the jurisdiction of a sexual offence committed outside it. See Chapter 17.
[234] Implementation date 27.8.1981.

Sentence

4.229 (i) On indictment: **10 YEARS.**[235]
(ii) Summarily: **6 months.**[236]

Sentencing Guidance

4.230 See the SGC guidelines at App C, pages 356–359.

Upon Conviction/Sentence

4.231 (i) Notification applies.[237]
(ii) Disqualification/barring from working with children/vulnerable adults. See paras 12.135 and 16.33.
(iii) SOPO applies.[238]

5. Other Offences Against Children

4.232 Not covered within this chapter but set out elsewhere:
(i) Incest/offences within the family (Familial Offences, Chapter 6).
(ii) Child prostitution (Prostitution and Trafficking, Chapter 8).
(iii) Indecent photographs of children (Obscene Publications, Chapter 9).

II. Offences committed by Children or Young Persons

4.233 The age of both the complainant and the defendant can make a difference to the maximum sentence. As such, the principle as enunciated in *R v Courtie*[239] applies.

When indicting such offences under the SOA 2003, consider the advantages and disadvantages of undertaking more elements to prove. In terms of sentence, an offence committed by a defendant under 18 will often attract higher maximum penalties if the sections specifying child offences are not used. For example, an allegation of sexual touching by a young man aged 17 on a complainant aged 12 will attract a maximum of 14 years if pleaded simply under s 7 (sexual assault); it would however only attract a 5-year maximum (even if the assault were penetrative) under s 13 (ss 9–12 committed by a defendant under 18).

4.234 By virtue of the SOA 2003, s 13 a person under the age of 18 who does an act which amounts to committing any of the following offences:
(i) sexual activity with a child (s 9);
(ii) causing or inciting a child to engage in sexual activity (s 10);
(iii) engaging in sexual activity in the presence of a child (s 11);
(iv) causing a child to watch a sexual act (s 12), is liable to conviction but will attract a lower maximum sentence on indictment: **5 YEARS** (summarily; still **6 [12] months/fine/both**).

4.235 These appear in this chapter together with the corresponding offence as set out for an adult defendant with amended particulars of indictments and information on available sentences, orders, etc.

---

235 SOA 2003, s 15(4).
236 SOA 2003, s 15(4). 12 months if CJA 2003, s 282(4) implemented.
237 SOA 2003, s 80(1) and Sch 3; see Chapter 14.
238 SOA 2003, s 104 and Sch 3; see Chapter 16.
239 [1984] AC 463; see para 1.38 (Indictments).

Note that in relation to these offences, neither consent nor belief in consent are defences.

Indictments: when indicting, it is suggested that it will be safer to aver both sections; both can be read together to establish the relevant age. It is also suggested that it will be better practice to aver s 13 first, as the principal section under which the count is averred or the charge brought. **4.236**

Youth Court Powers: the maximum available sentence available to the Youth Court is 2 years; however the PCC(S)A 2000, s 91 has been amended by the SOA 2003[240] to allow youths (who have not committed a 'grave crime') to be committed to the Crown Court for trial, where the youth has been charged with an offence under the SOA 2003, s 3, 13, 25, or 26. It is therefore possible for a youth charged under s 13 of the SOA 2003, to be committed to the Crown Court and receive a sentence of up to 5 years' imprisonment. **4.237**

III. Presumption and Determination of Age

A. *DOLI INCAPAX*

At common law there was a rebuttable presumption that a child aged not less than 10 but under 14 years was *doli incapax;* that is, incapable of committing a crime. The presumption was rebutted only if the prosecution proved beyond reasonable doubt, not only that the child caused an *actus reus* with *mens rea,* but also that he knew that the particular act was not merely naughty or mischievous, but 'seriously wrong'. This presumption was abolished on 30.9.1998 by the CDA 1998, s 34.[241] This was intended to put children aged 10 and above on the same footing as adults from the time of the implementation of s 34. The presumption still applies to historic abuse cases pre-dating the implementation of s 34.[242] However, the presumption is rebuttable by evidence that the child knew its actions were 'seriously wrong'.[243] **4.238**

B. PRESUMPTION THAT BOYS UNDER THE AGE OF 14 ARE INCAPABLE OF VAGINAL OR ANAL INTERCOURSE

Section 1 of the SOA 1993 abolished this presumption as from 20.9.1993. It follows that rape cannot be proved against a boy under 14 before 20.9.1993. This change was not retrospective.[244] However, the evidence of penetration can be adduced, and the case can be dealt with as an indecent assault. **4.239**

Note: *R v Claydon*;[245] conviction for buggery quashed on retrospective basis because D was under 14 (13 years old). **4.240**

240 Following Magistrates' Courts Act (MCA) 1980, s 24.

241 *R v JTB* [2009] UKHL 20. Confirms that the presumption and defence are abolished by s 34.

242 CDA 1998 Sch 9 para 1 'nothing in section 34 shall apply in relation to anything done before [its] commencement'. *Fethney* [2011] EWCA Crim 3096.

243 *Bevan* [2011] EWCA Crim 654.

244 *Fethney* [2011] EWCA Crim 3096.

245 [2005] EWCA Crim 2827.

C. DETERMINATION OF AGE

4.241 By s 99(1) of the Children and Young Persons Act (CYPA) 1933, where a person, whether charged with an offence or not, is brought before a court other than for the purpose of giving evidence, and it appears to the court that he is a child or young person, the court must make 'due inquiry' as to the age of that person. In so doing, the court shall take such evidence as may be forthcoming at the hearing of the case.[246]

4.242 Any order or judgment of the court is not invalidated by subsequent proof that the person's age was incorrectly stated.[247] The age of a defendant that is presumed or declared by the court shall, for the purposes of the CYPA 1933, apply.

4.243 Therefore, if subsequent information comes to light, that information has no effect on orders and determinations of the court.

4.244 A similar provision exists for determinations under the MCA 1980.[248]

D. PROVING AGE

4.245 Age can be proven by testimony of someone present at the time of birth. If a birth certificate is produced to prove age, evidence must also be adduced to positively identify the person as the person named in the certificate.[249]

E. DISCRETION TO REMIT CASES FROM THE ADULT MAGISTRATES' COURT TO THE YOUTH COURT

4.246 Adult magistrates' courts that have begun the trial of a defendant believing him to be over 18 have discretion to remit the case to the Youth Court or to continue the hearing in the adult court (if that belief is discovered to be incorrect).[250] The same discretion exists during Youth Court trials.

---

[246] CYPA 1933, s 99(1).
[247] CYPA 1933, s 99(1).
[248] MCA 1980, s 150(4).
[249] *R v Rogers* (1914) 10 Cr App R 276.
[250] CYPA 1933, s 46(1).

5

BUGGERY AND OFFENCES OF INDECENCY

Introduction

Over the years the offences of buggery, assault with intent to commit buggery, gross indecency and procurement have been the subject of review and gradual reform which has resulted in considerable limitation, in line with changes in public opinion. Most importantly, with the passing of the SOA 2000, homosexual acts in private between consenting adults over 16 no longer constituted an offence. The passing of the SOA 2003 repealed the offences featured in this chapter, and extinguished the offence of buggery. One effect of this has been the right of people previously subject to notification to be removed from the register upon application. **5.01**

1. Buggery: Categories of Offences and Related Sentences up to 30.4.2004

The implementation of the SOA 1967 heralded major retrospective changes to the offence of buggery, with its abolition of the criminalization of acts of private and consensual buggery between males over 21. Thereafter, piecemeal amendments to the law have taken place. This has resulted in there being a variety of ways in which the offence is made out, with criteria changing over the years and largely, since 1967, not being retrospective. As a result, a list of offences that may still be prosecuted has been compiled, uniquely for this chapter. See para 5.05. **5.02**

A separate sentencing table has been included. It is important to charge the correct factual scenario (ie specifying age/whether in private and/or consent was given) in order to attract the appropriate maximum sentence. See paras 5.07–5.08. **5.03**

5.04 When considering charge the following key points should be considered:

(i) Male rape ought to be charged as buggery until, and including 2.11.1994, and only as rape thereafter (from 3.11.1994).

(ii) In 1967 private and consensual acts of buggery between males over 21 were decriminalized. This change in the law was retrospective. Acts of consensual buggery by a male upon a female remained an offence up until, and including, 2.11.1994; thereafter no offence was committed. If there was no consent, rape should be charged.

(iii) The age of consent for males was later reduced to 18 in 1994,[1] and then to 16 in 2001.[2] These changes were not retrospective. It follows therefore that consenting 20-year-olds committing acts of buggery and gross indecency in private can still be said to have committed the offence of buggery until 1994, just as two consenting 17-year-old males can be said to have committed the offence of buggery or gross indecency until 2001. However, neither of these offences can be prosecuted as they are time-barred (see paras 5.43 and 5.62).

(iv) Consent to prosecute must be obtained from the DPP for offences of buggery, or for aiding or abetting, counselling or procuring its commission where either of those men were at the time under the age of consent, which by the year 2000 was reduced to 16 (SOA 1967, s 8 as amended by SO(A)A 2000, s 1(1)).

(v) Offences of gross indecency[3] and consensual buggery between males over 16 may not be prosecuted if 12 months or more has expired since the date of the offence.[4]

Offences (Pre-Sexual Offences Act 2003) which may be charged

5.05 (i) Buggery by a male aged 16 and over, with a boy or girl under 16 (where the other party consents), in public or in private.[5,6]

(ii) Buggery by a male aged 16 or over, of a boy or girl under 16 (where there is no consent by the other party) in public or in private.[7] From 3.11.1994 a rape charge is appropriate.

(iii) Buggery by a male aged 16 or over, of a man or woman over 16 without his or her consent, whether or not in private. From 3.11.1994, a rape charge is appropriate.

(iv) Buggery by a male aged under 16, of a person under 16 in public and in private.[8,9]

(v) Buggery of a male or female of any age, otherwise than in private.

(vi) Buggery of an animal (bestiality).

(vii) Buggery of a female over 16, with her consent, in private or public, until 2.11.1994. After which if the act is in private and the female consents, no offence is committed, if the female does not consent, rape ought to be charged.

5.06 In practical terms offences most commonly prosecuted before the change in the law (extending the offence of rape) on 3.11.1994 are (i) to (iii). (See paras 5.10, 5.48, 5.60, 5.63).

---

1 CJPOA 1994, s 145, commencement date 3.11.94.

2 SO(A)A 2000, s 1(1); commencement date 8.1.2001. SO(A)A 2000 (Commencement No 1) Order (SI 2000 No 3303).

3 SOA 1967, s 13.

4 SOA 1967, s 7.

5 Consent of DPP required.

6 If the defendant believes that the victim is 16 or over, then he has a defence. *R v Kumar* [2005] Crim LR CLR 470, [2004] EWCA Crim 3207.

7 Consent of DPP required.

8 Note that before 20.9.1993 males under 14 were presumed incapable of committing this offence. (SOA 1993, ss 1 and 2). Thereafter the presumption of incapability reverts to the age of 10 years (CYPA 1933, s 50). If committed upon a girl or boy under 14, the perpetrator alone is liable. (1 Hale 670; 3 Co Inst 59, 1 East PC 480).

9 Consent of DPP required.

Sentences

The punishment for buggery was defined by statute: 'penal servitude for life'—maximum.[10] In 1967 sentences were revised, these changes being retrospective.[11] 5.07

Table 5.1 Sentencing

5.08

Offence	Date	Max. sentence
Buggery with a boy under 16 (with his consent, whether or not in private)	1.1.1950–30.4.2004	LIFE
Buggery with a boy under 16 (without his consent)	1.1.1950–2.11.1994	LIFE
Buggery with a boy under 16 (without his consent)	3.11.1994–30.4.2004	Charge as rape:[12] LIFE
Bestiality	1.1.1950–30.4.2004	LIFE
Buggery of a female with or without her consent, in private or public	1.1.1950–2.11.1994	LIFE
Buggery of a female without her consent	3.11.1994–30.4.2004	Charge as rape:[13] LIFE
Buggery with a male aged 16 or over without his consent (whether or not in private)	1.1.1950–2.11.1994	10 YEARS
Buggery with a male aged 16 or over without his consent (whether or not in private)	3.11.1994–30.4.2004	Charge as rape: LIFE
Buggery if the accused is over 21 and the other party, male or female, is aged 16–20	1.1.1950–2.11.1994	5 YEARS
Buggery, where the accused is over 21 and the other male is aged 16–18	3.11.1994–30.4.2004	5 YEARS
Buggery, if the accused is under 21 and the other party, male or female, is aged 16–20 and consented (whether in public or private)	1.01.1950–2.11.1994	2 YEARS
Buggery committed between two males over the age of consent, otherwise than in private[14]	1.1.1950–30.4.2004 (offence is time-barred 12 months after commission)[15]	2 YEARS

Sentencing Guidance

Sentences of between three to five years, imprisonment for homosexual offences against boys,[16] 'when there are neither aggravating nor mitigating factors. The place in the bracket will depend on age, intelligence and education'.[17] The Court of Appeal identified aggravating features: 5.09

- physical injury;
- emotional and psychological damage;
- moral corruption;
- abuse of authority or trust;

[10] SOA 1861, s 61.
[11] SOA 1967, ss 3 and 10.
[12] SOA 1994, s 1.
[13] SOA 1994, s 1.
[14] The age of consent reducing to 18 on 2.11.1994, and 16 on 8.1.2001.
[15] SOA 1967, s 7.
[16] Under the age of consent.
[17] *R v Willis* (1974) 60 Cr App R 146, [1975] 1WLR 292 CA.

and in mitigation:
(i) mental imbalance or personality disorders;
(ii) emotional stress.

Offences committed pre-1.1.1957

2. Buggery

Offences Against the Person Act 1861, s 61

Definition

5.10 To commit buggery 'with mankind or with any animal'.

5.11 The essential elements of the offence were governed by common law. Buggery at common law is defined as sexual intercourse per anum:
(i) by a man, with a man;[18]
(ii) by a man with a woman;[19]
(iii) by a man or woman with an animal. An offence is committed if the animal is the perpetrator (the 'agent') or the other party (the 'patient'), and need not be per anum.[20]

Proof

5.12 As per Definition.

Notes

5.13 (i) Trial on indictment only.
(ii) Consent was no defence.[21] Both the perpetrator and the other party (if consenting) were equally guilty.
(iii) However, the SOA 1967 limited the offence substantially, in that buggery between consenting males over the age of 21 was de-criminalized, provided that the act takes place in private.[22] The changes were retrospective.[23]
(iv) It follows that once the Act was passed, such activity was no longer an offence, even if the act of buggery took place before 1967.[24]
(v) The act does not take place in private if more than two people take part or are present, or the act takes place in a lavatory to which the public have or are permitted to have access, whether on payment or otherwise.[25]
(vi) This limitation did not apply to homosexual acts on United Kingdom merchant ships by crew members, until 1994.[26]
(vii) Consent to such acts cannot be given by a man who is suffering from a severe mental handicap,[27] unless the accused proves that he did not know and had no reason to suspect that man to be suffering from such abnormality.

---

18 *R v Jacobs* (1817) Russ & Ry 331.
19 Including husband on wife, *R v Wiseman* (1718) Fortes KB 91.
20 *R v Bourne* (1952) 36 Cr App R 125.
21 *R v Jellyman* 8 C&P 604.
22 SOA 1967, s 1(1) and (2).
23 SOA 1967, s 10.
24 SOA 1967, s 10.
25 SOA 1967, s 1(1) and (2).
26 SOA 1967, s 2, CJPOA 1994, s 146(2).
27 As defined by SOA 1967, s 3A, as a state of arrested or incomplete development of mind which includes severe impairment of intelligence and social functioning.

Indictment

BUGGERY Pre-1.1.1957 **5.14**

> **Statement of Offence**
> BUGGERY, contrary to section 61 of the Offences against the Person Act 1861.
> **Particulars of Offence**
> D, a person of or over the age of 21 years on the..., day of...,...(in a public place, namely...) committed buggery with C (a male person under the age of 21 years, namely of the age of...years) or with X, a woman with/without X's consent.

5.15 The particulars should clarify which factual category of offence is charged and so should include the bracketed material above as appropriate, ie:
(i) ages of parties where relevant;[28]
(ii) whether or not the offence was otherwise than in private;
(iii) whether or not with consent (prior to 1994).

5.16 This is important in order to ensure that the offence attracts the appropriate sentence.[29] See paras 5.07–5.08.

5.17 Separate counts ought to be drafted catering for the relevant combination of factual ingredients which might attract a different maximum punishment. (See para 5.05 for alternative offences.)

Bestiality

5.18 An indictment for bestiality follows the previous example (excluding the bracketed material), but needs to specify in the particulars the type of animal involved. This offence was repealed by the SOA in 2004; a new offence of intercourse with an animal was created (new maximum penalty 2 years' imprisonment).

Alternative Offences

5.19 There are distinct categories for this offence; if the jury are not satisfied in relation to one category they could convict of another. The indictment should contain specific and if necessary separate counts to cater for this.[30] See para 5.05.

5.20 If the entire charge is not made out then attempted buggery may be charged.[31] This offence is also triable only on indictment.

5.21 The maximum sentence is **10 YEARS** if with an animal, a female or a boy under 16.[32] Otherwise the same maximum as for the full offence applies.[33]

ATTEMPTED BUGGERY Pre-1.1.57 **5.22**

> **Statement of Offence**
> ATTEMPTED BUGGERY, contrary to section 62 of the Offences against the Person Act 1861.
> **Particulars of Offence**
> D, on the...day of......attempted to commit buggery with C.

[28] *R v D* [1993] Crim LR 542.
[29] CLA 1967, s 6; *R v Reakes* [1974] Crim LR 615 CA; *R v Courtie* [1984] AC 463.
[30] CLA 1967, s 6; *R v Reakes, R v Courtie.*
[31] OAPA 1861, s 62.
[32] SOA 1967, s 3(4)(b).
[33] CLA 1967, s 7(2) and CAA 1981, s 4(5).

Sentence

5.23 See para 5.21.

Upon Conviction/Sentence

5.24 (i) Notification; not applicable.[34]
(ii) Disqualification/barring from working with children/vulnerable adults. See paras 12.135 and 16.33.
(iii) SOPO; not applicable.[35]

3. Assault with Intent to Commit Buggery

Offences Against the Person Act 1861, s 62

Definition

5.25 To '...commit any assault with intent to commit the same...' (that is, buggery).

Proof

5.26 As per Definition.

Notes

5.27 This offence is triable only on indictment.

Indictment

5.28 ASSAULT WITH INTENT TO COMMIT BUGGERY Pre-1.1.1957

Statement of Offence
ASSAULT WITH INTENT TO COMMIT BUGGERY, contrary to section 62 of the Offences against the Person Act 1861.
Particulars of Offence
D on the...day of...assaulted C with intent to commit buggery with the said C.

Sentence

5.29 On indictment: **10 YEARS.**

Upon Conviction/Sentence

5.30 (i) Notification; not applicable.[36]
(ii) Disqualification/barring from working with children/vulnerable adults. See paras 12.135 and 16.33.
(iii) SOPO: not applicable.[37]

5.31 *The SOA 1956 came into force on 1.1.1957. Section 16(1) covers this offence.*

---

[34] SOA 2003, s 80(1) (not listed in Sch 3): see Chapter 14.

[35] SOA 2003, s 104 (not listed in Sch 3); see Chapter 16.

[36] SOA 2003, s 80(1) (not listed in Sch 3): see Chapter 14.

[37] SOA 2003, s 104 (not listed in Sch 3); see Chapter 16.

4. Indecent Assault upon a Male Person

Offences Against the Person Act 1861, s 62

Definition

Any indecent assault upon any male person. **5.32**

This offence is defined by common law, as an assault in circumstances of indecency.[38] **5.33**

Proof

There was held to be an indecent assault in circumstances where a male forcibly pulled a boy's hand towards his penis,[39] but not when a young girl touched the penis of a male at his invitation.[40,41] **5.34**

Notes

(i) The offence is triable either way. **5.35**
(ii) An indecent assault under s 62 could be committed by a woman.[42]
(iii) Consent is a defence,[43] unless the male is under 16.[44]

Indictment

INDECENT ASSAULT UPON A MALE PERSON Pre-1.1.1957 **5.36**

Statement of Offence

INDECENT ASSAULT UPON A MALE PERSON, contrary to section 62 of the Offences against the Person Act 1861.

Particulars of Offence

D, on the... day of... indecently assaulted C, a male person (under the age of 16 years).

Alternative Offences

(i) An attempt should be charged under common law: **10 YEARS.**[45] **5.37**
(ii) Common assault.[46] This must be charged on the indictment.[47]

ATTEMPTED INDECENT ASSAULT UPON A MALE Pre-26.8.1981 **5.38**

Statement of Offence

ATTEMPTED INDECENT ASSAULT UPON A MALE, contrary to common law.

Particulars of Offence

D, on the... day of...... attempted to indecently assault C, a male person (under the age of 16 years).

Sentence

(i) On indictment: **10 YEARS.**[48] **5.39**
(ii) Summarily: **6 months.**

[38] *Beal v Kelley* (1951) 35 Cr App R 128. See para 3.05.
[39] *Beal v Kelley* (1951) 35 Cr App R 128.
[40] *Fairclough v Whipp* (1951) 35 Cr App R 138.
[41] Later the IwCA 1960 provides that this would be an offence under s 1. See paras 4.07–4.10.
[42] *R v Hare* [1934] 1 KB 354, 24 Cr App R 108.
[43] *R v Wollaston* 12 Cox CCR.
[44] CLAA 1922, s 1.
[45] OAPA 1861, s 62.
[46] *R v Bostock* (1893) 17 Cox 700.
[47] *R v Mearns* (1990) 91 Cr App R 312.
[48] OAPA 1861, s 62.

Upon Conviction/Sentence

5.40 (i) Notification; not applicable.[49]

(ii) Disqualification/barring from working with children/vulnerable adults. See paras 12.135 and 16.33.

(iii) SOPO; not applicable.

5. Gross Indecency between Males

Criminal Law Amendment Act 1885, s 11

Definition

5.41 Any male person who, in public or private, commits or is a party to the commission of, or who procures or attempts to procure the commission by any male person of, any act of gross indecency with another male person.

Proof

5.42 The offence is committed in one of two ways:

(i) committing an act of gross indecency;

(ii) procuring the commission by a man of an act of gross indecency.

Gross indecency is not defined by statute or common law, but would usually cover intercrural (leg or thigh) contact, mutual masturbation or oral–genital contact.[50] The behaviour has to be 'directed towards' or 'against' the other person.[51]

Notes

5.43 (i) These offences (gross indecency and procuring an offence of gross indecency) are triable either way.[52]

(ii) Historically, before the passing of the SOA 1967 consent of the other party was no defence and both parties were liable. However, the SOA 1967 limited the offence substantially, in that where the act takes place in private between consenting males over the age of 21, it is no longer an offence, nor is it an offence in those circumstances to procure the commission of the said act.[53] The changes were retrospective. No male can now be charged with the offence if it took place before 1967.

(iii) Either party is liable for conviction, but for both to be convicted it must be proved that one party committed the act with the other and that they both were acting in concert to behave in a grossly indecent manner (viewed from an objective point of view), even though there has been no physical contact.[54]

(iv) See para 5.13 for the definition of 'private'.

(v) See para 5.04 for restrictions on the defence of consent. This was later reduced to 18 in 1994[55] and 16 in 2000;[56] although these two amendments are not retrospective.

(vi) It follows that consenting 20 year olds committing acts of gross indecency in private can still be said to have committed such an offence until 1994, just as two consenting 17-year-old males can be said to have committed an offence until 2000.

---

49 SOA 2003, s 80(1) (not listed in Sch 3): see Chapter 14.

50 As recommended in the Wolfenden Committee Report.

51 *R v Hall* [1964] 1 QB 273, 47 Cr App R 253; *R v Preece and Howells* (1977) QB 370, 63 Cr App R 28 CA.

52 MCA 1980, s 17 and Sch 1.

53 SOA 1967, ss 1 and 4(3).

54 *R v Hunt* 34 Cr App R 135 CCA.

55 CJPOA 1994, s 43(1).

56 SO(A)A 2000, s (1)(a).

(vii) However these offences cannot be prosecuted as all offences of gross indecency over the age of 16 are time-barred; proceedings must be instituted within 12 months.[57]
(viii) Consent to prosecute must be obtained from the DPP where either of those two men were over the age of consent, which by 2000 had been reduced to 16.[58]

Indictment

GROSS INDECENCY Pre-1.1.1957 **5.44**

Statement of Offence

GROSS INDECENCY, contrary to section 11 of the Criminal Law Amendment Act 1885.

Particulars of Offence

D, a male person, committed or was party to the commission of or procured or attempted to procure the commission of an act of gross indecency with C (a male person under the age of 21, namely...).

Alternative Offences

Sexual Offences Act 1956, s 15

Indecent assault, where there is no consent: **10 YEARS**. See para 3.29. **5.45**

Procurement of gross indecency. Examples of when a charge of procuring (or attempting to procure) an act of gross indecency would be appropriate are where:
(i) a male persuaded, or attempted to persuade, a young boy to touch his penis;[59]
(ii) two individuals were talking about their desire to act indecently together.[60]

Sentence

On indictment: **5.46**
(i) an act of gross indecency by a male over the age of 21 with another male under the age of consent: **5 YEARS**;[61]
(ii) procuring or attempting to procure the commission by a male of gross indecency under the age of consent: **5 YEARS**;[62]
(iii) otherwise for an act of gross indecency (or attempting to procure the same) between males over the age of consent: **2 YEARS**;[63]
(iv) attempting to commit an act of gross indecency; as points (i) and (iii).[64]

Upon Conviction/Sentence

(i) Notification; not applicable.[65] **5.47**
(ii) Disqualification/barring from working with children/vulnerable adults. See paras 12.135 and 16.33.
(iii) SOPO: not applicable.[66]

---

57 SOA 1967, s 7.
58 SOA 1967, s 8.
59 *R v Burrows* 35 Cr App R 180.
60 *R v Miskell* 37 Cr App R 214.
61 SOA 1956, s 37, CJPOA 1994, s 144.
62 SOA 1956, s 37, CJPOA 1994, s 144.
63 SOA 1956, s 37, CJPOA 1994, s 144.
64 CAA 1981, ss 1 and 4.
65 SOA 2003, s 80(1) (not listed in Sch 3): see Chapter 14.
66 SOA 2003, s 104 (not listed in Sch 3); see Chapter 16.

Offences committed between 1.1.1957 and 30.4.2004

6. Buggery

Sexual Offences Act 1956, s 12

5.48 The SOA 1956 consolidated the law with regard to sexual offences and repealed s 61 of the OAPA 1861.

Section 12 of the SOA 1956 is substituted.[67]

Definition

5.49 It is an offence for a person to commit buggery with another person or with an animal.

Proof

5.50 As per Definition; also see paras 5.02–5.06.

Indictment

5.51 BUGGERY 1.1.1957 to 21.7.1967

Statement of Offence

BUGGERY, contrary to section 12(1) of the Sexual Offences Act 1956.

Particulars of Offence

D a person of or over the age of 21 years on the... day of... committed buggery with C (in a public place, namely...) or with C, a male person under the age of 21 years (namely of the age of... years), or with C, a male person, with/without his consent, or with C, a woman.

Alternative Offences

5.52 Attempted buggery. From 1.1.1957 until 26.8.1981 to indict an offence of attempted buggery; the Statement of Offence should read simply 'Attempted Buggery' and the particulars as above with the addition of the word 'attempted'. The maximum sentence is **10 YEARS**.

Sentence

5.53 See para 5.08.

Upon Conviction/Sentence

5.54 (i) Notification; applies if criteria met.[68]
(ii) Disqualification/barring from working with children/vulnerable adults. See paras 12.135 and 16.33.
(iii) SOPO: applies if criteria met.[69]

---

[67] SOA 1956, s 51 and Sch 4, commencement date 1.1.57.

[68] SOA 2003, s 80(1) and Sch 3; see Chapter 14.

[69] SOA 2003, s 104 and Sch 3; see Chapter 16.

22.7.1967 to 2.11.1994

Notes

For indictments during this period, the model for 1.1.1957 onwards (see para 5.51) should be used. In addition, the following might be added at the end of the Statement of Offence: 'and section 3(1)(a) of the Sexual Offences Act 1967'. **5.55**

Alternative Offences

Attempted Buggery. Pursuant to the enactment of the CAA 1981 (27.8.1981)[70] an attempted buggery ought to be framed as below from 27.8.1981 to 30.4.2004. **5.56**

ATTEMPTED BUGGERY 27.8.1981 to 30.4.2004 **5.57**

Statement of Offence

ATTEMPTED BUGGERY contrary to section 1(1) of the Criminal Attempts Act 1981.

Particulars of Offence

D on the... day of... attempted to commit buggery with C (in a public place, namely...) or with C, a male person under the age of 21 years (namely of the age of... years), or with C, a woman.

Sentence

As per maximum for full offence, see para 5.08. **5.58**

Upon Conviction/Sentence

(i) Notification; applies if criteria met.[71] **5.59**
(ii) Disqualification/barring from working with children/vulnerable adults. See paras 12.135 and 16.33.
(iii) SOPO: applies if criteria met.[72]

3.11.1994 to 7.1.2001

Definition

See para 5.49. **5.60**

Proof

See paras 5.02–5.06. **5.61**

Notes

The CJPOA 1994 (as of 3.11.94) reduced the age of consent for homosexual acts to 18.[73] This was not retrospective. However, acts of consensual buggery committed between males aged 18–20 before 3.11.1994, are time-barred after one year. **5.62**

---

[70] CAA 1981, s 11(1).
[71] SOA 2003, s 80(1) and Sch 3; see Chapter 14.
[72] SOA 2003, s 104 and Sch 3; see Chapter 16.
[73] Section 143(1) and (3) insert paras (1A) to (1C) into SOA 1956, s 12. As such, the charge does not need to state the 1967 Act.

5.63 Further, non-consensual acts of buggery are from 1994 defined as rape.[74] If there is a lack of consent then rape ought to be alleged. There is no longer any power for the judge to sentence an offence of buggery on the basis of there being a lack of consent.[75]

Indictment

5.64 BUGGERY 3.11.1994 to 7.1.2001

> **Statement of Offence**
> BUGGERY, contrary to section 12(1) of the Sexual Offences Act 1956.
> **Particulars of Offence**
> D (a person of, or over the age of 21) on the... day of..., committed buggery with C (a person under the age of 18 years, namely...) (in a public place, namely...) or with C, a woman.

Alternative Offences

5.65 See para 5.56.

Sentence

5.66 See para 5.08.

Upon Conviction/Sentence

5.67 (i) Notification; applies if criteria met.[76]
(ii) Disqualification/barring from working with children/vulnerable adults. See paras 12.135 and 16.33.
(iii) SOPO: applies if criteria met.[77]

8.1.2001 to 30.4.2004

Definition

5.68 See para 5.49.

Proof

5.69 See paras 5.02–5.06.

Notes

5.70 The SOA 2000 reduced the age of consent to 16.[78] This was not retrospective. However, acts of buggery between 16–17-year-old males before 3.11.1994 cannot be prosecuted as they are time-barred by one year.

From 1.5.2004

5.71 As of 1.5.2004 the SOA 2003 came into force.[79] This Act modernizes the law in relation to sexual offences and represents a complete overhaul of the law.

---

74 SOA 1956, s 1 as amended by CJPOA 1994, s 142.
75 *R v Davies* [1998] 1 Cr App R(S) 380 CA.
76 SOA 2003, s 80(1) and Sch 3; see Chapter 14.
77 SOA 2003, s 104 and Sch 3; see Chapter 16.
78 SOA 2003, s 1(1), commencement date 8.1.2001; SO(A)A 2000 (Commencement No 1) Order 2000 (SI 2000 No 3303).
79 (Commencement) Order 2004 (SI 2004 No 874).

Two offences under the old law no longer exist, that is consensual anal intercourse otherwise than in private,[80] and procuring a man to commit buggery in private.[81] For the former, depending on the facts, the common law offence of committing an act outraging public decency may be charged. See paras 10.03–10.13. **5.72**

Buggery of a child under the age of consent[82] is now covered by both: **5.73**

(i) SOA 2003, s 5—rape of a child under 13 (see paras 4.88–4.96).
(ii) SOA 2003, s 1—rape per anum (see paras 2.47–2.54).

Bestiality[83] is now covered by the SOA 2003, s 69—intercourse with an animal. This offence is triable either way and attracts a maximum sentence of **2 YEARS**. **5.74**

7. Assault with Intent to Commit Buggery

Sexual Offences Act 1956, s 16(1)

Definition

To 'assault another person with intent to commit buggery'. **5.75**

Proof

As per Definition. **5.76**

Notes

(i) This offence is triable only on indictment. **5.77**
(ii) The SOA 1956 consolidated the law with regard to sexual offences (as of 1.1.1957). OAPA 1861, s 62 was repealed and SOA 1956, s 16 substituted.

Indictment

ASSAULT WITH INTENT TO COMMIT BUGGERY 1.1.1957 to 30.4.2004 **5.78**

Statement of Offence
ASSAULT WITH INTENT TO COMMIT BUGGERY, contrary to section 16(1) of the Sexual Offences Act 1956.
Particulars of Offence
D on the…day of…assaulted C with intent to commit buggery with the said C.

Sentence

On indictment: **10 YEARS**. **5.79**

Upon Conviction/Sentence

(i) Notification; applicable if criteria met.[84] **5.80**
(ii) Disqualification/barring from working with children/vulnerable adults. See paras 12.135 and 16.33.
(iii) SOPO: applicable if criteria met.[85]

[80] SOA 1956, s 12.
[81] SOA 1956, s 4.
[82] SOA 1956, s 12.
[83] SOA 1956, s 12.
[84] SOA 2003, s 80(1) and Sch 3; see Chapter 14.
[85] SOA 2003, s 104 and Sch 3; see Chapter 16.

3.11.1994 to 30.4.2004

5.81 Once the CJPOA 1994 was passed, classifying non-consensual buggery as rape, an anomaly occurs. This offence was not re-classified to cover assault with intent to commit anal rape.[86] It is therefore an offence to assault another with intent to bugger, which includes the offence of anal rape post-1994. For offences committed after 3.11.1994 the offence would rarely in practice be charged. The sentence remained at 10 years' imprisonment.

5.82 *The SOA 2003 repeals this offence in its entirety.*

8. Indecent Assault on a Man

Sexual Offences Act 1956, s 15(1)

5.83 The SOA 1956 consolidated the law with regard to sexual offences and repealed the OAPA 1861, s 62. The SOA 1956, s 15(1) was substituted (as of 1.1.1957).

Definition

5.84 to make an indecent assault on a man.

Proof

5.85 Section 15(2) provided that a boy under 16 cannot give consent. However, if the defendant has a genuine belief that the victim is over 16 then, if the boy was in fact consenting or the defendant believed that he was, then there is no criminal liability.[87]

Notes

5.86 (i) This offence is triable either way.

(ii) Section 15(3) provided that a mentally disordered person cannot give consent and that the perpetrator would be guilty if he knew or had reason to suspect the person to be mentally disordered. See para 7.01.

Indictment

5.87 INDECENT ASSAULT UPON A MALE PERSON 1.1.1957 to 30.4.2004

Statement of Offence

INDECENT ASSAULT ON A MALE PERSON, contrary to section 15(1) of the Sexual Offences Act 1956.

Particulars of Offence

D on the... day of... indecently assaulted C, a male person (aged under 16 years).

Alternative Offences

5.88 Attempted indecent assault upon a male person. From 27.8.1981 to 30.4.2004 an attempt to commit this offence ought to be drafted with reference in the Statement of Offence to the CAA 1981, s 1(1). If the victim is aged under 16 then the age is usually averred.

[86] The common law offence of assault with intent to rape had fallen into disuse and OAPA 1861, s 38, which defined an offence of assault with intent to rape, had been abolished in 1967.

[87] *R v K* [2002] 1 AC 462 HL; *R v Fernandez* [2002] The Times 26 June.

Sentence

(i) On indictment: **10 YEARS.**[88] **5.89**
(ii) Summarily: **6 months.**

Upon Conviction/Sentence

(i) Notification; applicable if criteria met.[89] **5.90**
(ii) Disqualification/barring from working with children/vulnerable adults. See paras 12.135 and 16.33.
(iii) SOPO: applicable if criteria met.[90]

For offences after 1.5.2004: see paras 3.45–3.52. **5.91**

9. Gross Indecency with Another Man

Sexual Offences Act 1956, s 13

The SOA 1956 consolidated the law in relation to sexual offences. Section 11 of the CLAA 1885 was repealed. Section 13 of the SOA 1956 was substituted (as of 1.1.1957). **5.92**

Definition

> ...to commit an act of gross indecency with another man, whether in public or private, or to be a party to the commission by a man of an act of gross indecency with another man. **5.93**

Proof

As per Definition. **5.94**

Notes

After 1960 offences involving children (under 14) are best charged as offences under the IwCA 1960. See para 4.05. **5.95**

Indictment

GROSS INDECENCY 1.1.1957 to 30.4.2004 **5.96**

Statement of Offence

GROSS INDECENCY, contrary to section 13 of the Sexual Offences Act 1956.

Particulars of Offence

D, on the...day of...being a male person (over the age of 21 years/under the age of 21 years), committed/was party to the commission of/procured the commission of an act of gross indecency with C, a man (under the age of 16 years, namely...) (in a public place, namely...).

In addition if one of the parties is under the age of 21 then the age should be averred, in order to attract the appropriate maximum sentence.[91] **5.97**

88 SOA 1956, s 37 and Sch II18(i) and 19(i).
89 SOA 2003, s 80(1) and Sch 3; see Chapter 14.
90 SOA 2003, s 104 and Sch 3; see Chapter 16.
91 SOA 1956, s 3(4).

Alternative Offences

5.98 An attempt to commit the full offence. Sentence as per the full offence, see para 5.08.

ATTEMPTED GROSS INDECENCY 27.8.1861 to 26.8.1981

> **Statement of Offence**
>
> ATTEMPTED GROSS INDECENCY, contrary to common law.
>
> **Particulars of Offence**
>
> D, on the... day of......, being a male person (over the age of 21 years/under the age of 21 years) attempted to commit an act of gross indecency with C, a man (under the age of 21 years namely...).

5.99 If one of the parties is under the age of 21 then this ought to be averred in order to attract the appropriate maximum sentence.[92]

5.100 An indictment charging an attempt to procure the commission of a gross indecency should aver SOA 1956, s 37, and the word 'attempted' should be added to the Statement of Offence and Particulars (1956–81).

5.101 After the commencement of the CAA 1981 on 27.8.1981, attempted gross indecency should be indicted as stated previously, except delete 'contrary to common law', from the Statement of Offence and insert 'contrary to section 1(1) of the Criminal Attempts Act 1981'.

Sentence

5.102 See para 5.46.

Upon Conviction/Sentence

5.103 (i) Notification; applicable if criteria met.[93]

(ii) Disqualification/barring from working with children/vulnerable adults. See paras 12.135 and 16.33.

(iii) SOPO: applicable if criteria met.[94]

1.1.1961

5.104 The IwCA 1960, s 1(1) creates a separate offence of committing or inciting an act of gross indecency with or towards a child under 16 (the maximum sentence 2 years, until 1.10.97 when the sentence increased to 10 years.[95] (See para 4.05.)

1.5.2004

5.105 The offences of gross indecency[96] and procuring a man to commit buggery in private[97] were both repealed by the SOA 2003.

---

92 SOA 1967, s 3(2).
93 SOA 2003, s 80(1) and Sch 3; see Chapter 14.
94 SOA 2003, s 104 and Sch 3; see Chapter 16.
95 C(S)A 1997, s 52.
96 SOA 1956, s 13.
97 SOA 1967, s 4.

Offences committed between 27.7.1967 and 30.4.2004

10. Procuring Others to Commit Buggery

Sexual Offences Act 1967, s 4(1)

Definition

A man who procures another man to commit with a third man an act of buggery... **5.106**

Proof

Procurement requires a positive act, and that the defendant brought about a course of conduct which would not otherwise necessarily have been embarked upon.[98] **5.107**

The prosecution have to prove that the defendant: **5.108**
- (i) procured the second man to commit the offence of buggery;
- (ii) was aware that he was procuring the second male to commit an act of buggery with a third male;
- (iii) this offence can only be committed if one of the parties to the buggery is under 16 or otherwise than in private, or with two or more present.[99]

Notes

- (i) The offence is triable either way.[100] **5.109**
- (ii) The various amendments to the offence of buggery since 1967 apply; the age of consent was reduced to 18 in 1994,[101] and 16 in 2000[102] (see para 5.04).
- (iii) The extension of the offence of rape to include anal intercourse in 1994,[103] meant that from then on an offence of procurement is committed only if one of the parties to the buggery is under the age of consent or the buggery takes place otherwise than in private or more than two people are present.
- (iv) This offence was repealed by the SOA 2003.

Indictment

PROCURING AN ACT OF BUGGERY 27.7.1967 to 30.4.2004 **5.110**

Statement of Offence

PROCURING AN ACT OF BUGGERY, contrary to section 4(1) of the Sexual Offences Act 1967.

Particulars of Offence

D on the... day of... procured another man (namely) to commit with a third man (namely) an act of buggery.

Sentence

- (i) On indictment: **2 YEARS.** **5.111**
- (ii) Summarily: **6 months.**

[98] *R v Broadfoot* 64 Cr App R 71.
[99] SOA 1967, ss 1 and 4(1).
[100] MCA 1980, s 17(1).
[101] CJPOA 1994, s 143, from 3.11.1994.
[102] SO(A)A 2000, ss 1 and 2, as from 1.5.2004.
[103] CJPOA 1994, s 142.

5.112 Upon Conviction/Sentence

(i) Notification; not applicable.[104]
(ii) Disqualification/barring from working with children/vulnerable adults. See paras 12.135 and 16.33.
(iii) SOPO: not applicable.[105]

[104] SOA 2003, s 80(1) (not listed in Sch 3); see Chapter 14.

[105] SOA 2003, s 104 (not listed in Sch 3); see Chapter 16.

6

FAMILIAL OFFENCES

Introduction

Before the passing of the Punishment of Incest Act (PIA) 1908, incest was punishable in England and Ireland only by proceedings in the ecclesiastical courts. The 1908 Act created the offence of incest, which covered sexual intercourse with an immediate blood relative or half-sibling. It included offences by males upon females and females permitting with their consent a male blood relative to have sexual relations with them. **6.01**

Offences under the SOA 1956 had the same parameters. Again the all-important factor was blood relationships. Section 10(1) provided for it to be an offence for a man to have sexual intercourse with a woman whom he knew to be his granddaughter, daughter, sister or mother. Section 11(1) provided for it to be an offence for a woman aged 16 or over to permit a man whom she knew to be her grandfather, father, brother or son to have sexual intercourse with her by her consent. Section 54(1) of the CLA 1977 created an additional offence for a male to incite a girl under the age of 16 to have incestuous intercourse. **6.02**

The SOA 2003 made significant changes. It created two new gender-neutral offences designed to capture the sexual abuse and exploitation of children within the concept of the modern 'family unit'. Section 25 creates an offence of sexual activity with a child member, whilst s 26 covers inciting a child family member to engage in sexual activity. The scope of the proscribed sexual activity is extended to any form of touching, whilst the child 'family' member must be under 18. The Act also widens the category of family who can commit such offences by extending prohibited family relationships beyond blood relationships to include adoptive relationships, as well as past and present step-parents and foster parents. Although not specifically mentioned within s 27, adoptive parents who are in the role of parents who care for and live with the child will be included by virtue of their falling within the ambit of s 27(2). Adoptive parents are to be treated as being on a **6.03** par with biological parents. This is in keeping with the intention of the Sexual Offences Review in making its recommendations for changes to the law in this area, in stating that 'the kind of definition linked to bloodlines (alone)...was no longer tenable'.[1] Also included are cases where both parties live in the same household, and cases where a person is regularly involved in caring for, training, supervising or being in sole charge of the complainant. Excluded will be those related by adoption where there is no caring role falling within the terms of s 27(4), for example adoptive siblings over 18 who are not themselves related by blood. These new familial sex offences (that is, under ss 25 and 26) include all acts which would have been incest under the old law where the complainant is/was under 18.

6.04 In addition, the 2003 Act also created two offences to cover the situation where a person aged 16 or over sexually penetrates a relative aged 18 or over (s 64) or allows that adult relative to penetrate them (s 65). Penetration means penetration of another person's vagina or anus by any part of the defendant's body or with 'anything else', and penetration of another's mouth with his penis. In contrast to the familial offences, these offences (under ss 64 and 65) cover a limited circle of blood relationships, that is, parent, child, grandchild, brother, sister, half-brother, half-sister, uncle, aunt, nephew or niece. For the first time, uncles and aunts are included.

6.05 It should be borne in mind that the offences under ss 25 and 26 include within their ambit situations of sexual intercourse between an adult and a child too young to be able to give true consent, notwithstanding that the protection of such young people from both themselves and others must be the very purpose of a legislative minimum age of consent.

6.06 In drafting indictments generally for a familial offence it is important to remember the following:

(i) The maximum penalties such offences attract are usually significantly lower than the equivalent offence drafted outside the familial bracket because they are intended to reflect circumstances where there is consent. Where C is under 13, however, it will be appropriate to indict the non-familial offence either as the primary count with a familial offence in the alternative or to simply draft, for example, a count of rape of a child under 13 (life) rather than sexual activity with a child family member (5 years where the defendant is under 18 even when the child is under 13). This is the clear intention of Parliament and underpins the current CPS guidance for indicting such offences.[2]

(ii) Where possible, counts should relate to a specific incident with each count drafted to make clear what is alleged by giving sufficient detail. Where that is impossible because of, for example, several years of regular and repeated acts, it is now possible for multiple incident counts to be included in an indictment to both reflect the course of conduct and found a basis for sentencing on the full facts rather than for a single specimen. See paras 1.08–1.17.

(iii) If both parties to the sexual act are charged, it is possible for a guilty verdict against one only to stand; one party might be unaware of the relationship or there might not be true consent by the party alleged to have consented to the act.[3]

---

1 *Setting the Boundaries: Reforming the Law on Sex Offences* (Home Office, 2000), para 5.5.11.

2 See App B.

3 *R v Gordon* (1927) 19 Cr App R 20 CA; brother and sister both charged in same indictment but tried separately; she was acquitted—that did not make his conviction bad.

Offences committed pre-1.1.1957

1. Incest by Males

Punishment of Incest Act 1908, s 1

Definition

Carnal knowledge[4] by any male person of a female person, who is to his knowledge his grand-daughter, daughter, sister or mother. **6.07**

Proof

(i) Carnal knowledge (that is, penetration of vagina by penis; ejaculation unnecessary);[5] **6.08**
(ii) by any male person of his mother, sister, daughter or granddaughter. The term 'sister' includes a half-sibling.[6]
(iii) Consent is immaterial.[7] It is the blood relationship which is key; proof of lawful marriage linking D and C is not required.[8]

Notes

(i) Triable on indictment only.[9] **6.09**
(ii) Prosecution for any offence under the PIA had to be sanctioned prior to commencement by the Attorney General unless brought by the DPP,[10] similar to the current position.
(iii) For penetration of the anus, indict the offence as buggery (see para 5.10).
(iv) Where it is alleged that the female complainant is aged under 13 years that must be specifically alleged on the indictment in order for the higher sentencing power to be invoked.[11]

Indictment

INCEST BY A MALE PERSON Pre-1.1.1957 **6.10**

Statement of Offence
INCEST, contrary to section 1(1) of the Punishment of Incest Act 1908.
Particulars of Offence
D, being a male person, on the...day of... 19.., had carnal knowledge of C, who is and was to his knowledge his granddaughter/daughter/(half-)sister/mother (if she was under 13 years at the time, add C's age).

Alternative Offences

(i) Attempt to commit the full offence. When indicting offences of attempt, do so under common law. Aver the attempt in both the Statement and Particulars of Offence. **6.11**
(ii) Indecent assault: **2 YEARS** (see para 3.19).

Sentence

(i) On indictment for the full offence: **6.12**
- when averred and proved that C is under 13 **LIFE**, or not less than **3 YEARS**.[12]

[4] That is, vaginal sexual intercourse.
[5] OAPA 1861, s 63.
[6] PIA 1908, s 3.
[7] PIA 1908, s 1(2).
[8] PIA 1908, s 3.
[9] PIA 1908, s 4(2).
[10] PIA 1908, s 6.
[11] PIA 1908, s 1(1).
[12] PIA 1908, s 1(1) and CLAA 1885, s 4.

• Otherwise, not less than **3 YEARS** and not exceeding 7 **YEARS**.[13]

(ii) For an attempt: 2 **YEARS**.[14]

Upon Conviction/Sentence

6.13 (i) Notification; not applicable.[15]

(ii) Disqualification/barring from working with children/vulnerable adults. See paras 12.135 and 16.33.

(iii) SOPO; not applicable[16] as not on Sch 3 although the court had power under the 1908 Act where the girl/woman was under 21 to 'divest the defendant of all control over her and if he was her guardian to remove her from his guardianship and appoint another guardian.'[17]

6.14 *As of 1.1.1957 PIA, s 1 is repealed. From the 1.1.1957 SOA 1956, s 10 covers this offence (see para 6.23).*

2. Incest by Females

Punishment of Incest Act 1908, s 2

Definition

6.15 Permitting with her consent by any female person of or above the age of 16 by her grandfather, father, brother or son to have carnal knowledge[18] of her, knowing him to be her grandfather, father, brother or son as the case may be.

Proof

6.16 (i) A female over 16 years permitting with consent (not simply submitting to);

(ii) her grandfather, father, brother or son (the term 'brother' includes a half-sibling);[19]

(iii) to have carnal knowledge of her (that is, penetration of vagina by penis; ejaculation unnecessary).[20]

Notes

6.17 (i) Triable on indictment only.[21]

(ii) Prosecution for any offence under the PIA must be sanctioned prior to commencement by the Attorney General unless brought by the DPP.[22]

(iii) Proof of lawful marriage linking D and C is not required.[23]

Indictment

6.18 INCEST BY A FEMALE PERSON Pre-1.1.1957

Statement of Offence

INCEST, contrary to section 2 of the Punishment of Incest Act 1908.

Particulars of Offence

D, being a female person of the age of 16 or over, on the... day of... 19.., with her consent permitted C who is and was to her knowledge her grandfather/father/(half-)brother/son, to have carnal knowledge of her.

---

[13] PIA 1908, s 1(1).
[14] PIA 1908, s 1(3).
[15] SOA 2003, s 80(1) (not listed in Sch 3); see Chapter 14.
[16] SOA 2003, s 104 (not listed in Sch 3); see Chapter 16.
[17] PIA 1908, s 1(4).
[18] Sexual intercourse.
[19] PIA 1908, s 3.
[20] OAPA 1861, s 63.
[21] PIA 1908, s 4(2).
[22] PIA 1908, s 6.
[23] PIA 1908, s 3.

Alternative Offences

The PIA does not provide for the offence of attempt, perhaps not surprisingly, as it is difficult to envisage circumstances in which it would be charged. If, however, you are indicting an offence of attempt, do so under common law. Aver the attempt in both the Statement and Particulars of Offence. **6.19**

Sentence

On indictment: not less than **3 YEARS** and not exceeding 7 **YEARS**.[24] **6.20**

Upon Conviction/Sentence

(i) Notification; not applicable.[25] **6.21**
(ii) Disqualification/barring from working with children/vulnerable adults. See paras 12.135 and 16.33.
(iii) SOPO; not applicable.[26]

As of 1.1.1957 PIA, s 2 is repealed. From 1.1.1957 SOA 1956, s 11 covers this offence (see para 6.32). **6.22**

Offences committed between 1.1.1957 and 30.4.2004

3. Incest by Males

Sexual Offences Act 1956, s 10

Definition

For a man to have sexual intercourse with a woman or girl whom he knows to be his granddaughter, daughter, sister or mother. **6.23**

Proof

(i) Sexual intercourse (that is, penetration of vagina by penis; ejaculation unnecessary);[27] **6.24**
(ii) by any male person with his granddaughter, daughter, sister or mother. The term 'sister' includes a half-sibling.[28]
(iii) Consent is immaterial.

Notes

(i) Triable on indictment only. **6.25**
(ii) Prosecution for this offence, or an attempt to commit it, may not be commenced except with the consent of, or by, the DPP.[29]
(iii) A genuine mistake as to the identity of the woman provides D with a defence.[30]
(iv) For offences committed after the commencement of the SOA 1993,[31] a boy of 14 or over can be charged as the presumption of incapacity was abolished.[32]
(v) It is the blood relationship which is key; proof of lawful marriage linking D and C is not required.[33]

---

24 PIA 1908, s 2.
25 SOA 2003, s 80(1) (not listed in Sch 3); see Chapter 14.
26 SOA 2003, s 104 (not listed in Sch 3); see Chapter 16.
27 SOA 1956, s 44.
28 SOA 1956, s 10(2).
29 SOA 1956, s 37(2) and Sch 214(a) and (b).
30 *R v Baillie-Smith* (1977) 64 Cr App R 76 CA.
31 Commencement date 20.9.1993.
32 SOA 1993, ss 1, 2(2) and 3.
33 SOA 1956, s 10(2).

(vi) The legal adoption of the woman to another family does not provide the blood relative with a defence.[34]

Indictment

6.26 INCEST BY A MALE PERSON 1.1.1957 to 30.4.2004

Statement of Offence
INCEST, contrary to section 10(1) of the Sexual Offences Act 1956.
Particulars of Offence
D, being a male person, on the...day of... 19.., had sexual intercourse with C, whom he knew to be his grand-daughter, daughter, (half-)sister or mother (add C's age if under 13 at the time).

Alternative Offences

6.27 (i) Attempt to commit the full offence. When indicting offences of attempt after 27.8.1981, do so under the CAA 1981;[35] prior to that, under common law. Aver the attempt in both the Statement and Particulars of Offence.

(ii) Unlawful sexual intercourse with a girl under 13: **LIFE** (see para 4.70) (or under 16, **2 YEARS**; that will be academic on an historic offence, as prosecution is time-barred however, after 12 months on an offence under the SOA 1956, s 6).

(iii) Where C is under 16, indecent assault, even if not specifically averred; indecent assault is a specified alternative to ss 5 and 6 (the USI offences):[36] **2, 5 or 10 YEARS** (see paras 3.19 and 3.29).

Sentence

6.28 (i) On indictment:
- if C is under 13 years: **LIFE.**
- Otherwise 7 **YEARS.**[37]

(ii) An attempt attracts the same maximum.

Sentencing Guidance

6.29 Guidance is to be found in *A-G's Reference (No 1 of 1989)*[38] re father with daughter, giving assistance divided by her various potential age ranges and setting out aggravating features. It should be read subject to the Practice Statement (Crime: Sentencing).[39]

Upon Conviction/Sentence

6.30 (i) Notification applies if the victim or other party was under 18.[40]

(ii) Disqualification/barring from working with children/vulnerable adults. See paras 12.135 and 16.33.

(iii) SOPO applies if the victim or other party was under 18.[41]

6.31 *As of 1.5.2004, SOA 1956, s 10 is repealed. From 1.4.2004 SOA 2003, ss 64 and 25 cover this offence (see para 6.48).*

[34] Adoption Act (AA) 1976, s 47(1).
[35] Implementation date 27.8.1981.
[36] SOA 1956, s 37(5) and Sch 2.
[37] SOA 1956, s 37(3) and Sch 2, para 14(a) and (b).
[38] [1989] 3 WLR 1117.
[39] [1992] 1 WLR 948.
[40] SOA 2003, s 80(1) and Sch 3; see Chapter 14.
[41] SOA 2003, s 104 and Sch 3; see Chapter 16.

4. Incest by Females

Sexual Offences Act 1956, s 11

Definition

Sexual intercourse with her permission and consent between a man and a woman of 16 years or over, she knowing that he is her grandfather, father, brother, or son. 'Brother' includes a half-sibling. **6.32**

Proof

(i) A female over 16 years permitting with consent (not simply submitting to); **6.33**
(ii) her grandfather, father, brother or son (the term 'brother' includes a half-sibling);[42]
(iii) to have sexual intercourse with her (that is, penetration of vagina by penis; ejaculation unnecessary).[43]

Notes

(i) Triable only on indictment. **6.34**
(ii) Prosecution for this offence, or an attempt to commit it, may not be commenced except with the consent of or by the DPP.[44]
(iii) The common law presumption of incapacity is a boy of under 14 had no application where a woman was charged with incest.[45]
(iv) The legal adoption of either party to another family does not provide a defence; the criminality is in the fact of and knowledge of the blood relationship.[46]
(v) Proof of lawful marriage linking D and C is not required.[47]

Indictment

INCEST BY A FEMALE PERSON 1.1.1957 to 30.4.2004 **6.35**

Statement of Offence

INCEST, contrary to section 11(1) of the Sexual Offences Act 1956.

Particulars of Offence

D, being a female person of the age of..., on the...day of...19.., with her consent permitted C, whom she knew to be her grandfather/father/(half-)brother/son, to have sexual intercourse with her.

Alternative Offences

Attempt to commit the full offence. When indicting offences of attempt after 27.8.1981, do so under the CAA 1981;[48] prior to that, under common law. Aver the attempt in both the Statement and Particulars of Offence. **6.36**

Sentence

(i) The full offence on indictment: maximum **7 YEARS**.[49] **6.37**
(ii) Attempt on indictment: **2 YEARS**.[50]

---

42 SOA 1956, s 11(2).
43 OAPA 1861, s 63.
44 SOA 1956, s 37(2) and Sch 2.
45 *R v Pickford* [1995] 1 Cr App R 420 CA.
46 AA 1976, s 47(1).
47 SOA 1956, s 11(2).
48 Implementation date 27.8.1981.
49 SOA 1956, s 37(3) and Sch 215(a).
50 SOA 1956, s 37(3) and Sch 2, para 15(b).

Upon Conviction/Sentence

6.38 (i) Notification; not applicable.[51]
(ii) Disqualification/barring from working with children/vulnerable adults. See paras 12.135 and 16.33.
(iii) SOPO; not applicable.[52]

6.39 As of 30.4.2004, SOA 1956, s 11 is repealed. From 1.1.1957 SOA 2003, s 65 covers this offence directly (see para 6.56). Note, however, that the scope for familial offences by women is widened to include penetration by a woman using an object on another of either gender under s 64 because the section is gender non-specific.

6.40 *The SOA 2003 creates four offences of sexual activity either with a child within the 'family' or with adult relatives. Although the former category holds higher maximum sentences than the latter, they are still not as high as some other equivalent non-familial offences.* See para 6.03.

Offences committed between 1.2.1991 and 30.4.2004

5. Incitement of Girls under 16 to have Incestuous Intercourse

Criminal Law Act 1977, s 54

Definition

6.41 ... a man to incite to have sexual intercourse with him a girl under the age of sixteen whom he knows to be his granddaughter, daughter or sister.[53]

Proof

6.42 (i) Incitement or encouragement by D;
(ii) of his granddaughter, daughter, sister or half-sister;[54]
(iii) who is/was aged under 16 at the time;
(iv) to have sexual intercourse with him.

Notes

6.43 (i) This offence is triable either way.[55]
(ii) This section applies even if the relationship between the parties cannot be traced through lawful wedlock.[56]

Indictment

6.44 INCITEMENT OF A GIRL UNDER 16 TO COMMIT INCEST 8.9.1977 to 30.4.2004

Statement of Offence

INCITEMENT OF A GIRL UNDER 16 TO COMMIT INCEST, contrary to section 54 of the Criminal Law Act 1977.

Particulars of Offence

D, a boy/man, on the... day of... incited C, a girl under the age of 16, whom he knows to be his grand-daughter/daughter/(half-)sister, to have sexual intercourse with him.

[51] SOA 2003, s 80(1) (not listed in Sch 3); see Chapter 14.
[52] SOA 2003, s 104 (not listed in Sch 3); see Chapter 16.
[53] CLA 1977, s 54(1).
[54] CLA 1977, s 54(2).
[55] CLA 1977, s 54(4).
[56] CLA 1977, s 54 (2).

Sentence

(i) On indictment: 2 YEARS. 6.45
(ii) Summarily: **6 months.**

Upon Conviction/Sentence

(i) Notification: applicable if criteria met.[57] 6.46
(ii) Disqualification/barring from working with children/vulnerable adults. See paras 12.135 and 16.33.
(iii) SOPO applicable if criteria met.[58]

As of 1.5.2004, CLA 1977, s 54 is repealed. From 1.5.2004, SOA 2003, s 26 covers this offence (see para 6.74). Note the increase in the maximum sentence from 2 years to 14 years' imprisonment, as of 1.5.2004. 6.47

Offences committed from 1.5.2004 to date

6. Penetrative Sex with an Adult Relative

Sexual Offences Act 2003, s 64

Definition

As per Proof. 6.48

Proof

(i) Sexual[59] activity involving or including penetration of C's vagina or anus by D's penis or by D using anything else, or penetration of C's mouth by D's penis. 6.49
(ii) D is 16 years or over.
(iii) C is 18 years or over.
(iv) C is D's child, parent, grandchild, grandparent, brother, sister, half-brother, half-sister, niece, nephew, uncle or aunt. (Uncle/aunt has the ordinary meaning of brother/sister of a person's parent; likewise, niece/nephew means the child of a person's brother or sister.[60]) This now includes adoptive parents and relationships arising by virtue of a parental order (baby born to surrogate mother treated as child of couple whom one of them has contributed to the embryo).[61]
(v) Where the blood relationship is proved, D is to be taken to have known or to have been reasonably expected to have known of it unless sufficient evidence is adduced to raise an issue as to whether he knew or could reasonably have been expected to know that he was.[62]

Notes

(i) Triable either way. 6.50
(ii) This offence could be committed by a woman penetrating either a male or female's body using an object; this is a change from the previous legislation, which only contemplated penetration by males, but in keeping with the ambit of such offences under the SOA 2003.

---

57 SOA 2003, s 80(1) and Sch 3; see Chapter 14.
58 SOA 2003, s 104 and Sch 3; see Chapter 16.
59 SOA 2003, s 78 defines 'sexual'; either because of the nature of the act or its circumstances/purpose or both. See also *R v H* [2005] 2 All ER 859 CA for the two-stage approach required.
60 SOA 2003, s 64(3).
61 Human Fertilisation and Embryology Act 2008. Human Fertilisation and Embryology (Parental Orders) Regulations 2010 (SI 2010 No 985) Sch 4.
62 SOA 2003, s 64(4).

Indictment

6.51 PENETRATIVE SEXUAL ACTIVITY WITH AN ADULT RELATIVE 1.5.2004 to date

Statement of Offence

SEX WITH AN ADULT RELATIVE, contrary to section 64(1) of the Sexual Offences Act 2003.

Particulars of Offence

D, being a person of or over the age of 16 years, on the...day of...20.., intentionally and sexually penetrated the anus/vagina/mouth of C with his [penis] *or* [anything else if vagina/ anus (name object)], C was aged.../18 years or over at the time and the relationship of D to C was that of son/daughter/mother/father/grandson/granddaughter/grandfather/grandmother/(half-)brother/(half-)sister/niece/nephew/uncle/aunt.

An example of this might be:

Particulars of Offence

D, being a person then aged 17 years, on the...day of...20.., intentionally and sexually penetrated the anus of C with his penis, C was then aged (eg 19) years and the relationship of D to C was that of half-brothers.

Alternative Offences

6.52 Attempt to commit the full offence. When indicting offences of attempt, do so under the CAA 1981. Aver the attempt in both the Statement and Particulars of Offence.

Sentence

6.53 (i) On indictment: **2 YEARS.**[63]
(ii) Summarily: **6 months** or **fine** or **both.**[64]

Sentencing Guidance

6.54 See the SGC guidelines at App C, pages 414–417.

Upon Conviction/Sentence

6.55 (i) Notification applies[65] where D is either under 18 and has been sentenced to 12 months or more, or D is over 18 and has been sentenced either to a term of imprisonment or to be detained in a hospital.
(ii) Disqualification/barring from working with children/vulnerable adults. See paras 12.135 and 16.33.
(iii) SOPO applies where D is either under 18 and has been sentenced to 12 months or more, or D is over 18 and has been sentenced either to a term of imprisonment or to be detained in a hospital.[66]

7. Consenting to Penetrative Sex with an Adult Relative

Sexual Offences Act 2003, s 65

Definition

6.56 As per Proof.

---

63 SOA 2003, s 64(5).
64 SOA 2003, s 64(5), 12 months if CJA 2003, s 282(4) implemented.
65 SOA 2003, s 80(1) and Sch 3; see Chapter 14.
66 SOA 2003, s 104 and Sch 3; see Chapter 16.

Proof

(i) Sexual[67] activity involving or including consent to penetration of D's vagina or anus by A's penis or by A using anything else, or penetration of D's mouth by A's penis. **6.57**
(ii) D is 16 years or over.
(iii) A is 18 years or over.
(iv) D is A's child, parent, grandchild, grandparent, brother, sister, half-brother, half-sister, niece, nephew, uncle or aunt. (Uncle/aunt has the ordinary meaning of brother/sister of a person's parent; likewise, niece/nephew means the child of a person's brother or sister.[68]) This now includes adoptive parents and relationships arising by virtue of a parental order (baby born to surrogate mother treated as child of couple whom one of them has contributed to the embryo).[69]
(v) Where the blood relationship is proved, X is to be taken to have known or to be been reasonably expected to have known of it unless sufficient evidence is adduced to raise an issue as to whether he knew or could reasonably have been expected to know that he was.[70]

Notes

Triable either way. **6.58**

Indictment

CONSENTING TO PENETRATIVE SEX WITH AN ADULT RELATIVE 1.5.2004 to date **6.59**

Statement of Offence

CONSENTING TO SEX WITH AN ADULT RELATIVE, contrary to section 65(1) of the Sexual Offences Act 2003

Particulars of Offence

D, being a person of or over the age of 16 years, on the…day of…20.., consented to the sexual penetration of her vagina by A with his penis when A was 18 years or over, the relationship of D to A was that of son/daughter/mother/father/grandson/grand-daughter/grandfather/grandmother/ (half-)brother/(half-)sister/niece/nephew/uncle/aunt and the said D knew or could reasonably have been expected to know that he/she was so related to A.

An example of this might be:

Particulars of Offence

D, being a person of or over the age of 16 years, on the…day of…20.., consented to the sexual penetration of her vagina by A with his penis when A was 18 years or over, the relationship of D to A was that of niece and uncle and the said D knew or could reasonably have been expected to know that she was so related to A.

Alternative Offences

Attempt to commit the full offence. When indicting offences of attempt, do so under the CAA 1981. Aver the attempt in both the Statement and Particulars of Offence. **6.60**

Sentence

(i) On indictment: **2 YEARS.**[71] **6.61**

[67] SOA 2003, s 78 defines 'sexual'; either because of the nature of the act or its circumstances/purpose or both. See also *R v H* [2005] 2 All ER 859 CA for the two-stage approach required.
[68] SOA 2003, s 65(3).
[69] Human Fertilisation and Embryology Act 2008. Human Fertilisation and Embryology (Parental Orders) Regulations 2010 (SI 2010 No 985) Sch 4).
[70] SOA 2003, s 65(4).
[71] SOA 2003, s 65(5).

(ii) Summarily: **6 months** or **fine** or **both.**[72]

Sentencing Guidance

6.62 See the SGC guidelines at App C, pages 414–417.

Upon Conviction/Sentence

6.63 (i) Notification applies[73] where D is either under 18 and has been sentenced to 12 months or more, or D is over 18 and has been sentenced either to a term of imprisonment or to be detained in a hospital.

(ii) Disqualification/barring from working with children/vulnerable adults. See paras 12.135 and 16.33.

(iii) SOPO applies as where D is either under 18 and has been sentenced to 12 months or more, or D is over 18 and has been sentenced to either a term of imprisonment or to be detained in a hospital.[74]

8. Sexual Activity with a Child Family Member

Sexual Offences Act 2003, s 25

Definition

6.64 As per Proof.

Proof

6.65 (i) D intentionally and sexually touches C;

(ii) the relationship of D to C is within s 27; and

(iii) D knows or could reasonably be expected to know that and C is either under 18 (and D does not reasonably believe that C is 18 or over) or C is under 13.

(iv) Penetration; also indict under s 25(6) where any of the following are alleged:
- penetration of C's anus or vagina with a part of D's body or anything else;
- penetration of C's mouth with D's penis;
- penetration of D's anus or vagina with a part of C's body; or
- penetration of D's mouth with C's penis.

(v) Note the following:

(a) Where in proceedings for an offence under this section it is proved that C was under 18, D is to be taken not to have reasonably believed C was 18 or over unless sufficient evidence is adduced to raise an issue as to whether he reasonably believed it.[75]

(b) Where in proceedings for an offence under this section it is proved that the relation of D to C was of a description falling within s 27 (see para 6.66), it is to be taken that D knew or could reasonably have been expected to know that his relation to C was of that description unless sufficient evidence is adduced to raise an issue as to whether he knew or could reasonably have been expected to know that it was.[76]

6.66 Who is a family member is much wider under this section and is separately defined by s 27 for the purposes of this section of the Act. The relation of D to C is within this section if one of the following applies:

---

[72] SOA 2003, s 65(5). 12 months if CJA 2003, s 282(4) implemented. Section 282(4) is not retrospective.

[73] SOA 2003, s 80(1) and Sch 3; see Chapter 14.

[74] SOA 2003, s 104 and Sch 3; see Chapter 16.

[75] SOA 2003, s 25(2).

[76] SOA 2003, s 25(3).

(i) D or C is parent, grandparent, brother, sister, half-brother, half-sister, aunt or uncle to the other.[77]
(ii) D is or has been C's foster parent.[78]
(iii) If D and C live or have lived in the same household, or D has been regularly involved in caring for, training, supervising or being in sole charge of C; and[79]
- one of them is or has been the other's step-parent;
- D and C are cousins;
- one of them is or has been the other's stepbrother or stepsister; or
- the parent or present or former foster parent of one of them is or has been the other's foster parent.

(iv) If D and C live in the same household and D is regularly caring for, training, supervising or being in sole charge of D.[80]

Notes

(i) Triable only on indictment if defendant is over 18 and penetration is alleged; triable either way if non-penetrative.[81] **6.67**
(ii) Although it would be possible to prosecute under s 25(6) where C is under 13, it is perhaps more likely that the proper charge for this offence would be one of rape of a child under 13 (s 5 carries maximum of **LIFE**; see para 4.94). Consideration should perhaps be given to putting a s 5 charge/count as the primary one, with the familial offence as an alternative to it. See introductory remarks and notes at para 6.06.
(iii) It is not an offence where D is lawfully married to C, or they are civil partners,[82] at the time of the sexual conduct and C is over 16 at the time.[83]
(iv) A defence is afforded where the relationship is not one of blood relatives and a sexual relationship already existed immediately prior to the existence of the relationship bringing the couple within s 27.[84]
(v) Adoptive relations are excluded from the definition of family members under s 27. Arguably, however, adoptive parents could fit the description as primary carers living with the child.
(vi) Those who have been adopted away from the family are included if they fall into one of the categories in s 27, just as under the old law[85] where a blood relative could not escape prosecution because either party had been adopted away from the family.
(vii) The fact that D is/is not over 18 should be averred; it affects the maximum sentences which can be passed.
(viii) In dealing with a SOPO in respect of a sibling who is not the victim, it may be wise to involve the family court.[86]

Indictment

PENETRATIVE SEXUAL ACTIVITY WITH A CHILD FAMILY MEMBER, contrary to s 25(1) and (6) of the Sexual Offences Act 2003 1.5.2004 to date **6.68**

Statement of Offence
SEXUAL ACTIVITY WITH A CHILD FAMILY MEMBER, contrary to section 25(1) and (6) of the Sexual Offences Act 2003.

[77] SOA 2003, s 27(2)(a).
[78] SOA 2003, s 27(2)(b). Foster parent is itself defined under s 5(c)(i)(a) and (ii).
[79] SOA 2003, s 27(3)(a)–(d) inclusive.
[80] SOA 2003, s 27(4)(a) and (b).
[81] SOA 2003, s 25(4)–(6).
[82] Civil Partnership Act 2004, s 261(1), Sch 27, para 174.
[83] SOA 2003, s 28 (1)(a) and (b).
[84] SOA 2003, s 29.
[85] SOA 2003, s 27(1)(b).
[86] *R v D* [2005] EWCA Crim 2951, [2006] CLR 364.

Particulars of Offence

Examples of this might be:

D, on the... day of... 20.., being a person over the age of 18 years, intentionally and sexually touched his foster daughter by penetrating her mouth with his penis, when D either knew or could reasonably have been expected to have known that C was his foster daughter, and [where D did not reasonably believe that C was aged 18 or over at the time] *or* [where C was under 13 at the time].

Or:

D, on the... day of... 20.., being a person over the age of 18 years, intentionally and sexually touched her cousin by digitally penetrating her vagina when D either knew or could reasonably have been expected to have known that C was her cousin, and [where D did not reasonably believe that C was aged 18 or over at the time] *or* [where C was under 13 at the time].

6.69 **NON-PENETRATIVE SEXUAL ACTIVITY WITH A CHILD FAMILY MEMBER, contrary to s 25(1) of the Sexual Offences Act 2003** 1.5.2004 to date

Statement of Offence

SEXUAL ACTIVITY WITH A CHILD FAMILY MEMBER, contrary to section 25(1) of the Sexual Offences Act 2003.

Particulars of Offence

Examples of this might be:

D, on the... day of... 20.., a person of or over the age of 18 years, intentionally and sexually touched his daughter by kissing and stroking her breasts, when D either knew or could reasonably have been expected to have known that C was his daughter and where C was under 13 at the time.

Or

D, on the... day of... 20.., a person of the age of 18 years, intentionally and sexually touched her brother by performing oral sex upon him, when D either knew or could reasonably have been expected to have known that C was her brother and where D did not reasonably believe that C was aged 18 or over at the time.

Alternative Offences

6.70 Attempt to commit the full offence. When indicting offences of attempt, do so under the CAA 1981. Aver the attempt in both the Statement and Particulars of Offence.

Sentence

6.71 (i) On indictment:
- When D is over 18: **14 YEARS.**[87]
- In all other cases: **5 YEARS.**[88]

(ii) Summarily: **6 months.**[89]

Sentencing Guidance

6.72 See para 12.133; see also the SGC guidelines at App C, pages 423–424.

[87] SOA 2003, s 25(4).
[88] SOA 2003, s 25(5).
[89] SOA 2003, ss 25 (4)(b)(i) and (5)(a); 12 months if CJA 2003, s 282(4) implemented.

Upon Conviction/Sentence

(i) Notification applies[90] if D was over 18 at the time or is/has been sentenced to 12 months or more. **6.73**
(ii) Disqualification/barring from working with children/vulnerable adults. See paras 12.135 and 16.33.
(iii) SOPO applies[91] if D was over 18 at the time or is/has been sentenced to 12 months or more. In dealing with SOPO in respect of a sibling who is not the victim, it may be wise to involve the family court.[92]

9. Inciting a Child Family Member to Engage in Sexual Activity

Sexual Offences Act 2003, s 26

Definition

As per Proof. **6.74**

Proof

(i) C intentionally incites D to sexually touch him (C) or allows himself (D) to be sexually touched by C; **6.75**
(ii) the relationship of D to C is within s 27; and
(iii) D knows or could reasonably be expected to know that and C is either under 18 (and D does not reasonably believe that C is 18 or over) or D is under 13.
(iv) Penetration; also indict under s 26(6) where any of the following are alleged:
- penetration of D's anus or vagina with a part of C's body or anything else;
- penetration of C's mouth with D's penis;
- penetration of D's anus or vagina with a part of C's body; or
- penetration of D's mouth with C's penis.

(v) Note the following:
(a) Where in proceedings for an offence under this section it is proved that C was under 18, D is to be taken not to have reasonably believed C was 18 or over unless sufficient evidence is adduced to raise an issue as to whether he reasonably believed it.[93]
(b) Where in proceedings for an offence under this section it is proved that the relation of D to C was of a description falling within s 27 (set out under s 25 at para 6.64 *et seq*), it is to be taken that D knew or could reasonably have been expected to know that his relation to C was of that description unless sufficient evidence is adduced to raise an issue as to whether he knew or could reasonably have been expected to know that it was.[94]

Notes

(i) Triable only on indictment if D is 18 or over and penetration is alleged; triable either way if penetration is not alleged and if D is under 18 irrespective of whether penetration is alleged or not. **6.76**
(ii) Although it would be possible to prosecute under s 26(6) where C is under 13 and the activity is penetrative, it is perhaps more likely that the proper charge for this offence would be one of sexual activity with a child under 13 (s 8 carries maximum of life; see para 4.43). Consideration should at least be given to putting a s 8 charge/count as the primary one, with the familial offence as an alternative to it.

---

90 SOA 2003, s 80(1) and Sch 3; see Chapter 14.
91 SOA 2003, s 104 and Sch 3; see Chapter 16.
92 *R v D* [2005] EWCA Crim 2951, [2006] CLR 364.
93 SOA 2003, s 26(2).
94 SOA 2003, s 26(3).

(iii) There is an exception for a defendant who is lawfully married to or the civil partner[95] of D at the time of the sexual conduct and D is over 16 at the time.[96]
(iv) Those who have been adopted away from the family are included if they fall into one of the categories in s 27, just as under the old law[97] where a blood relative could not escape prosecution because either party had been adopted away from the family.
(v) Adoptive parents are to be viewed as on a par with biological parents.[98]
(vi) The fact that D is/is not over 18 should be averred; it affects the maximum sentences which can be passed.

Indictment

6.77 **INCITING A CHILD FAMILY MEMBER TO ENGAGE IN PENETRATIVE SEXUAL ACTIVITY contrary to s 26(1) and (6) of the Sexual Offences Act 2003** 1.5.2004 to date

Statement of Offence

INCITING A CHILD FAMILY MEMBER TO ENGAGE IN PENETRATIVE SEXUAL ACTIVITY, contrary to section 26(1) and (6) of the Sexual Offences Act 2003.

Particulars of Offence

D, on the...day of...20.., being a person of...years, intentionally incited C to sexually touch D/allow himself to be touched by D by encouraging or permitting her to perform oral sex upon him, where D either knew or could reasonably have been expected to have known that C was his daughter/granddaughter (anyone within s 27), and [where D did not reasonably believe that C was aged 18 or over at the time] *or* [where C was under 13 at the time].

6.78 **INCITING A CHILD FAMILY MEMBER TO ENGAGE IN NON-PENETRATIVE SEXUAL ACTIVITY contrary to s 26(1) of the Sexual Offences Act 2003** 1.5.2004 to date

Statement of Offence

INCITING A CHILD FAMILY MEMBER TO ENGAGE IN SEXUAL ACTIVITY, contrary to section 26(1) of the Sexual Offences Act 2003.

Particulars of Offence

D, on the...day of...20.., being a person of...years, intentionally incited C to sexually touch D by encouraging her to masturbate him, where D either knew or could reasonably have been expected to have known that C was his daughter/granddaughter (anyone within s 27), and [where D did not reasonably believe that C was aged 18 or over at the time] *or* [where C was under 13 at the time].

Alternative Offences

6.79 Attempt to commit the full offence. When indicting offences of attempt, do so under the CAA 1981. Aver the attempt in both the Statement and Particulars of Offence.

Sentence

6.80 (i) On indictment where D is 18 or over and offence is penetrative: **14 YEARS**,[99] summarily **6 months.**[100]

---

[95] Civil Partnership Act 2004, s 261(1) and Sch 27(174) implemented on 5.12.2005.
[96] SOA 2003, s 28(1)(a) and (b).
[97] SOA 2003, s 27(1)(b).
[98] *Setting the Boundaries*, para 5.6.1.
[99] SOA 2003, s 26(4).
[100] SOA 2003, s 26(5).

(ii) On indictment where D is under 18: **5 YEARS**, summarily **6 months.**[101]

Upon Conviction/Sentence

(i) Notification applies[102] if D was over 18 at the time or is/has been sentenced to 12 months or more. **6.81**
(ii) Disqualification/barring from working with children/vulnerable adults. See paras 12.135 and 16.33.
(iii) SOPO applies[103] if D was over 18 at the time or is/has been sentenced to 12 months or more. In dealing with SOPO in respect of a sibling who is not the victim, it may be wise to involve the family court.[104]

[101] The fact of penetration does not alter the maximum sentence.
[102] SOA 2003, s 80(1) and Sch 3; see Chapter 14.
[103] SOA 2003, s 104 and Sch 3; see Chapter 16.
[104] *R v D* [2005] EWCA Crim 2951, [2006] CLR 364.

7

OFFENCES INVOLVING THE MENTALLY DISORDERED

Introduction

7.01 This chapter deals principally with offences upon women. Mentally disordered males have in the past been provided with some protection (see paras 5.86 and 7.65[1]), but not extensively so, until the SOA 2003 was passed.

7.02 The SOA 2003 consolidated the law and provided offences against both mentally disordered males and females.

7.03 Before the passing of the SOA 1956 (commencement date 1.1.1957) there were several statutes dealing with offences against the mentally disordered. In each there was a separate definition of individuals, currently described as mentally disordered. In the main, terms used are offensive to the modern reader. They nevertheless have been included in order to cover the rare occasions that such a case (pre-dating 1957) would be prosecuted. However, judicial discretion may allow for an indictment to contain the term 'mental disorder' instead of 'idiot/imbecile/defective'.

A. SEXUAL ASSAULTS UPON THE MENTALLY DISORDERED

Offences committed pre-31.12.1956

1. Carnal Knowledge of a Mentally Disordered Female

Criminal Law Amendment Act 1885, s 5(2)

Definition

7.04 Any person who 'unlawfully and carnally knows, (that is, has vaginal intercourse with) or attempts to have unlawful carnal knowledge of any female idiot or imbecile woman or girl' in any circumstances not amounting to rape.

7.05 Proof

(i) Carnal knowledge, that is penetration of vagina by the penis, proof of ejaculation not necessary;[2]

---

[1] Indecent Assaults upon Males. SOA 1956, s 15(3) and Mental Health Act (MHA) 1959, s 128.

[2] *R v Marsden* [1891] 2 QB 149, and later OAPA 1861, s 63.

(ii) that the woman was an 'idiot or imbecile' as defined;
(iii) that the defendant knew the woman was an 'idiot or imbecile'.[3]

Notes

(i) The offence is triable only on indictment. **7.06**
(ii) An 'imbecile' was defined (by common law) as a woman incapable of appreciating the nature and quality of the act in question, or incapable of exercising an act of her own will in giving or withholding her consent; this incapacity must arise from want of understanding.[4]
(iii) An 'idiot' was defined as a person who has 'no mind' (whether or not from birth).[5]
(iv) Proof of consent is not required.

Indictment

CARNAL KNOWLEDGE OF AN 'IDIOT/IMBECILE' Pre-31.12.1956 **7.07**

Statement of Offence

CARNAL KNOWLEDGE OF AN IMBECILE WOMAN, contrary to section 5(2) of the Criminal Law Amendment Act 1885.

Particulars of Offence

D on a day between . . . had unlawful carnal knowledge of C, an imbecile woman, in circumstances not amounting to rape, knowing that the said C is an imbecile/idiot woman/girl.

Alternative Offences

Attempt to commit the full offence. When indicting offences of attempt do so under common law. Aver the attempt in both the Statement and Particulars of Offence. **7.08**

Sentence

On indictment: 2 YEARS. **7.09**

As of 1.1.1957, SOA 1956, s 7 covers this offence.[6] **7.10**

Offences committed between 1.1.1957 and 30.4.2004

2. Intercourse with an Idiot/Imbecile Woman

Sexual Offences Act 1956, s 7

Definition

. . . unlawful sexual intercourse with a woman whom he knows to be an idiot or imbecile. **7.11**

Proof

(i) Sexual intercourse—proof of penetration will suffice.[7] **7.12**
(ii) For the common law definition of 'imbecile' and 'idiot' see para 7.06.
(iii) That the defendant knew the female to be an 'idiot/imbecile'.

[3] CLAA 1885, s 5(2).
[4] *R v Turner* [1886] CCC Sess Papers.
[5] *R v F* 74 JP 384.
[6] The CLAA 1885 was repealed.
[7] SOA 1956, s 44.

Notes

7.13 (i) The offence is triable only on indictment.[8]
(ii) Consent to prosecute must be obtained from the DPP.[9]
(iii) If the maximum sentence of 2 years' imprisonment would not accurately reflect the gravity of the offence, and the complainant is not mentally capable of consenting, then a charge of rape would be appropriate (see para 2.04).
(iv) Severe impairment is to be measured as against the standard of ordinary persons, without any impairment.[10]
(v) Expert evidence as to impairment, whilst admissible, is not essential.[11]
(vi) The defendant is afforded a statutory defence, if he can prove that he did not believe, and had no reason to believe, that the complainant was a 'defective'.[12]
(vii) SOA 1956, s 7 provides a statutory alternative to:
  (a) rape;[13]
  (b) intercourse with a girl under 13;[14]
  (c) incest.[15]

Indictment

7.14 INTERCOURSE WITH AN 'IDIOT/IMBECILE' 1.1.1957 to 31.10.1960

Statement of Offence

INTERCOURSE WITH AN IDIOT/IMBECILE, contrary to section 7 of the Sexual Offences Act 1956.

Particulars of Offence

D on the... day of... 19.., had unlawful sexual intercourse with a woman whom he knew to be an idiot/imbecile.

Alternative Offences

7.15 Attempt to commit the full offence. When indicting offences of attempt, do so under common law. Aver the attempt in both the Statement and Particulars of Offence.

Sentence

7.16 (i) On indictment: **2 YEARS.**[16]
(ii) An attempt attracts the same sentence.

Upon Conviction/Sentence

7.17 (i) Notification; not applicable.[17]
(ii) Disqualification/barring from working with children/vulnerable adults. See paras 12.135 and 16.33.
(iii) SOPO: not applicable.[18]

---

[8] SOA 1956, s 37 and Sch II(11)(a).
[9] MHA 1959, s 128(4).
[10] *Hall* (1987) 86 Cr App R 159.
[11] *Hall* (1987) 86 Cr App R 162.
[12] SOA 1956, s 7(2) and SOA 1956, s 47.
[13] SOA 1956, s 37 and Sch II(1).
[14] SOA 1956, s 37 and Sch II(2).
[15] SOA 1957, s 37 and Sch II(14).
[16] SOA 1956, s 37 and Sch II(11)(b).
[17] SOA (not in Sch 3) 2003, s 80(1); see Chapter 14.
[18] SOA 2003, s 104; see Chapter 16.

1.11.1960 to 30.4.2004

Definition

See para 7.11. **7.18**

Proof

See para 7.12. **7.19**

Notes

(i) The term 'idiot/imbecile' was abandoned in 1960,[19] the term 'defective' was substituted. This was defined as 'a person suffering from severe subnormality within the meaning of the Mental Health Act 1959'.[20] **7.20**

(ii) This was soon after amended to 'a person suffering from a state of arrested or incomplete development of mind which includes severe impairment of intelligence and social functioning', by the Mental Health (Amendment) Act 1982.[21]

Indictment

As at para 7.14, except substitute 'defective' for 'idiot/imbecile'. **7.21**

Offences committed from 1.5.2004 to date

The SOA 2003 repealed the SOA 1956, s 7 in full. SOA 2003, s 30—sexual activity with a person with a mental disorder impeding choice covers this offence. Additional offences have been created, including: inciting a person with a mental disorder impeding choice to engage in sexual activity,[22] engaging in sexual activity in the presence of such persons[23] or causing them to watch.[24] **7.22**

3. Sexual Activity with a Person with Mental Disorder Impeding Choice

Sexual Offences Act 2003, s 30

Definition

(1) A person (A) commits an offence if— **7.23**
- (a) he intentionally touches another person (B),
- (b) the touching is sexual,
- (c) B is unable to refuse because of, or for a reason related to, a mental disorder, and
- (d) A knows or could reasonably be expected to know that B has a mental disorder and that because of it, or for a reason related to it, B is likely to be unable to refuse.

Proof

(i) See indictment particulars for elements of the offence. **7.24**

---

[19] MHA 1959. Commencement date 1.11.1960.
[20] MHA 1959, s 127(1)(b) (SOA 1956, s 45 substituted).
[21] Sch 3.
[22] SOA 2003, s 31.
[23] SOA 2003, s 32.
[24] SOA 2003, s 33.

(ii) Of particular note: for offences under ss 30–33 inclusive the prosecution must prove that C is unable to refuse because of, or for a reason related to, a mental disorder, and is unable to choose because he/she lacks the capacity to choose, whether because he/she lacks sufficient understanding of the nature or reasonably foreseeable consequences of what is being done, or for any other reason[25] or he/she is unable to communicate his/her choice to D.[26]

(iii) The case of *Cooper*[27] makes three key points:

(a) the inability to communicate choice must be linked to a mental and not physical disability;

(b) the capacity to choose is person and situation specific;

(c) a complainant may be robbed of the capacity to choose even though s/he can understand the information relevant to making the choice;

(iv) where the complainant's inability to communicate choice not to consent to the sexual act is due to a physical disability, the ordinary offences in ss 1–4 apply; where the inability to communicate choice is due to a mental disorder, the special offences in ss 30–33 apply[28] (per Lord Roger).

Notes

7.25 (i) If penetration is involved the offence is indictable only, except penetration of A's anus or vagina with an object.[29]

(ii) If penetration is not involved then the offence is triable either way.[30]

(iii) If the offence alleged falls within subsection (3), this ought to be averred in the indictment.

(iv) A woman suffering from cerebral palsy with a mental age well below that of her contemporaries, although able to speak, was held to be unable to communicate her choice as to sexual touching, as compared to the ability to do so of a woman the same age, not suffering from her disabilities.[31]

Indictment

7.26 SEXUAL ACTIVITY WITH MENTALLY DISORDERED PERSON IMPEDING CHOICE 1.5.2004 to date

Statement of Offence

SEXUAL ACTIVITY WITH A PERSON WITH A MENTAL DISORDER IMPEDING CHOICE, contrary to section 30(1) of the Sexual Offences Act 2003.

Particulars of Offence

D on the...day of...of 20.., intentionally touched C, by penetrating her mouth with his penis in sexual circumstances where C was unable to refuse because of or for a reason related to a mental disorder, and D knew or could reasonably be expected to know that C had a mental disorder and that because of it or for a reason related to it C was likely to be unable to refuse.

[25] These encompass a wide range of circumstances, including irrational fears, delusions and phobias (para 25) linked to a 'disorder, such as those which drive a person to refuse a life-saving injection or to refuse food in anorexia'. *Cooper* [2009] UKHL 42.

[26] SOA 2003, ss 30(2), 31(2), 32(2), 33(2).

[27] *Cooper* [2009] UKHL 42.

[28] *Cooper* [2009] UKHL 42, para 7.

[29] SOA 2003, s 30(3).

[30] SOA 2003, s 30(4).

[31] *Hulme v DPP* [2006] EWHC 1347 (Admin).

Alternative Offences

Attempt to commit the full offence. When indicting 2003 Act offences, the charge remains CAA 1981, s 1(1). Aver the attempt in both the Statement and Particulars of Offence. **7.27**

Sentence

(i) On indictment: **7.28**
- If penetration is involved: **LIFE.**
- If no penetration is involved: **14 YEARS.**[32]

(ii) Summarily: **6 months.**[33]

Upon Conviction/Sentence

(i) Notification applies.[34] **7.29**
(ii) Disqualification/barring from working with children/vulnerable adults. See paras 12.135 and 16.33.
(iii) SOPO applies.[35]

4. Causing or Inciting a Person with a Mental Disorder Impeding Choice to Engage in Sexual Activity

Sexual Offences Act 2003, s 31

Definition

(1) A person (A) commits an offence if— **7.30**
(a) he intentionally causes or incites another person (B) to engage in activity,
(b) the activity is sexual,
(c) B is unable to refuse because of or for a reason related to a mental disorder, and
(d) A knows or could reasonably be expected to know that B has a mental disorder and that because of it or for a reason related to it B is likely to be unable to refuse.

Proof

See Definition for elements of offence. **7.31**

Notes

(i) If penetration is involved the offence is indictable only.[36] **7.32**
(ii) If penetration is not involved then the offence is triable either way.[37]
(iii) If the offence falls within subsection (3) then this ought to be averred in the indictment.

Indictment

CAUSING/INCITING A PERSON WITH A MENTAL DISORDER IMPEDING CHOICE TO ENGAGE IN SEXUAL ACTIVITY 1.5.2004 to date **7.33**

Statement of Offence
CAUSING/INCITING A PERSON, WITH A MENTAL DISORDER IMPEDING CHOICE TO ENGAGE IN SEXUAL ACTIVITY, contrary to section 31(1) of the Sexual Offences Act 2003.

[32] SOA 2003, s 30(3) and (4).
[33] 12 months if CJA 2003, s 282(2) implemented.
[34] SOA 2003, s 80(1) and Sch 3, para 27; see Chapter 14.
[35] SOA 2003, s 104 and Sch 3, para 27; see Chapter 16.
[36] SOA 2003, s 31(3).
[37] SOA 2003, s 31(4).

Particulars of Offence

D on the... day of... intentionally caused/incited C, to engage in a sexual activity, namely..., and C was unable to refuse because of or for a reason related to a mental disorder, and D knew or could reasonably have been expected to have known that C had a mental disorder and that because of it or for a reason related to it C is likely to be unable to refuse.

Alternative Offences

7.34 Attempt to commit the full offence. When indicting SOA 2003 offences, the charge remains CAA 1981, s 1(1). Aver the attempt in the Statement and Particulars of Offence.

Sentence

7.35 (i) On indictment:
- If penetration is involved: **LIFE.**[38]
- If no penetration is involved: **14 YEARS.**[39]

(ii) Summarily: **6 months.**[40]

Upon Conviction/Sentence

7.36 (i) Notification requirements apply.[41]

(ii) Disqualification/barring from working with children/vulnerable adults. See paras 12.135 and 16.33.

(iii) SOPO applies.[42]

5. Engaging in Sexual Activity in the Presence of a Person with a Mental Disorder Impeding Choice

Sexual Offences Act 2003, s 32

Definition

7.37 (1) A person (A) commits an offence if—
- (a) he intentionally engages in an activity,
- (b) the activity is sexual,
- (c) for the purpose of obtaining sexual gratification, he engages in it—
  - (i) when another person (B) is present or is in a place from which A can be observed, and
  - (ii) knowing or believing that (B) is aware, or intending that B should be aware, that he is engaging in it,
- (d) B is unable to refuse because of or for a reason related to a mental disorder, and
- (e) A knows or could reasonably be expected to know that B has a mental disorder and that because of it or for a reason related to it B is likely to be unable to refuse.

Proof

7.38 See Definition for elements of the offence.

Notes

7.39 The offence is triable either way.[43]

[38] SOA 2003, s 31(3).
[39] SOA 2003, s 31(4).
[40] SOA 2003, s 31(4). 12 months if CJA 2003, s 282(2) implemented.
[41] SOA 2003, s 80 and Sch 3, para 27; see Chapter 14.
[42] SOA 2003, s 104 and Sch 4; see Chapter 16.
[43] SOA 2003, s 32(3).

Indictment

ENGAGING IN SEXUAL ACTIVITY IN THE PRESENCE OF A PERSON WITH A MENTAL DISORDER IMPEDING CHOICE 1.5.2004 to date 7.40

Statement of Offence

ENGAGING IN SEXUAL ACTIVITY IN THE PRESENCE OF A PERSON WITH A MENTAL DISORDER IMPEDING CHOICE, contrary to section 32 of the Sexual Offences Act 2003.

Particulars of Offence

D on the...day of...for the purpose of obtaining sexual gratification, intentionally engaged in sexual activity when C was [present] *or* [in a place from which D can be observed] and C being unable to refuse because of or for a reason related to a mental disorder, D [knowing or believing that C is aware] *or* [intending that C should be aware], that he was engaging in such activity, and where D knew or could reasonably have been expected to know that C had a mental disorder.

Alternative Offences

Attempt to commit the full offence. When indicting offences of attempt under SOA 2003, do so under the CAA 1981. Aver the attempt in the Particulars and Statement of Offence. 7.41

Sentence

(i) On indictment: **10 YEARS.**[44] 7.42
(ii) Summarily: **6 months.**[45]

Upon Conviction/Sentence

(i) Notification: applies.[46] 7.43
(ii) Disqualification/barring from working with children/vulnerable adults. See paras 12.135 and 16.33.
(iii) SOPO: applies if criteria met.[47]

6. Causing a Person with a Mental Disorder Impeding Choice to Watch a Sexual Act

Sexual Offences Act 2003, s 33

Definition

(1) A person (A) commits an offence if— 7.44
  (a) for the purpose of obtaining sexual gratification, he intentionally causes another person (B) to watch a third person engaging in an activity, or to look at an image of any person engaging in an activity.
  (b) The activity is sexual,
  (c) B is unable to refuse because of or for a reason related to a mental disorder, and
  (d) A knows or could reasonably be expected to know that B has a mental disorder and that because of it or for a reason related to it B is likely to be unable to refuse.

Proof

See Definition for elements of the offence. 7.45

[44] SOA 2003, s 32(3).
[45] 12 months if CJA 2003, s 282(2) implemented.
[46] SOA 2003, s 80(1) and Sch 3, para 27; see Chapter 14.
[47] SOA 2003, s 104 and Sch 3; see Chapter 16.

Notes

7.46 This offence is triable either way.[48]

Indictment

7.47 CAUSING A PERSON WITH A MENTAL DISORDER IMPEDING CHOICE TO WATCH A SEXUAL ACT 1.5.2004 to date

> **Statement of Offence**
> CAUSING A PERSON WITH A MENTAL DISORDER IMPEDING CHOICE, TO WATCH A SEXUAL ACT, contrary to section 33 of the Sexual Offences Act 2003.
>
> **Particulars of Offence**
> D on the... day of... for the purpose of obtaining sexual gratification, intentionally caused C [to watch X engaging in a sexual activity] *or* [to look at an image of a person engaging in a sexual activity], and C being unable to refuse because of or for a reason related to a mental disorder, and where D knew or could reasonably have been expected to know that C had a mental disorder.

Alternative Offences

7.48 Attempt to commit the full offence. When indicting offences of attempt under the SOA 2003, the charge remains CAA 1981, s 1(1). Aver the attempt in the Statement and Particulars of Offence.

Sentence

7.49 (i) On indictment: **10 YEARS.**[49]
(ii) Summarily: **6 months.**[50]

Upon Conviction/Sentence

7.50 (i) Notification: applies.[51]
(ii) Disqualification/barring from working with children/vulnerable adults. See paras 12.135 and 16.33.
(iii) SOPO: applies.[52]

B. ABUSE OF THE MENTALLY DISORDERED, AS PATIENTS OR BY THOSE WITH CERTAIN RESPONSIBILITY FOR THEM

Offences committed between 1.11.1913 and 31.12.1956

1. Carnal Knowledge of Female under Care/Treatment

Mental Deficiency Act 1913, s 56

Definition

7.51 Any person:

> 1(a) who unlawfully and carnally knows or attempts to have carnal knowledge of, any woman or girl under care or treatment in an institution or certified house or approved home, or whilst placed out on licence therefrom or under guardianship under this Act

---

[48] SOA 2003, s 33(3).
[49] SOA 2003, s 33(3).
[50] 12 months if CJA 2003, s 282(2) implemented.
[51] SOA 2003, s 80(1) and Sch 3(27); see Chapter 14.
[52] SOA 2003, s 104; see Chapter 16.

or...

(e) who with intent that any woman or girl who is a defective should be unlawfully and carnally known by any man whether such carnal knowledge is intended to be with any particular man or generally, takes or causes to be taken such woman or girl out of the possession and against the will of her parent, or any other person having the lawful care or charge of her.

Proof

As per Definition. Note the following: **7.52**

(i) Carnal knowledge is defined as 'proof of penetration'—without necessarily ejaculation.[53]

(ii) The defendant must be proven either not to have known or not to have had reason to suspect that the woman or girl was a defective.[54]

(iii) Defective is defined as a female idiot, imbecile, feeble minded or moral imbecile.[55]

Notes

(i) The offence is triable only on indictment.[56] **7.53**

(ii) This offence may be an alternative to an offence of rape.[57]

Alternative Offences

Section 56(1)(e): an attempt to commit the full offence. When indicting offences of attempt, do so under common law. Aver the attempt in both the Statement and Particulars of Offence. **7.54**

Sentence

On indictment: 2 YEARS.[58] **7.55**

As of 1.1.1957 the MDA 1913, s 56 is repealed. Separate offences are created by ss 8, 9, 21, 27 and 29 of the SOA 1956.[59] **7.56**

Offences committed between 1.1.1957 and 31.10.1960

2. Intercourse with Defectives Receiving Treatment

Sexual Offences Act 1956, s 8

Definition

(1)... unlawful sexual intercourse with a woman who is under care or treatment in an institution, certified house or approved home within the meaning of the Mental Deficiency Act 1913, or placed out on licence therefrom or under guardianship under that Act. **7.57**

Proof

As per Definition. In addition note: **7.58**

(i) Meaning of defective: '... mental defectiveness means a condition of arrested or incomplete development of mind existing before the age of 18, whether arising from inherent causes or induced by disease or injury'.[60]

---

53 *R v Marsden* [1891] 2 QB 149; OAPA 1861, s 63.

54 *R v Marsden* [1891] 2 QB 149; OAPA 1861, s 63, MDA 1913, s 56(1)(e).

55 MDA 1913, s 1.

56 MDA 1913, s 56(4).

57 MDA 1913, s 56(5).

58 MDA 1913, s 56(1)(e).

59 As of 1.1.1957.

60 SOA 1956, s 45(1).

(ii) Meaning of care or treatment: that the woman is under the care or treatment in an institution, certified house or approved home, or placed out on licence.[61] If the female has breached the terms of the licence, or run away, the offence is still committed.[62]

Notes

7.59 (i) The offence is triable only on indictment.[63]

(ii) The defendant is afforded a defence if he can prove that he did not believe and had no reason to believe that the woman was mentally disordered.[64]

(iii) This offence is an alternative to an offence of rape.

Indictment

7.60 INTERCOURSE WITH A MENTALLY DEFECTIVE PATIENT 1.1.1957 to 31.10.1960

Statement of Offence

INTERCOURSE WITH A DEFECTIVE, contrary to section 8 of the Sexual Offences Act 1956.

Particulars of Offence

D on the...day of...had unlawful sexual intercourse with C, a female [under the care/treatment in an institution/certified house/approved home within the meaning of the Mental Deficiency Act 1913] *or* [placed out on licence from...an institution/certified house/approved home within the meaning of the Mental Deficiency Act 1913] *or* [under guardianship of the Mental Deficiency Act 1913].

Alternative Offences

7.61 Attempt to commit the full offence. When indicting offences of attempt indict under common law until 27.8.1981 from which date the CAA 1981 is in force. Aver the attempt in the Statement and Particulars of Offence.

Sentence

7.62 (i) On indictment: **2 YEARS.**[65]

(ii) For an attempt the maximum is the same.[66]

Upon Conviction/Sentence

7.63 (i) Notification: not applicable.[67]

(ii) Disqualification/barring from working with children/vulnerable adults. See paras 12.135 and 16.33.

(iii) SOPO: not applicable.[68]

7.64 *As of 1.11.1960 the MHA 1959, s 128(1) repealed SOA 1956, s 8.*

[61] SOA 1956, s 8.
[62] *R v Balderstone* (1955) 39 Cr App R 97 CCA.
[63] SOA 1956, s 37 and Sch II(12).
[64] SOA 1956, s 47, s 8(1)(2).
[65] SOA 1956, s 37 and Sch II(12)(a).
[66] SOA 1956, s 37 and Sch II(12)(b).
[67] SOA 2003, s 80(1); see Chapter 14.
[68] SOA 2003, s 104; see Chapter 16.

Offences committed between 1.11.1960 and 30.4.2004

3. Intercourse with a Mentally Disordered Patient

Mental Health Act 1959, s 128(1)

Definition

It is an offence: **7.65**

(a) for a man who is an officer on the staff or is otherwise employed in, or is one of the managers of, a hospital or nursing home, to have unlawful sexual intercourse with a woman who is for the time being receiving treatment for mental disorder in that hospital or home, or to have such intercourse on the premises of which the hospital or home forms part with a woman who is for the time being receiving such treatment there as an outpatient;

(b) for a man to have unlawful sexual intercourse with a woman who is a mentally disordered patient and is subject to his guardianship under this Act or is otherwise in his custody or care under this Act or in pursuance of arrangements under the National Health Service Act 1946 or Part III of the National Assistance Act 1948, or as a resident in a residential home for mentally disordered persons within the meaning of Part III of this Act.

Proof

As per Definition. **7.66**

Note:

(i) Sexual intercourse must be proved (penile penetration of the vagina, without necessarily proof of ejaculation).[69]

(ii) This offence also covers buggery of such a female patient, or an act of gross indecency upon another man.[70] This is retrospective.[71]

(iii) It is a complete defence if the defendant proves that he did not know and had no reason to suspect that the complainant was a mentally disordered patient.[72]

Notes

(i) This offence is triable only on indictment. **7.67**

(ii) Consent to prosecute must be obtained from the DPP.[73]

Indictment

INTERCOURSE WITH A MENTALLY DISORDERED PATIENT 1.11.1960 to 30.4.2004 **7.68**

Statement of Offence

UNLAWFUL SEXUAL INTERCOURSE WITH A PATIENT, contrary to section 128(a) Mental Health Act 1959.

Particulars of Offence

D, a man who is an officer on the staff/employed in/a manager of...the...Hospital/the...mental nursing home, on the...day of...had unlawful sexual intercourse with C, a woman receiving treatment at the said...Hospital/...mental nursing home.

[69] SOA 1956, s 44.
[70] SOA 1967, s 1(4).
[71] SOA 1967, s 10(1).
[72] MHA 1959, s 128; SOA 1956, s 47(2).
[73] MHA 1959, s 128(4).

Alternative Offences

7.69 Attempt to commit the full offence. When indicting offences of attempt indict under common law. After 1981 indict under the CAA 1981. Aver the attempt in the Statement and Particulars of Offence.

Sentence

7.70 On indictment:
(i) For the full offence: **2 YEARS.**[74]
(ii) For an attempt: **2 YEARS.**

Upon Conviction/Sentence

7.71 (i) Notification: not applicable.[75]
(ii) Disqualification/barring from working with children/vulnerable adults. See paras 12.135 and 16.33.
(iii) SOPO: not applicable.[76]

Offences committed from 1.5.2004 to date

7.72 The SOA 2003 repealed the MHA 1959, s 128 in full. SOA 2003, s 38 sexual activity with a person with a mental disorder, now covers this offence. Additional offences are created including causing/inciting sexual activity,[77] sexual activity in the presence of a person with a mental disorder[78] or causing a person with a mental disorder to watch a sexual act.[79]

4. Sexual Activity with a Person who has a Mental Disorder by a Care Worker

Sexual Offences Act 2003, s 38

Definition

7.73 (1) A person (A) commits an offence if—
(a) he intentionally touches another person (B),
(b) the touching is sexual,
(c) B has a mental disorder,
(d) A knows or could reasonably be expected to know that B has a mental disorder, and
(e) A is involved in B's care in a way that falls within section 42.

Proof

7.74 (i) See Definition for elements of the offence.
(ii) In relation to ss 38–41 of the SOA 2003, once the prosecution have proved that the complainant had a mental disorder, it is to be taken that the defendant knew or could reasonably have been expected to have known that the complainant had such disorder, unless he adduces sufficient evidence to raise an issue in this regard.

---

[74] MHA 1959, s 128(3).
[75] SOA 2003, s 80(1); see Chapter 14.
[76] SOA 2003, s 104; see Chapter 16.
[77] SOA 2003, s 39.
[78] SOA 2003, s 40.
[79] SOA 2003, s 41.

Notes

(i) If the offence involves penetration then it is triable only on indictment.[80] If penetration is not alleged then the offence is triable either way.[81] **7.75**

(ii) Sections 38–41 are all subject to two exceptions: (a) if the parties are aged 16 or over and are civil partners[82] and (b) if the parties were in a lawful sexual relationship before one of them became the carer.[83]

(iii) Where the offence falls within subsection (3), then this ought to be alleged in the indictment.

(iv) In these cases, questions of the complainant's reliability will often be crucial to the case. If so, this is a question to be decided by a jury, in general.[84]

Indictment

SEXUAL ACTIVITY BY A CARE WORKER WITH A PERSON WITH A MENTAL DISORDER 1.5.2004 to date **7.76**

Statement of Offence

SEXUAL ACTIVITY WITH A PERSON WITH A MENTAL DISORDER BY A CARE WORKER, contrary to section 38(1) [and (3)] of the Sexual Offences Act 2003.

Particulars of Offence

D on the...day of...intentionally touched C, a person with a mental disorder, [by penetrating her mouth with his penis, in circumstances where the touching was sexual, where D knew or could reasonably have been expected to know that C had a mental disorder, and where D was a person involved in C's care in a way falling within section 42 of the Sexual Offences Act 2003.

Alternative Offences

Attempt to commit the full offence. When indicting offences of attempt indict under the CAA 1981. Aver the attempt in the Statement and Particulars of Offence. **7.77**

Sentence

(i) On indictment: **7.78**
- If penetration is involved: **14 YEARS.**[85]
- If no penetration is involved: **10 YEARS.**[86]

(ii) Summarily: **6 months.**[87]

(iii) Attempt: the same maximum.

Upon Conviction/Sentence

(i) Notification: applicable.[88] **7.79**

(ii) Disqualification/barring from working with children/vulnerable adults. See paras 12.135 and 16.33.

(iii) SOPO: applicable, if criteria met.[89]

---

[80] SOA 2003, s 38(3).
[81] SOA 2003, s 38(4).
[82] SOA 2003, s 43.
[83] SOA 2003, s 44.
[84] *R v Watts (James Michael)* [2010] EWCA Crim 1824, [2011] CLR 68.
[85] SOA 2003, s 38(3).
[86] SOA 2003, s 38(4).
[87] 12 months if CJA 2003, s 282(2) implemented.
[88] SOA 2003, s 80(1) and Sch 3, para 28; see Chapter 14.
[89] SOA 2003, s 104 and Sch 3, para (28); see Chapter 16.

5. Care Workers Causing or Inciting Sexual Activity with a Person with a Mental Disorder

Sexual Offences Act 2003, s 39

Definition

7.80 (1) A person (A) commits an offence if—
(a) he intentionally causes or incites another person (B) to engage in an activity,
(b) the activity is sexual,
(c) B has a mental disorder,
(d) A knows or could reasonably be expected to know that B has a mental disorder, and
(e) A is involved in B's care in a way that falls within section 42.

Proof

7.81 See Definition for elements of the offence.

Notes

7.82 (i) If the offence involves penetration then it is triable only on indictment.[90] If penetration is not alleged then the offence is triable either way.[91]
(ii) Sections 38–41 are all subject to two exceptions: (a) if the parties are aged 16 or over and are civil partners[92] and (b) if the parties were in a lawful sexual relationship before one of them became the carer.[93]
(iii) Where the offence falls within subsection (3), then this ought to be alleged in the indictment.

Indictment

7.83 CAUSING/INCITING SEXUAL ACTIVITY WITH A PERSON WITH A MENTAL DISORDER BY A CARE WORKER 1.5.2004 to date

Statement of Offence

CAUSING OR INCITING SEXUAL ACTIVITY WITH A PERSON WITH A MENTAL DISORDER BY A CARE WORKER, contrary to section 39(1) [and (3)] of the Sexual Offences Act 2003.

Particulars of Offence

D on the... day of... intentionally caused/incited C, a person with a mental disorder, to engage in sexual activity, [which involved penetration of C's...... with Z's......,] where D knew or could reasonably be expected to know that C had a mental disorder, and where D was a person involved in C's care in a way falling within section 42 of the Sexual Offences Act 2003.

Alternative Offences

7.84 Attempt to commit the full offence. Indict under s 1(1) of the CAA 1981. Aver the attempt in the Statement and Particulars of Offence.

Sentence

7.85 (i) On indictment:
- If penetration involved: **14 YEARS.**[94]

[90] SOA 2003, s 39(3).
[91] SOA 2003, s 39(4).
[92] SOA 2003, s 43.
[93] SOA 2003, s 44.
[94] SOA 2003, s 39(3).

- If no penetration: **10 YEARS.**[95]

(ii) Summarily: **6 months.**[96]
(iii) An attempt attracts the same sentences.

Upon Sentence/Conviction

(i) Notification requirements: applicable, subject to certain criteria being met.[97] **7.86**
(ii) Disqualification/barring from working with children/vulnerable adults. See paras 12.135 and 16.33.
(iii) SOPO: applicable, subject to certain criteria being met.[98]

6. Care Workers: Sexual Activity in the Presence of a Person with a Mental Disorder

Sexual Offences Act 2003, s 40

Definition

(1) A person (A) commits an offence if— **7.87**
(a) he intentionally engages in an activity,
(b) the activity is sexual,
(c) for the purpose of obtaining sexual gratification, he engages in it—
(i) when another person (B) is present or in a place from which A can be observed, and
(ii) knowing or believing that B is aware, or intending that B should be aware, that he is engaging in it,
(d) B has a mental disorder,
(e) A knows or could reasonably be expected to know that B has a mental disorder, and
(f) A is involved in B's care in a way that falls within section 42.

Proof

See Definition for elements of offence. **7.88**

Notes

(i) This offence is triable either way.[99] **7.89**
(ii) Sections 38–41 are all subject to two exceptions: (a) if the parties are aged 16 or over and are civil partners[100] and (b) if the parties were in a lawful sexual relationship before one of them became the carer.[101]

Indictment

SEXUAL ACTIVITY IN THE PRESENCE OF A PERSON WITH A MENTAL DISORDER 1.5.04 to date **7.90**

> **Statement of Offence**
> SEXUAL ACTIVITY IN THE PRESENCE OF A PERSON WITH A MENTAL DISORDER, contrary to section 40 of the Sexual Offences Act 2003.

[95] SOA 2003, s 39(4).
[96] 12 months if CJA 2003, s 282(3) implemented.
[97] SOA 2003, s 80(1) and Sch 3, para 28; see Chapter 14.
[98] SOA 2003, s 104 and Sch 3, para 28; see Chapter 16.
[99] SOA 2003, s 40(3).
[100] SOA 2003, s 43.
[101] SOA 2003, s 44.

Particulars of Offence

D on the . . . day of . . . for the purpose of obtaining sexual gratification, intentionally engaged in a sexual activity when C, who has a mental disorder [was present] *or* [was in a place from which D could be observed], [knowing or believing that C was aware] *or* [intending that C should be aware] that he was engaging in such activity, and where D knew or could reasonably be expected to have known that C had a mental disorder, and where D was a person involved in C's care in a way falling within section 42 of the Sexual Offences Act 2003.

Alternative Offences

7.91 Attempt to commit the full offence. Indict under s1(1) of the CAA 1981. Aver the attempt in the Statement and Particulars of Offence.

Sentence

7.92 (i) On indictment: **7 YEARS.**[102]
(ii) Summarily: **6 months.**[103]
(iii) Attempt: the same.

Upon Conviction/Sentence

7.93 (i) Notification applies, subject to certain criteria being met.[104]
(ii) Disqualification/barring from working with children/vulnerable adults. See paras 12.135 and 16.33.
(iii) SOPO applies, subject to certain criteria being met.[105]

7. Care Workers: Causing a Person with a Mental Disorder to Watch a Sexual Act

Sexual Offences Act 2003, s 41

Definition

7.94 (1) A person (A) commits an offence if—
(a) for the purpose of obtaining sexual gratification, he intentionally causes another person (B) to watch a third person engaging in an activity, or to look at an image of any person engaging in an activity,
(b) the activity is sexual,
(c) B has a mental disorder,
(d) A knows or could reasonably be expected to know that B has a mental disorder, and
(e) A is involved in B's care in a way that falls within section 42.

Proof

7.95 See Definition for elements of the offence.

---

102 SOA 2003, s 40(3).
103 12 months if CJA 2003, s 282(2) implemented.
104 SOA 2003, s 80 and Sch 3, para 28; see Chapter 14.
105 SOA 2003, s 104 and Sch 3, para 28; see Chapter 16.

Notes

(i) This offence is triable either way.[106] **7.96**

(ii) Sections 38–41 are all subject to two exceptions:
   (a) if the parties are aged 16 or over and are civil partners;[107] and
   (b) if the parties were in a lawful sexual relationship before one of them became the carer.[108]

Indictment

CAUSING A PERSON WITH A MENTAL DISORDER TO WATCH A SEXUAL ACT BY A CARE WORKER 1.5.2004 to date **7.97**

Statement of Offence

CAUSING A PERSON WITH A MENTAL DISORDER TO WATCH A SEXUAL ACT BY A CARE WORKER, contrary to section 41(1) of the Sexual Offences Act 2003.

Particulars of Offence

D on the...day of 20...for the purpose of obtaining sexual gratification, intentionally caused C, a person with a mental disorder, [to watch a third person engaging in a sexual activity] *or* [to look at an image of any person engaging in a sexual activity] where D knew or could reasonably be expected to have known that C had a mental disorder, and where D was a person involved in C's care in a way falling within section 42 of the Sexual Offences Act 2003.

Alternative Offences

Attempt to commit the full offence, charge under the CAA 1981, s 1(1). Aver the attempt in the Statement and Particulars of Offence. **7.98**

Sentence

(i) On indictment: **7 YEARS.**[109] **7.99**
(ii) Summarily: **6 months.**[110]
(iii) Attempt: the same.

Upon Conviction/Sentence

(i) Notification applies: subject to certain criteria being met.[111] **7.100**
(ii) Disqualification/barring from working with children/vulnerable adults. See paras 12.135 and 16.33.
(iii) SOPO applies, subject to certain criteria being met.[112]

---

106 SOA 2003, s 41(3).
107 SOA 2003, s 43.
108 SOA 2003, s 44.
109 SOA 2003, s 41(3).
110 12 months if CJA 2003, s 282(2) implemented.
111 SOA 2003, s 80(1) and Sch 3, para 28; see Chapter 14.
112 SOA 2003, s 104 and Sch 3, para 28; see Chapter 16.

C. OFFENCES DESIGNED TO PROTECT THE MENTALLY DISORDERED FROM PROCURATION

Offences committed pre-31.12.1956

1. Procuring a Female to have Carnal Connection

Mental Deficiency Act 1913, s 56

Definition

7.101 Any person who '. . . 1(b) who procures, or attempts to procure any woman or girl who is a defective to have unlawful carnal connection whether within or without the King's dominions, with any person or persons'.

Proof

7.102 As per Definition, in addition the prosecution must prove:
(i) sexual intercourse (penile penetration of the vagina), without necessarily ejaculation;[113]
(ii) that the female was defective within the definition (see para 7.52);
(iii) that the defendant knew or had reason to suspect that the woman or girl was a defective.[114]

Notes

7.103 (i) The offence is triable only on indictment.[115]
(ii) This offence may be an alternative to an offence of rape.[116]

Sentence

7.104 On indictment: 2 YEARS.[117]

7.105 *As of 1.1.1957, s 56 of the MDA 1913 is repealed. From 1.1.1957 s 9 of the SOA 1956 covers this offence.*

1.1.1957 to 30.4.2004

2. Procurement of a Defective

Sexual Offences Act 1956, s 9

Definition

7.106 (1)...to procure a woman who is a defective to have unlawful sexual intercourse in any part of the world.

Proof

7.107 (i) Procuration is proved by showing that the defendant 'set about to see that it [unlawful sexual intercourse] happens, and takes the appropriate steps to produce it happening'.[118]

---

113 *R v Marsden* [1891] 2 QB 149; and later OAPA 1861, s 63.

114 *R v Marsden* [1891] 2 QB 149; OAPA 1861, s 63, MDA 1913, s 56(1)(e).

115 MDA 1913, s 56(4).

116 MDA 1913, s 56(5).

117 MDA 1913, s 56(1)(e).

118 *AG's Reference (No 1 of 1975)* [1975] QB 773, 61 Cr App R 118 CA.

(ii) See para 7.58 for definition of mental defective.[119]
(iii) See para 7.66 for definition of sexual intercourse.[120]
(iv) The defendant is afforded a defence if he can prove that he did not know and had no reason to suspect that the female was defective.[121]

Notes

(i) Triable only on indictment.[122] 7.108
(ii) The offence may be committed by a male or female upon a female.

Indictment

PROCUREMENT OF A DEFECTIVE 1.1.1957 to 30.4.2004 7.109

Statement of Offence

PROCUREMENT OF A DEFECTIVE TO HAVE UNLAWFUL SEXUAL INTERCOURSE, contrary to section 9(1) of the Sexual Offences Act 1956.

Particulars of offence

D on the...day of...procured C, a woman who is a defective, to have unlawful sexual intercourse.

Alternative Offences

Attempt to commit the full offence. When indicting offences of attempt, until 26.8.1981, do so under common law, thereafter charge under s 1(1) of the CAA 1981. Aver the attempt in the Statement and Particulars of Offence. 7.110

Sentence

(i) On indictment: **2 YEARS.**[123] 7.111
(ii) An attempt carries the same maximum.[124]

Upon Conviction/Sentence

(i) Notification: not applicable.[125] 7.112
(ii) Disqualification/barring from working with children/vulnerable adults. See paras 12.135 and 16.33.
(iii) SOPO: not applicable.[126]

Offences committed from 1.5.2004 to date

The SOA 2003, Sch 7 repealed the SOA 1956, s 9(1) in full. A number of new offences in this area are created. These include procuring by inducement, threat or deception sexual activity with a mentally disordered person,[127] causing a person with a mental disorder to engage in or agree to engage in sexual activity by inducement, threat or deception,[128] engaging in sexual activity in the presence, procured by inducement, threat or deception of a mentally disordered person[129] or causing a mentally disordered person to watch sexual activity by inducement, threat or deception.[130] 7.113

119 SOA 1956, s 45.
120 SOA 1956, s 44.
121 SOA 1956, s 9(2) and s 47.
122 SOA 1956, s 37 and Sch II(13).
123 SOA 1956, s 37 and Sch II(13)(a).
124 SOA 1956, s 37 and Sch II(13)(b).
125 SOA 2003, s 80(1); see Chapter 14.
126 SOA 2003, s 104; see Chapter 16.
127 SOA 2003, s 34.
128 SOA 2003, s 35.
129 SOA 2003, s 36.
130 SOA 2003, s 37.

3. Procuring by Inducement, Threat or Deception Sexual Activity with a Mentally Disordered Person

Sexual Offences Act 2003, s 34

Definition

7.114 (1) A person (A) commits an offence if—
(a) with the agreement of another person (B) he intentionally touches that person,
(b) the touching is sexual,
(c) A obtains B's agreement by means of an inducement offered or given, a threat made or a deception practised by A for that purpose,
(d) B has a mental disorder, and
(e) A knows or could reasonably be expected to know that B has a mental disorder.

Proof

7.115 See Definition for elements of offence.

Notes

7.116 (i) If the offence involves penetration then it is triable only on indictment.[131] If penetration is not alleged then the offence is triable either way.[132]
(ii) Where the offence falls within subsection (2), then this ought to be alleged in the indictment.

Indictment

7.117 INDUCEMENT, THREAT OR DECEPTION TO PROCURE SEXUAL ACTIVITY WITH A PERSON WITH A MENTAL DISORDER 1.5.2004 to date

Statement of Offence

SEXUAL ACTIVITY WITH A PERSON WITH A MENTAL DISORDER WHOSE AGREEMENT THERTO IS PROCURED BY INDUCEMENT THREAT OR DECEPTION, contrary to section 34(1) and (2) of the Sexual Offences Act 2003.

Particulars of Offence

D on the... day of 20.., intentionally touched C, a person with a mental disorder, by penetrating her mouth with his penis, in circumstances where the touching was sexual, where C agreed to the touching, where D had obtained her agreement by [giving her an inducement] *or* [making a threat] or [practising deception], (namely...) and where D knew or could reasonably have been expected to know that C had a mental disorder.

Alternative Offences

7.118 Attempt to commit the full offence, charge under s 1(1) of the CAA 1981. Aver the attempt in the Statement and Particulars of Offence.

Sentence

7.119 (i) On indictment:
- If penetration is involved: **LIFE.**[133]
- If no penetration is involved: **14 YEARS.**[134]

[131] SOA 2003, s 34(2).
[132] SOA 2003, s 34(3).
[133] SOA 2003, s 34(2).
[134] SOA 2003, s 34(3)(b).

(ii) Summarily: **6 months.**[135]
(iii) Attempt: the same.

Upon Conviction/Sentence

(i) Notification: applicable.[136] **7.120**
(ii) Disqualification/barring from working with children/vulnerable adults. See paras 12.135 and 16.33.
(iii) SOPO: applies if the criteria are met.[137]

4. Causing a Person with a Mental Disorder to Engage in Sexual Activity by Inducement, Threat or Deception

Sexual Offences Act 2003, s 35

Definition

(1) A person (A) commits an offence if— **7.121**
 (a) by means of an inducement offered or given, a threat made or a deception practised by him for this purpose, he intentionally causes another person (B) to engage in, or to agree to engage in, an activity,
 (b) the activity is sexual,
 (c) B has a mental disorder, and
 (d) A knows or could reasonably be expected to know that B has a mental disorder.

Proof

See Definition for elements of the offence. **7.122**

Notes

(i) If the offence involves penetration then it is triable only on indictment.[138] If penetration is not alleged then the offence is triable either way.[139] **7.123**
(ii) Where the offence falls within subsection (2), then this ought to be alleged in the indictment.

Indictment

CAUSING A PERSON WITH A MENTAL DISORDER TO ENGAGE IN SEXUAL ACTIVITY 1.5.2004 to date **7.124**

Statement of Offence

CAUSING A PERSON WITH A MENTAL DISORDER TO ENGAGE IN OR AGREE TO ENGAGE IN SEXUAL ACTIVITY BY INDUCEMENT, THREAT OR DECEPTION, contrary to section 35(1) and (2) of the Sexual Offences Act 2003.

Particulars of Offence

D on the . . . day of 20 intentionally caused C to [engage in] *or* [agree to engage in] the pen etration of D's mouth/anus/vagina with C's penis a sexual activity, where C [agreed to the activity] *or* [engaged in the activity] and D had obtained her agreement by [giving her an inducement] *or* [making a threat] *or* [practising a deception] (namely. . .) and where D knew or could reasonably have been expected to know that C had a mental disorder.

---

[135] SOA 2003, s 34(3)(a). 12 months if CJA 2003, s 282(2) is implemented.
[136] SOA 2003, s 80(1) and Sch 3, para 27; see Chapter 14.
[137] SOA 2003, s 104 and Sch 3, para 27; see Chapter 16.
[138] SOA 2003, s 35(2).
[139] SOA 2003, s 35(3)(a).

Alternative Offences

7.125 Attempt to commit the full offence, charge under the CAA 1981, s 1(1). Aver the attempt in the Statement and Particulars of Offence.

Sentence

7.126 (i) On indictment:
- If penetration is involved: **LIFE.**[140]
- If no penetration is involved: **14 YEARS.**[141]

(ii) Summarily: **6 months.**[142]
(iii) Attempt: the same.

Upon Conviction/Sentence

7.127 (i) Notification: applies if criteria met.[143]
(ii) Disqualification/barring from working with children/vulnerable adults. See paras 12.135 and 16.33.
(iii) SOPO applies, if criteria met.[144]

5. Engaging in Sexual Activity in the Presence, Procured by Inducement, Threat or Deception, of a Person with a Mental Disorder

Sexual Offences Act 2003, s 36

Definition

7.128 (1) A person (A) commits an offence if—
(a) he intentionally engages in an activity,
(b) the activity is sexual,
(c) for the purpose of obtaining sexual gratification, he engages in it—
(i) when another person (B) is present or is in a place from which A can be observed, and
(ii) knowing or believing that B is aware, or intending that B should be aware, that he is engaging in it,
(d) B agrees to be present or in the place referred to in paragraph (c)(i) because of an inducement offered or given, a threat made or a deception practised by A for the purpose of obtaining that agreement,
(e) B has a mental disorder, and
(f) A knows or could reasonably be expected to know that B has a mental disorder.

Proof

7.129 See Definition for elements of offence.

Notes

7.130 This offence is triable either way.[145]

---

140 SOA 2003, s 35(2).
141 SOA 2003, s 35(3)(b).
142 SOA 2003, s 35(3). 12 months if CJA 2003, s 282(2) implemented.
143 SOA 2003, s 80(1) and Sch 3, para 27; see Chapter 14.
144 SOA 2003, s 104 and Sch 3, para 27; see Chapter 16.
145 SOA 2003, s 36(2).

Indictment

ENGAGING IN SEXUAL ACTIVITY IN THE PRESENCE, PROCURED BY INDUCEMENT, THREAT OR DECEPTION, OF A PERSON WITH A MENTAL DISORDER 1.5.2004 to date **7.131**

Statement of Offence

ENGAGING IN SEXUAL ACTIVITY IN THE PRESENCE, PROCURED BY INDUCEMENT, THREAT OR DECEPTION, OF A PERSON WITH A MENTAL DISORDER, contrary to section 36(1) of the Sexual Offences Act 2003.

Particulars of Offence

D on the...day of 20.., for the purpose of obtaining sexual gratification, intentionally engaged in an activity and that activity was sexual, [when C was present] or [in a place from which D could be observed], [knowing or believing that C was aware] *or* [intending that C be aware] that he is engaging in it, and D had obtained C's agreement by [giving her an inducement] *or* [making a threat] *or* [a deception practised by D] for the purpose of obtaining that agreement, and where D knew or could reasonably have been expected to know that C had a mental disorder.

Alternative Offences

Attempt to commit the full offence; charge under of the CAA 1981, s 1(1). Aver the attempt in the Statement and Particulars of Offence. **7.132**

Sentence

(i) On indictment: **10 YEARS.**[146] **7.133**
(ii) Summarily: **6 months.**[147]
(iii) Attempt: the same.

Upon Conviction/Sentence

(i) Notification: applies if criteria met.[148] **7.134**
(ii) Disqualification/barring from working with children/vulnerable adults. See paras 12.135 and 16.33.
(iii) SOPO applies if criteria met.[149]

6. Causing a Person with a Mental Disorder to Watch a Sexual Act by Inducement, Threat or Deception

Sexual Offences Act 2003, s 37

Definition

(1) A person (A) commits an offence if— **7.135**
(a) for the purpose of obtaining sexual gratification, he intentionally causes another person (B) to watch a third person engaging in an activity, or to look at an image of any person engaging in an activity,
(b) the activity is sexual,

146 SOA 2003, s 36(2).
147 SOA 2003, s 36(2)(a). 12 months if CJA 2003, s 282(2) implemented.
148 SOA 2003, s 80(1) and Sch 3, para 27; see Chapter 14.
149 SOA 2003, s 104 and Sch 3, para 27; see Chapter 16.

(c) B agrees to watch or look because of an inducement offered or given, a threat made or a deception practised by A for the purpose of obtaining that agreement,
(d) B has a mental disorder, and
(e) A knows or could reasonably be expected to know that B has a mental disorder.

Proof

7.136 See Definition for elements of offence.

Notes

7.137 This offence is triable either way.[150]

Indictment

7.138 CAUSING A PERSON WITH A MENTAL DISORDER TO WATCH A SEXUAL ACT BY INDUCEMENT, THREAT OR DECEPTION 1.5.2004 to date

Statement of Offence

CAUSING A PERSON WITH A MENTAL DISORDER TO WATCH A SEXUAL ACT BY INDUCEMENT, THREAT OR DECEPTION, contrary to section 37(1) of the Sexual Offences Act 2003.

Particulars of Offence

D on the…day of 20.., for the purpose of sexual gratification, intentionally caused C, a person with a mental disorder, [to watch X engaging in a sexual activity] *or* [to look at an image of any person engaging in sexual activity], and D had obtained C's agreement by [giving her an inducement] *or* [making a threat] *or* [a deception practised by D] for the purpose of obtaining that agreement, and where D knew or could reasonably have been expected to know that C had a mental disorder.

Alternative Offences

7.139 Attempt to commit the full offence, charge under of the CAA 1981, s 1(1). Aver the attempt in the Statement and Particulars of Offence.

Sentence

7.140 (i) On indictment: **10 YEARS.**[151]
(ii) Summarily: **6 months.**[152]
(iii) Attempt: the same.

Upon Conviction/Sentence

7.141 (i) Notification: applies if criteria met.[153]
(ii) Disqualification/barring from working with children/vulnerable adults. See paras 12.135 and 16.33.
(iii) SOPO applies if criteria met.[154]

---

150 SOA 2003, s 37(2).
151 SOA 2003, s 36(2).
152 SOA 2003, s 36(2). 12 months if CJA 2003, s 282(2) is implemented.
153 SOA 2003, s 80(1) and Sch 3, para 27; see Chapter 14.
154 SOA 2003, s 104 and Sch 3, para 27; see Chapter 16.

D. OFFENCES PROTECTING THE MENTALLY DISORDERED FROM PROSTITUTION OR ABUSE UPON PREMISES

Offences committed pre-1.1.1957

Section 56(1) of the Mental Deficiency Act 1913 created two offences. **7.142**
(i) Section 56(1)(c): causing or encouraging prostitution of a defective.
(ii) Section 56(1)(d): being the owner/occupier of premises used for sexual activity with a defective.

1. Causing or Encouraging Prostitution of a Defective

Mental Deficiency Act 1913, s 56(1)(c)

Definition

Any person '... causes or encourages prostitution whether within or without the King's dominions of any woman or girl who is defective'. **7.143**

Proof

(i) As per Definition. **7.144**
(ii) See para 7.52 for definition of defective.
(iii) The prosecution must prove that he did not know or have reason to suspect that the woman or girl was a defective.[155]

Notes

(i) The offence is triable only on indictment.[156] **7.145**
(ii) This offence may be an alternative to an offence of rape.[157]

Sentence

(i) On indictment: 2 YEARS.[158] **7.146**
(ii) Attempt: the same.

2. Permitting Premises to be Used for Sexual Intercourse with a Female Defective

Mental Deficiency Act 1913, s 56(1)(d)

Definition

Any person '... being the owner or occupier of any premises, or having or acting or assisting in the management or control thereof, induces or knowingly suffers any woman or girl who is a defective to resort to or be in or upon such premises for the purpose of being unlawfully and carnally known by any man whether such carnal knowledge is intended to be with any particular man or generally'. **7.147**

---

[155] MDA 1913, s 56(1)(e).
[156] MDA 1913, s 56(4).
[157] MDA 1913, s 56(5).
[158] MDA 1913, s 56(1)(e).

Proof

7.148 As per Definition. Of note is:

(i) Carnal knowledge is defined as penile penetration of the vagina, without necessarily ejaculation.[159]

(ii) The prosecution must prove that the defendant knew or had reason to suspect that the woman or girl was a defective.[160]

Notes

7.149 (i) The offence is triable only on indictment.[161]

(ii) This offence may be an alternative to an offence of rape.[162]

Sentence

7.150 On indictment: **2 YEARS.**[163]

Offences committed between 1.1.1957 to 30.4.2004

7.151 As of 1.1.1957 the MDA 1913, s 56 was repealed. Two offences were created.

7.152 The SOA 1956, s 29 covers the offence of causing or encouraging the prostitution of any woman or girl who is a defective.

7.153 The SOA 1956, s 27 covers the offence of permitting a defective to use premises for intercourse.

3. Causing or Encouraging the Prostitution of any Woman or Girl who is a Defective

Sexual Offences Act 1956, s 29

Definition

7.154 ...to cause or encourage the prostitution in any part of the world of any woman or girl who is a defective.

Proof

7.155 (i) As per Definition.

(ii) See para 7.58 for definition of mental defective.

(iii) It is a defence for the defendant to prove that he did not know and had no reason to suspect the female to be a defective.[164]

Notes

7.156 This offence is triable only on indictment.[165]

Indictment

7.157 CAUSING/ENCOURAGING PROSTITUTION OF A DEFECTIVE 1.1.1957 to 30.4.2004

---

[159] *R v Marsden* (1891) 2 QB 149; and later OAPA 1861, s 63.

[160] MDA 1913, s 56(1)(e).

[161] MDA 1913, s 56(4).

[162] MDA 1913, s 56(5).

[163] MDA 1913, s 56(1(e).

[164] SOA 1956, s 29(2).

[165] SOA 1956, s 37 and Sch 2, para 39.

Statement of Offence

CAUSING/ENCOURAGING PROSTITUTION OF A DEFECTIVE, contrary to section 29 of the Sexual Offences Act 1956.

Particulars of Offence

D on the... day of... caused/encouraged the prostitution of C, a woman who is a defective.

Sentence

(i) On indictment: **2 YEARS.**[166] **7.158**
(ii) Attempt: the same.

Upon Conviction/Sentence

(i) Notification; not applicable.[167] **7.159**
(ii) Disqualification/barring from working with children/vulnerable adults. See paras 12.135 and 16.33.
(iii) SOPO: not applicable.[168]

4. Permitting a Defective to Use Premises for Intercourse

Sexual Offences Act 1956, s 27

Definition

...a person who is the owner or occupier of any premises, or who has or acts or assists in the management or control of any premises, to induce or knowingly suffer a woman who is a defective to resort to or be on those premises for the purpose of having unlawful sexual intercourse with men or with a particular man. **7.160**

Proof

(i) See Definition. **7.161**
(ii) See para 7.58 for definition of mental defective.
(iii) It is a defence for the defendant to prove that he did not know nor had reason to suspect her to be defective.[169]

Notes

The offence is triable only on indictment.[170] **7.162**

Indictment

PERMITTING A DEFECTIVE TO USE PREMISES FOR INTERCOURSE 1.1.1957 to 30.4.2004 **7.163**

Statement of Offence

PERMITTING A DEFECTIVE TO USE PREMISES FOR INTERCOURSE, contrary to section 27 of the Sexual Offences Act 1956.

166 SOA 1956, s 37 and Sch II, para 29.
167 SOA 2003, s 80(1); see Chapter 14.
168 SOA 2003, s 104; see Chapter 16.
169 SOA 1956, s 27(2) and s 47.
170 SOA 1956, s 37 and Sch II, para 27.

Particulars of Offence

D, being an [owner/occupier of any premises] *or* [a person who acts/assists in the management/control of premises] namely..., on the...day of..., induced/knowingly suffered C, a woman who is a defective, to resort to/to be on those premises for the purpose of having unlawful sexual intercourse with men/a man.

Sentence

7.164 On indictment: 2 YEARS.[171]

Upon Conviction/Sentence

7.165 (i) Notification: not applicable.[172]
(ii) Disqualification from working with children applies if criteria met.[173]
(iii) SOPO: not applicable.[174]

Offences committed from 1.5.2004 to date

7.166 The SOA 2003 repealed the SOA 1956, ss 27 and 29. Section 52 covers the offence of causing or inciting prostitution for gain. Section 53 covers the offence of controlling prostitution for gain. In each case there is no requirement that the prostitution involved is that of a mentally disordered person.

5. Causing or Inciting Prostitution for Gain

Sexual Offences Act 2003, s 52

Definition

7.167 Any person who

(a) ...intentionally causes or incites another person to become a prostitute in any part of the world, and
(b) he does so for or in the expectation of gain for himself or a third person.

Proof

7.168 (i) See Definition for elements of offence.
(ii) 'Gain' is defined as 'any financial advantage...or...goodwill...which appears likely to bring financial advantage'.[175]
(iii) Prostitution covers the offer of sexual services to another in return for payment or promise of payment.[176]

Notes

7.169 This offence is triable either way.[177]

---

171 SOA 1956, s 37 and Sch II(39).
172 SOA 2003, s 80(1); see Chapter 14.
173 Criminal Justice and Courts Services Act 2000, s 26(1) and Sch 4, para 3(k); see para 12.135.
174 SOA 2003, s 104; see Chapter 16.
175 SOA 2003, s 54(1).
176 SOA 2003, ss 51(2) and 54(2).
177 SOA 2003, s 52(2).

Indictment

CAUSING OR INCITING PROSTITUTION FOR GAIN 1.5.2004 to date **7.170**

Statement of Offence

CAUSING OR INCITING PROSTITUTION FOR GAIN, contrary to section 52(1) of the Sexual Offences Act 2003.

Particulars of Offence

D on the... of 20.., intentionally incited C to become a prostitute and did so for or in the expectation of gain for himself or of a third person.

Alternative Offences

Attempt to commit the full offence; charge under of the CAA 1981, s 1(1). Aver the attempt in the Statement and Particulars of Offence. **7.171**

Sentence

(i) On indictment: **7 YEARS.**[178] **7.172**
(ii) Summarily: **6 months.**[179]
(iii) Attempt: the same.

Upon Conviction/Sentence

(i) Notification; not applicable.[180] **7.173**
(ii) Disqualification/barring from working with children/vulnerable adults. See paras 12.135 and 16.33.
(iii) SOPO: not applicable.[181]

6. Controlling Prostitution for Gain

Sexual Offences Act 2003, s 53(1)

Definition

Any person who **7.174**

(a) ...intentionally controls any of the activities of another person relating to that person's prostitution in any part of the world, and
(b) he does so for or in the expectation of gain for himself or a third person.

Proof

(i) Intentional control of activities relating to prostitution;[182] **7.175**
(ii) the expectation of (some) gain for himself or a third party;[183]
(iii) prostitution covers the mere offer on one occasion, of sexual services to another in return for payment/promise of payment.[184]

Notes

(i) This offence is triable either way.[185] **7.176**

[178] SOA 2003, s 5(2)(b).
[179] SOA 2003, s 52(2)(a). 12 months if CJA 2003, s 282(2) is implemented.
[180] SOA 2003, s 80(1); see Chapter 14.
[181] SOA 2003, s 104; see Chapter 16.
[182] SOA 2003, s 53(1)(a).
[183] SOA 2003, s 53(1)(b).
[184] SOA 2003, s 51(2).
[185] SOA 2003, s 53(2).

(ii) Control is to be given its ordinary English usage and covers instructing or directing a person to carry out the relevant activity or to do it in a certain way. The person may agree for a variety of reasons including even the simple hope of a better life. It does not require force or coercion.[186]

Indictment

7.177 **CONTROLLING PROSTITUTION FOR GAIN** 1.5.2004 to date

> **Statement of Offence**
>
> CONTROLLING PROSTITUTION FOR GAIN, contrary to section 53(1) of the Sexual Offences Act 2003.
>
> **Particulars of Offence**
>
> D on the... day of 20.., intentionally controlled the activities of C relating to the said C's prostitution.

Alternative Offences

7.178 Attempt to commit the full offence, charge under s 1(1) of the CAA 1981. Aver the attempt in the Statement and Particulars of Offence.

Sentence

7.179 (i) On indictment: **7 YEARS.**[187]
(ii) Summarily: **6 months.**[188]
(iii) Attempt: the same.

Upon Conviction/sentence

7.180 (i) Notification; not applicable.[189]
(ii) Disqualification/barring from working with children/vulnerable adults. See paras 12.135 and 16.33.
(iii) SOPO: not applicable.[190]

---

[186] *Massey* [2007] EWCA Crim 2664.
[187] SOA 2003, s 53(2)(b).
[188] SOA 2003, s 53(2)(a). 12 months if CJA 2003, s 282(2) implemented.
[189] SOA 2003, s 80(1); see Chapter 14.
[190] SOA 2003, s 104; see Chapter 16.

8

PROSTITUTION AND TRAFFICKING

Introduction

8.01 Before the SOA 1956 was passed, several offences relating to prostitution and trading in prostitution existed, in particular under the Vagrancy Act 1898.[1] Taking into account the rarity of these pre-1.1.1957 offences being prosecuted, only one, procuration of women under 21 into prostitution, has been included.[2]

8.02 After 1.1.1957 a great number of offences were created to deal with prostitution and the exploitation of prostitutes.

8.03 Until the passing of the SOA 2003 there were few statutory offences dealing with the exploitation of male prostitutes. Such offences as did exist dealt primarily with adult males/females living off the earnings of male prostitution[3] (except the offence of Solicitation by Men, contrary to the SOA 1956, s 32; see paras 8.96–8.102).

8.04 It was only after 1.5.2004 that the offences of procuring or causing prostitution of males were made offences.[4] Further, summary only offences of kerb crawling and soliciting were extended to cover male and female prostitutes.[5]

8.05 See paras 7.143–7.146 for offences involving prostitution and the mentally disordered.

8.06 Theses offences have been dealt with chronologically, in their categories:

A. Causing or encouraging prostitution of young women
B. Causing prostitution of women
C. Living on the earnings of prostitution
D. Trafficking of prostitutes

A. CAUSING OR ENCOURAGING PROSTITUTION OF YOUNG WOMEN OR GIRLS

Offences committed pre-31.12.1956

1. Procuration of Women under 21 into Prostitution

Criminal Law Amendment Act 1885, s 2

Definition

8.07 Procures or attempts to procure any girl or woman under 21 years of age to have unlawful carnal connection, either within or without the Queen's dominions with any other person or persons; or

(1) Procures or attempts to procure any woman or girl to become, either within or without the Queen's dominions, a common prostitute; or
(2) Procures or attempts to procure any woman or girl to leave the United Kingdom with intent that she may become an inmate of a brothel elsewhere; or
(3) Procures or attempts to procure any woman or girl to leave her usual place of abode in the United Kingdom (such place not being a brothel) with intent that she may, for the purposes of prostitution, become an inmate of or frequent a brothel within or without the Queen's dominions.

Proof

8.08 As per Definition.

---

[1] Vagrancy Act (VA) 1898, s 1: living off the earnings of prostitution. Commencement date 12.10.1898.
[2] CLAA 1885, s 2.
[3] SOA 1967, s 5.
[4] SOA 2003, ss 52 and 53.
[5] SOA 2003, s 56 and Sch 1.

In addition:

(i) 'common prostitute' covers the offer by a woman of her body for acts of 'lewdness' for payment in return.[6] The female has to be prepared to make such an offer to 'all and sundry' for any one who might hire her for that purpose, not just on one occasion.[7]

Notes

Triable on indictment only. 8.09

Indictment

PROCURING A WOMAN UNDER 21 TO BECOME A COMMON PROSTITUTE 8.10
Pre-31.12.1956

Statement of Offence

PROCURING A WOMAN TO BECOME A COMMON PROSTITUTE, contrary to section 2(1) of the Criminal Law Amendment Act 1885.

Particulars of Offence

D on the... day of... procured C, a woman, not being a common prostitute, aged under 21 years, to become a common prostitute.

Alternative Offences

An attempt to commit the full offence, contrary to common law. Aver attempt in both Statement 8.11
and Particulars of Offence. See para 2.10.

Sentence

On indictment: 2 YEARS. 8.12

Offences committed between 1.1.1957 and 30.4.2004

From 1.1.1957 the CLAA 1898, s 2 is repealed. Sections 28 (procuration of a girl under 16) and 8.13
23 (procuration of a girl under 21) of the SOA 1956 cover the offence previously covered by s 2 of the CLAA 1898. Other offences were created, including; causing prostitution,[8] detention of a woman in a brothel,[9] man living off the earnings of prostitution,[10] woman exercising control over a prostitute[11] and brothel keeping.[12]

2. Causing or Encouraging Prostitution of a Girl under 16

Sexual Offences Act 1956, s 28(1)

Definition

(1) To cause or encourage the prostitution of, or the commission of unlawful sexual intercourse with, or 8.14
of an indecent assault on, a girl under the age of 16 for whom he is responsible.

---

[6] *R v De Munck* 13 Cr App R 113 CCA, [1918–19] All ER Rep 499.

[7] *R v Morris-Lowe* [1985] 1 All ER 400.

[8] SOA 1956, s 22. See paras 8.57–8.65.

[9] SOA 1956, s 24. See paras 8.89–8.95.

[10] SOA 1956, s 30. See paras 8.75–8.82.

[11] SOA 1956, s 31. See paras 8.83–8.88.

[12] SOA 1956, s 33–36.

(2) Where a girl has become a prostitute, or has had unlawful sexual intercourse, or has been indecently assaulted, a person shall be deemed to have caused or encouraged it, if he knowingly allowed her to consort with, or to enter or to continue in the employment of, any prostitute or person of known immoral character.

Proof

8.15 As per Definition. In addition:

(i) It is sufficient for proof of causing/encouraging, to prove that the defendant does nothing to prevent the act when he is in a position to do so.[13]

(ii) Proof of those defined as responsible; this includes: a parent, legal guardian, any person with 'possession or control' of her (this was later amended to parental responsibility for)[14] or any person who has care for her.[15] A babysitter has been held to fall into this category.[16]

(iii) The definition of prostitute covers the offer of her body for lewdness for payment.[17] This includes passive acts of sexual activity; no physical contact is necessary, where the woman offers herself as a participant in physical acts of indecency for the sexual gratification of men.[18]

(iv) For unlawful sexual intercourse see para 7.12; for indecent assault see para 3.12.

(v) If the girl appears to have been under the age of 16 at the time, she is presumed to have been so, unless the contrary is proved.[19]

Notes

8.16 (i) Triable on indictment only.

(ii) Both males and females can commit this offence. The complainant must be female and under 16.[20]

Indictment

8.17 CAUSING OR ENCOURAGING PROSTITUTION OF A GIRL UNDER 16 1.1.1957 to 30.4.2004

Statement of Offence

CAUSING/ENCOURAGING PROSTITUTION OF A GIRL UNDER THE AGE OF 16, contrary to section 28(1) of the Sexual Offences Act 1956.

Particulars of Offence

D on the... day of... caused/encouraged [the prostitution of] *or* [commission of unlawful sexual intercourse on] *or* [indecent assault on] C, a girl under the age of 16 for whom he/she is responsible.

Alternative Offences

8.18 Until 26.8.1981 indict any attempt under common law. From 27.8.1981 onwards indict attempt under the CAA 1981, s 1(1). Aver the attempt in both Statement and Particulars of Offence. See paras 2.31–2.32.

[13] *Ralphs* (1913) 9 Cr App Rep 86 CCA.

[14] Children Act (CA) 1989, s 108(4) and Sch 12, para 14 (commencement date 16.11.1989). The parent is not to be treated as responsible if any residence order under the CA 1989 does not name him or her as the person with whom the child is to live, or if there is a care order in existence.

[15] SOA 1956, s 28(3).

[16] *R v Drury* (1975) 60 Cr App R 195 CA.

[17] *R v De Munck* 13 Cr App R 113 CCA.

[18] *R v Webb* [1964] 1 QB 357, [1963] 3 All ER 177 CCA.

[19] SOA 1956, s 28(5).

[20] SOA 1956, s 28(1).

Sentence

On indictment: **2 YEARS.** **8.19**

Upon Conviction/Sentence

(i) Notification applies, if criteria met.[21] **8.20**
(ii) Disqualification/barring from working with children/vulnerable adults. See paras 12.135 and 16.33.
(iii) SOPO applies, if criteria met.[22]

3. Procuring a Girl under 21 to have Unlawful Sexual Intercourse

Sexual Offences Act 1956, s 23

Definition

(1) to procure a girl under the age of 21 to have unlawful sexual intercourse in any part of the world with a third person. **8.21**

Proof

(i) To procure, that is to bring about a course of conduct, which the woman would not have embarked upon on her own;[23] **8.22**
(ii) a girl under 21;
(iii) to have unlawful sexual intercourse;
(iv) in any part of the world;
(v) that the accused intended that she would have intercourse with another man, and did not genuinely believe that the victim was 21 or over.[24]

Notes

(i) The offence is triable on indictment only. **8.23**
(ii) Unlawful sexual intercourse means 'illicit sexual intercourse', outside the bond of marriage.[25]
(iii) The offence may be committed by a male or female as principal.
(iv) The third person may not be tried as a party to the offence, but as a conspirator.
(v) Sexual intercourse with another party must take place.[26]

Indictment

PROCURING A GIRL UNDER 21 TO HAVE UNLAWFUL SEXUAL INTERCOURSE **8.24**
1.1.1957 to 30.4.2004

Statement of Offence

PROCURING A GIRL UNDER THE AGE OF 21 TO HAVE UNLAWFUL SEXUAL INTERCOURSE, contrary to section 23(1) of the Sexual Offences Act 1956.

Particulars of Offence

D on the... day of... procured C, a girl under the age of 21 years, and knowing that the said girl was under the age of 21, to have unlawful sexual intercourse with Z.

[21] SOA 2003, s 80(1) and Sch 3, para 10; see Chapter 14.
[22] SOA 2003, s 104 and Sch 3, para 10; see Chapter 16.
[23] *R v Broadfoot* (1977) 64 Cr App R 71 CA.
[24] *R v B (A Minor) v DPP* [2000] 2 Cr App R 65; *R v K* [2001] 3 All ER 897.
[25] *R v Chapman* 42 Cr App R 257 CCA.
[26] *R v Mackenzie and Higginson* (1910) 6 Cr App R 64 CCA.

Alternative Offences

8.25 An attempt to commit the full offence. Until 26.8.1981 indict the common law offence. Thereafter, do so under the CAA 1981. Aver the attempt in both the Statement and Particulars of Offence.

Sentence

8.26 (i) On indictment: 2 YEARS.
(ii) An attempt carries the same maximum.

Upon Conviction/Sentence

8.27 (i) Notification not applicable.[27]
(ii) Disqualification/barring from working with children/vulnerable adults. See paras 12.135 and 16.33.
(iii) SOPO not applicable.[28]

Offences committed from 1.5.2004 to date

8.28 The SOA 2003 repealed ss 23 and 28 of the SOA 1956 in full. Several offences relating to child prostitution are created: paying for sexual services of a child[29] (see para 8.29), causing or inciting child prostitution or pornography[30] (see para 8.36), controlling a child prostitute or a child involved in pornography[31] (see para 8.43).

4. Paying for Sexual Services of a Child

Sexual Offences Act 2003, s 47(1)

Definition

8.29 (1) A person (A) commits an offence if—
(a) he intentionally obtains for himself the sexual services of another person (B),
(b) before obtaining those services he has made or promised payment for those services to B or a third person, or knows that another person has made or promised such a payment, and
(c) either—
(i) B is under 18, and A does not reasonably believe that B is 18 or over, or
(ii) B is under 13.

Proof

8.30 As per Definition.

Notes

8.31 (i) If the offence is committed against a person under 16 and penetration is involved, the offence is triable only on indictment, otherwise triable either way.[32]
(ii) 'payment' means any financial advantage, including the discharge of an obligation to pay or the provision of goods and services (including sexual services) gratuitously or at a discount.[33]

---

27 SOA 2003, s 80(1) (not listed in Sch 3); see Chapter 14.
28 SOA 2003, s 104 (not listed in Sch 3); see Chapter 16.
29 SOA 2003, s 47.
30 SOA 2003, s 48.
31 SOA 2003, s 49.
32 SOA 2003, s 47(3)–(6).
33 SOA 2003, s 47(2).

(iii) Sexual services covers a wide variety of activities within the definition of 'sexual' under the SOA 2003, s 78.
(iv) Where the child is under 13 or under 16, this ought to be averred in the particulars. In addition, if penetration is involved, as per subsection (6), this ought to be averred.

Indictment

PAYING FOR SEXUAL SERVICES OF A CHILD 1.5.2004 to date **8.32**

Statement of Offence

PAYING FOR SEXUAL SERVICES OF A CHILD, contrary to section 47(1) of the Sexual Offences Act 2003.

Particulars of Offence

D, on the... day of... intentionally obtained for himself the sexual services of C, the said C being aged under 18 years, and the said D not reasonably believing that she was of or over the age of 18 years, and, before obtaining those services, the said D [promised payment for those services to C or another person X] *or* [knew that Y had made payment for those services to the said C or another person X].

Alternative Offences

If the payment or promise thereof is not proved under this section, then the following offences (carrying similar maximum sentences) may provide alternatives: **8.33**

(i) SOA 2003, s 5: rape of child under 13, see paras 4.88–4.96.
(ii) SOA 2003, s 6: assault of child under 13 by penetration, see paras 4.97–4.105.
(iii) SOA 2003, s 7: sexual assault of child under 13, see paras 4.119–4.127.
(iv) SOA 2003, s 9: sexual activity with a child, see paras 4.106–4.116.

Sentence

(i) On indictment: **8.34**
- where penetration involved and the child is under 13: **LIFE**;[34]
- where penetration involved and the child is aged 13–16: **14 YEARS**;[35]
- where penetration is not involved and the child is under 16: **14 YEARS**;[36]
- in any other case: **7 YEARS**.[37]

(ii) Summarily:
- **6 months** or a **fine** not exceeding the statutory maximum or **both**.[38]

Upon Conviction/Sentence

(i) Notification applies, if criteria met.[39] **8.35**
(ii) Disqualification/barring from working with children/vulnerable adults. See paras 12.135 and 16.33.
(iii) SOPO applies, if criteria met.[40]

[34] SOA 2003, s 47(3).
[35] SOA 2003, s 47(4)(a).
[36] SOA 2003, s 47(4)(b).
[37] SOA 2003, s 47(5)(b).
[38] 12 months if CJA 2003, s 282(4) implemented. Such cases not requiring proof of penetration of any sort.
[39] SOA 2003, s 80(1) and Sch 3, para 29; see Chapter 14.
[40] SOA 2003, s 104 and Sch 3; see Chapter 16.

5. Causing or Inciting Child Prostitution or Inciting Child Pornography

Sexual Offences Act 2003, s 48(1)

Definition

8.36 (1) A person commits an offence if—
(a) he intentionally causes or incites another person (B) to become a prostitute, or to be involved in pornography, in any part of the world, and
(b) either—
(i) B is under 18, and A does not reasonably believe that B is 18 or over, or
(ii) B is under 13.

Proof

8.37 As per Definition, in addition:
(i) 'prostitute'—is defined as a person (A) who on at least one occasion offers or provides sexual services in return for payment or promise of payment to A or a third person;[41]
(ii) 'payment' means any financial advantage, including an obligation to pay or the provision of goods or services gratuitously, or at a discount;[42]
(iii) 'involvement in pornography' if an indecent image of that person is recorded;[43]
(iv) 'causing'—the defendant must contemplate or desire that the act would ensue on his/her authority and as a result of his/her control/influence over the other person;
(v) 'inciting'—covers a suggestion, proposal, persuasion, inducement, threats or pressure.[44]

Notes

8.38 (i) Triable either way.[45]
(ii) The offence may be committed where the sexual activity does not for any reason take place.

Indictment

8.39 CAUSING OR INCITING CHILD PROSTITUTION OR PORNOGRAPHY 1.5.2004 to date

Statement of Offence

CAUSING OR INCITING CHILD PROSTITUTION/PORNOGRAPHY, contrary to section 48(1) of the Sexual Offences Act 2003.

Particulars of Offence

D on the...day of...intentionally incited C, a person under the age of 18 years, to become a prostitute, the said D not reasonably believing that C was aged 18 years or over.

Alternative Offences

8.40 Attempts should be indicted under CAA 1981, s 1(1). Aver attempt in the Statement and Particulars of Offence.

---

41 SOA 2003, s 51(2).
42 SOA 2003, s 51(3).
43 SOA 2003, s 51(1).
44 *R v Fitzmaurice* [1983] QB 1083; *Invicta Plastics Ltd v Clare* [1976] RTR 251.
45 SOA 2003, s 49(2).

Sentence

(i) On indictment: **14 YEARS.**[46] **8.41**
(ii) Summarily: **6 months** or a **fine** not exceeding the statutory maximum or **both.**[47]

Upon Conviction/Sentence

(i) Notification: applicable. **8.42**
(ii) Disqualification/barring from working with children/vulnerable adults. See paras 12.135 and 16.33.
(iii) SOPO: applicable.
(iv) Financial Reporting Order (FRO): applicable.[48]

6. Controlling a Child Prostitute or a Child Involved in Pornography

Sexual Offences Act 2003, s 49(1)

Definition

(1) A person (A) commits an offence if— **8.43**
(a) he intentionally controls any of the activities of another person (B) relating to B's prostitution or involvement in pornography in any part of the world, and
(b) either—
(i) B is under 18, and A does not reasonably believe that B is 18 or over, or
(ii) B is under 13.

Proof

As per Definition. In addition: **8.44**
(i) For proof of prostitution see para 8.37.
(ii) For proof of the term 'payment' see para 8.37.
(iii) For proof of the term 'involved in pornography' see para 8.37.

Notes

Triable either way. **8.45**

Indictment

CONTROLLING CHILD PROSTITUTION/PORNOGRAPHY 1.5.2004 to date **8.46**

Statement of Offence

CONTROLLING A CHILD PROSTITUTE OR A CHILD INVOLVED IN PORNOGRAPHY, contrary to section 49(1) of the Sexual Offences Act 2003.

Particulars of Offence

D on the... day of... intentionally controlled the activities of C relating to the said C's prostitution or involvement in pornography, [the said C being a person under the age of 18 years, and the said D not reasonably believing that the said C was aged 18 years or over] *or* [the said C being a person under the age of 13 years].

46 SOA 2003, s 48(2)(b).
47 SOA 2003, s 48(2)(a). 12 months if CJA 2003, s 282(4) implemented.
48 Proceeds of Crime Act (POCA) 2002, Sch 2 (defines lifestyle offences). Serious Organised Crime and Police Act (SOCPA) 2005, s 76.

Alternative Offences

8.47 Attempts should be indicted under the CAA 1981, s 1(1). Aver the attempt in the Statement and Particulars of Offence.

Sentence

8.48 (i) On indictment: **14 YEARS.**[49]
(ii) Summarily: **6 months** or a **fine** not exceeding the statutory maximum or **both.**[50]

Upon Conviction/Sentence

8.49 (i) Notification: applicable.
(ii) Disqualification/barring from working with children/vulnerable adults. See paras 12.135 and 16.33.
(iii) SOPO: applicable.
(iv) FRO: applicable.[51]

7. Arranging or Facilitating Child Prostitution or Pornography

Sexual Offences Act 2003, s 50(1)

Definition

8.50 (1) A person (A) commits an offence if—
(a) he intentionally arranges or facilitates the prostitution or involvement in pornography in any part of the world of another person (B), and
(b) either—
(i) B is under 18, and A does not reasonably believe that B is 18 or over, or
(ii) B is under 13.

Proof

8.51 As per Definition. In addition:
(i) For proof of prostitution see para 8.37.
(ii) For proof of the term 'payment' see para 8.37.
(iii) For proof of the term 'involved in pornography' see para 8.37.

Notes

8.52 Triable either way.

Indictment

8.53 ARRANGING/FACILITATING CHILD PROSTITUTION OR PORNOGRAPHY 1.5.2004 to date

Statement of Offence

ARRANGING (FACILITATING) CHILD PROSTITUTION (PORNOGRAPHY), contrary to section 50(1) of the Sexual Offences Act 2003.

Particulars of Offence

D on the... day of... intentionally arranged or facilitated the prostitution or involvement in pornography of C in..., [the said C being a person under the age of 18 years, and the said D not reasonably believing that the said C was aged 18 years or over] *or* [the said C being a person under the age of 13 years].

[49] SOA 2003, s 49(2)(b).
[50] SOA 2003, s 48(2)(a). 12 months if CJA 2003, s 282(4) implemented.
[51] POCA 2002, Sch 2; SOCPA 2005, s 76.

Alternative Offences

Attempts should be indicted under the CAA 1981, s 1(1). Aver the attempt in the Statement and Particulars of Offence. See para 8.25. **8.54**

Sentence

(i) On indictment: **14 YEARS.**[52] **8.55**
(ii) Summarily: **6 months** or a **fine** not exceeding the statutory maximum or **both.**[53]

Upon Conviction/Sentence

(i) Notification: applicable. **8.56**
(ii) Disqualification/barring from working with children/vulnerable adults. See paras 12.135 and 16.33.
(iii) SOPO: applicable.
(iv) FRO: applicable.[54]

B. PROCURING PROSTITUTION OF WOMEN

Offences committed between 1.1.1957 and 30.4.2004

See paras 7.154–7.159 for the SOA 1956, s 29; causing prostitution of a defective. **8.57**

1. Causing Prostitution of Women

Sexual Offences Act 1956, s 22(1)

Definition

(a) to procure a woman to become, in any part of the world, a common prostitute; or **8.58**
(b) to procure a woman to leave the United Kingdom, intending her to become an inmate of or frequent a brothel elsewhere; or
(c) to procure a woman to leave her usual place of abode in the United Kingdom, intending her to become an inmate of or frequent a brothel in any part of the world for the purposes of prostitution.

Proof

(i) To procure, that is to bring about a course of conduct, which the woman in question would not have embarked upon of her own volition;[55] **8.59**
(ii) a woman (this cannot apply to procuration of a male);
(iii) into becoming a common prostitute.
(iv) For s 22(1)(a) the defendant has to believe that the woman was not a prostitute before he procured her.[56]

Notes

(i) Triable on indictment only.[57] **8.60**
(ii) A female who is already a prostitute cannot be procured for the purposes of this offence.[58]

---

[52] SOA 2003, s 50(2)(b).
[53] SOA 2003, s 50(2)(a). 12 months if CJA 2003, s 282(4) implemented.
[54] POCA 2002, Sch 2; SOCPA 2005, s 76.
[55] *R v Broadfoot* 64 Cr App R 71 CA, *A-G's Reference (No 1 of 1975).*
[56] *R v Brown* [1984] 3 All ER 1013.
[57] SOA 1956, s 37(2) and Sch 2, para 23.
[58] SOA 1956. *R v Brown* [1984] 3 All ER 1013.

(iii) The term 'common prostitute' covers the offer of a woman's body commonly for acts of lewdness for payment, on more than one occasion.[59]

Indictment

8.61 PROCURING PROSTITUTION OF WOMEN 1.1.1957 to 30.4.2004

> **Statement of Offence**
> PROCURING A WOMAN TO BECOME A COMMON PROSTITUTE, contrary to section 22(1) of the Sexual Offences Act 1956.
>
> **Particulars of Offence**
> D on the...day of...at...procured C, a woman, to become a common prostitute.

Alternative Offences

8.62 Attempt to commit the full offence. When indicting offences of attempt, do so under common law until 26.8.1981, thereafter under the CAA 1981. Aver the attempt in both the Statement and Particulars of Offence.

Sentence

8.63 (i) On indictment: **2 YEARS.**[60]
(ii) An attempt attracts the same maximum.

Upon Conviction/Sentence

8.64 (i) Notification does not apply.[61]
(ii) Disqualification/barring from working with children/vulnerable adults. See paras 12.135 and 16.33.
(iii) SOPO does not apply.[62]

8.65 *From 1.5.2004 SOA 2003, s 52 covers this offence.*

Offences committed from 1.5.2004 to date

2. Causing or Inciting Prostitution for Gain

Sexual Offences Act 2003, s 52(1)

Definition

8.66 (1) A person (A) commits an offence if—
(a) he intentionally causes or incites another person to become a prostitute in any part of the world, and
(b) he does so for or in the expectation of gain for himself or a third person.

Proof

8.67 As per Definition.
(i) For proof of causing see para 8.37.
(ii) For proof of inciting see para 8.37.

---

59 *R v Morris-Lowe* [1985] 1 All ER 40.
60 SOA 1956, s 37(2) and Sch 2, para 23.
61 SOA 2003, s 80(1) (not listed in Sch 3); see Chapter 14.
62 SOA 2003, s 104 (not listed in Sch 3); see Chapter 16.

(iii) For proof of prostitute see para 8.37.
(iv) 'gain' includes any financial advantage, including the discharge of an obligation to pay or the provision of goods or services (including sexual services) gratuitously or at a discount; or the goodwill of any person which is or appears likely, in time, to bring financial advantage.[63]

Notes

8.68 This offence is triable either way.[64]

Indictment

8.69 CAUSING/INCITING PROSTITUTION FOR GAIN 1.5.2004 to date

Statement of Offence

CAUSING OR INCITING PROSTITUTION FOR GAIN, contrary to section 52(1) of the Sexual Offences Act 2003.

Particulars of Offence

D on the... day of... intentionally caused/incited C to become a prostitute in... in the expectation of gain for himself or a third person.

Alternative Offences

8.70 Attempt to commit the full offence. When indicting offences of attempt, do so under common law until 26.8.1981, thereafter under the CAA 1981. Aver the attempt in both the Statement and Particulars of Offence.

Sentence

8.71
(i) On indictment: 7 **YEARS.**[65]
(ii) Summarily: **6 months** or a **fine** not exceeding the statutory maximum or **both.**[66]

Upon Conviction/Sentence

8.72
(i) Notification: applicable.[67]
(ii) Disqualification/barring from working with children/vulnerable adults. See paras 12.135 and 16.33.
(iii) SOPO: applicable.
(iv) FRO applicable.[68]

C. LIVING ON THE EARNINGS OF PROSTITUTION

Offences committed between 1.1.1957 and 30.4.2004

8.73 The SOA 1956, ss 33–36 created three summary offences, covering the keeping of brothels or allowing premises to be so used. These summary only offences are not included. However, the SOA 2003,

[63] SOA 2003, s 54(1).
[64] SOA 2003, s 52(2).
[65] SOA 2003, s 52(2)(b).
[66] SOA 2003, s 52(2)(a). 12 months if CJA 2003, s 282(4) implemented.
[67] SOA 2003, s 80(1) (not listed in Sch 3 or 5); see Chapter 14.
[68] POCA 2002, Sch 2; SOCPA 2005, s 76.

s 55 amends the SOA 1956, s 33 and so creates a triable either way offence of brothel keeping[69] which has been included.

8.74 Other summary only offences of loitering,[70] soliciting (kerb crawling)[71] and persistent soliciting,[72] are not included in the text.

1. Man Living on Earnings of Prostitution

Sexual Offences Act 1956, s 30(1)

Definition

8.75 (1) For a man knowingly to live wholly or in part on the earnings of prostitution.
(2) For the purposes of this section a man who lives wholly or is habitually in the company of a prostitute, or who exercises control, direction, or influence over a prostitute's movements in a way which shows he is aiding, abetting, or compelling her prostitution with others, shall be presumed to be knowingly living on the earnings of prostitution, unless he proves the contrary.

Proof

8.76 As per Definition. In addition:
(i) Man covers man or boy.[73]
(ii) It must be proved that the woman on whose earnings the man was living was a prostitute; for proof of prostitute see paras 8.15.
(iii) Control, direction or influence.
(iv) Living on the earnings of prostitution covers payments received, not necessarily from the prostitutes themselves, for goods/services supplied to them for the purposes of prostitution.[74]
(v) The prosecution must prove that the defendant knew the female to be a prostitute, and knew that he was in part living on her earnings.

Notes

8.77 (i) This offence is triable either way.
(ii) If the prosecution proves that the defendant was either living with a prostitute, habitually in her company or exercising control, direction or influence over her movements which showed that he was aiding, abetting, compelling her prostitution, then the presumption in s 30(2) applies, that is, he is knowingly living on her earnings.[75]
(iii) Examples of living on the earnings of prostitution include selling a directory of prostitutes for which they pay to be included.[76] Letting premises for prostitution where the prostitute and the lessor are in the business of prostitution together.[77]
(iv) This offence may only be committed by a male as principal.
(v) The charge may relate to the commission of the offence on one day only, although evidence of their relations before or after the specified date may be adduced.[78]

Indictment

8.78 MAN LIVING ON EARNINGS OF PROSTITUTION 1.1.1957 to 30.4.2004

---

69 SOA 1956, s 33A. In force 1.5.2004.
70 Street Offences Act (StOA) 1959, s 1.
71 SOA 1985, s 1.
72 SOA 1985, s 2.
73 SOA 1956, s 46.
74 *Shaw v DPP* [1961] 2 All ER 446 HL.
75 *R v Clarke* 63 Cr App R 16 CA.
76 *Shaw v DPP* [1962] AC 220 HL.
77 *Stewart v DPP* (1986) 83 Cr App R 327 CA.
78 *R v Hill* 10 Cr App R 56 CCA.

Statement of Offence

LIVING ON PROSTITUTION, contrary to section 30(1) of the Sexual Offences Act 1956.

Particulars of Offence

D, a man, on the... day of... knowingly lived wholly or in part on the earnings of the prostitution of C.

Alternative Offences

There are a number of alternatives ways included within the definition of s 30(2), see para 8.75. **8.79**

Sentence

(i) On indictment: 7 **YEARS.**[79] **8.80**
(ii) Summarily: **6 months.**[80]

Sentencing Guidance

If there has been no element of coercion or corruption of the prostitute, then a sentence of **2 YEARS** would be appropriate.[81] **8.81**

Upon Conviction/Sentence

(i) Notification: not applicable.[82] **8.82**
(ii) Disqualification/barring from working with children/vulnerable adults. See paras 12.135 and 16.33.
(iii) SOPO: not applicable.[83]

2. Women Exercising Control over Prostitute

Sexual Offences Act 1956, s 31

Definition

> ...for a woman, for purposes of gain, to exercise control, direction or influence over a prostitute's movements in a way which shows she is aiding, abetting, or compelling her prostitution. **8.83**

Proof

As per Definition. In addition: **8.84**
(i) See para 8.15 for the meaning of prostitution.
(ii) Only a woman/girl may commit this offence upon a female prostitute.[84]
(iii) For proof of living on the earnings see paras 8.76.
(iv) For *mens rea* see para 8.76.

Notes

The offence is triable either way.[85] **8.85**

---

[79] SOA 1956, s 37(3) and Sch 2, para 30(i). The maximum of 2 years was increased on 16.8.1959 by StOA 1959, s 4.
[80] SOA 1956, s 37(3) and Sch 2, para 30(ii).
[81] *R v Farrugia and Others* (1979) 69 Cr App R 108 CA.
[82] SOA 2003, s 80(1) (not listed in Sch 3); see Chapter 14.
[83] SOA 2003, s 104 (not listed in Sch 3); see Chapter 16.
[84] The terms 'woman/girl' are interchangeable (SOA 1956, s 46).
[85] MCA 1980, s 17(1) and Sch 1.

Indictment

8.86 WOMEN EXERCISING CONTROL/DIRECTION/INFLUENCE OVER A PROSTITUTE
1.1.1957 to 30.4.2004

> **Statement of Offence**
> EXERCISING CONTROL/DIRECTION/INFLUENCE OVER A PROSTITUTE, contrary to section 31 of the Sexual Offences Act 1956.
>
> **Particulars of Offence**
> D a woman/girl,[86] on the... day of... exercised control/direction/influence over the movements of C, a prostitute, for purposes of gain, in a way which shows she is aiding, abetting or compelling her prostitution.

Sentence

8.87 (i) On indictment: 7 **YEARS.**[87]
(ii) Summarily: **6 months.**[88]

Upon Conviction/Sentence

8.88 (i) Notification: not applicable.[89]
(ii) Disqualification/barring from working with children/vulnerable adults. See paras 12.135 and 16.33.
(iii) SOPO: not applicable.[90]

3. Detention of a Woman in a Brothel or other Premises

Sexual Offences Act 1956, s 24

Definition

8.89 (1) ... to detain a woman against her will on any premises with the intention that she shall have unlawful sexual intercourse with men or with a particular man, or to detain a woman against her will in a brothel.
(2) Where a woman is on any premises for the purpose of having unlawful sexual intercourse or is in a brothel, a person shall be deemed... to detain her there if, with the intention of compelling or inducing her to remain there, he either withholds from her, her clothes or any other property belonging to her or threatens her with legal proceedings in the event of her taking away clothes provided for her by him or on his directions.

Proof

8.90 (i) As per Definition.
(ii) For unlawful sexual intercourse see para 2.17.
(iii) For the definition of brothel see para 8.112.
(iv) In addition, proof that the accused intended to detain the woman at the brothel/premises so that she would have unlawful sexual intercourse with a man/men.

---

[86] The terms 'woman/girl' are interchangeable (SOA 1956, s 46).
[87] SOA 2003, s 37(3) and Sch 2, para 31(i).
[88] SOA 2003, s 37(3) and Sch 2, para 31(ii).
[89] SOA 2003, s 80(1) (not listed in Sch 3); see Chapter 14.
[90] SOA 2003, s 104 (not listed in Sch 3 or 5); see Chapter 16.

Notes

(i) The offence is triable only on indictment. **8.91**
(ii) The detained woman who has taken clothes in order to leave these premises will not be liable to any legal proceedings.[91]
(iii) Both males and females may commit this offence.
(iv) The offence may be committed upon a girl, the words 'woman' and 'girl' are interchangeable.[92]

Indictment

DETENTION OF A WOMAN IN A BROTHEL OR OTHER PREMISES 1.1.1957 to 30.4.2004 **8.92**

> **Statement of Offence**
>
> DETAINING A WOMAN AGAINST HER WILL FOR UNLAWFUL SEXUAL INTERCOURSE (IN A BROTHEL), contrary to section 24(1) of the Sexual Offences Act 1956.
>
> **Particulars of Offence**
>
> D on the... day of... [detained C, a woman, against her will at... intending her to have unlawful sexual intercourse with men/with X, a man] *or* [detained C, a woman, against her will at,... a brothel].

Alternative Offences

(i) An attempt may be charged. Until 26.7.1981 charge an attempt under common law. Thereafter, under the CAA 1981. Aver the attempt in both the Statement and Particulars of Offence. **8.93**
(ii) CYPA 1933, s 3—allowing a child aged between the ages of 4 and 16 of whom they have custody, care or control to reside in or frequent a brothel. A summary offence only. Maximum: **6 months.**

Sentence

(i) On indictment: **2 YEARS.**[93] **8.94**
(ii) An attempt carries the same maximum.

Upon Conviction/Sentence

(i) Notification: not applicable.[94] **8.95**
(ii) Disqualification/barring from working with children/vulnerable adults. See paras 12.135 and 16.33.
(iii) SOPO: not applicable.[95]

4. Soliciting by Men for Immoral Purposes

Sexual Offences Act 1956, s 32

Definition

For a man persistently to solicit or importune in a public place for immoral purposes. **8.96**

---

91 SOA 1956, s 24(3).
92 SOA 1956, s 46.
93 SOA 1956, s 37(3) and Sch 2, para 25.
94 SOA 2003, s 80(1) (not listed in Sch 3); see Chapter 14.
95 SOA 2003, s 104 (not listed in Sch 3); see Chapter 16.

Proof

8.97 (i) Proof of 'persistently' requires at least two approaches.
(ii) 'Solicit' and 'importune' mean the same, that is, to allure and tempt for the purposes of sexual activity.[96]
(iii) The soliciting has to take place in a street or public place;
(iv) and must be done for the purposes of prostitution.

Notes

8.98 (i) The offence is triable either way.
(ii) Only males may be prosecuted for this offence. The person solicited may be male or female.[97]
(iii) Street and public place are widely defined[98] to include, for example, a passage, or any place to which the public have access.

Indictment

8.99 SOLICITATION FOR IMMORAL PURPOSES 1.1.1957 to 30.4.2004

Statement of Offence
SOLICITATION FOR IMMORAL PURPOSES, contrary to section 32 of the Sexual Offences Act 1956.
Particulars of Offence
D, a male, on... persistently solicited and importuned in a public place, namely... for immoral purposes.

Alternative Offences

8.100 Attempt to commit the full offence. When indicting offences of attempt, do so under common law until 26.8.1981, thereafter under the CAA 1981. Aver the attempt in both the Statement and Particulars of Offence.

Sentence

8.101 (i) On indictment: **2 YEARS.**[99]
(ii) Summarily: **6 months.**[100]

Upon Conviction/Sentence

8.102 (i) Notification: not applicable.[101]
(ii) Disqualification/barring from working with children/vulnerable adults. See paras 12.135 and 16.33.
(iii) SOPO: not applicable.[102]

96 *Behrendt v Burridge* (1976) 63 Cr App R 202 DC.
97 *R v Goddard* (1990) 92 Cr App R 185 CA.
98 SOA 1959, s 1(4).
99 SOA 1956, s 37(3) and Sch 2, para 32(i).
100 SOA 1956, s 37(3) and Sch 2, para 32(ii).
101 SOA 2003, s 80(1) (not listed in Sch 3); see Chapter 14.
102 SOA 2003, s 104 (not listed in Sch 3 or 5); see Chapter 16.

Offences committed between 27.7.1967 and 30.4.2004

5. Living on the Earnings of Male Prostitution

Sexual Offences Act 1967, s 5

Definition

A man or woman who knowingly lives wholly or in part on the earnings of prostitution of another man. **8.103**

Proof

As per definition. See para 8.15 for definition of prostitution. **8.104**

Notes

There is no presumption in this Act in relation to living on earnings.[103] See para 8.77. **8.105**

Indictment

LIVING ON THE EARNINGS OF MALE PROSTITUTION 27.7.1967 to 30.4.2004 **8.106**

Statement of Offence
LIVING ON PROSTITUTION, contrary to section 5 of the Sexual Offences Act 1967.
Particulars of Offence
D on the...day of...knowingly lived (in part) on the earnings of the prostitution of C, a male.

Alternative Offences

Attempt to commit the full offence. When indicting offences of attempt, do so under common law until 26.8.1981, thereafter under the CAA 1981. Aver the attempt in both the Statement and Particulars of Offence. **8.107**

Sentence

(i) On indictment: **7 YEARS.**[104] **8.108**
(ii) Summarily: **6 months.**[105]

Upon Conviction/Sentence

(i) Notification: not applicable.[106] **8.109**
(ii) Disqualification/barring from working with children/vulnerable adults. See paras 12.135 and 16.33.
(iii) SOPO: not applicable.[107]

---

[103] As in SOA 1956, s 30(2).
[104] SOA 1967, s 5(1)(b).
[105] SOA 1967, s 5(1)(a).
[106] SOA 2003, s 80(1) (not listed in Sch 3); see Chapter 14.
[107] SOA 2003, s 104 (not listed in Sch 3 or 5); see Chapter 16.

Offences committed from 1.5.2004 to date

6. Keeping a Brothel

Sexual Offences Act 1956, s 33A[108]

Definition

8.110 ...to keep or to manage, or act or assist in the management of, a brothel to which people resort for practices involving prostitution (whether or not also for other practices).

Proof

8.111 (i) For 'keeping a brothel' some significant control over the premises must be proved; or
(ii) for 'managing a brothel' the same must be proved, and evidence of an active part in the running of the business as a business;[109] or
(iii) for 'acting or assisting in the management of' duties that are more than menial must be proved.
(iv) That the premises was a brothel.

Notes

8.112 (i) This offence is triable either way.
(ii) Proof that joint use of premises by a team of women for the purposes of prostitution is sufficient, even where one was using it on a given day.[110]
(iii) This offence was created by virtue of an amendment of the SOA 1956, s 33.[111] Before 1.5.2004 it could be tried summarily only.

Indictment

8.113 KEEPING A BROTHEL USED FOR PROSTITUTION 1.5.2004 to date

Statement of Offence

KEEPING A BROTHEL USED FOR PROSTITUTION, contrary to section 33A(1) of the Sexual Offences Act 1956[112]

Particulars of Offence

D on the... day of... kept/managed/acted/assisted in the management of a brothel to which people resorted for practices involving prostitution.

Alternative Offences

8.114 Attempt to commit the full offence. When indicting offences of attempt do so under the CAA 1981. Aver both in the Statement and Particulars of Offence.

Sentence

8.115 (i) On indictment: **7 YEARS.**
(ii) Summarily: **6 months.**[113]

[108] SOA 1956, s 33 (a summary offence) as amended by SOA 2003, s 55.
[109] *Abbott v Smith* [1965] 2 QB 662n, [1964] 3 All ER 762.
[110] *Stevens v Christy* 85 Cr App R 249 DC, [1987] Crim LR 503.
[111] SOA 2003, s 55.
[112] As amended by s 55(1) and (2) SOA.
[113] 12 months if CJA 2003, s 282(4) implemented.

Upon Conviction/Sentence

(i) Notification; not applicable.[114] 8.116
(ii) Disqualification/barring from working with children/vulnerable adults. See paras 12.135 and 16.33.
(iii) SOPO: not applicable.[115]

7. Controlling Prostitution for Gain

Sexual Offences Act 2003, s 53(1)

Definition

(1) A person commits an offence if— 8.117
(a) he intentionally controls any of the activities of another person relating to that person's prostitution in any part of the world, and
(b) he does so for or in the expectation of gain for himself or a third person.

Proof

As per Definition. 8.118
(i) Control may cover such activities as the price charged, venue, diary, travel, bookings—even through a third party. See para 7.176(ii).
(ii) For proof of prostitution see para 8.37.
(iii) 'gain' includes any financial advantage, including the discharge of an obligation to pay or the provision of goods or services (including sexual services) gratuitously or at a discount; or goodwill likely to bring financial advantage.[116]

Notes

(i) This offence is triable either way. 8.119
(ii) This offence is more restricted than the old offence of living on the earnings of prostitution under the SOA 1956, s 30. See para 8.117 for requisite knowledge.
(iii) Article 26 of the Council of Europe Convention on Action against Human Trafficking 2005 requires careful consideration be given to whether public policy calls for a prosecution and punishment of victims of trafficking who have been compelled to become involved in unlawful activities.[117]

Indictment

CONTROLLING PROSTITUTION FOR GAIN 1.5.2004 to date 8.120

Statement of Offence

CONTROLLING PROSTITUTION FOR GAIN, contrary to section 53(1) of the Sexual Offences Act 2003.

Particulars of Offence

D on the... day of... intentionally controlled C's activities in relation to C's prostitution, in the expectation of gain for himself or a third person.

---

114 SOA 2003, s 80(1) (not listed in Sch 3); see Chapter 14.
115 SOA 2003, s 104 (not listed in Sch 3 or 5); see Chapter 16.
116 SOA 2003, s 54(1).
117 *R v LM* [2010] EWCA Crim 2327.

Sentence

8.121 (i) On indictment: 7 **YEARS.**[118]
(ii) Summarily: **6 months** or a **fine** not exceeding the statutory maximum or **both.**[119]

Upon Conviction/Sentence

8.122 (i) Notification; not applicable.[120]
(ii) Disqualification/barring from working with children/vulnerable adults. See paras 12.135 and 16.33.
(iii) SOPO: not applicable.[121]
(iv) FRO: applicable.[122]

D. TRAFFICKING FOR SEXUAL EXPLOITATION

Offences committed between 1.1.1957 and 30.4.2004

8.123 The SOA 1956 created a number of offences that were later used (with varying degrees of success) to prosecute those involved in people trafficking, dealt with in other sections of the book.

8.124 These include:
- SOA 1956, s 2: procurement of a woman by threats. See paras 11.04–11.10.
- SOA 1956, s 3: procurement of a woman by false pretences. See paras 11.11–11.18.
- SOA 1956, s 22: causing prostitution of women in any part of the world. See paras 8.58–8.65.
- SOA 1956, s 24: detention of a woman in a brothel. See paras 8.89–8.95.
- SOA 1956, s 28: causing prostitution of a girl under 16. See paras 8.14–8.20.
- SOA 1956, s 30: man living on the earnings of prostitution. See paras 8.75–8.82.
- SOA 1956, s 31: woman exercising control over a prostitute. See paras 8.83–8.88.

8.125 The SOA 2003 clarifies the position as to which offences ought to be charged.

Offences committed from 1.5.2004 to 5.4.2013

8.126 The SOA 2003 created three specific offences:
(i) s 57: trafficking into the UK for sexual exploitation;
(ii) s 58: trafficking within the UK for sexual exploitation;
(iii) s 59: trafficking out of the UK for sexual exploitation.

Note these have been repealed as of 5.4.2013.

118 SOA 2003, s 53(2)(b).
119 SOA 2003, s 52(2)(a); 12 months if CJA 2003, s 282 implemented.
120 SOA 2003, s 80(1) (not listed in Sch 3); see Chapter 14.
121 SOA 2003, s 104 (not listed in Sch 3); see Chapter 16.
122 POCA 2002, Sch 2; SOCPA 2005, s 76.

1. Trafficking into the UK for Sexual Exploitation

Sexual Offences Act 2003, s 57

Definition

(1) A person commits an offence if he intentionally arranges or facilitates the arrival in the United Kingdom of another person (B) and either— 8.127
- (a) he intends to do anything to or in respect of B, after B's arrival but in any part of the world, which if done will involve the commission of a relevant offence, or
- (b) he believes that another person is likely to do something to or in respect of B, after B's arrival but in any part of the world, which if done will involve the commission of a relevant offence.

Proof

As per Definition. In addition: 8.128

(i) Relevant offences include:
- SOA 2003, ss 1–79;
- PCA 1978, s 1(1)(a) (taking, permitting to be taken or making an indecent photograph or pseudo-photograph of a child under 18);
- an offence listed in Criminal Justice (Children) (Northern Ireland) Order 1988, Sch 1;
- an offence under the Protection of Children (Northern Ireland) Order 1978, Art 3(1)(a); or
- anything done outside England, Wales, Northern Ireland which is not an offence within paras (a)–(d) but would be if done in England and Wales or Northern Ireland.

(ii) 'Arranges or facilitates' may cover the provision of a ticket, or providing false papers.[123]

(iii) The facilitation or arrangement must be intentional, and the accused must have the necessary intention or belief in relation to s 57(1)(a) or (b).

Notes

(i) The offence is triable either way. 8.129

(ii) The accused and the victim may be male or female.

(iii) If the victim is under 18, a charge under the SOA 2003, s 50 (causing or inciting child prostitution or pornography) may be appropriate, see paras 8.36–8.42.

(iv) This section applies to anything done in the UK, and to anything done outside it by a body incorporated under the law of a part of the UK or by:
- a British citizen;
- a British overseas territories citizen;
- a British national (Overseas);
- a British overseas citizen;
- a person who is a British subject under the British Nationality Act 1981; or
- a British protected person within the meaning given by s 50(1) of that Act.

After 30.1.2008 this was simplified. Sections 57–59 apply to anything done whether inside or outside the United Kingdom.[124]

Indictment

TRAFFICKING INTO THE UK FOR SEXUAL EXPLOITATION 1.5.2004 to 5.4.2013 8.130

---

123 Cf Hansard, vol 648, col 210 (13.5.2003).

124 UK Borders Act 2007, s 31(4).

Statement of Offence

TRAFFICKING INTO THE UNITED KINGDOM FOR SEXUAL EXPLOITATION, contrary to section 57(1)(a) of the Sexual Offences Act 2003.

Particulars of Offence

D on the...day of...intentionally arranged/facilitated the arrival in the United Kingdom of C, D intending to do anything to or in respect of the said C, after C's arrival but in any part of the world which would involve the commission of a relevant offence, namely (...).

Alternative Offences

8.131 An attempt to commit the full offence. When indicting offences of attempt do so under the CAA 1981. Aver the attempt in the Statement and Particulars of Offence.

Sentence

8.132 (i) On indictment: **14 YEARS.**[125]

(ii) Summarily: **6 months** or a **fine** not exceeding the statutory maximum or **both.**[126]

Upon Conviction/Sentence

8.133 (i) Notification; not applicable.[127]

(ii) Disqualification/barring from working with children/vulnerable adults. See paras 12.135 and 16.33.

(iii) SOPO: applicable.

(iv) A Confiscation Order (CO) may be made if the accused has derived benefit from the offence.[128]

(v) From 12.2.2007: forfeiture of a relevant vehicle, ship or aircraft.[129]

2. Trafficking within the UK for Sexual Exploitation

Sexual Offences Act 2003, s 58

Definition

8.134 (1) A person commits an offence if he intentionally arranges or facilitates travel within the United Kingdom by another person (B) and either—

(a) he intends to do anything to or in respect of B, during or after the journey and in any part of the world, which if done will involve the commission of a relevant offence, or

(b) he believes that another person is likely to do something to or in respect of B during or after the journey and in any part of the world, which if done will involve the commission of a relevant offence.

Proof

8.135 As per Definition. In addition:

(i) See para 8.128 for 'arranges or facilitates'.

(ii) See para 8.128 for the definition of 'relevant offence'.

(iii) See para 8.128 for jurisdiction.

(iv) The facilitation or arrangement must be intentional and the accused must have the necessary intention or belief within s 58(1)(a) or (b).

---

[125] SOA 2003, s 57(2)(b).

[126] 12 months if CJA 2003, s 282(4) implemented.

[127] SOA 2003, s 80(1) (not listed in Sch 3); see Chapter 14.

[128] POCA 2002, para 4(2) and Sch 2, as amended by SOA 2003, s 139 and Sch 6, para 46.

[129] SOA 2003, s 60B, in force from 12.2.2007.

Notes

The offence is triable either way. **8.136**

Indictment

TRAFFICKING WITHIN THE UK FOR SEXUAL EXPLOITATION 1.5.2004 to 5.4.2013 **8.137**

> **Statement of Offence**
>
> TRAFFICKING WITHIN THE UNITED KINGDOM FOR SEXUAL EXPLOITATION, contrary to section 58(1)(a) of the Sexual Offences Act 2003.
>
> **Particulars of Offence**
>
> D on the... day of... intentionally arranged/facilitated travel within the United Kingdom by C, D intending to do anything to or in respect of C, during or after the journey in any part of the world, which would involve the commission of a relevant offence, namely (...).

Alternative Offences

An attempt to commit the full offence. When indicting offences of attempt do so under the CAA 1981. Aver the attempt in the Statement and Particulars of Offence. **8.138**

Sentence

(i) On indictment: **14 YEARS.**[130] **8.139**
(ii) Summarily: **6 months** or a **fine** not exceeding the statutory maximum or **both.**[131]

Upon Conviction/Sentence

(i) Notification; not applicable.[132] **8.140**
(ii) Disqualification/barring from working with children/vulnerable adults. See paras 12.135 and 16.33.
(iii) SOPO: applicable.
(iv) A CO may be made if the accused has derived benefit from the offence.[133]
(v) From 12.2.2007: forfeiture of a relevant vehicle, ship or aircraft.[134]

3. Trafficking out of the UK for Sexual Exploitation

Sexual Offences Act 2003, s 59(1)

Definition

A person commits an offence if he intentionally engages or facilitates the departure from the United Kingdom of another person (B) and either— **8.141**
(a) he intends to do anything to or in respect of B, after B's departure but in any part of the world, which if done will involve the commission of a relevant offence, or
(b) he believes that another person is likely to do something to or in respect of B, after B's departure but in any part of the world, which if done will involve the commission of a relevant offence.

Proof

(i) As per Definition. In addition: **8.142**
(ii) See para 8.128 for arranges or facilitates.

---

130 SOA 2003, s 58(2)(b).
131 12 months if CJA 2003, s 282(4) implemented.
132 SOA 2003, s 80(1) (not listed in Sch 3); see Chapter 14.
133 POCA 2002, Sch 2, para 4(2), as amended by SOA 2003, s 139 and Sch 6, para 46.
134 SOA 2003, s 60B, in force from 12.2.2007.

(iii) See para 8.128 for the definition of 'relevant offence'.
(iv) See para 8.128 for jurisdiction.
(v) The facilitation or arrangement must be intentional and the accused must have the necessary intention or belief within s 59(1)(a) or (b).

Notes

8.143 The offence is triable either way.

Indictment

8.144 TRAFFICKING OUT OF THE UK FOR SEXUAL EXPLOITATION 1.5.2004 to 5.4.2013.

Statement of Offence

TRAFFICKING OUT OF THE UNITED KINGDOM FOR SEXUAL EXPLOITATION, contrary to section 59(1)(a) of the Sexual Offences Act 2003.

Particulars of Offence

D on the... day of... intentionally arranged/facilitated the departure from the United Kingdom by C, D intending to do anything to or in respect of C, after C's departure but in any part of the world, which would involve the commission of a relevant offence, namely (...).

Alternative Offences

8.145 An attempt to commit the full offence. When indicting offences of attempt do so under the CAA 1981. Aver the attempt in the Statement and Particulars of Offence.

Sentence

8.146 (i) On indictment: **14 YEARS.**[135]
(ii) Summarily: **6 months** or a **fine** not exceeding the statutory maximum or **both.**[136]

Upon Conviction/Sentence

8.147 (i) Notification; not applicable.[137]
(ii) Disqualification/barring from working with children/vulnerable adults. See paras 12.135 and 16.33.
(iii) SOPO: applicable.
(iv) A CO may be made if the accused has derived benefit from the offence.[138]
(v) From 12.2.2007: forfeiture of a relevant vehicle, ship or aircraft.[139]

4. Trafficking People for Sexual Exploitation

Sexual Offences Act 2003, s 59A

Definition

8.148 Section 59A:

(1) A person (A) commits an offence if A intentionally arranges or facilitates—
(a) the arrival in, or entry into, the United Kingdom or another country of another person (B),
(b) the travel of B within the United Kingdom or another country, or
(c) the departure of B from the United Kingdom or another country,
with a view to the sexual exploitation of B.

---

135 SOA 2003, s 59(2)(b).
136 12 months if CJA 2003, s 282(4) implemented.
137 SOA 2003, s 80(1) (not listed in Sch 3); see Chapter 14.
138 POCA 2002, Sch 2, para 4(2), as amended by SOA 2003, s 139 and Sch 6, para 46.
139 SOA 2003, s 60B, in force from 12.2.2007.

(2) For the purposes of subsection (1)(a) and (c), A's arranging or facilitating is with a view to the sexual exploitation of B if, and only if— **8.149**
(a) A intends to do anything to or in respect of B, after B's arrival, entry or (as the case may be) departure but in any part of the world, which if done will involve the commission of a relevant offence, or
(b) A believes that another person is likely to do something to or in respect of B, after B's arrival, entry or (as the case may be) departure but in any part of the world, which if done will involve the commission of a relevant offence.

(3) For the purposes of subsection (1)(b) A's arranging or facilitating is with a view to the sexual exploitation of B if, and only if—
(a) A intends to do anything to or in respect of B, during or after the journey and in any part of the world, which if done will involve the commission of a relevant offence, or
(b) A believes that another person is likely to do something to or in respect of B, during or after the journey and in any part of the world, which if done will involve the commission of a relevant offence.

Proof

A person who is a UK national commits an offence under this section regardless of— **8.150**
(a) where the arranging or facilitating takes place, or
(b) which country is the country of arrival, entry, travel or (as the case may be) departure.

A person who is not a UK national commits an offence under this section if— **8.151**
(a) any part of the arranging or facilitating takes place in the United Kingdom, or
(b) the United Kingdom is the country of arrival, entry, travel or (as the case may be) departure.

- 'country' includes any territory or other part of the world;
- 'relevant offence' means—

(a) any offence under the law of England and Wales which is an offence under this Part or under section 1(1)(a) of the Protection of Children Act 1978, or
(b) anything done outside England and Wales which is not an offence within paragraph (a) but would be if done in England and Wales;

- 'UK national' means—

(a) a British citizen,
(b) a person who is a British subject by virtue of Part 4 of the British Nationality Act 1981 and who has the right of abode in the United Kingdom, or
(c) a person who is a British overseas territories citizen by virtue of a connection with Gibraltar.

Notes

The offence is triable either way. **8.152**

Indictment

TRAFFICKING PEOPLE FOR SEXUAL EXPLOITATION 6.4.2013 to date. **8.153**

Statement of Offence

TRAFFICKING PEOPLE FOR SEXUAL EXPLOITATION contrary to section 59A(1)(a) of the Sexual Offences Act 2003

Particulars of Offence

A on a day between . . . and the . . . day of . . . . . . intentionally arranged or facilitated the arrival in, or entry into the United Kingdom (or another country) of B with a view to the sexual exploitation of the said B, in that the said A intending to do anything to the said B after her arrival in the United Kingdom, which, if done, would involve the commission of a relevant offence.

Sentence

8.154 (i) On indictment: 14 YEARS.
(ii) Summarily: **12 months** or a **fine** not exceeding the statutory maximum or **both**;

Upon Conviction/Sentence

8.155 (i) Notification; not applicable
(ii) Disqualification/barring from working with children/vulnerable adults. See paras 12.135 and 16.33.
(iii) SOPO: not applicable.
(iv) Forfeiture of land vehicle, ship or aircraft: if the convicted person was the driver, owner or the director, manager or secretary of a company that owned the property or was in possession of the vehicle under a hire-purchase agreement.

9

OBSCENE PUBLICATIONS

Introduction

Child pornography

The Protection of Children Act (PCA) 1978 consolidated the law on child pornography, essentially legislating against the taking, showing, distribution and publishing of indecent photographs of children under 16. Before 1978 these categories of offences were prosecuted under obscenity laws, customs and excise legislation, offences of indecent assault and gross indecency with children. This Act is still in force. Section 160 of the CJA 1988 extended the PCA 1978 offences to include an offence of simple possession of such a photograph. The Criminal Justice and Public Order Act (CJPOA) 1994 extended these offences to computer data and computerized images of children. The SOA 2003 increased the age limit under the definition of 'child' to include those aged 16 and 17 (except those who are married or co-habiting). **9.01**

New offences created by the SOA 2003 include: SOA 2003, s 48—causing or inciting child prostitution or pornography (see para 8.36), SOA 2003, s 49—controlling a child involved in child pornography (see para 8.43), and s 50—arranging child pornography (see para 8.50). **9.02**

Obscene publications

For the readers of this book, the most common usages of these charges will be to cover the retail distribution of obscene material: in shops or by mail order. The Obscene Publications Act (OPA) 1959 and the extended offence under the OPA 1964 are still in force. The offence is time-barred (that is, there may be no prosecution under these sections more than two years after the commission of the offence).[1] The topic is not dealt with in its historical context. **9.03**

Section 2 of the OPA 1959 creates the offence of publication of an obscene article. In 1964,[2] the offence was extended to possessing an obscene article for gain. **9.04**

---

[1] OPA 1959, s 2(3).

[2] OPA 1964, s 1.

A. CHILD PORNOGRAPHY

Offences committed from 20.8.1978 to date

1. Taking, Making, Distributing, Publishing etc Photographs of Children

Protection of Children Act 1978, s 1

Definition[3]

9.05 (1) It is an offence for a person—

(a) to take, or permit to be taken [or to make][4] any indecent photograph [or pseudo-photograph as of] of a child (meaning in this Act); or
(b) to distribute or show such indecent photographs [or pseudo-photographs]; or
(c) to have in his possession such indecent photographs [or pseudo-photographs], with a view to their being distributed or shown by himself or others; or
(d) to publish or cause to be published any advertisement likely to be understood as conveying that the advertiser distributes or shows such indecent photographs [or pseudo-photographs] or intends to do so.

Proof

9.06 (i) '[P]hotograph' includes a film, copy of a photograph (negative or positive) or film, and a photograph comprised in a film.[5] Film includes any form of video recording. As from 3.2.1994, this definition is extended to include data stored on a computer disk or by other electronic means capable of conversion to a photograph.[6]

(ii) As from 3.2.1995: 'pseudo-photograph'[7] is defined as an image, whether made by computer graphics or otherwise, which appears to be a photograph.[8] This term includes a copy of a pseudo-photograph, and data stored on a computer disk or by other electronic means which is capable of conversion into a pseudo-photograph.[9] It is sufficient if the predominant impression given by the pseudo-photograph is that the person shown is a child.[10] This section covers the position where the image is created by computer graphics and gives the impression that the person shown is a child.[11]

(iii) References to photograph also include:

(a) a tracing or other image, whether made by electronic or other means (of whatever nature)—
   (i) which is not itself a photograph or pseudo-photograph, but
   (ii) which is derived from the whole or part of a photograph or pseudo-photograph (or a combination of either or both); and
(b) data stored on a computer disc or by other electronic means which is capable of conversion into an image within (a);

and subsection (8) applies in relation to such an image as it applies in relation to a pseudo-photograph.[12]

(iv) 'Indecent' is not defined in the Act, and is a matter for the tribunal of fact alone. The jury ought to be directed that they decide whether it would be considered indecent by right-thinking people.[13]

---

[3] Amendments in brackets in force from 3.2.1995. PCA 1978, s 1(1) as amended by CJPOA 1994 (commencement date 3.2.1995, SI 1995/127).
[4] PCA 1978, s 1(1).
[5] PCA 1978, s 7(2).
[6] PCA 1978, s 7(4).
[7] CJPOA 1994, s 84(1) and (2).
[8] PCA 1978, s 7(7).
[9] PCA 1978, s 7(9).
[10] PCA 1978, s 7(8).
[11] PCA 1978, s 7(7).
[12] Section 7(4A) (inserted by s 69 Criminal Justice and Immigration Act 2008).
[13] *R v Smethurst* [2002] 1 Cr App R 6 CA.

The photograph itself and the age of the child may be taken into account, but not the circumstances of the taking of the photograph or the defendant's motives for taking it.[14] If photographs show children and are indecent then they are indecent photographs.[15] This includes photographs of adults behaving in a highly indecent manner in which a child appears.[16]

(iv) Section 1(1)(a): as from 3.2.1995: 'to make' covers the following:
- downloading an image from the internet onto a computer or disk;[17]
- printing off an image downloaded from the internet;[18]
- opening an image attached to an e-mail;[19]
- storing an image on a computer directory.[20]
- accessing sites knowing that pop-ups of illegal material would occur.[21]

The act of making or taking the photograph has to be deliberate and intentional, made in the knowledge that the image is or is likely to be indecent.[22] The prosecution do not have to prove that the defendant intended the photograph or pseudo-photograph to be for an indecent purpose.[23]

(v) 'permit to be taken' covers the allowing of such photographs to be taken, being in a position to forbid it.[24]

(vi) Section 1(1)(b): 'distribute or show', a person is to be regarded as distributing an indecent photograph [or pseudo-photograph] if he parts with possession of it to, or exposes or offers it for acquisition by, another person.[25] Images kept on a computer and made available to people on the internet is sufficient.[26] Note the statutory defence: s 1(4), see (xi).

(vii) Section 1(1)(c): 'possession with a view to their being distributed or shown' requires some degree of control over the article in question, and knowledge of possession of the article (but not necessarily knowledge that the photograph or pseudo-photograph is of a child).[27] It is a matter for the jury to decide whether images may have been beyond the defendant's control. Lack of computer skills, or necessary software, may be relevant.[28] There is a specific requirement of intention. 'Shown' means to a third party, possession with a view to showing it to oneself is an offence contrary to the CJA 1988, s 160 (see para 9.18). Note the statutory defence: PCA 1978, s 1(4); see (xi).

(viii) Section 1(1)(d): 'publishing': the prosecution must prove that the defendant published the material intentionally.

(ix) 'Causing to be published': the prosecution must prove *mens rea*; where a statute creates an offence of causing something to be done, it is not to be construed as an absolute offence but as one requiring proof of the appropriate *mens rea*.[29]

(x) 'Child' is defined by the PCA 1978, s 1(1)(a) and (2), as a person under the age of 16. This was later amended by the SOA 2003 to increase the age to those aged 16 and 17[30] (unless married or living together; see (xiv)). In cases where the age of the child is unknown the question is one for the jury based on all evidence in the case. The prosecution may not call expert evidence as to likely age.[31] In cases before the 2003 Act was passed, prosecutors could rely on the rebuttable presumption in the CYPA 1933, s 99(2), based on appearance that a child be under 16. After 1.5.2004, s 2(3) creates a similar presumption in relation to those under 18.

---

14 *R v Owen* [1988] 1 WLR 134 and *R v Graham-Kerr* [1988] 1 WLR 1098.

15 PCA 1978, s 7(3), as amended by CJPOA 1994, s 84(1)(3) from 3.2.1995.

16 *R v Owen* [1988] 1 WLR 134.

17 *R v Smith; R v Jayson* [2003]1 Cr App R 13.

18 *R v Bowden* [2002] 2 Cr App R 438 CA.

19 *R v Smith; R v Jayson* [2003]1 Cr App R 13.

20 *Atkins v DPP; Goodland v DPP* [2000] 2 Cr App R 248 CA.

21 *Harrison* [2007] EWCA Crim 2976.

22 *R v Smith; R v Jayson* [2003]1 Cr App R 13.

23 *R v Smethurst* [2002] 1 Cr App R 6 CA.

24 *Thompson v Lodwick* [1983] RTR 76.

25 PCA 1978, s 1(2).

26 *R v Fellows and Arnold* [1997] Cr App R 244 CA. *Dooley* [2005] EWCA Crim 3093.

27 *R v Land* [1999] QB 65.

28 *R v Porter* [2006] EWCA Crim 560.

29 *Ross Hillman Ltd v Bond* [1974] QB 435 DC.

30 PCA, s 2, as amended by SOA 2003, s 45(2).

31 *R v Land* [1999] QB 65.

(xi) It is a defence to an offence under the PCA 1978, s 1(1)(b) or (c) if the defendant proves that he either had legitimate reasons for possessing, distributing or showing these photographs or pseudo-photographs, or did not know or have cause to suspect them to be indecent. The question of legitimate reason is one for the jury. If the defendant knew that he was in possession of the photographs or pseudo-photographs, but had not seen them and did not know or have reason to suspect that they were of children.
(xii) Section 1A (as amended on 1.5.2004[32]) provides a defence to offences under s 1(a), (b) or (c), where the image is a photograph (not a pseudo-photograph) and the child is proved, by the defendant, to be aged 16 or 17.
(xiii) Section 1(a) (taking or making): a defence is provided if the defendant proves they were married or living together at the time;[33] and
- there is sufficient to raise the question that she consented or he had a reasonable belief in her consent; and
- the child was either alone or with the defendant. This defence does not apply to permitting.

(xiv) Section 1(1)(b) (distributing or showing): a defence is provided if the defendant proves they were married or living together at the time, and the photograph shows only the child or the child and the defendant. The prosecution must prove that the showing or distribution was to someone other than the child.
(xv) Section 1(1)(c) (possessing with a view): a defence is provided if the defendant proves that they were married or living together at the time and that the photograph was of the child alone or with the defendant. There also has to be sufficient evidence adduced to raise the child's consent or the defendant's reasonable belief in her consent.
(xvi) Section 1B provides a defence to s 1(1)(a) where it can be proved that it was necessary for the defendant to make the images for the purpose of any criminal proceedings, or the prevention, detection or investigation of crime, or that he was a member of MI5 or GCHQ and it was necessary to make the photograph or pseudo-photograph.

Notes

9.07 (i) Triable either way.[34]
(ii) DPP consent is required.[35]
(iii) This offence may be committed by a male, female or a corporation. Where the offence has been committed by a body corporate with the consent of, connivance or neglect by any director, manager, secretary or officer (and any person purporting to be such)[36] that person shall be liable to prosecution.

Indictment

9.08 TAKING INDECENT PHOTOGRAPHS OF A CHILD 20.8.1978 to date

Statement of Offence

TAKING INDECENT PHOTOGRAPHS OF A CHILD, contrary to section 1(1)(a) of the Protection of Children Act 1978.

Particulars of Offence

X on a day between...and...took an indecent photograph or a pseudo-photograph of a child, (marked jpg...).

[32] SOA 2003, ss 45(1)(3) and 46(1).
[33] This does not include a 'one night stand'. *R v M* [2011] EWCA Crim 252.
[34] PCA 1978, s 6(1).
[35] PCA 1978, s 1(3).
[36] PCA 1978, s 3.

Where there are a large number of photographs or pseudo-photographs involved, the indictment should include: **9.09**

- specific counts to reflect a broad range of images (see sentencing at paras 9.13 and 12.03–12.12), these counts should clarify whether the image is a photograph or pseudo-photograph with reference to its 'jpg' number. If there is a dispute, alternative counts ought to be averred;
- a comprehensive count covering the remainder.

There ought to be agreement if possible as to the number of images at each level (see sentencing at paras 9.13 and 12.03–12.12) and the estimated age of the child in the images.[37] Where the defendant sends images to others a specific count ought to be included in the indictment.[38] **9.10**

Alternative Offences

(i) Attempt to commit the full offence. When indicting offences of attempt, do so under the CAA 1981. Aver the attempt in both the Statement and Particulars of Offence. **9.11**
(ii) Conspiracy (by A) with another (B) to distribute indecent photographs to himself (ie A) (CLA 1977, s 1): the indictment particulars must make it clear that the distribution is to A, in these circumstances.[39]
(iii) Incitement to distribute indecent photographs of children: does not require proof that the person incited intended to distribute the photographs.[40]

Sentence

(i) On indictment: **3 YEARS**. This was increased to **10 YEARS** on 11.1.2001.[41] **9.12**
(ii) Summarily: **6 months.**[42]
(iii) This offence is a specified offence within the CJA 2003, Sch 15.

Sentencing Guidance

See paras 12.03–12.12. The guideline case is *Oliver, Hartrey and Baldwin*.[43] Two factors determine seriousness: the nature of the indecent material and the defendant's involvement. **9.13**

The seriousness relies upon the categorization of these images into five levels: **9.14**
(1) erotic posing, with no sexual activity;
(2) sexual activity between children, or solo masturbation by a child;
(3) non-penetrative sexual activity between adults and children;
(4) penetrative sexual activity between adults and children;
(5) sadism or bestiality.

The level of involvement is determined by assessing the defendant's proximity to the abuse of the child. The following sentences apply to cases where the defendant is an adult, after a contested trial: **9.15**
(1) In a case where the offender was merely in possession of or had downloaded such material (without distribution) solely for his own use, and where the images were mainly pseudo-photographs, or there was a small number of level 1 photographs, accompanied by a guilty plea with no previous convictions, a conditional discharge or a fine would normally be appropriate. This applies to cases of possession of levels 1, 2 and 3 for personal use where the child is 16 or 17.[44]
(2) Where the defendant was in possession of a large amount of level 1 and/or a small number of level 2 images (with no distribution), then a community sentence (and if appropriate a sex offender treatment programme) may be appropriate.

---

37 *Thompson (Richard)* [2004] 2 Cr App R 262.
38 *Wild* [2002] 1 Cr App R(S) 156.
39 *Barker* (unreported), 27 March 1998 CA (No 9705014 Z5).
40 *DPP v Armstrong* [2000] Crim LR 379.
41 Criminal Justice and Courts Services Act (CJCSA) 2000, s 41(1) commencement date 11.1.2001 (SI 2000 No 3302).
42 12 months if CJA 2003, s 282(4) implemented.
43 [2003] 1 Cr App R 28.
44 Consultation Paper on the Sexual Offences Act 2003—the Exploitation of Offences, 22.4.2004, <http://sentencingcouncil.judiciary.gov.uk>.

(3) Where there was a large amount of level 2 or a small amount of level 3 material, or the defendant had shown, distributed or exchanged indecent material at level 1 or 2 on a limited scale, with no financial benefit, a sentence of up to 6 months might be appropriate.
(4) Where there was the distribution or showing of a large number of images at level 2 or 3, or possession of a small number of images at level 4 or 5, a sentence of between 6 to 12 months would be appropriate.
(5) Where the defendant is in possession of large quantities of level 4 or 5 material, or the defendant has shown or distributed a large number of level 3 material, or produced or traded in level 1 to 3 material, a sentence of between 12 months and 3 years would be appropriate.
(6) In cases where level 4 or 5 material has been shown, distributed, commissioned, produced or encouraged to be produced, perhaps with a breach of trust or some commercial gain, then a sentence of over 3 years would be appropriate.
(7) Sentences approaching 10 years' imprisonment would be reserved for very serious cases where the defendant has a previous conviction for violence, dealing in child pornography or sexually abusing children.

Aggravating features

9.16 (i) The showing or distributing of these images to a child.
(ii) Large numbers of images.
(iii) The organization of the material on a computer, which may reflect trading or a higher level of personal interest in the material.
(iv) Any posting of the images on the internet, or distribution which makes it more likely that others will accidentally find it.
(v) If the defendant was in a position of trust or was responsible for the original production or if the children involved were members of the defendant's family, or if the children were particularly vulnerable.
(vi) Age and likely/visible distress to the victim.

Mitigating features

(i) Good character, although not much weight ought to be attached.
(ii) Guilty plea.

For those falling to be sentenced on or after 14.5.2007 see the SGC guiidelines at App C, pages 366–369.

Upon Conviction/Sentence

9.17 (i) Notification applies.[45]
(ii) Disqualification/barring from working with children/vulnerable adults. See paras 12.135 and 16.33.
(iii) SOPO applies.[46]

Offences committed from 29.9.1988 to date

2. Possession of Indecent Photograph of a Child

Criminal Justice Act 1988, s 160

9.18 The CJA 1988, s 160(1) was designed to supplement provisions in the PCA 1978 in order to provide for the simple possession of indecent photographs of children. The offence was similarly extended to computerized data and pseudo-photographs in 1995.[47] This offence was originally summary only until

[45] SOA 2003, s 80(1) and Sch 3; see Chapter 14.
[46] SOA 2003, s 104 and Sch 3; see Chapter 16.
[47] CJPOA 1994, s 84(4), commencement date 03.2.1995 (SI 1995 No 127).

11.1.2001.[48] On 1.5.2003 the definition of child was extended to include a child aged 16 or 17 subject to exceptions.[49]

Definition

It is an offence for a person to have an indecent photograph [or pseudo-photograph][50] of a child in his possession. **9.19**

Proof

(i) For the definition of photograph (and pseudo-photograph)[51] see para 9.06. **9.20**
(ii) For the definition of indecent see para 9.06.
(iii) For the definition of child see para 9.06.[52]
(iv) Possession requires some degree of knowledge and control over the image.[53]
(v) Section 160(2) provides a defence if the defendant had a legitimate reason for possession of the image, or had not seen it, or did not know or have cause to suspect it to be indecent, or that it had been sent to him without request and had not been kept for an unreasonable length of time.
(vi) A statutory defence is provided for offences committed after 1.5.2003 if the defendant proves that the child is 16 or 17 and that at the time of the offence charged or when he obtained the image they were married or living together. This defence applies only if the photograph shows the child alone or with the defendant.
(vii) If the defendant adduces sufficient evidence of consent or reasonable belief in consent, the prosecution must prove that the child did not consent and that the defendant did not reasonably believe that the child consented.[54]

Notes

(i) Summary only until 10.1.2001, thereafter triable either way.[55] **9.21**
(ii) DPP consent is required.[56]
(iii) This offence may be committed by a male, female or a corporation.

Indictment

POSSESSION OF INDECENT PHOTOGRAPH OF A CHILD 29.9.1988 to date **9.22**

Statement of Offence

POSSESSION OF AN INDECENT PHOTOGRAPH OF A CHILD, contrary to section 160(1) of the Criminal Justice Act 1988.

Particulars of Offence

X on a day between . . . and . . . was in possession of an indecent photograph/pseudo-photograph of a child, (marked jpg . . .).

Where there are a large number of photographs or pseudo-photographs involved, the indictment should include **9.23**

- specific counts to reflect a broad range of images (see sentencing at paras 9.13 and 12.03–12.12), these counts should clarify whether the image is a photograph or pseudo-photograph with reference to its 'jpg' number. If there is a dispute, alternative counts ought to be averred;
- a comprehensive count to cover the remainder.

---

[48] CJCSA 2000, s 41(3) (SI 2000 No 3302).
[49] SOA 2003, s 45(2).
[50] Amended by CJPOA 1994, s 84(1) and (2) and commencement date 3.2.1995.
[51] CJA 1988, s 160(1) and (4).
[52] CJA 1988, s 160(1) and (4).
[53] *R v Porter* [2006] 2 Cr App R 25.
[54] CJA 1988, s 160A.
[55] CJA 1988, s 160(2A) and (3), as amended by CJCSA 2000, s 41(3).
[56] CJA 1988, s 160(4).

9.24 There ought to be agreement if possible as to the number of images and their level of indecency (see sentencing at para 9.13) and the estimated age of the child in the images.[57]

Alternative Offences

9.25 Attempt to commit the full offence. When indicting offences of attempt, do so under the CAA 1981. Aver the attempt in both the Statement and Particulars of Offence.

Sentence

9.26 See paras 12.03–12.12; see also the SGC guidelines at App C, pages 366–369. From 11.1.01:[58]
(i) On indictment: **5 YEARS.**
(ii) Summarily: **6 months.**

Upon Conviction/Sentence

9.27 (i) Notification applies.[59]
(ii) Disqualification/barring from working with children/vulnerable adults. See paras 12.135 and 16.33.
(iii) SOPO applies.[60]

B. POSSESSION OF PROHIBITED AND EXTREME PORNOGRAPHIC IMAGES OF CHILDREN

1. Possession of a Prohibited Image of a Child

Coroners and Justice Act 2009

Definition

9.28 To be in possession of:
(i) a pornographic image;[61]
(ii) that focuses solely or principally on a child's genitals or anal region;[62] or
(iii) that portrays any of the following:[63]
(a) the performance by a person of an act of intercourse or oral sex with or in the presence of a child;
(b) an act of masturbation by, of, involving or in the presence of a child;
(c) an act which involves penetration of the vagina or anus of a child with a part of a person's body or with anything else;
(d) an act of penetration, in the presence of a child, of the vagina or anus of a person with a part of a person's body or with anything else;
(e) the performance by a child of an act of intercourse or oral sex with an animal (whether dead or alive or imaginary);
(f) the performance by a person of an act of intercourse or oral sex with an animal (whether dead or alive or imaginary) in the presence of a child (penetation is a continuing act from entry to withdrawal (s 62(8));
(iv) and that is grossly offensive, disgusting or otherwise of an obscene character.[64]

[57] *Thompson (Richard)* [2004] 2 Cr App R 262.
[58] Previously summary only.
[59] SOA 2003, s 80(1) and Sch 3; see Chapter 14.
[60] SOA 2003, s 104 and Sch 3; see Chapter 16.
[61] Section 62(2)(a).
[62] Section 62(2)(b); (6)(a).
[63] Section 62(2)(b); (6)(b); (7).
[64] Section 62(2)(c).

Proof

(i) A 'child' is a person under 18.[65] 9.29
(ii) It also includes pictures of a person over 18 where:[66]
  (a) the impression conveyed by the image is that the person shown is a child; or
  (b) the predominant impression conveyed is that the person shown is a child despite the fact that some of the physical characteristics shown are not those of a child.
(iii) The image can be of an imaginary person or child.
(iv) 'Image' includes—
  (a) a moving or still image (produced by any means); or
  (b) data (stored by any means) which is capable of conversion into a moving or still image;
  (c) 'Image' does not include an indecent photograph, or indecent pseudo-photograph, of a child.
(v) The image is 'pornographic' if it is produced solely or principally for the purpose of sexual arousal.[67] This must be judged in the context of the whole where it forms part of a series of images.[68]
(vi) Excluded images include images that fall within a 'classified work'[69] such as films that have been issued a classification certificate. The Act expressly excludes from the exemption images extracted from classified works for the purpose of sexual arousal.[70]

Notes

(i) The offence is triable either way. 9.30
(ii) DPP consent is required.
(iii) It is a defence if the person had a legitimate reason for being in possession of the image concerned; had not seen the image concerned and did not know, nor had any cause to suspect, it to be a prohibited image of a child; or that the person was sent the image concerned without any prior request having been made by or on behalf of the person, and did not keep it for an unreasonable time.[71]

Indictment

POSSESSION OF PROHIBITED IMAGES OF CHILDREN 6.4.2010 to date 9.31

Statement of Offence

POSSESSION OF PROHIBITED IMAGES OF CHILDREN, contrary to section 62(1) and (6)(a) of the Coroners and Justice Act 2009.

Particulars of Offence

A on a day between...... and the... day of...., was in possession of a pornographic image of a child, which focuses solely or principally on a child's genitals or anal region, the said image being grossly offensive, disgusting or otherwise of an obscene character.

Alternative Offences

Attempt to commit the full offence. When indicting offences of attempt, do so under the CAA 1981. Aver the attempt in both the Statement and Particulars of Offence. 9.32

65 Section 65(5)
66 Section 65(6).
67 Section 62(3).
68 Section 62(4), (5).
69 Section 63(7).
70 Section 63(3)(b).
71 Section 64(1).

Sentence

9.33 (i) On indictment: **3 YEARS**, a **fine** or **both**.
(ii) Summarily: **6 months**, a **fine** or **both**.[72]

Upon Conviction/Sentence

9.34 (i) SOPO: applicable
(ii) Notification: applicable[73]
(iii) Disqualification/barring from working with children/vulnerable adults. See paras 12.135 and 16.33.

2. Possession of an Extreme Pornographic Image, 26.1.2009 to date

Criminal Justice and Immigration Act 2008, s 63

Definition

9.35 (i) To be in possession of an extreme pornographic image.
(ii) An image is 'pornographic' if it is of such a nature that it must reasonably be assumed to have been produced solely or principally for the purpose of sexual arousal. This must be judged in the context of the whole where it forms part of a series of images.[74]
(iii) An 'extreme image' is an image which:
  (a) is grossly offensive, disgusting or otherwise of an obscene character; and
  (b) portrays in an explicit and realistic way, any of the following
    (a) an act which threatens a person's life,
    (b) an act which results, or is likely to result, in serious injury to a person's anus, breasts or genitals,
    (c) an act which involves sexual interference with a human corpse, or
    (d) a person performing an act of intercourse or oral sex with an animal (whether dead or alive), and
    (e) a reasonable person looking at the image would think that any such person or animal was real.

Proof

9.36 (i) References to a part of the body include references to a part surgically constructed (in particular through gender reassignment surgery).[75]
(ii) 'Image' means—
  (a) a moving or still image (produced by any means); or
  (b) data (stored by any means) which is capable of conversion into such an image.[76]
(iii) Excluded images include images that fall within a 'classified work'[77] such as films that have been issued a classification certificate, unless, for the purpose of sexual arousal.[78]

Notes

9.37 (i) This offence is triable either way.
(ii) Consent of the DPP is required.

---

[72] Coroners and Justice Act 2009, s 66.
[73] Sch 3, s 35B SOA 2003: if the offender was 18 or over and receives a 2-year prison sentence or more.
[74] Section 63(4), (5).
[75] Section 63(7).
[76] Section 63(8).
[77] Section 64(7).
[78] Section 64(3)(b).

(iii) It is a defence if there is a legitimate reason for being in possession of the image concerned;[79] or if the person had not seen the image concerned and did not know, nor had any cause to suspect, it to be an extreme pornographic image; or that the person was sent the image concerned without any prior request having been made by or on behalf of the person, and did not keep it for an unreasonable time.

Participation in Consensual Acts: Sexual Offences Act, s 66

Where D is charged with an offence under s 63 that relates to an act or acts within s 7(a)–(c), only s 66(1)(b), it is a defence for D to prove— **9.38**

Section 66(2):

(a) that D directly participated in the act or any of the acts portrayed, and
(b) that the act or acts did not involve the infliction of any non-consensual harm on any person, and
(c) if the image portrays an act within section 63(7)(c), that what is portrayed as a human corpse was not in fact a corpse.

(3) For the purposes of this section harm inflicted on a person is 'non-consensual' harm if—
(a) the harm is of such a nature that the person cannot, in law, consent to it being inflicted on himself or herself; or
(b) where the person can, in law, consent to it being so inflicted, the person does not in fact consent to it being so inflicted.

Sentence

(i) If the offence portrays an act within s 63(7)(a) or (b): summarily 12 **months,**[80] on indictment **3 YEARS:** **9.39**
(a) an act which threatens a person's life,
(b) an act which results, or is likely to result, in serious injury to a person's anus, breasts or genitals,
(ii) If the offence is committed before the CJA 2003, the maximum summarily is 6 **months.**
iii) If the offence does not portray an act within s 63(7)(a) or (b).
Summarily 12 **months,**[81] on indictment 2 **YEARS.**

Upon Sentence/Conviction

(i) Notification applies. **9.40**
(ii) Disqualification/barring from working with children/vulnerable adults. See paras 12.135 and 16.33.
(iii) SOPO: applicable.

C. OBSCENE PUBLICATIONS

As stated (see Introduction) the most commonly charged offences will relate to the retail distribution of obscene material: in shops or by mail order. The OPA 1959 and the OPA 1964 are still in force. The offence is time-barred (that is, there may be no prosecution under these sections more than two years after the commission of the offence).[82] The topic is not dealt with in its historical context. **9.41**

Section 2 of the OPA 1959 created the offence of publishing an obscene article. **9.42**

In 1964,[83] the offence was extended to having obscene articles for gain. **9.43**

---

[79] Section 65(2).
[80] Section 154(1): 2008 Act, s 148(2) and Sch 27, para 23.
[81] Criminal Justice and Immigration Act 2008, s 67.
[82] OPA 1959, s 2(3).
[83] OPA 1964, s 1.

1. Publishing an Obscene Article or Having an Obscene Article for Publication for Gain

Obscene Publications Act 1959, s 2

Definition

9.44 any person who, whether for gain or not publishes an obscene article or who has an obscene article for publication for gain (whether gain to himself or to another).

Proof

9.45 (i) 'Publishes' is defined by statute as the distribution, circulation, selling, hiring, giving, lending or offering for sale,[84] or the showing, playing, projecting (data), an article containing matter to be looked at.[85] This includes the uploading or downloading of a web page, the electronic transmission of data[86] and providing another with a password to enable access to a computer.[87]

(ii) 'Obscene' is defined as any article which tends to deprave and corrupt persons who are likely, having regard to all relevant circumstances, to read, see or hear the matter contained or embodied in it.[88]

(iii) 'Article' is defined as any description or article containing or embodying matter to be read or looked at or both, any sound record and any film or other record of a picture or pictures.[89] This includes negatives,[90] pictures produced by a video cassette[91] or a computer disk.[92]

(iv) 'Having' an article for publication for gain covers where the defendant has the article in his ownership, possession or control.[93]

Notes

9.46 (i) The offence is triable either way.[94]

(ii) DPP consent is required in certain cases.[95]

(iii) This offence may be committed by a male, female or a corporation.

(iv) 'Deprave' has been held to mean make morally bad, to pervert, to debase or to corrupt morally.

(v) 'Corrupt' has been defined as to render morally unsound or rotten, to destroy the moral purity or chastity, to pervert or ruin a good quality, to debase, to defile.[96]

(vi) Once the prosecution have proved that the article is obscene, if the defence can prove that the publication of the article is justified as being for the public good on the ground that it is in the interest of science, literature, art or learning, or of other objects of general concern, then he/she is afforded a defence.[97] Expert evidence is admissible on whether the article is in the interest of science, literature, art or learning.

(vii) It is a complete defence to publishing an obscene article, if the defendant proves that he has not examined the article and had no reasonable cause to suspect that it was such that his publication of it would make him liable to be convicted of an offence.[98]

(viii) It is a complete defence of an offence of having an obscene article for publication for gain if the defendant proves that he had not examined the article and had no reasonable cause to suspect that it was such and that his having it would make him liable to be convicted.[99]

---

[84] OPA 1959, s 1(3)(a).
[85] OPA 1959, s 1(3)(b).
[86] *R v Perrin* [2002] 4 Archbold News 2 CA.
[87] *R v Fellows and Arnold* [1997] 1 Cr App R 244 CA.
[88] OPA 1959, s 1(1).
[89] OPA 1959, s 1(2).
[90] OPA 1964, s 2.
[91] *A-G Reference (No 5 of 1980)* 72 Cr App R 71 CA.
[92] *R v Fellows and Arnold* [1997] Cr App R 244 CA.
[93] OPA 1964, s 1(2).
[94] OPA 1959, s 2.
[95] OPA 1959, s 2, s 2(3A).
[96] *R v Penguin Books Ltd* [1961] Crim LR 176 at 177.
[97] OPA 1959, s 4(1).
[98] OPA 1959, s 2(6).
[99] OPA 1964, s 1(3).

(iv) Where the essence of the offence is that the material is obscene, the prosecution must prosecute under the OPA 1959, and not charge the common law offence of publishing an obscene libel.[100] This provision ensures that the defences available under the OPA 1959 are not evaded by the prosecution. However, the common law offence of outraging public decency (and conspiracy) is not barred by s 2(4).[101] (See paras 10.03–10.13.)

(x) The offence is time-barred. A prosecution for this offence may only be brought within 2 years of the commission of the offence.[102]

Indictment

PUBLISHING AN OBSCENE ARTICLE 29.8.1959 to date 9.47

Statement of Offence

PUBLISHING AN OBSCENE ARTICLE, contrary to section 2(1) of the Obscene Publications Act 1959.

Particulars of Offence

X on a day between... and... [sold] *or* [let on hire or gave or lent] *or* [distributed or circulated] *or* [offered for sale or for letting on hire] an obscene article, namely... (adding where necessary) the particulars of which are attached to this indictment.

Particulars should specify pages and lines complained of when necessary as in a book which may be in the following form:

Particulars of Obscene Articles Contained in the Book Entitled...

Count 1 of indictment. A book entitled the... beginning at... line... and ending at... line..., with the words...

HAVING AN OBSCENE ARTICLE FOR PUBLICATION FOR GAIN 31.8.1964 to date 9.48

Statement of Offence

HAVING AN OBSCENE ARTICLE FOR PUBLICATION FOR GAIN, contrary to section 2(1) of the Obscene Publications Act 1959.

Particulars of Offence

X on a day between the... and... had an obscene article, namely... for publication for gain.
(If appropriate on the facts of the case, particulars—as in above example)

Alternative Offences

Attempt to commit the full offence. When indicting offences of attempt, do so under the CAA 1981. Aver the attempt in both the Statement and Particulars of Offence. 9.49

Sentence

(i) On indictment: **3 YEARS.**[103] 9.50
(ii) Summarily: **6 months.**[104]

Upon Conviction/Sentence

(i) Notification does not apply.[105] 9.51
(ii) Disqualification/barring from working with children/vulnerable adults. See paras 12.135 and 16.33.
(iii) SOPO: not applicable.

[100] OPA 1959, s 2(4).
[101] *R v Gibson* [1990] 2 QB 619.
[102] OPA 1959, s 2(3).
[103] OPA 1959, s 2(1)(b).
[104] OPA 1959, s 2(1)(a).
[105] SOA 2003, s 80(1) (not listed in Sch 3); see Chapter 14.

10

OFFENCES AGAINST PUBLIC DECENCY

These offences deal with indecent acts which offend public decency. The old common law offence of outraging public decency is the most wide-ranging of offences in this section. This offence was not repealed by the SOA 2003; in addition, its use was effectively extended by the CJA 2003, s 320. The offence is no longer indictable only, but triable either way.[1] Offences of indecent exposure and voyeurism created by the SOA 2003 replace and extend certain old offences, in particular under the Vagrancy Act (VA) 1824. **10.01**

New offences such as intercourse with an animal[2] and sexual penetration of a corpse[3] were created. **10.02**

Offences committed from 1.1.1950 to date

1. Outraging Public Decency

Introduction

This offence is a common law offence and covers lewd, disgusting or obscene acts performed in public. In practice most cases have tended to involve acts of public masturbation, sexual intercourse in public places and prostitutes advertising in public places. A conviction for this offence was upheld where the defendants had made earrings from dried human foetuses and displayed them, as hanging from a sculpted human head in a gallery.[4] **10.03**

This offence was not repealed by the SOA 2003. New legislation covering sexual activity in a public lavatory,[5] voyeurism[6] and indecent exposure,[7] will often cover the criminality alleged. Where a statutory offence covers the conduct in question, that statutory offence should be preferred to the common law. **10.04**

---

1 CJA 2003, s 320.
2 SOA 2003, s 69.
3 SOA 2003, s 70.
4 *R v Gibson and Sylveire* [1990] 2 QB 619, 91 Cr App R 341 CA.
5 SOA 2003, s 71.
6 SOA 2003, s 67.
7 SOA 2003, s 66.

10.05 This offence will be reserved for offences of a more serious and unusual nature that do not readily fall within other sections of the Act; the maximum sentence is life imprisonment as opposed to, for example, 2 years' imprisonment for cases of exposure.

Definition

10.06 All open lewdness, grossly scandalous, and whatever openly outrages decency or is offensive and disgusting, or is injurious to public morals, by tending to corrupt the mind and destroy the love of decency, morality and good order[8] (common law).

Proof

10.07 The prosecution must prove:

(i) a deliberate act (it is arguable that the prosecution must also prove that the perpetrator was at least reckless as to whether his act could be seen by two or more[9]);

(ii) that this act was of such a lewd, obscene or disgusting character as constitutes an outrage on public decency. This evidence can be given by a police officer. It is not necessary to prove that the act did disgust or annoy individuals who were present.[10] The test for this is objective.

(iii) This act must be committed in public so that more than one person has the opportunity to have seen it. The act (or exposure) does not of itself have to take place in public but must be visible from a place to which the public have access.[11] It is sufficient for just one person to have seen it, as long as at least one other (present) might have witnessed it at the time.[12]

Notes

10.08 (i) The offence is triable either way,[13] but not before 20.1.2004;[14] offences of this nature committed before 20.1.2004 are on indictment only.

(ii) The particulars must aver the element of indecency.[15]

(iii) This offence can be committed by a male or female upon a male or female.[16]

Indictment

10.09 **OUTRAGING PUBLIC DECENCY** 1.1.1950 to date

Statement of Offence

Committing an act outraging public decency.

Particulars of Offence

D on the...day of...committed an act of a lewd, obscene and disgusting nature and outraging public decency, by indecently...

Sentence

10.10 (i) On indictment: **fine or imprisonment** or both. As this offence is a common law offence there is no maximum sentence, so long as neither is 'inordinate'.[17]

(ii) On summary conviction: **6 months** or a **fine** not exceeding the prescribed sum (currently £5000), or **both.**[18]

---

8 2 Russ Cr 12th edn.
9 *R v Rowley* [1991] Crim LR 785.
10 *R v Clayton and Halsey* [1963] 1 QB 163, 46 Cr App R 450.
11 *Walker* [1996] Cr App R 111 CA.
12 *R v Mayling* [1963] 2 QB 717, 47 Cr App R 102.
13 CJA 2003, s 320.
14 SOA 2003 (SI 2004 No 81).
15 *R v Clifford* (1988) 8 CL 86.
16 *Evans v Ewells* [1972] 2 All ER 22, [1972] 1WLR 671.
17 *R v Morris* [1951] 1 KB 394, 34 Cr App R 210.
18 MCA 1980, s 32(1).

Sentencing Guidance

See the SGC guidelines at App C, pages 411–414. **10.11**

Upon Conviction/Sentence

(i) Notification requirements: not applicable.[19] **10.12**
(ii) Disqualification/barring from working with children/vulnerable adults. See paras 12.135 and 16.33.
(iii) SOPO: not applicable.[20]

The SOA 2003 did not repeal the common law offence of outraging public decency. However most offences that might previously have been charged under this Act, will be now be charged as: **10.13**
(a) *exposure:* [21]*exposure of genitals intending someone to see them and that someone would be caused alarm and distress; maximum 2 years; or*
(b) *voyeurism:* [22]*observing someone doing a private act knowing there is no consent, for the purpose of sexual gratification; maximum 2 years; or*
(c) *threatening behaviour;*[23]
(d) *disorderly conduct.*[24]

Offences committed pre-30.4.2004

2. Indecent Exposure

Vagrancy Act 1824, s 4

In practice, most cases of indecent exposure are prosecuted under: **10.14**
(a) VA 1824, s 4 and dealt with summarily (until 2004); or
(b) SOA 2003, s 66.

Definition

Wilfully, openly, lewdly, and obscenely exposing his person with intent to insult any female… **10.15**

Proof

(i) This offence can only be committed by a male, and the exposure has to be of the penis.[25] **10.16**
(ii) The exposure does not have to take place in public but must be capable of being seen by the public.[26]
(iii) The man must have at least been reckless as to whether he was indecently exposing himself.

Notes

(i) These offences were summary offences only. Accordingly, a 6-month time limit to prosecute applied. **10.17**
(ii) This offence can only be committed upon a woman. Cases of indecent exposure to a male may be prosecuted summarily under the Town and Police Clauses Act 1847, s 28. The maximum sentence is one of 14 days' imprisonment or a fine on the level 3 standard scale. In such cases the act must take place in public and a person was likely to have been annoyed. This offence was repealed and abolished by the SOA 2003.

---

[19] SOA 2003, s 80 (not listed in Sch 3); see Chapter 14.
[20] SOA 2003, s 104 (not listed in Sch 3); see Chapter 16.
[21] SOA 2003, s 66.
[22] SOA 2003, s 67.
[23] Public Order Act (POA) 1986, s 4.
[24] POA 1986, s 5.
[25] *Evans v Ewells* [1972] 2 All ER 22.
[26] *Hunt v DPP* [1990] Crim LR 812.

Sentence

10.18 (i) Maximum sentence: **3 months** and a **fine**: level 3 standard scale.[27]

(ii) **12 months** (if further offences under VA 1824, s 4 are committed and the defendant is committed to the Crown Court to be sentenced).[28]

Upon Conviction/Sentence

10.19 (i) Notification requirements: not applicable.[29]

(ii) Disqualification/barring from working with children/vulnerable adults. See paras 12.135 and 16.33.

(iii) SOPO: not applicable.[30]

10.20 *This offence has been repealed under the SOA 2003. The following offences may now be charged.*

Offences committed from 1.5.2004 to date

3. Exposure

Sexual Offences Act 2003, s 66(1)

Definition

10.21 (1) (a) he intentionally exposes his genitals and
(b) intends that someone will see them and be caused alarm or distress.

Proof

10.22 The prosecution must prove

(i) exposure of the genitalia;

(ii) intention to expose genitals and that someone will see them and be caused harassment, alarm or distress.

Notes

10.23 (i) This offence is triable either way.[31]

(ii) The offence may be committed as principal by males or females.

Indictment

10.24 INDECENT EXPOSURE 1.5.2004 to date

Statement of Offence

EXPOSURE, contrary to section 66(1) of the Sexual Offences Act 2003.

Particulars of Offence

D on the... day of 20.., intentionally exposed his genitals, intending that someone would see them and be caused alarm or distress.

---

[27] MCA 1980, s 34(3).
[28] VA 1824, s 5.
[29] SOA 2003, s 80(1) (not in Sch 3); see Chapter 14.
[30] SOA 2003, s 104 (not in Sch 3). See Chapter 16.
[31] CJA 2003, s 66(2).

Sentence

(i) On indictment: **2 YEARS.**[32] **10.25**
(ii) Summarily: **6 months** or a **fine** (not exceeding the maximum, currently £5000) or **both.**[33]

Sentencing Guidance

See the SGC guidelines at App C, pages 408–411. **10.26**

Upon Conviction/Sentence

(i) Notification requirements apply, if criteria met.[34] **10.27**
(ii) Disqualification/barring from working with children/vulnerable adults. See paras 12.135 and 16.33.
(iii) SOPO: applicable if criteria met.[35]

4. Voyeurism

Sexual Offences Act 2003, s 67

Definition

(1) A person commits an offence if— **10.28**
   (a) for the purposes of obtaining sexual gratification, he observes another person doing a private act, and
   (b) he knows that the other person does not consent to being observed for his sexual gratification.
(2) A person commits an offence if—
   (a) he operates equipment with the intention of enabling another person to observe, for the purpose of obtaining sexual gratification, a third person (B) doing a private act, and
   (b) he knows that B does not consent to his operating equipment with that intention.
(3) A person commits an offence if—
   (a) he records another person (B) doing a private act,
   (b) he does so with the intention that he or a third person will, for the purpose of obtaining sexual gratification, look at an image of B doing the act, and
   (c) he knows that B does not consent to his recording the act with that intention.
(4) A person commits an offence if he instals equipment, or constructs or adapts a structure or part of a structure, with the intention of enabling himself or another person to commit an offence under subsection (1).

Notes

The offence is triable either way.[36] **10.29**

Indictment

VOYEURISM 1.5.2004 to date **10.30**

Statement of Offence
VOYEURISM, contrary to section 67(1) of the Sexual Offences Act 2003.
Particulars of Offence
D on the... day of 20.., for the purpose of obtaining sexual gratification, observed C doing a private act, C being in a place which, in the circumstances, would reasonably be expected to provide privacy and (state nature of C's act/state of undress) the said D knowing that C did not consent to being so observed.

[32] SOA 2003, s 66(2).
[33] SOA 2003, s 66(2).
[34] SOA 2003, s 80(1) and Sch 3; see Chapter 14.
[35] SOA 2003, s 104 and Sch 3; see Chapter 16.
[36] SOA 2003, s 67(5).

Sentence

10.31 (i) On indictment: **2 YEARS.**[37]

(ii) Summarily: **6 months** or a **fine** not exceeding the statutory maximum (£5,000) or both.

Sentencing Guidance

10.32 See the SGC guidelines at App C, pages 411–441.

Upon Conviction/ Sentence

10.33 (i) Notification requirements apply, if criteria met.[38]

(ii) Disqualification/barring from working with children/vulnerable adults. See paras 12.135 and 16.33.

(iii) SOPO: applicable if criteria met.[39]

---

[37] SOA 2003.

[38] SOA 2003, s 80(1) and Sch 3; see Chapter 14.

[39] SOA 2003, s 104 and Sch 3; see Chapter 16.

11

PREPARATORY OFFENCES

Introduction

This chapter includes: **11.01**

(a) offences of procurement (those not dealt with in Chapter 8), and
(b) other preparatory offences.

The SOA 1956 in the main followed earlier legislation, the Criminal Law Amendment Act (CLAA) **11.02** 1885, which was largely concerned with the 'white slave market'. By the time the SOA 2003 was passed these offences were rarely charged. For this reason the pre-1956 Act offences have not been included.

- For SOA 1956, s 22: procuration of a woman to become a prostitute, see para 8.58.
- For SOA 1956, s 23: procurement of girl under 21, see para 8.21.
- For SOA 1967, s 4: procurement to commit homosexual acts, see para 5.106.

Other preparatory offences: **11.03**

- For SOA 1956, s 16: assault with intent to commit buggery, see para 5.75.
- For assault with intent to commit rape (common law offence—fallen into disuse).

Offences committed between 1.1.1957 and 30.4.2004

1. Procurement of a Woman by Threats or Intimidation

Sexual Offences Act 1956, s 2(1)

Definition

...to procure a woman by threats or intimidation, to have unlawful sexual intercourse in any part of the world. **11.04**

Proof

11.05 (i) For definition of procuring, see para 8.22.
(ii) The threats and intimidation must relate to the procuring.
(iii) Until 1994[1] there was a requirement that sexual intercourse was unlawful, that is, outside marriage; thereafter the word has been deleted from the definition.
(iv) The accused must have an intention to procure the female to have sexual intercourse with him or another man.

Notes

11.06 (i) The offence is triable on indictment only.
(ii) The offence can be committed upon a girl or woman
(iii) The sexual intercourse relates to penetration of the vagina by the penis.
(iv) A male or female may commit this offence. The victim can only be female.

Indictment

11.07 PROCUREMENT OF A WOMAN BY THREATS 1.1.1957 to 30.4.2004

Statement of Offence

PROCURATION BY THREATS OR INTIMIDATION, contrary to section 2(1) of the Sexual Offences Act 1956.

Particulars of Offences

D on the...day of...procured C, a woman to have (unlawful) sexual intercourse with himself (or another), by threats or intimidation (state the nature of the alleged threats/intimidation).

Alternative Offences

11.08 An attempt to commit this offence. Until (and including) 2.11.1981, indict the attempt under common law. Thereafter charge under the CAA 1981. Aver the attempt in both the Statement and Particulars of Offence.

Sentence

11.09 On indictment: 2 YEARS.[2]

Upon Conviction/Sentence

11.10 (i) Notification: not applicable.[3]
(ii) Disqualification/barring from working with children/vulnerable adults. See paras 12.135 and 16.33.
(iii) SOPO: not applicable.[4]

2. Procurement of Intercourse by False Pretences

Sexual Offences Act 1956, s 3(1)

Definition

11.11 ...to procure a woman by false pretences or false representations, to have unlawful sexual intercourse in any part of the world.

---

[1] CJPOA 1994, s 168(1) and (3) and Sch 9, para 2, Sch 11.
[2] SOA 1956, Sch 2, para 8.
[3] SOA 2003, s 80(1) (not listed in Sch 3); see Chapter 14.
[4] SOA 2003, s 104 (not listed in Sch 3 or 5); see Chapter 16.

Proof

(i) For definition of procuring: see para 8.22. **11.12**
(ii) The false pretences or representations must relate to the procuring.
(iii) Until 1994[5] there was a requirement that sexual intercourse was unlawful, that is outside marriage; thereafter the word has been deleted from the definition.
(iv) The accused must have an intention to procure the female to have sexual intercourse with him or another man.

Notes

(i) The offence is triable on indictment only. **11.13**
(ii) The offence can be committed upon a girl or woman.
(iii) The sexual intercourse relates to penetration of the vagina by the penis.
(iv) A male or female may commit this offence. The victim can only be female.

Indictment

PROCUREMENT OF A WOMAN BY FALSE PRETENCES OR REPRESENTATIONS **11.14**
1.1.1957 to 30.4.2004

Statement of Offence

PROCURATION BY FALSE PRETENCES OR FALSE REPRESENTATIONS, contrary to section 3(1) of the Sexual Offences Act 1956.

Particulars of Offences

D on the... day of... procured C, a woman to have (unlawful) sexual intercourse with himself (or X), by falsely pretending or representing to her that (state the nature of the alleged pretence or representation).

Alternative Offences

An attempt to commit this offence. Until (and including) 2.11.1981, indict the attempt under common law. Thereafter charge under the CAA 1981. Aver the attempt in both the Statement and Particulars of Offence. **11.15**

Sentence

On indictment: **2 YEARS.**[6] **11.16**

Upon Conviction/Sentence

(i) Notification: not applicable.[7] **11.17**
(ii) Disqualification/barring from working with children/vulnerable adults. See paras 12.135 and 16.33.
(iii) SOPO: not applicable.[8]

The SOA 2003 repealed both ss 2 and 3 of the SOA 1956, without replacing either offence. **11.18**

---

[5] CJPOA 1994, s 168 (1) and (3) and Sch 9, para 2, Sch 11.
[6] SOA 2003, Sch 2, para 8.
[7] SOA 2003, s 80(1) (not listed in Sch 3); see Chapter 14.
[8] SOA 2003, s 104 (not listed in Schs 3 and 5); see Chapter 16.

3. Administering Drugs to Obtain or Facilitate Intercourse

Sexual Offences Act 1956, s 4(1)

Definition

11.19 . . . to apply or administer to, or cause to be taken by a woman any drug, matter or thing with intent to stupefy or overpower her so as thereby to enable any man to have unlawful sexual intercourse with her.

Proof

11.20 (i) 'Apply or administer to' covers any action which leads to the drug being taken and having an effect.

(ii) 'Drug' covers anything capable of having the effect of overpowering or stupefying the victim, as per the Definition.

(iv) The accused must have an intention whilst administering the drug, that the female would be overpowered or stupefied and that a man could have sexual intercourse with her.

Notes

11.21 (i) The offence is triable on indictment only.

(ii) The offence can be committed upon a girl or woman

(iii) The sexual intercourse relates to penetration of the vagina by the penis.

(iv) A male or female may commit this offence. The victim can only be female.

Indictment

11.22 ADMINISTERING DRUGS TO OBTAIN OR FACILITATE INTERCOURSE 1.1.1957 to 30.4.2004

Statement of Offence

ADMINISTRATION OF DRUGS TO OBTAIN OR FACILITATE (UNLAWFUL) SEXUAL INTERCOURSE, contrary to section 4(1) of the Sexual Offences Act 1956.

Particulars of Offences

D on the. . . day of. . . administered (state the drug/thing) a drug/matter/thing to C (caused a drug/matter/thing to be taken by C), with intent to stupefy or overpower her so as thereby to enable any man to have (unlawful) sexual intercourse with her.

Alternative Offences

11.23 An attempt to commit this offence. Until (and including) 2.11.1981, indict the attempt under common law. Thereafter charge under the CAA 1981. Aver the attempt in both the Statement and Particulars of Offence.

Sentence

11.24 On indictment: **2 YEARS.**[9]

Upon Conviction/Sentence

11.25 (i) Notification: not applicable.[10]

[9] SOA 1956, Sch 2, para 9.

[10] SOA 2003, s 80(1) (not listed in Sch 3); see Chapter 14.

(ii) Disqualification/barring from working with children/vulnerable adults. See paras 12.135 and 16.33.
(iii) SOPO: not applicable.[11]

The SOA repealed SOA 1956, s 4 in full. Section 61 of the SOA 2003 covers this offence (see para 11.35). **11.26**

Offences committed between 1.1.1969 and 30.4.2004

4. Burglary with Intent to Commit Rape

Theft Act 1968, s 9(1)

Definition

...A person is guilty of burglary if— **11.27**

(a) he enters any building or part of a building as a trespasser and with intent to commit any such offence as is mentioned in subsection (2) below;...

This includes '(2) ... raping any woman [from 3.11.1994: changes to person] therein'.

Proof

(i) Entry of a building or part of a building, as a trespasser. Trespass is defined as any intentional, reckless or negligent entry into a building in possession of another without that person's consent, and the defendant must know or be reckless as to the facts which make the entry a trespass.[12] **11.28**
(ii) Intent to commit the offence of rape.

Notes

(i) The offence is triable on indictment only. **11.29**
(ii) From 3.11.1994 the offence can be committed upon a male or female. Before this date the offence could only be committed upon a female.
(iii) The rape covers penetration of the vagina by the penis, up until (and including) 2.11.1994. Thereafter the offence also covers penile penetration of the anus without consent.[13]
(iv) From 3.11.1994 a male or female may commit this offence and the victim may be male or female.

Indictment

BURGLARY WITH INTENT TO COMMIT RAPE 1.1.1969 to 30.4.2004 **11.30**

Statement of Offence

BURGLARY WITH INTENT TO COMMIT RAPE, contrary to section 9(1)(a) of the Theft Act 1968.

Particulars of Offences

D on the...day of...entered as a trespasser a building (part of a building) (being a dwelling) known as...with intent to rape C, a female (male).

[11] SOA 2003, s 104 (not listed in Sch 3); see Chapter 16.
[12] *R v Smith and Jones* (1976) 63 Cr App R 47 CA.
[13] SOA 1956, s 1 as amended by CJPOA 1994, s 142.

Alternative Offences

11.31 An attempt to commit this offence. Until 2.11.1981, indict the attempt under common law. After this date charge under the CAA 1981. Aver the attempt in both the Statement and Particulars of Offence.

Sentence

11.32 On indictment:
- if the building was a dwelling: **14 YEARS**;[14]
- otherwise: **10 YEARS**.[15]

Upon Conviction/Sentence

11.33 (i) Notification: not applicable.[16]
(ii) Disqualification/barring from working with children/vulnerable adults. See paras 12.135 and 16.33.
(iii) SOPO: not applicable.[17]

11.34 *The SOA 2003 repealed that part of the Theft Act (TA) 1968, s 9(2) that referred to the intention of 'raping any person therein'. Section 63 of the SOA 2003 (trespass with intent to commit a sexual offence) now covers this offence, and extends the offence to include an intent to commit any sexual offence. Section 62 covers the commission of an offence with intent to commit any sexual offence (see para 11.42).*

Offences committed from 1.5.2004 to date

5. Administering a Substance with Intent

Sexual Offences Act 2003, s 61(1)

Definition

11.35 (1) A person commits an offence if he intentionally administers a substance to, or causes a substance to be taken by another person (B)—
(a) knowing that B does not consent, and
(b) with the intention of stupefying or overpowering B, so as to enable any person to engage in a sexual activity that involves B.

Proof

11.36 As per Definition. In addition:
(i) For 'administering or causing to be taken', see para 11.20.
(ii) 'Substance' covers both alcohol and drugs.
(iii) Intention that the substance be administered, knowing that B does not consent, and with intent to stupefy or overpower B so as to enable any person to engage in sexual activity.

Notes

11.37 (i) The offence is triable either way.[18]
(ii) SOA 2003, s 74 applies in relation to consent, which qualifies as consent if the person had the freedom and capacity to make that choice.

---

[14] TA 1968, s 9(3)(a).
[15] TA 1968, s 9(3)(b).
[16] SOA 2003, s 80(1) (not listed in Sch 3); see Chapter 14.
[17] SOA 2003, s 104 (not listed in Sch 3 or 5); see Chapter 16.
[18] SOA 2003, s 61(2).

Indictment

ADMINISTERING A SUBSTANCE WITH INTENT 1.5.2004 to date 11.38

Statement of Offence

ADMINISTERING A SUBSTANCE WITH INTENT, contrary to section 61(1) of the Sexual Offences Act 2003.

Particulars of Offence

D on the... day of... intentionally administered a substance to C (caused a substance to be taken by C) knowing that C did not consent and with the intention of stupefying or overpowering C so as to enable D (or X) to engage in sexual activity that involved C.

Alternative Offences

An attempt to commit the offence. This should be charged under the CAA 1981, s 1(1). Aver the attempt in both the Statement and Particulars of Offence. This will be appropriate, for example, where 'administration' as defined by case law is in issue. 11.39

Sentence

(i) On indictment: **10 YEARS.** 11.40
(ii) Summarily: **6 months**[19] or a **fine** not exceeding the statutory maximum or **both.**

Upon Conviction/Sentence

(i) Notification: applicable.[20] 11.41
(ii) Disqualification/barring from working with children/vulnerable adults. See paras 12.135 and 16.33.
(iii) SOPO: applicable.[21]

6. Committing an Offence with Intent to Commit a Sexual Offence

Sexual Offences Act 2003, s 62(1)

Definition

(1) A person commits any offence under this section if he commits an offence with the intention of committing a relevant sexual offence. 11.42
(2) In this section, 'relevant sexual offence' means any offence under this Part (including an offence of aiding, abetting, counselling, or procuring such an offence).

Proof

As per Definition. In addition: 11.43
(i) Relevant sexual offence relates to any offence within the SOA 2003, ss 1–79.
(ii) Intent to commit a relevant sexual offence covers the situation whereby the defendant hoped that the sexual activity would be consensual, but intended to rape her if there was no consent.

---

19 12 months if CJA 2003, s 282(4) implemented.
20 SOA 2003, s 80(1) and Sch 3, para 30; see Chapter 14.
21 SOA 2003, s 104 and Sch 3, para 30; see Chapter 16.

Notes

11.44 The offence is triable on indictment only if the initial offence is false imprisonment or kidnapping.[22] Otherwise the offence is triable either way.[23]

Indictment

11.45 COMMITTING AN OFFENCE WITH INTENT TO COMMIT A SEXUAL OFFENCE
1.5.2004 to date

> **Statement of Offence**
> COMMITTING AN OFFENCE WITH INTENT TO COMMIT A SEXUAL OFFENCE, contrary to section 62(1) of the Sexual Offences Act 2003.
>
> **Particulars of Offence**
> D on the... day of... committed the offence of [kidnapping] *or* [false imprisonment] particularised in Count 1, and did so with the intention of committing a relevant sexual offence.

The commission of the offence, in the above example: kidnapping or false imprisonment, ought to be drafted as an additional separate count on the indictment.

The particular sexual activity intended does not have to be averred.

Alternative Offences

11.46 (i) The initial offence, whatever that may be.
(ii) An attempt to commit the offence. This should be charged under the CAA 1981, s 1(1) Aver the attempt in both the Statement and Particulars of Offence.

Sentence

11.47 (i) On indictment:
- if the initial offence is kidnapping or false imprisonment: **LIFE;**[24]
- otherwise: **10 YEARS.**[25]

(ii) Summarily: **6 months**[26] or a **fine** not exceeding the statutory maximum or **both**.

Sentencing Guidance

11.48 See App C, p. 420.

Upon Conviction/ Sentence

11.49 (i) Notification: applicable.[27]
(ii) Disqualification/barring from working with children/vulnerable adults. See paras 12.135 and 16.33.
(iii) SOPO: applicable.[28]

---

[22] SOA 2003, s 62(3).
[23] SOA 2003, s 62(4).
[24] SOA 2003, s 62(3).
[25] SOA 2003, s 62(4)(b).
[26] 12 months if CJA 2003, s 282(4) implemented.
[27] SOA 2003, s 80(1) and Sch 3, para 31; see Chapter 14.
[28] SOPA 2003, s 104 and Sch 3; see Chapter 16.

12

SENTENCING

Introduction

Offences must be sentenced according to the sentencing regime in place at the time the offence was committed. The maximum sentences available are set out within the chapters at the sentencing paragraph for each offence. The different types of sentence available under the Criminal Justice Act (CJA) 2003 and as amended by the Legal Aid, Sentencing and Punishment of Offenders Act (LASPO) 2012 will apply to offences committed on or after 4.4.2005 and 3.12.2013 respectively **12.01** and appear from para 12.28. In addition, there are a number of ancillary orders which need to be considered when sentencing as well as the automatic notification requirement and the likelihood of barring from working with children/vulnerable adults. These are set out within this chapter from para 12.135 and in the Appendices. Guideline authorities, insofar as they are now of assistance, are set out in App C. The Sexual Offences Definitive Guideline, issued by the Sentencing Council (SC) in December 2013 and in force from 1.4.2014, is reproduced in large part at App C with the kind permission of the SC.

Indications of Sentence (Goodyear Indications)

12.02 Where a defendant is charged with a specified offence to which the dangerousness provisions apply (most sexual offences; see the list at para 12.96), a judge should be cautious about giving an indication as to the likely sentence because the question of dangerousness remains undetermined. The issue did not arise in the guideline case of *Goodyear*,[1] but in *R v Kulah*[2] the Court of Appeal judged the assessment of dangerousness in most such cases not to be clear-cut. A judge who had not been provided with reports might well feel disinclined to give an indication. A renewed request of a second judge uninformed by defence counsel of the refusal (regarded as proper) from the first was deprecated by the court. Similarly, a judge should be slow to give an indication of sentence in the absence of a victim personal statement; the SC Definitive Guideline at para 1.23 for sexual offences provides that 'if a victim personal statement has not been produced, the court should enquire whether the victim had been given the opportunity to make one. In the absence of a victim personal statement, the court should not assume the offence had no impact on the victim.'

A. SENTENCING MULTIPLE OFFENCES

12.03 The Sentencing Council Guidelines on Totality[3] provide comprehensive and clear guidance for sentencing more than one offence. The new Sexual Offences Guidelines are based on a sentence for a single offence; see para 12.113.

Dangerous Offenders: Aggregate Concurrent Terms

12.04 Whilst it is not permissible to add together shorter sentences in order to arrive at the required four-year term, it is proper to consider the seriousness of all offences when deciding the correct term for a qualifying (specified) offence.

12.05 In *R v Pinnell* [2010],[4] the Court of Appeal held that, when an offender has been convicted of a specified offence and the court has concluded that he is dangerous, but none of the associated offences for which he was being sentenced justified a four-year term, the seriousness of the aggregate offending must be considered. If a four-year term results from aggregating the shortest terms commensurate with the seriousness of each offence, then that four-year term can be imposed in relation to the specified offence.

12.06 In *R v Brown* [2007],[5] the Court of Appeal had held that it was undesirable to pass an extended sentence(s) followed by a determinate term but in *Pinnell* the court said the 2008 amendments to early release provisions applicable to extended sentences had altered the position. It was now

---

1 *R v Goodyear* [2005] 3 All ER 117.
2 *R v Kulah* [2008] 1 All ER 16.
3 Offences Taken Into Consideration and Totality: Definitive Guideline.
4 *R v Pinnell* [2010] EWCA Crim 2848.
5 *R v Brown* [2007] 1 Cr App R(S) 468.

permissible to pass a determinate term to follow an extended sentence if there was a particular reason to do so because at that time the early release provisions meant release had to occur at the half-way point and so the date of release was known at the time of passing sentence.

The LASPO 2012 provisions have altered the date of release for those serving an extended sentence. Early release is now 'normally to be at the two-thirds point of the custodial term', unless the term is 10 years or more or the sentence was imposed for an offence listed under Sch 15B, when the case must be referred to the Parole Board for consideration as to whether the offender still needs to be detained for the protection of the public. **12.07**

It would seem, therefore, that if at the time of sentence the offender's date of release is known (not at the two-thirds point) then *Pinnell* will continue to apply, but that if the case must be referred to the Parole Board then the date of release is uncertain at the time of sentence then *Pinnell* can no longer apply. The problem was recognized by the Court of Appeal in *Saunders*[6] but as it did not arise on the facts of that appeal, the court declined to provide guidance. **12.08**

Associated Offences

Section 161(1) Sentencing Act 2000: an offence is associated with another offence if the offender is convicted of it in the same proceedings as the other offence or is sentenced for it at the same time as the other offence. **12.09**

In deciding what the appropriate sentence to be passed is, the court may take account of all the offences for which an offender is to be sentenced on the same occasion, as long as they are 'associated offences'. Associated offences are limited to offences of which a defendant has been convicted, or which he has asked the court to take into consideration. They must therefore be both individually identified and admitted. Sample counts are not 'associated offences' for the purpose of determining sentence. **12.10**

Sample Counts and Multiple Incident Counts

Indictments reflecting a course of conduct may contain either sample counts or multiple incident counts;[7] see paras 1.08–1.17. In sentencing upon conviction of sample counts, the judge will be restricted to what is contained within the indictment unless more than that is both identified and admitted. **12.11**

Whilst, therefore, sample counts do not, without more, allow the sentencing judge to pass a longer sentence to reflect that course of conduct, multiple incident counts do and consequently may be a better method of achieving justice. **12.12**

B. SENTENCING HISTORIC OFFENCES

Offenders must be sentenced according to the sentencing regime in place at the time the offence was committed. The maximum sentences available at the relevant time for offences appear at each sentencing paragraph within Chapters 2–11 inclusive. The new SC Guidelines provide assistance in sentencing historic offences at its Annexes B and C; the latter is based on the table which appears in Chapter 1 of both editions of this work. **12.13**

When sentencing in an historic sex case, it is important to have two critical dates in mind: **12.14**

(i) 1.5.2004, when the SOA 2003 came into force; and
(ii) 4.4.2005, when the sentencing provisions of the CJA 2003 came into force.

---

[6] *R v Saunders* [2013] EWCA Crim 1027.

[7] See para 1.03 *et seq*, including the new rules allowing one count to reflect a continuing course of conduct.

The court should then make the appropriate 'measured reference'[8] to the current sentencing guideline.

12.15 In *R v H(J) and Others* [2011][9] the then Lord Chief Justice, Lord Judge, provided guidance in sentencing historic sexual offences. His review of numerous such cases revealed that the Court of Appeal had at different times adopted conflicting approaches to the critical sentencing issues, not least because of the changes in both the substantive law and sentencing provisions, under evolving sentencing regimes.

12.16 Lord Judge identified that specific guidance was required about the extent to which, if any, the sentencing court should reflect the level(s) of sentence which would have been likely to have been imposed if the defendant had been convicted at a trial shortly after the offences were committed and, by contrast, the extent to which the events during the long period between the commission of the crime and the sentencing decision may be relevant.

12.17 Lord Judge suggested at [46] that reference to earlier decisions should be generally discouraged as unlikely to be helpful and said that, with the exception of *Millberry*[10] and the definitive sentencing guideline (used in a measured way), the following considerations should be treated as guidance. He further said that subsequent decisions of the Court of Appeal, unless specifically stated as intending to provide guidance, should be regarded as fact-specific only.

12.18 At [47] he summarized the principles to be followed:

(a) Sentence will be imposed at the date of the sentencing hearing, on the basis of the legislative provisions then current, and by measured reference to any definitive sentencing guidelines relevant to the situation revealed by established facts.

(b) Although sentence must be limited to the maximum sentence at the date when the offence was committed, it is wholly unrealistic to attempt an assessment of sentence by seeking to identify in [the present day] what the sentence for the individual offence was likely to have been if the offence had come to light at or shortly after the date when it was committed.[11]

(c) As always, the particular circumstances in which the offence was committed and its seriousness must be the main focus. Due allowance for the passage of time may be appropriate. The date may have a considerable bearing upon the offender's culpability. If, for example, the offender was very young and immature at the time when the case was committed, that remains a continuing feature of the sentencing decision.[12] Similarly if the allegations had come to light many years earlier, and when confronted with them the defendant admitted them, but, for whatever reason, the complaint had not been drawn to the attention of, or investigated by, the police, or had been investigated and not then pursued to trial, these too would be relevant features.

(d) In some cases it may be safe to assume that the fact that, notwithstanding the passage of years, the victim has chosen spontaneously to report what happened to him or her in his or her childhood or younger years would be an indication of continuing inner turmoil. However the circumstances in which the facts come to light varies, and careful judgment of the harm done to the victim is always a critical feature of the sentencing decision. Simultaneously, equal care needs to be taken to assess the true extent of the defendant's criminality by reference to what he actually did and the circumstances in which he did it.

---

[8] *R v H(J) and Others* [2011] EWCA Crim 2753. In *P* (one of the conjoined appeals in *R v H(J)*) the sentencing court overlooked that the maximum sentence for attempted rape was seven years at the time.

[9] *R v (H(J) and Others* [2011] EWCA Crim 2753, [2012] 1WLR, [2012] 2 All ER 340.

[10] *R v Milberry* [2003] 1 WLR 546.

[11] See *R v S (Paul Martin)* [2012] EWCA Crim 2668 where the judge erred in sentencing on the basis of authorities existing at the time of the offence in 2000. However, the sentence under the current regime would not have been significantly different so it was not manifestly excessive.

[12] It follows that the historic nature of the case is not necessarily irrelevant to the sentencing decision. *R v O* (Unreported; Court of Appeal 4 December 2012) is good example of a case where the defendant's mental age of 8 at the time when he had raped his 17-year-old-sister in 1977 was of relevance to the sentencing decision. The offender was 82 at the time of the appeal. The court when reducing a sentence of 7 years to 5½ years also took into account the impact of imprisonment upon his wife, who also had mental health difficulties. See also *R v Robert Clarke* [2012] EWCA Crim 9.

(e) The passing of the years may demonstrate aggravating features if, for example, the defendant has continued to commit sexual crime or he represents a continuing risk to the public. On the other hand, mitigation may be found in an unblemished life over the years since the offences were committed, particularly if accompanied by evidence of positive good character.
(f) Early admissions and a guilty plea are of particular importance in historic cases. Just because they relate to facts which are long passed, the defendant will inevitably be tempted to lie his way out of allegations. It is greatly to his credit if he makes early admissions. Even more powerful mitigation is available to the offender who out of a sense of guilt and remorse reports himself to the authorities. Considerations like these provide the victim with vindication, often a feature of great importance to them.

It follows from (a) above that when passing sentence for an offence committed on or after 6.4.2010, the sentencer must follow the relevant guideline unless satisfied that it would be contrary to the interests of justice to do so.[13] To apply a current guideline to an offence committed before it came into force does not offend the rule against retrospectivity as enshrined in Article 7.[14] In respect of historic offences, as long as sentences fall within or do not exceed the maximum sentence which could lawfully be imposed at that date when the offence was committed, neither the restrospectivity principle nor Article 7 are contravened.[15] **12.19**

The subsequent judgment of the Court of Appeal when increasing the total sentences passed on Stuart Hall[16] from 15 to 30 months is illustrative of this approach. **12.20**

Per Lord Judge CJ:

> [3] For a period of years, and indeed at the time he committed the offences with which we are concerned, through radio and television he had become a well-known, popular and successful public figure. Without seeking to minimise the offences or their impact on the victims, which we shall address later in the judgment, it is the unfortunate reality that children and teenagers are sometimes subjected to indecent assaults, which take a more extreme form than those suffered by the offender's victims. However, we are here concerned with indecent assaults on thirteen female victims over a period of almost 20 years, between 1967 and 1985/1986. The ages of the victims ranged from 9 years to 17 years. At the time when they took place the offender was aged between 38 and his mid-50s. From the point of view of the victims, he was, and must have seemed, a figure of power, authority and influence. That is a feature of the case which involves significant breach of trust which seriously aggravates the offences that he committed. He is now an elderly, frail man.

Lord Judge then took time to set out the circumstances of the offences, acknowledging the levels of their individual seriousness, and concluded: **12.21**

> [82] ... We must keep the seriousness of the offences in proper perspective, as the Attorney General did. Some were more serious than others. Taken in isolation, some would not have required a custodial sentence. Some, as time went by and as the offender escaped detection, seem to us to have started to be marked with an increasing degree of thought and premeditation. The result of the offending taken as a whole is that a multiplicity of young girls were sexually molested over an 18-year period, some when they were very young, all when they were in one way or another vulnerable, and all when the offender was in a position to misbehave as he did just because he was who he was—trusted as a friend, trusted as somebody to whose home it was safe to send a child, or to invite into a home, or trusted as a public figure. All of the offences were real assaults. There was no question of any of the victims consenting to anything. These were not just technical assaults because the victims were too young to have, if they had, consented in law. There was no such question; they were all assaults—technically, legally and as a matter of fact.

---

[13] Coroners and Justice Act 2009, s 125(1).

[14] *R v Bao* [2008] 2 Cr App R(S) 10. Article 7 prevents a sentence from being imposed which could not have been passed at the time because the maximum was lower.

[15] *R v H and Others* [2012] 2 Cr App R(S) 21, paras 17 *et seq*. Privy Council in *Fynn v HM Advocate* [2004] UKPC 1; *R (On the Application of Uttley) v Secretary of State for the Home Department* [2004] UKHL 38, [2005] 1 Cr App R(S) 91.

[16] A-G Ref; *James Stuart Hall* [2013] EWCA Crim 1450.

12.22 The Court of Appeal also concluded that the offender's position of trust created by his public position as one of the most celebrated television personalities of the time and his reputation as a decent man had caused certainly two of his victims' parents not to pursue a complaint to the police.

12.23 The court regarded the offender's public denials on the steps of the magistrates' court in which he proclaimed his innocence as a serious aggravating feature of the case, knowing as he did his guilt whatever legal advice he had by then received. The court referred to the known effects on his victims of hearing those denials and whilst acknowledging it meant they would not have to give evidence, did not regard his guilty pleas at the Plea and Case Management Hearing (PCMH) as tendered at the first opportunity.

12.24 A critical feature of determining such a sentence, in keeping with *H*[17] and adopted as central in the new Definitive Guideline, will be the effect of the offender's actions on his victim(s):

> [83.] The impact on the victims has been lifelong. They have resulted in different manifestations. Indeed, the breadth of the manifestations, as we have set out in the judgment, highlight that although it is possible to predict that this kind of sexual misbehaviour will always cause some permanent consequences, it is not always easy to predict precisely what they will be in the case of each individual victim. Difficulty in forming a lasting sexual relationship may be obvious in some cases of indecent assault; but a deep resentment of a father's reaction may sour what should be a natural, loving relationship of a quite different kind between father and daughter, to the disadvantage of both the father and the daughter.

12.25 Other examples of the application of *H* include *R v Wendell Baker* [2014],[18] *Clarke* [2012],[19] *Wheller* [2012][20] and *D* [2013].[21] See paras 12.64–12.65 for *Wendell Baker* and *D*, both of which attracted life sentences for historic cases of rape by burglars.

12.26 When an historic case attracts a low maximum sentence it is permissible for the sentencing judge to pass consecutive sentences in order to have regard to current sentencing practice: *R v Woods* [2012].

C. SENTENCES FOR OFFENCES UNDER A PRE-CRIMINAL JUSTICE ACT 2003 LICENSING REGIME

12.27 It is not appropriate to make a reduction in an otherwise appropriate sentence on the basis that since the time of the offence the early release provisions have been changed and/or the licensing system made more severe.[22]

D. SUSPENDED SENTENCES AND COMMUNITY ORDERS: HISTORIC AND CURRENT

Suspended Sentences

12.28 The history:

1967 Suspended sentences were first introduced (CJA 1967, s 39), despite two reviews rejecting them; a term of up to 2 years could be suspended.

---

17 A-G Ref; *R v James Stuart Hall* [2013] EWCA Crim 1450.

18 *R v Wendell Baker* [2013] EWCA Crim 242.

19 *R v Clarke* [2012] EWCA Crim 9.

20 *R v Wheller* [2012] EWCA.

21 *D* [2013] 1 Cr App R(S) 674.

22 *Matthews (Alex Joseph)* [2011] EWCA Crim 3110; *Round, Dunn and Others* [2009] EWCA Crim 2667; [2010], referred to in *R v H(J)* at para 19 and *A-G's Reference (No 27 of 2013)* [2014] EWCA Crim 334.

1982 The power to partly suspend a sentence was introduced (CLA 1977).
1991 The power to partly suspend a sentence was removed and suspended sentences were restricted to cases where 'exceptional circumstances' could be shown (CJA 1991, s 5(1)).

4.5.2005–3.12.2013

Criminal Justice Act 2003, s 190

The maximum period of imprisonment (or detention in a Young Offender Institution (YOI)) which could be suspended was 12 months. The maximum operational period was 2 years. **12.29**

For the first time an order was required to be attached; those available included supervision of up to 2 years with a requirement that the offender attend a nationally credited Sexual Offender Treatment Programme (SOTP), curfew, residence, unpaid work, mental health treatment order. **12.30**

3.12.2013 to date

Legal Aid, Sentencing and Punishment of Offenders Act 2012, ss 68 and 69

The maximum period of imprisonment (or detention in a YOI) which could be suspended was increased to 2 years. The maximum operational period is 2 years. **12.31**

Section 189(1A) of the CJA 2003: the requirement to attach an order was removed, although they remain available. This opens the suspended sentence up to the pre-CJA 2003 criticism of there being no penalty for a serious offence, save in the event of conviction for a further offence. **12.32**

Sexual Offender Treatment Programmes: Completion within the Period of Suspension

For an effective SOTP, a term longer than that available under a suspended sentence is sometimes argued to be necessary. The reason historically was more likely to be founded in a backlog or a delay in forming groups of offenders. The Community SOTP is identical to the programme prisoners attend apart from the format and each takes 12–18 months to complete, dependent upon the offender as assessed once the programme has begun. It is possible for an offender in custody to complete the programme more quickly once it has begun because of his improved availability.[23] **12.33**

Community Orders

Section 177 of the CJA 2003 governs community orders for offenders aged over 16. The maximum period is 3 years. Similar requirements and programmes are available as for suspended sentences, including a SOTP. In cases where the sentence would be measured in months it is arguable that a community order will be more appropriate, particularly having regard to the absence of any extended licence provisions. The maximum period of supervision is usually preferred by the Probation Service when a SOTP is imposed as part of a community order, in order to allow for ongoing risk management and to monitor change.[24] **12.34**

Section 70 of the LASPO 2012: programme requirements no longer have to be accredited, nor is the consent of anyone involved in the programme necessary. **12.35**

[23] With thanks to Jerry Thomas and Sean McMillan, Senior Probation Officers.

[24] With thanks to Jerry Thomas, Senior Probation Officer.

E. SENTENCING OFFENCES STRADDLING THE IMPLEMENTATION DATES OF DIFFERENT ACTS

12.36 When the allegations made straddle the implementation dates of Acts which create two different sentencing regimes, the indictment should be drafted in such a way as to reflect the differing sentencing powers which attach to the different time frame; see paras 1.21–1.31.

Section 55 of the Violent Crime Reduction Act (VCRA) 2006 provides the mechanism for offences which span the SOA 2003 and earlier, repealed legislation.[25] If this has not been done and an indictment spans two sentencing regimes without reflecting the differing powers, then unless it is clear from the evidence under which regime the offence was committed,[26] the court should sentence as if the offence was committed under the preceding legislation assuming that this will be more favourable to the defendant.[27]

1. Offences Straddling the Implementation of the Criminal Justice Act 2003

12.37 If an indictment spans the implementation of the CJA 2003,[28] it is usually possible to sentence under the current provisions.

Note the Court of Appeal's ruling in *R v Harries and Others* [2007]:[29]

> The Court considered the dangerous offender provisions contained in the Criminal Justice Act 2003 in relation to (various child sex) offences which straddled the commencement date. Where offences were committed after the commencement date, the provisions should be applied and any other offences, including those committed prior to the commencement date, could be considered by the sentencing judge in making an assessment of dangerousness under s 229 of the 2003 Act. Per Sir Igor Judge:
>
> > 'Where a count on an indictment spanned the April 4, 2005 commencement date, sentencing courts should not impose a sentence under the 2003 Act unless satisfied that one of the offences was committed after the commencement date. However, where an offence was not subject to the dangerous offender provisions, the sentencing court could consider that offence in relation to the assessment of dangerousness for offences that were subject to the provisions. Those offences did not cease to be relevant because the provisions did not apply to them.'

2. Offences Straddling the Implementation of the Sexual Offences Act 2003

12.38 Following the repeal of the SOA 1956 on 1.5.2004, any sexual offence occurring from this date onwards must be prosecuted under the SOA 2003. The lacuna which existed because no transitional provision had been implemented[30] to deal with the situation where the prosecution could not prove whether the offence occurred before, on or after 1 May, leading to the decisions in *R v Newbon*[31] and *R v C*,[32] has now been filled by s 55 of the VCRA 2006. This section came into force on 12.2.2007.[33]

---

25 See also from 12.38 and para 1.25.

26 *R v R (Paul Brian)* [1993] Crim LR 541.

27 However, see CJA 2003 (Commencement No 8 and Transitional and Saving Provisions) Order 2005 (SI No 950); in particular, 'where an offence is found to have been committed over a period of two or more days, or at some time during a period of two or more days, it shall be taken . . . to have been committed on the last of those days'.

28 Commencement date CJA 2003: 4.4.2005.

29 *R v Harries and Others* [2007] EWCA Crim 1622.

30 Despite provision being made by SOA 2003, s 141.

31 *R v Newbon* [2005] Crim LR 738.

32 [2005] EWCA Crim 3533.

33 By virtue of the VCRA 2006 (Commencement No 1) Order 2007 (SI 2006 No 74). See para 12.42 for list of offences it applies to.

Section 55 provides for the situation where a defendant is charged in respect of the same conduct with both an offence under the SOA 2003 and an offence under the old law, and the only thing preventing him being found guilty of the 2003 Act offence or the offence under the old law is the fact that it has not been proved beyond a reasonable doubt that the time when the conduct took place was either after the coming into force of the enactment providing for the offence or before the repeal of the old law. **12.39**

In such circumstances, for the purpose of determining guilt, it will be conclusively presumed that the time when the conduct took place was when the old law applied if the offence attracted a lesser maximum penalty; otherwise it will be presumed the conduct took place after the implementation of the new law.[34]

For s 55 to have effect, both the SOA 2003 and the earlier legislation must be pleaded in the alternative[35] in the indictment. See also para 1.26. **12.40**

To apply s 55 of the VCRA 2006,[36] consider: **12.41**

- Is the offence charged an offence under the SOA 2003?
- Does the conduct alleged also amount to an offence under one of the repealed offences listed in subsection (2) see para 12.42 or the inchoate offences specified in subsection (5) (see para 12.43)?
- Is the *only thing* preventing D being found guilty that it cannot be proved beyond reasonable doubt whether the conduct took place before or after the commencement of the SOA 2003?

If so:

- Consider whether the maximum penalty of imprisonment available was lower under the old law or the new law.
- Whichever version carries the lower penalty will be conclusively presumed to apply.
- If the penalties are the same, then it shall be conclusively presumed that the conduct took place after the commencement of the SOA 2003.

Offences Listed in the Violent Crime Reduction Act 2006, s 55(2)

(a) Any offence under the SOA 1956 (c. 69) **12.42**
(b) an offence under the VA 1824, s 4 (c. 83) (obscene exposure)
(c) an offence under the Town Police Clauses Act 1847, s 28 (c. 89) (indecent exposure)
(d) an offence under the OPA 1861, s 61 or 62 (c. 100) (buggery etc)
(e) an offence under the MHA 1959, s 128 (c. 72) (sexual intercourse with patients)
(f) an offence under the IwCA 1960, s 1 (c. 33) (indecency with children)
(g) an offence under the SOA 1967, s 4 or 5 (procuring a man to commit buggery and living on the earnings of male prostitution)
(h) an offence under the TA 1968, s 9 (c. 60) (burglary, including entering premises with intent to commit rape)
(i) an offence under the CLA 1977, s 54 (c. 45) (incitement of girl under 16 to commit incest)
(j) an offence under the PCA 1978, s 1 (c. 37) (indecent photographs of children)
(k) an offence under the SO(A)A 2000, s 3 (c. 44) (abuse of position of trust)
(l) an offence under the Nationality, Immigration and Asylum Act 2002, s 145 (c. 41) (traffic in prostitution).

Offences Listed in the Violent Crime Reduction Act 2006, s 55(5)

A reference in s 55 to an offence under the SOA 2003 or to an offence specified in subsection (2) includes a reference to— **12.43**

(a) inciting the commission of that offence;
(b) conspiracy to commit that offence;
(c) attempting to commit that offence.

---

34 VCRA 2006, s 55(1).
35 *R v Chaney* [2009] EWCA Crim 52.
36 With thanks to David Ormerod QC.

F. SENTENCING REGIMES FOR DANGEROUS OFFENDERS

Pre-Sentence Reports

12.44 When considering dangerousness a pre-sentence report 'should usually be obtained'.[37] See also *Attorney General's Reference (No 145 of 2006)*;[38] in most cases, a sentencing judge should obtain a pre-sentence report before deciding whether a sexual offender posed a significant risk to members of the public of serious harm occasioned by the commission by him of further specified offences. However, in *R v PH*[39] the judge at first instance had been correct to impose life sentences for two rapes where he found there was a continuing significant risk to the public; no reports were before the court, but the defendant had a previous conviction for firearms offences. The offences revealed the defendant's dominant and aggressive attitude towards women:

> The sentencer will be guided, but not bound by, the assessment of risk in such reports. A sentencer who contemplates differing from the assessment in such a report should give both counsel the opportunity of addressing the point.[40]

Only in exceptional circumstances would a judge permit cross-examination of the author of the pre-sentence report.[41]

Dangerousness Test

12.45 The definition for dangerousness has not altered. *R v Lang and Others* [2005]:[42] the test to be applied is twofold:

- Is there a significant risk that D will commit further specified offences?

and

- Is there a significant risk that such offences will cause *serious* harm?

Section 229 of the CJA 2003 deals with the assessment of dangerousness and the evidence required to make the assessment. The court must take into account all such information as is available to it about the nature and circumstances of the offence...any information about any pattern of behaviour of which the offence forms part...any information about the offender which is before it.

12.46 Section 229 is not relevant where the court is considering the application of s 224A (life term for second listed offence); see para 12.78.

12.47 If at the time the offence was committed the offender was over 18 and has a conviction for a specified offence the court *must assume* that there is such a risk *unless* after taking into account...The nature and circumstances of each of the offences...where appropriate, any pattern of behaviour...information about the offender which is before it...the court considers *it would be unreasonable to conclude there is such a risk.*

12.48 In *Considine* and *Davies*[43] the Court of Appeal dealt with the ambit of information which a sentencing court may have regard to when assessing dangerousness:

> On any view, an assessment based on 'information' is not restricted to 'evidence', and the information to be taken into account when making the assessment is not limited to the offender's previous convictions or a pattern of behaviour established by them, or indeed information about the offender which is limited to them. If it were otherwise, section 229(2)(b) and (c) would not have been made to apply to the offender without previous convictions. Accordingly, as a matter of statutory construction, relevant information bearing on the assessment of dangerousness may take the form of material adverse to the offender which is not substantiated or proved by criminal convictions.

---

[37] Per Rose LJ; *Lang* [2005] EWCA Crim 2864 at para 17(iii) and ss 156(3) CJA 2003.

[38] [2007] EWCA Crim 692.

[39] [2006] EWCA Crim 2394.

[40] Per Rose LJ; *Lang* at para 17.

[41] *R v Burt* [2005] EWCA Crim 3616 at para 100.

[42] Per Rose LJ; *Lang* at para 17.

[43] [2007] EWCA Crim 1166.

This includes a 'Synopsis of Material' prepared by prosecution counsel for the judge's use when D came to be sentenced for the present offence. It set out assertions that formed the basis on which an anti-social behavior order (ASBO) was made against D without objection by him. Although the incidents were not tested in adversarial judicial proceedings, they may be regarded as hard information (*Hillman* [2006] EWCA Crim 690). **12.49**

In deciding whether an offender convicted of possession or distribution of indecent images of children is dangerous, regard should be had to *R v Terrell* [2007][44] and *R v Hicks* [2009].[45] Both cases arose under the pre-LASPO regime but provide valuable guidance for assessing dangerousness in such cases. At first instance Ian Watkins (of Lostprophets fame) was sentenced in December 2013 to an extended sentence of 29 years with an extended licence period of 6 years; offences included the attempted rape of a baby and possession of indecent images. The evidence showed that he was an entrenched paedophile. **12.50**

1. Historic Dangerousness Provisions: Offences committed prior to the Criminal Justice Act 2003

The following sentences are the options when dealing with a dangerous offender for an offence committed before 4.4.2005: **12.51**

- automatic life sentence;
- 'old-style' discretionary life sentence;[46]
- extended sentence;
- longer than commensurate sentence under s 80(2)(b) of the PCC(S)A 2000;
- determinate sentence combined with appropriate ancillary orders.

Automatic Life Sentence

Powers of Criminal Courts (Sentencing) Act 2000, s 109

Available for a second serious offence committed after 30.9.1997 and before 4.4.2005. The sexual offences included in s 109 are rape, attempted rape and SOA 1956, s 5 intercourse with a girl under 13.[47] In addition, this will apply to the following offences if committed between 1.5.2004 and 4.4.2005, by virtue of s 109(5)(fa)–(fg):[48] **12.52**

- (fa) SOA 2003, s 1 or 2 (in this section, 'the 2003 Act') (rape, assault by penetration);
- (fb) SOA 2003, s 4 (causing a person to engage in sexual activity without consent), where the activity caused involved penetration within subsection (4)(a)–(d) of that section;
- (fc) SOA 2003, s 5 (rape of a child under 13, assault of a child under 13 by penetration);
- (fd) SOA 2003, s 8 (causing or inciting a child under 13 to engage in sexual activity), where an activity involving penetration within subsection (3)(a)–(d) of that section was caused;
- (fe) SOA 2003, s 30 (sexual activity with a person with a mental disorder impeding choice), where the touching involved penetration within subsection (3)(a)–(d) of that section;
- (ff) SOA 2003, s 31 (causing or inciting a person, with a mental disorder impeding choice, to engage in sexual activity), where an activity involving penetration within subsection (3)(a)–(d) of that section was caused;
- (fg) an attempt to commit an offence within any of (fa)–(ff).

---

44 *Terrell* [2007] EWCA Crim 3079.

45 *Hicks* [2009] EWCA Crim 733.

46 So described by the late Dr Thomas QC in his commentary on *Red Saunders and Others* [2013] EWCA Crim 1027, at [2013] Crim LR 935.

47 PCC(S)A 2000, s 109(5)(e) and (f).

48 Inserted by the SOA 2003, Sch 6, para 43(3) (repealed by CJA 2003, s 303(d)(iv) and s 332; hence its brief ambit). The authors are grateful to Iestyn Morgan, Barrister, for drawing this to their attention.

12.53 To apply the PCCSA 2000, s 109, consider:

- Was the second serious offence committed after 30.9.1997 and before 4.4.2005?

If so:

- Was the defendant 18 or over?

and

- Had he been convicted in the UK of another serious offence?

If so:

- The court shall impose a life sentence

unless:

- the court is of the opinion that there are exceptional circumstances relating to either the offences or the offender which justify its not doing so.[49] When not imposing life that opinion and the exceptional circumstances shall be stated in open court.[50]

Guideline Authority

R v Offen [2001] 1 Cr App R 372

12.54 The guidance (in *Offen*) is equally applicable to cases falling under both the C(S)A 1997 and PCC(S)A 2000,[51] notwithstanding it was decided before the implementation of the PCC(S)A 2000 (appeal heard in October 2000). *Offen* involved five conjoined appeals against life sentences being imposed for a second qualifying offence under the C(S)A 1997, s 2; Court of Appeal guidance in respect of 'exceptional circumstances' and, within that, 'dangerousness' was given. Also dealt with was whether s 2 was compatible with the European Convention on Human Rights.

Discretionary Life Sentence

12.55 The law remains unchanged in respect of 'old style' discretionary life sentences for offences committed before 4.4.2005.[52]

12.56 The criteria for the imposition of such a sentence are set out in *Hodgson*[53] and *Attorney General's Reference (No 32 of 1996) (R v Whittaker)*:[54]

- First, the offender must have been convicted of a 'very serious offence'. The meaning of 'very serious offence' was considered in *R v D*[55] where the Court of Appeal took the view that the *Hodgson/Whittaker* criteria were satisfied where the offender as a youth had broken into his grandmother's home and raped her.
- Second, there should be good grounds for believing that the offender might remain a serious danger to the public for a period which could not be reliably estimated at the date of sentence. It was explained in *Whittaker* that by 'serious danger' the court had in mind particularly serious offences of violence and serious sexual offences.

12.57 Dangerousness should be central to the court's consideration: the greater the risk of re-offending and the more grave such offending might be, the less emphasis the court might place on the gravity of the first offence; however, the first pre-condition is indispensable and should not be watered down.

---

49 Section 109(1)(b) and (2).

50 Section 109(3).

51 C(S)A 1997, s 2 was replaced by PCC(S)A 2000, s 109.

52 *Red Saunders and Others* [2013] EWCA Crim 1027. For a fuller discussion of this important case, see paras 12.58–12.59.

53 *R v Hodgson* (1968) 52 Cr App R 113, [1968] Crim LR 46.

54 *R v Whittaker* [1997] 1 Cr App R(S) 261, [1996] Crim LR 917.

55 *R v D* [2012] EWCA Crim 2370, [2013] 1 Cr App R(S) 127 (p. 674). See also para 12.65.

The Demise of Imprisonment for the Protection of the Public

The changes to the dangerous offender provisions under the CJA 2003,[56] effected by ss 122–124 of the LASPO 2012, means that from 3.12.2012 sentences of Imprisonment for the Protection of the Public (IPPs) are no longer available. **12.58**

Shortly before his retirement as Lord Chief Justice, Lord Judge addressed the potential difficulty this repeal created for sentencing courts and provided the remedy in *Saunders and Others v R* [2013].[57] In *Saunders* the Court of Appeal made clear that an offender who would otherwise have been properly sentenced to an IPP could now be sentenced to a discretionary life sentence, bearing in mind that such a sentence is one of last resort. **12.59**

Per Lord Judge:

> [15] The new statutory life sentence has not replaced the IPP. Many offenders who represent a danger to the public may not 'qualify' for the statutory life sentence. Yet, for some offenders, the imperative of public protection continues undiminished, and is not wholly met by the 'new' extended sentence. Very long term public protection must therefore be provided by the imposition of a discretionary life sentence. That is consequent on s 225(1) and (2) which, in the context of the discretionary life sentence for serious offences continue, as we have explained, in full force.

Section 82A of the PCC(S)A 2000[58] applies in determining the tariff for a discretionary life sentence. **12.60**

The court is permitted to look at both the totality of the associated offences and whether they would have been consecutive to the main term had a life sentence not been passed, rather than only considering the seriousness of the offence attracting the life term in determining the tariff for it.[59] **12.61**

Remand time is deducted from the minimum term and not from the notional determinate sentence, so the number of days served on remand should not be doubled.[60] **12.62**

Recent examples of discretionary life for historic offences

A recent illustration of a discretionary life sentence is *R v DP* [2013],[61] in which the appellant pleaded guilty to a number of sexual offences, including a sexual assault on a child under 13 by penetration (SOA 2003, 6(1)), committed between December 2004 and March 2005. It was accepted by the judge and the Court of Appeal that the appellant should be sentenced by reference to the law which existed before 4.4.2005, the relevant legislation being the PCC(S)A 2000 and the early release provisions of the CJA 1991. The complainants were the children of a woman with whom the appellant had formed a relationship. The appellant had a long record of sexual offences against children. He was sentenced to life imprisonment in respect of the s 6 offence with various concurrent determinate sentences for other offences. The Court of Appeal concluded that (i) the offending was of sufficient gravity to warrant a sentence of imprisonment for life and (ii) the appellant was a serial predatory paedophile, had been so for many years, and at the time of sentence it could not be estimated how long he would remain a danger to younger children. **12.63**

R v Wendell Baker [2014] EWCA Crim 242; a discretionary life sentence was upheld for a pre-CJA 2003 offence of the brutal rape of an elderly woman after he forced entry into her home. **12.64**

---

56 As amended by the Criminal Justice and Immigration Act 2008.
57 *R v Saunders and Others* [2013] EWCA Crim 1027.
58 Inserted by CJCSA 2000, s 6.
59 *A G's Reference (No 3 of 2004)* [2005] 1 Cr App R(S) 230.
60 *R v Taylor* [2008] 2 Cr App R(S) 480.
61 *R v DP* [2013] EWCA Crim 1143.

12.65 *D* [2013][62] is an example of an historic case which is unlikely to have attracted a life sentence at the time, but in which a discretionary life sentence for the rape by her grandson who broke in of a woman alone in her home at night was upheld.

Extended Sentence

Criminal Justice Act, s 225

12.66 The new LASPO extended sentence will apply when sentencing historic cases which otherwise meet the qualifying criteria. Sections 26A and B1(a) state:

> This section applies where a person . . . is convicted of a specified offence (**whether the offence was committed before or after this section came into force**).

It has therefore replaced the old extended sentence under s 85 of the PCC(S)A 2000 with retrospective effect from 3.12.2012. (The s 85 extended sentence had replaced the extended sentence available under s 35 of the CJA 1967, which was itself repealed by the CJA 1991.)

12.67 Although in respect of the qualifying criteria the new extended sentence is similar to the old one, there is a significant difference in the release provisions.

Per Lord Judge in *Saunders*:

> [16] Section 123 of LASPO abolished the extended sentence created by s 227 of the 2003 Act. It is unfortunate that the description 'extended sentence' has been retained by LASPO for the purposes of a sentence which is much more onerous, and therefore in significant respects different, to the 'extended sentence', as created in the 2003 Act.

See from para 12.69 for the statutory provisions and para 12.77 for *Burinskas*[63] in relation to its implementation.

Longer Than Commensurate Sentence

12.68 Where the threshold for a life sentence has not been crossed, and if necessary to protect the public from harm in the future, a court may impose a longer than commensurate sentence together with an extended licence period. The harm anticipated must be by the commission of future sexual or violent offences which must be 'serious' but may be either physical or psychological.

12.69 Section 80(2)(b) of the PCC(S)A 2000[64] provides the power to pass such a sentence 'for such longer term not exceeding the maximum as is necessary to protect the public from serious harm from the offender', from 25.8.2000 to 3.4.2005.

12.70 Section 161 of the PCC(S)A 2000 sets out the offences to which s 80 applies. The sexual offences include:

- any offence under the SOA 1956, except ss 30, 31 or 33–6;
- any offence under the IwCA 1960;
- burglary with intent to commit rape (TA 1968, s 9);
- an offence under the MHA 1959, s 128;
- an offence under the CLA 1977;
- an offence under the PCA 1978;
- an offence under the SO(A)A 2000, s 3;
- an offence of CLA 1977, s 1 conspiracy to commit, CAA 1981, s 1 attempting to commit or inciting the commission of any of the above.

Note: abduction of a child is not included.

---

[62] *D* [2013] 1 Cr App R(S) 674.

[63] *A-G's Ref (No 27 of 2013)* [2014] EWCA Crim 334 (*R v Burinskas*).

[64] Implemented 25.8.2000. In force until 3.4.2005.

In addition, this will apply to the following offences if committed between 1.5.2004 and 4.4.2005, by virtue of s 109(5)(fa)–(ff):[65] **12.71**

- (fa) SOA 2003, s 1 or 2 (in this section, 'the 2003 Act') (rape, assault by penetration);
- (fb) SOA 2003, s 4 (causing a person to engage in sexual activity without consent), where the activity caused involved penetration within subsection (4)(a)–(d) of that section;
- (fc) SOA 2003, s 5 (rape of a child under 13, assault of a child under 13 by penetration);
- (fd) SOA 2003, s 8 (causing or inciting a child under 13 to engage in sexual activity), where an activity involving penetration within subsection (3)(a)–(d) of that section was caused;
- (fe) SOA 2003, s 30 (sexual activity with a person with a mental disorder impeding choice), where the touching involved penetration within subsection (3)(a)–(d) of that section;
- (ff) SOA 2003, s 31 (causing or inciting a person, with a mental disorder impeding choice, to engage in sexual activity), where an activity involving penetration within subsection (3)(a)–(d) of that section was caused;
- (fg) an attempt to commit an offence within any of (fa)–(ff).

Sentencing Offences which Straddle the Sexual Offences Act 2003

When dealing with dangerous offenders whose offences either do or may straddle 4.4.2005, see para 12.38 (and para 1.26). **12.72**

2. Current Dangerousness Provisions: Offences committed post the CJA 2003 and LASPO 2012

These powers will only apply to offences committed after 4.4.2005 (CJA 2003 implementation date). This needs to be borne in mind when dealing with offences committed between 1.5.2004 (SOA 2003) and 3.4.2005; they must be sentenced under the regime in place for the Act against which they were committed. **12.73**

Life Sentence

The four situations in which a life sentence may currently arise for consideration were identified by Lord Judge, then Lord Chief Justice, in *Saunders*.[66] The court made clear that a discretionary life sentence may be appropriate in cases which previously would properly have attracted an IPP; see para 12.59, bearing in mind that such a sentence is one of last resort. All but a mandatory life sentence may apply to rape and other serious sexual offences with a maximum term of life imprisonment. **12.74**

(1) **Mandatory life** sentence; following conviction for murder.
(2) **Statutory life** sentence; following conviction for a second listed offence under s 224A, of the 2003 Act, inserted by s 122 of LASPO 2012, a sentence of imprisonment for life '*must*' be imposed, unless the particular circumstances would make it unjust.[67]
(3) **Discretionary life** sentence; available following conviction for a 'specified offence' under s 225 of the CJA 2003.
(4) **Discretionary life** sentence; available following conviction for both a 'specified' and a 'non-specified offence'. This may be appropriate in a case where an IPP would have been imposed. The question will be whether or not the current, more onerous, form of extended sentence will provide adequate protection for the public.

---

[65] Inserted by the SOA 2003, Sch 6, para 43(3) (repealed by s 303(d)(iv) and CJA 2003, s 332; hence its brief ambit). The authors are grateful to Iestyn Morgan, Barrister, for drawing this to their attention.

[66] *R v Saunders and Others* [2013] EWCA Crim 1027.

[67] See s 224A(2). In short, there is a discretionary power in the court to disapply what would otherwise be a provision requiring an obligatory sentence. See also *A-G's Ref (No 55 of 2008)* [2008] EWCA Crim 2790.

12.75 Per Lord Judge CJ in *Saunders*:

> [11.] This leaves open the further question (addressed in the Criminal Law Review at (2013) Crim LR 508 in commentary on *R v Cardwell* [2012] EWCA Crim 3030) whether a sentence of life imprisonment may be imposed when the case does not fall within either the statutory life sentence or the discretionary life sentence analysed in the previous paragraphs. The jurisdiction to impose a life sentence in an appropriate case has survived the enactment of the 2003 Act and the changes to the sentencing regime affected by LASPO. If it had been intended to abolish it, the appropriate legislative change could readily have been made by provisions restricting the life sentence (other than the mandatory sentence) to the statutory sentence or the discretionary sentence under s 225(1) and (2). As it is, neither the 2003 Act, nor LASPO, imposed any limit on the power of the court to impose a sentence of life imprisonment in such cases. Some of these offences may involve a significant risk of serious harm to the public, but are not included within the list of 'specified' offences in the dangerousness provisions in the 2003 Act. One obvious example is the offender who commits repeated offences of very serious drug supplying which justifies the imposition of the life sentence. In circumstances like these the court is not obliged to impose the sentence in accordance with s 225(2), but its discretion to do so is unaffected.
>
> [12.] In reality, the occasions when this second form of discretionary life sentence is likely to be imposed will be rare, and no inconvenience has yet resulted from applying the description 'discretionary' to both forms of sentence. We have reflected whether any advantages might accrue to sentencing courts if we were able to offer alternative descriptions which would identify the distinction between these two forms of discretionary life sentence. In reality, none is needed.
>
> [13.] For those convicted after 3 December 2012, as a result of s 123 of LASPO the sentence of imprisonment for public protection (IPP) created for serious offences by s 225(1) and (3) of the 2003 Act will no longer be available. As we have explained, for dangerous offenders the statutory life sentence under s 224A of the 2003 Act has been abated and the discretionary life sentence remains. In relation to convictions returned before 3 December 2012 the protection of the public from dangerous offenders was achieved either by the discretionary life sentence or IPP. There are relatively minor distinctions between the two sentences which have no direct bearing on the issue of public protection. In relation to the discretionary life sentence, the court was theoretically able to make a whole life order, but, as far as we are aware, no such orders have been made or, if made, upheld. In relation to the IPP there was a supplementary jurisdiction in the Parole Board to give a direction that supervision under licence should come to an end 10 years after release.
>
> [14.] In the overwhelming majority of cases these distinctions were irrelevant, and so the IPP was normally sufficient to address the protection of the public from a dangerous offender who would, if made subject to the order, continue to be detained until the Parole Board was satisfied that he no longer represented a risk to the public. (See *R v Kehoe* [2009] 1 Cr App R(S) 9.) As the court observed in *R v Wilkinson* [2010] 1 Cr App R(S) 100:
>
>> '... as a matter of principle a discretionary life sentence under s 225 should continue to be reserved for offences of the utmost gravity. Without being prescriptive, we suggest that the sentence should come into contemplation when the judgment of the court is that the seriousness is such that the life sentence would have... a "denunciatory" value, reflective of public abhorrence of the offence, and where, because of its seriousness, the notional determinate sentence would be very long, measured in very many years.'
>
> [15.] The new statutory life sentence has not replaced the IPP. Many offenders who represent a danger to the public may not 'qualify' for the statutory life sentence. Yet, for some offenders, the imperative of public protection continues undiminished, and is not wholly met by the 'new' extended sentence. Very long term public protection must therefore be provided by the imposition of a discretionary life sentence. That is consequent on s 225(1) and (2) which, in the context of the discretionary life sentence for serious offences continue, as we have explained, in full force.

Discretionary Life Sentence

12.76 In *R v Saunders* [2013] EWCA Crim 1027 Lord Judge CJ expressed the view that discretionary life sentences could still be passed in addition to life sentences passed under ss 224A and 225 of the CJA 2003.

The Court of Appeal in *Attorney General's Reference (No 27 of 2013)* (*R v Burinskas*) rejected criticism of the court in *Saunders* on this point, observing that in its view the approach of the court was correct and pointed to the current SGC Guidelines (para 1, p. 24) in support of that view: **12.77**

> Life imprisonment is the maximum for the offence [of rape]. Such a sentence may be imposed either as a result of the offence itself where a number of aggravating factors are present, or because the offender meets the dangerousness criterion.

Statutory Life Sentence

Section 224A of the CJA 2003 (inserted by s 122 of the LASPO 2012) creates the new sentence of 'life sentence for second listed offence'. It applies to a defendant convicted on or after 3.12.2012. **12.78**

As per Lord Judge at [15] in *Saunders* at para 12.75, it does not replace IPPs but has its own qualifying criteria: **12.79**

- (i) a person aged 18 or over is convicted of an offence listed in Part 1 of Sch 15B to the CJA 2003;
- (ii) the offence is such that the court would have imposed a determinate sentence of 10 years or more (including an extended sentence where the custodial term would have been 10 years or more); and
- (iii) the offender has a previous conviction for an offence listed in Sch 15B (not just in Part 1) for which he received a life sentence (with a minimum term of at least 5 years) or a determinate sentence of 10 years or more (including an extended sentence where the custodial term was 10 years or more);
- (iv) the court must impose a life sentence if all the conditions in s 122 apply, unless there are particular circumstances relating to either the current offence or the previous relevant offence, or to the offender which 'would make it unjust to do so in all the circumstances': s 224A(2).

The sexual offences listed in Part 1, Sch 15B are: **12.80**

SOA 2003 s 1
SOA 2003 s 2
SOA 2003 ss 4–12
SOA 2003 s 14
SOA 2003 s 15
SOA 2003 s 25
SOA 2003 s 26 (if D is over 18), and
SOA 2003 ss 47–50

and where the offence is punishable with life imprisonment:

SOA 2003 s 30
SOA 2003 s 31
SOA 2003 s 34
SOA 2003 s 35, and
SOA 2003 s 62.

Also included are attempts to commit any of these offences, conspiracy or incitement to commit a listed offence and aiding, abetting, counselling or procuring the commission of a listed offence.

Note that whilst the new offence must be listed in Part 1 of Sch 15B, the previous offence can be listed anywhere in the schedule. This is intended to allow within the qualifying previous conviction for offences which have been repealed (such as those under the SOA 1956) but replaced with broadly equivalent offences. **12.81**

It is suggested that an offender who qualifies under the criteria would most likely be subject to a discretionary life sentence for the new offence in any event. However, it should be remembered **12.82** that whilst to pass a discretionary life sentence a judge would have to find an offender to be dangerous within the statutory test, it is not necessary to apply that test in passing a statutory life sentence.

(i) Section 224A of the CJA applies where an offender is convicted of a second listed offence; the judge must pass a life sentence unless the particular circumstances make it unjust.

(ii) Section 225 of the CJA applies where a person is convicted of a serious offence after 3.12.2013, is dangerous and the seriousness of the offence justifies the imposition of a life sentence. Where the offender is judged to be dangerous and the conditions under s 225(2)(a) and (b) are met, there is no judicial discretion; a life sentence must be passed.

12.83 *Attorney General's Reference (No 27 of 2013)* [2014] EWCA Crim 334 (*R v Burinskas*) deals with life sentences and extended sentences under the CJA 2003 as amended by the LASPO 2012.

12.84 This was a judgment following consideration of eight appeals (only one a prosecution reference) involving dangerous sexual offenders; in six, life sentences had been imposed under the LASPO provisions (s 224A or 225 CJA 2003 following the abolition of IPPs); in two, extended sentences were imposed under the LASPO 2012.

12.85 The court considered the effect of the new provisions under LASPO on sentencing dangerous offenders, that is, the new route to a life sentence under s 224A and the correct interpretation of s 225 after the abolition of IPPs.

12.86 Delivering his judgment, Lord Thomas CJ said:

> [8] i) For a life sentence to be imposed under s 224A there is no requirement of a finding that the offender is dangerous within the meaning of the CJA 2003, although it is likely that in most cases he will be. It follows that the fact that an offender is not dangerous is not something that of itself would make it unjust to pass a life sentence under this section.
>
> ii) s 225(2)(b) does not apply to the relevant offence in s 224A. There is no requirement to consider whether the 'seriousness' threshold has been passed.
>
> iii) s 224A could lead in cases that may be rare to the imposition of a life sentence in respect of an offence which does not carry life as a maximum.
>
> ...
>
> [12] The critical issue is the interpretation of the condition in s 225(2)(b).
>
> ...
>
> [15] ... decisions about the circumstances in which a life sentence was appropriate handed down during the currency of the version of the CJA which was in force between 3 April 2005 and 3 December 20012 are now of limited assistance.
>
> [16] Although the provisions of s 225 ... remain the same, the statutory context in which they are to be interpreted is fundamentally changed ... IPP no longer exists.
>
> [17] We interpret [s 225] in the light of the new regime which includes s 224A and the new extended sentences.
>
> ...
>
> [18] Save where imposed under s 224A a life sentence remains a sentence of last resort ... [Given the abolition of IPPs] it is inevitable that sentences of life imprisonment will be imposed more frequently than before [LASPO].
>
> [19] We agree with the view of Lord Judge in *Saunders* that the new extended sentence cannot be treated as a direct replacement for the old IPP ... where the court is faced with facts which ... [pre-LASPO] would have led the court to pass an IPP, it may well be necessary to pass a life sentence.
>
> ...
>
> [22] ... taking into account the law prior to the coming into force of the CJA 2003 and the whole of the new statutory provisions, the question in s 225(2)(b) as to whether the seriousness of the offence (or the offence and one or more offences associated with it) is such as to justify a life sentence requires consideration of—
>
> i) The seriousness of the offence itself, on its own or with other offences associated with it (s 143(1)) ... This is always a matter for the judgment of the court.

ii) The defendant's previous convictions (s 142(2)).
iii) The level of danger posed to the public by the defendant and whether there is a reliable time estimate of the length of time he will remain a danger.
iv) The available alternative sentences.

See para 12.67 for the court's judgment in relation to extended sentences.

Whole Life Sentence

Whilst whole life sentences have been upheld by the Supreme Court,[68] whole life sentences have been judged rarely appropriate for sexual offences without more. **12.87**

Oakes [2012]:[69] absent accompanying murder, it is unlikely to include sexual cases. **12.88**

Hogg [2007]:[70] the Court of Appeal set a minimum term for the life sentences properly passed, rather than the whole life term imposed by the trial judge. The criteria for deciding whether whole life is necessary relate to the offences themselves, not the question of future risk. It is for the Parole Board to determine the latter. **12.89**

Extended Sentence

The new LASPO extended sentence is available in respect of historic cases, transcending the pre-existing extended sentences because of its wording. See para 12.66 in relation to sentencing historic cases. **12.90**

It seems likely that wide use will be made of the new extended sentence to deal with offenders who pose a continuing risk of serious harm from the commission of further specified offences, but where the offence(s) committed are not so serious that a life sentence can be justified. **12.91**

Defendant 18 or over

Criminal Justice Act 2003, s 226A

(1) This section applies where— **12.92**
 (a) a person aged 18 or over is convicted of a specified offence (whether the offence was committed before or after this section comes into force),
 the court considers that there is a significant risk to members of the public of serious harm occasioned by the commission of further specified offences,
 the court is not required by s 224A or s 225(2) to impose a sentence of imprisonment for life, and
 (b) condition A or B is met.
(2) Condition (a) is that, at the time the offence was committed, the offender had been convicted of an offence in Schedule 15B.
(3) Condition (b) is that, if the court were to impose an extended sentence, the term that it would specify as the appropriate custodial term would be at least 4 years.
(4) The court may impose an extended sentence of imprisonment on the offender.

---

[68] *McLoughlin & Newell* [2014] EWCA Crim 188. The question was whether a whole life term is lawful, bearing in mind the domestic statutory regime in place governing the hope or possibility of release. The Court of Appeal found that the provision for release by the Secretary of State in exceptional circumstances (C(S)A 1997, s 30) means that the power to impose a whole life sentence is not incompatible Article 3 ECHR.

[69] *Oakes* [2012] EWCA Crim 2435. Suggestion that the whole life order will only be for the most exceptional cases. Absent accompanying murder, it is unlikely to include sexual cases.

[70] *Hogg* [2007] EWCA Crim 1357.

(5) An extended sentence of imprisonment is a sentence of imprisonment the term of which is equal to the aggregate of—
  (a) the appropriate custodial term, and
  (b) a further period (the 'extension period') for which the offender is to be subject to a licence.
(6) The appropriate custodial term is the term of imprisonment that would (apart from this section) be imposed in compliance with section 153(2).
(7) The extension period must be a period of such length as the court considers necessary for the purpose of protecting members of the public from serious harm occasioned by the commission by the offender of further specified offences, subject to subsections (8) and (9).
(8) The extension period must not exceed—
  (a) 5 years in the case of a specified violent offence, and
  (b) 8 years in the case of a specified sexual offence.

The term of an extended sentence of imprisonment imposed under this section in respect of an offence must not exceed the term that, at the time the offence was committed, was the maximum term permitted for the offence.

Defendant under 18

Criminal Justice Act 2003, s 226B

12.93 (1) This section applies where—
  (a) a person aged under 18 is convicted of a specified offence (whether the offence was committed before or after this section comes into force),
  (b) the court considers that there is a significant risk to members of the public of serious harm occasioned by the commission of further specified offences,
  (c) the court is not required by section 226(2) to impose a sentence of detention for life under section 91 of the Sentencing Act, and
  (d) if the court were to impose an extended sentence of detention, the term it would specify as the appropriate custodial term would be at least 4 years.
(2) The court may impose an extended sentence of detention on the offender.
(3) An extended sentence of detention is a sentence of detention the term of which is equal to the aggregate of—
  (a) the appropriate custodial term, and
  (b) a further period (the 'extension period') for which the offender is to be subject to a licence.
(4) The appropriate custodial term is the term of detention that would (apart from this section) be imposed in compliance with section 153(2).
(5) The extension period must be a period of such length as the court considers necessary for the purpose of protecting members of the public from serious harm occasioned by the commission by the offender of further specified offences, subject to subsections (6) and (7).
(6) The extension period must not exceed—
  (a) 5 years in the case of a specified violent offence, and
  (b) 8 years in the case of a specified sexual offence.
(7) The term of an extended sentence of detention imposed under this section in respect of an offence may not exceed the term that, at the time the offence was committed, was the maximum term permitted for the offence in the case of a person aged 18 or over.

Release on licence

12.94 The post-LASPO extended sentence release is normally at the two-thirds point of the sentence, rather than the previous system of half-way under the pre-LASPO extended sentence unless the custodial term is 10 years or more or the sentence is imposed for an offence listed in Sch 15B. If either (or both) of these conditions apply, the case will be referred at the two-thirds point to the Parole Board, which will consider whether it is no longer necessary for the protection of the public for the offender to be imprisoned/detained.

It is therefore certainly true that at least in respect of such cases, the new extended sentence is 'much more onerous': *Saunders* [2013].[71] **12.95**

Offences listed in the Criminal Justice Act 2003, Sch 15B

The offences listed in Sch 15B are: **12.96**
Sexual Offences Act 2003, s 1
Sexual Offences Act 2003, s 2
Sexual Offences Act 2003, ss 4–12
Sexual Offences Act 2003, s 14
Sexual Offences Act 2003, s 15
Sexual Offences Act 2003, s 25
Sexual Offences Act 2003, s 26 (if D is over 18), and
Sexual Offences Act 2003, ss 47–50;

and where the offence is punishable with life imprisonment:
Sexual Offences Act 2003, s 30
Sexual Offences Act 2003, s 31
Sexual Offences Act 2003, s 34
Sexual Offences Act 2003, s 35
Sexual Offences Act 2003, s 62, and
Protection of Children Act 1978, s 1 (indecent images of children).

Also included are attempts to commit any of these offences, conspiracy or incitement to commit a listed offence and aiding, abetting, counselling or procuring the commission of a listed offence.

Attorney General's Reference (No 27 of 2013) [2014] EWCA Crim 334 (*R v Burinskas*) deals with life sentences and extended sentences under the CJA 2003 as amended by the LASPO 2012. See para 12.77 for the judgment in relation to life sentences. **12.97**

This was a judgment following consideration of eight appeals (only one a prosecution reference) involving dangerous sexual offenders; in six, life sentences had been imposed under the LASPO provisions (s 224A or 225 of the CJA 2003 following the abolition of IPPs); in two, extended sentences were imposed under the LASPO 2012.

The court considered the effect of the new provisions under LASPO on sentencing dangerous offenders, that is, the new route to a life sentence under s 224A and the correct interpretation of s 225 after the abolition of IPPs.

Dealing with extended sentences under s 226A, Lord Thomas noted that it is in effect a new provision for extended sentences although it remains a discretionary sentence even where there is a finding of dangerousness; whilst it will usually be the appropriate sentence where a life term is not justified for a dangerous offender, a determinate sentence is not only available (as it was pre-LASPO), but may be appropriate. The fact that it is the extended licence period rather than the custodial period which provides public protection is what differentiates the LASPO extended sentence from the position of consideration by the Parole Board for a sentence of IPP. **12.98**

It should be noted, however, that s 246A of the CJA (as amended by s 125 of the LASPO 2012) means that time spent in custody has increased for those subject to an extended sentence passed for an offence committed on or after 3.12.2013. **12.99**

Where the custodial term is 10 years or more or the offence is listed in Sch 15B the offender is not entitled to be released until the end of that term. He may be released after serving two thirds, at which point he is eligible to be considered for parole. **12.100**

[71] *Hogg* [2007] EWCA Crim 1357.

12.101 Where the custodial term is under 10 years and the offence is not listed in Sch 15B, the offender is entitled to release after serving two-thirds. There is no requirement for an assessment by the Parole Board. He will then be subject to the licence period, as extended.

12.102 The court also dealt (at [35]–[39]) with the argument that the early release provisions might result in an offender being released earlier from a life sentence that an extended sentence.

12.103 At [40] the court made clear that no reduction in sentence may be made to reflect (that is, compensate for) the new early release regime for extended sentences.

12.104 At [41] *et seq.*, Lord Thomas set out the general approach to sentencing when consideration of dangerousness arises following the amendment of the CJA 2003 by LASPO. The court warned against moving straight to sentencing under s 224A if the criteria apply.

12.105 At [43] the order in which a judge should approach sentencing in a case of this type is this:

> (i) Consider the question of dangerousness. If the offender is not dangerous and section 224A does not apply, a determinate sentence should be passed. If the offender is not dangerous and the conditions in section 224A are satisfied then (subject to s 2(a) and (b)), a life sentence must be imposed.
> (ii) If the offender is dangerous, consider whether the seriousness of the offence and offences associated with it justify a life sentence. Seriousness is to be considered as we have set out at paragraph 22.
> (iii) If a life sentence is justified then the judge must pass a life sentence in accordance with s 225. If s 224A also applies, the judge should record that fact in open court.
> (iv) If a life sentence is not justified, then the sentencing judge should consider whether s 224A applies. If it does then (subject to the terms of s 224A) a life sentence must be imposed.
> (v) If section 224A does not apply, the judge should then consider the provisions of section 226A. Before passing an extended sentence the judge should consider a determinate sentence.

12.106 *R v C and Others* [2007] EWCA Crim 680 provides guidance in relation to the interaction between extended and determinate sentences and Sexual Offences Prevention Orders. Its principles will now apply to discretionary life sentences as they did to the sentences of IPP available at the time:

> The court is entitled to and should have in mind all the alternative and cumulative methods of providing the necessary public protection against the risk posed by the individual offender. For example, structured around a determinate sentence, or indeed an extended sentence under the Act, a Sexual Offences Prevention Order, with appropriate conditions attached could form part of what we may colloquially describe as the total protective sentencing package.
>
> ...We re-emphasise that the primary question is the nature and the extent of the risk posed by the individual offender, and the most appropriate method of addressing that risk and providing public protection.

Multiple offences; seriousness of the aggregate offending and consecutive extended sentences

12.107 The question of whether sentences can be added together to arrive at a term sufficiently long to attract an extended sentence was considered in *Pinnell* [2010] EWCA Crim 2848:

> [47] If no one offence would justify a four year custodial term on ordinary principles, the seriousness of the aggregate offending must be considered. If a four-year custodial term results from aggregating the shortest terms commensurate with the seriousness of each offence, then that four year term can be imposed in relation to the specified offence. If there is more than one specified offence that aggregate term should be passed for the lead specified offence, or, if appropriate, concurrently on more than one specified offence. If appropriate a concurrent determinate term may be imposed for other offences. The combination of the custodial term and extension period cannot exceed the maximum statutory sentence for the offence to which the extended sentence is attached. If the maximum period for the offence is 5 years, the extension period is therefore limited to a year.
>
> [48] There is no objection to imposing an extended sentence consecutive to another sentence, or to imposing consecutive extended sentences, although we suggest that it should be done only where there

is a particular reason for doing so. The extension periods in the case of consecutive extended sentences will themselves be consecutive. In a case of consecutive extended sentences, each offence for which such a sentence is imposed must itself be a specified offence. Most importantly, each offence for which an extended sentence is imposed must also justify, on ordinary principles, including the aggregation of associated offences, a custodial term of at least 4 years. It is not possible to pass separate sentences of less than 4 years to meet this condition to the imposition of an extended sentence, even if their total is more than 4 years.

Multiple offences; concurrent terms for non-specified

Where only some of the offences are specified, shorter concurrent sentences should be imposed for the other offences. 12.108

G. SEXUAL OFFENCES DEFINITIVE GUIDELINE: APPLICATION

See App C for the Guideline.

The new guideline applies to all sentencing decisions in sex cases after its implementation on 1.4.2014, whenever the offence was committed. The old guideline applies to cases sentenced up until then.[72] 12.109

The guideline applies only to offenders aged 18 and older; offenders under 18 will be covered by a separate youth guideline which it is expected the Council will begin to devise in 2014. 12.110

The Sentencing Council Guidelines remain guidelines which should usually, but not exclusively, be followed.[73] To depart from the 'offence range' requires a finding that to do otherwise 'would be contrary to the interests of justice'; CAJA 2009. S125(1). Such a finding is not necessary in order to move outside the 'category range'.[74] 12.111

Section 125(1) of the CAJA 2009 provides that when sentencing offences committed on or after 6.4.2012: 12.112

> Every court—
> (a) must, in sentencing an offender, follow any sentencing guideline which is relevant to the offender's case, and
> (b) must, in exercising any other function relating to the sentencing of offenders, follow any sentencing guidelines which are relevant to the exercise of the function,
> unless the court is satisfied that it would be contrary to the interests of justice to do so.[75]

See also at para 12.18; Lord Judge CJ at [47] in *H(J)*.

The new guideline for sexual offences resembles the decision-making process for sentencing that was developed for the current assault guideline. It sets out nine steps to be followed for each offence. In applying the guideline, it is important to bear in mind that it is concerned with sentence levels for a single offence. It follows that in respect of cases involving more than one offence sentencers should ensure this is adequately reflected by the overall sentence, subject to the principle of totality. 12.113

The Sentencing Council has updated its guidelines in respect of sexual offences; the new guidelines were implemented on 1.4.2014. They represent a significant change of approach for the sentencing 12.114

---

72 *Boakye and Others* [2012] EWCA Crim 838.

73 *A-G's Reference (No 21 of 2007)* (*R v Oakes*) [2007] All ER (D) 281 May 9.

74 Martin Wasik, Sentencing: Recent Developments (2014).

75 But see [2013] Crim LR 998, in which the late Dr David Thomas QC criticizes the Court of Appeal in *Karam (Mawawe Ibrahim)* [2013] EWCA Crim 138 for failing to have regard for s 125(3) of the Act, which qualifies the obligation to 'follow' the guidelines by making clear that the court is under an obligation to impose a sentence within the offence range but not within the category range. Dr Thomas argues that 'the effect of s 125(3) when read as a whole is to preserve the critical discretion of the judge to achieve a just sentence, based upon the detailed facts of the case rather than the increasingly mechanistic application of quasi-statutory guidelines'.

judge; the guidelines are now tailored to deal with the specific offending behaviour. This is intended to be achieved by the new structure for determining the level of harm caused and the level of culpability varying according to the offence(s) being considered.

12.115 Part 1 of the guideline contains the Overarching Principles, which should not be overlooked when sentencing non-consensual offences, although they are set out within Part 2. Many factors may be relevant to the level of culpability and the degree of harm suffered, including sexual offences committed by gangs or groups which is relevant to and increases both.

Harm and Culpability

12.116 The new guideline provides a different approach to addressing harm and culpability. For most offences (including rape and sexual assault), harm and culpability are assumed, from which lowest level one or more factors can move it to a higher category of harm or culpability with a higher staring point.

12.117 A different approach is adopted for offences such as meeting a child following sexual grooming (s 15); administering a substance with intent (s 61); trespass with intent to commit a sexual offence (s 63); sex with an adult relative (ss 64 and 65); exposure (s 66); and voyeurism (s 67); here, factors are identified which indicate a level of raised harm and/or culpability. Where both exist, they attract the highest starting points.

12.118 For offences involving indecent images of children, harm is assessed on the basis of the level of images involved. The Sentencing Council reduced the levels provided in *Oliver* from five to three. Culpability is assessed on the basis of what the offender was doing with the images and is split into three categories: possession, distribution and production. The categories are:

Category A: this broadly coincides with *Oliver* levels 4 and 5 (images involving penetrative sexual activity, sexual activity with an animal and sadism).

Category B: this broadly coincides with *Oliver* level 3 (images involving non-penetrative activity).

Category C: this covers other indecent images not falling within either A or B.

Good Character and/or Exemplary Conduct

12.119 The guideline divides the approach into two categories of case:

(i) For offences attracting a maximum sentence of under 14 years:

> Previous good character/exemplary conduct is different from having no previous convictions. The more serious the offence, the less the weight which should normally be attributed to this factor. Where previous good character/exemplary conduct has been used to facilitate the offence, this mitigation should not normally be allowed and such conduct may constitute an aggravating factor.

(ii) For offences attracting a maximum sentence of under 14 years the guideline additionally states:

> In the context of this offence previous good character/exemplary conduct should not normally be given any significant weight and will not normally justify a reduction in what would otherwise be the appropriate sentence.

Greater focus on harm to the victim whether physical and/or psychological

12.120 Vulnerability of the victim is treated as a major indicator of harm. Whilst every child is vulnerable, the personal circumstances of some will render them acutely so. This would place them in the highest category for a s 5 rape of a child under 13 offence.

Grooming

12.121 An appreciation of the greater culpability of an offender who grooms his victim(s) and/or uses the internet to facilitate sex offending is reflected by the guideline.

Ostensible or apparent consent

The Sentencing Council agreed with the statement of Pitchford LJ in *Attorney General's References (Nos 11 and 12 of 2012) (Channer and Monteiro)*,[76] that '"ostensible consent" and "willingness" are terms which, in the context of offences against the young in particular, are susceptible to misunderstanding and, even if accurately used, are liable to obscure the true nature of the encounter between the offender and the victim'. The new guideline moves away from the language of 'ostensible consent' so that the focus in relation to children aged between 13 and 15 is placed not on the behaviour of the victim but on the behaviour and culpability of the offender. Accordingly, harm is determined by the nature of the sexual activity involved, so avoiding the need to consider the child's behaviour or their understanding of their 'relationship' with the offender. The guideline places more emphasis on how the offender has persuaded the child to engage in the activity and obtained their apparent consent. Following on from the consideration given to 'remote offending' in *Prince*,[77] the guideline confirms that the approach to sentencing and the starting points and ranges apply equally where the offender commits the offence remotely over the internet. **12.122**

Rape of child under 13

The guideline says that the majority of offences of a rape of a child under 13 will attract significant custodial sentences, but it acknowledges that the courts may be faced with a wide range of offending behaviour. Exploitative behaviour towards a child should be considered to indicate high culpability even where the child is not subjected to force or fear of force. In wholly exceptional cases, a lengthy community order with a requirement to participate in a sex offender programme may be the best way of changing the offender's behaviour and of protecting the public by preventing any repetition of the offence. **12.123**

Increase in sentencing levels for some offences of rape and assault by penetration

Where an offender is convicted of a campaign of rape, against single or multiple victims, a sentence of 20 years or more should now be passed. In addition, the starting point for a single offence will be 15 years if its nature reflects Category 1 harm together with higher culpability. The most serious cases of s 2 assault by penetration may attract similar levels of sentence as rape because of the physical harm that will be caused when large or dangerous objects have been used by the offender. **12.124**

The Overall Picture

Whilst it should be appreciated that under the new guidelines a higher starting point would have been likely, an example of the need to look at the overall picture can be found in *Attorney General's Reference (No 107 of 2007)*.[78] The unpleasant threats and violence, accompanied by multiple acts of penetration, distinguished the case from a single offence of rape for which a 5-year sentence remained the appropriate starting point after a trial. The court sympathized with the trial judge in his conscientious attempt to make the case fit into one or more of the boxes provided by the guidelines. The court considered that the sentencing judge might not have stood back and looked at the overall picture. Whatever was the appropriate pigeonhole starting point, the court was satisfied that the appropriate sentence following a trial would have been in the region of 9 years. **12.125**

[76] [2012] EWCA Crim 1119, at 34.
[77] [2013] EWCA Crim 1768.
[78] [2008] EWCA Crim 198.

Facts Not Envisaged by the Sentencing Council Guidelines

12.126 When a SC Guideline presumes, for example, consensual sexual activity but the facts demonstrate otherwise, the guideline will not apply. Although the question of consent is not expressly dealt with in the new guideline (presumably because it is not an ingredient of the offence), Category 1 provides a higher starting point and range. An example of this is to be found (using the old guideline) in *R v Jones* [2009].[79] The defendant was convicted of sexual activity with a person with a mental disorder by a care worker (s 38 of the SOA 2003). He was a 22-year-old male care worker working in a care home, the victim was a woman aged 76 with severe dementia. The offender had taken the victim to her bedroom for the purposes of putting her to bed and shortly afterwards activated an emergency alarm. The victim was removed to hospital where it was found that she had severe tears to the perineum. The medical evidence was that the injuries had most likely been caused by the insertion into her vagina of a penis or similar object. D denied that he was responsible. He was a man of previous good character with significant learning difficulties. Sentenced to 9 years' imprisonment. Held:

The sentencing judge had considered the (then) Sentencing Guidelines Council Guidelines in relation to sexual offences. The guidelines proceeded on the basis that the sexual activity was essentially consensual, while in the present case it plainly was not; the guidelines were therefore of no particular assistance. The maximum penalty for the offence was 14 years' imprisonment. The sentencing judge made it clear that the guidelines were not applicable to the offence with which he was dealing. In the court's judgment, the sentencing judge was correct to conclude that the guidelines did not apply. The question for the court was whether in all the circumstances the sentence of nine years was manifestly excessive. In the court's view, the proper sentence, reflecting to the gravity of the offending balanced against the factors in favour of the appellant, would have been 7 years' imprisonment and a sentence of 7 years' imprisonment would be substituted.

12.127 Cultural differences provide no mitigation of rape; *MA* [2012] EWCA Crim 1646. The fact that the offender had been brought up in Pakistan to believe that he had a right to rape his wife was no basis for leniency.

Sentencing Young Offenders

12.128 The Sexual Offences Definitive Guideline applies only to offenders aged 18 and over; offenders under 18 will be covered by a separate youth guideline which it is expected the Council will begin to consider in 2014.

12.129 The current guideline provides that the youth and immaturity of an offender may provide personal mitigation in an historic case (SC Definitive Guideline; Annex B (10)).

12.130 The SC Overarching Principles for Sentencing Young Offenders should be borne in mind in determining the relevant factors which may affect the correct level of reduction in sentence, especially the offender's level of immaturity as well as chronological age (see also *R v N* [2010][80]), generally decreasing the closer the offender is to 18.

12.131 For young offenders, the sentence for rape should normally be significantly shorter than that for an adult.[81] However, this approach is not intended to be of invariable and inevitable application; where the facts of the case are particularly serious, the youth of the offender will not necessarily mitigate the appropriate sentence; for example, *Asi-Akram*;[82] *Patrick M*.[83]

12.132 *B* (2006)[84] is an example of where the Court of Appeal upheld an indeterminate sentence detaining the 15-year-old offender for life where, as a pupil, he had forced a teacher to perform oral

79 [2009] EWCA Crim 237.
80 [2010] EWCA Crim 941.
81 Per Lord Woolf in *Milberry*.
82 [2006] 1 Cr App R(S) 47.
83 [2005] 1 Cr App R(S) 49.
84 [2006] EWCA Crim 330.

sex twice, having dragged her from the classroom and told her he would kill her. The sentencing judge fixed a notional sentence of 9 years with a specific term of 3 years and 8 months. The Court of Appeal held that the case was unique and exceptional violence had been used and that the offender's young age had to be balanced against the seriousness of the offence. While the age of the offender was something a court had to take strongly into account, it could not be a matter that prevented an appropriate sentence on particular facts.

Child Victims and Young Offenders

Guideline authority

R v Corran and Others [2006][85] provides non-prescriptive guidance to sentencers in respect of young offenders and child victims which it is suggested will remain of assistance in relation to offenders under 18 at least until the sexual offences guideline for young offenders is published. The SC (at p. 28) acknowledges that the new guideline may not be appropriate where the sentencer is satisfied that on the available evidence, and in the absence of exploitation, a young or particularly immature defendant genuinely believed, on reasonable grounds, that the victim was aged 16 or over and that they were engaging in lawful sexual activity. **12.133**

Per Rose LJ: **12.134**

> [3] ...The 2003 Act has greatly expanded the circumstances in which sexual penetration can give rise to an offence punishable by life imprisonment...
>
> [4] It is apparent that rape can now be committed in a much wider variety of circumstances than before the Act. The age of the offender is immaterial. In all cases the maximum punishment available is life imprisonment. But the level of punishment appropriate will depend on the circumstances of the particular case.
>
> [5] This Court has given guidance on sentencing in relation to rape as defined in section 1 and assault by penetration as defined in section 2, in Attorney-General's Reference (No 104 of 2004) *(R v Garvey)* [2005] 1 Cr App R(S) 117, where it was concluded, in paragraph 28, that the aggravating and mitigating features identified in *R v Millberry* [2003] 2 Cr App R(S) 142, continue to be of assistance, though the starting point for non-penile penetration should generally be lower than for penile penetration. The Court also indicated that, following *Millberry*, for young offenders the sentence for rape and assault by penetration should be significantly shorter than for an adult.
>
> [6] ...There will be very few cases in which immediate custody is not called for, even in relation to a young offender because the purpose of the legislation is to protect children under 13 from themselves, as well as from others minded to prey upon them.
>
> [7] ...Where there is no question of consent and where significant aggravating features, as identified in *Millberry*, are present...a long determinate sentence, or a life sentence, will be called for, in accordance with existing authority on seriousness and dangerousness...
>
> [8] Although absence of consent is not an ingredient of the offence, presence of consent is material in relation to sentence, particularly in relation to young defendants.
>
> The age of the defendant, both of itself and when compared with the age of the victim, is also an important factor. A very short period of custody is likely to suffice for a teenager where the other party consents. In exceptional cases...a non-custodial sentence may be appropriate for a young defendant. If the offender is much older than the victim, a substantial term of imprisonment will usually be called for.
>
> [9] Other factors include the nature of the relationship between the two and their respective characters and maturity, the number of occasions when penetration occurred, the circumstances of the penetration, including whether contraception was used, the consequences for the victim, emotionally and physically, the degree of remorse shown by the defendant and the likelihood of repetition. A reasonable belief that the victim was 16 will also be a mitigating factor, particularly where the defendant is young. A plea of guilty will of course be pertinent...

[85] [2005] 2 Cr App R(S) 73, [2005] EWCA Crim 192.

H. ORDERS AND REQUIREMENTS AFTER CONVICTION

Disqualification

Disqualification from working with children and vulnerable adults

12.135 Sections 26–34 of the CJCSA have been fully repealed and replaced with effect from 17 June 2013 (Safeguarding Vulnerable Groups Act 2006 (Commencement No 8 and Saving) Order 2012 No 2231). The role of disqualifying an offender from working with children or vulnerable adults now lies with the Disclosure and Barring Service (the replacement to the Independent Safeguarding Authority) (s 87(1) of the Protection of Freedoms Act 2012).[86]

12.136 The role of the judge[87] is now to inform the offender that the Disclosure and Barring Service (DBS) either *will* or *may* be barred, depending on where the offence is found within Part 2 of the Safeguarding Vulnerable Groups Act 2006 (Prescribed Criteria and Miscellaneous Provisions) Regulations 2009 (SI 2009 No 37). For some offences (known as automatic inclusion offences, as opposed to automatic barring offences) the offender is able to make representations to the DBS after conviction/caution, but before he or she is placed on the list; hence, *may* be barred. See para 12.137 for offences which attract automatic barring without the right to make representations (*will* be barred) and for offences in respect of which an offender can make representations (*may* be barred). The court should inform the defendant which list he or she will be included on and under what legislation. In addition, a defendant should be told whether or not they can make representations to be removed from the list.

Suggested form of words: 'You (may/)will be made subject to the barring regulations under the Safeguarding Vulnerable Groups Act 2006 and (may/)will be placed on the adult/children's list (subject to your right to make representations to be removed from that list).'

The Lists of Offences Attracting Automatic Inclusion

12.137 There are four lists; two in relation to working with children and two in relation to working with adults. All offences listed are 'automatically included' but not all attract automatic barring. Each pair is divided between those offences in respect of which the offender can make representations as to why he or she should not be placed on the list and those in respect of which they cannot and so barring is automatic.

Note: these lists are subject to change as the legislation is amended and updated.

Automatically included in the children's barred list with no right to make representations to be removed (Will be Barred)

12.138 An offender will be barred automatically from working with children in a regulated activity with no right to make representations to the DBS if convicted of an offence falling within Sch 1, para 1 of the Regulation, namely:[88]

s 4 CLA 1885 Carnal knowledge of a girl under 13
s 1 SOA 1956 Rape (where the victim was a child)
s 5 SOA 1956 Sexual intercourse with a girl under 13
s 128 MH 1959 Sexual intercourse with patients (where the victim was a child)
s 1 SOA 2003 Rape (where the victim was a child)
s 2 SOA 2003 Assault by penetration (where the victim was a child)
s 5 SOA 2003 Rape of a child under 13
s 6 SOA 2003 Assault of a child under 13 by penetration

86 (Commencement No 4) Order 2012 (SI 2012 No 2521).

87 CPR 2013, r 42.3(1)

88 Safeguarding Vulnerable Groups Act 2006 (Prescribed Criteria and Miscellaneous Provisions) Regulations 2009/37, reg 3 and Sch 1, para 1.

s 7 SOA 2003 Sexual assault of a child under 13
s 8 SOA 2003 Causing or inciting a child under 13 to engage in sexual activity
s 30 SOA 2003 Sexual activity with a person with a mental disorder impeding choice (where the victim was a child)
s 31 SOA 2003 Causing or inciting a person with a mental disorder impeding choice, to engage in sexual activity (where the victim was a child)
s 32 SOA 2003 Engaging in sexual activity in the presence of a person with a mental disorder impeding choice (where the victim was a child)
s 33 SOA 2003 Causing a person, with a mental disorder impeding choice, to watch a sexual act (where the victim was a child)
s 34 SOA 2003 Inducement, threat or deception to procure sexual activity with a person with a mental disorder (where the victim was a child)
s 35 SOA 2003 Causing a person with a mental disorder to engage in or agree to engage in sexual activity by inducement, threat or deception (where the victim was a child)
s 36 SOA 2003 Engaging in sexual activity in the presence, procured by inducement, threat or deception, of a person with a mental disorder (where the victim was a child)
s 37 SOA 2003 Causing a person with a mental disorder to watch a sexual act by inducement, threat or deception (where the victim was a child)
s 38 SOA 2003 Care workers: sexual activity with a person with a mental disorder (where the victim was a child)
s 39 SOA 2003 Care workers: causing or inciting sexual activity (where the victim was a child)
s 40 SOA 2003 Care workers: sexual activity in the presence of a person with a mental disorder (where the victim was a child)
s 41 SOA 2003 Care workers: causing a person with a mental disorder to watch a sexual act (where the victim was a child)

Automatically included in the children's barred list with right to make representations to be removed (May be Barred)

An offender will be barred automatically from working with children in a regulated activity, but with a right to make representations to the DBS if convicted of an offence falling within Sch 1, para 2 of the Regulation, namely:[89] **12.139**

Common Law Offences:
Murder
Kidnap
Infanticide

s 21 OAPA 1861 Attempt to choke, suffocate/strangle in order to commit or assist in the commission of any indictable offence
s 52 OAPA 1861 Indecent assault upon a female
s 53 OAPA 1861 Fraudulent abduction of a girl under age against the will of her father
s 54 OAPA 1861 Forcible abduction of any woman with intent to marry or carnally know her
s 55 OAPA 1861 Abduction of a girl under 16 years of age
s 61 OAPA 1861 Buggery (where the victim was under 16 or did not consent)
s 62 OAPA 1861 Indecent assault upon a male, attempt to commit buggery, assault with intent to commit buggery (where the victim was under 16 or did not consent)
s 2 CLAA 1885 Procuration
s 3 CLAA 1885 Procuring defilement of a woman by threats or fraud or administering drugs
s 5 CLAA 1885 Defilement of a girl under 17 years of age
s 6 CLAA 1885 Householder permitting defilement of young girl on his premises

[89] Safeguarding Vulnerable Groups Act 2006 (Prescribed Criteria and Miscellaneous Provisions) Regulations 2009 (SI 2009 No 37), reg 4 and Sch 1, para 2.

s 7 CLAA 1885 Abduction of a girl under 18 with intent to have carnal knowledge
s 8 CLAA 1885 Unlawful detention with intent to have carnal knowledge
s 11 CLAA 1885 Outrages on decency (where the victim was under 16 or did not consent, and the conviction has not been disregarded under Chapter 4 of Part 5 of the Protection of Freedoms Act 2012)
s 1 Vagrancy Act 1898 Trading in prostitution
s 1 Punishment of Incest Act 1908 Incest by males (where the victim was a child)
s 2 Punishment of Incest Act 1908 Incest by females aged 16 or over (where the victim was a child)
s 1 C&YPA 1933 Cruelty to children
s 1 Infanticide Act 1938 Infanticide
s 1 SOA 1956 Rape (where the victim was an adult)
s 2 SOA 1956 Procurement of a woman by threats
s 3 SOA 1956 Procurement of a woman by false pretences
s 4 SOA 1956 Administering drugs to obtain or facilitate intercourse
s 6 SOA 1956 Sexual intercourse with a girl under 16
s 7 SOA 1956 Intercourse with a defective
s 9 SOA 1956 Procurement of a defective
s 10 SOA 1956 Incest by a man (where the victim was a child)
s 11 SOA 1956 Incest by a woman (where the victim was a child)
s 12 SOA 1956 Buggery (where the victim was under 16 or did not consent, and the conviction has not been disregarded under Chapter 4 of Part 5 of the Protection of Freedoms Act 2012)
s 13 SOA 1956 Indecency between men (where the victim was under 16 or did not consent, and the conviction has not been disregarded under Chapter 4 of Part 5 of the Protection of Freedoms Act 2012)
s 14 SOA 1956 Indecent assault on a woman
s 15 SOA 1956 Indecent assault on a man
s 16 SOA 1956 Assault with intent to commit buggery
s 17 SOA 1956 Abduction of a woman by force or for the sake of her property
s 19 SOA 1956 Abduction of unmarried girl under 18
s 20 SOA 1956 Abduction of unmarried girl under 16
s 21 SOA 1956 Abduction of defective from parent or guardian
s 22 SOA 1956 Causing prostitution of women
s 23 SOA 1956 Procurement of girl under 21
s 24 SOA 1956 Detention of a woman in a brothel or other premises
ss 25 and 26 SOA 1956 Permitting girl, under 13, or between 13 and 16, to use premises for intercourse
s 27 SOA 1956 Permitting defective to use premises for intercourse
s 28 SOA 1956 Causing or encouraging prostitution of, intercourse with or indecent assault on girl under 16
s 29 SOA 1956 Causing or encouraging prostitution of defective
s 30 SOA 1956 Man living on earnings of prostitution
s 31 SOA 1956 Woman exercising control over prostitute
s 128 MHA 1959 Sexual intercourse with patients
s 1 IwCA 1960 Indecency with children under 16
s 4 SOA 1967 Procuring others to commit homosexual acts
s 5 SOA 1967 Living on the earnings of male prostitution
s 9(1)(a) Theft Act 1968 Burglary (with intent to commit rape)
s 4(3) Misuse of Drugs Act 1971 Production or supply of controlled drugs (where the victim was a child)
s 54 CLA 1977 Inciting girl under 16 to have incestuous sexual intercourse
s 1 Protection of Children Act 1978 Distribution or possession of indecent photograph of a child
s 170 Customs and Excise Management Act 1979 Fraudulent evasion of duty re importation of obscene material

s 127 MHA 1983 Ill-treatment or wilful neglect of a patient with a mental disorder
s 1 Child Abduction Act 1984 Abduction of a child by parent
s 2 Child Abduction Act 1984 Abduction of child by other persons
s 160 CJA 1988 Possession of indecent photographs of children
s 3 SO(A)A 2000 Sex in abuse of trust with person under 18
s 145 Nationality, Immigration and Asylum Act 2002 Traffic in prostitution
s 1 Female Genital Mutilation Act 2003 Carrying out female genital mutilation (where the victim was a child)
s 2 Female Genital Mutilation Act 2003 Aiding, abetting, counselling or procuring a girl to mutilate her own genitals (where the victim was a child)
s 3 Female Genital Mutilation Act 2003 Aiding, abetting, counselling or procuring a non-UK person to mutilate overseas a girl's genitals (where the victim was a child)
s 1 SOA 2003 Rape (where the victim was an adult)
s 2 SOA 2003 Assault by penetration (where the victim was an adult)
s 3 SOA 2003 Sexual assault
s 4 SOA 2003 Causing a person to engage in sexual activity without consent
s 4(1A) SOA 2003 Trafficking people for labour and other exploitation
s 9 SOA 2003 Sexual activity with a child
s 10 SOA 2003 Causing or inciting a child to engage in sexual activity
s 11 SOA 2003 Engaging in sexual activity in the presence of a child
s 12 SOA 2003 Causing a child to watch a sexual act
s 14 SOA 2003 Arranging or facilitating commission of a child sex offence
s 15 SOA 2003 Meeting a child following sexual grooming
s 16 SOA 2003 Abuse of a position of trust: sexual activity with a child
s 17 SOA 2003 Abuse of a position of trust: causing or inciting a child to engage in sexual activity
s 18 SOA 2003 Abuse of position of trust: sexual activity in the presence of a child
s 19 SOA 2003 Abuse of position of trust: causing a child to watch a sexual act
s 25 SOA 2003 Sexual activity with a child family member
s 26 SOA 2003 Inciting a child family member to engage in sexual activity
s 30 SOA 2003 Sexual activity with a person with a mental disorder impeding choice (where the victim was an adult)
s 31 SOA 2003 Causing or inciting a person, with a mental disorder impeding choice, to engage in sexual activity (where the victim was an adult)
s 32 SOA 2003 Engaging in sexual activity in the presence of a person with a mental disorder impeding choice (where the victim was an adult)
s 33 SOA 2003 Causing a person, with a mental disorder impeding choice, to watch a sexual act (where the victim was a adult)
s 34 SOA 2003 Inducement, threat or deception to procure sexual activity with a person with a mental disorder (where the victim was an adult)
s 35 SOA 2003 Causing a person with a mental disorder to engage in/ agree to engage in sexual activity by inducement, threat or deception (where the victim was an adult)
s 36 SOA 2003 Engaging in sexual activity in the presence, procured by inducement, threat or deception, of a person with a mental disorder (where the victim was an adult)
s 37 SOA 2003 Causing a person with a mental disorder to watch a sexual act by inducement, threat or deception (where the victim was an adult)
s 38 SOA 2003 Care workers: sexual activity with a person with a mental disorder (where the victim was an adult)
s 39 SOA 2003 Care workers: causing or inciting sexual activity (where the victim was an adult)
s 40 SOA 2003 Care workers: sexual activity in the presence of a person with a mental disorder (where the victim was an adult)
s 41 SOA 2003 Care workers: causing a person with a mental disorder to watch a sexual act (where the victim was an adult)

s 47 SOA 2003 Paying for sexual services of a child
s 48 SOA 2003 Causing or inciting child prostitution or pornography
s 49 SOA 2003 Controlling a child prostitute or a child involved in pornography
s 50 SOA 2003 Arranging or facilitating child prostitution or pornography
s 52 SOA 2003 Causing or inciting prostitution for gain
s 53 SOA 2003 Controlling prostitution for gain
s 57 SOA 2003 Trafficking into the UK for sexual exploitation
s 58 SOA 2003 Trafficking within the UK for sexual exploitation
s 59 SOA 2003 Trafficking out of the UK for sexual exploitation
s 59A SOA 2003 Trafficking people for sexual exploitation
s 61 SOA 2003 Administering a substance with intent
ss 62 and 63 SOA 2003 Committing an offence or trespassing with intent to commit a sexual offence (where that offence leads to automatic barring)
s 66 SOA 2003 Exposure (where the victim was under 16)
s 67 SOA 2003 Voyeurism (where the victim was under 16)
s 72 SOA 2003 Sexual offences committed outside the UK (corresponding to an offence which leads to automatic barring from work with children with the right to make representations)
s 4 Asylum and Immigration (Treatment of Claimants) Act 2004 Trafficking people for exploitation
s 5 Domestic Violence, Crime and Victims Act 2004 Causing or allowing a child or vulnerable adult to die, or suffer serious physical harm
s 44 Mental Capacity Act 2005 Ill-treatment or wilful neglect
s 63 Criminal Justice and Immigration Act 2008 Possession of extreme pornographic images
s 62 CAJA 2009 Possession of prohibited images of children

Automatic inclusion in the adults' barred list with no right to make representations to be removed (Will be Barred)

12.140 An offender will be barred automatically from working in a regulated activity related to vulnerable adults with no right to make representations to the DBS if convicted of an offence falling within Sch 1, para 3 of the Regulation, namely:[90]

s 30 SOA 2003 Sexual activity with a person with a mental disorder impeding choice
s 31 SOA 2003 Causing or inciting a person, with a mental disorder impeding choice, to engage in sexual activity
s 32 SOA 2003 Engaging in sexual activity in the presence of a person with a mental disorder impeding choice
s 33 SOA 2003 Causing a person, with a mental disorder impeding choice, to watch a sexual act
s 34 SOA 2003 Inducement, threat or deception to procure sexual activity with a person with a mental disorder
s 35 SOA 2003 Causing a person with a mental disorder to engage in or agree to engage in sexual activity by inducement, threat or deception
s 36 SOA 2003 Engaging in sexual activity in the presence, procured by inducement, threat or deception, of a person with a mental disorder
s 37 SOA 2003 Causing a person with a mental disorder to watch a sexual act by inducement, threat or deception
s 38 SOA 2003 Care workers: sexual activity with a person with a mental disorder
s 39 SOA 2003 Care workers: causing or inciting sexual activity
s 40 SOA 2003 Care workers: sexual activity in the presence of a person with a mental disorder
s 41 SOA 2003 Care workers: causing a person with a mental disorder to watch a sexual act

[90] Safeguarding Vulnerable Groups Act 2006 (Prescribed Criteria and Miscellaneous Provisions) Regulations 2009 (SI 2009 No 37), reg 5 and Sch 1, para 3.

Automatic inclusion in the adults' barred list with the right to make representations to be removed (May be Barred)

An offender will be barred automatically from working with vulnerable adults, but with a right to make representations to the DBS if convicted of an offence falling within Sch 1, para 4 of the Regulation, namely:[91] **12.141**

As per the children's list with the right to make representations at para 12.139 with the following additions (which offences appear in the children's list of offences in respect of which no representations can be made):

s 4 CLAA 1885 Defilement of a girl under 14 years of age
s 6 SOA 1956 Sexual intercourse with a girl under 16
s 5 SOA 2003 Rape of a child under 13
s 6 SOA 2003 Assault of a child under 13 by penetration
s 7 SOA 2003 Sexual assault of a child under 13
s 8 SOA 2003 Causing a inciting a child under 13 to engage in sexual activity

but not including *the following offences (which offences do appear at para 12.139):*

s 30 SOA 2003 Sexual activity with a person with a mental disorder impeding choice (where the victim was an adult)
s 31 SOA 2003 Causing or inciting a person, with a mental disorder impeding choice, to engage in sexual activity (where the victim was an adult)
s 32 SOA 2003 Engaging in sexual activity in the presence of a person with a mental disorder impeding choice (where the victim was an adult)
s 33 SOA 2003 Causing a person, with a mental disorder impeding choice, to watch a sexual act (where the victim was a adult)
s 34 SOA 2003 Inducement, threat or deception to procure sexual activity with a person with a mental disorder (where the victim was an adult)
s 35 SOA 2003 Causing a person with a mental disorder to engage in/agree to engage in sexual activity by inducement, threat or deception (where the victim was an adult)
s 36 SOA 2003 Engaging in sexual activity in the presence, procured by inducement, threat or deception, of a person with a mental disorder (where the victim was an adult)
s 37 SOA 2003 Causing a person with a mental disorder to watch a sexual act by inducement, threat or deception (where the victim was an adult)
s 38 SOA 2003 Care workers: sexual activity with a person with a mental disorder (where the victim was an adult)
s 39 SOA 2003 Care workers: causing or inciting sexual activity (where the victim was an adult)
s 40 SOA 2003 Care workers: sexual activity in the presence of a person with a mental disorder (where the victim was an adult)
s 41 SOA 2003 Care workers: causing a person with a mental disorder to watch a sexual act (where the victim was an adult)

Restraining Orders

Sex Offenders Act 1997, s 5A, as inserted by Criminal Justice and Courts Services Act 2000, s 66 and Sch 5, para 6

Restraining Orders under s 5A of the Sexual Offenders Act 1997 have been replaced by SOPOs—s 5A was repealed by the SOA 2003. **12.142**

---

[91] Safeguarding Vulnerable Groups Act 2006 (Prescribed Criteria and Miscellaneous Provisions) Regulations 2009 (SI 2009 No 37), reg 6, Sch 1, para 4.

However, the Domestic Violence, Crime and Victims Act (DVCVA) 2004 amended the Protection from Harassment Act 1997 (from 30.9.2009 (SI 2009 No 2501)) to allow a restraining order to be made under s 5 on conviction for any offence. The order must protect 'the victim or victims of the offence, or any other person mentioned in the order, from conduct which—
(a) amounts to harassment, or
(b) will cause a fear of violence.'

12.143 In most sexual cases a SOPO would seem to continue to be the most appropriate way of restraining the defendant from further prohibited activity.

12.144 By s 12 of the DVCVA 2004 there is now a s 5A of the Protection from Harassment Act 1997. This permits the court to make a restraining order against a defendant who has been acquitted in order to protect a person from harassment by the defendant. The order is a civil order and the civil standard of proof applies. Further evidence can be called (*Major* [2010] EWCA Crim 3016).

Sexual Offences Prevention Orders

12.145 See Chapter 16.

Notification

12.146 See Chapter 14; not an order but the judge should deal with the requirement expressly.[92]

A right of review for those subject to indefinite requirements was upheld by the Supreme Court, having been found to breach Article 8: *R (F and T) v Secretary of State for Justice*.[93]

12.147 It is wrong in principle to pass a lower sentence in order to avoid the operation of the notification requirements: *R v F* [2009].[94]

Forfeiture under the Sexual Offences Act 2003, s 60A

12.148 See para 8.155.

Recommendation for Deportation

12.149 The Secretary of State is under a duty to make a deportation order in respect of a person who is not a British citizen and who has been sentenced to imprisonment for a period of at least 12 months. This includes indeterminate sentences and detention in a Young Offenders Institution (ss 23–39 UK Borders Act 2007). Judges should not seek to avoid this provision by reducing what would have otherwise been an appropriate sentence of 12 months or more; *Gebru* [2011].[95] The circumstances in which a judge will now have to make a recommendation for deportation are limited. The approach to be followed was set out in *Kluxen* [2010]:[96]

i) In cases to which the 2007 Act applies, it is no longer necessary or appropriate to recommend the deportation of the offender concerned.
ii) In cases to which the 2007 Act does not apply, it will rarely be appropriate to recommend the deportation of the offender concerned, whether or not the offender is a citizen of the EU.
iii) If in a case to which the 2007 Act does not apply a Court is, exceptionally, considering recommending the deportation of the offender concerned, it should apply the *Nazari* test in tandem with the *Bouchereau* test, there being no practical difference between the two. This is so whether the offender is or is not a citizen of the EU. The test:

> [25] Is there a genuine and sufficiently serious threat to the requirements of public policy affecting one of the fundamental interests of society? In other words, would the appellant's continued presence in the United Kingdom be to its detriment?

iv) However, the Court should not take into account the Convention Rights of the offender; the political situation in the country to which the offender may be deported; the effect that a recommendation might have on innocent persons not before the Court; the provisions of Article 28 of Directive 2004/38; or the 2006 Regulations.

---

[92] CPR 2013.
[93] [2010] UKSC 17.
[94] [2009] CLR 462.
[95] [2011] EWCA Crim 3321.
[96] [2010] EWCA Crim 1081.

Immigration Act 1971, s 3(6)

Where there is power to deport a person under either the Immigration Act 1971 or the UK Borders Act 2007, the European Citizens Directive (2004/38/EC) makes further requirements before that power may be exercised in the cases of European Economic Area nationals or their family members. **12.150**

Nazari 1980: the starting point is whether in the light of the nature of the offence and other material the continued presence of D is detrimental to the country. However, this is reconsidered in *Carmona* (2006). The basic test remains unaltered. **12.151**

I. PROSECUTION REVIEWS OF SENTENCE (ATTORNEY GENERAL'S REFERENCES)

In *Johnson and Others* Judge LJ dealt with references from cases where the rebuttable presumption of an indeterminate sentence applies: **12.152**

> In cases to which section 229(3) applies, where the sentencer has applied the statutory assumption, to succeed the appellant should demonstrate that it was unreasonable not to disapply it. Equally, where the Attorney General has referred such a case because the sentencer has decided to disapply the assumption, the Reference will not succeed unless it is shown that the decision was one which the sentencer could not properly have reached.

Offences Referable to the Court of Appeal by the Attorney General

Listed below are all those offences in respect of which it is currently possible for the Attorney General to refer the sentence to the Court of Appeal for its consideration. Included as of April 2006 are a number of offences under the SOA 2003. **12.153**

1. All offences triable only on indictment.
2. Any case tried on indictment following a notice of transfer under the CJA 1987, s 4.
3. Any case where one or more of the counts in respect of which sentence was passed relates to a charge which was dismissed at committal (under CJA 1987, s 6(1)) and further proceedings then brought by means of preferment of a voluntary bill.
4. Any sentence passed for any of the following offences under the SOA 1956:

Legislative Provision	Offence
SOA 1956, s 6	unlawful sexual intercourse with girl under 13
SOA 1956, s 14	Indecent assault on a female
SOA 1956, s 15	Indecent assault on a male

5. Any sentence passed for one of the following either way offences under the SOA 2003:

Legislative Provision	Offence
SOA 2003, s 3	Sexual assault
SOA 2003, s 4	Causing a person to engage in sexual activity without consent
SOA 2003, s 7	Sexual assault of a child under 13
SOA 2003, s 8	Causing or inciting a child under 13 to engage in sexual activity
SOA 2003, s 9	Sexual activity with a child
SOA 2003, s 10	Causing or inciting a child to engage in sexual activity
SOA 2003, s 11	Engaging in sexual activity in the presence of a child
SOA 2003, s 12	Causing a child to watch a sexual act

Legislative Provision	Offence
SOA 2003, s 14	Arranging/facilitating commission of a child sex offence
SOA 2003, s 15	Meeting a child following sexual grooming
SOA 2003, s 25	Sexual activity with a child family member
SOA 2003, ss 47–50 incl	Child prostitution offences
SOA 2003, ss 57–59 SOA 2003, s 59A	Trafficking offences
SOA 2003, s 61	Administering a substance with intent

6. Any sentence passed for any of the following offences:

Legislative Provision	Offence
IwCA, s 1	Gross indecency with/towards a child
CLA 1977, s 54	Incitement by man of daughter, granddaughter, daughter or sister to commit incest with him
CLAA 1885, s 5(1)	Defilement of a girl under 17
OAPA 1861, s 16	Threats to kill
CYPA 1933, s 1	Cruelty to persons under 16

7. Any offence for either attempting to commit or inciting the commission of any of the above offences (conspiracy to commit any offence is triable only on indictment and so automatically referable).

12.154 Note: referable offences under the Misuse of Drugs Act 1971 and the Customs and Excise Management Act 1979 are not set out above.

Checklist of Matters to be Included[97]

12.155 The Attorney General's References are dealt with in the Court of Appeal by treasury counsel. Prior to that it is necessary for trial counsel to prepare an advice for consideration. This should be done immediately after sentence as a notice of an application for leave to refer a case to the Court of Appeal must be submitted within 28 days of sentence and is the initial step in the process.

12.156 The following is a list of those matters with which trial counsel should deal in submitting an advice for consideration by treasury counsel.

12.157 Checklist:

(1) Chronology of proceedings
(2) Details of any basis of plea/concessions by the prosecution
(3) Name of sentencing judge and court
(4) Outline of facts (include case summary or opening if available)
(5) Details of previous convictions/breach of bail/licence, etc.
(6) Pre-sentence report
(7) Address the question whether the offender is subject to the 'dangerousness' provisions of the 2003 Act and what the prosecution's submissions were on the subject
(8) List the aggravating features
(9) List the mitigating features
(10) Refer to any guideline authority and any authority which the judge was referred to. Resist the temptation to quote reams of old authorities which are not similar on the facts
(11) Explain in a final paragraph why the sentence is unduly lenient. For example, it may be because the judge has misdirected himself as to his sentencing powers or that he has not followed the guideline authority or given too great a reduction for a guilty plea.

[97] With thanks to Zoe Johnson QC, senior treasury counsel, for compiling this list.

SENTENCING TABLE [sentencing maximum and changes to applicable regime for persistent/dangerous offenders]

S.	OFFENCE	FROM	UNTIL	MAXIMUM SENTENCE	EXTENDED TERM OF IMPRISONMENT Section 37[1] Criminal Justice Act 1967[2] [Offences committed on or after 21 July 1967– 30 September 1992][3]	EXTENDED LICENCE Sexual offences for the purposes of s 86[4] Powers of Criminal Courts (Sentencing) Act 2000 [Offences committed before 30 September 1998]	LONGER THAN COMMENSURATE SENTENCE/ EXTENDED SENTENCE Specified sexual offences for the purposes of s 80[5] and s 85[6] Powers of Criminal Courts (Sentencing) Act 2000 [Offences committed before 4 April 2005[7]]	AUTOMATIC LIFE SENTENCE Specified serious offences for purposes of s 109[8] Powers of Criminal Courts (Sentencing) Act 2000 [Offences committed on or after 30 September 1998 – 3 April 2005][9]	IMPRISONMENT FOR PUBLIC PROTECTION[10] [IPP] EXTENDED SENTENCES FOR PUBLIC PROTECTION[11] [EPP]/LIFE SENTENCE[12] Specified sexual offences for purposes of Schedule 15 CJA 2003[13] [Offences Committed on or after 4 April 2005 – 3 December 2012	IPP[14]/ EPP/[15]LIFE SENTENCE Specified sexual offences for purposes of Schedule 15A CJA 2003 [inserted by CJIA 2008[16] applicable 14 July 2008 – 3 December 2012]	EXTENDED DETERMINATE SENTENCE[17] [EDS]/LIFE SENTENCE[18] Specified sexual offences for the purposes of Schedule 15 CJA 2003 (as amended by LASPOA 2012)[19] [Offences committed on or after 3 December 2012 to date]	LIFE SENTENCE FOR SECOND LISTED OFFENCE[20] Listed (sexual) offences for the purposes of Schedule 15B CJA 2003 (as amended by LASPOA 2012) [Offences committed on or after 3 December 2012 to date][21]
Contrary to Common Law												
	Outraging public decency	1.1.1950	To date	No maximum	•							
Sexual Offences Act 1956[22]												
1	Rape	1.1.1957	30.4.2004	Life	•	•	•	•	•	•	•	
	Attempt Rape	1.1.1957	15.9.1985	7 years	•	•	•	•	•	•	•	
		16.9.1985[23]	30.4.2004	Life								
2	Procurement of a woman by threats	1.1.1957	30.4.2004	2 years	•	•	•		•		•	

(*continued*)

S.	OFFENCE	FROM	UNTIL	MAXIMUM SENTENCE	EXTENDED TERM OF IMPRISONMENT Section 37 Criminal Justice Act 1967 [Offences committed on or after 21 July 1967– 30 September 1992]	EXTENDED LICENCE Sexual offences for the purposes of s 86 Powers of Criminal Courts (Sentencing) Act 2000 [Offences committed before 30 September 1998]	LONGER THAN COMMENSURATE SENTENCE/ EXTENDED SENTENCE Specified sexual offences for the purposes of s 80 and s 85 Powers of Criminal Courts (Sentencing) Act 2000 [Offences committed before 4 April 2005]	AUTOMATIC LIFE SENTENCE Specified serious offences for purposes of s 109 Powers of Criminal Courts (Sentencing) Act 2000 [Offences committed on or after 30 September 1998 – 3 April 2005]	IMPRISONMENT FOR PUBLIC PROTECTION [IPP] EXTENDED SENTENCES FOR PUBLIC PROTECTION [EPP]/LIFE SENTENCE Specified sexual offences for purposes of Schedule 15 CJA 2003 [Offences Committed on or after 4 April 2005 – 3 December 2012	IPP/EPP/ LIFE SENTENCE Specified sexual offences for purposes of Schedule 15A CJA 2003 [inserted by CJIA 2008 applicable 14 July 2008 – 3 December 2012]	EXTENDED DETERMINATE SENTENCE [EDS]/LIFE SENTENCE Specified sexual offences for the purposes of Schedule 15 CJA 2003 (as amended by LASPOA 2012) [Offences committed on or after 3 December 2012 to date]	LIFE SENTENCE FOR SECOND LISTED OFFENCE Listed (sexual) offences for the purposes of Schedule 15B CJA 2003 (as amended by LASPOA 2012) [Offences committed on or after 3 December 2012 to date]
3	Procurement of a woman by false pretences or representations	1.1.1957	30.4.2004	2 years	•	•	•		•		•	
4	Administering drugs to obtain or facilitate intercourse	1.1.1957	30.4.2004	2 years	•	•	•		•		•	
5	Sexual intercourse with a girl under 13 Attempt sexual intercourse with a girl under 13	1.1.1957 1.1.1957	30.4.2004 30.4.2004	Life 7 years	•	•	•	•	•	•	•	
6[24]	Sexual intercourse with a girl under 16	1.1.1957	30.4.2004	2 years	•	•	•		•		•	

7	Intercourse with an idiot/ imbecile	1.1.1957	31.10.1960[25]	2 years	•	•	•		•		•	
8	Intercourse with a defective	1.1.1957	31.10.1960[26]	2 years	•	•	•					
9	Procurement of a defective	1.1.1957	30.4.2004	2 years	•	•	•		•		•	
10	Incest by a male person	1.1.1957	30.4.2004	Life where C under 13 otherwise 7 years	•	•	•		•		•	
11	Incest by a female person	1.1.1957	30.4.2004	7 years	•	•	•		•		•	
12	Buggery with boy under 16 with his consent	1.1.1957	30.4.2004	Life	•[27]	•	•					
	Buggery with boy under 16 without his consent	1.1.1957	2.11.1994	Life								
	Buggery with an animal	1.1.1957	30.4.2004	Life								
	Buggery of a female with or without consent	1.1.1957	2.11.1994	Life								
	Buggery of male under 16 or female without consent AND Buggery of male over 16 with or without consent now becomes Rape under s 1	3.11.1994[28]										

(continued)

S.	OFFENCE	FROM	UNTIL	MAXIMUM SENTENCE	EXTENDED TERM OF IMPRISONMENT Section 37 Criminal Justice Act 1967 [Offences committed on or after 21 July 1967– 30 September 1992]	EXTENDED LICENCE Sexual offences for the purposes of s 86 Powers of Criminal Courts (Sentencing) Act 2000 [Offences committed before 30 September 1998]	LONGER THAN COMMENSURATE SENTENCE/ EXTENDED SENTENCE Specified sexual offences for the purposes of s 80 and s 85 Powers of Criminal Courts (Sentencing) Act 2000 [Offences committed before 4 April 2005]	AUTOMATIC LIFE SENTENCE Specified serious offences for purposes of s 109 Powers of Criminal Courts (Sentencing) Act 2000 [Offences committed on or after 30 September 1998 – 3 April 2005]	IMPRISONMENT FOR PUBLIC PROTECTION [IPP] EXTENDED SENTENCES FOR PUBLIC PROTECTION [EPP]/LIFE SENTENCE Specified sexual offences for purposes of Schedule 15 CJA 2003 [Offences Committed on or after 4 April 2005 – 3 December 2012	IPP/EPP/ LIFE SENTENCE Specified sexual offences for purposes of Schedule 15A CJA 2003 [inserted by CJIA 2008 applicable 14 July 2008 – 3 December 2012]	EXTENDED DETERMINATE SENTENCE [EDS]/LIFE SENTENCE Specified sexual offences for the purposes of Schedule 15 CJA 2003 (as amended by LASPOA 2012) [Offences committed on or after 3 December 2012 to date]	LIFE SENTENCE FOR SECOND LISTED OFFENCE Listed (sexual) offences for the purposes of Schedule 15B CJA 2003 (as amended by LASPOA 2012) [Offences committed on or after 3 December 2012 to date]
	Buggery of male over 16 with or without consent	1.1.1957	2.11.1994	10 years								
	Buggery where D aged over 21 and C aged between 16 and 20	1.1.1957	2.11.1994	5 years								
	Buggery where D aged 21 and C between 16 and 18	3.11.1994	30.4.2004	5 years								
	Buggery where D aged under 21 and C aged between 16 and 20 were consenting	1.1.1957	2.11.1994	2 years								

	Buggery between males over the age of consent other than in private[29]	1.1.1957	30.4.2004	2 years								
13	Gross indecency with another man (D over 21, C under 16)	1.1.1957	30.4.2004	5 years	• [30]	•	•					
14	Indecent assault upon a woman	1.1.1957 1.1.1961[31] 16.9.1985[32]	31.12.1960 15.9.1985 30.4.2004	2 years 5 years where C under 13 and age averred otherwise 2 years 10 years	•	•	•		•		•	
15	Indecent assault upon a man	1.1.1957	30.4.2004	10 years	•	•	•		•		•	
16	Assault with intent to commit buggery	1.1.1957	30.4.2004	10 years	•	•	•		•		•	
22	Procuring prostitution of women	1.1.1957	30.4.2004	2 years	•	•	•		•		•	
23	Procuring a girl under 21 to have unlawful sexual intercourse	1.1.1957	30.4.2004	2 years	•	•	•		•		•	

(continued)

S.	OFFENCE	FROM	UNTIL	MAXIMUM SENTENCE	EXTENDED TERM OF IMPRISONMENT Section 37 Criminal Justice Act 1967 [Offences committed on or after 21 July 1967– 30 September 1992]	EXTENDED LICENCE Sexual offences for the purposes of s 86 Powers of Criminal Courts (Sentencing) Act 2000 [Offences committed before 30 September 1998]	LONGER THAN COMMENSURATE SENTENCE/ EXTENDED SENTENCE Specified sexual offences for the purposes of s 80 and s 85 Powers of Criminal Courts (Sentencing) Act 2000 [Offences committed before 4 April 2005]	AUTOMATIC LIFE SENTENCE Specified serious offences for purposes of s 109 Powers of Criminal Courts (Sentencing) Act 2000 [Offences committed on or after 30 September 1998 – 3 April 2005]	IMPRISONMENT FOR PUBLIC PROTECTION [IPP] EXTENDED SENTENCES FOR PUBLIC PROTECTION [EPP]/LIFE SENTENCE Specified sexual offences for purposes of Schedule 15 CJA 2003 [Offences Committed on or after 4 April 2005 – 3 December 2012	IPP/EPP/ LIFE SENTENCE Specified sexual offences for purposes of Schedule 15A CJA 2003 [inserted by CJIA 2008 applicable 14 July 2008 – 3 December 2012]	EXTENDED DETERMINATE SENTENCE [EDS]/LIFE SENTENCE Specified sexual offences for the purposes of Schedule 15 CJA 2003 (as amended by LASPOA 2012) [Offences committed on or after 3 December 2012 to date]	LIFE SENTENCE FOR SECOND LISTED OFFENCE Listed (sexual) offences for the purposes of Schedule 15B CJA 2003 (as amended by LASPOA 2012) [Offences committed on or after 3 December 2012 to date]
24	Detention of a woman in a brothel or other premises	1.1.1957	30.4.2004	2 years	•	•	•		•		•	
27	Permitting a defective to use premises for intercourse	1.1.1957	30.4.2004	2 years	•	•	•		•		•	
28	Causing or encouraging prostitution of a girl under 16	1.1.1957	30.4.2004	2 years	•	•	•		•		•	
29	Causing/ encouraging prostitution of a defective	1.1.1957	30.4.2004	2 years	•	•	•		•		•	
30	Male living on the earnings of prostitution	1.1.1957	30.4.2004	7 years	•							

31	Women exercising control/ direction/ influence over a prostitute	1.1.1957	30.4.2004	7 years	•							
32	Solicitation for immoral purposes	1.1.1957	30.4.2004	2 years	•	•	•		•		•	
33A[33]	Keeping a brothel used for prostitution	1.5.2004	To date	7 years	•				•[34]		•	
Obscene Publications Act 1959[35]												
2	Having an obscene article	29.8.1959	To date	3 years	•							
2	Having an obscene article for publication for gain	31.8.1964[36]	To date	3 years	•							
Mental Health Act 1959[37]												
128	Intercourse with a mentally disordered patient	1.11.1960	30.4.2004	2 years	•	•	•		•		•	
Indecency with Children Act 1960[38]												
1	Indecency with a child	2.7.1960 1.10.1997[39] 11.1.2001[40]	30.9.1997 10.1.2001 30.4.2004	2 years where C under 14 10 years where C under 14 10 years where C under 16	•	•	•		•		•	
Sexual Offences Act 1967[41]												
4	Procuring an act of buggery	27.7.1967	30.4.2004	2 years	•	•			•		•	

(continued)

S.	OFFENCE	FROM	UNTIL	MAXIMUM SENTENCE	EXTENDED TERM OF IMPRISONMENT Section 37 Criminal Justice Act 1967 [Offences committed on or after 21 July 1967– 30 September 1992]	EXTENDED LICENCE Sexual offences for the purposes of s 86 Powers of Criminal Courts (Sentencing) Act 2000 [Offences committed before 30 September 1998]	LONGER THAN COMMENSURATE SENTENCE/ EXTENDED SENTENCE Specified sexual offences for the purposes of s 80 and s 85 Powers of Criminal Courts (Sentencing) Act 2000 [Offences committed before 4 April 2005]	AUTOMATIC LIFE SENTENCE Specified serious offences for purposes of s 109 Powers of Criminal Courts (Sentencing) Act 2000 [Offences committed on or after 30 September 1998 – 3 April 2005]	IMPRISONMENT FOR PUBLIC PROTECTION [IPP] EXTENDED SENTENCES FOR PUBLIC PROTECTION [EPP]/LIFE SENTENCE Specified sexual offences for purposes of Schedule 15 CJA 2003 [Offences Committed on or after 4 April 2005 – 3 December 2012	IPP/EPP/ LIFE SENTENCE Specified sexual offences for purposes of Schedule 15A CJA 2003 [inserted by CJIA 2008 applicable 14 July 2008 – 3 December 2012]	EXTENDED DETERMINATE SENTENCE [EDS]/LIFE SENTENCE Specified sexual offences for the purposes of Schedule 15 CJA 2003 (as amended by LASPOA 2012) [Offences committed on or after 3 December 2012 to date]	LIFE SENTENCE FOR SECOND LISTED OFFENCE Listed (sexual) offences for the purposes of Schedule 15B CJA 2003 (as amended by LASPOA 2012) [Offences committed on or after 3 December 2012 to date]
5	Living on the earnings of male prostitution	27.7.1967	30.4.2004	7 years	•	•			•		•	
Theft Act 1968												
9	Burglary with intent to rape	1.1.1969	30.4.2004	14 years	•		•		•		•	
Criminal Law Act 1977												
54[42]	Inciting a girl under 16 to commit incest	8.9.1977	30.4.2004	2 years	•	•	•		•		•	
Protection of Children Act 1978[43]												
1	Taking indecent photographs of a child	20.8.1978 11.1.2001[44]	10.1.2001 To date	3 years 10 years	•	•	•		•		•	•

Criminal Justice Act 1988[45]												
160	Possession of indecent photographs of a child	29.9.1988 11.1.2001[46]	10.1.2001 To date	Summary only max 6 months 5 years					•		•	
Sexual Offences (Amendment) Act 2000[47]												
3	Abuse of a position of trust	8.1.2001	30.4.2004	5 years		•	•					
Sexual Offences Act 2003[48, 49]												
1	Rape	1.5.2004	To date	Life		•	•	•	•	•	•	•
2	Assault by penetration	1.5.2004	To date	Life		•	•	•	•	•	•	•
3	Sexual assault	1.5.2004	To date	10 years					•		•	
4	Causing a person to engage in sexual activity without consent	1.5.2004 To date		Life if involves penetration otherwise 10 years		•	•	•	•	•		•
5	Rape of a child under 13	1.5.2004	To date	Life		•	•	•	•	•	•	•
6	Assault of a child under 13 by penetration	1.5.2004	To date	Life					•	•	•	•
7	Sexual assault of a child under 13	1.5.2004	To date	14 years					•		•	•
8	Causing or inciting a child under 13 to engage in sexual activity	1.5.2004	To date	Life if involves penetration otherwise 14 years		•	•	•	•	•	•	•

(continued)

S.	OFFENCE	FROM	UNTIL	MAXIMUM SENTENCE	EXTENDED TERM OF IMPRISONMENT Section 37 Criminal Justice Act 1967 [Offences committed on or after 21 July 1967– 30 September 1992]	EXTENDED LICENCE Sexual offences for the purposes of s 86 Powers of Criminal Courts (Sentencing) Act 2000 [Offences committed before 30 September 1998]	LONGER THAN COMMENSURATE SENTENCE/ EXTENDED SENTENCE Specified sexual offences for the purposes of s 80 and s 85 Powers of Criminal Courts (Sentencing) Act 2000 [Offences committed before 4 April 2005]	AUTOMATIC LIFE SENTENCE Specified serious offences for purposes of s 109 Powers of Criminal Courts (Sentencing) Act 2000 [Offences committed on or after 30 September 1998 – 3 April 2005]	IMPRISONMENT FOR PUBLIC PROTECTION [IPP] EXTENDED SENTENCES FOR PUBLIC PROTECTION [EPP]/LIFE SENTENCE Specified sexual offences for purposes of Schedule 15 CJA 2003 [Offences Committed on or after 4 April 2005 – 3 December 2012	IPP/EPP/ LIFE SENTENCE Specified sexual offences for purposes of Schedule 15A CJA 2003 [inserted by CJIA 2008 applicable 14 July 2008 – 3 December 2012]	EXTENDED DETERMINATE SENTENCE [EDS]/LIFE SENTENCE Specified sexual offences for the purposes of Schedule 15 CJA 2003 (as amended by LASPOA 2012) [Offences committed on or after 3 December 2012 to date]	LIFE SENTENCE FOR SECOND LISTED OFFENCE Listed (sexual) offences for the purposes of Schedule 15B CJA 2003 (as amended by LASPOA 2012) [Offences committed on or after 3 December 2012 to date]
9	Sexual activity with a child	1.5.2004	To date	14 years or 5 years if D under 18					•		•	•
10	Causing or inciting a child to engage in sexual activity	1.5.2004	To date	14 years or 5 years if D under 18					•		•	•
11	Engaging in sexual activity in the presence of a child	1.5.2004	To date	10 years or 5 years if D under 18 [s. 13]					• [50]		• [51]	• [52]
12	Causing a child to watch a sexual act	1.5.2004	To date	10 years or 5 years if D under 18 [s. 13]					• [53]		• [54]	• [55]

14	Arranging or facilitating the commission of a child sex offence			14 years					•		•	•
15	Meeting a child following sexual grooming	1.5.2004	To date	10 years					•		•	•
16	Abuse of trust: sexual activity with a child	1.5.2004	To date	5 years					•		•	
17	Abuse of trust: causing or inciting a child to engage in sexual activity	1.5.2004	To date	5 years					•		•	
18	Abuse of trust: sexual activity in the presence of a child	1.5.2004	To date	5 years					•		•	
19	Abuse of position of trust: causing a child to watch a sexual act	1.5.2004	To date	5 years					•		•	
25	Sexual activity with a child family member	1.5.2004	To date	14 years where D over 18 otherwise 5 years					•		•	where D 18 or over
26	Inciting a child family member to engage in sexual activity	1.5.2004	To date	14 years where D over 18 otherwise 5 years					•		•	where D 18 or over

(continued)

S.	OFFENCE	FROM	UNTIL	MAXIMUM SENTENCE	EXTENDED TERM OF IMPRISONMENT Section 37 Criminal Justice Act 1967 [Offences committed on or after 21 July 1967– 30 September 1992]	EXTENDED LICENCE Sexual offences for the purposes of s 86 Powers of Criminal Courts (Sentencing) Act 2000 [Offences committed before 30 September 1998]	LONGER THAN COMMENSURATE SENTENCE/ EXTENDED SENTENCE Specified sexual offences for the purposes of s 80 and s 85 Powers of Criminal Courts (Sentencing) Act 2000 [Offences committed before 4 April 2005]	AUTOMATIC LIFE SENTENCE Specified serious offences for purposes of s 109 Powers of Criminal Courts (Sentencing) Act 2000 [Offences committed on or after 30 September 1998 – 3 April 2005]	IMPRISONMENT FOR PUBLIC PROTECTION [IPP] EXTENDED SENTENCES FOR PUBLIC PROTECTION [EPP]/LIFE SENTENCE Specified sexual offences for purposes of Schedule 15 CJA 2003 [Offences Committed on or after 4 April 2005 – 3 December 2012	IPP/EPP/ LIFE SENTENCE Specified sexual offences for purposes of Schedule 15A CJA 2003 [inserted by CJIA 2008 applicable 14 July 2008 – 3 December 2012]	EXTENDED DETERMINATE SENTENCE [EDS]/LIFE SENTENCE Specified sexual offences for the purposes of Schedule 15 CJA 2003 (as amended by LASPOA 2012) [Offences committed on or after 3 December 2012 to date]	LIFE SENTENCE FOR SECOND LISTED OFFENCE Listed (sexual) offences for the purposes of Schedule 15B CJA 2003 (as amended by LASPOA 2012) [Offences committed on or after 3 December 2012 to date]
30	Sexual activity with a person with a mental disorder impeding choice	1.5.2004	To date	Life if involves penetration otherwise 14 years		•	•	•	•	•	•	where D liable to life
31	Causing or inciting a person with a mental disorder impeding choice to engage in sexual activity	1.5.2004	To date	Life if involves penetration otherwise 14 years		•	•	•	•	•	•	where D liable to life
32	Engaging in sexual activity in the presence of a person with a mental disorder impeding choice	1.5.2004	To date	10 years					•		•	

33	Causing a person with a mental disorder impeding choice, to watch a sexual act	1.5.2004	To date	10 years					•		•	
34	Inducement, threat or deception to procure sexual activity with a person with a mental disorder	1.5.2004	To date	Life if involves penetration otherwise 14 years					•	•	•	where D liable to life
35	Causing a person with a mental disorder to engage in, or agree to engage in, sexual activity by inducement, threat or deception	1.5.2004	To date	Life if involves penetration otherwise 14 years					•	•	•	where D liable to life
36	Engaging in sexual activity in the presence, secured by inducement, threat or deception, of a person with a mental disorder	1.5.2004	To date	10 years					•		•	
37	Causing a person with a mental disorder to watch a sexual act by inducement, threat or deception	1.5.2004	To date	10 years					•		•	

(*continued*)

S.	OFFENCE	FROM	UNTIL	MAXIMUM SENTENCE	EXTENDED TERM OF IMPRISONMENT Section 37 Criminal Justice Act 1967 [Offences committed on or after 21 July 1967– 30 September 1992]	EXTENDED LICENCE Sexual offences for the purposes of s 86 Powers of Criminal Courts (Sentencing) Act 2000 [Offences committed before 30 September 1998]	LONGER THAN COMMENSURATE SENTENCE/ EXTENDED SENTENCE Specified sexual offences for the purposes of s 80 and s 85 Powers of Criminal Courts (Sentencing) Act 2000 [Offences committed before 4 April 2005]	AUTOMATIC LIFE SENTENCE Specified serious offences for purposes of s 109 Powers of Criminal Courts (Sentencing) Act 2000 [Offences committed on or after 30 September 1998 – 3 April 2005]	IMPRISONMENT FOR PUBLIC PROTECTION [IPP] EXTENDED SENTENCES FOR PUBLIC PROTECTION [EPP]/LIFE SENTENCE Specified sexual offences for purposes of Schedule 15 CJA 2003 [Offences Committed on or after 4 April 2005 – 3 December 2012	IPP/EPP/ LIFE SENTENCE Specified sexual offences for purposes of Schedule 15A CJA 2003 [inserted by CJIA 2008 applicable 14 July 2008 – 3 December 2012]	EXTENDED DETERMINATE SENTENCE [EDS]/LIFE SENTENCE Specified sexual offences for the purposes of Schedule 15 CJA 2003 (as amended by LASPOA 2012) [Offences committed on or after 3 December 2012 to date]	LIFE SENTENCE FOR SECOND LISTED OFFENCE Listed (sexual) offences for the purposes of Schedule 15B CJA 2003 (as amended by LASPOA 2012) [Offences committed on or after 3 December 2012 to date]
38	Care workers: sexual activity with a person with a mental disorder	1.5.2004	To date	14 years if involves penetration otherwise 10 years					•		•	
39	Care workers: causing or inciting sexual activity	1.5.2004	To date	14 years if involves penetration otherwise 10 years					•		•	
40	Care workers: sexual activity in the presence of a person with a mental disorder	1.5.2004	To date	7 years					•		•	

41	Care workers: causing a person with a mental disorder to watch a sexual act	1.5.2004	To date	7 years					•		•	
47	Paying for sexual services of a child	1.5.2004	To date	Life where penetration and C under 13 14 years where penetration and C 13-16 14 years where C under 16 and no penetration Otherwise 7 years					•	• Where D liable to life	•	• Where C under 16
48	Causing or inciting child prostitution of pornography	1.5.2004	To date	14 years					•		•	•
49	Controlling child prostitution/ pornography	1.5.2004	To date	14 years					•		•	•
50	Arranging/ facilitating child prostitution or pornography	1.5.2004	To date	14 years					•		•	•
52	Causing or inciting prostitution for gain	1.5.2004	To date	7 years					•		•	

(*continued*)

S.	OFFENCE	FROM	UNTIL	MAXIMUM SENTENCE	EXTENDED TERM OF IMPRISONMENT Section 37 Criminal Justice Act 1967 [Offences committed on or after 21 July 1967– 30 September 1992]	EXTENDED LICENCE Sexual offences for the purposes of s 86 Powers of Criminal Courts (Sentencing) Act 2000 [Offences committed before 30 September 1998]	LONGER THAN COMMENSURATE SENTENCE/ EXTENDED SENTENCE Specified sexual offences for the purposes of s 80 and s 85 Powers of Criminal Courts (Sentencing) Act 2000 [Offences committed before 4 April 2005]	AUTOMATIC LIFE SENTENCE Specified serious offences for purposes of s 109 Powers of Criminal Courts (Sentencing) Act 2000 [Offences committed on or after 30 September 1998 – 3 April 2005]	IMPRISONMENT FOR PUBLIC PROTECTION [IPP] EXTENDED SENTENCES FOR PUBLIC PROTECTION [EPP]/LIFE SENTENCE Specified sexual offences for purposes of Schedule 15 CJA 2003 [Offences Committed on or after 4 April 2005 – 3 December 2012	IPP/EPP/ LIFE SENTENCE Specified sexual offences for purposes of Schedule 15A CJA 2003 [inserted by CJIA 2008 applicable 14 July 2008 – 3 December 2012]	EXTENDED DETERMINATE SENTENCE [EDS]/LIFE SENTENCE Specified sexual offences for the purposes of Schedule 15 CJA 2003 (as amended by LASPOA 2012) [Offences committed on or after 3 December 2012 to date]	LIFE SENTENCE FOR SECOND LISTED OFFENCE Listed (sexual) offences for the purposes of Schedule 15B CJA 2003 (as amended by LASPOA 2012) [Offences committed on or after 3 December 2012 to date]
53	Controlling prostitution for gain	1.5.2004	To date	7 years					•		•	
57	Trafficking into the UK for sexual exploitation	1.5.2004	05.04.12	14 years					•		•	
58	Trafficking within the UK for sexual exploitation	1.5.2004	5.4.2012	14 years					•		•	
59	Trafficking out of the UK for sexual exploitation	1.5.2004	5.4.2012	14 years					•		•	
59A	Trafficking people for sexual exploitation	6.4.2013[56]	To date	14 years							•[57]	

61	Administering a substance with intent	1.5.2004	To date	10 years					•		•	
62	Committing an offence with intent to commit a sexual offence	1.5.2004	To date	Life is kidnapping or false imprisonment otherwise 10 years					•	• Where D liable to life	•	where D liable to life
63	Trespass with intent to commit a sexual offence	1.5.2004	To date	10 years					•	•	•	
64	Sex with an adult relative: penetration	1.5.2004	To date	2 years					•	•	•	
65	Sex with an adult relative: consenting to penetration	1.5.2004	To date	2 years					•	•	•	
66	Indecent exposure	1.5.2004	To date	2 years					•	•	•	
67	Voyeurism	1.5.2004	To date	2 years					•	•	•	
69	Intercourse with an animal	1.5.2004	To date	2 years					•	•	•	
Coroners and Justice Act 2009												
62	Possession of Prohibited images of children	6.4.2010	To date	3 years								

Notes

[1] Imposition of an extended term for persistent offenders, applies to offences punishable with imprisonment for a term of two years or more.

[2] As amended by section 28 Powers of Criminal Courts Act 1973.

[3] Section 37 commenced on 21 July 1967 and repealed on 30 September 1992 by the Criminal Justice Act 1991.

[4] Section 86 implemented on 1 October 1992. Section 86 creates a power to extend the licence period.

[5] Power to pass a sentence 'for such longer term not exceeding the maximum as is necessary to protect the public from serious harm from the offender'.

[6] Power to extend sexual offender's licence for up to ten years only for offences committed on or after 30 September 1998 and not later than 3 April 2005.

[7] Includes attempted offences, conspiracy to commit such offences and inciting the commission of such offences other than offences under the 2003 Act which applies to attempted offences.

[8] Automatic life for a second serious offence. See Act for applicability of offences committed in other jurisdictions.

[9] Includes attempted offences under the 2003 Act.

[10] Sections 225 and 226 CJA 2003.

[11] Sections 227 and 228 CJA 2003.

[12] Section 225 CJA 2003.

[13] CJA 2003 introduced provisions in relation to 'dangerous offenders' and provided for Indeterminate Sentences of Imprisonment for Public Protection (IPP) and Extended Sentences for Public Protection [EPP].

[14] See footnote 10.

[15] See footnote 11.

[16] Sections 13 to 18 of the Criminal Justice and Immigration Act 2008 amended CJA 2003 by introducing a new seriousness threshold for the dangerousness provisions; introducing an exception to the seriousness threshold for adult offenders; removing the rebuttable presumption of risk; allowing the courts increased discretion and changing the structure of extended sentences.

[17] Sections 226A and 226B CJA 2003 (as inserted by section 124 of the 2012 Act).

[18] Section 225, life sentence for 'serious offences' applies to offences which are specified offences punishable in the case of a person over 18 years (apart from section 224A Life sentence for second listed offence) with imprisonment for life or imprisonment for a determinate period of ten years of more (section 224(2)).

[19] LASPOA 2012 abolished IPP (Imprisonment for Public Protection) and EPP (Extended Sentences for Public Protection) and replaced with a new Extended Determinate Sentence (EDS).

[20] Section 224A CJA 2003.

[21] Includes attempt/conspiracy/incitement or aiding, abetting, counseling, or procuring a listed offence.

[22] Sexual Offences Act 1956 came into force on 1 January 1957.

[23] Increased by section 3(2) Sexual Offences Act 1985.

[24] Maximum sentence academic as offences under section 6 are time barred from prosecution 12 months after the offence.

[25] Repealed by the Mental Health Act 1959 which came into force on 1 November 1960.

[26] Repealed by the Mental Health Act 1959 which came into force on 1 November 1960.

[27] Applies to offences under section 12 other than those which would not be an offence but for section 2 Sexual Offences Act 1967.

[28] Criminal Justice and Public Order Act section 145 came into force on 3 November 1994 reducing the age of consent to 18; amending the statutory definition; converting non-consensual buggery of a man or woman to rape, and revising the penalties for buggery and indecency between men. The age of consent was subsequently reduced to 16 on 8 January 2001 by the Sexual Offences (Amendment) Act 2000.

[29] Offence is time barred 12 months after commission.

30 Applies to offences under section 13 other than those which would not be an offence but for section 2 Sexual Offences Act 1967.
31 Indecency with Children Act 1960 increased maximum to five years where C under 13 and age stated in indictment.
32 Section 3(3) Sexual Offences Act 1985 increased maximum sentence to ten years.
33 Inserted into the 1956 Act by the Sexual Offences Act 2003.
34 Applies to offence under section 33, then to offence under amended section 33A from 1 May 2004.
35 Obscene Publications Act 1959 came into force on 29 August 1959.
36 Wording amended by the Obscene Publications Act 1964, section 1(1).
37 Mental Health Act 1959 came into force on 1 November 1960.
38 Indecency with Children Act came into force on 2 July 1960.
39 Increased by section 52 Crime (Sentences) Act 1997.
40 Amended by section 41 Criminal Justice and Court Services Act 2000.
41 Sexual Offences Act 1967 came into force on 27 July 1967.
42 Section 54 came into force on 8 September 1977 [SI 1977/1365].
43 Protection of Children Act 1978 came into force on 20 August 1978.
44 Increased by section 41 Criminal Justice and Court Services Act 2000.
45 Criminal Justice Act 1988 came into force on 29 September 1988.
46 Increased by section 41 Criminal Justice and Court Services Act 2000.
47 Sexual Offences (Amendment) Act 2000 came into force on 8 January 2001.
48 Sexual Offences Act 2003 came into force on 1 May 2004.
49 Only applies to offences under the 2003 Act when committed between 1.5.2004 and 1.4.2005.
50 Applies to offences under section 13.
51 Applies to offences under section 13.
52 Does not apply to offences under section 13.
53 Applies to offences under section 13.
54 Applies to offences under section 13.
55 Does not apply to offences under section 13.
56 Section 59A inserted by section 109 Protection of Freedoms Act 2012 which repealed sections 57, 58 and 59 SOA 2003 on 6 April 2013.
57 Inserted from 6 April 2004.
58 Section 62 came into force on 6 April 2010 [SI 2010/816].

13

SPECIAL MEASURES

A. WHO IS ELIGIBLE FOR SPECIAL MEASURES?

There are two categories of witness eligible for special measures:[1] **13.01**

(1) Witnesses who are eligible for assistance on grounds of age or incapacity.[2]
(2) Witnesses eligible for assistance on the ground of fear or distress about testifying.[3]

1. Witnesses Eligible for Assistance on the Grounds of Age or Incapacity

These witnesses fall into three subcategories: **13.02**

(a) Witnesses under 18 *at the time of the hearing.*[4]
(b) Witnesses under 18 *at the time of the making of their video-recorded interview.*[5]
(c) Witnesses whose evidence the court considers is likely to be *diminished in quality*[6] by reason of the witness suffering from a mental disorder,[7] significant impairment of intelligence and social functioning;[8] or where the witness has a physical disability or disorder.[9]

Quality of Evidence

References to the quality of a witness's evidence are to its quality in terms of completeness, coherence and accuracy; and for this purpose 'coherence' refers to a witness's ability in giving evidence to give answers which address the questions put to the witness and can be understood both individually and collectively.[10] **13.03**

---

1 This chapter is limited to special measures issues relevant to sexual offences.
2 Youth Justice and Criminal Evidence Act (YJCEA) 1999 (as amended by Coroners and Justice Act (CAJA) 2009), s 16.
3 YJCEA 1999, s 17.
4 YJCEA 1999, s 16(1)(a).
5 YJCEA 1999, s 22(1)(a).
6 YJCEA 1999, s 16(1)(b).
7 Within the meaning of the MHA 1983 (YJCEA 1999, s 16(2)(a)(i)).
8 YJCEA 1999, s 16(2)(a)(ii).
9 YJCEA 1999, s 16(2)(b).
10 YJCEA 1999, s 16(5).

Witnesses Aged under 18 and 'Qualifying' Witnesses

13.04 Witnesses under 18 at the time of the court's determination of eligibility for special measures,[11] or witnesses who were under 18 at the time of the making of their video-recorded interview (known as 'qualifying witnesses')[12] are automatically eligible for special measures.[13]

13.05 The 'Primary Rule'[14] in the case of a child or qualifying witness is that the court must give a special measures direction which:

(a) provides for any video-recorded interview to be admitted (YJCEA 1999, s 27);[15]
(b) for any other evidence to be given by means of a live link (YJCEA 1999, s 24).[16]

13.06 These special measures are presumed to be likely to maximize, so far as practicable, the quality of the witness's evidence.[17]

13.07 The primary rule can be displaced if the special measures are unavailable at the court in question,[18] it is not in the interests of justice to admit the recording[19] or the court is satisfied that these measures would not maximize the quality of the witness's evidence, for example because another type of special measure would also have that effect.[20]

13.08 The child or qualifying witness may also ask the court to disapply the primary rule.[21] In acceding to the request the court must be satisfied that the quality of the witness's evidence would not be diminished, taking into account (a) the age and maturity of the witness; (b) the ability of the witness to understand the consequences of giving evidence using other (or no) special measures; (c) the relationship between the witness and the accused; (d) the witness's social and cultural background and ethnic origins; and (e) the nature and alleged circumstances of the offence to which the proceedings relate.[22]

13.09 If the court disapplies the primary rule it must make an order for the use of screens, pursuant to the YJCEA 1999, s 23.[23] However, this provision may also be displaced if, again, the witness informs the court that they do not wish to give evidence using a screen and the court is satisfied that the quality of evidence would not be diminished if a screen is not used.[24]

13.10 The court may also refuse to order screens to be used on the basis that it would not be likely to maximize the quality of the evidence, for example because another type of special measure would also have that effect.[25]

13.11 There are therefore three stages to the court's consideration of appropriate special measures in the case of a witness who is under 18 or a qualifying witness:

(1) Consideration of the use of video recording and live link. In the absence of a request from the witness, the court should compare other available special measures with the efficacy of using video recording and live link in maximizing the quality of the witness's evidence.
(2) If the court disapplies the primary rule, it should conduct a similar comparison exercise using screens as the benchmark.
(3) If, having conducted the comparison, the court decides that a particular special measure (or combination, or none) will be more effective than screens at maximizing the quality of evidence, the court should order that those special measures (or none) to be used.

[11] YJCEA 1999, ss 16(3); 19(2).
[12] YJCEA 1999, s 22(1)(a).
[13] YJCEA 1999, ss 21, 22.
[14] YJCEA 1999, s 21(3).
[15] YJCEA 1999, s 21(3)(a).
[16] YJCEA 1999, s 21(3)(b).
[17] YJCEA 1999, s 21(2).
[18] YJCEA 1999, s 21(4)(a).
[19] YJCEA 1999, ss 21(4)(b); 27(2).
[20] YJCEA 1999, s 21(4)(c).
[21] YJCEA 1999, s 21(4)(ba).
[22] YJCEA 1999, s 21(4C).
[23] YJCEA 1999, s 21(4A).
[24] YJCEA 1999, s 21(4B)(a).
[25] YJCEA 1999, s 21(4B)(b).

2. Witnesses Eligible for Assistance on the Ground of Fear or Distress about Testifying

The court must be satisfied that (a) the complainant is in fear or distress, and (b) that this fear or distress would diminish the quality of evidence. 13.12

Quality of Evidence

Quality of evidence refers to its quality in terms of completeness, coherence and accuracy.[26] 13.13

Fear or Distress

In assessing whether the court is satisfied that the quality of evidence given by the witness is likely to be diminished by reason of fear or distress on the part of the witness in connection with testifying in the proceedings,[27] the court must take into account: (a) the nature and alleged circumstances of the offence; (b) the age of the witness; (c) the social, cultural and ethnic origins of the witness (where relevant); (d) the domestic and employment circumstances of the witness (where relevant); (e) any religious or political beliefs of the witness; (f) any behaviour of the accused (or their family or associates), co-accused (actual or potential) or other witnesses (actual or potential) in the proceedings towards the witness.[28] 13.14

Further, the court must take into account any views expressed by the witness.[29]

Fear or Distress in Cases of Sexual Offences

In cases of sexual offences where the complainant is to be a witness, that complainant is automatically eligible for special measures under the YJCEA, s 17(4) unless that witness informs the court that they do not wish to avail themselves of such measures. 13.15

In Crown Court[30] trials of sexual offences, where the complainant is over 18 at the time of the hearing,[31] the complainant may request video-recorded evidence-in-chief as the relevant special measure.[32] A direction that video-recorded evidence-in-chief pursuant to the YJCEA, s 27 must then be made,[33] unless it would not be likely to maximize the quality of the complainant's evidence or it would not be in the interests of justice to admit it.[34] 13.16

B. APPLYING FOR SPECIAL MEASURES

Applications for special measures may be made by any party to the proceedings or may be raised by the court of its own motion.[35] The content of an application for a special measures direction is prescribed by the Criminal Procedure Rules.[36] A pro forma is available on the Ministry of Justice website (<http://www.justice.gov.uk/courts/procedure-rules/criminal/formspage>). 13.17

The application must be filed with the court and served on every other party to the proceedings. The application must made as soon as reasonably practicable, and in any event no later than 28 days after the defendant pleads not guilty in a magistrates' court or 14 days after of a not guilty plea in the Crown Court.[37] 13.18

---

[26] YJCEA 1999, s 16(5).
[27] YJCEA 1999, s 17(1).
[28] YJCEA 1999, s 17(2).
[29] YJCEA 1999, s 17(3).
[30] YJCEA 1999, s 22A(2).
[31] YJCEA 1999, s 22A(3).
[32] YJCEA 1999, s 22A(4).
[33] YJCEA 1999, s 22A(7).
[34] YJCEA 1999, ss 22A(8); 27(2).
[35] YJCEA 1999, s 19(1).
[36] CPR 2013, r 29.10.
[37] CPR 2013, r 29.3.

13.19 Objections must be made within 14 days of the application in writing, stating whether eligibility or likelihood to improve the quality of evidence is contested.[38]

13.20 Where no objection is received, the application may be dealt with administratively.[39] However, the court must announce, at a hearing in public before the witness gives evidence, the reasons for a decision to either make, vary, discharge or refuse to make an order.[40]

13.21 Applications for extension of the application period may be made in writing, and be accompanied by a statement setting out the reasons why the applicant was unable to make the application within that period.[41] Alternatively, late applications may be made orally at trial;[42] or the court may of its own motion raise the issue.[43] If a party makes an oral application, the reasons for this late application must be stated.[44]

Youths or Qualifying Witnesses

13.22 There is additional content specific to special measures applications for youths and qualifying witnesses. A party seeking to introduce the evidence of such a witness must, as soon as reasonably practicable, (a) notify the court that the witness is eligible for assistance; (b) provide the court with any information that the court may need to assess the witness's views, if the witness does not want the primary rule to apply; and (c) file with the court and serve on any other party any video-recorded evidence.[45]

C. WHAT ARE THE SPECIAL MEASURES PROVISIONS IN FORCE?

13.23 Table 13.1 sets out the special measures provisions directions available as of 1.8.2013.

Table 13.1 Special Measures Provisions

Special Measure (YJCEA 1999)	Section 16 Witnesses (children and vulnerable adults)	Section 17 Witnesses (intimidated/fear or distress)	Qualification to Applicability
s 23 Screening the witness from the accused	Yes	Yes	The screen must not prevent the witness from being able to see, and to be seen by, (a) the judge or justices and the jury; (b) at least one of the legal representatives acting for each party in the proceedings; (c) any interpreter or other person appointed to assist the witness.
s 24 Giving evidence via live link	Yes	Yes	The witness may be supported in the live-link room, and the judge must have the regard to the wishes of the witness as to who the supporter is.

[38] CPR 2013, r 29.13.
[39] CPR 2013, r 29.8.
[40] CPR 2013, r 29.4(2).
[41] CPR 2013, r 29.5.
[42] CPR 2013, r 29.5(1)(b).
[43] CPR 2013, r 29.1(a).
[44] CPR 2013, r 29.5(2).
[45] CPR 2013, r 29.9.

s 25 Giving evidence in private	Yes	Yes	This provision only applies to: (a) proceedings for sexual offences under SOA 2003, Part 1; or (b) where there are reasonable grounds for believing that there has been or will be witness intimidation by someone other than the accused. The persons to be excluded must be specified. This may not include: (a) the accused; (b) legal representatives acting in the proceedings; (c) any interpreter or other person appointed to assist the witness.
s 26 Removing wigs and gowns	Yes	Yes	This provision has no applicability to the magistrates' court because wigs and gowns are not worn.
s 27 Video recorded evidence-in-chief	Yes	Yes	The presumption that this is the most appropriate measure for both adult complainants and child witnesses can be displaced by the court either: (a) acceding to the witness's request to use a different measure; or (b) determining that playing the video recording would not maximize the quality of the evidence.
s 28 Video-recorded cross-examination re-examination	No	No	This provision is not yet in force, save for piloted areas.
s 29 Examination through an intermediary	Yes	No	(a) The judge or justices, legal representatives and the jury should be able to hear the examination of the witness. (b) The judge or justices and legal representatives should be able to communicate with the intermediary.
s 30 Aids to communication	Yes	No	

D. WHAT SPECIAL MEASURES APPLY TO DEFENDANTS?

Defendants have only limited access to two special measures,[46] namely live link and the use of an intermediary. **13.24**

Live Link for Defendants under 18

Defendants who are under 18 when the special measures application is made are eligible to give evidence over a live link if the court is satisfied that (a) their ability to participate in the proceedings as a witness is compromised by their level of intellectual ability or social functioning; and (b) that the use of a live link would enable them to participate more effectively as a witness, whether by improving the quality of their evidence or otherwise.[47] **13.25**

---

[46] YJCEA 1999, ss 16(1), 17(1), 19(1).

[47] YCJEA 1999, s 33A(4).

Live Link for Defendants over 18

13.26 Defendants who are over 18 at the time of application are eligible to give evidence over a live link if (a) they suffer from a mental disorder[48] or otherwise have a significant impairment of intelligence or social function; (b) they therefore are unable to participate effectively in the proceedings as a witness giving oral evidence in court; and (c) the live link would enable the defendant to participate more effectively in the proceedings as a witness, whether by improving the quality of his evidence or otherwise.[49]

Intermediaries

13.27 The CAJA 2009 inserted new ss 33BA–BB into the YJCEA 1999.[50] The effect of s 33BA is that a defendant will be eligible to give evidence with the assistance of an intermediary if the court is satisfied that the same conditions set out earlier for live links are met,[51] and that such a direction is necessary to ensure that the accused has a fair trial.[52] However, these provisions will only come into force on a date yet to be appointed. A defendant must therefore rely upon the court exercising its inherent power to take such steps as are necessary to enable a defendant to participate effectively in a trial by directing the use of an intermediary.[53]

Applying for a Defendant's Evidence Direction

13.28 The application for a defendant's evidence direction must: (a) explain how the proposed direction meets the conditions prescribed by the YJCEA 1999; and (b) in a case in which the applicant proposes that the defendant give evidence by live link (i) identify a person to accompany the defendant while the defendant gives evidence, and (ii) explain why that person is appropriate.[54]

13.29 The application must be filed with the court and served on every other party to the proceedings. The application must made as soon as reasonably practicable, and in any event no later than 28 days after the defendant pleads not guilty in a magistrates' court or 14 days after a not guilty plea in the Crown Court.[55]

13.30 Objections must be made within 14 days of the service of the application.[56]

13.31 Where no objection is received, the application may be dealt with administratively.[57] However, the court must announce, at a hearing in public before the defendant gives evidence, the reasons for a decision to either make, vary, discharge or refuse to make an order.[58]

---

48 Within the meaning of the MHA 1983.
49 YJCEA 1999, s 33A(5).
50 CAJA 2009, s 104.
51 YJCEA 1999, s 33BA(5), (6).
52 YJCEA 1999, s 33BA(2).
53 *C v Sevenoaks Youth Court* [2009] EWHC 3088 (Admin).
54 CPR 2013, r 29.15.
55 CPR 2013, r 29.3.
56 CPR 2013, r 29.17.
57 CPR 2013, r 29.14.
58 CPR 2013, r 29.4.

14

NOTIFICATION REQUIREMENTS

Notification requirements have applied since 1.9.1997, falling within the ambit of Part 1 of the SOA 1997.[1] Notification is now governed by Part 2 of the SOA 2003,[2] which came into force on 1.5.2004. The provisions have retrospective application[3] to those who were previously subject to a notification requirement under the 1997 Act. It is important to note therefore that these requirements are now the same for any offence committed after 1.9.1997. Notification requirements do not apply to those individuals who were convicted of Sch 3 offences before 1.9.1997. **14.01**

A. APPLICABILITY

Notification requirements apply to those who are either convicted of an offence specified in Sch 3 to the 2003 Act;[4] found not guilty of such an offence by reason of insanity;[5] are found to be under a disability and to have done the act charged against them in respect of such an offence;[6] or are cautioned in respect of such an offence.[7] **14.02**

The notification requirements also apply where any of the above conditions are found to be met in a foreign jurisdiction and the chief police officer for the area in which the offender lives or is intending to live applies to the magistrates' court for a notification order.[8] **14.03**

---

1 Hereafter 'the 1997 Act'.
2 Hereafter 'the 2003 Act'.
3 SOA 2003, s 81.
4 SOA 2003, s 80(1)(a); see Tables 14.1–14.4.
5 SOA 2003, s 80(1)(b).
6 SOA 2003, s 80(1)(c).
7 SOA 2003, s 80(1)(d).
8 SOA 2003, s 97.

B. ROLE OF THE COURT

14.04 A notification requirement is not a 'penalty'.[9] It is therefore unnecessary, except in the case of a notification order following conviction abroad, for the court to order notification. Instead, the requirement is automatic. The role of the court is only to state in open court that one of the eligibility criteria in s 80(1) has been satisfied[10] and to certify that fact.[11]

14.05 A defendant having been required to notify upon conviction, the judge should state at the sentencing hearing how long the defendant will be subject to the requirements for. If notification is indefinite, that is the term which should be used, not 'for life'; it is possible for an offender to apply to be removed from the Sex Offender Register.[12]

14.06 Where the period will be indeterminate the fact of the defendant's youth may found a reason for cessation of the notification requirement if full rehabilitation can be argued.

C. YOUNG DEFENDANTS

14.07 The court has a further discretionary role with regard to defendants under 18 at the date of conviction or finding, namely that it may direct that the notification obligation transfers to an individual with parental responsibility for the offender.[13]

14.08 Where a Detention and Training Order has been imposed, the period of actual 'detention and training' (as opposed to the overall sentence which also includes a period of supervision)[14] is equivalent to a 'sentence of imprisonment' for the purposes of calculating the length of a notification requirement.[15]

14.09 The length of any notification requirement for a young defendant is half of that imposed on an adult.[16]

D. INITIAL NOTIFICATION

14.10 Unless a defendant is already subject to a notification requirement,[17] within 3 days of conviction (or the finding), the defendant must notify the police of the following information: (a) the relevant offender's date of birth; (b) his national insurance number; (c) his name on the relevant date and, where he used one or more other names on that date, each of those names; (d) his home address on the relevant date; (e) his name on the date on which notification is given and, where he uses one or more other names on that date, each of those names; (f) his home address on the date on which notification is given; (g) the address of any other premises in the United Kingdom at which, at the time the notification is given, he regularly resides or stays.[18]

14.11 The defendant must also notify the police of any information prescribed by regulations made by the Secretary of State.[19] This includes the defendant's passport details.[20] It also includes details of

---

[9] *Ibbotson v UK* [1999] Crim LR 153.

[10] SOA 2003, s 92(2)(a); Criminal Procedure Rules 2013, r 42.3.

[11] SOA 2003, s 92(2)(b).

[12] *R (on the application of F (by his litigation friend F) and Thompson (FC) (Respondents)) v Secretary of State for the Home Department (Appellant)* [2010] UKSC 17 E.

[13] SOA 2003, s 89.

[14] *R v Slocombe* [2005] EWCA Crim 2297.

[15] SOA 2003, s 131(a).

[16] SOA 2003, s 82(1), (2).

[17] SOA 2003, s 83(2).

[18] SOA 2003, s 83(5).

[19] SOA 2003, s 83(5)(h), s 83(5A).

[20] Sexual Offences Act 2003 (Notification Requirements) (England and Wales) Regulations 2012 (hereafter 'SI 2012/1876'), r 14.

the defendant's bank accounts, credit and debit cards, whether solely or jointly held.[21] Where a defendant resides or stays for at least 12 hours at a household at which a child resides or stays, the defendant must provide: (a) the date on which the residence or stay begins; (b) the address of the relevant household; and (c) the period for which he intends to reside or stay at the address.[22]

E. UPDATING DETAILS

Any changes in name, address, passport details,[23] debit, credit card or bank account details[24] must be notified to the police within 3 days.[25] The defendant must also notify the police when residing or staying (or ceasing to reside or stay) for at least 12 hours at a household at which a child resides or stays. The defendant must provide: (a) the date on which the residence or stay begins; (b) the address of the relevant household; and (c) the period for which he intends to reside or stay at the address.[26] **14.12**

In any event, at least once every 12 months the offender must update the information provided to the police.[27] If the offender's sole or main residence is outside the United Kingdom they must give notification of their address to the police every 7 days.[28] **14.13**

F. METHOD OF NOTIFICATION

A defendant fulfils his notification obligation by attending his prescribed police station and giving an oral notification to any authorized officer at the station.[29] A person who is changing address may give notification at the police station that would be the prescribed police station had the change of address already occurred.[30] **14.14**

G. FAILURE TO NOTIFY

A failure to notify without reasonable excuse is an offence triable either way. It is punishable summarily with a maximum of 6 months' imprisonment or a fine not exceeding the statutory maximum. The maximum sentence on indictment is imprisonment for a term not exceeding 5 years.[31] **14.15**

H. CONDITIONAL DISCHARGES

Anyone conditionally discharged for an offence to which the 2003 Act applies is, by virtue of the express provision of that Act, liable to the notification requirements of that Act for the period of the conditional discharge. **14.16**

A person conditionally discharged before 1.5.2004 (implementation date for the SOA 2003), for an offence to which the 1997 Act applies, is not liable for notification.[32] **14.17**

21 SI 2012/1876, r 12.
22 SI 2012/1876, r 10.
23 SI 2012/1876, r 14.
24 SI 2012/1876, r 13.
25 SOA 2003, s 84.
26 SI 2012/1876, r 11.
27 SOA 2003, s 85(b).
28 SOA 2003, s 85(a); SI 2012/1876, r 11.
29 SOA 2003 s 87(1).
30 SOA 2003, s 87(2).
31 SOA 2003, s 91.
32 *R v Longworth* [2006] UKHL 1.

14.18 A conviction resulting in an absolute discharge[33] or a conditional discharge deemed not to be a conviction[34] under the PCC(S)A 2000, s 12 does not trigger the requirement to notify.[35]

I. REMOVAL OF DETAILS

Offences since Decriminalized

14.19 Anyone convicted of an offence which has since been decriminalized has the right to have his name and details removed from the list of those required to notify. This will include those convicted of some homosexual offences which are no longer offences by virtue of the lowering of the age of consent, first from 21 to 18[36] and then from18 to 16.[37]

Defendants Subject to an Indefinite Notification Requirement

14.20 A defendant who is subject to an indefinite notification period may apply in writing for a determination by the relevant chief officer of police that the notification requirements should cease to apply in their case.[38] The defendant must not be subject to a Sexual Offences Prevention Order.[39]

14.21 The defendant may only apply after the qualifying date. The qualifying date is 15 years after initial notification for a defendant who was over 18 and 8 years for a defendant under 18 at the time of the date of conviction, finding or caution.[40]

14.22 The chief officer of police must determine the application within 6 weeks of acknowledging receipt,[41] taking into account the factors set out in s 91D of the 2003 Act. Any appeal against a determination must be made to the magistrates' court within 21 days of receipt.[42]

14.23 If a defendant's application is unsuccessful the notification requirements will continue without eligibility for further review for a further period of 8 years, rising to a maximum of 15 years dependent upon the chief officer of police's assessment of the risk of sexual harm posed.[43]

J. NOTIFICATION PERIOD[44]

14.24 **Table 14.1 Notification Periods**

Description of relevant offender	Notification period
A person who, in respect of the offence, is or has been sentenced to imprisonment for life, for public protection or for a term of 30 months or more	An indefinite period beginning with the date of conviction or finding
A person who, in respect of the offence or finding, is or has been admitted to a hospital subject to a restriction order	An indefinite period beginning with that date

33 PCC(S)A 2000, s 12(1)(a).
34 PCC(S)A 2000, s 12(1)(b).
35 PCC(S)A 2000, ss 134(1)(a) and 14(1).
36 CJPOA 1994, s 145 commencement date 3.11.1994.
37 SO(A)A 2000, s 1(1) commencement date 8.1.2001.
38 SOA 2003, s 91A.
39 SOA 2003, s 91A(2b).
40 SOA 2003, s 91B(2).
41 SOA 2003, s 91C.
42 SOA 2003, s 91E.
43 SOA 2003, s 91B(3)–(5).
44 SOA 2003, s 82.

Description of relevant offender	Notification period
A person who, in respect of the offence, is or has been sentenced to imprisonment for a term of more than 6 months but less than 30 months	10 years beginning with that date
A person who, in respect of the offence, is or has been sentenced to imprisonment for a term of 6 months or less	7 years beginning with that date
A person who, in respect of the offence or finding, is or has been admitted to a hospital without being subject to a restriction order	7 years beginning with that date
A person within s 80(1)(d) (cautioned in respect of the offence)	2 years beginning with that date
A person in whose case an order for conditional discharge is made in respect of the offence	The period of conditional discharge
A person of any other description	5 years beginning with the date of conviction or finding

K. SEXUAL OFFENCES ACT 2003, SCH 3

1. Offences Subject to Notification Requirements under the Sexual Offences Act 1956

Table 14.2 Offences Subject to Notification Requirements under the Sexual Offences Act 1956 14.25

	Offence	Qualification to applicability of notification requirement *Notification requirements only apply . . .*
s 1	Rape	
s 5	Intercourse with a girl under 13	
s 6	Intercourse with a girl under 16	If the offender is 20 or over
s 10	Incest by a man	If the victim or other party was under 18
s 12	Buggery	(a) If the offender was 20 or over, **and** (b) the victim or other party was under 18
s 13	Indecency between men	(a) If the offender was 20 or over, **and** (b) the victim or other party was under 18
s 14	Indecent assault on a woman	(a) The victim or other party was under 18, **or** (b) the offender, in respect of the offence or finding, is or has been— (i) sentenced to imprisonment for a term of at least 30 months; **or** (ii) admitted to a hospital subject to a restriction order.

	Offence	Qualification to applicability of notification requirement *Notification requirements only apply…*
s 15	Indecent assault on a man	(a) The victim or other party was under 18, **or** (b) the offender, in respect of the offence or finding, is or has been— (i) sentenced to imprisonment for a term of at least 30 months; **or** (ii) admitted to a hospital subject to a restriction order
s 16	Assault with intent to commit buggery	If the victim or other party was under 18
s 28	Causing or encouraging the prostitution of, intercourse with or indecent assault on girl under 16	

2. Offences Subject to Notification Requirements under Miscellaneous Acts 1957–2002

14.26 **Table 14.3 Offences Subject to Notification Requirements under Miscellaneous Acts 1957–2002**

	Offence	Qualification to applicability of notification requirement *Notification requirements only apply…*
IwCA 1960, s 1	Indecent conduct towards young child	
CLA 1977, s 54	Inciting girl under 16 to have incestuous sexual intercourse	
PCA 1978, s 1	Indecent photographs of children	If the indecent photographs or pseudo-photographs showed persons under 16, **and** (a) the conviction, finding or caution was before 1 May 2004 (the commencement of this Part) **or** (b) the offender— (i) was 18 or over, **or** (ii) is sentenced in respect of the offence to imprisonment for a term of at least 12 months
Customs and Excise Management Act 1979, s 170	Penalty for fraudulent evasion of duty etc. in relation to goods prohibited to be imported under of the Customs Consolidation Act 1876, s 42 (indecent or obscene articles)	If the prohibited goods included indecent photographs of persons under 16, **and** (a) the conviction, finding or caution was before 1 May 2004 (the commencement of this Part) **or** (b) the offender— (i) was 18 or over, or (ii) is sentenced in respect of the offence to imprisonment for a term of at least 12 months

	Offence	Qualification to applicability of notification requirement *Notification requirements only apply…*
CJA 1988, s 160	Possession of indecent photograph of a child	If the indecent photographs or pseudo-photographs showed persons under 16, **and** (a) the conviction, finding, or caution was before 1 May 2004 (the commencement of this Part) **or** (b) the offender— (i) was 18 or over, **or** (ii) is sentenced in respect of the offence to imprisonment for a term of at least 12 months
SO(A)A 2000, s 3	Abuse of position of trust	If the offender was 20 or over

3. Offences Subject to Notification Requirements under the Sexual Offences Act 2003

Table 14.4 Offences Subject to Notification Requirements under the Sexual Offences Act 2003 14.27

	Offence	Qualification to applicability of notification requirement *Notification requirements only apply…*
s 1	Rape	
s 2	Assault by penetration	
s 3	Sexual assault	If: (a) **where the offender was under 18**, he is or has been sentenced, in respect of the offence, to imprisonment for a term of at least 12 months; (b) **in any other case** (i) the victim was under 18, **or** (ii) the offender, in respect of the offence or finding, is or has been (a) sentenced to a term of imprisonment, (b) detained in a hospital, **or** (c) made the subject of a community sentence of at least 12 months
s 4	Causing sexual activity without consent	
s 5	Rape of a child under 13	
s 6	Assault of a child under 13 by penetration	
s 7	Sexual assault of a child under 13	If the offender (a) was 18 or over, **or** (b) is or has been sentenced in respect of the offence to imprisonment for a term of at least 12 months
s 8	Causing or inciting a child under 13 to engage in sexual activity	

	Offence	Qualification to applicability of notification requirement *Notification requirements only apply...*
s 9	Sexual activity with a child	
s 10	Causing or inciting a child to engage in sexual activity	
s 11	Engaging in sexual activity in the presence of a child	
s 12	Causing a child to watch a sexual act	
s 13	Child sex offences committed by children or young persons	If the offender is or has been sentenced, in respect of the offence, to imprisonment for a term of at least 12 months
s 14	Arranging or facilitating the commission of a child sex offence	If the offender (a) was 18 or over, **or** (b) is or has been sentenced, in respect of the offence, to imprisonment for a term of at least 12 months
s 15	Meeting a child following sexual grooming etc.	
s 16	Abuse of position of trust: sexual activity with a child	If the offender, in respect of the offence, is or has been (a) sentenced to a term of imprisonment, **or** (b) detained in a hospital, **or** (c) made the subject of a community sentence of at least 12 months
s 17	Abuse of position of trust: causing or inciting a child to engage in sexual activity	If the offender, in respect of the offence, is or has been (a) sentenced to a term of imprisonment, **or** (b) detained in a hospital, **or** (c) made the subject of a community sentence of at least 12 months
s 18	Abuse of position of trust: sexual activity in the presence of a child	If the offender, in respect of the offence, is or has been (a) sentenced to a term of imprisonment, **or** (b) detained in a hospital, **or** (c) made the subject of a community sentence of at least 12 months
s 19	Abuse of position of trust: causing a child to watch a sexual act	If the offender, in respect of the offence, is or has been (a) sentenced to a term of imprisonment, **or** (b) detained in a hospital, **or** (c) made the subject of a community sentence of at least 12 months
s 25	Sexual activity with a child family member	If the offender (a) was 18 or over, **or** (b) is or has been sentenced in respect of the offence to imprisonment for a term of at least 12 months
s 26	Inciting a child family member to engage in sexual activity	If the offender (a) was 18 or over, **or** (b) is or has been sentenced in respect of the offence to imprisonment for a term of at least 12 months
s 30	Sexual activity with a person with a mental disorder impeding choice	
s 31	Causing or inciting a person, with a mental disorder impeding choice, to engage in sexual activity	

	Offence	Qualification to applicability of notification requirement *Notification requirements only apply...*
s 32	Engaging in sexual activity in the presence of a person with a mental disorder impeding choice	
s 33	Causing a person, with a mental disorder impeding choice, to watch a sexual act	
s 34	Inducement, threat or deception to procure sexual activity with a person with a mental disorder	
s 35	Causing a person with a mental disorder to engage in or agree to engage in sexual activity by inducement, threat or deception	
s 36	Engaging in sexual activity in the presence, procured by inducement, threat or deception, of a person with a mental disorder	
s 37	Causing a person with a mental disorder to watch a sexual act by inducement, threat or deception	
s 38	Care workers: sexual activity with a person with a mental disorder	If: (a) **where the offender was under 18**, he is or has been sentenced, in respect of the offence, to imprisonment for a term of at least 12 months; (b) **in any other case,** the offender, in respect of the offence or finding, is or has been (i) sentenced to a term of imprisonment (ii) detained in a hospital, **or** (iii) made the subject of a community sentence of at least 12 months
s 39	Care workers: causing or inciting sexual activity	If: (a) **where the offender was under 18**, he is or has been sentenced, in respect of the offence, to imprisonment for a term of at least 12 months; (b) **in any other case,** the offender, in respect of the offence or finding, is or has been (i) sentenced to a term of imprisonment, (ii) detained in a hospital, **or** (iii) made the subject of a community sentence of at least 12 months
s 40	Care workers: sexual activity in the presence of a person with a mental disorder	If: (a) **where the offender was under 18**, he is or has been sentenced, in respect of the offence, to imprisonment for a term of at least 12 months; (b) **in any other case,** the offender, in respect of the offence or finding, is or has been (i) sentenced to a term of imprisonment (ii) detained in a hospital, **or** (iii) made the subject of a community sentence of at least 12 months

	Offence	Qualification to applicability of notification requirement *Notification requirements only apply…*
s 41	Care workers: causing a person with a mental disorder to watch a sexual act	If: (a) **where the offender was under 18**, he is or has been sentenced, in respect of the offence, to imprisonment for a term of at least 12 months; (b) **in any other case**, the offender, in respect of the offence or finding, is or has been (i) sentenced to a term of imprisonment (ii) detained in a hospital, **or** (iii) made the subject of a community sentence of at least 12 months
s 47	Paying for sexual services of a child	If the victim or other party was under 16, **and** the offender (a) was 18 or over, **or** (b) is or has been sentenced in respect of the offence to imprisonment for a term of at least 12 months
s 48	Causing or inciting child prostitution or pornography	If the offender (a) was 18 or over, **or** (b) is or has been sentenced in respect of the offence to imprisonment for a term of at least 12 months
s 49	Controlling a child prostitute or a child involved in pornography	If the offender (a) was 18 or over, **or** (b) is or has been sentenced in respect of the offence to imprisonment for a term of at least 12 months
s 50	Arranging or facilitating child prostitution or pornography	If the offender (a) was 18 or over, **or** (b) is or has been sentenced in respect of the offence to imprisonment for a term of at least 12 months
s 61	Administering a substance with intent	
s 62	Committing an offence with intent to commit a sexual offence	If: (a) **where the offender was under 18**, he is or has been sentenced, in respect of the offence, to imprisonment for a term of at least 12 months; (b) **in any other case** (i) the intended victim was under 18, **or** (ii) the offender, in respect of the offence or finding, is or has been (a) sentenced to a term of imprisonment, (b) detained in a hospital, **or** (c) made the subject of a community sentence of at least 12 months
s 63	Trespass with intent to commit a sexual offence	If: (a) **where the offender was under 18**, he is or has been sentenced, in respect of the offence, to imprisonment for a term of at least 12 months; (b) **in any other case** (i) the intended victim was under 18, **or** (ii) the offender, in respect of the offence or finding, is or has been (a) sentenced to a term of imprisonment, (b) detained in a hospital, **or** (c) made the subject of a community sentence of at least 12 months

	Offence	Qualification to applicability of notification requirement *Notification requirements only apply...*
s 64	Sex with an adult relative: penetration	If: (a) **where the offender was under 18**, he is or has been sentenced, in respect of the offence, to imprisonment for a term of at least 12 months; (b) **in any other case**, the offender, in respect of the offence or finding, is or has been (i) sentenced to a term of imprisonment (ii) detained in a hospital
s 65	Sex with an adult relative: consenting to penetration	If: (a) **where the offender was under 18**, he is or has been sentenced, in respect of the offence, to imprisonment for a term of at least 12 months; (b) **in any other case**, the offender, in respect of the offence or finding, is or has been (i) sentenced to a term of imprisonment, (ii) detained in a hospital
s 66	Exposure	If: (a) **where the offender was under 18**, he is or has been sentenced, in respect of the offence, to imprisonment for a term of at least 12 months; (b) **in any other case** (i) the victim was under 18, **or** (ii) the offender, in respect of the offence or finding, is or has been (a) sentenced to a term of imprisonment, (b) detained in a hospital, or (c) made the subject of a community sentence of at least 12 months
s 67	Voyeurism	If: (a) **where the offender was under 18**, he is or has been sentenced, in respect of the offence, to imprisonment for a term of at least 12 months; (b) **in any other case** (i) the victim was under 18, **or** (ii) the offender, in respect of the offence or finding, is or has been (a) sentenced to a term of imprisonment, (b) detained in a hospital, or (c) made the subject of a community sentence of at least 12 months
s 69	Intercourse with an animal	If: (a) **where the offender was under 18**, he is or has been sentenced, in respect of the offence, to imprisonment for a term of at least 12 months; (b) **in any other case**, the offender, in respect of the offence or finding, is or has been (i) sentenced to a term of imprisonment, (ii) detained in a hospital

	Offence	Qualification to applicability of notification requirement *Notification requirements only apply…*
s 70	Sexual penetration of a corpse	If: (a) **where the offender was under 18**, he is or has been sentenced, in respect of the offence, to imprisonment for a term of at least 12 months; (b) **in any other case**, the offender, in respect of the offence or finding, is or has been (i) sentenced to a term of imprisonment, (ii) detained in a hospital

15

PUBLICITY

A. ANONYMITY OF COMPLAINANTS

Where a complainant makes an allegation of any offence specified under s 2 of the Sexual Offences (Amendment) Act (SO(A)A) 1992, *no matter* relating to the complainant *during the complainant's lifetime* should be published if it is likely to lead members of the public to identify the complainant.[1] **15.01**

This includes, specifically, the complainant's name; address; identity of any school or education establishment attended by the complainant; the identity of any place of work; and any still or moving picture of the person.[2] **15.02**

In relation to a complainant who is deceased, there is no protection provided by statute. In a case where the evidence of that complainant is not challenged, with the agreement of defence counsel, the deceased witness could be referred to as Witness A in order to protect his/her identity. (Such a measure was adopted in *R v Delroy Grant* (March 2011)—The 'Night Stalker' trial—where the defence was identification.) **15.03**

1. Offences to which the Anonymity Requirement Applies

15.04

1. Rape (under any legislative provision).
2. Burglary with intent to commit rape (under any legislative provision).
3. Any attempt, conspiracy, incitement, aiding, abetting, counselling or procuring of either of the above or any of the offences specified below.
4. Any of the offences below.

Table 15.1 Offences to which the Anonymity Requirement Applies

Legislative Provision	Offence
SOA 1956, s 2	Procurement of woman by threats
SOA 1956, s 3	Procurement of woman by false pretences
SOA 1956, s 4	Administering drugs to obtain or facilitate intercourse

[1] SO(A)A 1992, s 1(1).

[2] SO(A)A 1992, s 1(3A).

Legislative Provision	Offence
SOA 1956, s 5	Intercourse with a girl under 13
SOA 1956, s 6	Intercourse with a girl under 16
SOA 1956, s 7	Intercourse with a defective
SOA 1956, s 9	Procurement of a defective
SOA 1956, s 10	Incest by a man. Except where the complainant is alleged to have committed incest under s 11 against the defendant at the time of the s 10 offence[3]
SOA 1956, s 11	Incest by a woman. Except where the complainant is alleged to have committed incest under s 10 against the defendant at the time of the s 11 offence[4]
SOA 1956, s 12	Buggery. Except where the complainant is alleged to have committed buggery under s 12 against the defendant at the time of the s 12 offence[5]
SOA 1956, s 14	Indecent assault on a woman
SOA 1956, s 15	Indecent assault on a man
SOA 1956, s 16	Assault with intent to commit buggery
SOA 1956, s 17	Abduction of woman by force or for the sake of her property
MHA 1959, s 128	Sexual intercourse with patients
IwCA 1960, s 1	Indecent conduct towards young child
CLA 1977, s 54	Inciting girl under 16 to have incestuous sexual intercourse

2. Offences *Not* Subject to Reporting under the Sexual Offences Act 2003

15.05 *All offences* under the SOA 2003 are subject to the anonymity provisions of the SO(A)A 1992, except for the following.[6]

Table 15.2 Offences *Not* Subject to Reporting under the Sexual Offences Act 2003

SOA 2003, s 64	Sex with an adult relative: penetration
SOA 2003, s 65	Sex with an adult relative: consenting to penetration
SOA 2003, s 69	Intercourse with an animal
SOA 2003, s 71	Sexual activity in a public lavatory

3. When Can Anonymity be Waived?

15.06 (i) *Before trial:* if the defendant applies to the judge for a direction and satisfies the judge: (a) that such direction is required for the purpose of inducing persons who are likely to be needed as

[3] SO(A)A 1992, s 4(2), (5).
[4] SO(A)A 1992, s 4(3), (6).
[5] SO(A)A 1992, s 4(4), (7).
[6] SO(A)A 1992, s 2(1).

witnesses at the trial to come forward; and (b) that the conduct of the defendant's defence at the trial is likely to be substantially prejudiced if the direction is not given.[7]

(ii) *At trial:* if: (a) the effect of a reporting restriction is to impose a substantial and unreasonable restriction on the reporting of proceedings at the trial; and (b) it is in the public interest to remove or relax the restriction.[8]

(iii) *After trial:* the outcome of the trial is not reason enough to remove or relax the restriction.[9] If a defendant is convicted and applies to appeal that conviction, the defendant may apply to the appellate court for a direction under the SOA(A) 1992, s 3(4) to displace reporting restrictions. The restrictions shall be displaced if the court is satisfied: (a) that the direction is required for the purpose of obtaining evidence in support of the appeal; and (b) that the applicant is likely to suffer substantial injustice if the direction is not given.[10]

B. ANONYMITY OF WITNESSES

The YJCEA 1999 sets out detailed provisions regarding the anonymity of witnesses. To date, only the provisions relating to adult witnesses[11] are in force. Those relating to young witnesses are to come into force on a day to be appointed under s 68(3). Young persons therefore still fall within the ambit of the Children and Young Persons Act 1933, s 39. **15.07**

1. Adult Witnesses Aged 18 or Over

Section 46 of the YJCEA 1999 gives the court the power to make a 'reporting direction' where an application is made in relation to a witness who is 18 or over.[12] This provision came into force on 7.10.2004.[13] Breach of such a reporting direction is a summary offence, the maximum penalty for which is a fine not exceeding level 5 on the standard scale.[14] **15.08**

Eligibility of Adult Witnesses for Reporting Restrictions

The court may make such an order if it considers (a) that the witness is eligible for protection and (b) that giving a reporting direction is likely to improve the quality of evidence given by the witness or the level of cooperation given by the witness to any party in connection with the case.[15] **15.09**

When determining eligibility, the court must take into account the nature and alleged circumstances of the offence; the age of the witness; the social, cultural and ethnic origins of the witness (where relevant); the domestic and employment circumstances of the witness (where relevant); and the religious or political beliefs of the witness (where relevant). Further, the court may take into account any behaviour towards the witness by either the accused, members or associates of the accused's family or any other person who is likely to be an accused or witness to the proceedings.[16] The court must also consider any views expressed by the witness.[17] **15.10**

---

[7] SO(A)A 1992, s 3(1).
[8] SO(A)A 1992, s 3(2).
[9] SO(A)A 1992, s 3(3).
[10] SO(A)A 1992, s 3(4). A complainant can waive anonymity (with written consent if done through a third party) s 4(5A) SOA(A)1976 and s 5 SOA(A)1992. With thanks to HHJ Stephen Gullick.
[11] YJCEA 1999, s 46.
[12] YJCEA 1999, s 46(1).
[13] YJCEA 1999 (Commencement Order No 10) (England and Wales) Order 2004 (SI 2004 No 2428).
[14] YJCEA 1999, s 49.
[15] YJCEA 1999, s 46(2).
[16] YJCEA 1999, s 46(4).
[17] YJCEA 1999, s 46(5).

Applying for Reporting Restrictions

15.11 The procedure for application and objection is set out in rule 16 of the CPR 2013. The CPR does not specify whether the application must be oral or in writing, leaving the form of the application to the court.[18] However, the content of the application is specified. The application must: (a) specify the proposed terms of the order; (b) explain the court's power to make the order; (c) explain why the order is necessary; (d) explain, in the case of adult witnesses, how s 46 of the YJCEA 1999 is satisfied both in terms of the witness's eligibility for assistance and why a reporting direction would be likely to improve the witness's quality of evidence or their cooperation in preparing the case.[19]

15.12 The application should be made as soon as reasonably practicable.[20] Any other party to the proceedings and such other persons as the court directs should be notified.[21]

15.13 Any representations in response must be filed and served as soon as reasonably practicable after the notice of application. The reasons for any objection must be explained and any alternative terms proposed must be specified. If a hearing is required, it must be requested and an explanation given as to why it is needed.[22]

15.14 The application can either be dealt with administratively or at a hearing.[23] It may only be dealt with after all parties to the proceedings and any other person directly affected have been afforded the opportunity to either attend a hearing or make representations.[24] When dealing with the application the court must have regard to the importance of open justice.[25]

Nature and Duration of Reporting Restrictions

15.15 Reporting restrictions last for the lifetime of the witness and apply to any matter that is likely to lead members of the public to identify the witness as being such in the proceedings.[26] This includes, in particular, their name; address; the identity of any educational establishment or place of work attended by the witness; and any still or moving picture of the witness.[27]

Dispensing with Reporting Restrictions

15.16 The court or an appellate court may make an 'excepting direction' to dispense with the restrictions, provided: (a) it is satisfied that it is necessary in the interest of justice to do so; or (b) it is satisfied the effect of the restrictions is to impose a substantial and unreasonable restriction on the reporting of proceedings, and that it is in the public interest to remove or relax that restriction.[28] The relaxation can be to any extent specified by the court.[29]

15.17 The abandonment or determination of the criminal proceedings is not a good ground for the making of an excepting direction.[30]

2. Young Persons Aged Under 18

15.18 The provisions of the YJCEA 1999 relating to young witnesses are to come into force on a day to be appointed pursuant to s 68(3). Children[31] and young persons[32] therefore still fall within the ambit of the Children and Young Persons Act (CYPA) 1933, s 39.

---

18 CPR 2013, r 16.3.
19 CPR 2013, r 16.5(3)(c)–(e).
20 CPR 2013, r 16.5(3)(a).
21 CPR 2013, r 16.5(3)(b).
22 CPR 2013, r 16.7.
23 CPR 2013, r 16.2(2).
24 CPR 2013, r 16.2(3).
25 CPR 2013, r 16.2(1).
26 YJCEA 1999, s 46(6).
27 YJCEA 1999, s 46(7).
28 YJCEA 1999, s 46(9).
29 YJCEA 1999, s 46(9).
30 YJCEA 1999, s 46(9).
31 Aged under 14 (CYPA 1933, s 107).
32 Aged between 14 and under 18 (CYPA 1933, s 107).

Current Provisions

The court has the power to direct that no newspaper report or sound or television broadcast[33] of the proceedings should reveal the name, address, school or include any particulars calculated to lead to the identification of any child or young person concerned in the proceedings as a defendant, complainant or witness.[34] **15.19**

Provisions under the Youth Justice and Criminal Evidence Act 1999

The provisions under the YJCEA 1999 will supersede those of the CYPA 1933 in relation to criminal proceedings from a day to be appointed under the YJCEA 1999, s 68(3). **15.20**

Witnesses under 18 during the course of the investigation: no matter relating to any person involved in the offence while he is under the age of 18 is to be included in any publication if it is likely to lead members of the public to identify him as a person involved in the offence as a defendant, complainant or *witness.*[35] These provisions only apply until the institution of criminal proceedings. **15.21**

Witnesses under 18 once proceedings have been instituted: the court may direct that no matter relating to any person concerned in the proceedings while he is under 18 be included in any publication if it is likely to lead members of the public to identify him as a person concerned as a defendant, complainant or witness in the court proceedings. **15.22**

The court or an appellate court may make an 'excepting direction' to dispense with the restrictions provided: (a) it is satisfied that it is necessary in the interest of justice to do so;[36] or (b) it is satisfied the effect of the restrictions is to impose a substantial and unreasonable restriction on the reporting of proceedings, and that it is in the public interest to remove or relax that restriction.[37] The relaxation can be to any extent specified by the court. **15.23**

---

33 Inserted by the CYPA 1963, s 57(4).
34 CYPA 1933, s 39.
35 YJCEA 1999, s 44(2) and (4).
36 YJCEA 1999, s 45(4).
37 YJCEA 1999, s 45(5).

16

SEXUAL OFFENCES PREVENTION ORDERS

General

16.01 Since its repeal by the implementation of the SOA 2003, the court's power to impose a s 5A restraining order[1] has been replaced by the power to impose a Sexual Offences Prevention Order (SOPO); see also para 12.142. SOPOs have a wide ambit. A SOPO may be imposed if the offence was sexual and falls within Sch 3 to the 2003 Act.[2] Further, a SOPO may be imposed for a number of non-sexual offences falling within Sch 5 to the 2003 Act.[3]

16.02 The court must, before granting a SOPO following an offence under either schedule, be satisfied that such an order is necessary for the purpose of protecting the public or any particular members of the public from serious sexual harm from the defendant.[4]

16.03 In dealing with a SOPO in respect of a sibling who is not the victim, it may be wise to involve the family court.[5]

A. APPLICABILITY

Within Criminal Court Proceedings

16.04 If a SOPO is to be imposed during criminal court proceedings, such an order may be made in relation to those who are either convicted of an offence specified in Sch 3 or 5 to the 2003 Act;[6] found not guilty of such an offence by reason of insanity;[7] or are found to be under a disability and to have done the act charged against them in respect of such an offence.[8]

Procedure

16.05 Rule 50 of the CPR now governs the application for a SOPO, requiring 2 days' written notice of a draft application. It reflects the Court of Appeal's emphasis in *Smith* 'that it is essential that there is a written draft, properly considered in advance of the sentencing hearing. The normal requirement should be that it is served on the court and the defendant before the sentencing hearing...not less than two clear days before but in any event not *at* the hearing...Because the draft is likely to require amendment before it is issued by the court staff, it is sensible for it to be available in electronic as well as paper form'.[9] The court may then grant a SOPO if it is satisfied that such an order is necessary for the purpose of protecting the public or any particular members of the public from serious sexual harm from the defendant.[10]

16.06 If further time is needed for proper consideration of the proposed SOPO, it is permissible for the sentencing court to make the order on a date subsequent to sentence, but not outside the 56-day slip rule.[11]

1 SOA 1997, s 5A.
2 SOA 2003, s 104(2).
3 SOA 2003, s 104(2).
4 SOA 2003, s 104(1)(b).
5 *R v D* [2005] EWCA Crim 2591.
6 SOA 2003, s 104(2); see tables at the end of this chapter.
7 SOA 2003, s 104(3)(a).
8 SOA 2003, s 104(3)(b).
9 *R v Smith and Others* [2011] EWCA Crim 1772, at [26].
10 SOA 2003, s 104(1)(b).
11 Criminal Courts (Sentencing) Act, s 155.

Civil Orders

SOPOs may also be imposed as a civil order at another date upon complaint to a magistrates' court.[12] The effect of imposing a subsequent SOPO is that an existing SOPO is revoked; care therefore needs to be taken to ensure that terms from an original order are included if still appropriate.[13] 16.07

The ambit of such an application is wider, extending to all 'qualifying offenders'.[14] 16.08

A 'qualifying offender' means a person who has been either: (a) convicted of an offence specified in Sch 3 or 5 of the 2003 Act[15] in the UK or an equivalent offence abroad;[16] (b) found not guilty of such an offence by reason of insanity;[17] (c) found to be under a disability and to have done the act charged against them in respect of such an offence;[18] or (d) cautioned for such an offence.[19] 16.09

Such later application must be made by a chief police officer in respect of a person who resides in his police area or who that officer believes intends to come to his police area.[20] It must appear to that chief police officer: (a) that the offender is a 'qualifying offender' and; (b) that since being dealt with for the original offence the offender has acted in such a way as to give reasonable cause to believe that it is necessary for an order to be made.[21] 16.10

The court may grant a SOPO if it is satisfied that the defendant's behaviour since the date of dealing makes such an order necessary for the purpose of protecting the public or any particular members of the public from serious sexual harm from the defendant.[22] 16.11

B. RISK OF SERIOUS SEXUAL HARM

For the purposes of a SOPO, 'protecting the public or any particular members of the public from serious sexual harm from the defendant' means protecting the public in the United Kingdom or any particular members of that public from serious physical or psychological harm, caused by the defendant committing one or more of the offences specified in Sch 3.[23] 16.12

C. INTERIM SOPOs

Interim SOPOs may be ordered to cover the period leading up to determination of the main application.[24] Such application may be granted if the court considers it just to do so.[25] The order has effect only for a fixed period that must be specified.[26] It will cease to have effect, at the latest, on determination of the main application.[27] 16.13

12 SOA 2003, s 104(5).
13 SOA 2003, s 107(6).
14 SOA 2003, s 104(5)(a).
15 SOA 2003, s 106(6)(a).
16 SOA 2003, s 106(7)(a).
17 SOA 2003, s 106(6)(b) and (7)(b).
18 SOA 2003, s 106(6)(c) and (7)(c).
19 SOA 2003, s 106(6)(d) and (6)(d).
20 SOA 2003, s 104(5).
21 SOA 2003, s 104(5)(b).
22 SOA 2003, s 104(1)(a).
23 SOA 2003, s 106(3).
24 SOA 2003, s 109(1).
25 SOA 2003, s 109(3).
26 SOA 2003, s 109(4)(a).
27 SOA 2003, s 109(4)(b).

D. AMBIT AND CONTENT OF A SOPO, INCLUDING REPEAL OF/CHANGES TO DISQUALIFICATION ORDERS AND THE BARRING AUTHORITIES

16.14 The SOPO has effect for a fixed period (not less than 5 years) specified in the order or until a further order is made.[28]

16.15 The SOPO prohibits the offender from doing anything described in the order.[29] The only prohibitions that may be included in the order are those necessary for the purpose of protecting the public or any particular members of the public from serious sexual harm from the defendant.[30]

Clarity of the SOPO

16.16 A SOPO must be sufficiently clear on its face for the defendant, those who have to deal with him in ordinary daily life and those who have to consider enforcement, to understand without real difficulty or the need for expert legal advice exactly what he can and cannot do. Real risk of unintentional breach must be avoided.[31] Such orders need to be carefully drafted and 'bearing in mind that... they are often made against those of limited education, simplicity is a virtue'.[32]

SOPOs and Other Regimes

16.17 No SOPO is needed if it merely duplicates or interferes with another regime, such as the notification requirements[33] and a bar from working with children or vulnerable adults.[34]

16.18 An indeterminate sentence needs no SOPO, at least unless there is some very unusual feature which means that such an order could add something useful and does not run the risk of undesirably tying the hands of the offender managers later.[35] Licence conditions should suffice.

Computer Access

16.19 The case of *Smith* lays down a number of propositions about terms limiting computer use.[36]

(a) A blanket prohibition on computer use or internet access is impermissible.
(b) Restricting internet access to 'job search, study, work, lawful recreation and purchases' prevents a defendant from legitimate use of the internet.
(c) A requirement to notify the police of the possession of any device giving access to the internet is also onerous and of little value, given the proliferation of internet-ready devices such as mobile phones.
(d) A prohibition on internet access without filtering software risks uncertainty about precisely what is required.
(e) The most effective formulation is likely to be the preservation of readable internet history coupled with a submission to inspection on request.
(f) Where the risk includes the use of chat rooms or similar networks for grooming, suitable terms include a prohibition on communicating via the internet with any young person known or believed to be under the age of 16, coupled with an internet history provision.

---

28 SOA 2003, s 107(1)(b).
29 SOA 2003, s 107(1)(a).
30 SOA 2003, s 107(2).
31 *R v Smith and Others* [2011] EWCA Crim 1772, per Hughes LJ at [4].
32 *Hemsley* [2010] EWCA Crim 225, per HHJ Cooke QC at [4].
33 *R v Smith and Others* [2011] EWCA Crim 1772, at [9] and [17].
34 *R v Smith and Others* [2011] EWCA Crim 1772, at [9].
35 *R v Smith and Others* [2011] EWCA Crim 1772, at [13].
36 *R v Smith and Others* [2011] EWCA Crim 1772, at [20].

Personal Contact with Children

When prohibiting contact with children, the age should be commensurate with the *actus reus* of the offence. Most SOPOs with such a provision will therefore prohibit contact with children under 16. Offences under ss 16–19, 21, 25 and 26 of the SOA 2003 are defined with reference to a child under 18 and any prohibition following the commission of such offences should relate to children under 18.[37] **16.20**

The court should consider carefully whether it is appropriate to restrict contact with children generally. There should be an identifiable risk of 'contact offences'. If such a condition is imposed it should include a saving for incidental contact inherent in everyday life.[38] **16.21**

E. VARIATIONS, RENEWALS AND DISCHARGES

The defendant,[39] a chief police officer for the area in which the defendant resides[40] or intends to reside,[41] or the chief police officer that made the original application[42] may apply to the court for an order varying, renewing or discharging a SOPO.[43] **16.22**

The court may make any order varying, renewing or discharging the SOPO that the court considers appropriate.[44] Any varied or renewed conditions, including any additional conditions, must be necessary to protect the public or any particular members of the public from serious sexual harm from the defendant.[45] **16.23**

Care must be taken in the event of a further SOPO once an order is in place. A new SOPO has the effect of revoking the original SOPO,[46] therefore it may, depending on the circumstances and reasons for the new order, be necessary to include the original terms. **16.24**

The application to vary should be to the Crown Court where the original application was granted in a Crown Court or in the Court of Appeal.[47] The application, if made in a youth or magistrates' court, should be to a youth or magistrates' court for the area where the defendant lives or, if made by a chief police officer, to a youth or magistrates' court whose commission area includes any part of the chief police officer's area.[48] **16.25**

The court must not discharge an order before the end of 5 years, beginning with the day on which the order was made, without the consent of the defendant and: **16.26**

(a) where the application is made by a chief officer of police, that chief officer; or
(b) in any other case, the chief officer of police for the area in which the defendant resides.[49]

F. APPEALS AGAINST THE MAKING OF SOPOs AND INTERIM SOPOs

A defendant may appeal against the making of a SOPO.[50] This effectively takes the form of an appeal against sentence,[51] even where the defendant was found not guilty by reason of insanity or **16.27**

---

[37] *R v Smith and Others* [2011] EWCA Crim 1772, at [21].
[38] *R v Smith and Others* [2011] EWCA Crim 1772, at [24].
[39] SOA 2003, s 108(2)(a).
[40] SOA 2003, s 108(2)(b).
[41] SOA 2003, s 108(2)(c).
[42] SOA 2003, s 108(2)(d).
[43] SOA 2003, s 108(1).
[44] SOA 2003, s 108(4).
[45] SOA 2003, s 108(5).
[46] SOA 2003, s 107(6).
[47] SOA 2003, s 108(7)(a).
[48] SOA 2003, s 108(7)(b) and (c).
[49] SOA 2003, s 108(6).
[50] SOA 2003, s 110(1).
[51] SOA 2003, s 110(1)(a).

suffering from a disability.[52] Where the SOPO was granted in the Crown Court, appeal is to the Court of Appeal.[53] In any other case, appeal is to the Crown Court.[54]

16.28 Where the SOPO was made on application to a magistrates' court by a chief police officer, the appeal is to the Crown Court.[55]

16.29 Appeal against the making of an interim SOPO is to the Crown Court.[56]

G. RELATIONSHIP WITH NOTIFICATION REQUIREMENTS

16.30 Where a defendant was subject to notification requirements immediately before the making of the SOPO, and would ordinarily cease to be subject to the notification requirements, the defendant remains subject to the notification requirements throughout the period of the SOPO.[57]

16.31 Where a defendant was not subject to notification requirements but is made subject to a SOPO (this would arise essentially when a defendant is convicted of an offence under the SOA 2003, Sch 5), the making of a SOPO triggers the notification requirements throughout the period of the SOPO.[58]

16.32 The terms of a SOPO should not duplicate the notification requirements and should not be used as a device to extend the notification requirements.[59]

H. RELATIONSHIP WITH BARRING FROM WORKING WITH CHILDREN AND VULNERABLE ADULTS

16.33 Amendments to the Safeguarding and Vulnerable Groups Act (SVGA) 2006 have resulted in an amended test for inclusion onto the Barred List(s) applicable to some offenders. The consequence of the new test is that a number of sexual offenders who would previously have been included on the List(s) no longer meet the criteria for inclusion. In those cases, it will be necessary to consider applying for an additional prohibition as part of a SOPO. There will also be a number of offenders previously on the List(s) who are entitled to make representations as to their removal from the List(s) and offenders who have already been removed from the List(s). These offenders will need to be identified by the police or prosecution if consideration is to be given as to whether applications for SOPOs or variations to existing SOPOs are required.

The Original Regime under the Safeguarding and Vulnerable Groups Act 2006

16.34 The SVGA 2006 introduced the Independent Barring Board which was subsequently renamed the Independent Safeguarding Authority (ISA). The role of the ISA was to prevent unsuitable people from working with children and vulnerable adults by establishing and maintaining the 'children's barred list' and the 'adults barred list'.[60]

The Regime under the Safeguarding and Vulnerable Groups Act 2006 (as amended)

16.35 On 1 December 2012 sections of the Protection of Freedoms Act (PFA) 2012 came into force to form the Disclosure and Barring Service (DBS). The PFA also made amendments to the SVGA. Section 67 of the PFA made specific amendments to Sch 3 to the SVGA 2006 which altered

[52] SOA 2003, s 110(1)(b).
[53] SOA 2003, s 110(3)(a).
[54] SOA 2003, s 110(3)(b).
[55] SOA 2003, s 110(1)(c).
[56] SOA 2003, s 110(2).
[57] SOA 2003, s 107(3).
[58] SOA 2003, s 107(4).
[59] *R v Smith and Others* [2011] EWCA Crim 1772.
[60] SGVA 2006, s 2 and Sch 3.

the test for barring decisions. Following the amendments, the DBS can now only bar a person from working within a regulated activity with children or adults if they have reason to believe that the person is or has been, or might in the future be, engaged in regulated activity. The only exception to this is where a person is cautioned or convicted for a relevant (automatic barring) offence (under para 1 or 7) and is not eligible to submit representations against their inclusion in a Barred List(s).

Additionally, where a person is cautioned for or convicted of a relevant offence with the right to make representations (para 2 or 8), the DBS will ask the person to submit their representations and consider them *before* making a final barring decision. **16.36**

The consequences of these changes are that only those convicted of the most serious offences (paras 1 and 7) will be certain to be placed on the List(s). Those convicted of less serious offences (para 2 or 8) who do not meet the new test because they have not, do not or will not carry out regulated activities will no longer qualify to be considered for inclusion on the List(s). Those who do qualify under the new test and have been convicted of less serious offences may be placed on the List(s) subject to the consideration of representations *before* they are entered onto the List(s). **16.37**

A further relevant change is that, whereas previously the ISA's decision would not be subject to review for a period of 10 years, the position has now been altered so that a review may take place at any time if new information emerges, or there has been a change of circumstances, or it becomes apparent that the DBS has made an error.[61] **16.38**

There will be a number of offenders who would previously have been placed on the List(s) who do not fulfil the new criteria and will not now be included on the List(s), as a result of the amendments to the Act. **16.39**

See paras 12.138–12.141 for the list of barred offences. **16.40**

However, this lacuna can be addressed by applying, in appropriate cases, for a SOPO prohibition at the time of sentence prohibiting them from working with children. This is particularly pertinent given that Disqualification Orders under the CJCSA 2000 are no longer available as an alternative to SOPO prohibitions as of 17.6.2013.[62] **16.41**

The prohibition could be along the lines of: **16.42**

> Not to seek or undertake any employment (including voluntary work), paid or otherwise, which will or is likely to bring him/her into unsupervised contact with children [specify target gender where appropriate, although arguably a sex offender who targets very young children does so regardless of gender] under the age of 16 years.

Such a prohibition should be tailored to the individual facts of the offence and may not be suitable in all cases. **16.43**

It is important that those who draft, apply for and make SOPOs are aware of the important changes to the SVGA 2006 and that there are cases which would previously have been 'caught' by the SVGA which no longer are and therefore careful consideration needs to be given, in appropriate cases, as to whether a further prohibition in a SOPO is required. **16.44**

There may well be cases where even though the offender is placed on the Barring List(s), there are risks envisaged which fall outside the remit of the List(s). In those circumstances it is not only permissible (see *R v Smith & Others* [2011] EWCA Crim 1772 per Hughes LJ at para 25) but necessary to consider imposing SOPO prohibitions to address those risks provided there is justification for doing so. **16.45**

In the same way that a judge must inform a defendant being sentenced that he will be subject to the Notification Requirements, the judge must inform a defendant of future restrictions imposed upon him by the DBS.[63] The court should inform the defendant which list he or she **16.46**

---

[61] SVGA 2006, s 18A, as inserted by the PFA 2012.

[62] SI 2009 No 2611; SI 2012 No 2231.

[63] CPR 2013, r 42.3(1).

will be included on and under what legislation. In addition, a defendant should be told whether or not they can make representations to be removed from the list. See paras 16.35–16.40.

I. OFFENCES: BREACH OF SOPO OR INTERIM SOPO

16.47 A person subject to a SOPO or interim SOPO commits an offence if, without reasonable excuse, he does anything that he is prohibited from doing by that SOPO or interim SOPO.[64]

16.48 Breach of a SOPO or interim SOPO renders the offender liable: (a) on summary conviction, to imprisonment for a term not exceeding 6 months, or a fine not exceeding the statutory maximum, or both;[65] (b) on conviction on indictment, to imprisonment for a term not exceeding 5 years.[66]

J. SEXUAL OFFENCES ACT 2003, SCH 3

16.49

Offences Which may be Subject to a SOPO under the Sexual Offences Act 1956

	Offence	Qualification to applicability of a SOPO *A SOPO may only be ordered...*
s 1	Rape	
s 5	Intercourse with a girl under 13	
s 6	Intercourse with a girl under 16	If the offender is 20 or over
s 10	Incest by a man	If the victim or other party was under 18
s 12	Buggery	(a) If the offender was 20 or over, and (b) the victim or other party was under 18.
s 13	Indecency between men	(a) If the offender was 20 or over, and (b) the victim or other party was under 18.
s 14	Indecent assault on a woman	(a) The victim or other party was under 18, or (b) the offender, in respect of the offence or finding, is or has been— (i) sentenced to imprisonment for a term of at least 30 months; or (ii) admitted to a hospital subject to a restriction order.
s 15	Indecent assault on a man	(a) The victim or other party was under 18, or (b) the offender, in respect of the offence or finding, is or has been— (i) sentenced to imprisonment for a term of at least 30 months; or (ii) admitted to a hospital subject to a restriction order.

[64] SOA 2003, s 113(1)(a) and (b).
[65] SOA 2003, s 113(2)(a).
[66] SOA 2003, s 113(2)(b).

	Offence	Qualification to applicability of a SOPO *A SOPO may only be ordered...*
s 16	Assault with intent to commit buggery	If the victim or other party was under 18.
s 28	Causing or encouraging the prostitution of, intercourse with or indecent assault on girl under 16	

Offences Which may be Subject to a SOPO under Miscellaneous Acts 1957–2002 16.50

	Offence	Qualification to applicability of a SOPO *A SOPO may only be ordered...*
s 1 Indecency with Children Act 1960	Indecent conduct towards young child	
s 54 Criminal Law Act 1977	Inciting girl under 16 to have incestuous sexual intercourse	
s 1 Protection of Children Act 1978	Indecent photographs of children	If the indecent photographs or pseudo-photographs showed persons under 16, and (a) the conviction, finding or caution was before 1 May 2004 (the commencement of this Part) or (b) the offender— (i) was 18 or over, or (ii) is sentenced in respect of the offence to imprisonment for a term of at least 12 months.
s 170 Customs and Excise Management Act 1979	Penalty for fraudulent evasion of duty etc in relation to goods prohibited to be imported under s 42 of the Customs Consolidation Act 1876 (indecent or obscene articles)	If the prohibited goods included indecent photographs of persons under 16, and (a) the conviction, finding or caution was before 1 May 2004 (the commencement of this Part) or (b) the offender— (i) was 18 or over, or (ii) is sentenced in respect of the offence to imprisonment for a term of at least 12 months.
s 160 Criminal Justice Act 1988	Possession of indecent photograph of a child	If the indecent photographs or pseudo-photographs showed persons under 16, and (a) the conviction, finding or caution was before 1 May 2004 (the commencement of this Part) or (b) the offender— (i) was 18 or over, or (ii) is sentenced in respect of the offence to imprisonment for a term of at least 12 months.
s 3 Sexual Offences (Amendment) Act 2000	Abuse of position of trust	If the offender was 20 or over.

16.51
Offences Which may be Subject to a SOPO under the Sexual Offences Act 2003

	Offence	Qualification to applicability of a SOPO *A SOPO may only be ordered...*
s 1	Rape	
s 2	Assault by penetration	
s 3	Sexual assault	If:— (a) where the offender was under 18, he is or has been sentenced, in respect of the offence, to imprisonment for a term of at least 12 months; (b) in any other case (i) the victim was under 18, or (ii) the offender, in respect of the offence or finding, is or has been (a) sentenced to a term of imprisonment (b) detained in a hospital, or (c) made the subject of a community sentence of at least 12 months.
s 4	Causing sexual activity without consent	
s 5	Rape of a child under 13	
s 6	Assault of a child under 13 by penetration	
s 7	Sexual assault of a child under 13	If the offender (a) was 18 or over, or (b) is or has been sentenced in respect of the offence to imprisonment for a term of at least 12 months.
s 8	Causing or inciting a child under 13 to engage in sexual activity	
s 9	Sexual activity of a child	
s 10	Causing or inciting a child to engage in sexual activity	
s 11	Engaging in sexual activity in the presence of a child	
s 12	Causing a child to watch a sexual act	
s 13	Child sex offences committed by children or young persons	If the offender is or has been sentenced, in respect of the offence, to imprisonment for a term of at least 12 months.
s 14	Arranging or facilitating the commission of a child sex offence	If the offender (a) was 18 or over, or (b) is or has been sentenced, in respect of the offence, to imprisonment for a term of at least 12 months.
s 15	Meeting a child following sexual grooming etc	

	Offence	Qualification to applicability of a SOPO *A SOPO may only be ordered...*
s 16	Abuse of position of trust: sexual activity with a child	If the offender, in respect of the offence, is or has been (a) sentenced to a term of imprisonment, or (b) detained in a hospital, or (c) made the subject of a community sentence of at least 12 months.
s 17	Abuse of position of trust: causing or inciting a child to engage in sexual activity	If the offender, in respect of the offence, is or has been (a) sentenced to a term of imprisonment, or (b) detained in a hospital, or (c) made the subject of a community sentence of at least 12 months.
s 18	Abuse of position of trust: sexual activity in the presence of a child	If the offender, in respect of the offence, is or has been (a) sentenced to a term of imprisonment, or (b) detained in a hospital, or (c) made the subject of a community sentence of at least 12 months.
s 19	Abuse of position of trust: causing a child to watch a sexual act	If the offender, in respect of the offence, is or has been (a) sentenced to a term of imprisonment, or (b) detained in a hospital, or (c) made the subject of a community sentence of at least 12 months.
s 25	Sexual activity with a child family member	If the offender (a) was 18 or over, or (b) is or has been sentenced in respect of the offence to imprisonment for a term of at least 12 months.
s 26	Inciting a child family member to engage in sexual activity	If the offender (a) was 18 or over, or (b) is or has been sentenced in respect of the offence to imprisonment for a term of at least 12 months.
s 30	Sexual activity with a person with a mental disorder impeding choice	
s 31	Causing or inciting a person, with a mental disorder impeding choice, to engage in sexual activity	
s 32	Engaging in sexual activity in the presence of a person with a mental disorder impeding choice	
s 33	Causing a person, with a mental disorder impeding choice, to watch a sexual act	
s 34	Inducement, threat or deception to procure sexual activity with a person with a mental disorder	
s 35	Causing a person with a mental disorder to engage in or agree to engage in sexual activity by inducement, threat or deception	

	Offence	Qualification to applicability of a SOPO *A SOPO may only be ordered...*
s 36	Engaging in sexual activity in the presence, procured by inducement, threat or deception, of a person with a mental disorder	
s 37	Causing a person with a mental disorder to watch a sexual act by inducement, threat or deception	
s 38	Care workers: sexual activity with a person with a mental disorder	If:— (a) where the offender was under 18, he is or has been sentenced, in respect of the offence, to imprisonment for a term of at least 12 months; (b) in any other case, the offender, in respect of the offence or finding, is or has been (i) sentenced to a term of imprisonment (ii) detained in a hospital, or (iii) made the subject of a community sentence of at least 12 months.
s 39	Care workers: causing or inciting sexual activity	If:— (a) where the offender was under 18, he is or has been sentenced, in respect of the offence, to imprisonment for a term of at least 12 months; (b) in any other case,the offender, in respect of the offence or finding, is or has been (i) sentenced to a term of imprisonment (ii) detained in a hospital, or (iii) made the subject of a community sentence of at least 12 months.
s 40	Care workers: sexual activity in the presence of a person with a mental disorder	If:— (a) where the offender was under 18, he is or has been sentenced, in respect of the offence, to imprisonment for a term of at least 12 months; (b) in any other case,the offender, in respect of the offence or finding, is or has been (i) sentenced to a term of imprisonment (ii) detained in a hospital, or (iii) made the subject of a community sentence of at least 12 months.
s 41	Care workers: causing a person with a mental disorder to watch a sexual act	If:— (a) where the offender was under 18, he is or has been sentenced, in respect of the offence, to imprisonment for a term of at least 12 months; (b) in any other case,the offender, in respect of the offence or finding, is or has been (i) sentenced to a term of imprisonment (ii) detained in a hospital, or (iii) made the subject of a community sentence of at least 12 months.

	Offence	Qualification to applicability of a SOPO *A SOPO may only be ordered...*
s 47	Paying for sexual services of a child	If the victim or other party was under 16, and the offender (a) was 18 or over, or (b) is or has been sentenced in respect of the offence to imprisonment for a term of at least 12 months. *Note that where V or other party was over 16 Sch 5 applies.*
s 48	Causing or inciting child prostitution or pornography	If the offender (a) was 18 or over, or (b) is or has been sentenced in respect of the offence to imprisonment for a term of at least 12 months.
s 49	Controlling a child prostitute or a child involved in pornography	If the offender (a) was 18 or over, or (b) is or has been sentenced in respect of the offence to imprisonment for a term of at least 12 months.
s 50	Arranging or facilitating child prostitution or pornography	If the offender (a) was 18 or over, or (b) is or has been sentenced in respect of the offence to imprisonment for a term of at least 12 months.
s 61	Administering a substance with intent	
s 62	Committing an offence with intent to commit a sexual offence	If:— (a) where the offender was under 18, he is or has been sentenced, in respect of the offence, to imprisonment for a term of at least 12 months; (b) in any other case (i) the victim was under 18, or (ii) the offender, in respect of the offence or finding, is or has been (a) sentenced to a term of imprisonment (b) detained in a hospital, or (c) made the subject of a community sentence of at least 12 months.
s 63	Trespass with intent to commit a sexual offence	If:— (a) where the offender was under 18, he is or has been sentenced, in respect of the offence, to imprisonment for a term of at least 12 months; (b) in any other case (i) the victim was under 18, or (ii) the offender, in respect of the offence or finding, is or has been (a) sentenced to a term of imprisonment (b) detained in a hospital, or (c) made the subject of a community sentence of at least 12 months.

	Offence	Qualification to applicability of a SOPO *A SOPO may only be ordered…*
s 64	Sex with an adult relative: penetration	If:— (a) where the offender was under 18, he is or has been sentenced, in respect of the offence, to imprisonment for a term of at least 12 months; (b) in any other case,the offender, in respect of the offence or finding, is or has been (i) sentenced to a term of imprisonment (ii) detained in a hospital.
s 65	Sex with an adult relative: consenting to penetration	If:— (a) where the offender was under 18, he is or has been sentenced, in respect of the offence, to imprisonment for a term of at least 12 months; (b) in any other case,the offender, in respect of the offence or finding, is or has been (i) sentenced to a term of imprisonment (ii) detained in a hospital.
s 66	Exposure	If:— (a) where the offender was under 18, he is or has been sentenced, in respect of the offence, to imprisonment for a term of at least 12 months; (b) in any other case (i) the victim was under 18, or (ii) the offender, in respect of the offence or finding, is or has been (a) sentenced to a term of imprisonment (b) detained in a hospital or (c) made the subject of a community sentence of at least 12 months.
s 67	Voyeurism	If:— (a) where the offender was under 18, he is or has been sentenced, in respect of the offence, to imprisonment for a term of at least 12 months; (b) in any other case (i) the victim was under 18, or (ii) the offender, in respect of the offence or finding, is or has been (a) sentenced to a term of imprisonment (b) detained in a hospital or (c) made the subject of a community sentence of at least 12 months.
s 69	Intercourse with an animal	If:— (a) where the offender was under 18, he is or has been sentenced, in respect of the offence, to imprisonment for a term of at least 12 months; (b) in any other case,the offender, in respect of the offence or finding, is or has been (i) sentenced to a term of imprisonment (ii) detained in a hospital.

	Offence	Qualification to applicability of a SOPO *A SOPO may only be ordered...*
s 70	Sexual penetration of a corpse	If:— (a) where the offender was under 18, he is or has been sentenced, in respect of the offence, to imprisonment for a term of at least 12 months; (b) in any other case,the offender, in respect of the offence or finding, is or has been (i) sentenced to a term of imprisonment (ii) detained in a hospital.

Note that ss 47, 51–53 and 57–59A of the SOA 2003 are found under Sch 5; see from para 16.54. **16.52**

Offences Which may be Subject to a SOPO under Miscellaneous Acts after 2003 **16.53**

	Offence	Qualification to applicability of a SOPO *A SOPO may only be ordered...*
s 63 Criminal Justice and Immigration Act 2008	Possession of extreme pornographic images	If the offender (a) was 18 or over; and (b) is sentenced to a term of imprisonment of at least 2 years.
s 62(1) Coroners and Justice Act 2009	Possession of prohibited images of children	If the offender (a) was 18 or over; and (b) is sentenced to a term of imprisonment of at least 2 years.

K. SEXUAL OFFENCES ACT 2003, SCH 5

References to an offence include attempts, conspiracy or incitement to commit that offence,[67] and aiding, abetting, counselling or procuring the commission of that offence.[68] **16.54**

Common Law Offences Which may be Subject to a SOPO

These comprise murder; manslaughter; kidnapping; false imprisonment; and outraging public decency. **16.55**

[67] SOA 2003, Sch 5, s 173(a).

[68] SOA 2003, s 173(b).

16.56 Offences under the Offences against the Person Act 1861 Which may be Subject to a SOPO

Provision	Offence
s 4	Soliciting murder
s 16	Threats to kill
s 18	Wounding with intent to cause grievous bodily harm
s 20	Malicious wounding
s 21	Attempting to choke, suffocate, or strangle in order to commit or assist in committing an indictable offence
s 22	Using chloroform etc. to commit or assist in the committing of any indictable offence
s 23	Maliciously administering poison etc. so as to endanger life or inflict grievous bodily harm
s 27	Abandoning children
s 28	Causing bodily injury by explosives
s 29	Using explosives etc. with intent to do grievous bodily harm
s 30	Placing explosives with intent to do bodily injury
s 31	Setting spring guns etc. with intent to do grievous bodily harm
s 32	Endangering the safety of railway passengers
s 35	Injuring persons by furious driving
s 37	Assaulting officer preserving wreck
s 38	Assault with intent to resist arrest
s 47	Assault occasioning actual bodily harm

16.57 Offences under Miscellaneous Acts 1883 to 1938 Which may be Subject to a SOPO

Provision	Offence
Explosive Substances Act 1883, s 2	Causing explosion likely to endanger life or property
Explosive Substances Act 1883, s 3	Attempt to cause explosion, or making or keeping explosive with intent to endanger life or property
Infant Life (Preservation) Act 1929, s 1	Child destruction
Children and Young Persons Act 1933, s 1	Cruelty to children
Infanticide Act 1938, s 1	Infanticide

Offences under the Firearms Act 1968 Which may be Subject to a SOPO 16.58

Provision	Offence
s 16	Possession of firearm with intent to endanger life
s 16A	Possession of firearm with intent to cause fear of violence
s 17(1)	Use of firearm to resist arrest
s 17(2)	Possession of firearm at time of committing or being arrested for offence specified in Schedule 1 to that Act
s 18	Carrying a firearm with criminal intent

Offences under the Theft Act 1968 Which may be Subject to a SOPO 16.59

Provision	Offence
s 8	Robbery or assault with intent to rob
s 9(1)(a)	Burglary with intent to— (a) steal; (b) inflict grievous bodily harm on a person; or (c) do unlawful damage to a building or anything in it
s 10	Aggravated burglary
s 12A	Aggravated vehicle-taking involving an accident which caused the death of any person

Offences under Miscellaneous Acts 1971 to 1982 Which may be Subject to a SOPO 16.60

Criminal Damage Act 1971, s 1	Arson
Criminal Damage Act 1971, s 1(2)	Destroying or damaging property other than an offence of arson
Taking of Hostages Act 1982, s 1	Hostage-taking

Offences under the Aviation Security Act 1982 Which may be Subject to a SOPO 16.61

s 1	Hijacking
s 2	Destroying, damaging or endangering safety of aircraft
s 3	Other acts endangering or likely to endanger safety of aircraft
s 4	Offences in relation to certain dangerous articles

16.62 Offences under Miscellaneous Acts 1983 to 1985 Which may be Subject to a SOPO

Mental Health Act 1983, s 127	Ill-treatment of patients
Child Abduction Act 1984, s1	Abduction of child by parent, etc
Child Abduction Act 1984, s 2	Abduction of child by other persons
Prohibition of Female Circumcision Act 1985, s 1	Prohibition of female circumcision

16.63 Offences under the Public Order Act 1986 Which may be Subject to a SOPO

s 1	Riot
s 2	Violent disorder
s 3	Affray

16.64 Offences under Miscellaneous Acts 1988 (including Causing Death by Driving) Which may be Subject to a SOPO

Criminal Justice Act 1988, s 134	Torture
Road Traffic Act 1988, s 1	Causing death by dangerous driving
Road Traffic Act 1988, s 3A	Causing death by careless driving (when under influence of drink or drugs)

16.65 Offences under the Aviation and Maritime Security Act 1990 Which may be Subject to a SOPO

s 1	Endangering safety at aerodromes
s 9	Hijacking of ships
s 10	Seizing or exercising control of fixed platforms
s 11	Destroying fixed platforms or endangering their safety
s 12	Other acts endangering or likely to endanger safe navigation
s 13	Offences involving threats

Offences under the Protection from Harassment Act 1997 Which may be Subject to a SOPO 16.66

s 2	Harassment
s 2A	Stalking
s 4	Putting people in fear of violence
S 4A	Stalking involving fear of violence or serious alarm or distress

Miscellaneous Acts 1994 to 2004 Which may be Subject to a SOPO 16.67

Part II Channel Tunnel (Security) Order 1994 (SI 1994 No 570)	Offences relating to Channel Tunnel trains and the tunnel system
Crime and Disorder Act 1998, s 29	Racially or religiously aggravated assaults
Crime and Disorder Act 1998, s 31(1)(a) or (b)	Racially or religiously aggravated offences under the Public Order Act 1986, s 4 or 4A
Regulation of Investigatory Powers Act 2000, s 53	Failure to comply with a notice relating to encrypted information
Regulation of Investigatory Powers Act 2000, s 54	Tipping off in connection with such a notice
Postal Services Act 2000, s 85(3)	Sending a postal package with obscene contents
Postal Services Act 2000, s 85(4)	Sending a postal package with obscene words, marks or designs
International Criminal Court Act 2001, s 51	Genocide, crimes against humanity or war crimes
International Criminal Court Act 2001, s 52	Conduct ancillary to genocide etc committed outside the jurisdiction
Communications Act 2003, s 127(1)	Sending or causing to be sent a message or other matter that is grossly offensive or of an indecent, obscene or menacing character
Domestic Violence, Crime and Victims Act 2004, s 5	Causing or allowing the death of a child or vulnerable adult

Offences under the Sexual Offences Act 2003 listed under Sch 5 16.68

s 47	Paying for sexual services of a child, where the victim or (as the case may be) other party was 16 or over. *See Sch 3 for victims under 16*
s 52	Causing or inciting prostitution for gain
s 53	Controlling prostitution for gain
s 57	Trafficking into the UK for sexual exploitation
s 58	Trafficking within the UK for sexual exploitation
s 59	Trafficking out of the UK for sexual exploitation
s 59A	(When brought into force) Trafficking people for sexual exploitation

L. SUGGESTED FORMS OF WORDS FOR SOPOs

16.69 With thanks to HHJ Martin Picton, Director, Serious Sexual Offences Course for his generosity in allowing us to include here his work for the Judicial College.

In a 'typical' internet browsing case it is highly unlikely that anything more than the *Smith and Ors* formulation will be necessary or justifiable	
Smith compliant suggested form of wording	Comment
The defendant is prohibited from: (1) using any device capable of accessing the internet unless (i) it has the capacity to retain and display the history of internet use (and is at all times set to do so[69]), and (ii) he makes the device available on request for inspection by a police officer; (2) deleting such history; (3) possessing any device capable of storing digital images unless he makes it available on request for inspection by a police officer.	The words in brackets 'and is at all times set to do so' were suggested in *Warbutton* in appreciation of the ease with which the prohibition might otherwise be sidestepped. The judgment did not refer to the even easier method by which the *Smith* formulation can be defeated, ie the use of a standard 'in private' setting. In *Kimpriktzis*[70] the court held that the inclusion of the words 'for removal and inspection by a police officer' after 'makes the device available' was 'too Draconian'.
	Query the inclusion of a 'net nanny' program and/or any other police monitoring software. In *Smith* it was suggested that there may be 'fewer difficulties' with such a provision but a danger of uncertainty. Make sure you have evidence that the police in your area use such software—the majority do not. Require there to be evidence of the effectiveness of any such program—there is unlikely to be any software that effectively blocks access to indecent images of children. In monitoring terms SECURUS (where available—only a limited number of forces have approved its use thus far) would appear to have the greatest potential for effectiveness. Bear in mind the difficulties that can arise, however, re mobile and tablet devices on which such software cannot currently be installed. Query a prohibition against owning or possessing or installing any history deletion software—they are popular programs amongst the 'browsing' fraternity. Query whether the enforced installation of software which prevents an offender from accessing 'legal' pornography would be regarded as oppressive and disproportionate—there is clearly some risk of that being the conclusion. In *Smith* the practice of including a prohibition framed as a requirement that an offender inform the police of all the devices owned or possessed that have the capacity for accessing the internet was disapproved of on the basis that it imposed too great a burden on the police.

[69] [2012] EWCA Crim 3146.

[70] [2013] EWCA Crim 734.

My researches suggest that police officers tasked with monitoring offenders disagree and would welcome such an order—breach is a great deal easier to establish than can be achieved by some occasional inspection of a computer's 'history' which provides little by way of insight into criminal usage.

Bear in mind that the more complicated the order the greater the potential for it to offend the *Smith* strictures.

If the risk consists of or includes the use of chatlines or similar networks to groom young people for sexual purposes, an additional clause to cover that may be permissible.

Bear in mind that file-sharing sites are the most common route by which offenders obtain indecent images of children—consider prohibiting an offender from using such sites but the terminology of such a prohibition will require careful thought and benefit from evidence from officers responsible for offender monitoring in this field. The breach of such a prohibition does at least have some potential for being discovered on a fairly cursory examination of the 'history' which is all that is ever likely to be undertaken by an officer tasked with monitoring a particular offender.

Using the internet to contact or to attempt to contact any female/male/child known or believed to be under the age of 16

Ensure appropriate gender specificity and guard against the risk of unintentional breach. In an extreme case it may be justifiable to extend the prohibition on internet contact to cover social networking generally, eg in the case of an offender who has been in contact with other paedophiles via such sites.

In a case that merits a non-contact prohibition anything more complicated than that set out below is going to be susceptible to legitimate objection.

The defendant is prohibited from:

(1) living in the same household as any female/male/child under the age of 16/18 unless with the express approval of Social Services for the area;

(2) having any unsupervised contact or communication of any kind with any female/male/child under the age of 16/18, other than

  (i) such as is inadvertent and not reasonably avoidable in the course of lawful daily life, or

  (ii) with the consent of the child's parent or guardian (who has knowledge of his convictions) *and* with the express approval of Social Services for the area.

The appropriate age and gender restrictions will depend on whether the offender's sexual attraction toward children is gender-specific and whether the risk to be catered for can legitimately be said to encompass familial and/or breach of trust type offending in which case the older age limit would be appropriate. Any non-contact restriction should only be imposed where there is an identifiable risk of contact offences. There *must* be an inadvertent contact exception included in any prohibition. A failure to include such an exception will almost certainly result in a successful appeal. The case of *Turner*[71] suggests that the Court of Appeal may be more prepared to sanction a non-contact prohibition in a 'browsing' case than has been the case previously.

In *R (on the application of Paul Richards) v Teeside Magistrates Court and the Chief Constable of Cleveland*[72] the court approved the use of an electronic tag in order to monitor compliance with a non-contact framed by way of an exclusion from a particular area.

[71] Decided on 30.1.2013.

[72] [2013] EWHC 2208 (QB).

There may be cases where the particular circumstances of the offending can be indicative of specific 'risk' situations, eg engaging in occupations or activities with children, or frequenting schools or parks. An additional condition specifically catering for that may be justified, but note in particular Practical Tips (3) and (4) above.

Victim-specific prohibitions remain of potential value and should be worded as with any other restraint order type provision. A map delineating particular areas from which the defendant is excluded may be desirable.

In a case where an offender has made use of a camera in order to offend there may be a justification in prohibiting him from owning or possessing one in the future but care will have to be taken not to impose a prohibition that is overly restrictive in the context of modern communications devices. It *may* still be possible to acquire a mobile phone that lacks the capacity to take still and/or video images but the vast majority do possess such a capacity.

Not to seek or undertake any employment (including voluntary work, paid or otherwise, which will or is likely to bring him/her into unsupervised contact with children [specify target gender where appropriate] under the age of 16 years	Clauses such as this have not, since *Smith*, been routinely made (even in cases where non-contact prohibitions may be justified) by judges aware of the direction in *Smith* that SOPOs must avoid duplication with other statutory controls that may impact on an offender's freedom of behaviour by reference, inter alia, to the maintenance of barred lists under the SVGA 2006 and/or disqualification under the CJCSA 2000. Subsequent to *Smith*, disqualification under the 2000 Act has been abolished and the regimes under the SVGA amended. The more serious sexual offences will result in an offender being placed upon either the children's barred list (or adult barred list) dependent upon the nature of the offence charged as set out in s 2 and Sch 3 to the Act and the Safeguarding Vulnerable Groups Act 2006 (Prescribed and Miscellaneous Provisions) Regulations 2009 (SI 2009 No 37) and an offender caught by the relevant provision will have no right to make representations. Other offences, including 'browsing', will result in inclusion in the children's (or adult) list but with the right to make representations before inclusion and only if there is reason to believe that the offender is or has been, or might in the future be, engaged in a regulated activity. The body now responsible for administering the scheme, the Disclosure and Barring Service, will have to make an assessment in the case of all those not caught by the automatic inclusion offences. It is suggested that any court considering a SOPO will have to establish whether the offender is subject to automatic inclusion on a list and if not whether a clause such as this is 'necessary' in SOPO terms.

17

SEXUAL OFFENCES COMMITTED OUTSIDE THE JURISDICTION

17.01 The Criminal Justice and Immigration Act 2008 amended the provisions relating to the commission of sexual offences outside the jurisdiction from 14.7.2008.[1] Accordingly, it is necessary to know the date of the alleged offending so that charges may be brought under the appropriate version of the SOA 2003, s 72.

A. OFFENCES PRIOR TO 14 JULY 2008

17.02 A person who on or after 1.4.2004 is a British citizen or United Kingdom resident[2] is liable to prosecution for a sexual offence committed outside the jurisdiction if the offence is recognized as a sexual offence both in the country in which it is committed[3] and within the jurisdiction of England, Wales or Northern Ireland.[4]

17.03 The offence committed is that sexual offence with which the defendant would have been charged had the offence been committed in the jurisdiction.[5]

1. Establishing the Offence committed in the Foreign Jurisdiction

17.04 The court should presume that the defendant's alleged actions constitute an offence under the law in force in the foreign country or territory unless the defendant serves a notice upon the prosecution disputing that this condition has been met.[6]

17.05 The notice must: (a) state that, on the facts as alleged, the condition is not in the defendant's opinion met;[7] (b) show the defendant's grounds for that opinion;[8] and (c) require the prosecution to prove that it is met.[9] The court can, however, waive the condition to serve such a notice.[10]

1 Criminal Justice and Immigration Act 2008 (Commencement No 2 and Transitional and Savings Provisions) Order 2008 (SI 2008 No 1586).
2 SOA 2003 prior to amendment, s 72(2).
3 SOA 2003, s 72(1)(a).
4 SOA 2003, s 72(1)(b).
5 SOA 2003, s 72(1)(b).
6 SOA 2003, s 72(4).
7 SOA 2003, s 72(4)(a).
8 SOA 2003, s 72(4)(b).
9 SOA 2003, s 72(4)(c).
10 SOA 2003, s 72(5).

17.06 The extra-territorial sexual offence need not be described identically to the offence under the law of England, Wales or Northern Ireland. All that is necessary is that the *actus reus* of an offence under both sets of laws is satisfied.[11] This is a question for the judge alone.[12]

2. Relevant Offences

17.07 Paragraph 1 of Sch 2 to the SOA 2003 lists the sexual offences to which s 72 applies.[13]

Offences under the Sexual Offences Act 2003

17.08 *All* offences under the SOA 2003, ss 1–63 fall within the ambit of s 72 where the complainant (or intended complainant in the case of ss 62 and 63)[14] was *under 16 at the time of the offence.*[15] By their very nature, ss 5–15 involve complainants under 16 (or under 13).[16]

Offences under Miscellaneous Acts

17.09 Offences under:

(i) the Protection of Children Act 1978, s 1 (indecent photographs of children);[17] or

(ii) the Criminal Justice Act 1988, s 160 (possession of indecent photograph of a child);[18]

where the photograph or pseudo-photograph showing a child under 16 falls within the ambit of s 72.

B. OFFENCES ON OR AFTER 14 JULY 2008

17.10 A new s 72 was inserted into the SOA 2003 by the Criminal Justice and Immigration Act 2008. It creates an offence that can be committed in three different ways.

(1) If a UK national does an act in a country outside the United Kingdom (even if legal in that country) that, if done in England and Wales, would constitute a sexual offence listed in Sch 2.[19]

(2) If a UK national does an act in a country outside the United Kingdom that constitutes an offence under the law in force in that country, and the act, if done in England and Wales, would constitute a sexual offence listed in Sch 2.[20]

(3) If a person commits an offence in another country that, if done in England and Wales, would have constituted a sexual offence to which this section applies, and that person was not a UK national or resident at the time, but met the residence or nationality criteria.[21]

1. Establishing the Offence committed in the Foreign Jurisdiction

17.11 For the purposes of offences (2) and (3), the court should presume that the defendant's alleged actions constitute an offence under the law in force in the foreign country or territory unless the defendant serves a notice upon the prosecution disputing that this condition has been met.[22]

[11] SOA 2003, s 72(3).
[12] SOA 2003, s 72(6).
[13] SOA 2003, s 72(7).
[14] Committing an offence with intent to commit a sexual offence (s 62); trespass with intent to commit a sexual offence (s 63); SOA 2003, Sch 2, s 1(c).
[15] SOA 2003, Sch 2, s 1(b).
[16] SOA 2003, s 1(a).
[17] SOA 2003, s 1(d)(i).
[18] SOA 2003, s 1(d)(ii).
[19] SOA 2003 following amendment, s 72(1).
[20] SOA 2003, s 72(2).
[21] SOA 2003, s 72(3), s 72(9).
[22] SOA 2003, s 72(6).

The notice must: (a) state that, on the facts as alleged, the condition is not in the defendant's opinion met;[23] (b) show the defendant's grounds for that opinion;[24] and (c) require the prosecution to prove that it is met.[25] The court can, however, waive the condition to serve such a notice.[26] **17.12**

For the purposes of offences (2) and (3), the extra-territorial sexual offence need not be described identically to the offence under the law of England and Wales. All that is necessary is that the *actus reus* of an offence under both sets of laws is satisfied.[27] This is a question for the judge alone.[28] **17.13**

2. Relevant Offences

The relevant offences are set out in Sch 2 to the Sexual Offences Act 2003, as amended by the Criminal Justice and Immigration Act 2008. **17.14**

Offences under the Sexual Offences Act 2003

(i) An offence under any of ss 5–19, 25, 26 and 47–50. **17.15**
(ii) An offence under any of ss 1–4, 30–41 and 61 where the victim of the offence was under 18 at the time of the offence.
(iii) An offence under s 62 or 63 where the intended offence was an offence against a person under 18.

Offences under miscellaneous acts

(i) Protection of Children Act 1978, s 1 (indecent photographs of children), or **17.16**
(ii) Criminal Justice Act 1988, s 160 (possession of indecent photograph of child).

[23] SOA 2003, s 72(6)(a).
[24] SOA 2003, s 72(6)(b).
[25] SOA 2003, s 72(6)(c).
[26] SOA 2003, s 72(7).
[27] SOA 2003, s 72(5).
[28] SOA 2003, s 72(8).

APPENDIX A

Specified Sexual Offences

Schedule 15 of Part II of the Criminal Justice Act 2003 provides a definitive list of 'specified' sexual offences for the purposes of assessing 'dangerousness' when sentencing. Aiding, abetting, counselling, procuring, inciting, conspiring or attempting to commit any of the specified offences also falls within the ambit of Sch 15.[1]

A. Specified Sexual Offences under the Sexual Offences Act 1956

Legislative Provision	Offence
SOA 1956, s 1	Rape
SOA 1956, s 2	Procurement of woman by threats
SOA 1956, s 3	Procurement of woman by false pretences
SOA 1956, s 4	Administering drugs to obtain or facilitate intercourse
SOA 1956, s 5	Intercourse with a girl under 13
SOA 1956, s 6	Intercourse with a girl under 16
SOA 1956, s 7	Intercourse with a defective
SOA 1956, s 9	Procurement of a defective
SOA 1956, s 10	Incest by a man
SOA 1956, s 11	Incest by a woman
SOA 1956, s 14	Indecent assault on a woman
SOA 1956, s 15	Indecent assault on a man
SOA 1956, s 16	Assault with intent to commit buggery
SOA 1956, s 17	Abduction of woman by force or for the sake of her property
SOA 1956, s 19	Abduction of unmarried girl under 18 from parent or guardian
SOA 1956, s 20	Abduction of unmarried girl under 16 from parent or guardian
SOA 1956, s 21	Abduction of defective from parent or guardian
SOA 1956, s 22	Causing prostitution of women
SOA 1956, s 23	Procuration of girl under 21
SOA 1956, s 24	Detention of woman in brothel
SOA 1956, s 25	Permitting girl under 13 to use premises for intercourse
SOA 1956, s 26	Permitting girl under 16 to use premises for intercourse

[1] CJA 2003, Sch 15, Part II, para 153.

Legislative Provision	Offence
SOA 1956, s 27	Permitting defective to use premises for intercourse
SOA 1956, s 28	Causing or encouraging the prostitution of, intercourse with, or indecent assault on girl under 16
SOA 1956, s 29	Causing or encouraging prostitution of defective
SOA 1956, s 32	Soliciting by men
SOA 1956, s 33	Keeping a brothel

B. Specified Sexual Offences under Miscellaneous Acts 1957–2002

Legislative Provision	Offence
MHA 1959, s 128	Sexual intercourse with patients
IwCA 1960, s 1	Indecent conduct towards young child
SOA 1967, s 4	Procuring others to commit homosexual acts
SOA 1967, s 5	Living on earnings of male prostitution
TA 1968, s 9	Burglary with intent to commit rape
CLA 1977, s 54	Inciting girl under 16 to have incestuous sexual intercourse
PCA 1978, s 1	Indecent photographs of children
Customs and Excise Management Act 1979, s 170	Penalty for fraudulent evasion of duty etc in relation to goods prohibited to be imported under the Customs Consolidation Act 1876, s 42 (indecent or obscene articles)
CJA 1988, s 160	Possession of indecent photograph of a child

C. Specified Sexual Offences under the Sexual Offences Act 2003

Legislative Provision	Offence
SOA 2003, s 1	Rape
SOA 2003, s 2	Assault by penetration
SOA 2003, s 3	Sexual assault
SOA 2003, s 4	Causing a person to engage in sexual activity without consent
SOA 2003, s 5	Rape of a child under 13
SOA 2003, s 6	Assault of a child under 13 by penetration
SOA 2003, s 7	Sexual assault of a child under 13
SOA 2003, s 8	Causing or inciting a child under 13 to engage in sexual activity
SOA 2003, s 9	Sexual activity with a child
SOA 2003, s 10	Causing or inciting a child to engage in sexual activity
SOA 2003, s 11	Engaging in sexual activity in the presence of a child
SOA 2003, s 12	Causing a child to watch a sexual act
SOA 2003, s 13	Child sex offences committed by children or young persons
SOA 2003, s 14	Arranging or facilitating commission of a child sex offence
SOA 2003, s 15	Meeting a child following sexual grooming etc

SOA 2003, s 16	Abuse of position of trust: sexual activity with a child
SOA 2003, s 17	Abuse of position of trust: causing or inciting a child to engage in sexual activity
SOA 2003, s 18	Abuse of position of trust: sexual activity in the presence of a child
SOA 2003, s 19	Abuse of position of trust: causing a child to watch a sexual act
SOA 2003, s 25	Sexual activity with a child family member
SOA 2003, s 26	Inciting a child family member to engage in sexual activity
SOA 2003, s 30	Sexual activity with a person with a mental disorder impeding choice
SOA 2003, s 31	Causing or inciting a person, with a mental disorder impeding choice, to engage in sexual activity
SOA 2003, s 32	Engaging in sexual activity in the presence of a person with a mental disorder impeding choice
SOA 2003, s 33	Causing a person, with a mental disorder impeding choice, to watch a sexual act
SOA 2003, s 34	Inducement, threat, or deception to procure sexual activity with a person with a mental disorder
SOA 2003, s 35	Causing a person with a mental disorder to engage in or agree to engage in sexual activity by inducement, threat, or deception
SOA 2003, s 36	Engaging in sexual activity in the presence, procured by inducement, threat or deception, of a person with a mental disorder
SOA 2003, s 37	Causing a person with a mental disorder to watch a sexual act by inducement, threat or deception
SOA 2003, s 38	Care workers: sexual activity with a person with a mental disorder
SOA 2003, s 39	Care workers: causing or inciting sexual activity
SOA 2003, s 40	Care workers: sexual activity in the presence of a person with a mental disorder
SOA 2003, s 41	Care workers: causing a person with a mental disorder to watch a sexual act
SOA 2003, s 47	Paying for sexual services of a child
SOA 2003, s 48	Causing or inciting child prostitution or pornography
SOA 2003, s 49	Controlling a child prostitute or a child involved in pornography
SOA 2003, s 50	Arranging or facilitating child prostitution or pornography
SOA 2003, s 52	Causing or inciting prostitution for gain
SOA 2003, s 53	Controlling prostitution for gain
SOA 2003, s 57	Trafficking into the UK for sexual exploitation
SOA 2003, s 58	Trafficking within the UK for sexual exploitation
SOA 2003, s 59	Trafficking out of the UK for sexual exploitation
SOA 2003, s 59A	Trafficking for sexual exploitation
SOA 2003, s 61	Administering a substance with intent
SOA 2003, s 62	Committing an offence with intent to commit a sexual offence
SOA 2003, s 63	Trespass with intent to commit a sexual offence
SOA 2003, s 64	Sex with an adult relative: penetration
SOA 2003, s 65	Sex with an adult relative: consenting to penetration
SOA 2003, s 66	Exposure
SOA 2003, s 67	Voyeurism
SOA 2003, s 69	Intercourse with an animal
SOA 2003, s 70	Sexual penetration of a corpse

APPENDIX B

CPS Guidance on Prosecuting Rape and Sexual Offences

Edited by Charlotte Triggs OBE, Senior Policy Advisor

Introduction

Rape cases are notoriously difficult to prosecute and by their very nature require sensitive and careful handling. The provision of accurate information to the victim throughout the life of the case, together with quality witness care, and careful consideration of Special Measures are all important factors in raising the quality of evidence given.

CPS Policy Statement

The Policy Statement explains how the CPS deals with allegations of rape. It is a public document available on the CPS external website in English at <http://www.cps.gov.uk/publications/docs/rape_policy_2012.pdf> and in Welsh at <http://www.cps.gov.uk/publications/docs/rape_policy_2012_welsh.pdf>.

The decision to prosecute—the Code for Crown Prosecutors

When deciding whether to prosecute a rape allegation, the two-stage Full Code Test must be satisfied. In terms of the evidence, there must be a realistic prospect of conviction. However, see *R (On the Application of B) v Director of Public Prosecutions* [2009] EWHC 106 on the 'Merits-Based' Approach to prosecuting rape.

The Policy Statement emphasizes the need for a proactive approach to case building working with investigators from early in the investigation to build evidentially strong cases. Rather than merely spotting the evidential failings, prosecutors are encouraged to think 'well, there is a problem here but is there any way that we can improve the evidence so that the Code standard is met?'

Victims and Witnesses

Giving evidence can be a traumatic experience for victims of rape. The Statement deals with:

- Special Measures, including the need to involve the victim in the decision to apply for a particular Special Measures Direction.
- A commitment to instruct advocates who have the right skills including their ability to deal sensitively with victims and witnesses.
- The rules preventing questioning about victims' previous sexual behaviour.
- Communication with the victim in the event that a charge is dropped or substantially reduced. This will include offering the victim a meeting with the prosecutor.

In addition the Policy Statement provides information and guidance on:

- The procedures to be adopted where the victim withdraws support or no longer wishes to give evidence.
- Accepting alternative pleas.
- Bail issues.
- Sentencing issues.
- Groups and organizations offering support to victims of rape.

Sexual Offences Act 2003

Selecting Charges

The variety of available offences frequently provides prosecutors with a choice of charges. Prosecutors should choose the most appropriate charge to fit the circumstances of the case, taking account of the courts' sentencing powers. As a general rule, where the circumstances of a case match a particular offence specified in the Act, that offence should be charged. For example, section 25 (familial child sex offence) where the victim is 14 should be charged rather than section 9 (sexual activity with a child), so long as the elements can be proved. Adopting this approach makes clear the context in which an offence is committed.

Offences against children under 13, where age can be proved, should be charged under sections 5–8, where the elements can be proved. For example, section 5 (rape of a child under 13) should be preferred to section 1 rape, to reflect the victim was a child.

Conversely, when reviewing cases involving children under 16 and under 18, prosecutors should select more serious charges involving proof of absence of consent over those in sections 9 to 12, where all the elements can be proved. So, for example, section 1 rape should be preferred to section 9 sexual activity with a child under 16 where the elements of rape are satisfied.

Rape (section 1)

Charging practice

Prosecutors should specify in the indictment whether the vagina, anus or mouth was penetrated. Where penetration of more than one orifice occurs, separate counts of rape should be preferred. The Court of Appeal in *R v K* [2008] EWCA Crim 1923 held that where it is unclear whether penetration was of the vagina or of the anus, it is permissible to allege penetration of 'the vagina or the anus'. The jury will be entitled to convict if they are sure that there was non-consensual penetration of one or the other by the defendant with his penis.

Rape is so serious that a prosecution is almost certainly required in the public interest.

Assault by penetration (section 2)

Key points:

- There has to be penetration of the vagina or anus but not the mouth.
- Penetration is by any part of A's body (e.g. finger, tongue, toe) or by anything else (e.g. bottle).
- Offence can be committed by either gender.
- This offence should be charged where there is insufficient evidence to charge rape, for example, if the victim is unsure if penetration was by a penis or something else.

This offence is in essence similar to rape and a prosecution is almost certainly required in the public interest.

Sexual Assault (section 3)

- If touching does not occur, then consider an attempt.
- The exact nature of the sexual activity involved will be a key factor in assessing the seriousness of the offence e.g. on the upper end of the scale, using one's naked genital organs to stroke, rub, press or touch the naked genital organs of another to at the lower end of the scale of patting someone on the bottom through clothing. There may be the presence of aggravating features that make the offence significantly more serious, such as, abuse of position, use of drugs or other substances, use of violence/coercion, use of a weapon in the offence, repeated offending, etc.

Causing Sexual Activity without Consent (section 4)

- Can be committed by words alone, e.g. defendant makes his victim carry out a sexual act, such as masturbation, that only involves the victim.
- The mode of trial and sentence varies depending on whether there is or is not penetration.
- One of the purposes of this offence, in addition to the wider range of sexual activity, is to create a female equivalent of the offence of rape, which carries the same level of punishment for what amounts to the same type of offending behaviour.

In determining the seriousness of the offence, the two main factors are the nature of the sexual activity and the level of the offender's culpability. In addition there may be aggravating factors present, e.g. force, coercion, use of a weapon, etc.

This section creates two separate offences because the maximum sentence differs depending on proving penetrative or non-penetrative activity: *R v Courtie* [1984] AC 463. In drafting charges and indictments, prosecutors should specify whether the sexual activity is penetrative or non-penetrative.

Offences Against Children

The 2003 Sexual Offences Act identifies three categories of offences against children, namely:

- under 13;
- under 16;
- under 18.

Offences Against Children under 13 (sections 5–8)

- Sections 5–8 apply the main non-consensual offences to children under 13, except that consent in these offences is irrelevant. A child under 13 does not, under any circumstances, have the legal capacity to consent to any form of sexual activity.
- The under-13 offences overlap with the child sex offences (ss 9 to 15 of the 2003 Act), which are designed to protect children under 16. However, the intention of parliament is that anyone who engages in sexual activity with a child under 13 should be prosecuted with one of the offences specifically designed to protect such children. This is to ensure the availability of the higher maximum penalties for the under-13 offences.
- These are offences of strict liability as to age. The prosecution has to prove only the intentional sexual activity and the age of the complainant at the relevant date.
- Note: *R v G* [2008] UKHL 37; [2009] Offences of strict liability are compatible with A6.2 European Convention on Human Rights (ECHR).

Section 5: Rape of a child under 13

- Where a defendant admits sexual activity with a child under 13 but states that the victim consented, the proper course is to invite the court to hold a Newton hearing. On no account should a section 1 rape count be added as an alternative.

Section 6: Assault of a child under 13 by penetration

- A defendant indicted for assault of a child under 13 by penetration may be acquitted and convicted in the alternative of the lesser offence of sexual assault.

Section 7: Sexual assault of a child under 13

Section 8: Causing or inciting a child under 13 to engage in sexual activity

- Section 8 creates two separate offences because the maximum sentence differs depending on proving penetrative or non-penetrative activity: *R v Courtie* [1984] AC 463.

Charges and indictments should specify whether the sexual activity is penetrative or non-penetrative.

In determining the level of sentence, the same degree of seriousness should apply whether a person 'causes' or 'incites' the activity.

Code for Crown Prosecutors—Considerations

Adult defendant

Where the defendant is an adult, notwithstanding the wide nature of the activity in sections 5–8, a prosecution will normally be required in the public interest.

Child defendant (under 18)

The overriding public concern is to protect children. It was not parliament's intention to punish children unnecessarily or for the criminal law to intervene where it is wholly inappropriate.

There are two important points to note:

(i) The Directors Guidance on Charging (5th edition: May 2013) states that offences under the Sexual Offences Act 2003 committed by or upon persons under the age of 18 years must always be referred to the CPS for a charging decision, whether admitted or not.
(ii) Youth Offender Specialists should review all files involving youth offenders and take all major decisions in relation to those cases, in particular, whether or not a prosecution should take place.

In addition:

- Chief Crown Prosecutors must be notified of any case where at least one of the complainants and at least one of the suspects are under the age of 13. This includes cases which are diverted from prosecution, whether on evidential or public interest grounds.
- All such cases must be reviewed by a prosecutor who is both a rape specialist and a youth specialist. All advocates conducting these cases must have a rape specialism and should also have a youth specialism.

Where a sexual offence committed by a child passes the evidential stage of the Full Code Test, it is essential that when considering the public interest, prosecutors have as much information as possible from sources including the police, Youth Offending Teams (YOTs), and any professionals assisting those agencies, about the defendant's background and the circumstances surrounding the alleged offence, as well as information about the victim. Failure to do so may lead to judicial review of any decision: *R v Chief Constable of Kent ex parte L* and *R v DPP ex parte B* [1991] 93 Cr App R 416.

Views expressed by the victim, and where appropriate the victim's family, should be taken into account in accordance with the Code.

Furthermore prosecutors must consider the interests of the youth when deciding whether it is in the public interest to prosecute (paragraph 4.12d) of the Code for Crown Prosecutors.

Factors: whether or not to prosecute young defendants

The weight to be attached to a particular factor will vary depending on the circumstances of each case. The factors are:

- The age and understanding of the offender, including whether the offender has been subjected to exploitation, coercion, threat, deception, grooming or manipulation by another which has led him or her to commit the offence;
- The relevant ages and levels of maturity of the parties, i.e. the same or no significant disparity in age;
- Whether the complainant entered into sexual activity willingly, i.e. did the complainant understand the nature of his or her actions and that (s)he was able to communicate his or her willingness freely;
- Parity between the parties in regard to sexual, physical, emotional and educational development;

- The relationship between the parties, its nature and duration and whether this represents a genuine transitory phase of adolescent development;
- Whether there is any element of exploitation, coercion, threat, deception, grooming, seduction, manipulation or breach of trust in the relationship;
- Whether the child under 13 freely consented (even though in law this is not a defence) or a genuine mistake as to his/her age was in fact made;
- The nature of the activity, e.g. penetrative or non-penetrative activity;
- The sexual and emotional maturity of the parties and any emotional or physical effects resulting from the conduct; and
- The likely impact of any prosecution on the parties.

In *R v G* and the *Secretary State for the Home Department*, G was a 15-year-old boy who had been charged with section 5 rape of a girl aged 12 years. The defence argued that a charge under section 5 amounted to a disproportionate interference with the defendant's right to privacy under Article 8 and that a charge under section 9 SOA 2003 (sexual activity with a child) or section 13 SOA 2003 (child sex offences committed by a child or young person) would have been correct.

The Court held Article 8.1 may be infringed if a child is prosecuted for an offence under section 5 and such interference may not be justified under Article 8.2. Any infringement will turn on the individual facts of each case and in this matter, the initial section 5 charge was correct and there was no duty on the judge to substitute a section 13 charge.

However, in many cases the issue of consent will not be resolved until after a Newton hearing has been held. If the facts are found to be not as serious as initially presented to the court, the judge can pass an appropriate sentence. This will ensure that there is no illegal interference with a defendant's Article 8 rights.

Offences Against Children under 16 (sections 9–13)

The 2003 Act provides that the age of consent is 16. Sections 9–13 clarify that any sexual activity involving consenting children under 16 is unlawful.

Sections 9–12 cover adult defendants.

Section 9: Sexual activity with a child

Section 10: Causing or inciting a child to engage in sexual activity

Section 11: Engaging in sexual activity in the presence of a child

Section 12: Causing a child to watch a sexual act

Key points:

- Consent is irrelevant.
- There is a defence of reasonable belief that the child is 16 or over. This does not apply where the child is under 13.
- No defence for lawfully married couples (foreign nationals) where one party is under 16.
- There is a defence for aiding and abetting or counselling the commission of an offence under section 9 only where the conditions of section 73 apply.
- Under section 11, there is no requirement that (B) is actually aware of the activity, although there is a requirement that (B) is present or can observe. Observation can be via a web-cam. Observation includes an image (section 79).

The factors in assessing the seriousness of the offences in sections 9–12 will be the:

- nature of the sexual activity;
- age and vulnerability of the victim;
- age gap between the child and offender;
- any breach of trust in the relationship; and
- any aggravating features, such as, covert use of drugs, use of force, exploitation, etc.

Charging Practice

The same set of circumstances may support a prosecution for offences requiring proof of lack of consent. Where this situation arises, and it is clear that there is an absence of consent, it would be appropriate to charge a non-consensual offence.

If, however, there are difficulties in proving the non-consensual offences, then an offence under section 9 may be appropriate (where the elements can be proved).

Offences under sections 25 and 26 (familial child sex offences) may also come within sections 9 and 10. Where there is clear evidence of the family relationship, prosecutors should charge the familial child sex offence.

Sections 9 and 10 apply where a child is under 13, which means that the activity may also be an offence under sections 5–8 (rape of a child under 13, assault of a child under 13 by penetration, sexual assault of a child under 13, and causing of inciting a child under 13 to engage in sexual activity). If it can be proved that the child is under 13 prosecutors should charge an offence, if appropriate, under sections 5–8. If there is difficulty in proving the victim is under 13, then a child sex offence should be charged. This approach is consistent with the intention of parliament.

Section 13: Child sex offences committed by children or young persons

It is an offence if a person under 18 commits an offence if (s)he does anything which would be an offence under sections 9–12.

Code for Crown Prosecutors—Adult/Child Defendants

Guidance set out above in relation to sections 5–8 also applies to sections 9–12. However, prosecutors may exercise greater discretion in relation to cases where the victim is aged 13–15 than where the victim is under 13.

It is not in the public interest to prosecute children of the same or similar age and understanding that engage in sexual activity, where the activity is truly consensual and there are no aggravating features, such as coercion or corruption.

Other Related Offences Against Children (Under 16)

Arranging and facilitating a child sex offence (section 14)

This offence is to prevent people making it possible for a child under 16 to be sexually abused.

Meeting a child following sexual grooming (section 15, as amended by section 73(a) Criminal Justice and Immigration Act 2008):

- The offence only applies to adults
- There must be communication (a meeting or any other form of communication) on at least two previous occasions. It need not be of a sexual nature.
- The communication can occur anywhere in the world.
  - i) The offender must either meet the child or travel to the pre-arranged meeting, or arrange to meet the child, or the child must travel to meet the offender.
  - ii) The meeting or at least part of the travel must take place within the jurisdiction.
  - iii) The person must have an intention to commit any offence under Part 1 of the 2003 Act or any act done outside England and Wales, which would be an offence in the jurisdiction. This may be evident from the previous communications or other circumstances e.g. an offender travels in possession of ropes, condoms or lubricants, etc.
  - iv) The child is under 16 and the adult does not reasonably believe that the child is over 16. However, if this is not the case e.g. the child's place has been taken by an undercover police officer, an attempt could be charged.

Offences Against Children Under 18

These offences are primarily concerned with the child giving ostensible consent, but that consent is not relevant because of their relationship with the abuser.

Abuse of position of trust (sections 16–24)

These offences are designed to protect 16- and 17-year-olds from being persuaded to engage in sexual activity, which would not be criminal except for (A's) position of trust in relation to the victim.

Where lack of consent can be proved, sections 1–4 should be charged where the child is 16 or 17. Notwithstanding that the sections apply to under 16s where (B) is under 16, prosecutors should charge an offence(s) under the child sex offences (sections 9–12), or the under 13s offences (sections 5–8), if appropriate, where the penalties are significantly higher to reflect the fact that (B) is below the age of consent and that the sexual activity is, of itself unlawful. It may be appropriate to charge an abuse of trust offence where the victim is under 16 when it is likely that the person in a position of trust reasonably believed that the child was 16 or over, but it is less probable that (s)he reasonably believed the child to be 18 or over.

Familial child sex offences (sections 25 and 26)

These offences reflect the modern family unit and take account of situations where someone is living within the same household as a child and assuming a position of trust or authority over that child, as well as relationships defined by blood ties, adoption, fostering, marriage or living together as partners.

Sections 25 and 26 create two separate offences because the maximum sentence differs depending on proving penetrative or non-penetrative activity: *R v Courtie* [1984] AC 463. In drafting charges and indictments, you should specify whether the sexual activity is either penetrative or non-penetrative sexual activity.

Where the offender is under 18 the offence (whether penetration occurred or not) is either way with a maximum penalty of 5 years on indictment (subsection (5) of each section).

In determining the seriousness of the offences relevant factors may include:
- the nature of the sexual activity;
- age and degree of vulnerability of the victim;
- the age gap between the victim and the offender; and
- the breach of trust arising from the family relationship;
- the same degree of seriousness should apply to section 26 (incites) as to engaging in the activity.

Where a child is under 13, prosecutors should charge an under 13 offence, if appropriate, notwithstanding that sections 25 and 26 apply to a child under 13. If there is difficulty in proving age under 13, then these sections should be charged, so long as the other elements of the offence can be proved.

Some cases involving children between 13 and 15 offences may fall within the familial offences as well as offences such as sections 9 and 10. In these circumstances, where there is sufficient evidence, prosecutors should charge a familial offence rather than a child sex offence. Where a child is 16 or 17 this will be the only charge available.

Offences (Children—Prostitution or Pornography)

Indecent photographs of children (sections 45 and 46)

Sections 45 and 46 of the Act introduced amendments to the Protection of Children Act 1978.

Abuse of children through prostitution or pornography (sections 47–50)

Sections 47–50 provide offences specifically to tackle the use of children in the sex industry, where a child is under 18.

These offences are:
- Section 47—paying for sexual services of a child;
- Section 48—causing or inciting child prostitution or pornography;
- Section 49—controlling a child prostitute or a child involved in pornography;
- Section 50—arranging or facilitating child prostitution or pornography.

Key points:
- Applies to children under 18.
- Consent is not in issue.
- There is a defence that a person reasonably believed that the child was over 18 providing the child was not under 13.
- 'Payment' is widely defined.
- A person is involved in pornography if an image of the child is recorded.

Charging practice

Where a child is under 13, prosecutors should charge sections 5–8 offences.

Where there are problems in proving that the defendant did not have a reasonable belief that the child was over 18, prosecutors may consider an offence under section 52 or section 53 (adult prostitution offences) provided the elements of the offence could be proved (e.g. the activity was done for an expectation of gain).

Code for Crown Prosecutors—Considerations

Although the legal age of consent for sexual activity is 16, parliament considered that persons should be protected from sexual exploitation up until the age of 18. These are very serious offences in which the public interest will normally require a prosecution.

Offences against Persons with a Mental Disorder

The legislation distinguishes between:

i) persons with a mental disorder impeding choice, whose mental functioning is so impaired at the time of the sexual activity that they are unable to make any decision about their involvement in that activity, i.e. they are 'unable to refuse',

ii) those who have the capacity to consent to sexual activity but who have a mental disorder that makes them vulnerable to inducement, threat or deception; and

iii) those who have the capacity to consent to sexual activity but who have a mental disorder and are in a position of dependency upon the carer.

Mental disorder is defined as in section 1 of the Mental Health Act 1983, as amended by the Mental Health Act 2007, as 'any disorder or disability of the mind'. As well as including serious mental illness this definition ensures the protection of those with a lifelong learning disability and persons who develop dementia in later life.

Medical evidence will usually be required to prove that a person has a mental disorder.

Offences Against Persons with a Mental Disorder Impeding Choice (sections 30–33)

Key points are:
- The sexual activity in sections 30–33 is the same activity as for the child sex offences (sections 9–12).
- The victim is, regardless of age, unable to refuse because of or for a reason related to a mental disorder.

- The offender knows or could reasonably be expected to know of the disorder and therefore the victim is likely to be unable to refuse.
- The victim is unable to refuse if (s)he lacks the capacity to choose to agree to the activity, e.g. sufficient understanding of the nature of the activity, or is unable to communicate such a choice to the offender (subsection (2) of sections 30–33).

In determining the seriousness of the offence, relevant factors include the:

- nature of the activity;
- relationship between the victim and the offender; and
- age and vulnerability of the victim.

Given the seriousness of these offences a prosecution will almost certainly be required in the public interest.

Offences where there are Inducements etc. to Persons with a Mental Disorder (sections 34–37)

Key points are:

- This category of offences is designed to protect persons with a mental disorder, whose mental impairment is not so severe that they are unable to refuse but who are vulnerable to inducement, threat or deception.
- The structure of sections 34–37 is the same as for sections 30–33 and the offences against children (sections 9–12).
- The victim purports to agree to the activity, but (s)he has a mental disorder.
- The defendant knows or could reasonably be expected to know that; and
- The agreement to the activity is obtained by the defendant by means of an inducement, threat or deception.

Refer to sections 30–33 above

Offences by Care Workers Against Persons with a Mental Disorder (sections 38–41)

These offences relate to the protection of those who have the capacity to consent but who, for reasons associated with their mental disorder, may agree to sexual activity solely because they are influenced by their familiarity with and/or dependency upon the carer.

Charging practice

Sections 38 and 39 carry a high maximum penalty because it is designed as a 'catch all' offence. The prosecution is not required to prove (sections 38–41) that the victim has either 'an inability to refuse' or has been given an inducement, threat or deception. Where these elements cannot be proved or are difficult to prove and the defendant is in a position of care, these offences should be charged.

Given the seriousness of these offences a prosecution will normally be required.

Sex with an Adult Relative (sections 64 and 65 Sexual Offences Act 2003)

Charging practice

These offences should primarily be reserved for situations where a history of abuse against a child family member continues into adulthood or where a suspect sexually exploits an adult relative who is vulnerable. To this end it will be useful to consider the circumstances in which the relationship first arose and how long it has existed.

Where a history of exploitation and grooming can be shown, at least in the early stages of the relationship, a prosecution for historic offences of rape, sexual assault or similar may be appropriate in addition to any offence committed under sections 64 and 65.

The introduction of blood uncles and aunts into the list of proscribed relationships raises the possibility of a lawful relationship pre-dating the Act subsequently becoming unlawful. In the absence of any history of exploitation a prosecution in these circumstances is unlikely to be in the public interest.

When considering a case involving sex with an adult relative, prosecutors should bear in mind that all adult parties will commit an offence providing they either commit or consent to the act, regardless of whether or not they are the 'victim'. Prosecutors should always consider the position of the parties individually and identify any issues of exploitation and victimization. Although both may have committed an offence, different factors may apply to each, especially in relation to the public interest.

Victims and Witnesses

It is vital that victims are treated with dignity and respect and provided with the opportunity to influence how their case is handled. Whilst sexual violence can rob victims of the feeling of 'being in control', being kept informed and given choices, can help them 'take back control'. This may contribute to their recovery and avoid their re-victimization.

Information and Support for Victims and Witnesses

Multi-agency Witness Care Units staffed by police and CPS Witness Care Officers in every Criminal Justice System (CJS) Area provide information and support throughout the criminal justice process, tailored to the individual needs of the victim or witness.

Sexual Assault Referral Centres

The Sexual Assault Referral Centre (SARC) concept involves an integrated multi-agency response to sexual violence including specialist clinical intervention with defined care pathways that promote recovery and health following sexual violence irrespective of whether the victim wishes to report to the police.

Independent Sexual Violence Advisors

Independent Sexual Violence Advisors (ISVAs) provide professional support to victims of sexual violence, whether they report to the police or not.

ISVAs work alongside victims and provide practical advice and information ranging from how the CJS works to how to access housing benefit. Where a victim's case is going through the CJS the ISVA will work with him/her throughout the legal process and beyond, including accompanying the victim when they give evidence at court.

The support provided by ISVAs (as set out in Box 4.1(a) of *Achieving Best Evidence in Criminal Proceedings; Guidance on Interviewing Victims and Witnesses, and Guidance on Using Special Measures*) includes:

- Understanding the witness's views, wishes, concerns, and any particular vulnerabilities that might affect them during the criminal process (including the witness's views on Special Measures), and convey these to the relevant criminal justice system agency;
- Agreeing the manner and frequency of the provision of information;
- Familiarizing the witness with the court and its procedures, and with the responsibilities of the criminal justice system;
- Supporting the witness through interviews and court hearings;
- Exploring with the witness their preferences in respect of Special Measures and if it is relevant who they would want to accompany them into the live link room and relay that information to the Witness Care Unit or CPS Prosecutor;
- Undertaking court preparation and passing on information about the forthcoming trial;
- Accompanying the witness on a pre-trial visit to court;

- Accompanying the witness when their memory is to be refreshed (this should not be undertaken by a supporter who will accompany the witness while giving evidence);
- Accompanying the witness while they give evidence in court or the live link room (where the court approves this).

Witnesses who Withdraw Support for the Prosecution or Indicate that they are No Longer Willing to Give Evidence

When a victim or witness decides they no longer wish to give evidence, it is essential that the police enquire fully about why support for the prosecution has been withdrawn. Prosecutors may need to consider further charges of, for example, witness intimidation and should liaise with the Witness Care Officer, ISVA, or local specialist support service to establish what support the victim has already and whether to offer such services if not already provided.

Continuing a Case where the Victim Indicates a Withdrawal of Support

In some cases, a Special Measures application may provide sufficient reassurance to the victim for them to reconsider and to support a prosecution. If an application is not possible or the victim remains unwilling to give evidence, consideration must be given to the following options:

- proceeding without using the victim's evidence;
- making a hearsay application under section 116 of the Criminal Justice Act 2003;
- compelling the victim to give evidence; or
- discontinuing the case.

Background information is crucial when deciding how to proceed after the victim has withdrawn their support for the prosecution. This includes:

- the victim's ability to testify;
- any ongoing relationship between victim and defendant;
- if there is an ongoing relationship, its history and any previous incidents;
- the likelihood of the defendant re-offending;
- the likely impact on the victim of proceeding or not proceeding with the case; and
- any threats made since the incident.

Before deciding to issue a summons requiring the victim to give evidence, prosecutors must be satisfied that the safety of the victim will not be endangered. Factors to consider when assessing the victim's safety include:

- the victim's views on the impact on their safety of supporting the prosecution;
- whether a witness summons would make it safer for the victim to attend by effectively making it clear that the decision to proceed is that of the CPS rather than that of the victim;
- the police views on the safety of the victim and the likelihood of further harm; and
- whether the victim has support from a specialist service outside the CJS.

Prosecutors should request a risk assessment when making decisions about how to proceed. The final decision is the prosecutor's, but any decision to compel a witness to give evidence may be construed negatively, so every attempt should be made to regain the victim's or witness's support.

Visually Recorded Interviews with Witnesses

Prosecutors reviewing the video should be alert to any technical issues. Poor sound quality may have resulted from the copying process and a fresh copy may solve the problem.

Where the sound quality is especially poor, subtitles may be added. However, they must be easily removed since the leave of the court will be required before the jury can view the recording with subtitles. (By analogy with *R v Welstead* [1996] 1 Cr App R 59, the judge will have a discretion whether to allow the jury to follow the video recording by reference to the transcript in front of them.)

If the picture quality is poor it might it be possible to enhance it or re-arrange the configuration/layout of the screen image to give more prominence to the face of the witness.

It is essential that prosecutors, in consultation with counsel, ensure that interviews are edited so that they are an acceptable length. Inadmissible and irrelevant evidence (including sensitive information that does not form part of the case) should be edited out.

Special Measures Meeting with Witness

An early Special Measures discussion between the police and prosecutor should take place in every case.

It is good practice for the prosecutor and the trial advocate to meet the witness at a Special Measures meeting. Meeting the advocate in advance will better prepare the witness for court and provide an opportunity to discuss his/her Special Measures requirements. A full record must be maintained of matters discussed at the meeting, and there must be no discussion as to the evidence in the case.

Forensic Medical Evidence

CPS policy requires the Forensic Physician (FP) be included at the conference with the prosecutor, trial advocate and the investigating officer unless there are particular reasons for not doing so. Similarly, the FP should be called as a live witness at trial unless there are considered reasons for not so doing. FPs often work as GPs or hospital consultants. Efforts should be made for them to give evidence at a time that causes as little disruption as possible to them and their patients. Prosecutors should be aware of the impact when a busy clinic is cancelled.

FPs' statements should never be reduced to section 10 admissions without first consulting the FP to check that their meaning has not been diminished or misinterpreted.

One of the myths around rape is that victims will always have genital injuries. This is incorrect with many victims sustaining no genital injuries. Also, even where they may at the time have been injuries, if the allegation is historical, healing may have occurred. Prosecutors need to ensure that evidence about the incidence of injuries is included by the FP in their statement. Also a statement about whether the medical evidence supports, refutes or is neutral in relation to the victim's account, should be included in the FP's evidence.

Charging Practice

Alternative Charges

Prosecutors should use alternative counts sparingly and only where there are doubts concerning the issues, e.g. if evidence is unclear whether the victim was penetrated by a penis or other object, an alternative of assault by penetration would be appropriate.

Similarly where a complainant between the ages of 13 and 15 makes a clear and credible complaint of rape, prosecutors should charge rape rather than a section 9 sexual activity with a child offence.

Charging an alternative section 9 offence is not regarded as good practice. It may send a signal to the jury that the prosecution is not confident of its case, and may thereby weaken the prosecution's position. It may also serve to give a jury an easy option of convicting of section 9, rather than rape.

Youths

If an allegation of sexual abuse committed by a youth offender passes the evidential stage of the full Code test, the public interest stage must always be carefully considered before any prosecution is commenced. In reaching any decision to pursue an out-of-court disposal, the police and CPS must take into account other agencies' views and in particular Social Services. The consequences for the victim of the decision to prosecute and any views expressed by the victim or the victim's family should also be taken into account.

If the sexual act or activity was genuinely consensual and the youth and the child victim under 13 are close in age and development, a prosecution is unlikely to be appropriate. There is a fine line between sexual experimentation and offending and in general, children under the age of 13 should not be criminalized for sexual behaviour in the absence of coercion, exploitation or abuse of trust.

However, if a very young child has been seduced by a youth, or a babysitter in a position of responsibility has taken advantage of a child under 13 in his/her care, prosecution is likely to be in the public interest. Where a child under 13 has not given ostensible consent to the activity, a prosecution contrary to sections 5 to 8 is likely to be the appropriate course of action. Where the Full Code Test is satisfied in a case in which a youth is suspected of committing a sexual offence involving a child under the age of 13, the appropriate charge will be an offence contrary to sections 5 to 8 depending on the act, and not the lesser offence contrary to section 13 Sexual Offences Act 2003.

It is an offence contrary to section 13 Sexual Offences Act 2003 if a person under 18 does anything which would be an offence under sections 9–12 Sexual Offences Act 2003. These offences are punishable on indictment with imprisonment for a term not exceeding 5 years. They are 'grave crimes' for the purposes of section 24 Magistrates' Courts Act 1980 and section 91 Powers of Criminal Courts (Sentencing) Act 2000. Section 13(2)(a) purports to restrict the maximum penalty on summary conviction to a maximum of 6 months' imprisonment, although this should be read in the light of section 101(2) Powers of Criminal Courts (Sentencing) Act 2000 to allow a Detention and Training Order of up to 24 months.

Where both parties to sexual activity are under 16, they may both have committed a criminal offence. However, the overriding purpose of the legislation is to protect children and it was not parliament's intention to punish children unnecessarily or for the criminal law to intervene where it was wholly inappropriate. Consensual sexual activity between, for example, a 14- or 15-year-old and a teenage partner would not normally require criminal proceedings in the absence of aggravating features. The relevant considerations include:

- the respective ages of the parties;
- the existence and nature of any relationship
- their level of maturity;
- whether any duty of care existed;
- whether there was a serious element of exploitation.

Familial Sexual Offences Committed by Young People

Sections 25 and 26 Sexual Offences Act 2003 create the offences of sexual activity with a child family member and inciting a child family member to engage in sexual activity. These offences are punishable on indictment with imprisonment for a term not exceeding 5 years. They are 'grave crimes' for the purposes of section 24 Magistrates' Courts Act 1980 and section 91 Powers of Criminal Courts (Sentencing) Act 2000. Section 25(5)(b) and 26(5)(b) purport to restrict the maximum penalty on summary conviction to a maximum of 6 months' imprisonment, although this should be read in the light of section 101(2) Powers of Criminal Courts (Sentencing) Act 2000 to allow a Detention and Training Order of up to 24 months.

Sections 64 and 65 Sexual Offences Act 2003 make it an offence for a person aged 16 or over to penetrate or consent to penetration by a family member who is aged 18 or over. The maximum penalty is imprisonment for a term not exceeding 2 years (sections 64 (5) and 65 (5)).

In cases of sexual activity between siblings, care should be taken to balance the public interest in prosecuting such conduct with the interests and welfare of the victim and the family unit. As a general rule, alternatives to prosecution should be sought where the sexual activity was wholly consensual. The welfare agencies will normally intervene.

Prosecution should be considered where there is evidence of:

- seduction;
- coercion;
- exploitation or violence;
- a significant disparity in age.

In all cases the effect of prosecution on a victim and family should be taken into account and if the views of the welfare agencies are not included with the file they should be sought.

Rape of a child under 13 (section 5), assault of a child under 13 by penetration (section 6) and causing or inciting a child under 13 to engage in sexual activity that involves penetration (section 8) are indictable only offences with a maximum sentence of life imprisonment. The offences of sexual assault of a child under 13 (section 7), causing or inciting a child under 13 to engage in sexual activity where there has been no penetration (section 8) are punishable on indictment with imprisonment for a term not exceeding 14 years. They are all 'grave crimes' for the purposes of section 24 Magistrates' Courts Act 1980 and s 91 Powers of Criminal Courts (Sentencing) Act 2000.

A 'grave crime' is defined in section 91(1) Powers of Criminal Courts (Sentencing) Act 2000 as:

(a) an offence punishable in the case of a person aged 21 or over with imprisonment of 14 years or more, not being an offence for which the sentence is fixed by law; OR
(b) an offence of sexual assault contrary to section 3 Sexual Offences Act 2003; OR
(c) an offence of child sexual offences committed by children or young persons under 18 contrary to section 13 Sexual Offences Act 2003; OR
(d) an offence of sexual activity with a child family member contrary to section 25 Sexual Offences Act 2003; OR
(e) an offence of inciting a child family member to engage in sexual activity contrary to section 26 Sexual Offences Act 2003.

If a youth is convicted on indictment of a 'grave crime', the Crown Court may pass a sentence of detention under section 91(3) Powers of Criminal Courts (Sentencing) Act 2000 for a period that does not exceed the maximum period of imprisonment that can be imposed on a person aged 21 or over.

The Crown Court may only impose a sentence of detention under section 91 Powers of Criminal Courts (Sentencing) Act 2000 if none of the other available sentences are suitable (section 91 (3) Powers of Criminal Courts (Sentencing) Act 2000.

In all cases involving a grave crime, the magistrates should be invited to consider the question of venue (Archbold 5-286), before a plea is taken.

The reviewing lawyer should bear in mind the principles set out by Leveson J with the approval of the Vice President of the Court of Appeal in *R (On the Application of H, A and O) v Southampton Youth Court* [2004] EWHC 2912 Admin when the issue of venue is considered:

1. The general policy of the legislature is that those who are under 18 years of age and in particular children of under 15 years of age should, wherever possible, be tried in the youth court. It is the court which is best designed to meet their specific needs. A trial in the Crown Court with the inevitably greater formality and greatly increased number of people involved (including a jury and the public) should be reserved for the most serious cases.
2. It is a further policy of the legislature that, generally speaking, first time offenders aged 12 to 14 and all offenders under 12 should not be detained in custody and decisions as to jurisdiction should have regard to the fact that the exceptional power to detain for grave offences should not be used to water down the general principle. Those under 15 will rarely attract a period of detention and, even more rarely, those who are under 12.

3. In each case the court should ask itself whether there is a real prospect, having regard to his or her age, that this defendant whose case they are considering might require a sentence of, or in excess of, two years or, alternatively, whether although the sentence might be less than two years, there is some unusual feature of the case which justifies declining jurisdiction, bearing in mind that the absence of a power to impose a detention and training order because the defendant is under 15 is not an unusual feature.

Disclosure

Third Party Material

A third party has no obligation under the Criminal Procedure and Investigations Act (CPIA) to reveal material to the police or to the prosecutor. Furthermore, for example in the case of social services records, there may be a duty to claim public interest immunity (PII).

Nor is there any duty on the third party to retain material which may be relevant to the investigation and, in some circumstances, the third party may not be aware of the investigation or prosecution.

Third parties commonly encountered in rape/sexual offence investigations include:
- Social services departments
- Forensic Physicians
- Counsellors/therapists
- Schools
- Medical Practitioners
- Hospitals
- Owners of CCTV.

Reasonable lines of enquiry may include enquiries about relevant material in the possession of a third party. It is not necessary to make speculative enquiries, but frequently the existence of the material can be deduced from the circumstances. For example, where a child witness is in the care of the local authority, the social services may have relevant material.

In *R v Alibhai* [2004] EWCA Crim 681, the Court of Appeal held that before taking steps to obtain third party material, it must be shown that there was not only a suspicion that the third party had relevant material but also that the material was likely to satisfy the disclosure test.

Furthermore, *R v Alibhai* states that the prosecutor has a 'margin of consideration' as to what steps to take and was not under an absolute obligation to obtain material.
- Where having received a request from the investigator or prosecutor the third party refuses to co-operate, the matter should not be left. If criminal proceedings have commenced, the prosecutor should consider making an application for a witness summons, under section 97 of the Magistrates' Courts Act 1980 or section 2 of the Criminal Procedure (Attendance of Witnesses) Act 1965.
- Part 28 Criminal Procedure Rules 2010 applies to witness summons procedures.

If the prosecutor decides that unused material obtained from a third party passes the disclosure test (because it might reasonably be considered capable of undermining the prosecution case or assisting the accused), the prosecutor should take account of the Article 8 ECHR rights of the person to whom confidential material relates and consult with the third party before disclosure is made. See *R v Stafford Crown Court* [2006] EWHC 1645.

There may be public interest reasons which justify withholding disclosure, in which case the prosecutor will seek a PII ruling from the Court. Only material satisfying the disclosure test should be brought before the court for the purposes of seeking PII (*R v H and C* [2004] 2 AC 134).

Consent to Disclosure of Medical Records and Counselling Notes

Prosecutors must satisfy themselves that consent to disclosure of the medical records/counselling notes has been obtained by the police from the person to whom the notes refer.

If police enquiries indicate that there may be material in the records which falls within the CPIA disclosure test, the prosecutor should request the police to secure access to such records having first obtained the witness's informed consent. Such material as meets the test should then be disclosed to the defence with the witness's informed consent.

When obtaining consent, the victim or witness should be informed why the request is being made and what might happen to the record. The victim or witness has the right to decline consent if he or she so wishes but must also be told about the possible consequences as far as the case outcome is concerned.

Protocols for Disclosure

The 2013 Protocol and Good Practice Model—Disclosure of Information in cases of alleged child abuse and linked criminal and care directions hearings—came into force on 1 January 2014 and although not binding on local authorities includes very strong encouragement to operate in accordance with the good practice model.

Police and prosecutors are expected to share and seek appropriate information about vulnerable children and young people from social services, schools and family courts in accordance with the protocol and good practice model.

Disclosure—Miscellaneous

The disclosure regime set out in CPIA must be scrupulously followed. This means that only material satisfying the disclosure test should be disclosed to the defence. Under no circumstances should there be B 'blanket disclosure'. The disclosure of material that does not satisfy the disclosure test is a breach of the CPIA.

Newton Hearings

A Newton hearing (also known as the trial of an issue) is held following a plea of guilty to resolve factual conflicts between the prosecution and defence. In *R v Newton* (1982) 4 Cr App R (S) 388, Lord Lane CJ identified the methods by which such disputes can be resolved: in some cases by jury verdict, by the judge trying the issue or by hearing counsel (which generally meant that the defence version would be accepted).

The need for a Newton hearing commonly arises in prosecutions involving child sexual offences, particularly under sections 5, 6 and 7 of the SOA 2003. Although the child's consent is not an element of the offence it may become relevant to sentencing, where the defendant says that the child consented and the complainant says otherwise. A Newton hearing will enable the judge to determine the basis on which he will pass sentence.

When prosecuting sexual offences and the complainant and the defendant provide conflicting accounts, it may nonetheless be appropriate to accept a plea of guilty and to resolve the outstanding issues by holding a Newton hearing.

Prosecutors dealing with a Newton hearing must comply with the Attorney General's Guidelines on the Acceptance of Pleas and the Prosecutor's Role in the Sentencing Exercise [2009].

Societal Myths

Myth 1: Rape Occurs Between Strangers in Dark Alleys

- Domestic or acquaintance rape is 'real rape' and as serious as stranger rape;
- the psychological impact of being raped by a person the victim trusted can be greater;

- if the offence occurred at home the victim may have nowhere they feel safe; and
- they may self-blame and lose confidence in their own judgement.

Myth 2: Women Provoke Rape By The Way They Dress or Act

- It is the rapist who is at fault;
- women are entitled to dress how they wish.

Myth 3: Women Who Drink Alcohol or Use Drugs Are Asking to Be Raped

- Women have the same right to consume alcohol as men;
- being vulnerable does not imply consent;
- if a woman is unable to give consent because she is drunk, drugged or unconscious, it is rape; and
- only the rapist is responsible for the rape.

Myth 4: Rape is a Crime of Passion

- Rape is about power and control.

Myth 5: If She Didn't Scream, Fight or Get Injured, It Wasn't Rape

- Victims often fear serious injury or death and so co-operate with the rapist to save their lives;
- victims in a rape situations often become physically paralysed with terror or shock and are unable to move or fight; and
- non-consensual intercourse doesn't always leave visible signs on the body or the genitals.

Myth 6: You Can Tell if She's 'Really' Been Raped by How She Acts

- Reactions to rape are varied and individual; and
- many women experience shock after rape leaving them emotionally numb and apparently calm;
- others may be in self-denial or confused about what happened and carry on as normal.

Myth 7: Women Cry Rape When They Regret Having Sex or Want Revenge

- Studies have indicated that few reported rapes are false.

Myth 8: Only Gay Men Get Raped/Only Gay Men Rape Men

- Men of all sexual orientations get raped;
- men who rape other men are often heterosexual—they usually have a relationship with a woman; and
- rapists rape other men as part of their violence and need for power, dominance and control.

Myth 9: Prostitutes Cannot be Raped

- Sex workers negotiate with clients for consensual activities, not rape.

Myth 10: If the victim didn't complain immediately, it wasn't rape

- The trauma of rape can cause feelings of shame and guilt which might inhibit a victim from reporting. It was recognized by the Court of Appeal in *R v D (JA)* October 24 2008, that 'a late complaint does not necessarily mean that it's a false complaint'.

APPENDIX C

Sentencing Guidelines Council—Sexual Offences Act 2003 Definitive Guidelines

Applicability of guideline

In accordance with section 120 of the Coroners and Justice Act 2009, the Sentencing Council issues this definitive guideline. It applies to all offenders aged 18 and older, who are sentenced on or after 1 April 2014.

Section 125(1) of the Coroners and Justice Act 2009 provides that when sentencing offences committed on or after 6 April 2010:

"Every court—

(a) must, in sentencing an offender, follow any sentencing guideline which is relevant to the offender's case, and
(b) must, in exercising any other function relating to the sentencing of offenders, follow any sentencing guidelines which are relevant to the exercise of the function,

unless the court is satisfied that it would be contrary to the interests of justice to do so."

This guideline applies only to offenders aged 18 and older. General principles to be considered in the sentencing of youths are in the Sentencing Guidelines Council's definitive guideline, *Overarching Principles—Sentencing Youths.*

Structure, ranges and starting points

For the purposes of section 125(3)–(4) of the Coroners and Justice Act 2009, the guideline specifies *offence ranges*—the range of sentences appropriate for each type of offence. Within each offence, the Council has specified different *categories* which reflect varying degrees of seriousness. The offence range is split into *category ranges*—sentences appropriate for each level of seriousness. The Council has also identified a starting point within each category.

Starting points define the position within a category range from which to start calculating the provisional sentence. **Starting points apply to all offences within the corresponding category and are applicable to all offenders, in all cases.** Once the starting point is established, the court should consider further aggravating and mitigating factors and previous convictions so as to adjust the sentence within the range. Starting points and ranges apply to all offenders, whether they have pleaded guilty or been convicted after trial. Credit for a guilty plea is taken into consideration only at step four in the decision making process, after the appropriate sentence has been identified.

Information on ancillary orders is set out at Annex A on page 424. Information on historic offences is set out at annexes B and C on pages 425 and 426.

Information on community orders and fine bands is set out at Annex D on page 428.

Rape

Sexual Offences Act 2003 (section 1)

Triable only on indictment

Maximum: Life imprisonment

Offence range: 4–19 years' custody

This is a serious specified offence for the purposes of sections 224 and 225(2) (life sentence for serious offences) of the Criminal Justice Act 2003.

For offences committed on or after 3 December 2012, this is an offence listed in Part 1 of Schedule 15B for the purposes of sections 224A (life sentence for second listed offence) of the Criminal Justice Act 2003.

For convictions on or after 3 December 2012 (irrespective of the date of commission of the offence), this is a specified offence for the purposes of section 226A (extended sentence for certain violent or sexual offences) of the Criminal Justice Act 2003.

STEP ONE

Determining the offence category

The court should determine which categories of harm and culpability the offence falls into by reference **only** to the tables below.

Offences may be of such severity, for example involving a campaign of rape, that sentences of 20 years and above may be appropriate.

HARM	
Category 1	• The extreme nature of one or more category 2 factors or the extreme impact caused by a combination of category 2 factors **may** elevate to category 1
Category 2	• Severe psychological or physical harm • Pregnancy or STI as a consequence of offence • Additional degradation/humiliation • Abduction • Prolonged detention/sustained incident • Violence or threats of violence (beyond that which is inherent in the offence) • Forced/uninvited entry into victim's home • Victim is particularly vulnerable due to personal circumstances* *for children under 13 please refer to the guideline on page 331
Category 3	Factor(s) in categories 1 and 2 not present

CULPABILITY	
A	B
• Significant degree of planning • Offender acts together with others to commit the offence • Use of alcohol/drugs on victim to facilitate the offence • Abuse of trust • Previous violence against victim • Offence committed in course of burglary • Recording of the offence • Commercial exploitation and/or motivation • Offence racially or religiously aggravated • Offence motivated by, or demonstrating, hostility to the victim based on his or her sexual orientation (or presumed sexual orientation) or transgender identity (or presumed transgender identity) • Offence motivated by, or demonstrating, hostility to the victim based on his or her disability (or presumed disability)	Factor(s) in category A not present

STEP TWO

Starting point and category range

Having determined the category, the court should use the corresponding starting points to reach a sentence within the category range below. The starting point applies to all offenders irrespective of plea or previous convictions. Having determined the starting point, step two allows further adjustment for aggravating or mitigating features set out below.

A case of particular gravity, reflected by multiple features of culpability or harm in step one, could merit upward adjustment from the starting point before further adjustment for aggravating or mitigating features, set out below.

	A	B
Category 1	**Starting point** 15 years' custody **Category range** 13–19 years' custody	**Starting point** 12 years' custody **Category range** 10–15 years' custody
Category 2	**Starting point** 10 years' custody **Category range** 9–13 years' custody	**Starting point** 8 years' custody **Category range** 7–9 years' custody
Category 3	**Starting point** 7 years' custody **Category range** 6–9 years' custody	**Starting point** 5 years' custody **Category range** 4–7 years' custody

The table below contains a **non-exhaustive** list of additional factual elements providing the context of the offence and factors relating to the offender. Identify whether any combination of these, or other relevant factors, should result in an upward or downward adjustment from the starting point. **In particular, relevant recent convictions are likely to result in an upward adjustment.** In some cases, having considered these factors, it may be appropriate to move outside the identified category range.

Aggravating factors

Statutory aggravating factors

- Previous convictions, having regard to a) the nature of the offence to which the conviction relates and its relevance to the current offence; and b) the time that has elapsed since the conviction
- Offence committed whilst on bail

Other aggravating factors

- Specific targeting of a particularly vulnerable victim
- Ejaculation (where not taken into account at step one)
- Blackmail or other threats made (where not taken into account at step one)
- Location of offence
- Timing of offence
- Use of weapon or other item to frighten or injure
- Victim compelled to leave their home (including victims of domestic violence)
- Failure to comply with current court orders
- Offence committed whilst on licence
- Exploiting contact arrangements with a child to commit an offence
- Presence of others, especially children
- Any steps taken to prevent the victim reporting an incident, obtaining assistance and/or from assisting or supporting the prosecution
- Attempts to dispose of or conceal evidence
- Commission of offence whilst under the influence of alcohol or drugs

Mitigating factors

- No previous convictions **or** no relevant/recent convictions
- Remorse
- Previous good character and/or exemplary conduct*
- Age and/or lack of maturity where it affects the responsibility of the offender
- Mental disorder or learning disability, particularly where linked to the commission of the offence

*Previous good character/exemplary conduct is different from having no previous convictions. The more serious the offence, the less the weight which should normally be attributed to this factor. Where previous good character/exemplary conduct has been used to facilitate the offence, this mitigation should not normally be allowed and such conduct may constitute an aggravating factor.

In the context of this offence, previous good character/exemplary conduct should not normally be given any significant weight and will not normally justify a reduction in what would otherwise be the appropriate sentence.

STEP THREE

Consider any factors which indicate a reduction, such as assistance to the prosecution

The court should take into account sections 73 and 74 of the Serious Organised Crime and Police Act 2005 (assistance by defendants: reduction or review of sentence) and any other rule of law by virtue of which an offender may receive a discounted sentence in consequence of assistance given (or offered) to the prosecutor or investigator.

STEP FOUR

Reduction for guilty pleas

The court should take account of any potential reduction for a guilty plea in accordance with section 144 of the Criminal Justice Act 2003 and the *Guilty Plea* guideline.

STEP FIVE

Dangerousness

The court should consider whether having regard to the criteria contained in Chapter 5 of Part 12 of the Criminal Justice Act 2003 it would be appropriate to award a life sentence (section 224A or section 225(2)) or an extended sentence (section 226A). When sentencing offenders to a life sentence under these provisions, the notional determinate sentence should be used as the basis for the setting of a minimum term.

STEP SIX

Totality principle

If sentencing an offender for more than one offence, or where the offender is already serving a sentence, consider whether the total sentence is just and proportionate to the offending behaviour.

STEP SEVEN

Ancillary orders

The court must consider whether to make any ancillary orders. The court must also consider what other requirements or provisions may *automatically* apply. Further information is included at Annex A on page 424.

STEP EIGHT

Reasons

Section 174 of the Criminal Justice Act 2003 imposes a duty to give reasons for, and explain the effect of, the sentence.

STEP NINE

Consideration for time spent on bail

The court must consider whether to give credit for time spent on bail in accordance with section 240A of the Criminal Justice Act 2003.

Assault by penetration

Sexual Offences Act 2003 (section 2)

Triable only on indictment

Maximum: Life imprisonment

Offence range: Community order–19 years' custody

This is a serious specified offence for the purposes of sections 224 and 225(2) (life sentence for serious offences) of the Criminal Justice Act 2003.

For offences committed on or after 3 December 2012, this is an offence listed in Part 1 of Schedule 15B for the purposes of sections 224A (life sentence for second listed offence) of the Criminal Justice Act 2003.

For convictions on or after 3 December 2012 (irrespective of the date of commission of the offence), this is a specified offence for the purposes of section 226A (extended sentence for certain violent or sexual offences) of the Criminal Justice Act 2003.

STEP ONE

Determining the offence category

The court should determine which categories of harm and culpability the offence falls into by reference **only** to the tables below.

HARM	
Category 1	• The extreme nature of one or more category 2 factors or the extreme impact caused by a combination of category 2 factors **may** elevate to category 1

CULPABILITY	
A	B
• Significant degree of planning • Offender acts together with others to commit the offence • Use of alcohol/drugs on victim to facilitate the offence • Abuse of trust • Previous violence against victim • Offence committed in course of burglary • Recording of the offence • Commercial exploitation and/or motivation • Offence racially or religiously aggravated	Factor(s) in category A not present

Category 2	• Severe psychological or physical harm • Penetration using large or dangerous object(s) • Additional degradation/humiliation • Abduction • Prolonged detention/sustained incident • Violence or threats of violence (beyond that which is inherent in the offence) • Forced/uninvited entry into victim's home • Victim is particularly vulnerable due to personal circumstances* *for children under 13 please refer to the guideline on page 334	• Offence motivated by, or demonstrating, hostility to the victim based on his or her sexual orientation (or presumed sexual orientation) or transgender identity (or presumed transgender identity) • Offence motivated by, or demonstrating, hostility to the victim based on his or her disability (or presumed disability)
Category 3	Factor(s) in categories 1 and 2 not present	

STEP TWO

Starting point and category range

Having determined the category, the court should use the corresponding starting points to reach a sentence within the category range below. The starting point applies to all offenders irrespective of plea or previous convictions.

Having determined the starting point, step two allows further adjustment for aggravating or mitigating features, set out below.

A case of particular gravity, reflected by multiple features of culpability or harm in step one, could merit upward adjustment from the starting point before further adjustment for aggravating or mitigating features, set out below.

Where there is a sufficient prospect of rehabilitation, a community order with a sex offender treatment programme requirement under section 202 of the Criminal Justice Act 2003 can be a proper alternative to a short or moderate length custodial sentence.

	A	B
Category 1	**Starting point** 15 years' custody **Category range** 13–19 years' custody	**Starting point** 12 years' custody **Category range** 10–15 years' custody
Category 2	**Starting point** 8 years' custody **Category range** 5–13 years' custody	**Starting point** 6 years' custody **Category range** 4–9 years' custody
Category 3	**Starting point** 4 years' custody **Category range** 2–6 years' custody	**Starting point** 2 years' custody **Category range** High level community order–4 years' custody

The table below contains a **non-exhaustive** list of additional factual elements providing the context of the offence and factors relating to the offender. Identify whether any combination of these, or other relevant factors, should result in an upward or downward adjustment from the starting point. **In particular, relevant recent convictions are likely to result in an upward adjustment.** In some cases, having considered these factors, it may be appropriate to move outside the identified category range.

When sentencing appropriate **category 3** offences, the court should also consider the custody threshold as follows:

- has the custody threshold been passed?
- if so, is it unavoidable that a custodial sentence be imposed?
- if so, can that sentence be suspended?

Aggravating factors

Statutory aggravating factors

- Previous convictions, having regard to a) the nature of the offence to which the conviction relates and its relevance to the current offence; and b) the time that has elapsed since the conviction
- Offence committed whilst on bail

Other aggravating factors

- Specific targeting of a particularly vulnerable victim
- Blackmail or other threats made (where not taken into account at step one)
- Location of offence
- Timing of offence
- Use of weapon or other item to frighten or injure
- Victim compelled to leave their home (including victims of domestic violence)
- Failure to comply with current court orders
- Offence committed whilst on licence
- Exploiting contact arrangements with a child to commit an offence
- Presence of others, especially children
- Any steps taken to prevent the victim reporting an incident, obtaining assistance and/or from assisting or supporting the prosecution
- Attempts to dispose of or conceal evidence
- Commission of offence whilst under the influence of alcohol or drugs

Mitigating factors

- No previous convictions **or** no relevant/recent convictions
- Remorse
- Previous good character and/or exemplary conduct*
- Age and/or lack of maturity where it affects the responsibility of the offender
- Mental disorder or learning disability, particularly where linked to the commission of the offence

*Previous good character/exemplary conduct is different from having no previous convictions. The more serious the offence, the less the weight which should normally be attributed to this factor. Where previous good character/exemplary conduct has been used to facilitate the offence, this mitigation should not normally be allowed and such conduct may constitute an aggravating factor. In the context of this offence, previous good character/exemplary conduct should not normally be given any significant weight and will not normally justify a reduction in what would otherwise be the appropriate sentence.

STEP THREE

Consider any factors which indicate a reduction, such as assistance to the prosecution

The court should take into account sections 73 and 74 of the Serious Organised Crime and Police Act 2005 (assistance by defendants: reduction or review of sentence) and any other rule of law by virtue of which an offender may receive a discounted sentence in consequence of assistance given (or offered) to the prosecutor or investigator.

STEP FOUR

Reduction for guilty pleas

The court should take account of any potential reduction for a guilty plea in accordance with section 144 of the Criminal Justice Act 2003 and the *Guilty Plea* guideline.

STEP FIVE

Dangerousness

The court should consider whether having regard to the criteria contained in Chapter 5 of Part 12 of the Criminal Justice Act 2003 it would be appropriate to award a life sentence (section 224A or section 225(2)) or an extended sentence (section 226A). When sentencing offenders to a life sentence under these provisions, the notional determinate sentence should be used as the basis for the setting of a minimum term.

STEP SIX

Totality principle

If sentencing an offender for more than one offence, or where the offender is already serving a sentence, consider whether the total sentence is just and proportionate to the offending behaviour.

STEP SEVEN

Ancillary orders

The court must consider whether to make any ancillary orders. The court must also consider what other requirements or provisions may *automatically* apply. Further information is included at Annex A on page 424.

STEP EIGHT

Reasons

Section 174 of the Criminal Justice Act 2003 imposes a duty to give reasons for, and explain the effect of, the sentence.

STEP NINE

Consideration for time spent on bail

The court must consider whether to give credit for time spent on bail in accordance with section 240A of the Criminal Justice Act 2003.

Sexual assault

Sexual Offences Act 2003 (section 3)

Triable either way

Maximum: 10 years' custody

Offence range: Community order–7 years' custody

For convictions on or after 3 December 2012 (irrespective of the date of commission of the offence), this is a specified offence for the purposes of section 226A (extended sentence for certain violent or sexual offences) of the Criminal Justice Act 2003.

STEP ONE

Determining the offence category

The court should determine which categories of harm and culpability the offence falls into by reference **only** to the tables below.

HARM	
Category 1	• Severe psychological or physical harm • Abduction • Violence or threats of violence • Forced/uninvited entry into victim's home
Category 2	• Touching of naked genitalia or naked breasts • Prolonged detention/sustained incident • Additional degradation/humiliation • Victim is particularly vulnerable due to personal circumstances* *for children under 13 please refer to the guideline on page 338
Category 3	Factor(s) in categories 1 and 2 not present

CULPABILITY	
A	**B**
• Significant degree of planning • Offender acts together with others to commit the offence • Use of alcohol/drugs on victim to facilitate the offence • Abuse of trust • Previous violence against victim • Offence committed in course of burglary • Recording of offence • Commercial exploitation and/or motivation • Offence racially or religiously aggravated • Offence motivated by, or demonstrating, hostility to the victim based on his or her sexual orientation (or presumed sexual orientation) or transgender identity (or presumed transgender identity) • Offence motivated by, or demonstrating, hostility to the victim based on his or her disability (or presumed disability)	Factor(s) in category A not present

STEP TWO

Starting point and category range

Having determined the category, the court should use the corresponding starting points to reach a sentence within the category range below. The starting point applies to all offenders irrespective of plea or previous convictions. Having determined the starting point, step two allows further adjustment for aggravating or mitigating features, set out below.

A case of particular gravity, reflected by multiple features of culpability or harm in step one, could merit upward adjustment from the starting point before further adjustment for aggravating or mitigating features, set out below.

Where there is a sufficient prospect of rehabilitation, a community order with a sex offender treatment programme requirement under section 202 of the Criminal Justice Act 2003 can be a proper alternative to a short or moderate length custodial sentence.

	A	B
Category 1	**Starting point** 4 years' custody **Category range** 3–7 years' custody	**Starting point** 2 years 6 months' custody **Category range** 2–4 years' custody
Category 2	**Starting point** 2 years' custody **Category range** 1–4 years' custody	**Starting point** 1 year's custody **Category range** High level community order–2 years' custody
Category 3	**Starting point** 26 weeks' custody **Category range** High level community order–1 year's custody	**Starting point** High level community order **Category range** Medium level community order–26 weeks' custody

The table below contains a **non-exhaustive** list of additional factual elements providing the context of the offence and factors relating to the offender. Identify whether any combination of these, or other relevant factors, should result in an upward or downward adjustment from the starting point. **In particular, relevant recent convictions are likely to result in an upward adjustment.** In some cases, having considered these factors, it may be appropriate to move outside the identified category range.

When sentencing appropriate **category 2 or 3 offences**, the court should also consider the custody threshold as follows:

- has the custody threshold been passed?
- if so, is it unavoidable that a custodial sentence be imposed?
- if so, can that sentence be suspended?

Aggravating factors

Statutory aggravating factors

- Previous convictions, having regard to a) the nature of the offence to which the conviction relates and its relevance to the current offence; and b) the time that has elapsed since the conviction
- Offence committed whilst on bail

Other aggravating factors

- Specific targeting of a particularly vulnerable victim
- Blackmail or other threats made (where not taken into account at step one)
- Location of offence
- Timing of offence
- Use of weapon or other item to frighten or injure
- Victim compelled to leave their home (including victims of domestic violence)
- Failure to comply with current court orders
- Offence committed whilst on licence

- Exploiting contact arrangements with a child to commit an offence
- Presence of others, especially children
- Any steps taken to prevent the victim reporting an incident, obtaining assistance and/or from assisting or supporting the prosecution
- Attempts to dispose of or conceal evidence
- Commission of offence whilst under the influence of alcohol or drugs

Mitigating factors

- No previous convictions **or** no relevant/recent convictions
- Remorse
- Previous good character and/or exemplary conduct*
- Age and/or lack of maturity where it affects the responsibility of the offender
- Mental disorder or learning disability, particularly where linked to the commission of the offence
- Demonstration of steps taken to address offending behaviour

*Previous good character/exemplary conduct is different from having no previous convictions. The more serious the offence, the less the weight which should normally be attributed to this factor. Where previous good character/exemplary conduct has been used to facilitate the offence, this mitigation should not normally be allowed and such conduct may constitute an aggravating factor.

STEP THREE

Consider any factors which indicate a reduction, such as assistance to the prosecution

The court should take into account sections 73 and 74 of the Serious Organised Crime and Police Act 2005 (assistance by defendants: reduction or review of sentence) and any other rule of law by virtue of which an offender may receive a discounted sentence in consequence of assistance given (or offered) to the prosecutor or investigator.

STEP FOUR

Reduction for guilty pleas

The court should take account of any potential reduction for a guilty plea in accordance with section 144 of the Criminal Justice Act 2003 and the *Guilty Plea* guideline.

STEP FIVE

Dangerousness

The court should consider whether having regard to the criteria contained in Chapter 5 of Part 12 of the Criminal Justice Act 2003 it would be appropriate to award an extended sentence (section 226A).

STEP SIX

Totality principle

If sentencing an offender for more than one offence, or where the offender is already serving a sentence, consider whether the total sentence is just and proportionate to the offending behaviour.

STEP SEVEN

Ancillary orders

The court must consider whether to make any ancillary orders. The court must also consider what other requirements or provisions may *automatically* apply. Further information is included at Annex A on page 424.

STEP EIGHT

Reasons

Section 174 of the Criminal Justice Act 2003 imposes a duty to give reasons for, and explain the effect of, the sentence.

STEP NINE

Consideration for time spent on bail

The court must consider whether to give credit for time spent on bail in accordance with section 240A of the Criminal Justice Act 2003.

Causing a person to engage in sexual activity without consent

Sexual Offences Act 2003 (section 4)

Triable only on indictment (if penetration involved)—otherwise, triable either way

Maximum: Life imprisonment (if penetration involved)—otherwise, 10 years

Offence range: Community order–7 years' custody (if no penetration involved)/19 years' custody (if penetration involved)

This is a serious specified offence for the purposes of section 224 and, where the offence involved penetration, section 225(2) (life sentence for serious offences) of the Criminal Justice Act 2003.

For offences involving penetration, committed on or after 3 December 2012, this is an offence listed in Part 1 of Schedule 15B for the purposes of sections 224A (life sentence for second listed offence) of the Criminal Justice Act 2003.

For convictions on or after 3 December 2012 (irrespective of the date of commission of the offence), this is a specified offence for the purposes of section 226A (extended sentence for certain violent or sexual offences) of the Criminal Justice Act 2003.

STEP ONE

Determining the offence category

The court should determine which categories of harm and culpability the offence falls into by reference **only** to the tables below.

HARM	
Category 1	• The extreme nature of one or more category 2 factors or the extreme impact caused by a combination of category 2 factors **may** elevate to category 1
Category 2	• Severe psychological or physical harm • Penetration using large or dangerous object(s) • Pregnancy or STI as a consequence of offence

CULPABILITY	
A	B
• Significant degree of planning • Offender acts together with others to commit the offence • Use of alcohol/drugs on victim to facilitate the offence • Abuse of trust • Previous violence against victim • Offence committed in course of burglary • Recording of the offence • Commercial exploitation and/or motivation	Factor(s) in category A not present

	• Additional degradation/ humiliation • Abduction • Prolonged detention/sustained incident• Violence or threats of violence • Forced/uninvited entry into victim's home • Victim is particularly vulnerable due to personal circumstances* *for children under 13 please refer to the guideline on page 341	• Offence racially or religiously aggravated • Offence motivated by, or demonstrating, hostility to the victim based on his or her sexual orientation (or presumed sexual orientation) or transgender identity (or presumed transgender identity) • Offence motivated by, or demonstrating, hostility to the victim based on his or her disability (or presumed disability)
Category 3	Factor(s) in categories 1 and 2 not present	

STEP TWO

Starting point and category range

Having determined the category, the court should use the corresponding starting points to reach a sentence within the category range below. The starting point applies to all offenders irrespective of plea or previous convictions.

Having determined the starting point, step two allows further adjustment for aggravating or mitigating features, set out below.

A case of particular gravity, reflected by multiple features of culpability or harm in step one, could merit upward adjustment from the starting point before further adjustment for aggravating or mitigating features, set out below.

Where there is a sufficient prospect of rehabilitation, a community order with a sex offender treatment programme requirement under section 202 of the Criminal Justice Act 2003 can be a proper alternative to a short or moderate length custodial sentence.

Where offence involved penetration

	A	B
Category 1	**Starting point** 15 years' custody **Category range** 13–19 years' custody	**Starting point** 12 years' custody **Category range** 10–15 years' custody
Category 2	**Starting point** 8 years' custody **Category range** 5–13 years' custody	**Starting point** 6 years' custody **Category range** 4–9 years' custody
Category 3	**Starting point** 4 years' custody **Category range** 2–6 years' custody	**Starting point** 2 years' custody **Category range** High level community order–4 years' custody

Where offence did not involve penetration

	A	B
Category 1	**Starting point** 4 years' custody **Category range** 3–7 years' custody	**Starting point** 2 years 6 months' custody **Category range** 2–4 years' custody
Category 2	**Starting point** 2 years' custody **Category range** 1–4 years' custody	**Starting point** 1 year's custody **Category range** High level community order–2 years' custody
Category 3	**Starting point** 26 weeks' custody **Category range** High level community order–1 year's custody	**Starting point** High level community order **Category range** Medium level community order–26 weeks' custody

The table below contains a **non-exhaustive** list of additional factual elements providing the context of the offence and factors relating to the offender. Identify whether any combination of these, or other relevant factors, should result in an upward or downward adjustment from the starting point. **In particular, relevant recent convictions are likely to result in an upward adjustment.** In some cases, having considered these factors, it may be appropriate to move outside the identified category range.

When sentencing appropriate **category 2 or 3** offences, the court should also consider the custody threshold as follows:

- has the custody threshold been passed?
- if so, is it unavoidable that a custodial sentence be imposed?
- if so, can that sentence be suspended?

Aggravating factors

Statutory aggravating factors

- Previous convictions, having regard to a) the nature of the offence to which the conviction relates and its relevance to the current offence; and b) the time that has elapsed since the conviction
- Offence committed whilst on bail

Other aggravating factors

- Specific targeting of a particularly vulnerable victim
- Ejaculation (where not taken into account at step one)
- Blackmail or other threats made (where not taken into account at step one)
- Location of offence
- Timing of offence
- Use of weapon or other item to frighten or injure
- Victim compelled to leave their home (including victims of domestic violence)
- Failure to comply with current court orders
- Offence committed whilst on licence
- Exploiting contact arrangements with a child to commit an offence
- Presence of others, especially children

- Any steps taken to prevent the victim reporting an incident, obtaining assistance and/or from assisting or supporting the prosecution
- Attempts to dispose of or conceal evidence
- Commission of offence whilst under the influence of alcohol or drugs

Mitigating factors

- No previous convictions **or** no relevant/recent convictions
- Remorse
- Previous good character and/or exemplary conduct*
- Age and/or lack of maturity where it affects the responsibility of the offender
- Mental disorder or learning disability, particularly where linked to the commission of the offence

*Previous good character/exemplary conduct is different from having no previous convictions. The more serious the offence, the less the weight which should normally be attributed to this factor. Where previous good character/exemplary conduct has been used to facilitate the offence, this mitigation should not normally be allowed and such conduct may constitute an aggravating factor. In the context of this offence, previous good character/exemplary conduct should not normally be given any significant weight and will not normally justify a reduction in what would otherwise be the appropriate sentence.

STEP THREE

Consider any factors which indicate a reduction, such as assistance to the prosecution

The court should take into account sections 73 and 74 of the Serious Organised Crime and Police Act 2005 (assistance by defendants: reduction or review of sentence) and any other rule of law by virtue of which an offender may receive a discounted sentence in consequence of assistance given (or offered) to the prosecutor or investigator.

STEP FOUR

Reduction for guilty pleas

The court should take account of any potential reduction for a guilty plea in accordance with section 144 of the Criminal Justice Act 2003 and the *Guilty Plea* guideline.

STEP FIVE

Dangerousness

The court should consider whether having regard to the criteria contained in Chapter 5 of Part 12 of the Criminal Justice Act 2003 it would be appropriate to award a life sentence (section 224A or section 225(2)) or an extended sentence (section 226A). When sentencing offenders to a life sentence under these provisions, the notional determinate sentence should be used as the basis for the setting of a minimum term.

STEP SIX

Totality principle

If sentencing an offender for more than one offence, or where the offender is already serving a sentence, consider whether the total sentence is just and proportionate to the offending behaviour.

STEP SEVEN

Ancillary orders

The court must consider whether to make any ancillary orders. The court must also consider what other requirements or provisions may *automatically* apply. Further information is included at Annex A on page 424.

STEP EIGHT

Reasons

Section 174 of the Criminal Justice Act 2003 imposes a duty to give reasons for, and explain the effect of, the sentence.

STEP NINE

Consideration for time spent on bail

The court must consider whether to give credit for time spent on bail in accordance with section 240A of the Criminal Justice Act 2003.

Rape of a child under 13

Sexual Offences Act 2003 (section 5)

Triable only on indictment

Maximum: Life imprisonment

Offence range: 6–19 years' custody

This is a serious specified offence for the purposes of sections 224 and 225(2) (life sentence for serious offences) of the Criminal Justice Act 2003.

For offences committed on or after 3 December 2012, this is an offence listed in Part 1 of Schedule 15B for the purposes of section 224A (life sentence for second listed offence) of the Criminal Justice Act 2003.

For convictions on or after 3 December 2012 (irrespective of the date of commission of the offence), this is a specified offence for the purposes of section 226A (extended sentence for certain violent or sexual offences) of the Criminal Justice Act 2003.

STEP ONE

Determining the offence category

The court should determine which categories of harm and culpability the offence falls into by reference **only** to the tables below.

Offences may be of such severity, for example involving a campaign of rape, that sentences of 20 years and above may be appropriate.

When dealing with the statutory offence of rape of a child under 13, the court may be faced with a wide range of offending behaviour.

Sentencers should have particular regard to the fact that these offences are not only committed through force or fear of force but may include exploitative behaviour towards a child which should be considered to indicate high culpability.

This guideline is designed to deal with the majority of offending behaviour which deserves a significant custodial sentence; the starting points and ranges reflect the fact that such offending merits such an approach. There may also be **exceptional** cases, where a lengthy community order with a requirement to participate in a sex offender treatment programme may be the best way of changing the offender's behaviour and of protecting the public by preventing any repetition of the offence. This guideline may not be appropriate where the sentencer is satisfied that on the available evidence, and in the absence of exploitation, a young or particularly immature defendant genuinely believed, on reasonable grounds, that the victim was aged 16 or over and that they were engaging in lawful sexual activity.

Sentencers are reminded that if sentencing outside the guideline they must be satisfied that it would be contrary to the interests of justice to follow the guideline.

HARM	
Category 1	• The extreme nature of one or more category 2 factors or the extreme impact caused by a combination of category 2 factors **may** elevate to category 1
Category 2	• Severe psychological or physical harm • Pregnancy or STI as a consequence of offence • Additional degradation/ humiliation • Abduction • Prolonged detention /sustained incident • Violence or threats of violence • Forced/uninvited entry into victim's home • Child is particularly vulnerable due to extreme youth and/or personal circumstances
Category 3	Factor(s) in categories 1 and 2 not present

CULPABILITY	
A	B
• Significant degree of planning • Offender acts together with others to commit the offence • Use of alcohol/drugs on victim to facilitate the offence • Grooming behaviour used against victim • Abuse of trust • Previous violence against victim • Offence committed in course of burglary • Sexual images of victim recorded, retained, solicited or shared • Deliberate isolation of victim • Commercial exploitation and/ or motivation • Offence racially or religiously aggravated • Offence motivated by, or demonstrating, hostility to the victim based on his or her sexual orientation (or presumed sexual orientation) or transgender identity (or presumed transgender identity) • Offence motivated by, or demonstrating, hostility to the victim based on his or her disability (or presumed disability)	Factor(s) in category A not present

STEP TWO

Starting point and category range

Having determined the category, the court should use the corresponding starting points to reach a sentence within the category range below. The starting point applies to all offenders irrespective of plea or previous convictions. Having determined the starting point, step two allows further adjustment for aggravating or mitigating features, set out below.

A case of particular gravity, reflected by multiple features of culpability or harm in step one, could merit upward adjustment from the starting point before further adjustment for aggravating or mitigating features, set out below.

Sentencers should also note the wording set out at step one which may be applicable in exceptional cases.

	A	B
Category 1	**Starting point** 16 years' custody **Category range** 13–19 years' custody	**Starting point** 13 years' custody **Category range** 11–17 years' custody

Category 2	**Starting point** 13 years' custody **Category range** 11–17 years' custody	**Starting point** 10 years' custody **Category range** 8–13 years' custody
Category 3	**Starting point** 10 years' custody **Category range** 8–13 years' custody	**Starting point** 8 years' custody **Category range** 6–11 years' custody

The table below contains a **non-exhaustive** list of additional factual elements providing the context of the offence and factors relating to the offender. Identify whether any combination of these, or other relevant factors, should result in an upward or downward adjustment from the starting point. **In particular, relevant recent convictions are likely to result in an upward adjustment.** In some cases, having considered these factors, it may be appropriate to move outside the identified category range.

Aggravating factors

Statutory aggravating factors

- Previous convictions, having regard to a) the nature of the offence to which the conviction relates and its relevance to the current offence; and b) the time that has elapsed since the conviction
- Offence committed whilst on bail

Other aggravating factors

- Specific targeting of a particularly vulnerable child
- Ejaculation (where not taken into account at step one)
- Blackmail or other threats made (where not taken into account at step one)
- Location of offence
- Timing of offence
- Use of weapon or other item to frighten or injure
- Victim compelled to leave their home, school, etc
- Failure to comply with current court orders
- Offence committed whilst on licence
- Exploiting contact arrangements with a child to commit an offence
- Presence of others, especially other children
- Any steps taken to prevent the victim reporting an incident, obtaining assistance and/or from assisting or supporting the prosecution
- Attempts to dispose of or conceal evidence
- Commission of offence whilst offender under the influence of alcohol or drugs
- Victim encouraged to recruit others

Mitigating factors

- No previous convictions **or** no relevant/recent convictions
- Remorse
- Previous good character and/or exemplary conduct*
- Age and/or lack of maturity where it affects the responsibility of the offender
- Mental disorder or learning disability, particularly where linked to the commission of the offence

*Previous good character/exemplary conduct is different from having no previous convictions. The more serious the offence, the less the weight which should normally be attributed to this factor. Where previous good character/exemplary conduct has been used to facilitate the offence, this mitigation should not normally be allowed and such conduct may constitute an aggravating factor. In the context of this offence, previous good character/exemplary conduct should not normally be given any significant weight and will not normally justify a reduction in what would otherwise be the appropriate sentence.

STEP THREE

Consider any factors which indicate a reduction, such as assistance to the prosecution

The court should take into account sections 73 and 74 of the Serious Organised Crime and Police Act 2005 (assistance by defendants: reduction or review of sentence) and any other rule of law by virtue of which an offender may receive a discounted sentence in consequence of assistance given (or offered) to the prosecutor or investigator.

STEP FOUR

Reduction for guilty pleas

The court should take account of any potential reduction for a guilty plea in accordance with section 144 of the Criminal Justice Act 2003 and the *Guilty Plea* guideline.

STEP FIVE

Dangerousness

The court should consider whether having regard to the criteria contained in Chapter 5 of Part 12 of the Criminal Justice Act 2003 it would be appropriate to award a life sentence (section 224A or section 225(2)) or an extended sentence (section 226A). When sentencing offenders to a life sentence under these provisions, the notional determinate sentence should be used as the basis for the setting of a minimum term.

STEP SIX

Totality principle

If sentencing an offender for more than one offence, or where the offender is already serving a sentence, consider whether the total sentence is just and proportionate to the offending behaviour.

STEP SEVEN

Ancillary orders

The court must consider whether to make any ancillary orders. The court must also consider what other requirements or provisions may *automatically* apply. Further information is included at Annex A on page 424.

STEP EIGHT

Reasons

Section 174 of the Criminal Justice Act 2003 imposes a duty to give reasons for, and explain the effect of, the sentence.

STEP NINE

Consideration for time spent on bail

The court must consider whether to give credit for time spent on bail in accordance with section 240A of the Criminal Justice Act 2003.

Assault of a child under 13 by penetration

Sexual Offences Act 2003 (section 6)

Triable only on indictment

Maximum: Life imprisonment

Offence range: 2–19 years' custody

This is a serious specified offence for the purposes of sections 224 and 225(2) (life sentence for serious offences) of the Criminal Justice Act 2003.

For offences committed on or after 3 December 2012, this is an offence listed in Part 1 of Schedule 15B for the purposes of section 224A (life sentence for second listed offence) of the Criminal Justice Act 2003.

For convictions on or after 3 December 2012 (irrespective of the date of commission of the offence), this is a specified offence for the purposes of section 226A (extended sentence for certain violent or sexual offences) of the Criminal Justice Act 2003.

STEP ONE

Determining the offence category

The court should determine which categories of harm and culpability the offence falls into by reference **only** to the tables below.

HARM	
Category 1	The extreme nature of one or more category 2 factors or the extreme impact caused by a combination of category 2 factors **may** elevate to category 1
Category 2	• Severe psychological or physical harm • Penetration using large or dangerous object(s) • Additional degradation/ humiliation • Abduction • Prolonged detention / sustained incident • Violence or threats of violence • Forced/uninvited entry into victim's home • Child is particularly vulnerable due to extreme youth and/or personal circumstances
Category 3	Factor(s) in categories 1 and 2 not present

CULPABILITY	
A	B
• Significant degree of planning • Offender acts together with others to commit the offence • Use of alcohol/drugs on victim to facilitate the offence • Grooming behaviour used against victim • Abuse of trust • Previous violence against victim • Offence committed in course of burglary • Sexual images of victim recorded, retained, solicited or shared • Deliberate isolation of victim • Commercial exploitation and/or motivation • Offence racially or religiously aggravated • Offence motivated by, or demonstrating, hostility to the victim based on his or her sexual orientation (or presumed sexual orientation) or transgender identity (or presumed transgender identity) • Offence motivated by, or demonstrating, hostility to the victim based on his or her disability (or presumed disability)	Factor(s) in category A not present

STEP TWO

Starting point and category range

Having determined the category, the court should use the corresponding starting points to reach a sentence within the category range below. The starting point applies to all offenders irrespective of plea or previous convictions. Having determined the starting point, step two allows further adjustment for aggravating or mitigating features, set out below.

A case of particular gravity, reflected by multiple features of culpability or harm in step one, could merit upward adjustment from the starting point before further adjustment for aggravating or mitigating features, set out below.

	A	B
Category 1	**Starting point** 16 years' custody **Category range** 13–19 years' custody	**Starting point** 13 years' custody **Category range** 11–17 years' custody
Category 2	**Starting point** 11 years' custody **Category range** 7–15 years' custody	**Starting point** 8 years' custody **Category range** 5–13 years' custody
Category 3	**Starting point** 6 years' custody **Category range** 4–9 years' custody	**Starting point** 4 years' custody **Category range** 2–6 years' custody

The table below contains a **non-exhaustive** list of additional factual elements providing the context of the offence and factors relating to the offender. Identify whether any combination of these, or other relevant factors, should result in an upward or downward adjustment from the starting point. **In particular, relevant recent convictions are likely to result in an upward adjustment.** In some cases, having considered these factors, it may be appropriate to move outside the identified category range.

Aggravating factors

Statutory aggravating factors

- Previous convictions, having regard to a) the nature of the offence to which the conviction relates and its relevance to the current offence; and b) the time that has elapsed since the conviction
- Offence committed whilst on bail

Other aggravating factors

- Specific targeting of a particularly vulnerable child
- Blackmail or other threats made (where not taken into account at step one)
- Location of offence
- Timing of offence
- Use of weapon or other item to frighten or injure
- Victim compelled to leave their home, school etc
- Failure to comply with current court orders
- Offence committed whilst on licence
- Exploiting contact arrangements with a child to commit an offence
- Presence of others, especially other children
- Any steps taken to prevent the victim reporting an incident, obtaining assistance and/or from assisting or supporting the prosecution
- Attempts to dispose of or conceal evidence
- Commission of offence whilst under the influence of alcohol or drugs
- Victim encouraged to recruit others

Mitigating factors

- No previous convictions **or** no relevant/recent convictions
- Remorse
- Previous good character and/or exemplary conduct*
- Age and/or lack of maturity where it affects the responsibility of the offender
- Mental disorder or learning disability, particularly where linked to the commission of the offence

*Previous good character/exemplary conduct is different from having no previous convictions. The more serious the offence, the less the weight which should normally be attributed to this factor. Where previous good character/ exemplary conduct has been used to facilitate the offence, this mitigation should not normally be allowed and such conduct may constitute an aggravating factor. In the context of this offence, previous good character/exemplary conduct should not normally be given any significant weight and will not normally justify a reduction in what would otherwise be the appropriate sentence.

STEP THREE

Consider any factors which indicate a reduction, such as assistance to the prosecution

The court should take into account sections 73 and 74 of the Serious Organised Crime and Police Act 2005 (assistance by defendants: reduction or review of sentence) and any other rule of law by virtue of which an offender may receive a discounted sentence in consequence of assistance given (or offered) to the prosecutor or investigator.

STEP FOUR

Reduction for guilty pleas

The court should take account of any potential reduction for a guilty plea in accordance with section 144 of the Criminal Justice Act 2003 and the *Guilty Plea* guideline.

STEP FIVE

Dangerousness

The court should consider whether having regard to the criteria contained in Chapter 5 of Part 12 of the Criminal Justice Act 2003 it would be appropriate to award a life sentence (section 224A or section 225(2)) or an extended sentence (section 226A). When sentencing offenders to a life sentence under these provisions, the notional determinate sentence should be used as the basis for the setting of a minimum term.

STEP SIX

Totality principle

If sentencing an offender for more than one offence, or where the offender is already serving a sentence, consider whether the total sentence is just and proportionate to the offending behaviour.

STEP SEVEN

Ancillary orders

The court must consider whether to make any ancillary orders. The court must also consider what other requirements or provisions may *automatically* apply. Further information is included at Annex A on page 424.

STEP EIGHT

Reasons

Section 174 of the Criminal Justice Act 2003 imposes a duty to give reasons for, and explain the effect of, the sentence.

STEP NINE

Consideration for time spent on bail

The court must consider whether to give credit for time spent on bail in accordance with section 240A of the Criminal Justice Act 2003.

Sexual assault of a child under 13

Sexual Offences Act 2003 (section 7)

Triable either way

Maximum: 14 years' custody

Offence range: Community order–9 years' custody

For offences committed on or after 3 December 2012, this is an offence listed in Part 1 of Schedule 15B for the purposes of section 224A (life sentence for second listed offence) of the Criminal Justice Act 2003.

For convictions on or after 3 December 2012 (irrespective of the date of commission of the offence), this is a specified offence for the purposes of section 226A (extended sentence for certain violent or sexual offences) of the Criminal Justice Act 2003.

STEP ONE

Determining the offence category

The court should determine which categories of harm and culpability the offence falls into by reference **only** to the tables below.

HARM	
Category 1	• Severe psychological or physical harm • Abduction • Violence or threats of violence • Forced/uninvited entry into victim's home •
Category 2	• Touching of naked genitalia or naked breast area • Prolonged detention/sustained incident • Additional degradation/humiliation • Child is particularly vulnerable due to extreme youth and/or personal circumstances
Category 3	Factor(s) in categories 1 and 2 not present

CULPABILITY	
A	B
• Significant degree of planning • Offender acts together with others to commit the offence • Use of alcohol/drugs on victim to facilitate the offence • Grooming behaviour used against victim • Abuse of trust • Previous violence against victim • Offence committed in course of burglary • Sexual images of victim recorded, retained, solicited or shared • Deliberate isolation of victim • Commercial exploitation and/or motivation • Offence racially or religiously aggravated	Factor(s) in category A not present

- Offence motivated by, or demonstrating, hostility to the victim based on his or her sexual orientation (or presumed sexual orientation) or transgender identity (or presumed transgender identity)
- Offence motivated by, or demonstrating, hostility to the victim based on his or her disability (or presumed disability)

STEP TWO

Starting point and category range

Having determined the category, the court should use the corresponding starting points to reach a sentence within the category range below. The starting point applies to all offenders irrespective of plea or previous convictions. Having determined the starting point, step two allows further adjustment for aggravating or mitigating features, set out below.

A case of particular gravity, reflected by multiple features of culpability or harm in step one, could merit upward adjustment from the starting point before further adjustment for aggravating or mitigating features, set out below.

Where there is a sufficient prospect of rehabilitation, a community order with a sex offender treatment programme requirement under section 202 of the Criminal Justice Act 2003 can be a proper alternative to a short or moderate length custodial sentence.

	A	B
Category 1	**Starting point** 6 years' custody **Category range** 4–9 years' custody	**Starting point** 4 years' custody **Category range** 3–7 years' custody
Category 2	**Starting point** 4 years' custody **Category range** 3–7 years' custody	**Starting point** 2 years' custody **Category range** 1–4 years' custody
Category 3	**Starting point** 1 year's custody **Category range** 26 weeks'–2 years' custody	**Starting point** 26 weeks' custody **Category range** High level community order–1 year's custody

The table below contains a **non-exhaustive** list of additional factual elements providing the context of the offence and factors relating to the offender. Identify whether any combination of these, or other relevant factors, should result in an upward or downward adjustment from the starting point. **In particular, relevant recent convictions are likely to result in an upward adjustment.** In some cases, having considered these factors, it may be appropriate to move outside the identified category range.

Aggravating factors

Statutory aggravating factors

- Previous convictions, having regard to a) the nature of the offence to which the conviction relates and its relevance to the current offence; and b) the time that has elapsed since the conviction
- Offence committed whilst on bail

Other aggravating factors

- Specific targeting of a particularly vulnerable child
- Blackmail or other threats made (where not taken into account at step one)
- Location of offence
- Timing of offence
- Use of weapon or other item to frighten or injure
- Victim compelled to leave their home, school, etc
- Failure to comply with current court orders
- Offence committed whilst on licence
- Exploiting contact arrangements with a child to commit an offence
- Presence of others, especially other children
- Any steps taken to prevent the victim reporting an incident, obtaining assistance and/or from assisting or supporting the prosecution
- Attempts to dispose of or conceal evidence
- Commission of offence whilst under the influence of alcohol or drugs
- Victim encouraged to recruit others

Mitigating factors

- No previous convictions **or** no relevant/recent convictions
- Remorse
- Previous good character and/or exemplary conduct*
- Age and/or lack of maturity where it affects the responsibility of the offender
- Mental disorder or learning disability, particularly where linked to the commission of the offence

*Previous good character/exemplary conduct is different from having no previous convictions. The more serious the offence, the less the weight which should normally be attributed to this factor. Where previous good character/exemplary conduct has been used to facilitate the offence, this mitigation should not normally be allowed and such conduct may constitute an aggravating factor. In the context of this offence, previous good character/exemplary conduct should not normally be given any significant weight and will not normally justify a reduction in what would otherwise be the appropriate sentence.

STEP THREE

Consider any factors which indicate a reduction, such as assistance to the prosecution

The court should take into account sections 73 and 74 of the Serious Organised Crime and Police Act 2005 (assistance by defendants: reduction or review of sentence) and any other rule of law by virtue of which an offender may receive a discounted sentence in consequence of assistance given (or offered) to the prosecutor or investigator.

STEP FOUR

Reduction for guilty pleas

The court should take account of any potential reduction for a guilty plea in accordance with section 144 of the Criminal Justice Act 2003 and the *Guilty Plea* guideline.

STEP FIVE

Dangerousness

The court should consider whether having regard to the criteria contained in Chapter 5 of Part 12 of the Criminal Justice Act 2003 it would be appropriate to award a life sentence (section 224A) or an extended sentence (section 226A). When sentencing offenders to a life sentence under these provisions, the notional determinate sentence should be used as the basis for the setting of a minimum term.

STEP SIX

Totality principle

If sentencing an offender for more than one offence, or where the offender is already serving a sentence, consider whether the total sentence is just and proportionate to the offending behaviour.

STEP SEVEN

Ancillary orders

The court must consider whether to make any ancillary orders. The court must also consider what other requirements or provisions may *automatically* apply. Further information is included at Annex A on page 424.

STEP EIGHT

Reasons

Section 174 of the Criminal Justice Act 2003 imposes a duty to give reasons for, and explain the effect of, the sentence.

STEP NINE

Consideration for time spent on bail

The court must consider whether to give credit for time spent on bail in accordance with section 240A of the Criminal Justice Act 2003.

Causing or inciting a child under 13 to engage in sexual activity

Sexual Offences Act 2003 (section 8)

Triable only on indictment (if penetration involved)—otherwise, triable either way

Maximum: Life imprisonment (if penetration involved)—otherwise, 14 years' custody

Offence range: 1–17 years' custody

This is a serious specified offence for the purposes of sections 224 and, where the offence involved penetration, 225(2) (life sentence for serious offences) of the Criminal Justice Act 2003.

For offences committed on or after 3 December 2012, this is an offence listed in Part 1 of Schedule 15B for the purposes of section 224A (life sentence for second listed offence) of the Criminal Justice Act 2003.

For convictions on or after 3 December 2012 (irrespective of the date of commission of the offence), this is a specified offence for the purposes of section 226A (extended sentence for certain violent or sexual offences) of the Criminal Justice Act 2003.

STEP ONE

Determining the offence category

The court should determine which categories of harm and culpability the offence falls into by reference **only** to the tables below.

HARM	
Category 1	• The extreme nature of one or more category 2 factors or the extreme impact caused by a combination of category 2 factors **may** elevate to category 1
Category 2	• Severe psychological or physical harm • Penetration of vagina or anus (using body or object) by, or of, victim • Penile penetration of mouth by, or of, victim • Additional degradation/ humiliation • Abduction • Prolonged detention /sustained incident • Violence or threats of violence • Forced/uninvited entry into victim's home • Child is particularly vulnerable due to extreme youth and/or personal circumstances
Category 3	Factor(s) in categories 1 and 2 not present

CULPABILITY	
A	B
• Significant degree of planning • Offender acts together with others to commit the offence • Use of alcohol/drugs on victim to facilitate the offence • Grooming behaviour used against victim • Abuse of trust • Previous violence against victim • Offence committed in course of burglary • Sexual images of victim recorded, retained, solicited or shared • Deliberate isolation of victim • Commercial exploitation and/or motivation • Offence racially or religiously aggravated • Offence motivated by, or demonstrating hostility to the victim based on his or her sexual orientation (or presumed sexual orientation) or transgender identity (or presumed transgender identity) • Offence motivated by, or demonstrating, hostility to the victim based on his or her disability (or presumed disability)	Factor(s) in category A not present

STEP TWO

Starting point and category range

Having determined the category, the court should use the corresponding starting points to reach a sentence within the category range below. The starting point applies to all offenders irrespective of plea or previous convictions. Having determined the starting point, step two allows further adjustment for aggravating or mitigating features, set out below.

A case of particular gravity, reflected by multiple features of culpability or harm in step one, could merit upward adjustment from the starting point before further adjustment for aggravating or mitigating features, set out below.

	A	B
Category 1	**Starting point** 13 years' custody **Category range** 11–17 years' custody	**Starting point** 11 years' custody **Category range** 10–15 years' custody
Category 2	**Starting point** 8 years' custody **Category range** 5–10 years' custody	**Starting point** 6 years' custody **Category range** 3–9 years' custody
Category 3	**Starting point** 5 years' custody **Category range** 3–8 years' custody	**Starting point** 2 years' custody **Category range** 1–4 years' custody

The table below contains a **non-exhaustive** list of additional factual elements providing the context of the offence and factors relating to the offender. Identify whether any combination of these, or other relevant factors, should result in an upward or downward adjustment from the starting point. **In particular, relevant recent convictions are likely to result in an upward adjustment.** In some cases, having considered these factors, it may be appropriate to move outside the identified category range.

Aggravating factors

Statutory aggravating factors

- Previous convictions, having regard to a) the nature of the offence to which the conviction relates and its relevance to the current offence; and b) the time that has elapsed since the conviction
- Offence committed whilst on bail

Other aggravating factors

- Specific targeting of a particularly vulnerable child
- Ejaculation (where not taken into account at step one)
- Blackmail or other threats made (where not taken into account at step one)
- Pregnancy or STI as a consequence of offence
- Location of offence
- Timing of offence
- Use of weapon or other item to frighten or injure
- Victim compelled to leave their home, school, etc
- Failure to comply with current court orders
- Offence committed whilst on licence
- Exploiting contact arrangements with a child to commit an offence
- Presence of others, especially other children
- Any steps taken to prevent the victim reporting an incident, obtaining assistance and/or from assisting or supporting the prosecution
- Attempts to dispose of or conceal evidence
- Commission of offence whilst offender under the influence of alcohol or drugs
- Victim encouraged to recruit others

Mitigating factors

- No previous convictions **or** no relevant/recent convictions
- Remorse
- Previous good character and/or exemplary conduct*
- Age and/or lack of maturity where it affects the responsibility of the offender
- Mental disorder or learning disability, particularly where linked to the commission of the offence
- Sexual activity was incited but no activity took place because the offender voluntarily desisted or intervened to prevent it

*Previous good character/exemplary conduct is different from having no previous convictions. The more serious the offence, the less the weight which should normally be attributed to this factor. Where previous good character/exemplary conduct has been used to facilitate the offence, this mitigation should not normally be allowed and such conduct may constitute an aggravating factor. In the context of this offence, previous good character/exemplary conduct should not normally be given any significant weight and will not normally justify a reduction in what would otherwise be the appropriate sentence.

STEP THREE

Consider any factors which indicate a reduction, such as assistance to the prosecution

The court should take into account sections 73 and 74 of the Serious Organised Crime and Police Act 2005 (assistance by defendants: reduction or review of sentence) and any other rule of law by virtue of which an offender may receive a discounted sentence in consequence of assistance given (or offered) to the prosecutor or investigator.

STEP FOUR

Reduction for guilty pleas

The court should take account of any potential reduction for a guilty plea in accordance with section 144 of the Criminal Justice Act 2003 and the *Guilty Plea* guideline.

STEP FIVE

Dangerousness

The court should consider whether having regard to the criteria contained in Chapter 5 of Part 12 of the Criminal Justice Act 2003 it would be appropriate to award a life sentence (section 224A or section 225(2)) or an extended sentence (section 226A). When sentencing offenders to a life sentence under these provisions, the notional determinate sentence should be used as the basis for the setting of a minimum term.

STEP SIX

Totality principle

If sentencing an offender for more than one offence, or where the offender is already serving a sentence, consider whether the total sentence is just and proportionate to the offending behaviour.

STEP SEVEN

Ancillary orders

The court must consider whether to make any ancillary orders. The court must also consider what other requirements or provisions may *automatically* apply. Further information is included at Annex A on page 424.

STEP EIGHT

Reasons

Section 174 of the Criminal Justice Act 2003 imposes a duty to give reasons for, and explain the effect of, the sentence.

STEP NINE

Consideration for time spent on bail

The court must consider whether to give credit for time spent on bail in accordance with section 240A of the Criminal Justice Act 2003.

Sexual activity with a child

Sexual Offences Act 2003 (section 9)

Causing or inciting a child to engage in sexual activity

Sexual Offences Act 2003 (section 10)

Triable only on indictment (if penetration involved)—otherwise, triable either way

Maximum: 14 years' custody

Offence range: Community order–10 years' custody
For offences committed on or after 3 December 2012, these are offences listed in Part 1 of Schedule 15B for the purposes of section 224A (life sentence for second listed offence) of the Criminal Justice Act 2003.

For convictions on or after 3 December 2012 (irrespective of the date of commission of the offence), these are specified offences for the purposes of section 226A (extended sentence for certain violent or sexual offences) of the Criminal Justice Act 2003.

> Arranging or facilitating the commission of a child offence (section 14 of the Sexual Offences Act 2003—page 356)
>
> The starting points and ranges in this guideline are also applicable to offences of arranging or facilitating the commission of a child offence. In such cases, the level of harm should be determined by reference to the type of activity arranged or facilitated. Sentences commensurate with the applicable starting point and range will ordinarily be appropriate. For offences involving significant commercial exploitation and/or an international element, it may, in the interests of justice, be appropriate to increase a sentence to a point above the category range. In exceptional cases, such as where a vulnerable offender performed a limited role, having been coerced or exploited by others, sentences below the starting point and range may be appropriate.

STEP ONE

Determining the offence category

The court should determine which categories of harm and culpability the offence falls into by reference **only** to the tables below.

THIS GUIDLINE [sic] ALSO APPLIES TO OFFENCES COMMITTED REMOTELY/ ONLINE

HARM	
Category 1	• Penetration of vagina or anus (using body or object) • Penile penetration of mouth In either case by, or of, the victim

CULPABILITY	
A	B
• Significant degree of planning • Offender acts together with others to commit the offence • Use of alcohol/drugs on victim to facilitate the offence • Grooming behaviour used against victim	Factor(s) in category A not present

Category 2	Touching, or exposure, of naked genitalia or naked breasts by, or of, the victim	• Abuse of trust • Use of threats (including blackmail) • Sexual images of victim recorded, retained, solicited or shared • Specific targeting of a particularly vulnerable child • Offender lied about age • Significant disparity in age • Commercial exploitation and/or motivation • Offence racially or religiously aggravated • Offence motivated by, or demonstrating, hostility to the victim based on his or her sexual orientation (or presumed sexual orientation) or transgender identity (or presumed transgender identity) • Offence motivated by, or demonstrating, hostility to the victim based on his or her disability (or presumed disability)
Category 3	Other sexual activity	

STEP TWO

Starting point and category range

Having determined the category, the court should use the corresponding starting points to reach a sentence within the category range below. The starting point applies to all offenders irrespective of plea or previous convictions. Having determined the starting point, step two allows further adjustment for aggravating or mitigating features, set out below.

A case of particular gravity, reflected by multiple features of culpability or harm in step one, could merit upward adjustment from the starting point before further adjustment for aggravating or mitigating features, set out below.

Where there is a sufficient prospect of rehabilitation, a community order with a sex offender treatment programme requirement under section 202 of the Criminal Justice Act 2003 can be a proper alternative to a short or moderate length custodial sentence.

	A	B
Category 1	**Starting point** 5 years' custody **Category range** 4–10 years' custody	**Starting point** 1 year's custody **Category range** High level community order–2 years' custody
Category 2	**Starting point** 3 years' custody **Category range** 2–6 years' custody	**Starting point** 26 weeks' custody **Category range** High level community order–1 year's custody
Category 3	**Starting point** 26 weeks' custody **Category range** High level community order–3 years' custody	**Starting point** Medium level community order **Category range** Low level community order–High level community order

The table below contains a **non-exhaustive** list of additional factual elements providing the context of the offence and factors relating to the offender. Identify whether any combination of these, or other relevant factors, should result in an upward or downward adjustment from the starting point. **In particular, relevant recent convictions are likely to result in an upward adjustment.** In some cases, having considered these factors, it may be appropriate to move outside the identified category range.

When sentencing appropriate **category 2 or 3 offences**, the court should also consider the custody threshold as follows:

- has the custody threshold been passed?
- if so, is it unavoidable that a custodial sentence be imposed?
- if so, can that sentence be suspended?

Aggravating factors

Statutory aggravating factors

- Previous convictions, having regard to a) the nature of the offence to which the conviction relates and its relevance to the current offence; and b) the time that has elapsed since the conviction
- Offence committed whilst on bail

Other aggravating factors

- Severe psychological or physical harm
- Ejaculation
- Pregnancy or STI as a consequence of offence
- Location of offence
- Timing of offence
- Victim compelled to leave their home, school, etc
- Failure to comply with current court orders
- Offence committed whilst on licence
- Exploiting contact arrangements with a child to commit an offence
- Presence of others, especially other children
- Any steps taken to prevent the victim reporting an incident, obtaining assistance and/or from assisting or supporting the prosecution
- Attempts to dispose of or conceal evidence
- Failure of offender to respond to previous warnings
- Commission of offence whilst under the influence of alcohol or drugs
- Victim encouraged to recruit others
- Period over which offence committed

Mitigating factors

- No previous convictions **or** no relevant/recent convictions
- Remorse
- Previous good character and/or exemplary conduct*
- Age and/or lack of maturity where it affects the responsibility of the offender
- Mental disorder or learning disability, particularly where linked to the commission of the offence
- Sexual activity was incited but no activity took place because the offender voluntarily desisted or intervened to prevent it

*Previous good character/exemplary conduct is different from having no previous convictions. The more serious the offence, the less the weight which should normally be attributed to this factor. Where previous good character/exemplary conduct has been used to facilitate the offence, this mitigation should not normally be allowed and such conduct may constitute an aggravating factor.

In the context of this offence, previous good character/exemplary conduct should not normally be given any significant weight and will not normally justify a reduction in what would otherwise be the appropriate sentence.

STEP THREE

Consider any factors which indicate a reduction, such as assistance to the prosecution

The court should take into account sections 73 and 74 of the Serious Organised Crime and Police Act 2005 (assistance by defendants: reduction or review of sentence) and any other rule of law by virtue of which an offender may receive a discounted sentence in consequence of assistance given (or offered) to the prosecutor or investigator.

STEP FOUR

Reduction for guilty pleas

The court should take account of any potential reduction for a guilty plea in accordance with section 144 of the Criminal Justice Act 2003 and the *Guilty Plea* guideline.

STEP FIVE

Dangerousness

The court should consider whether having regard to the criteria contained in Chapter 5 of Part 12 of the Criminal Justice Act 2003 it would be appropriate to award a life sentence (section 224A) or an extended sentence (section 226A). When sentencing offenders to a life sentence under these provisions, the notional determinate sentence should be used as the basis for the setting of a minimum term.

STEP SIX

Totality principle

If sentencing an offender for more than one offence, or where the offender is already serving a sentence, consider whether the total sentence is just and proportionate to the offending behaviour.

STEP SEVEN

Ancillary orders

The court must consider whether to make any ancillary orders. The court must also consider what other requirements or provisions may ***automatically*** apply. Further information is included at Annex A on page 424.

STEP EIGHT

Reasons

Section 174 of the Criminal Justice Act 2003 imposes a duty to give reasons for, and explain the effect of, the sentence.

STEP NINE

Consideration for time spent on bail

The court must consider whether to give credit for time spent on bail in accordance with section 240A of the Criminal Justice Act 2003.

Sexual activity with a child family member

Sexual Offences Act 2003 (section 25)

Inciting a child family member to engage in sexual activity

Sexual Offences Act 2003 (section 26)

Triable only on indictment (if penetration involved)—otherwise, triable either way

Maximum: 14 years' custody

Offence range: Community order–10 years' custody

For offences committed on or after 3 December 2012, these are offences listed in Part 1 of Schedule 15B for the purposes of section 224A (life sentence for second listed offence) of the Criminal Justice Act 2003.

For convictions on or after 3 December 2012 (irrespective of the date of commission of the offence), these are specified offences for the purposes of section 226A (extended sentence for certain violent or sexual offences) of the Criminal Justice Act 2003.

STEP ONE

Determining the offence category

The court should determine which categories of harm and culpability the offence falls into by reference **only** to the tables below. This offence involves those who have a family relationship with the victim and it should be assumed that the greater the abuse of trust within this relationship the more grave the offence.

HARM	
Category 1	• Penetration of vagina or anus (using body or object) • Penile penetration of mouth In either case by, or of, the victim
Category 2	Touching of naked genitalia or naked breasts by, or of, the victim
Category 3	Other sexual activity

CULPABILITY	
A	B
• Significant degree of planning • Offender acts together with others to commit the offence • Use of alcohol/drugs on victim to facilitate the offence • Grooming behaviour used against victim • Use of threats (including blackmail) • Sexual images of victim recorded, retained, solicited or shared • Specific targeting of a particularly vulnerable child • Significant disparity in age • Commercial exploitation and/or motivation • Offence racially or religiously aggravated • Offence motivated by, or demonstrating, hostility to the victim based on his or her sexual orientation (or presumed sexual orientation) or transgender identity (or presumed transgender identity) • Offence motivated by, or demonstrating, hostility to the victim based on his or her disability (or presumed disability)	Factor(s) in category A not present

STEP TWO

Starting point and category range

Having determined the category, the court should use the corresponding starting points to reach a sentence within the category range below. The starting point applies to all offenders irrespective of plea or previous convictions. Having determined the starting point, step two allows further adjustment for aggravating or mitigating features, set out below.

A case of particular gravity, reflected by multiple features of culpability or harm in step one, could merit upward adjustment from the starting point before further adjustment for aggravating or mitigating features, set out below.

Where there is a sufficient prospect of rehabilitation, a community order with a sex offender treatment programme requirement under section 202 of the Criminal Justice Act 2003 can be a proper alternative to a short or moderate length custodial sentence.

	A	B
Category 1	**Starting point** 6 years' custody **Category range** 4–10 years' custody	**Starting point** 3 years 6 months' custody **Category range** 2 years 6 months'–5 years' custody
Category 2	**Starting point** 4 years' custody **Category range** 2–6 years' custody	**Starting point** 18 months' custody **Category range** 26 weeks'–2 years 6 months' custody
Category 3	**Starting point** 1 year's custody **Category range** High level community order–3 years' custody	**Starting point** Medium level community order **Category range** Low level community order–High level community order

The table below contains a **non-exhaustive** list of additional factual elements providing the context of the offence and factors relating to the offender. Identify whether any combination of these, or other relevant factors, should result in an upward or downward adjustment from the starting point. **In particular, relevant recent convictions are likely to result in an upward adjustment.** In some cases, having considered these factors, it may be appropriate to move outside the identified category range.

When sentencing appropriate **category 3 offences**, the court should also consider the custody threshold as follows:

- has the custody threshold been passed?
- if so, is it unavoidable that a custodial sentence be imposed?
- if so, can that sentence be suspended?

Aggravating factors

Statutory aggravating factors

- Previous convictions, having regard to a) the nature of the offence to which the conviction relates and its relevance to the current offence; and b) the time that has elapsed since the conviction
- Offence committed whilst on bail

Other aggravating factors

- Severe psychological or physical harm
- Ejaculation
- Pregnancy or STI as a consequence of offence
- Location of offence
- Timing of offence
- Victim compelled to leave their home, school, etc
- Failure to comply with current court orders

- Offence committed whilst on licence
- Exploiting contact arrangements with a child to commit an offence
- Presence of others, especially other children
- Any steps taken to prevent the victim reporting an incident, obtaining assistance and/or from assisting or supporting the prosecution
- Attempts to dispose of or conceal evidence
- Failure of offender to respond to previous warnings
- Commission of offence whilst under the influence of alcohol or drugs
- Victim encouraged to recruit others
- Period over which offence committed

Mitigating factors

- No previous convictions **or** no relevant/recent convictions
- Remorse
- Previous good character and/or exemplary conduct*
- Age and/or lack of maturity where it affects the responsibility of the offender
- Mental disorder or learning disability, particularly where linked to the commission of the offence
- Sexual activity was incited but no activity took place because the offender voluntarily desisted or intervened to prevent it

*Previous good character/exemplary conduct is different from having no previous convictions. The more serious the offence, the less the weight which should normally be attributed to this factor. Where previous good character/exemplary conduct has been used to facilitate the offence, this mitigation should not normally be allowed and such conduct may constitute an aggravating factor.

In the context of this offence, previous good character/exemplary conduct should not normally be given any significant weight and will not normally justify a reduction in what would otherwise be the appropriate sentence.

STEP THREE

Consider any factors which indicate a reduction, such as assistance to the prosecution

The court should take into account sections 73 and 74 of the Serious Organised Crime and Police Act 2005 (assistance by defendants: reduction or review of sentence) and any other rule of law by virtue of which an offender may receive a discounted sentence in consequence of assistance given (or offered) to the prosecutor or investigator.

STEP FOUR

Reduction for guilty pleas

The court should take account of any potential reduction for a guilty plea in accordance with section 144 of the Criminal Justice Act 2003 and the *Guilty Plea* guideline.

STEP FIVE

Dangerousness

The court should consider whether having regard to the criteria contained in Chapter 5 of Part 12 of the Criminal Justice Act 2003 it would be appropriate to award a life sentence (section 224A) or an extended sentence (section 226A). When sentencing offenders to a life sentence under these provisions, the notional determinate sentence should be used as the basis for the setting of a minimum term.

STEP SIX

Totality principle

If sentencing an offender for more than one offence, or where the offender is already serving a sentence, consider whether the total sentence is just and proportionate to the offending behaviour.

STEP SEVEN

Ancillary orders

The court must consider whether to make any ancillary orders. The court must also consider what other requirements or provisions may *automatically* apply. Further information is included at Annex A on page 424.

STEP EIGHT

Reasons

Section 174 of the Criminal Justice Act 2003 imposes a duty to give reasons for, and explain the effect of, the sentence.

STEP NINE

Consideration for time spent on bail

The court must consider whether to give credit for time spent on bail in accordance with section 240A of the Criminal Justice Act 2003.

Engaging in sexual activity in the presence of a child

Sexual Offences Act 2003 (section 11)

Causing a child to watch a sexual act

Sexual Offences Act 2003 (section 12)

Triable either way

Maximum: 10 years' custody

Offence range: Community order–6 years' custody

For offences committed on or after 3 December 2012, these are offences listed in Part 1 of Schedule 15B for the purposes of section 224A (life sentence for second listed offence) of the Criminal Justice Act 2003.

For convictions on or after 3 December 2012 (irrespective of the date of commission of the offence), these are specified offences for the purposes of section 226A (extended sentence for certain violent or sexual offences) of the Criminal Justice Act 2003.

> Arranging or facilitating the commission of a child offence (section 14 of the Sexual Offences Act 2003–guidance on page 356)
>
> The starting points and ranges in this guideline are also applicable to offences of arranging or facilitating the commission of a child offence. In such cases, the level of harm should be determined by reference to the type of activity arranged or facilitated. Sentences commensurate with the applicable starting point and range will ordinarily be appropriate. For offences involving significant commercial exploitation and/or an international element, it may, in the interests of justice, be appropriate to increase a sentence to a point above the category range. In exceptional cases, such as where a vulnerable offender performed a limited role, having been coerced or exploited by others, sentences below the starting point and range may be appropriate.

STEP ONE

Determining the offence category

The court should determine which categories of harm and culpability the offence falls into by reference **only** to the tables below.

HARM	
Category 1	• Causing victim to view extreme pornography • Causing victim to view indecent/ prohibited images of children • Engaging in, or causing a victim to view live, sexual activity involving sadism/violence/sexual activity with an animal/a child
Category 2	Engaging in, or causing a victim to view images of or view live, sexual activity involving: • penetration of vagina or anus (using body or object) • penile penetration of the mouth • masturbation
Category 3	Factor(s) in categories 1 and 2 not present

CULPABILITY	
A	B
• Significant degree of planning • Offender acts together with others in order to commit the offence • Use of alcohol/drugs on victim to facilitate the offence • Grooming behaviour used against victim • Abuse of trust • Use of threats (including blackmail) • Specific targeting of a particularly vulnerable child • Significant disparity in age • Commercial exploitation and/ or motivation • Offence racially or religiously aggravated • Offence motivated by, or demonstrating, hostility to the victim based on his or her sexual orientation (or presumed sexual orientation) or transgender identity (or presumed transgender identity) • Offence motivated by, or demonstrating, hostility to the victim based on his or her disability (or presumed disability)	Factor(s) in category A not present

STEP TWO

Starting point and category range

Having determined the category, the court should use the corresponding starting points to reach a sentence within the category range below. The starting point applies to all offenders irrespective of plea or previous convictions. Having determined the starting point, step two allows further adjustment for aggravating or mitigating features, set out below.

A case of particular gravity, reflected by multiple features of culpability or harm in step one, could merit upward adjustment from the starting point before further adjustment for aggravating or mitigating features, set out below.

Where there is a sufficient prospect of rehabilitation, a community order with a sex offender treatment programme requirement under section 202 of the Criminal Justice Act 2003 can be a proper alternative to a short or moderate length custodial sentence.

	A	B
Category 1	**Starting point** 4 years' custody **Category range** 3–6 years' custody	**Starting point** 2 years' custody **Category range** 1–3 years' custody
Category 2	**Starting point** 2 years' custody **Category range** 1–3 years' custody	**Starting point** 1 year's custody **Category range** High level community order–18 months' custody
Category 3	**Starting point** 26 weeks' custody **Category range** High level community order–1 year's custody	**Starting point** Medium level community order **Category range** Low level community order–Medium level community order

The table below contains a **non-exhaustive** list of additional factual elements providing the context of the offence and factors relating to the offender. Identify whether any combination of these, or other relevant factors, should result in an upward or downward adjustment from the starting point. **In particular, relevant recent convictions are likely to result in an upward adjustment.** In some cases, having considered these factors, it may be appropriate to move outside the identified category range.

When sentencing appropriate **category 2 or 3 offences**, the court should also consider the custody threshold as follows:

- has the custody threshold been passed?
- if so, is it unavoidable that a custodial sentence be imposed?
- if so, can that sentence be suspended?

Aggravating factors

Statutory aggravating factors

- Previous convictions, having regard to a) the nature of the offence to which the conviction relates and its relevance to the current offence; and b) the time that has elapsed since the conviction
- Offence committed whilst on bail

Other aggravating factors

- Location of offence
- Timing of offence
- Victim compelled to leave their home, school, etc
- Failure to comply with current court orders
- Offence committed whilst on licence
- Exploiting contact arrangements with a child to commit an offence
- Presence of others, especially other children
- Any steps taken to prevent the victim reporting an incident, obtaining assistance and/or from assisting or supporting the prosecution
- Attempts to dispose of or conceal evidence
- Failure of offender to respond to previous warnings
- Commission of offence whilst offender under the influence of alcohol or drugs
- Victim encouraged to recruit others

Mitigating factors

- No previous convictions **or** no relevant/recent convictions
- Remorse
- Previous good character and/or exemplary conduct*
- Age and/or lack of maturity where it affects the responsibility of the offender
- Mental disorder or learning disability, particularly where linked to the commission of the offence
- Demonstration of steps taken to address offending behaviour

*Previous good character/exemplary conduct is different from having no previous convictions. The more serious the offence, the less the weight which should normally be attributed to this factor. Where previous good character/exemplary conduct has been used to facilitate the offence, this mitigation should not normally be allowed and such conduct may constitute an aggravating factor.

STEP THREE

Consider any factors which indicate a reduction, such as assistance to the prosecution

The court should take into account sections 73 and 74 of the Serious Organised Crime and Police Act 2005 (assistance by defendants: reduction or review of sentence) and any other rule of law by virtue of which an offender may receive a discounted sentence in consequence of assistance given (or offered) to the prosecutor or investigator.

STEP FOUR

Reduction for guilty pleas

The court should take account of any potential reduction for a guilty plea in accordance with section 144 of the Criminal Justice Act 2003 and the *Guilty Plea* guideline.

STEP FIVE

Dangerousness

The court should consider whether having regard to the criteria contained in Chapter 5 of Part 12 of the Criminal Justice Act 2003 it would be appropriate to award a life sentence (section 224A) or an extended sentence (section 226A). When sentencing offenders to a life sentence under these provisions, the notional determinate sentence should be used as the basis for the setting of a minimum term.

STEP SIX

Totality principle

If sentencing an offender for more than one offence, or where the offender is already serving a sentence, consider whether the total sentence is just and proportionate to the offending behaviour.

STEP SEVEN

Ancillary orders

The court must consider whether to make any ancillary orders. The court must also consider what other requirements or provisions may *automatically* apply. Further information is included at Annex A on page 424.

STEP EIGHT

Reasons

Section 174 of the Criminal Justice Act 2003 imposes a duty to give reasons for, and explain the effect of, the sentence.

STEP NINE

Consideration for time spent on bail

The court must consider whether to give credit for time spent on bail in accordance with section 240A of the Criminal Justice Act 2003.

Arranging or facilitating the commission of a child sex offence

Sexual Offences Act 2003 (section 14)

Triable either way

Maximum: 14 years' custody

For offences committed on or after 3 December 2012, these are offences listed in Part 1 of Schedule 15B for the purposes of section 224A (life sentence for second listed offence) of the Criminal Justice Act 2003.

For convictions on or after 3 December 2012 (irrespective of the date of commission of the offence), these are specified offences for the purposes of section 226A (extended sentence for certain violent or sexual offences) of the Criminal Justice Act 2003.

Sentencers should refer to the guideline for the applicable, substantive offence of arranging or facilitating under sections 9 to 10. See pages 345–348. The level of harm should be determined by reference to the type of activity arranged or facilitated. Sentences commensurate with the applicable starting point and range will ordinarily be appropriate. For offences involving significant commercial exploitation and/or an international element, it may, in the interests of justice, be appropriate to increase a sentence to a point above the category range. In exceptional cases, such as where a vulnerable offender performed a limited role, having been coerced or exploited by others, sentences below the starting point and range may be appropriate.

Meeting a child following sexual grooming

Sexual Offences Act 2003 (section 15)

Triable either way

Maximum: 10 years' custody

Offence range: 1–7 years' custody

For offences committed on or after 3 December 2012, this is an offence listed in Part 1 of Schedule 15B for the purposes of section 224A (life sentence for second listed offence) of the Criminal Justice Act 2003.

For convictions on or after 3 December 2012 (irrespective of the date of commission of the offence), this is a specified offence for the purposes of section 226A (extended sentence for certain violent or sexual offences) of the Criminal Justice Act 2003.

STEP ONE

Determining the offence category

The court should determine the offence category using the table below.

Category 1	Raised harm **and** raised culpability
Category 2	Raised harm **or** raised culpability
Category 3	Grooming **without** raised harm or culpability factors present

The court should determine culpability and harm caused or intended, by reference **only** to the factors below, which comprise the principal factual elements of the offence. Where an offence does not fall squarely into a category, individual factors may require a degree of weighting before making an overall assessment and determining the appropriate offence category.

Factors indicating raised harm

- Continued contact despite victim's attempts to terminate contact
- Sexual images exchanged
- Victim exposed to extreme sexual content for example, extreme pornography
- Child is particularly vulnerable due to personal circumstances

Factors indicating raised culpability

- Offender acts together with others to commit the offence
- Communication indicates penetrative sexual activity is intended
- Offender lied about age/persona
- Use of threats (including blackmail), gifts or bribes
- Abuse of trust
- Specific targeting of a particularly vulnerable child
- Abduction/detention
- Commercial exploitation and/or motivation
- Offence racially or religiously aggravated
- Offence motivated by, or demonstrating, hostility to the victim based on his or her sexual orientation (or presumed sexual orientation) or transgender identity (or presumed transgender identity)
- Offence motivated by, or demonstrating, hostility to the victim based on his or her disability (or presumed disability)

STEP TWO

Starting point and category range

Having determined the category, the court should use the corresponding starting points to reach a sentence within the category range below. The starting point applies to all offenders irrespective of plea or previous convictions. Having determined the starting point, step two allows further adjustment for aggravating or mitigating features, set out below.

A case of particular gravity, reflected by multiple features of culpability or harm in step one, could merit upward adjustment from the starting point before further adjustment for aggravating or mitigating features, set out below.

Category 1	**Starting point** 4 years' custody **Category range** 3–7 years' custody
Category 2	**Starting point** 2 years' custody **Category range** 1–4 years' custody
Category 3	**Starting point** 18 months' custody **Category range** 1 year–2 years 6 months' custody

The table below contains a **non-exhaustive** list of additional factual elements providing the context of the offence and factors relating to the offender. Identify whether any combination of these, or other relevant factors, should result in an upward or downward adjustment from the starting point. **In particular, relevant recent convictions are likely to result in an upward adjustment.** In some cases, having considered these factors, it may be appropriate to move outside the identified category range.

Aggravating factors

Statutory aggravating factors

- Previous convictions, having regard to a) the nature of the offence to which the conviction relates and its relevance to the current offence; and b) the time that has elapsed since the conviction
- Offence committed whilst on bail

Other aggravating factors

- Failure to comply with current court orders
- Offence committed whilst on licence
- Any steps taken to prevent the victim reporting an incident, obtaining assistance and/or from assisting or supporting the prosecution
- Attempts to dispose of or conceal evidence
- Victim encouraged to recruit others

Mitigating factors

- No previous convictions **or** no relevant/recent convictions
- Remorse
- Previous good character and/or exemplary conduct*
- Age and/or lack of maturity where it affects the responsibility of the offender
- Mental disorder or learning disability, particularly where linked to the commission of the offence
- Demonstration of steps taken to address offending behaviour

*Previous good character/exemplary conduct is different from having no previous convictions. The more serious the offence, the less the weight which should normally be attributed to this factor. Where previous good character/exemplary conduct has been used to facilitate the offence, this mitigation should not normally be allowed and such conduct may constitute an aggravating factor.

STEP THREE

Consider any factors which indicate a reduction, such as assistance to the prosecution

The court should take into account sections 73 and 74 of the Serious Organised Crime and Police Act 2005 (assistance by defendants: reduction or review of sentence) and any other rule of law by virtue of which an offender may receive a discounted sentence in consequence of assistance given (or offered) to the prosecutor or investigator.

STEP FOUR

Reduction for guilty pleas

The court should take account of any potential reduction for a guilty plea in accordance with section 144 of the Criminal Justice Act 2003 and the *Guilty Plea* guideline.

STEP FIVE

Dangerousness

The court should consider whether having regard to the criteria contained in Chapter 5 of Part 12 of the Criminal Justice Act 2003 it would be appropriate to award a life sentence (section 224A) or an extended sentence (section 226A). When sentencing offenders to a life sentence under these provisions, the notional determinate sentence should be used as the basis for the setting of a minimum term.

STEP SIX

Totality principle

If sentencing an offender for more than one offence, or where the offender is already serving a sentence, consider whether the total sentence is just and proportionate to the offending behaviour.

STEP SEVEN

Ancillary orders

The court must consider whether to make any ancillary orders. The court must also consider what other requirements or provisions may *automatically* apply. Further information is included at Annex A on page 424.

STEP EIGHT

Reasons

Section 174 of the Criminal Justice Act 2003 imposes a duty to give reasons for, and explain the effect of, the sentence.

STEP NINE

Consideration for time spent on bail

The court must consider whether to give credit for time spent on bail in accordance with section 240A of the Criminal Justice Act 2003.

Abuse of position of trust: sexual activity with a child

Sexual Offences Act 2003 (section 16)

Abuse of position of trust: causing or inciting a child to engage in sexual activity

Sexual Offences Act 2003 (section 17)

Triable either way

Maximum: 5 years' custody

Offence range: Community order–2 years' custody

For convictions on or after 3 December 2012 (irrespective of the date of commission of the offence), these are specified offences for the purposes of section 226A (extended sentence for certain violent or sexual offences) of the Criminal Justice Act 2003.

STEP ONE

Determining the offence category

The court should determine which categories of harm and culpability the offence falls into by reference **only** to the tables below.

THIS GUIDLINE [sic] ALSO APPLIES TO OFFENCES COMMITTED REMOTELY/ONLINE

HARM	
Category 1	• Penetration of vagina or anus (using body or object) • Penile penetration of mouth In either case by, or of, the victim
Category 2	• Touching, or exposure, of naked genitalia or naked breasts by, or of, the victim
Category 3	Factor(s) in categories 1 and 2 not present

CULPABILITY	
A	B
• Significant degree of planning • Offender acts together with others to commit the offence • Use of alcohol/drugs on victim to facilitate the offence • Grooming behaviour used against victim • Use of threats (including blackmail) • Sexual images of victim recorded, retained, solicited or shared • Specific targeting of a particularly vulnerable child • Commercial exploitation and/or motivation • Offence racially or religiously aggravated • Offence motivated by, or demonstrating, hostility to the victim based on his or her sexual orientation (or presumed sexual orientation) or transgender identity (or presumed transgender identity) • Offence motivated by, or demonstrating, hostility to the victim based on his or her disability (or presumed disability)	Factor(s) in category A not present

STEP TWO

Starting point and category range

Having determined the category, the court should use the corresponding starting points to reach a sentence within the category range below. The starting point applies to all offenders irrespective of plea or previous convictions. Having determined the starting point, step two allows further adjustment for aggravating or mitigating features, set out below.

A case of particular gravity, reflected by multiple features of culpability or harm in step one, could merit upward adjustment from the starting point before further adjustment for aggravating or mitigating features, set out below.

Where there is a sufficient prospect of rehabilitation, a community order with a sex offender treatment programme requirement under section 202 of the Criminal Justice Act 2003 can be a proper alternative to a short or moderate length custodial sentence.

	A	B
Category 1	**Starting point** 18 months' custody **Category range** 1–2 years' custody	**Starting point** 1 year's custody **Category range** 26 weeks'–18 months' custody
Category 2	**Starting point** 1 year's custody **Category range** 26 weeks'–18 months' custody	**Starting point** 26 weeks' custody **Category range** High level community order–1 year's custody
Category 3	**Starting point** 26 weeks' custody **Category range** High level community order–1 year's custody	**Starting point** Medium level community order **Category range** Low level community order–High level community order

The table below contains a **non-exhaustive** list of additional factual elements providing the context of the offence and factors relating to the offender. Identify whether any combination of these, or other relevant factors, should result in an upward or downward adjustment from the starting point. **In particular, relevant recent convictions are likely to result in an upward adjustment.** In some cases, having considered these factors, it may be appropriate to move outside the identified category range.

When sentencing appropriate **category 2 or 3 offences**, the court should also consider the custody threshold as follows:

- has the custody threshold been passed?
- if so, is it unavoidable that a custodial sentence be imposed?
- if so, can that sentence be suspended?

Aggravating factors

Statutory aggravating factors

- Previous convictions, having regard to a) the nature of the offence to which the conviction relates and its relevance to the current offence; and b) the time that has elapsed since the conviction
- Offence committed whilst on bail

Other aggravating factors

- Ejaculation
- Pregnancy or STI as a consequence of offence
- Location of offence
- Timing of offence
- Victim compelled to leave their home, school, etc
- Failure to comply with current court orders
- Offence committed whilst on licence
- Presence of others, especially other children
- Any steps taken to prevent the victim reporting an incident, obtaining assistance and/or from assisting or supporting the prosecution
- Attempts to dispose of or conceal evidence
- Failure of offender to respond to previous warnings
- Commission of offence whilst under the influence of alcohol or drugs
- Victim encouraged to recruit others

Mitigating factors

- No previous convictions **or** no relevant/recent convictions
- Remorse
- Previous good character and/or exemplary conduct*
- Age and/or lack of maturity where it affects the responsibility of the offender
- Mental disorder or learning disability, particularly where linked to the commission of the offence
- Sexual activity was incited but no activity took place because the offender voluntarily desisted or intervened to prevent it
- Demonstration of steps taken to address offending behaviour

*Previous good character/exemplary conduct is different from having no previous convictions. The more serious the offence, the less the weight which should normally be attributed to this factor. Where previous good character/exemplary conduct has been used to facilitate the offence, this mitigation should not normally be allowed and such conduct may constitute an aggravating factor.

STEP THREE

Consider any factors which indicate a reduction, such as assistance to the prosecution

The court should take into account sections 73 and 74 of the Serious Organised Crime and Police Act 2005 (assistance by defendants: reduction or review of sentence) and any other rule of law by virtue of which an offender may receive a discounted sentence in consequence of assistance given (or offered) to the prosecutor or investigator.

STEP FOUR

Reduction for guilty pleas

The court should take account of any potential reduction for a guilty plea in accordance with section 144 of the Criminal Justice Act 2003 and the *Guilty Plea* guideline.

STEP FIVE

Dangerousness

The court should consider whether having regard to the criteria contained in Chapter 5 of Part 12 of the Criminal Justice Act 2003 it would be appropriate to award an extended sentence (section 226A).

STEP SIX

Totality principle

If sentencing an offender for more than one offence, or where the offender is already serving a sentence, consider whether the total sentence is just and proportionate to the offending behaviour.

STEP SEVEN

Ancillary orders

The court must consider whether to make any ancillary orders. The court must also consider what other requirements or provisions may *automatically* apply. Further information is included at Annex A on page 424.

STEP EIGHT

Reasons

Section 174 of the Criminal Justice Act 2003 imposes a duty to give reasons for, and explain the effect of, the sentence.

STEP NINE

Consideration for time spent on bail

The court must consider whether to give credit for time spent on bail in accordance with section 240A of the Criminal Justice Act 2003.

Abuse of position of trust: sexual activity in the presence of a child

Sexual Offences Act 2003 (section 18)

Abuse of position of trust: causing a child to watch a sexual act

Sexual Offences Act 2003 (section 19)

Triable either way

Maximum: 5 years' custody

Offence range: Community order–2 years' custody

For convictions on or after 3 December 2012 (irrespective of the date of commission of the offence), these are specified offences for the purposes of section 226A (extended sentence for certain violent or sexual offences) of the Criminal Justice Act 2003.

STEP ONE

Determining the offence category

The court should determine which categories of harm and culpability the offence falls into by reference **only** to the tables below.

HARM	
Category 1	• Causing victim to view extreme pornography • Causing victim to view indecent/prohibited images of children • Engaging in, or causing a victim to view live, sexual activity involving sadism/violence/sexual activity with an animal/a child
Category 2	Engaging in, or causing a victim to view images of or view live, sexual activity involving: • penetration of vagina or anus (using body or object) • penile penetration of mouth • masturbation
Category 3	Factor(s) in categories 1 and 2 not present

CULPABILITY	
A	B
• Significant degree of planning • Offender acts together with others to commit the offence • Use of alcohol/drugs on victim to facilitate the offence • Grooming behaviour used against victim • Use of threats (including blackmail) • Specific targeting of a particularly vulnerable child • Commercial exploitation and/or motivation • Offence racially or religiously aggravated • Offence motivated by, or demonstrating, hostility to the victim based on his or her sexual orientation (or presumed sexual orientation) or transgender identity (or presumed transgender identity) • Offence motivated by, or demonstrating, hostility to the victim based on his or her disability (or presumed disability)	Factor(s) in category A not present

STEP TWO

Starting point and category range

Having determined the category, the court should use the corresponding starting points to reach a sentence within the category range below. The starting point applies to all offenders irrespective of plea or previous convictions. Having determined the starting point, step two allows further adjustment for aggravating or mitigating features, set out below.

A case of particular gravity, reflected by multiple features of culpability or harm in step one, could merit upward adjustment from the starting point before further adjustment for aggravating or mitigating features, set out below.

Where there is a sufficient prospect of rehabilitation, a community order with a sex offender treatment programme requirement under section 202 of the Criminal Justice Act 2003 can be a proper alternative to a short or moderate length custodial sentence.

	A	B
Category 1	**Starting point** 18 months' custody **Category range** 1–2 years' custody	**Starting point** 1 year's custody **Category range** 26 weeks'–18 months' custody
Category 2	**Starting point** 1 year's custody **Category range** 26 weeks'–18 months' custody	**Starting point** 26 weeks' custody **Category range** High level community order–1 year's custody
Category 3	**Starting point** 26 weeks' custody **Category range** High level community order–1 year's custody	**Starting point** Medium level community order **Category range** Low level community order–High level community order

The table below contains a **non-exhaustive** list of additional factual elements providing the context of the offence and factors relating to the offender. Identify whether any combination of these, or other relevant factors, should result in an upward or downward adjustment from the starting point. **In particular, relevant recent convictions are likely to result in an upward adjustment.** In some cases, having considered these factors, it may be appropriate to move outside the identified category range.

When sentencing appropriate **category 2 or 3 offences**, the court should also consider the custody threshold as follows:

- has the custody threshold been passed?
- if so, is it unavoidable that a custodial sentence be imposed?
- if so, can that sentence be suspended?

Aggravating factors
Statutory aggravating factors
• Previous convictions, having regard to a) the nature of the offence to which the conviction relates and its relevance to the current offence; and b) the time that has elapsed since the conviction • Offence committed whilst on bail

Other aggravating factors

- Location of offence
- Timing of offence
- Victim compelled to leave their home, school, etc
- Failure to comply with current court orders
- Offence committed whilst on licence
- Presence of others, especially other children
- Any steps taken to prevent the victim reporting an incident, obtaining assistance and/or from assisting or supporting the prosecution
- Attempts to dispose of or conceal evidence
- Failure of offender to respond to previous warnings
- Commission of offence whilst under the influence of alcohol or drugs
- Victim encouraged to recruit others

Mitigating factors

- No previous convictions **or** no relevant/recent convictions
- Remorse
- Previous good character and/or exemplary conduct*
- Age and/or lack of maturity where it affects the responsibility of the offender
- Mental disorder or learning disability, particularly where linked to the commission of the offence
- Demonstration of steps taken to address offending behaviour

*Previous good character/exemplary conduct is different from having no previous convictions. The more serious the offence, the less the weight which should normally be attributed to this factor. Where previous good character/ exemplary conduct has been used to facilitate the offence, this mitigation should not normally be allowed and such conduct may constitute an aggravating factor.

STEP THREE

Consider any factors which indicate a reduction, such as assistance to the prosecution

The court should take into account sections 73 and 74 of the Serious Organised Crime and Police Act 2005 (assistance by defendants: reduction or review of sentence) and any other rule of law by virtue of which an offender may receive a discounted sentence in consequence of assistance given (or offered) to the prosecutor or investigator.

STEP FOUR

Reduction for guilty pleas

The court should take account of any potential reduction for a guilty plea in accordance with section 144 of the Criminal Justice Act 2003 and the *Guilty Plea* guideline.

STEP FIVE

Dangerousness

The court should consider whether having regard to the criteria contained in Chapter 5 of Part 12 of the Criminal Justice Act 2003 it would be appropriate to award an extended sentence (section 226A).

STEP SIX

Totality principle

If sentencing an offender for more than one offence, or where the offender is already serving a sentence, consider whether the total sentence is just and proportionate to the offending behaviour.

STEP SEVEN

Ancillary orders

The court must consider whether to make any ancillary orders. The court must also consider what other requirements or provisions may *automatically* apply. Further information is included at Annex A on page 424.

STEP EIGHT

Reasons

Section 174 of the Criminal Justice Act 2003 imposes a duty to give reasons for, and explain the effect of, the sentence.

STEP NINE

Consideration for time spent on bail

The court must consider whether to give credit for time spent on bail in accordance with section 240A of the Criminal Justice Act 2003.

Possession of indecent photograph of child

Criminal Justice Act 1988 (section 160)

Triable either way

Maximum: 5 years' custody

Offence range: Community order–3 years' custody

Indecent photographs of children

Protection of Children Act 1978 (section 1)

Triable either way

Maximum: 10 years' custody

Offence range: Community order–9 years' custody

For section 1 offences committed on or after 3 December 2012, this is an offence listed in Part 1 of Schedule 15B for the purposes of section 224A (life sentence for second listed offence) of the Criminal Justice Act 2003.

For convictions on or after 3 December 2012 (irrespective of the date of commission of the offence), these are specified offences for the purposes of section 226A (extended sentence for certain violent or sexual offences) of the Criminal Justice Act 2003.

STEP ONE

Determining the offence category

The court should determine the offence category using the table below.

	Possession	Distribution*	Production**
Category A	Possession of images involving penetrative sexual activity Possession of images involving sexual activity with an animal or sadism	Sharing images involving penetrative sexual activity Sharing images involving sexual activity with an animal or sadism	Creating images involving penetrative sexual activity Creating images involving sexual activity with an animal or sadism

Category B	Possession of images involving non-penetrative sexual activity	Sharing of images involving non-penetrative sexual activity	Creating images involving non-penetrative sexual activity
Category C	Possession of other indecent images not falling within categories A or B	Sharing of other indecent images not falling within categories A or B	Creating other indecent images not falling within categories A or B

*Distribution includes possession with a view to distributing or sharing images.

**Production includes the taking or making of any image at source for instance. the original image. Making an image by simple downloading should be treated as possession for the purposes of sentencing. In most cases the intrinsic character of the most serious of the offending images will initially determine the appropriate category. If, however, the most serious images are unrepresentative of the offender's conduct a lower category may be appropriate. A lower category will not, however, be appropriate if the offender has produced or taken (for example photographed) images of a higher category.

STEP TWO

Starting point and category range

Having determined the category, the court should use the corresponding starting points to reach a sentence within the category range below. The starting point applies to all offenders irrespective of plea or previous convictions. Having determined the starting point, step two allows further adjustment for aggravating or mitigating features, set out below.

Where there is a sufficient prospect of rehabilitation, a community order with a sex offender treatment programme requirement under section 202 of the Criminal Justice Act 2003 can be a proper alternative to a short or moderate length custodial sentence.

	Possession	**Distribution**	**Production**
Category A	**Starting point** 1 year's custody **Category range** 26 weeks–3 years' custody	**Starting point** 3 years' custody **Category range** 2–5 years' custody	**Starting point** 6 years' custody **Category range** 4–9 years' custody
Category B	**Starting point** 26 weeks' custody **Category range** High level community order–18 months' custody	**Starting point** 1 year's custody **Category range** 26 weeks–2 years' custody	**Starting point** 2 years' custody **Category range** 1–4 years' custody
Category C	**Starting point** High level community order **Category range** Medium level community order–26 weeks' custody	**Starting point** 13 weeks' custody **Category range** High level community order–26 weeks' custody	**Starting point** 18 months' custody **Category range** 1–3 years' custody

The table below contains a **non-exhaustive** list of additional factual elements providing the context of the offence and factors relating to the offender. Identify whether any combination of these, or other relevant factors, should result in an upward or downward adjustment from the starting point. **In particular, relevant recent convictions are likely to result in an upward adjustment.** In some cases, having considered these factors, it may be appropriate to move outside the identified category range.

When sentencing appropriate **category 2 or 3 offences**, the court should also consider the custody threshold as follows:

- has the custody threshold been passed?
- if so, is it unavoidable that a custodial sentence be imposed?
- if so, can that sentence be suspended?

Aggravating factors

Statutory aggravating factors

- Previous convictions, having regard to a) the nature of the offence to which the conviction relates and its relevance to the current offence; and b) the time that has elapsed since the conviction
- Offence committed whilst on bail

Other aggravating factors

- Failure to comply with current court orders
- Offence committed whilst on licence
- Age and/or vulnerability of the child depicted^
- Discernable pain or distress suffered by child depicted
- Period over which images were possessed, distributed or produced
- High volume of images possessed, distributed or produced
- Placing images where there is the potential for a high volume of viewers
- Collection includes moving images
- Attempts to dispose of or conceal evidence
- Abuse of trust
- Child depicted known to the offender
- Active involvement in a network or process that facilitates or commissions the creation or sharing of indecent images of children
- Commercial exploitation and/or motivation
- Deliberate or systematic searching for images portraying young children, category A images or the portrayal of familial sexual abuse
- Large number of different victims
- Child depicted intoxicated or drugged

^Age and/or vulnerability of the child should be given significant weight. In cases where the actual age of the victim is difficult to determine sentencers should consider the development of the child (infant, pre-pubescent, post-pubescent)

Mitigating factors

- No previous convictions **or** no relevant/recent convictions
- Remorse
- Previous good character and/or exemplary conduct*
- Age and/or lack of maturity where it affects the responsibility of the offender
- Mental disorder or learning disability, particularly where linked to the commission of the offence
- Demonstration of steps taken to address offending behaviour

*Previous good character/exemplary conduct is different from having no previous convictions. The more serious the offence, the less the weight which should normally be attributed to this factor. Where previous good character/exemplary conduct has been used to facilitate the offence, this mitigation should not normally be allowed and such conduct may constitute an aggravating factor.

STEP THREE

Consider any factors which indicate a reduction, such as assistance to the prosecution

The court should take into account sections 73 and 74 of the Serious Organised Crime and Police Act 2005 (assistance by defendants: reduction or review of sentence) and any other rule of law by virtue of which an offender may receive a discounted sentence in consequence of assistance given (or offered) to the prosecutor or investigator.

STEP FOUR

Reduction for guilty pleas

The court should take account of any potential reduction for a guilty plea in accordance with section 144 of the Criminal Justice Act 2003 and the *Guilty Plea* guideline.

STEP FIVE

Dangerousness

The court should consider whether having regard to the criteria contained in Chapter 5 of Part 12 of the Criminal Justice Act 2003 it would be appropriate to award a life sentence (section 224A) or an extended sentence (section 226A). When sentencing offenders to a life sentence under these provisions, the notional determinate sentence should be used as the basis for the setting of a minimum term.

STEP SIX

Totality principle

If sentencing an offender for more than one offence, or where the offender is already serving a sentence, consider whether the total sentence is just and proportionate to the offending behaviour.

STEP SEVEN

Ancillary orders

The court must consider whether to make any ancillary orders. The court must also consider what other requirements or provisions may *automatically* apply. Further information is included at Annex A on page 424.

STEP EIGHT

Reasons

Section 174 of the Criminal Justice Act 2003 imposes a duty to give reasons for, and explain the effect of, the sentence.

STEP NINE

Consideration for time spent on bail

The court must consider whether to give credit for time spent on bail in accordance with section 240A of the Criminal Justice Act 2003.

Causing or inciting prostitution for gain

Sexual Offences Act 2003 (section 52)

Controlling prostitution for gain

Sexual Offences Act 2003 (section 53)

Triable either way

Maximum: 7 years' custody

Offence range: Community order–6 years' custody

For convictions on or after 3 December 2012 (irrespective of the date of commission of the offence), these are specified offences for the purposes of section 226A (extended sentence for certain violent or sexual offences) of the Criminal Justice Act 2003.

The terms "prostitute" and "prostitution" are used in this guideline in accordance with the statutory language contained in the Sexual Offences Act 2003.

STEP ONE

Determining the offence category

The court should determine which categories of harm and culpability the offence falls into by reference **only** to the tables below.

HARM	
Category 1	• Abduction/detention • Violence or threats of violence • Sustained and systematic psychological abuse • Individual(s) forced or coerced to participate in unsafe/degrading sexual activity • Individual(s) forced or coerced into seeing many "customers" • Individual(s) forced/coerced/deceived into prostitution
Category 2	Factor(s) in category 1 not present

CULPABILITY

A	B	C
• Causing, inciting or controlling prostitution on significant commercial basis • Expectation of significant financial or other gain • Abuse of trust • Exploitation of those known to be trafficked • Significant involvement in limiting the freedom of prostitute(s) • Grooming of individual(s) to enter prostitution including through cultivation of a dependency on drugs or alcohol	• Close involvement with prostitute(s) for example control of finances, choice of clients, working conditions, etc (where offender's involvement is not as a result of coercion)	• Performs limited function under direction • Close involvement but engaged by coercion/intimidation/ exploitation

STEP TWO

Starting point and category range

Having determined the category, the court should use the corresponding starting points to reach a sentence within the category range below. The starting point applies to all offenders irrespective of plea or previous convictions. Having determined the starting point, step two allows further adjustment for aggravating or mitigating features, set out below.

A case of particular gravity, reflected by multiple features of culpability or harm in step one, could merit upward adjustment from the starting point before further adjustment for aggravating or mitigating features, set out below.

Where there is a sufficient prospect of rehabilitation, a community order with a sex offender treatment programme requirement under section 202 of the Criminal Justice Act 2003 can be a proper alternative to a short or moderate length custodial sentence.

	A	B	C
Category 1	**Starting point** 4 years' custody **Category range** 3–6 years' custody	**Starting point** 2 years 6 months' custody **Category range** 2–4 years' custody	**Starting point** 1 year's custody **Category range** 26 weeks'–2 years' custody
Category 2	**Starting point** 2 years' 6 months' custody **Category range** 2–5 years' custody	**Starting point** 1 year's custody **Category range** High level community order–2 years' custody	**Starting point** Medium level community Order **Category range** Low level community order–High level community order

The table below contains a **non-exhaustive** list of additional factual elements providing the context of the offence and factors relating to the offender. Identify whether any combination of these, or other relevant factors, should result in an upward or downward adjustment from the starting point. **In particular, relevant recent convictions are likely to result in an upward adjustment.** In some cases, having considered these factors, it may be appropriate to move outside the identified category range.

When sentencing appropriate **category 2 offences**, the court should also consider the custody threshold as follows:

- has the custody threshold been passed?
- if so, is it unavoidable that a custodial sentence be imposed?
- if so, can that sentence be suspended?

Aggravating factors
Statutory aggravating factors
• Previous convictions, having regard to a) the nature of the offence to which the conviction relates and its relevance to the current offence; and b) the time that has elapsed since the conviction • Offence committed whilst on bail

Other aggravating factors

- Failure to comply with current court orders
- Offence committed whilst on licence
- Deliberate isolation of prostitute(s)
- Threats made to expose prostitute(s) to the authorities (for example, immigration or police), family/friends or others
- Harm threatened against the family/friends of prostitute(s)
- Passport/identity documents removed
- Prostitute(s) prevented from seeking medical treatment
- Food withheld
- Earnings withheld/kept by offender or evidence of excessive wage reduction or debt bondage, inflated travel or living expenses or unreasonable interest rates
- Any steps taken to prevent the reporting of an incident, obtaining assistance and/or from assisting or supporting the prosecution
- Attempts to dispose of or conceal evidence
- Prostitute(s) forced or coerced into pornography
- Timescale over which operation has been run

Mitigating factors

- No previous convictions **or** no relevant/recent convictions
- Remorse
- Previous good character and/or exemplary conduct*
- Age and/or lack of maturity where it affects the responsibility of the offender
- Mental disorder or learning disability, particularly where linked to the commission of the offence
- Demonstration of steps taken to address offending behaviour

*Previous good character/exemplary conduct is different from having no previous convictions. The more serious the offence, the less the weight which should normally be attributed to this factor. Where previous good character/exemplary conduct has been used to facilitate the offence, this mitigation should not normally be allowed and such conduct may constitute an aggravating factor.

STEP THREE

Consider any factors which indicate a reduction, such as assistance to the prosecution

The court should take into account sections 73 and 74 of the Serious Organised Crime and Police Act 2005 (assistance by defendants: reduction or review of sentence) and any other rule of law by virtue of which an offender may receive a discounted sentence in consequence of assistance given (or offered) to the prosecutor or investigator.

STEP FOUR

Reduction for guilty pleas

The court should take account of any potential reduction for a guilty plea in accordance with section 144 of the Criminal Justice Act 2003 and the *Guilty Plea* guideline.

STEP FIVE

Dangerousness

The court should consider whether having regard to the criteria contained in Chapter 5 of Part 12 of the Criminal Justice Act 2003 it would be appropriate to award an extended sentence (section 226A).

STEP SIX

Totality principle

If sentencing an offender for more than one offence, or where the offender is already serving a sentence, consider whether the total sentence is just and proportionate to the offending behaviour.

STEP SEVEN

Ancillary orders

The court must consider whether to make any ancillary orders. The court must also consider what other requirements or provisions may *automatically* apply. Further information is included at Annex A on page 424.

STEP EIGHT

Reasons

Section 174 of the Criminal Justice Act 2003 imposes a duty to give reasons for, and explain the effect of, the sentence.

STEP NINE

Consideration for time spent on bail

The court must consider whether to give credit for time spent on bail in accordance with section 240A of the Criminal Justice Act 2003.

Keeping a brothel used for prostitution

Sexual Offences Act 1956 (section 33A)

Triable either way

Maximum: 7 years' custody

Offence range: Community order–6 years' custody

The terms "prostitute" and "prostitution" are used in this guideline in accordance with the statutory language contained in the Sexual Offences Act 2003.

STEP ONE

Determining the offence category

The court should determine which categories of harm and culpability the offence falls into by reference **only** to the tables below.

HARM	
Category 1	• Under 18 year olds working in brothel • Abduction/detention • Violence or threats of violence • Sustained and systematic psychological abuse • Those working in brothel forced or coerced to participate in unsafe/degrading sexual activity • Those working in brothel forced or coerced into seeing many "customers" • Those working in brothel forced/coerced/deceived into prostitution • Established evidence of community impact
Category 2	Factor(s) in category 1 not present

CULPABILITY		
A	**B**	**C**
• Keeping brothel on significant commercial basis • Involvement in keeping a number of brothels • Expectation of significant financial or other gain • Abuse of trust • Exploitation of those known to be trafficked • Significant involvement in limiting freedom of those working in brothel • Grooming of a person to work in the brothel including through cultivation of a dependency on drugs or alcohol	• Keeping/managing premises • Close involvement with those working in brothel e.g. control of finances, choice of clients, working conditions, etc. (where offender's involvement is not as a result of coercion)	• Performs limited function under direction • Close involvement but engaged by coercion/intimidation/ exploitation

STEP TWO

Starting point and category range

Having determined the category, the court should use the corresponding starting points to reach a sentence within the category range below. The starting point applies to all offenders irrespective of plea or previous convictions. Having determined the starting point, step two allows further adjustment for aggravating or mitigating features, set out below.

A case of particular gravity, reflected by multiple features of culpability or harm in step one, could merit upward adjustment from the starting point before further adjustment for aggravating or mitigating features, set out below.

Where there is a sufficient prospect of rehabilitation, a community order with a sex offender treatment programme requirement under section 202 of the Criminal Justice Act 2003 can be a proper alternative to a short or moderate length custodial sentence.

	A	B	C
Category 1	**Starting point** 5 years' custody **Category range** 3–6 years' custody	**Starting point** 3 years' custody **Category range** 2–5 years' custody	**Starting point** 1 year's custody **Category range** High level community order–18 months' custody
Category 2	**Starting point** 3 years' custody **Category range** 2–5 years' custody	**Starting point** 12 months' custody **Category range** 26 weeks'–2 years' custody	**Starting point** Medium level community order **Category range** Low level community order–High level community order

The table below contains a **non-exhaustive** list of additional factual elements providing the context of the offence and factors relating to the offender. Identify whether any combination of these, or other relevant factors, should result in an upward or downward adjustment from the starting point. **In particular, relevant recent convictions are likely to result in an upward adjustment.** In some cases, having considered these factors, it may be appropriate to move outside the identified category range.

When sentencing appropriate **category 1 offences**, the court should also consider the custody threshold as follows:

- has the custody threshold been passed?
- if so, is it unavoidable that a custodial sentence be imposed?
- if so, can that sentence be suspended?

Aggravating factors
Statutory aggravating factors
• Previous convictions, having regard to a) the nature of the offence to which the conviction relates and its relevance to the current offence; and b) the time that has elapsed since the conviction • Offence committed whilst on bail
Other aggravating factors
• Failure to comply with current court orders • Offence committed whilst on licence • Deliberate isolation of those working in brothel • Threats made to expose those working in brothel to the authorities (for example, immigration or police), family/friends or others • Harm threatened against the family/friends of those working in brothel • Passport/identity documents removed • Those working in brothel prevented from seeking medical treatment • Food withheld • Those working in brothel passed around by offender and moved to other brothels • Earnings of those working in brothel withheld/kept by offender or evidence of excessive wage reduction or debt bondage, inflated travel or living expenses or unreasonable interest rates • Any steps taken to prevent those working in brothel reporting an incident, obtaining assistance and/or from assisting or supporting the prosecution • Attempts to dispose of or conceal evidence • Those working in brothel forced or coerced into pornography • Timescale over which operation has been run

Mitigating factors
• No previous convictions **or** no relevant/recent convictions • Remorse • Previous good character and/or exemplary conduct* • Age and/or lack of maturity where it affects the responsibility of the offender • Mental disorder or learning disability, particularly where linked to the commission of the offence • Demonstration of steps taken to address offending behaviour

*Previous good character/exemplary conduct is different from having no previous convictions. The more serious the offence, the less the weight which should normally be attributed to this factor. Where previous good character/ exemplary conduct has been used to facilitate the offence, this mitigation should not normally be allowed and such conduct may constitute an aggravating factor.

STEP THREE

Consider any factors which indicate a reduction, such as assistance to the prosecution

The court should take into account sections 73 and 74 of the Serious Organised Crime and Police Act 2005 (assistance by defendants: reduction or review of sentence) and any other rule of law by virtue of which an offender may receive a discounted sentence in consequence of assistance given (or offered) to the prosecutor or investigator.

STEP FOUR

Reduction for guilty pleas

The court should take account of any potential reduction for a guilty plea in accordance with section 144 of the Criminal Justice Act 2003 and the *Guilty Plea* guideline.

STEP FIVE

Totality principle

If sentencing an offender for more than one offence, or where the offender is already serving a sentence, consider whether the total sentence is just and proportionate to the offending behaviour.

STEP SIX

Ancillary orders

The court must consider whether to make any ancillary orders. The court must also consider what other requirements or provisions may *automatically* apply. Further information is included at Annex A on page 424.

STEP SEVEN

Reasons

Section 174 of the Criminal Justice Act 2003 imposes a duty to give reasons for, and explain the effect of, the sentence.

STEP EIGHT

Consideration for time spent on bail

The court must consider whether to give credit for time spent on bail in accordance with section 240A of the Criminal Justice Act 2003.

Causing or inciting child prostitution or pornography

Sexual Offences Act 2003 (section 48)

Controlling a child prostitute or child involved in pornography

Sexual Offences Act 2003 (section 49)

Arranging or facilitating child prostitution or pornography

Sexual Offences Act 2003 (section 50)

Triable either way

Maximum: 14 years' custody

Offence range: Victim aged under 13 1–13 years' custody

Victim aged 13–15 26 weeks'–11 years' custody

Victim aged 16–17 Community order–7 years' custody

For offences committed on or after 3 December 2012, these are offences listed in Part 1 of Schedule 15B for the purposes of sections 224A (life sentence for second listed offence) of the Criminal Justice Act 2003.

For convictions on or after 3 December 2012 (irrespective of the date of commission of the offence), these are specified offences for the purposes of section 226A (extended sentence for certain violent or sexual offences) of the Criminal Justice Act 2003.

The terms "child prostitute", "child prostitution" and "child involved in pornography" are used in this guideline in accordance with the statutory language contained in the Sexual Offences Act 2003.

STEP ONE

Determining the offence category

The court should determine which categories of harm and culpability the offence falls into by reference **only** to the tables below.

> For offences that involve wide scale commercial and/or international activity sentences above the category range may be appropriate.

HARM	
Category 1	• Victims involved in penetrative sexual activity • Abduction/detention • Violence or threats of violence • Sustained and systematic psychological abuse • Victim(s) participated in unsafe/degrading sexual activity beyond that which is inherent in the offence • Victim(s) passed around by the offender to other "customers" and/or moved to other brothels
Category 2	Factor(s) in category 1 not present

CULPABILITY

A	B	C
• Directing or organising child prostitution or pornography on significant commercial basis • Expectation of significant financial or other gain • Abuse of trust • Exploitation of victim(s) known to be trafficked • Significant involvement in limiting the freedom of the victim(s) • Grooming of a victim to enter prostitution or pornography including through cultivation of a dependency on drugs or alcohol	• Close involvement with inciting, controlling, arranging or facilitating child prostitution or pornography (where offender's involvement is not as a result of coercion)	• Performs limited function under direction • Close involvement but engaged by coercion/intimidation / exploitation

STEP TWO

Starting point and category range

Having determined the category, the court should use the corresponding starting points to reach a sentence within the category range below. The starting point applies to all offenders irrespective of plea or previous convictions. Having determined the starting point, step two allows further adjustment for aggravating or mitigating features, set out below.

A case of particular gravity, reflected by multiple features of culpability or harm in step one, could merit upward adjustment from the starting point before further adjustment for aggravating or mitigating features, set out below.

Where there is a sufficient prospect of rehabilitation, a community order with a sex offender treatment programme requirement under section 202 of the Criminal Justice Act 2003 can be a proper alternative to a short or moderate length custodial sentence.

		A	B	C
Category 1	U13	**Starting point**10 years' custody **Category range** 8 -13 years' custody	**Starting point**8 years' custody **Category range** 6 -11 years' custody	**Starting point**5 years' custody **Category range** 2–6 years' custody
	13-15	**Starting point** 8 years' custody **Category range** 6–11 years' custody	**Starting point** 5 years' custody **Category range** 4–8 years' custody	**Starting point** 2 years 6 months' custody **Category range** 1–4 years' custody
	16-17	**Starting point** 4 years' custody **Category range** 3–7 years' custody	**Starting point** 2 years' custody **Category range** 1–4 years' custody	**Starting point** 1 year's custody **Category range** 26 weeks'–2 years' custody
Category 2	U13	**Starting point** 8 years' custody **Category range** 6 -11 years' custody	**Starting point** 6 years' custody **Category range** 4–9 years' custody	**Starting point** 2 years' custody **Category range** 1–4 years' custody
	13-15	**Starting point** 6 years' custody **Category range** 4–9 years' custody	**Starting point** 3 years' custody **Category range** 2–5 years' custody	**Starting point** 1 year's custody **Category range** 26 weeks'–2 years' custody
	16-17	**Starting point** 3 years' custody **Category range** 2–5 years' custody	**Starting point** 1 year's custody **Category range** 26 weeks'–2 years' custody	**Starting point** 26 weeks' custody **Category range** High level community order- 1 year's custody

The table below contains a **non-exhaustive** list of additional factual elements providing the context of the offence and factors relating to the offender. Identify whether any combination of these, or other relevant factors, should result in an upward or downward adjustment from the starting point. **In particular, relevant recent convictions are likely to result in an upward adjustment.** In some cases, having considered these factors, it may be appropriate to move outside the identified category range.

When sentencing appropriate **category 2 offences**, the court should also consider the custody threshold as follows:

- has the custody threshold been passed?
- if so, is it unavoidable that a custodial sentence be imposed?
- if so, can that sentence be suspended?

Aggravating factors

Statutory aggravating factors

- Previous convictions, having regard to a) the nature of the offence to which the conviction relates and its relevance to the current offence; and b) the time that has elapsed since the conviction
- Offence committed whilst on bail

Other aggravating factors

- Failure to comply with current court orders
- Offence committed whilst on licence
- Deliberate isolation of victim(s)
- Vulnerability of victim(s)
- Threats made to expose victim(s) to the authorities (for example immigration or police), family/friends or others
- Harm threatened against the family/friends of victim(s)
- Passport/identity documents removed
- Victim(s) prevented from seeking medical treatment
- Victim(s) prevented from attending school
- Food withheld
- Earnings withheld/kept by offender or evidence of excessive wage reduction or debt bondage, inflated travel or living expenses or unreasonable interest rates
- Any steps taken to prevent the victim reporting an incident, obtaining assistance and/or from assisting or supporting the prosecution
- Attempts to dispose of or conceal evidence
- Timescale over which the operation has been run

Mitigating Factors

- No previous convictions **or** no relevant/recent convictions
- Remorse
- Previous good character and/or exemplary conduct*
- Age and/or lack of maturity where it affects the responsibility of the offender
- Mental disorder or learning disability, particularly where linked to the commission of the offence

*Previous good character/exemplary conduct is different from having no previous convictions. The more serious the offence, the less the weight which should normally be attributed to this factor. Where previous good character/exemplary conduct has been used to facilitate the offence, this mitigation should not normally be allowed and such conduct may constitute an aggravating factor. In the context of this offence, previous good character/exemplary conduct should not normally be given any significant weight and will not normally justify a reduction in what would otherwise be the appropriate sentence.

STEP THREE

Consider any factors which indicate a reduction, such as assistance to the prosecution

The court should take into account sections 73 and 74 of the Serious Organised Crime and Police Act 2005 (assistance by defendants: reduction or review of sentence) and any other rule of law by virtue of which an offender may receive a discounted sentence in consequence of assistance given (or offered) to the prosecutor or investigator.

STEP FOUR

Reduction for guilty pleas

The court should take account of any potential reduction for a guilty plea in accordance with section 144 of the Criminal Justice Act 2003 and the *Guilty Plea* guideline.

STEP FIVE

Dangerousness

The court should consider whether having regard to the criteria contained in Chapter 5 of Part 12 of the Criminal Justice Act 2003 it would be appropriate to award a life sentence (section 224A) or an extended sentence (section 226A). When sentencing offenders to a life sentence under these provisions, the notional determinate sentence should be used as the basis for the setting of a minimum term.

STEP SIX

Totality principle

If sentencing an offender for more than one offence, or where the offender is already serving a sentence, consider whether the total sentence is just and proportionate to the offending behaviour.

STEP SEVEN

Ancillary orders

The court must consider whether to make any ancillary orders. The court must also consider what other requirements or provisions may ***automatically*** apply. Further information is included at Annex A on page 424.

STEP EIGHT

Reasons

Section 174 of the Criminal Justice Act 2003 imposes a duty to give reasons for, and explain the effect of, the sentence.

STEP NINE

Consideration for time spent on bail

The court must consider whether to give credit for time spent on bail in accordance with section 240A of the Criminal Justice Act 2003.

Paying for the sexual services of a child

Sexual Offences Act 2003 (section 47)

Triable only on indictment (if involving penetration against victim under 16) -otherwise triable either way

Maximum:	**Victim under 13 (penetrative) Life imprisonment** **Victim under 13 (non-penetrative) 14 years' custody** **Victim aged 13-15 14 years' custody** **Victim aged 16-17 7 years' custody**
Offence range:	**Victim aged 16-17 Community order–5 years' custody**

This guideline should only be used where the victim is aged 16 or 17 years old. If the victim is under 13 please refer to the guidelines for rape of a child under 13, assault by penetration of a child under 13, sexual assault of a child under 13 or causing or inciting a child under 13 to engage in sexual activity, depending on the activity involved in the offence.

If the victim is aged 13-15 please refer to the sexual activity with a child guideline.

Where the victim is 16 or 17 years old–for convictions on or after 3 December 2012 (irrespective of the date of commission of the offence), this is a specified offence for the purposes of section 226A (extended sentence for certain violent or sexual offences) of the Criminal Justice Act 2003.

STEP ONE

Determining the offence category

The court should determine which categories of harm and culpability the offence falls into by reference **only** to the tables below.

This guideline should only be used where the victim was aged 16 or 17 years old.

HARM	
Category 1	• Penetration of vagina or anus (using body or object) by, or of, the victim • Penile penetration of mouth by, or of, the victim • Violence or threats of violence • Victim subjected to unsafe/degrading sexual activity (beyond that which is inherent in the offence)
Category 2	• Touching of naked genitalia or naked breasts by, or of, the victim
Category 3	• Other sexual activity

CULPABILITY	
A	B
• Abduction/detention • Sexual images of victim recorded, retained, solicited or shared • Offender acts together with others to commit the offence • Use of alcohol/drugs on victim • Abuse of trust • Previous violence against victim • Sexual images of victim recorded, retained, solicited or shared • Blackmail or other threats made (including to expose victim to the authorities, family/friends or others) • Offender aware that he has a sexually transmitted disease • Offender aware victim has been trafficked	Factor(s) in category A not present

STEP TWO

Starting point and category range

Having determined the category, the court should use the corresponding starting points to reach a sentence within the category range below **for victims aged 16 or 17**. The starting point applies to all offenders irrespective of plea or previous convictions. Having determined the starting point, step two allows further adjustment for aggravating or mitigating features, set out below.

A case of particular gravity, reflected by multiple features of culpability in step one, could merit upward adjustment from the starting point before further adjustment for aggravating or mitigating features, set out below.

Where there is a sufficient prospect of rehabilitation, a community order with a sex offender treatment programme requirement under section 202 of the Criminal Justice Act 2003 can be a proper alternative to a short or moderate length custodial sentence.

	A	B
Category 1	**Starting point** 4 years' custody **Category range** 2–5 years' custody	**Starting point** 2 years' custody **Category range** 1–4 years' custody
Category 2	**Starting point** 3 years' custody **Category range** 1–4 years' custody	**Starting point** 1 year's custody **Category range** 26 weeks'–2 years' custody
Category 3	**Starting point** 1 year's custody **Category range** 26 weeks'–2 years' custody	**Starting point** 26 weeks' custody **Category range** High level community order–1 year's custody

The table below contains a **non-exhaustive** list of additional factual elements providing the context of the offence and factors relating to the offender. Identify whether any combination of these, or other relevant factors, should result in an upward or downward adjustment from the starting point. **In particular, relevant recent convictions are likely to result in an upward adjustment.** In some cases, having considered these factors, it may be appropriate to move outside the identified category range.

When sentencing appropriate **category 3 offences**, the court should also consider the custody threshold as follows:

- has the custody threshold been passed?
- if so, is it unavoidable that a custodial sentence be imposed?
- if so, can that sentence be suspended?

Aggravating factors

Statutory aggravating factors

- Previous convictions, having regard to a) the nature of the offence to which the conviction relates and its relevance to the current offence; and b) the time that has elapsed since the conviction
- Offence committed whilst on bail

Other aggravating factors

- Ejaculation
- Failure to comply with current court orders
- Offence committed whilst on licence
- Any steps taken to prevent the victim reporting an incident, obtaining assistance and/or from assisting or supporting the prosecution
- Attempts to dispose of or conceal evidence

Mitigating factors

- No previous convictions **or** no relevant/recent convictions
- Remorse
- Previous good character and/or exemplary conduct*
- Age and/or lack of maturity where it affects the responsibility of the offender
- Mental disorder or learning disability, particularly where linked to the commission of the offence
- Demonstration of steps taken to address offending behaviour

*Previous good character/exemplary conduct is different from having no previous convictions. The more serious the offence, the less the weight which should normally be attributed to this factor. Where previous good character/exemplary conduct has been used to facilitate the offence, this mitigation should not normally be allowed and such conduct may constitute an aggravating factor.

STEP THREE

Consider any factors which indicate a reduction, such as assistance to the prosecution

The court should take into account sections 73 and 74 of the Serious Organised Crime and Police Act 2005 (assistance by defendants: reduction or review of sentence) and any other rule of law by virtue of which an offender may receive a discounted sentence in consequence of assistance given (or offered) to the prosecutor or investigator.

STEP FOUR

Reduction for guilty pleas

The court should take account of any potential reduction for a guilty plea in accordance with section 144 of the Criminal Justice Act 2003 and the *Guilty Plea* guideline.

STEP FIVE

Dangerousness

The court should consider whether having regard to the criteria contained in Chapter 5 of Part 12 of the Criminal Justice Act 2003 it would be appropriate to award an extended sentence (section 226A).

STEP SIX

Totality principle

If sentencing an offender for more than one offence, or where the offender is already serving a sentence, consider whether the total sentence is just and proportionate to the offending behaviour.

STEP SEVEN

Ancillary orders

The court must consider whether to make any ancillary orders. The court must also consider what other requirements or provisions may *automatically* apply. Further information is included at Annex A on page 424.

STEP EIGHT

Reasons

Section 174 of the Criminal Justice Act 2003 imposes a duty to give reasons for, and explain the effect of, the sentence.

STEP NINE

Consideration for time spent on bail

The court must consider whether to give credit for time spent on bail in accordance with section 240A of the Criminal Justice Act 2003.

Trafficking people for sexual exploitation

Sexual Offences Act 2003 (sections 59A)

(This guideline also applies to offences, committed before 6 April 2013, of trafficking into/within/out of the UK for sexual exploitation contrary to sections 57 to 59 of the Sexual Offences Act 2003)

Triable either way

Maximum: 14 years' custody

Offence range: Community order–12 years' custody

For convictions on or after 3 December 2012 (irrespective of the date of commission of the offence), this is a specified offence for the purposes of section 226A (extended sentence for certain violent or sexual offences) of the Criminal Justice Act 2003.

The term "prostitution" is used in this guideline in accordance with the statutory language contained in the Sexual Offences Act 2003.

STEP ONE

Determining the offence category

The court should determine which categories of harm and culpability the offence falls into by reference **only** to the tables below.

HARM	
Category 1	• Abduction/detention • Violence or threats of violence • Sustained and systematic psychological abuse • Victim(s) under 18 • Victim(s) forced or coerced to participate in unsafe/degrading sexual activity • Victim(s) forced/coerced into prostitution • Victim(s) tricked/deceived as to purpose of visit
Category 2	• Factor(s) in category 1 not present

CULPABILITY		
A	B	C
• Directing or organising trafficking on significant commercial basis • Expectation of significant financial or other gain • Significant influence over others in trafficking organisation/hierarchy • Abuse of trust	• Operational or management function within hierarchy • Involves others in operation whether by coercion/ intimidation/ exploitation or reward (and offender's involvement is not as a result of coercion)	• Performs limited function under direction • Close involvement but engaged by coercion/ intimidation/ exploitation

STEP TWO

Starting point and category range

Having determined the category of harm and culpability, the court should use the corresponding starting points to reach a sentence within the category range below. The starting point applies to all offenders irrespective of plea or previous convictions. Having determined the starting point, step two allows further adjustment for aggravating or mitigating features, set out below.

A case of particular gravity, reflected by multiple features of culpability or harm in step one, could merit upward adjustment from the starting point before further adjustment for aggravating or mitigating features, set out below.

Where there is a sufficient prospect of rehabilitation, a community order with a sex offender treatment programme requirement under section 202 of the Criminal Justice Act 2003 can be a proper alternative to a short or moderate length custodial sentence.

	A	B	C
Category 1	**Starting point** 8 years' custody **Category range** 6 -12 years' custody	**Starting point** 6 years' custody **Category range** 4–8 years' custody	**Starting point** 18 months' custody **Category range** 26 weeks'–2 years' custody
Category 2	**Starting point** 6 years' custody **Category range** 4–8 years' custody	**Starting point** 4 years' custody **Category range** 2- 6 years' custody	**Starting point** 26 weeks' custody **Category range** High level community order–18 months' custody

The table below contains a **non-exhaustive** list of additional factual elements providing the context of the offence and factors relating to the offender. Identify whether any combination of these, or other relevant factors, should result in an upward or downward adjustment from the starting point. **In particular, relevant recent convictions are likely to result in an upward adjustment.** In some cases, having considered these factors, it may be appropriate to move outside the identified category range.

When sentencing appropriate **category 2 offences**, the court should also consider the custody threshold as follows:

- has the custody threshold been passed?
- if so, is it unavoidable that a custodial sentence be imposed?
- if so, can that sentence be suspended?

Aggravating factors
Statutory aggravating factors
• Previous convictions, having regard to a) the nature of the offence to which the conviction relates and its relevance to the current offence; and b) the time that has elapsed since the conviction • Offence committed whilst on bail

Other aggravating factors

- Failure to comply with current court orders
- Offence committed whilst on licence
- Deliberate isolation of victim(s)
- Children of victim(s) left in home country due to trafficking
- Threats made to expose victim(s) to the authorities (for example immigration or police), family/friends or others
- Harm threatened against the family/friends of victim
- Exploitation of victim(s) from particularly vulnerable backgrounds
- Victim(s) previously trafficked/sold/passed around
- Passport/identity documents removed
- Victim(s) prevented from seeking medical treatment
- Food withheld
- Use of drugs/alcohol or other substance to secure victim's compliance
- Earnings of victim(s) withheld/kept by offender or evidence of excessive wage reduction, debt bondage, inflated travel or living expenses, unreasonable interest rates
- Any steps taken to prevent the victim reporting an incident, obtaining assistance and/or from assisting or supporting the prosecution
- Attempts to dispose of or conceal evidence
- Timescale over which operation has been run

Mitigating factors

- No previous convictions **or** no relevant/recent convictions
- Remorse
- Previous good character and/or exemplary conduct*
- Age and/or lack of maturity where it affects the responsibility of the offender
- Mental disorder or learning disability, particularly where linked to the commission of the offence

*Previous good character/exemplary conduct is different from having no previous convictions. The more serious the offence, the less the weight which should normally be attributed to this factor. Where previous good character/exemplary conduct has been used to facilitate the offence, this mitigation should not normally be allowed and such conduct may constitute an aggravating factor. In the context of this offence, previous good character/exemplary conduct should not normally be given any significant weight and will not normally justify a reduction in what would otherwise be the appropriate sentence.

STEP THREE

Consider any factors which indicate a reduction, such as assistance to the prosecution

The court should take into account sections 73 and 74 of the Serious Organised Crime and Police Act 2005 (assistance by defendants: reduction or review of sentence) and any other rule of law by virtue of which an offender may receive a discounted sentence in consequence of assistance given (or offered) to the prosecutor or investigator.

STEP FOUR

Reduction for guilty pleas

The court should take account of any potential reduction for a guilty plea in accordance with section 144 of the Criminal Justice Act 2003 and the *Guilty Plea* guideline.

STEP FIVE

Dangerousness

The court should consider whether having regard to the criteria contained in Chapter 5 of Part 12 of the Criminal Justice Act 2003 it would be appropriate to award an extended sentence (section 226A).

STEP SIX

Totality principle

If sentencing an offender for more than one offence, or where the offender is already serving a sentence, consider whether the total sentence is just and proportionate to the offending behaviour.

STEP SEVEN

Ancillary orders

The court must consider whether to make any ancillary orders. The court must also consider what other requirements or provisions may *automatically* apply. Further information is included at Annex A on page 424.

STEP EIGHT

Reasons

Section 174 of the Criminal Justice Act 2003 imposes a duty to give reasons for, and explain the effect of, the sentence.

STEP NINE

Consideration for time spent on bail

The court must consider whether to give credit for time spent on bail in accordance with section 240A of the Criminal Justice Act 2003.

Sexual activity with a person with a mental disorder impeding choice

Sexual Offences Act 2003 (section 30)

Causing or inciting a person, with a mental disorder impeding choice, to engage in sexual activity

Sexual Offences Act 2003 (section 31)

Triable only on indictment (if penetration involved)—otherwise, triable either way

Maximum: Life imprisonment (if penetration involved)—otherwise 14 years' custody

Offence range: Community order–19 years' custody

These are serious specified offences for the purposes of section 224 and, where the offence involved penetration, section 225(2) (life sentence for serious offences) of the Criminal Justice Act 2003.

For offences involving penetration, committed on or after 3 December 2012, these are offences listed in Part 1 of Schedule 15B for the purposes of section 224A (life sentence for second listed offence) of the Criminal Justice Act 2003.

For convictions on or after 3 December 2012 (irrespective of the date of commission of the offence), these are specified offences for the purposes of section 226A (extended sentence for certain violent or sexual offences) of the Criminal Justice Act 2003.

STEP ONE

Determining the offence category

The court should determine which categories of harm and culpability the offence falls into by reference **only** to the tables below.

Harm	
Category 1	• The extreme nature of one or more category 2 factors or the extreme impact caused by a combination of category 2 factors **may** elevate to category 1
Category 2	• Severe psychological or physical harm • Pregnancy or STI as a consequence of offence • Additional degradation/ humiliation • Abduction • Prolonged detention / sustained incident • Violence or threats of violence • Forced/uninvited entry into victim's home or residence
Category 3	Factor(s) in categories 1 and 2 not present

Culpability	
A	**B**
• Significant degree of planning • Offender acts together with others to commit the offence • Use of alcohol/drugs on victim to facilitate the offence • Grooming behaviour used against victim • Abuse of trust • Previous violence against victim • Offence committed in course of burglary • Sexual images of victim recorded, retained, solicited or shared • Deliberate isolation of victim • Commercial exploitation and/or motivation • Offence racially or religiously aggravated • Offence motivated by, or demonstrating, hostility to the victim based on his or her sexual orientation (or presumed sexual orientation) or transgender identity (or presumed transgender identity) • Offence motivated by, or demonstrating, hostility to the victim based on the victim's disability (or presumed disability)	Factor(s) in category A not present

STEP TWO

Starting point and category range

Having determined the category of harm and culpability, the court should use the corresponding starting points to reach a sentence within the category range below. The starting point applies to all offenders irrespective of plea or previous convictions. Having determined the starting point, step two allows further adjustment for aggravating or mitigating features, set out below.

A case of particular gravity, reflected by multiple features of culpability or harm in step one, could merit upward adjustment from the starting point before further adjustment for aggravating or mitigating features, set out below.

Where there is a sufficient prospect of rehabilitation, a community order with a sex offender treatment programme requirement under section 202 of the Criminal Justice Act 2003 can be a proper alternative to a short or moderate length custodial sentence.

Where offence involved penetration

	A	B
Category 1	**Starting point** 16 years' custody **Category range** 13–19 years' custody	**Starting point** 13 years' custody **Category range** 11–17 years' custody
Category 2	**Starting point** 13 years' custody **Category range** 11–17 years' custody	**Starting point** 10 years' custody **Category range** 8–13 years' custody
Category 3	**Starting point** 10 years' custody **Category range** 8–13 years' custody	**Starting point** 8 years' custody **Category range** 6–11 years' custody

Where offence did not involve penetration

	A	B
Category 1	**Starting point** 6 years' custody **Category range** 4–9 years' custody	**Starting point** 4 years' custody **Category range** 3–7 years' custody
Category 2	**Starting point** 4 years' custody **Category range** 3–7 years' custody	**Starting point** 2 years' custody **Category range** 1–4 years' custody
Category 3	**Starting point** 1 year's custody **Category range** 26 weeks' – 2 years' custody	**Starting point** 26 weeks' custody **Category range** High level community order – 1 year's custody

The table below contains a **non-exhaustive** list of additional factual elements providing the context of the offence and factors relating to the offender. Identify whether any combination of these, or other relevant factors, should result in an upward or downward adjustment from the starting point. **In particular, relevant recent convictions are likely to result in an upward adjustment.** In some cases, having considered these factors, it may be appropriate to move outside the identified category range.

When appropriate, the court should also consider the custody threshold as follows:

- has the custody threshold been passed?
- if so, is it unavoidable that a custodial sentence be imposed?
- if so, can that sentence be suspended?

Aggravating factors

Statutory aggravating factors

- Previous convictions, having regard to a) the nature of the offence to which the conviction relates and its relevance to the current offence; and b) the time that has elapsed since the conviction
- Offence committed whilst on bail

Other aggravating factors

- Ejaculation (where not taken into account at step one)
- Blackmail or other threats made (where not taken into account at step one)
- Location of offence
- Timing of offence
- Use of weapon or other item to frighten or injure
- Victim compelled to leave their home or institution (including victims of domestic violence)
- Failure to comply with current court orders
- Offence committed whilst on licence
- Presence of others, especially children
- Any steps taken to prevent the victim reporting an incident, obtaining assistance and/or from assisting or supporting the prosecution
- Attempts to dispose of or conceal evidence
- Commission of offence whilst under the influence of alcohol or drugs

Mitigating factors

- No previous convictions **or** no relevant/recent convictions
- Remorse
- Previous good character and/or exemplary conduct*
- Age and/or lack of maturity where it affects the responsibility of the offender
- Mental disorder or learning disability, particularly where linked to the commission of the offence
- Sexual activity was incited but no activity took place because the offender voluntarily desisted or intervened to prevent it

*Previous good character/exemplary conduct is different from having no previous convictions. The more serious the offence, the less the weight which should normally be attributed to this factor. Where previous good character/exemplary conduct has been used to facilitate the offence, this mitigation should not normally be allowed and such conduct may constitute an aggravating factor. In the context of this offence, previous good character/exemplary conduct should not normally be given any significant weight and will not normally justify a reduction in what would otherwise be the appropriate sentence.

STEP THREE

Consider any factors which indicate a reduction, such as assistance to the prosecution

The court should take into account sections 73 and 74 of the Serious Organised Crime and Police Act 2005 (assistance by defendants: reduction or review of sentence) and any other rule of law by virtue of which an offender may receive a discounted sentence in consequence of assistance given (or offered) to the prosecutor or investigator.

STEP FOUR

Reduction for guilty pleas

The court should take account of any potential reduction for a guilty plea in accordance with section 144 of the Criminal Justice Act 2003 and the *Guilty Plea* guideline.

STEP FIVE

Dangerousness

The court should consider whether having regard to the criteria contained in Chapter 5 of Part 12 of the Criminal Justice Act 2003 it would be appropriate to award a life sentence (section 224A or section 225(2)) or an extended sentence (section 226A). When sentencing offenders to a life sentence under these provisions, the notional determinate sentence should be used as the basis for the setting of a minimum term.

STEP SIX

Totality principle

If sentencing an offender for more than one offence, or where the offender is already serving a sentence, consider whether the total sentence is just and proportionate to the offending behaviour.

STEP SEVEN

Ancillary orders

The court must consider whether to make any ancillary orders. The court must also consider what other requirements or provisions may *automatically* apply. Further information is included at Annex A on page 424.

STEP EIGHT

Reasons

Section 174 of the Criminal Justice Act 2003 imposes a duty to give reasons for, and explain the effect of, the sentence.

STEP NINE

Consideration for time spent on bail

The court must consider whether to give credit for time spent on bail in accordance with section 240A of the Criminal Justice Act 2003.

Engaging in sexual activity in the presence of a person with mental disorder impeding choice

Sexual Offences Act 2003 (section 32)

Causing a person, with mental disorder impeding choice, to watch a sexual act

Sexual Offences Act 2003 (section 33)

Triable either way

Maximum: 10 years' custody

Offence range: Community order–6 years' custody

For convictions on or after 3 December 2012 (irrespective of the date of commission of the offence), these are specified offences for the purposes of section 226A (extended sentence for certain violent or sexual offences) of the Criminal Justice Act 2003.

STEP ONE

Determining the offence category

The court should determine which categories of harm and culpability the offence falls into by reference **only** to the tables below.

Harm	
Category 1	• Causing victim to view extreme pornography • Causing victim to view indecent/prohibited images of children • Engaging in, or causing a victim to view live, sexual activity involving sadism/violence/sexual activity with an animal/a child
Category 2	Engaging in, or causing a victim to view images of or view live, sexual activity involving: • penetration of vagina or anus (using body or object) • penile penetration of mouth • masturbation
Category 3	Factor(s) in categories 1 and 2 not present

Culpability	
A	B
• Significant degree of planning • Offender acts together with others in order to commit the offence • Use of alcohol/drugs on victim to facilitate the offence • Grooming behaviour used against victim • Abuse of trust • Use of threats (including blackmail) • Commercial exploitation and/or motivation • Offence racially or religiously aggravated • Offence motivated by, or demonstrating, hostility to the victim based on his or her sexual orientation (or presumed sexual orientation) or transgender identity (or presumed transgender identity) • Offence motivated by, or demonstrating, hostility to the victim based on his or her disability (or presumed disability)	Factor(s) in category A not present

STEP TWO

Starting point and category range

Having determined the category of harm and culpability, the court should use the corresponding starting points to reach a sentence within the category range below. The starting point applies to all offenders irrespective of plea or previous convictions.

Having determined the starting point, step two allows further adjustment for aggravating or mitigating features, set out below.

A case of particular gravity, reflected by multiple features of culpability or harm in step one, could merit upward adjustment from the starting point before further adjustment for aggravating or mitigating features, set out below.

Where there is a sufficient prospect of rehabilitation, a community order with a sex offender treatment programme requirement under section 202 of the Criminal Justice Act 2003 can be a proper alternative to a short or moderate length custodial sentence.

	A	B
Category 1	**Starting point** 4 years' custody **Category range** 3–6 years' custody	**Starting point** 2 years' custody **Category range** 1–3 years' custody
Category 2	**Starting point** 2 years' custody **Category range** 1–3 years' custody	**Starting point** 1 year's custody **Category range** High level community order–18 months' custody
Category 3	**Starting point** 26 weeks' custody **Category range** High level community order–1 year's custody	**Starting point** Medium level community order **Category range** Low level community order–Medium level community order

The table below contains a **non-exhaustive** list of additional factual elements providing the context of the offence and factors relating to the offender. Identify whether any combination of these, or other relevant factors, should result in an upward or downward adjustment from the starting point. **In particular, relevant recent convictions are likely to result in an upward adjustment.** In some cases, having considered these factors, it may be appropriate to move outside the identified category range.

When sentencing appropriate **category 2 or 3 offences**, the court should also consider the custody threshold as follows:

- has the custody threshold been passed?
- if so, is it unavoidable that a custodial sentence be imposed?
- if so, can that sentence be suspended?

Aggravating factors
Statutory aggravating factors
• Previous convictions, having regard to a) the nature of the offence to which the conviction relates and its relevance to the current offence; and b) the time that has elapsed since the conviction • Offence committed whilst on bail

Other aggravating factors
• Location of offence • Timing of offence • Failure to comply with current court orders • Offence committed whilst on licence • Any steps taken to prevent the victim reporting an incident, obtaining assistance and/or from assisting or supporting the prosecution • Attempts to dispose of or conceal evidence • Commission of offence whilst under the influence of alcohol or drugs

Mitigating factors

- No previous convictions **or** no relevant/recent convictions
- Remorse
- Previous good character and/or exemplary conduct*
- Age and/or lack of maturity where it affects the responsibility of the offender
- Mental disorder or learning disability, particularly where linked to the commission of the offence
- Demonstration of steps taken to address offending behaviour

*Previous good character/exemplary conduct is different from having no previous convictions. The more serious the offence, the less the weight which should normally be attributed to this factor. Where previous good character/exemplary conduct has been used to facilitate the offence, this mitigation should not normally be allowed and such conduct may constitute an aggravating factor.

STEP THREE

Consider any factors which indicate a reduction, such as assistance to the prosecution

The court should take into account sections 73 and 74 of the Serious Organised Crime and Police Act 2005 (assistance by defendants: reduction or review of sentence) and any other rule of law by virtue of which an offender may receive a discounted sentence in consequence of assistance given (or offered) to the prosecutor or investigator.

STEP FOUR

Reduction for guilty pleas

The court should take account of any potential reduction for a guilty plea in accordance with section 144 of the Criminal Justice Act 2003 and the *Guilty Plea* guideline.

STEP FIVE

Dangerousness

The court should consider whether having regard to the criteria contained in Chapter 5 of Part 12 of the Criminal Justice Act 2003 it would be appropriate to award an extended sentence (section 226A).

STEP SIX

Totality principle

If sentencing an offender for more than one offence, or where the offender is already serving a sentence, consider whether the total sentence is just and proportionate to the offending behaviour.

STEP SEVEN

Ancillary orders

The court must consider whether to make any ancillary orders. The court must also consider what other requirements or provisions may *automatically* apply. Further information is included at Annex A on page 424.

STEP EIGHT

Reasons

Section 174 of the Criminal Justice Act 2003 imposes a duty to give reasons for, and explain the effect of, the sentence.

STEP NINE

Consideration for time spent on bail

The court must consider whether to give credit for time spent on bail in accordance with section 240A of the Criminal Justice Act 2003.

Inducement, threat or deception to procure sexual activity with a person with a mental disorder

Sexual Offences Act 2003 (section 34)

Causing a person with a mental disorder to engage in or agree to engage in sexual activity by inducement, threat or deception

Sexual Offences Act 2003 (section 35)

Triable only on indictment (if penetration involved)—otherwise

Triable either way

Maximum: Life imprisonment (if penetration involved)—otherwise

14 years' custody

Offence range: Community order–10 years' custody

These are serious specified offences for the purposes of section 224 and, where the offence involved penetration, section 225(2) (life sentence for serious offences) of the Criminal Justice Act 2003.

For offences involving penetration, committed on or after 3 December 2012, these are offences listed in Part 1 of Schedule 15B for the purposes of section 224A (life sentence for second listed offence) of the Criminal Justice Act 2003.

For convictions on or after 3 December 2012 (irrespective of the date of commission of the offence), these are specified offences for the purposes of section 226A (extended sentence for certain violent or sexual offences) of the Criminal Justice Act 2003.

STEP ONE

Determining the offence category

The court should determine which categories of harm and culpability the offence falls into by reference **only** to the tables below.

THIS GUIDLINE [sic] ALSO APPLIES TO OFFENCES COMMITTED REMOTELY/ONLINE

Harm	
Category 1	• Penetration of vagina or anus (using body or object) • Penile penetration of mouth In either case by, or of, the victim
Category 2	Touching, or exposure, of naked genitalia or naked breasts by, or of, the victim
Category 3	Other sexual activity

Culpability	
A	**B**
• Significant degree of planning • Offender acts together with others to commit the offence • Use of alcohol/drugs on victim to facilitate the offence • Abuse of trust • Sexual images of victim recorded, retained, solicited or shared • Commercial exploitation and/or motivation • Offence racially or religiously aggravated • Offence motivated by, or demonstrating, hostility to the victim based on his or her sexual orientation (or presumed sexual orientation) or transgender identity (or presumed transgender identity)	Factor(s) in category A not present

- Offence motivated by, or demonstrating, hostility to the victim based on his or her disability (or presumed disability)

STEP TWO

Starting point and category range

Having determined the category of harm and culpability, the court should use the corresponding starting points to reach a sentence within the category range below. The starting point applies to all offenders irrespective of plea or previous convictions. Having determined the starting point, step two allows further adjustment for aggravating or mitigating features, set out below.

A case of particular gravity, reflected by multiple features of culpability or harm in step one, could merit upward adjustment from the starting point before further adjustment for aggravating or mitigating features, set out below.

Where there is a sufficient prospect of rehabilitation, a community order with a sex offender treatment programme requirement under section 202 of the Criminal Justice Act 2003 can be a proper alternative to a short or moderate length custodial sentence.

	A	B
Category 1	**Starting point** 5 years' custody **Category range** 4–10 years' custody	**Starting point** 1 year's custody **Category range** High level community order–2 years' custody
Category 2	**Starting point** 3 years' custody **Category range** 2–6 years' custody	**Starting point** 26 weeks' custody **Category range** High level community order–1 year's custody
Category 3	**Starting point** 26 weeks' custody **Category range** High level community order–3 years' custody	**Starting point** Medium level community order **Category range** Low level community order–High level community order

The table below contains a **non-exhaustive** list of additional factual elements providing the context of the offence and factors relating to the offender. Identify whether any combination of these, or other relevant factors, should result in an upward or downward adjustment from the starting point. **In particular, relevant recent convictions are likely to result in an upward adjustment.** In some cases, having considered these factors, it may be appropriate to move outside the identified category range.

When sentencing appropriate **category 2 or 3 offences**, the court should also consider the custody threshold as follows:

- has the custody threshold been passed?
- if so, is it unavoidable that a custodial sentence be imposed?
- if so, can that sentence be suspended?

Aggravating factors

Statutory aggravating factors

- Previous convictions, having regard to a) the nature of the offence to which the conviction relates and its relevance to the current offence; and b) the time that has elapsed since the conviction
- Offence committed whilst on bail

Other aggravating factors

- Severe psychological or physical harm
- Ejaculation
- Pregnancy or STI as a consequence of offence
- Location of offence
- Timing of offence
- Victim compelled to leave their home or institution (including victims of domestic violence)
- Failure to comply with current court orders
- Offence committed whilst on licence
- Any steps taken to prevent the victim reporting an incident, obtaining assistance and/or from assisting or supporting the prosecution
- Attempts to dispose of or conceal evidence
- Commission of offence whilst under the influence of alcohol or drugs

Mitigating factors

- No previous convictions **or** no relevant/recent convictions
- Remorse
- Previous good character and/or exemplary conduct*
- Age and/or lack of maturity where it affects the responsibility of the offender
- Mental disorder or learning disability, particularly where linked to the commission of the offence

*Previous good character/exemplary conduct is different from having no previous convictions. The more serious the offence, the less the weight which should normally be attributed to this factor. Where previous good character/exemplary conduct has been used to facilitate the offence, this mitigation should not normally be allowed and such conduct may constitute an aggravating factor. In the context of this offence, previous good character/exemplary conduct should not normally be given any significant weight and will not normally justify a reduction in what would otherwise be the appropriate sentence.

STEP THREE

Consider any factors which indicate a reduction, such as assistance to the prosecution

The court should take into account sections 73 and 74 of the Serious Organised Crime and Police Act 2005 (assistance by defendants: reduction or review of sentence) and any other rule of law by virtue of which an offender may receive a discounted sentence in consequence of assistance given (or offered) to the prosecutor or investigator.

STEP FOUR

Reduction for guilty pleas

The court should take account of any potential reduction for a guilty plea in accordance with section 144 of the Criminal Justice Act 2003 and the *Guilty Plea* guideline.

STEP FIVE

Dangerousness

The court should consider whether having regard to the criteria contained in Chapter 5 of Part 12 of the Criminal Justice Act 2003 it would be appropriate to award a life sentence (section 224A or section 225(2)) or an extended sentence (section 226A). When sentencing offenders to a life sentence under these provisions, the notional determinate sentence should be used as the basis for the setting of a minimum term.

STEP SIX

Totality principle

If sentencing an offender for more than one offence, or where the offender is already serving a sentence, consider whether the total sentence is just and proportionate to the offending behaviour.

STEP SEVEN

Ancillary orders

The court must consider whether to make any ancillary orders. The court must also consider what other requirements or provisions may *automatically* apply. Further information is included at Annex A on page 424.

STEP EIGHT

Reasons

Section 174 of the Criminal Justice Act 2003 imposes a duty to give reasons for, and explain the effect of, the sentence.

STEP NINE

Consideration for time spent on bail

The court must consider whether to give credit for time spent on bail in accordance with section 240A of the Criminal Justice Act 2003.

Engaging in sexual activity in the presence, procured by inducement, threat or deception, of a person with a mental disorder

Sexual Offences Act 2003 (section 36)

Causing a person with a mental disorder to watch a sexual act by inducement, threat or deception

Sexual Offences Act 2003 (section 37)

Triable either way

Maximum: 10 years' custody

Offence range: Community order–6 years' custody

For convictions on or after 3 December 2012 (irrespective of the date of commission of the offence), these are specified offences for the purposes of section 226A (extended sentence for certain violent or sexual offences) of the Criminal Justice Act 2003.

STEP ONE

Determining the offence category

The court should determine which categories of harm and culpability the offence falls into by reference **only** to the tables below.

Harm	
Category 1	• Causing victim to view extreme pornography • Causing victim to view indecent/prohibited images of children • Engaging in, or causing a victim to view live, sexual activity involving sadism/violence/sexual activity with an animal/a child
Category 2	Engaging in, or causing a victim to view images of or view live, sexual activity involving: • penetration of vagina or anus (using body or object) • penile penetration of mouth • masturbation
Category 3	Factor(s) in categories 1 and 2 not present

Culpability	
A	B
• Significant degree of planning • Offender acts together with others in order to commit the offence • Use of alcohol/drugs on victim to facilitate the offence • Abuse of trust • Commercial exploitation and/or motivation • Offence racially or religiously aggravated • Offence motivated by, or demonstrating, hostility to the victim based on his or her sexual orientation (or presumed sexual orientation) or transgender identity (or presumed transgender identity) • Offence motivated by, or demonstrating, hostility to the victim based on his or her disability (or presumed disability)	Factor(s) in category A not present

STEP TWO

Starting point and category range

Having determined the category of harm and culpability, the court should use the corresponding starting points to reach a sentence within the category range below. The starting point applies to all offenders irrespective of plea or previous convictions. Having determined the starting point, step two allows further adjustment for aggravating or mitigating features, set out below.

A case of particular gravity, reflected by multiple features of culpability or harm in step one, could merit upward adjustment from the starting point before further adjustment for aggravating or mitigating features, set out below.

Where there is a sufficient prospect of rehabilitation, a community order with a sex offender treatment programme requirement under section 202 of the Criminal Justice Act 2003 can be a proper alternative to a short or moderate length custodial sentence.

	A	B
Category 1	**Starting point** 4 years' custody **Category range** 3–6 years' custody	**Starting point** 2 years' custody **Category range** 1–3 years' custody

Category 2	**Starting point** 2 years' custody **Category range** 1–3 years' custody	**Starting point** 1 year's custody **Category range** High level community order–18 months' custody
Category 3	**Starting point** 26 weeks' custody **Category range** High level community order–1 year's custody	**Starting point** Medium level community order **Category range** Low level community order–Medium level community order

The table below contains a **non-exhaustive** list of additional factual elements providing the context of the offence and factors relating to the offender. Identify whether any combination of these, or other relevant factors, should result in an upward or downward adjustment from the starting point. **In particular, relevant recent convictions are likely to result in an upward adjustment.** In some cases, having considered these factors, it may be appropriate to move outside the identified category range.

When sentencing appropriate **category 2 or 3 offences**, the court should also consider the custody threshold as follows:

- has the custody threshold been passed?
- if so, is it unavoidable that a custodial sentence be imposed?
- if so, can that sentence be suspended?

Aggravating factors

Statutory aggravating factors

- Previous convictions, having regard to a) the nature of the offence to which the conviction relates and its relevance to the current offence; and b) the time that has elapsed since the conviction
- Offence committed whilst on bail

Other aggravating factors

- Location of offence
- Timing of offence
- Failure to comply with current court orders
- Offence committed whilst on licence
- Any steps taken to prevent the victim reporting an incident, obtaining assistance and/or from assisting or supporting the prosecution
- Attempts to dispose of or conceal evidence
- Commission of offence whilst under the influence of alcohol or drugs

Mitigating factors

- No previous convictions **or** no relevant/recent convictions
- Remorse
- Previous good character and/or exemplary conduct*
- Age and/or lack of maturity where it affects the responsibility of the offender
- Mental disorder or learning disability, particularly where linked to the commission of the offence
- Demonstration of steps taken to address offending behaviour

*Previous good character/exemplary conduct is different from having no previous convictions. The more serious the offence, the less the weight which should normally be attributed to this factor. Where previous good character/exemplary conduct has been used to facilitate the offence, this mitigation should not normally be allowed and such conduct may constitute an aggravating factor.

STEP THREE

Consider any factors which indicate a reduction, such as assistance to the prosecution

The court should take into account sections 73 and 74 of the Serious Organised Crime and Police Act 2005 (assistance by defendants: reduction or review of sentence) and any other rule of law by virtue of which an offender may receive a discounted sentence in consequence of assistance given (or offered) to the prosecutor or investigator.

STEP FOUR

Reduction for guilty pleas

The court should take account of any potential reduction for a guilty plea in accordance with section 144 of the Criminal Justice Act 2003 and the *Guilty Plea* guideline.

STEP FIVE

Dangerousness

The court should consider whether having regard to the criteria contained in Chapter 5 of Part 12 of the Criminal Justice Act 2003 it would be appropriate to award an extended sentence (section 226A).

STEP SIX

Totality principle

If sentencing an offender for more than one offence, or where the offender is already serving a sentence, consider whether the total sentence is just and proportionate to the offending behaviour.

STEP SEVEN

Ancillary orders

The court must consider whether to make any ancillary orders. The court must also consider what other requirements or provisions may *automatically* apply. Further information is included at Annex A on page 424.

STEP EIGHT

Reasons

Section 174 of the Criminal Justice Act 2003 imposes a duty to give reasons for, and explain the effect of, the sentence.

STEP NINE

Consideration for time spent on bail

The court must consider whether to give credit for time spent on bail in accordance with section 240A of the Criminal Justice Act 2003.

Care workers: sexual activity with a person with a mental disorder

Sexual Offences Act 2003 (section 38)

Care workers: causing or inciting sexual activity

Sexual Offences Act 2003 (section 39)

Triable only on indictment (if penetration involved)—otherwise triable either way

Maximum: 14 years' custody (if penetration involved)—otherwise 10 years' custody

Offence range: Community order–10 years' custody

For convictions on or after 3 December 2012 (irrespective of the date of commission of the offence), these are specified offences for the purposes of section 226A (extended sentence for certain violent or sexual offences) of the Criminal Justice Act 2003.

STEP ONE

Determining the offence category

The court should determine which categories of harm and culpability the offence falls into by reference **only** to the tables below.

THIS GUIDLINE [sic] ALSO APPLIES TO OFFENCES COMMITTED REMOTELY/ONLINE

Harm	
Category 1	• Penetration of vagina or anus (using body or object) • Penile penetration of mouth In either case by, or of, the victim
Category 2	• Touching, or exposure, of naked genitalia or naked breasts by, or of, the victim
Category 3	Factor(s) in categories 1 and 2 not present

Culpability	
A	**B**
• Significant degree of planning • Offender acts together with others to commit the offence • Use of alcohol/drugs on victim to facilitate the offence • Grooming behaviour used against victim • Use of threats (including blackmail) • Sexual images of victim recorded, retained, solicited or shared • Commercial exploitation and/or motivation • Offence racially or religiously aggravated • Offence motivated by, or demonstrating, hostility to the victim based on his or her sexual orientation (or presumed sexual orientation) or transgender identity (or presumed transgender identity) • Offence motivated by, or demonstrating, hostility to the victim based on his or her disability (or presumed disability)	Factor(s) in category A not present

STEP TWO

Starting point and category range

Having determined the category of harm and culpability, the court should use the corresponding starting points to reach a sentence within the category range below. The starting point applies to all offenders irrespective of plea or previous convictions. Having determined the starting point, step two allows further adjustment for aggravating or mitigating features, set out below.

A case of particular gravity, reflected by multiple features of culpability or harm in step one, could merit upward adjustment from the starting point before further adjustment for aggravating or mitigating features, set out below.

Where there is a sufficient prospect of rehabilitation, a community order with a sex offender treatment programme requirement under section 202 of the Criminal Justice Act 2003 can be a proper alternative to a short or moderate length custodial sentence.

	A	B
Category 1	**Starting point** 5 years' custody **Category range** 4–10 years' custody	**Starting point** 18 months' custody **Category range** 1–2 years' custody
Category 2	**Starting point** 3 year's custody **Category range** 2–6 years' custody	**Starting point** 26 weeks' custody **Category range** Medium level community order–1 year's custody
Category 3	**Starting point** 26 weeks' custody **Category range** High level community order–3 years' custody	**Starting point** Medium level community order **Category range** Low level community order–High level community order

The table below contains a **non-exhaustive** list of additional factual elements providing the context of the offence and factors relating to the offender. Identify whether any combination of these, or other relevant factors, should result in an upward or downward adjustment from the starting point. **In particular, relevant recent convictions are likely to result in an upward adjustment.** In some cases, having considered these factors, it may be appropriate to move outside the identified category range.

When sentencing appropriate **category 2 or 3 offences**, the court should also consider the custody threshold as follows:

- has the custody threshold been passed?
- if so, is it unavoidable that a custodial sentence be imposed?
- if so, can that sentence be suspended?

Aggravating factors

Statutory aggravating factors

- Previous convictions, having regard to a) the nature of the offence to which the conviction relates and its relevance to the current offence; and b) the time that has elapsed since the conviction
- Offence committed whilst on bail

Other aggravating factors

- Ejaculation
- Pregnancy or STI as a consequence of offence
- Location of offence
- Timing of offence
- Victim compelled to leave their home or institution (including victims of domestic violence)
- Failure to comply with current court orders
- Offence committed whilst on licence

- Any steps taken to prevent the victim reporting an incident, obtaining assistance and/or from assisting or supporting the prosecution
- Attempts to dispose of or conceal evidence
- Failure of offender to respond to previous warnings
- Commission of offence whilst under the influence of alcohol or drugs

Mitigating factors

- No previous convictions **or** no relevant/recent convictions
- Remorse
- Previous good character and/or exemplary conduct*
- Age and/or lack of maturity where it affects the responsibility of the offender
- Mental disorder or learning disability, particularly where linked to the commission of the offence
- Sexual activity was incited but no activity took place because the offender voluntarily desisted or intervened to prevent it

*Previous good character/exemplary conduct is different from having no previous convictions. The more serious the offence, the less the weight which should normally be attributed to this factor. Where previous good character/exemplary conduct has been used to facilitate the offence, this mitigation should not normally be allowed and such conduct may constitute an aggravating factor. In the context of this offence, previous good character/exemplary conduct should not normally be given any significant weight and will not normally justify a reduction in what would otherwise be the appropriate sentence.

STEP THREE

Consider any factors which indicate a reduction, such as assistance to the prosecution

The court should take into account sections 73 and 74 of the Serious Organised Crime and Police Act 2005 (assistance by defendants: reduction or review of sentence) and any other rule of law by virtue of which an offender may receive a discounted sentence in consequence of assistance given (or offered) to the prosecutor or investigator.

STEP FOUR

Reduction for guilty pleas

The court should take account of any potential reduction for a guilty plea in accordance with section 144 of the Criminal Justice Act 2003 and the *Guilty Plea* guideline.

STEP FIVE

Dangerousness

The court should consider whether having regard to the criteria contained in Chapter 5 of Part 12 of the Criminal Justice Act 2003 it would be appropriate to award an extended sentence (section 226A).

STEP SIX

Totality principle

If sentencing an offender for more than one offence, or where the offender is already serving a sentence, consider whether the total sentence is just and proportionate to the offending behaviour.

STEP SEVEN

Ancillary orders

The court must consider whether to make any ancillary orders. The court must also consider what other requirements or provisions may *automatically* apply. Further information is included at Annex A on page 424.

STEP EIGHT

Reasons

Section 174 of the Criminal Justice Act 2003 imposes a duty to give reasons for, and explain the effect of, the sentence.

STEP NINE

Consideration for time spent on bail

The court must consider whether to give credit for time spent on bail in accordance with section 240A of the Criminal Justice Act 2003.

Care workers: sexual activity in the presence of a person with a mental disorder

Sexual Offences Act 2003 (section 40)

Care workers: causing a person with a mental disorder to watch a sexual act

Sexual Offences Act 2003 (section 41)

Triable either way

Maximum: 7 years' custody

Offence range: Community order–2 years' custody

For convictions on or after 3 December 2012 (irrespective of the date of commission of the offence), these are specified offences for the purposes of section 226A (extended sentence for certain violent or sexual offences) of the Criminal Justice Act 2003.

STEP ONE

Determining the offence category

The court should determine which categories of harm and culpability the offence falls into by reference **only** to the tables below.

Harm	
Category 1	• Causing victim to view extreme pornography • Causing victim to view indecent/prohibited images of children • Engaging in, or causing a victim to view live, sexual activity involving sadism/violence/sexual activity with an animal/a child
Category 2	Engaging in, or causing a victim to view images of or view live, sexual activity involving: • penetration of vagina or anus (using body or object) • penile penetration of mouth • masturbation
Category 3	Factor(s) in categories 1 and 2 not present

Culpability	
A	**B**
• Significant degree of planning • Offender acts together with others to commit the offence • Use of alcohol/drugs on victim to facilitate the offence • Grooming behaviour used against victim • Use of threats (including blackmail) • Commercial exploitation and/or motivation • Offence racially or religiously aggravated • Offence motivated by, or demonstrating, hostility to the victim based on his or her sexual orientation (or presumed sexual orientation) or transgender identity (or presumed transgender identity) • Offence motivated by, or demonstrating, hostility to the victim based on his or her disability (or presumed disability)	Factor(s) in category A not present

STEP TWO

Starting point and category range

Having determined the category of harm and culpability, the court should use the corresponding starting points to reach a sentence within the category range below. The starting point applies to all offenders irrespective of plea or previous convictions. Having determined the starting point, step two allows further adjustment for aggravating or mitigating features, set out below.

A case of particular gravity, reflected by multiple features of culpability or harm in step one, could merit upward adjustment from the starting point before further adjustment for aggravating or mitigating features, set out below.

Where there is a sufficient prospect of rehabilitation, a community order with a sex offender treatment programme requirement under section 202 of the Criminal Justice Act 2003 can be a proper alternative to a short or moderate length custodial sentence.

	A	B
Category 1	**Starting point** 18 months' custody **Category range** 1–2 years' custody	**Starting point** 1 year's custody **Category range** 26 weeks'–18 months' custody
Category 2	**Starting point** 1 year's custody **Category range** 26 weeks'–18 months' custody	**Starting point** 26 weeks' custody **Category range** High level community order–1 year's custody
Category 3	**Starting point** 26 weeks' custody **Category range** High level community order–1 year's custody	**Starting point** Medium level community order **Category range** Low level community order–High level community order

The table below contains a **non-exhaustive** list of additional factual elements providing the context of the offence and factors relating to the offender. Identify whether any combination of these, or other relevant factors, should result in an upward or downward adjustment from the starting point. **In particular, relevant recent convictions are likely to result in an upward adjustment.** In some cases, having considered these factors, it may be appropriate to move outside the identified category range.

When sentencing appropriate **category 2 or 3 offences**, the court should also consider the custody threshold as follows:

- has the custody threshold been passed?
- if so, is it unavoidable that a custodial sentence be imposed?
- if so, can that sentence be suspended?

Aggravating factors
Statutory aggravating factors
• Previous convictions, having regard to a) the nature of the offence to which the conviction relates and its relevance to the current offence; and b) the time that has elapsed since the conviction • Offence committed whilst on bail

Other aggravating factors

- Location of the offence
- Timing of the offence
- Any steps taken to prevent the victim reporting an incident, obtaining assistance and/or from assisting or supporting the prosecution
- Failure to comply with current court orders
- Offence committed whilst on licence
- Commission of offence whilst under the influence of alcohol or drugs
- Presence of others, especially children

Mitigating factors

- No previous convictions **or** no relevant/recent convictions
- Remorse
- Previous good character and/or exemplary conduct*
- Age and/or lack of maturity where it affects the responsibility of the offender
- Mental disorder or learning disability, particularly where linked to the commission of the offence
- Demonstration of steps taken to address offending behaviour

*Previous good character/exemplary conduct is different from having no previous convictions. The more serious the offence, the less the weight which should normally be attributed to this factor. Where previous good character/exemplary conduct has been used to facilitate the offence, this mitigation should not normally be allowed and such conduct may constitute an aggravating factor.

STEP THREE

Consider any factors which indicate a reduction, such as assistance to the prosecution

The court should take into account sections 73 and 74 of the Serious Organised Crime and Police Act 2005 (assistance by defendants: reduction or review of sentence) and any other rule of law by virtue of which an offender may receive a discounted sentence in consequence of assistance given (or offered) to the prosecutor or investigator.

STEP FOUR

Reduction for guilty pleas

The court should take account of any potential reduction for a guilty plea in accordance with section 144 of the Criminal Justice Act 2003 and the *Guilty Plea* guideline.

STEP FIVE

Dangerousness

The court should consider whether having regard to the criteria contained in Chapter 5 of Part 12 of the Criminal Justice Act 2003 it would be appropriate to award an extended sentence (section 226A).

STEP SIX

Totality principle

If sentencing an offender for more than one offence, or where the offender is already serving a sentence, consider whether the total sentence is just and proportionate to the offending behaviour.

STEP SEVEN

Ancillary orders

The court must consider whether to make any ancillary orders. The court must also consider what other requirements or provisions may *automatically* apply. Further information is included at Annex A on page 424.

STEP EIGHT

Reasons

Section 174 of the Criminal Justice Act 2003 imposes a duty to give reasons for, and explain the effect of, the sentence.

STEP NINE

Consideration for time spent on bail

The court must consider whether to give credit for time spent on bail in accordance with section 240A of the Criminal Justice Act 2003.

Exposure

Sexual Offences Act 2003 (section 66)

Triable either way

Maximum: 2 years' custody

Offence range: Fine–1 year's custody

For convictions on or after 3 December 2012 (irrespective of the date of commission of the offence), this is a specified offence for the purposes of section 226A (extended sentence for certain violent or sexual offences) of the Criminal Justice Act 2003.

STEP ONE

Determining the offence category

The court should determine the offence category using the table below.

Category 1	Raised harm **and** raised culpability
Category 2	Raised harm **or** raised culpability
Category 3	Exposure **without** raised harm or culpability factors present

The court should determine culpability and harm caused or intended, by reference **only** to the factors below, which comprise the principal factual elements of the offence. Where an offence does not fall squarely into a category, individual factors may require a degree of weighting before making an overall assessment and determining the appropriate offence category.

Factors indicating raised harm
• Victim followed/pursued • Offender masturbated

Factors indicating raised culpability
• Specific or previous targeting of a particularly vulnerable victim • Abuse of trust • Use of threats (including blackmail) • Offence racially or religiously aggravated • Offence motivated by, or demonstrating, hostility to the victim based on his or her sexual orientation (or presumed sexual orientation) or transgender identity (or presumed transgender identity) • Offence motivated by, or demonstrating, hostility to the victim based on his or her disability (or presumed disability)

STEP TWO

Starting point and category range

Having determined the category, the court should use the corresponding starting points to reach a sentence within the category range below. The starting point applies to all offenders irrespective of plea or previous convictions. Having determined the starting point, step two allows further adjustment for aggravating or mitigating features, set out below.

A case of particular gravity, reflected by multiple features of culpability or harm in step one, could merit upward adjustment from the starting point before further adjustment for aggravating or mitigating features, set out below.

Where there is a sufficient prospect of rehabilitation, a community order with a sex offender treatment programme requirement under section 202 of the Criminal Justice Act 2003 can be a proper alternative to a short or moderate length custodial sentence.

Category 1	**Starting point** 26 weeks' custody **Category range** 12 weeks'–1 year's custody
Category 2	**Starting point** High level community order **Category range** Medium level community order–26 weeks' custody
Category 3	**Starting point** Medium level community order **Category range** Band A fine–High level community order

The table below contains a **non-exhaustive** list of additional factual elements providing the context of the offence and factors relating to the offender. Identify whether any combination of these, or other relevant factors, should result in an upward or downward adjustment from the starting point. **In particular, relevant recent convictions are likely to result in an upward adjustment.** In some cases, having considered these factors, it may be appropriate to move outside the identified category range.

When sentencing **category 2 offences**, the court should also consider the custody threshold as follows:

- has the custody threshold been passed?
- if so, is it unavoidable that a custodial sentence be imposed?
- if so, can that sentence be suspended?

When sentencing **category 3 offences**, the court should also consider the community order threshold as follows:

- has the community order threshold been passed?

Aggravating factors
Statutory aggravating factors
• Previous convictions, having regard to a) the nature of the offence to which the conviction relates and its relevance to the current offence; and b) the time that has elapsed since the conviction • Offence committed whilst on bail

Other aggravating factors

- Location of offence
- Timing of offence
- Failure to comply with current court orders
- Offence committed whilst on licence
- Any steps taken to prevent the victim reporting an incident, obtaining assistance and/or from assisting or supporting the prosecution
- Attempts to dispose of or conceal evidence
- Failure of offender to respond to previous warnings
- Commission of offence whilst under the influence of alcohol or drugs

Mitigating factors

- No previous convictions **or** no relevant/recent convictions
- Remorse
- Previous good character and/or exemplary conduct*
- Age and/or lack of maturity where it affects the responsibility of the offender
- Mental disorder or learning disability, particularly where linked to the commission of the offence
- Demonstration of steps taken to address offending behaviour

*Previous good character/exemplary conduct is different from having no previous convictions. The more serious the offence, the less the weight which should normally be attributed to this factor. Where previous good character/exemplary conduct has been used to facilitate the offence, this mitigation should not normally be allowed and such conduct may constitute an aggravating factor.

STEP THREE

Consider any factors which indicate a reduction, such as assistance to the prosecution

The court should take into account sections 73 and 74 of the Serious Organised Crime and Police Act 2005 (assistance by defendants: reduction or review of sentence) and any other rule of law by virtue of which an offender may receive a discounted sentence in consequence of assistance given (or offered) to the prosecutor or investigator.

STEP FOUR

Reduction for guilty pleas

The court should take account of any potential reduction for a guilty plea in accordance with section 144 of the Criminal Justice Act 2003 and the *Guilty Plea* guideline.

STEP FIVE

Dangerousness

The court should consider whether having regard to the criteria contained in Chapter 5 of Part 12 of the Criminal Justice Act 2003 it would be appropriate to award an extended sentence (section 226A).

STEP SIX

Totality principle

If sentencing an offender for more than one offence, or where the offender is already serving a sentence, consider whether the total sentence is just and proportionate to the offending behaviour.

STEP SEVEN

Ancillary orders

The court must consider whether to make any ancillary orders. The court must also consider what other requirements or provisions may *automatically* apply. Further information is included at Annex A on page 424.

STEP EIGHT

Reasons

Section 174 of the Criminal Justice Act 2003 imposes a duty to give reasons for, and explain the effect of, the sentence.

STEP NINE

Consideration for time spent on bail

The court must consider whether to give credit for time spent on bail in accordance with section 240A of the Criminal Justice Act 2003.

Voyeurism

Sexual Offences Act 2003 (section 67)

Triable either way

Maximum: 2 years' custody

Offence range: Fine–18 months' custody

For convictions on or after such date (irrespective of the date of commission of the offence), these are specified offences for the purposes of section 226A (extended sentence for certain violent or sexual offences) of the Criminal Justice Act 2003.

STEP ONE

Determining the offence category

The court should determine the offence category using the table below.

Category 1	Raised harm **and** raised culpability
Category 2	Raised harm **or** raised culpability
Category 3	Voyeurism **without** raised harm or culpability factors present

The court should determine culpability and harm caused or intended, by reference **only** to the factors below, which comprise the principal factual elements of the offence. Where an offence does not fall squarely into a category, individual factors may require a degree of weighting before making an overall assessment and determining the appropriate offence category.

Factors indicating raised harm
• Image(s) available to be viewed by others • Victim observed or recorded in their own home or residence

Factors indicating raised culpability
• Significant degree of planning • Image(s) recorded • Abuse of trust • Specific or previous targeting of a particularly vulnerable victim • Commercial exploitation and/or motivation • Offence racially or religiously aggravated • Offence motivated by, or demonstrating, hostility to the victim based on his or her sexual orientation (or presumed sexual orientation) or transgender identity (or presumed transgender identity) • Offence motivated by, or demonstrating, hostility to the victim based on his or her disability (or presumed disability)

STEP TWO

Starting point and category range

Having determined the category, the court should use the corresponding starting points to reach a sentence within the category range below. The starting point applies to all offenders irrespective of plea or previous convictions. Having determined the starting point, step two allows further adjustment for aggravating or mitigating features, set out below.

A case of particular gravity, reflected by multiple features of culpability or harm in step one, could merit upward adjustment from the starting point before further adjustment for aggravating or mitigating features, set out below.

Where there is a sufficient prospect of rehabilitation, a community order with a sex offender treatment programme requirement under section 202 of the Criminal Justice Act 2003 can be a proper alternative to a short or moderate length custodial sentence.

Category 1	**Starting point** 26 weeks' custody **Category range** 12 weeks'–18 months' custody
Category 2	**Starting point** High level community order **Category range** Medium level community order–26 weeks' custody
Category 3	**Starting point** Medium level community order **Category range** Band A fine–High level community order

The table below contains a **non-exhaustive** list of additional factual elements providing the context of the offence and factors relating to the offender. Identify whether any combination of these, or other relevant factors, should result in an upward or downward adjustment from the starting point. **In particular, relevant recent convictions are likely to result in an upward adjustment.** In some cases, having considered these factors, it may be appropriate to move outside the identified category range.

When sentencing **category 2 offences**, the court should also consider the custody threshold as follows:

- has the custody threshold been passed?
- if so, is it unavoidable that a custodial sentence be imposed?
- if so, can that sentence be suspended?

When sentencing **category 3 offences**, the court should also consider the community order threshold as follows:

- has the community order threshold been passed?

Aggravating factors

Statutory aggravating factors

- Previous convictions, having regard to a) the nature of the offence to which the conviction relates and its relevance to the current offence; and b) the time that has elapsed since the conviction
- Offence committed whilst on bail

Other aggravating factors

- Location of offence
- Timing of offence
- Failure to comply with current court orders
- Offence committed whilst on licence
- Distribution of images, whether or not for gain
- Placing images where there is the potential for a high volume of viewers
- Period over which victim observed
- Period over which images were made or distributed
- Any steps taken to prevent victim reporting an incident, obtaining assistance and/or from assisting or supporting the prosecution
- Attempts to dispose of or conceal evidence

Mitigating factors

- No previous convictions **or** no relevant/recent convictions
- Remorse
- Previous good character and/or exemplary conduct*
- Age and/or lack of maturity where it affects the responsibility of the offender
- Mental disorder or learning disability, particularly where linked to the commission of the offence
- Demonstration of steps taken to address offending behaviour

*Previous good character/exemplary conduct is different from having no previous convictions. The more serious the offence, the less the weight which should normally be attributed to this factor. Where previous good character/exemplary conduct has been used to facilitate the offence, this mitigation should not normally be allowed and such conduct may constitute an aggravating factor.

STEP THREE

Consider any factors which indicate a reduction, such as assistance to the prosecution

The court should take into account sections 73 and 74 of the Serious Organised Crime and Police Act 2005 (assistance by defendants: reduction or review of sentence) and any other rule of law by virtue of which an offender may receive a discounted sentence in consequence of assistance given (or offered) to the prosecutor or investigator.

STEP FOUR

Reduction for guilty pleas

The court should take account of any potential reduction for a guilty plea in accordance with section 144 of the Criminal Justice Act 2003 and the *Guilty Plea* guideline.

STEP FIVE

Dangerousness

The court should consider whether having regard to the criteria contained in Chapter 5 of Part 12 of the Criminal Justice Act 2003 it would be appropriate to award an extended sentence (section 226A).

STEP SIX

Totality principle

If sentencing an offender for more than one offence, or where the offender is already serving a sentence, consider whether the total sentence is just and proportionate to the offending behaviour.

STEP SEVEN

Ancillary orders

The court must consider whether to make any ancillary orders. The court must also consider what other requirements or provisions may *automatically* apply. Further information is included at Annex A on page 424.

STEP EIGHT

Reasons

Section 174 of the Criminal Justice Act 2003 imposes a duty to give reasons for, and explain the effect of, the sentence.

STEP NINE

Consideration for time spent on bail

The court must consider whether to give credit for time spent on bail in accordance with section 240A of the Criminal Justice Act 2003.

Sex with an adult relative: penetration

Sexual Offences Act 2003 (section 64)

Sex with an adult relative: consenting to penetration

Sexual Offences Act 2003 (section 65)

Triable either way

Maximum: 2 years' custody

Offence range: Fine–2 years' custody

For convictions on or after 3 December 2012 (irrespective of the date of commission of the offence), these are specified offences for the purposes of section 226A (extended sentence for certain violent or sexual offences) of the Criminal Justice Act 2003.

STEP ONE

Determining the offence category

The court should determine the offence category using the table below.

Category 1	Raised harm **and** raised culpability
Category 2	Raised harm **or** raised culpability
Category 3	Sex with an adult relative **without** raised harm or culpability factors present

The court should determine culpability and harm caused or intended, by reference **only** to the factors below, which comprise the principal factual elements of the offence. Where an offence does not fall squarely into a category, individual factors may require a degree of weighting before making an overall assessment and determining the appropriate offence category.

Factors indicating raised harm
• Victim is particularly vulnerable due to personal circumstances • Child conceived

Factors indicating raised culpability
• Grooming behaviour used against victim • Use of threats (including blackmail)

STEP TWO

Starting point and category range

Having determined the category, the court should use the corresponding starting points to reach a sentence within the category range below. The starting point applies to all offenders irrespective of plea or previous convictions. Having determined the starting point, step two allows further adjustment for aggravating or mitigating features, set out below.

A case of particular gravity, reflected by multiple features of culpability or harm in step one, could merit upward adjustment from the starting point before further adjustment for aggravating or mitigating features, set out below.

Where there is a sufficient prospect of rehabilitation, a community order with a sex offender treatment programme requirement under section 202 of the Criminal Justice Act 2003 can be a proper alternative to a short or moderate length custodial sentence.

Category 1	**Starting point** 1 year's custody **Category range** 26 weeks'- 2 years' custody
Category 2	**Starting point** High level community order **Category range** Medium level community order– 1 year's custody
Category 3	**Starting point** Medium level community order **Category range** Band A fine–High level community order

The table below contains a **non-exhaustive** list of additional factual elements providing the context of the offence and factors relating to the offender. Identify whether any combination of these, or other relevant factors, should result in an upward or downward adjustment from the starting point. **In particular, relevant recent convictions are likely to result in an upward adjustment.** In some cases, having considered these factors, it may be appropriate to move outside the identified category range.

When sentencing **category 2 offences**, the court should also consider the custody threshold as follows:

- has the custody threshold been passed?
- if so, is it unavoidable that a custodial sentence be imposed?
- if so, can that sentence be suspended?

When sentencing **category 3 offences**, the court should also consider the community order threshold as follows:

- has the community order threshold been passed?

Aggravating factors

Statutory aggravating factors

- Previous convictions, having regard to a) the nature of the offence to which the conviction relates and its relevance to the current offence; and b) the time that has elapsed since the conviction
- Offence committed whilst on bail

Other aggravating factors

- Failure to comply with current court orders
- Offence committed whilst on licence
- Failure of offender to respond to previous warnings
- Any steps taken to prevent reporting an incident, obtaining assistance and/or from assisting or supporting the prosecution
- Attempts to dispose of or conceal evidence

Mitigating factors

- No previous convictions **or** no relevant/recent convictions
- Remorse
- Previous good character and/or exemplary conduct*
- Age and/or lack of maturity where it affects the responsibility of the offender
- Mental disorder or learning disability, particularly where linked to the commission of the offence
- Demonstration of steps taken to address offending behaviour

*Previous good character/exemplary conduct is different from having no previous convictions. The more serious the offence, the less the weight which should normally be attributed to this factor. Where previous good character/exemplary conduct has been used to facilitate the offence, this mitigation should not normally be allowed and such conduct may constitute an aggravating factor.

STEP THREE

Consider any factors which indicate a reduction, such as assistance to the prosecution

The court should take into account sections 73 and 74 of the Serious Organised Crime and Police Act 2005 (assistance by defendants: reduction or review of sentence) and any other rule of law by virtue of which an offender may receive a discounted sentence in consequence of assistance given (or offered) to the prosecutor or investigator.

STEP FOUR

Reduction for guilty pleas

The court should take account of any potential reduction for a guilty plea in accordance with section 144 of the Criminal Justice Act 2003 and the *Guilty Plea* guideline.

STEP FIVE

Dangerousness

The court should consider whether having regard to the criteria contained in Chapter 5 of Part 12 of the Criminal Justice Act 2003 it would be appropriate to award an extended sentence (section 226A).

STEP SIX

Totality principle

If sentencing an offender for more than one offence, or where the offender is already serving a sentence, consider whether the total sentence is just and proportionate to the offending behaviour.

STEP SEVEN

Ancillary orders

The court must consider whether to make any ancillary orders. The court must also consider what other requirements or provisions may ***automatically*** apply. Further information is included at Annex A on page 424.

STEP EIGHT

Reasons

Section 174 of the Criminal Justice Act 2003 imposes a duty to give reasons for, and explain the effect of, the sentence.

STEP NINE

Consideration for time spent on bail

The court must consider whether to give credit for time spent on bail in accordance with section 240A of the Criminal Justice Act 2003.

Administering a substance with intent

Sexual Offences Act 2003 (section 61)

Triable either way

Maximum: 10 years' custody

Offence range: 1–9 years' custody

For convictions on or after 3 December 2012 (irrespective of the date of commission of the offence), this is a specified offence for the purposes of section 226A (extended sentence for certain violent or sexual offences) of the Criminal Justice Act 2003.

STEP ONE

Determining the offence category

The court should determine the offence category using the table below.

Category 1	Raised harm **and** raised culpability
Category 2	Raised harm **or** raised culpability
Category 3	Administering a substance with intent **without** raised harm or culpability factors present

The court should determine culpability and harm caused or intended, by reference **only** to the factors below, which comprise the principal factual elements of the offence. Where an offence does not fall squarely into a category, individual factors may require a degree of weighting before making an overall assessment and determining the appropriate offence category. Where no substantive sexual offence has been committed the main consideration for the court will be the offender's conduct as a whole including, but not exclusively, the offender's intention.

Factors indicating raised harm

- Severe psychological or physical harm
- Prolonged detention /sustained incident
- Additional degradation/humiliation

Factors indicating raised culpability

- Significant degree of planning
- Specific targeting of a particularly vulnerable victim
- Intended sexual offence carries a statutory maximum of life
- Abuse of trust
- Recording of offence
- Offender acts together with others to commit the offence
- Commercial exploitation and/or motivation
- Offence racially or religiously aggravated
- Offence motivated by, or demonstrating, hostility to the victim based on his or her sexual orientation (or presumed sexual orientation) or transgender identity (or presumed transgender identity)
- Offence motivated by, or demonstrating, hostility to the victim based on his or her disability (or presumed disability)

STEP TWO

Starting point and category range

Having determined the category, the court should use the corresponding starting points to reach a sentence within the category range below. The starting point applies to all offenders irrespective of plea or previous convictions. Having determined the starting point, step two allows further adjustment for aggravating or mitigating features, set out below.

A case of particular gravity, reflected by multiple features of culpability or harm in step one, could merit upward adjustment from the starting point before further adjustment for aggravating or mitigating features, set out below.

Category 1	**Starting point** 6 years' custody **Category range** 4–9 years' custody
Category 2	**Starting point** 4 years' custody **Category range** 3–7 years' custody
Category 3	**Starting point** 2 years' custody **Category range** 1–5 years' custody

The table below contains a **non-exhaustive** list of additional factual elements providing the context of the offence and factors relating to the offender. Identify whether any combination of these, or other relevant factors, should result in an upward or downward adjustment from the starting point. **In particular, relevant recent convictions are likely to result in an upward adjustment.** In some cases, having considered these factors, it may be appropriate to move outside the identified category range.

Aggravating factors

Statutory aggravating factors

- Previous convictions, having regard to a) the nature of the offence to which the conviction relates and its relevance to the current offence; and b) the time that has elapsed since the conviction
- Offence committed whilst on bail

Other aggravating factors

- Location of offence
- Timing of offence
- Any steps taken to prevent reporting an incident, obtaining assistance and/or from assisting or supporting the prosecution
- Attempts to dispose of or conceal evidence
- Failure to comply with current court orders
- Offence committed whilst on licence

Mitigating factors

- No previous convictions **or** no relevant/recent convictions
- Remorse
- Previous good character and/or exemplary conduct*
- Age and/or lack of maturity where it affects the responsibility of the offender
- Mental disorder or learning disability, particularly where linked to the commission of the offence
- Demonstration of steps taken to address offending behaviour

*Previous good character/exemplary conduct is different from having no previous convictions. The more serious the offence, the less the weight which should normally be attributed to this factor. Where previous good character/exemplary conduct has been used to facilitate the offence, this mitigation should not normally be allowed and such conduct may constitute an aggravating factor.

STEP THREE

Consider any factors which indicate a reduction, such as assistance to the prosecution

The court should take into account sections 73 and 74 of the Serious Organised Crime and Police Act 2005 (assistance by defendants: reduction or review of sentence) and any other rule of law by virtue of which an offender may receive a discounted sentence in consequence of assistance given (or offered) to the prosecutor or investigator.

STEP FOUR

Reduction for guilty pleas

The court should take account of any potential reduction for a guilty plea in accordance with section 144 of the Criminal Justice Act 2003 and the *Guilty Plea* guideline.

STEP FIVE

Dangerousness

The court should consider whether having regard to the criteria contained in Chapter 5 of Part 12 of the Criminal Justice Act 2003 it would be appropriate to award an extended sentence (section 226A).

STEP SIX

Totality principle

If sentencing an offender for more than one offence, or where the offender is already serving a sentence, consider whether the total sentence is just and proportionate to the offending behaviour.

STEP SEVEN

Ancillary orders

The court must consider whether to make any ancillary orders. The court must also consider what other requirements or provisions may *automatically* apply. Further information is included at Annex A on page 424.

STEP EIGHT

Reasons

Section 174 of the Criminal Justice Act 2003 imposes a duty to give reasons for, and explain the effect of, the sentence.

STEP NINE

Consideration for time spent on bail

The court must consider whether to give credit for time spent on bail in accordance with section 240A of the Criminal Justice Act 2003.

Committing an offence with intent to commit a sexual offence

Sexual Offences Act 2003 (section 62)

Triable only on indictment (if kidnapping or false imprisonment committed)

- otherwise, triable either way

Maximum: Life imprisonment (if kidnapping or false imprisonment committed)

- otherwise, 10 years

This is a serious specified offence for the purposes of section 224 and, where kidnapping or false imprisonment was committed, section 225(2) (life sentence for serious offences) of the Criminal Justice Act 2003.

For offences committed by kidnapping or false imprisonment, on or after 3 December 2012, this is an offence listed in Part 1 of Schedule 15B for the purposes of sections 224A (life sentence for second listed offence) of the Criminal Justice Act 2003.

For convictions on or after 3 December 2012 (irrespective of the date of commission of the offence), this is a specified offence for the purposes of section 226A (extended sentence for certain violent or sexual offences) of the Criminal Justice Act 2003.

The starting point and range should be commensurate with that for the preliminary offence actually committed, but with an enhancement to reflect the intention to commit a sexual offence.

The enhancement will vary depending on the nature and seriousness of the intended sexual offence, but 2 years is suggested as a suitable enhancement where the intent was to commit rape or assault by penetration.

Trespass with intent to commit a sexual offence

Sexual Offences Act 2003 (section 63)

Triable either way

Maximum: 10 years' custody

Offence range: 1–9 years' custody

For convictions on or after 3 December 2012 (irrespective of the date of commission of the offence), this is a specified offence for the purposes of section 226A (extended sentence for certain violent or sexual offences) of the Criminal Justice Act 2003.

STEP ONE

Determining the offence category

The court should determine the offence category using the table below.

Category 1	Raised harm **and** raised culpability
Category 2	Raised harm **or** raised culpability
Category 3	Trespass with intent to commit a sexual offence **without** raised harm or culpability factors present

The court should determine culpability and harm caused or intended, by reference **only** to the factors below, which comprise the principal factual elements of the offence. Where an offence does not fall squarely into a category, individual factors may require a degree of weighting before making an overall assessment and determining the appropriate offence category. Where no substantive sexual offence has been committed the main consideration for the court will be the offender's conduct as a whole including, but not exclusively, the offender's intention.

Factors indicating raised harm

- Prolonged detention/sustained incident
- Additional degradation/humiliation
- Offence committed in victim's home

Factors indicating raised culpability

- Significant degree of planning
- Specific targeting of a particularly vulnerable victim
- Intended sexual offence attracts a statutory maximum of life imprisonment
- Possession of weapon or other item to frighten or injure
- Abuse of trust
- Offender acts together with others to commit the offence
- Commercial exploitation and/or motivation
- Offence racially or religiously aggravated
- Offence motivated by, or demonstrating, hostility to the victim based on his or her sexual orientation (or presumed sexual orientation) or transgender identity (or presumed transgender identity)
- Offence motivated by, or demonstrating, hostility to the victim based on his or her disability (or presumed disability)

STEP TWO

Starting point and category range

Having determined the category, the court should use the corresponding starting points to reach a sentence within the category range below. The starting point applies to all offenders irrespective of plea or previous convictions. Having determined the starting point, step two allows further adjustment for aggravating or mitigating features, set out below.

A case of particular gravity, reflected by multiple features of culpability or harm in step one, could merit upward adjustment from the starting point before further adjustment for aggravating or mitigating features, set out below.

Category 1	**Starting point** 6 years' custody **Category range** 4–9 years' custody
Category 2	**Starting point** 4 years' custody **Category range** 3–7 years' custody
Category 3	**Starting point** 2 years' custody **Category range** 1–5 years' custody

The table below contains a **non-exhaustive** list of additional factual elements providing the context of the offence and factors relating to the offender. Identify whether any combination of these, or otherrelevant factors, should result in an upward or downward adjustment from the starting point. **In particular, relevant recent convictions are likely to result in an upward adjustment.** In some cases, having considered these factors, it may be appropriate to move outside the identified category range.

Aggravating factors

Statutory aggravating factors

- Previous convictions, having regard to a) the nature of the offence to which the conviction relates and its relevance to the current offence; and b) the time that has elapsed since the conviction
- Offence committed whilst on bail

Other aggravating factors

- Location of offence
- Timing of offence
- Any steps taken to prevent reporting an incident, obtaining assistance and/or from assisting or supporting the prosecution
- Attempts to dispose of or conceal evidence
- Failure to comply with current court orders
- Offence committed whilst on licence

Mitigating factors

- No previous convictions **or** no relevant/recent convictions
- Remorse
- Previous good character and/or exemplary conduct*
- Age and/or lack of maturity where it affects the responsibility of the offender
- Mental disorder or learning disability, particularly where linked to the commission of the offence
- Demonstration of steps taken to address offending behaviour

*Previous good character/exemplary conduct is different from having no previous convictions. The more serious the offence, the less the weight which should normally be attributed to this factor. Where previous good character/ exemplary conduct has been used to facilitate the offence, this mitigation should not normally be allowed and such conduct may constitute an aggravating factor.

STEP THREE

Consider any factors which indicate a reduction, such as assistance to the prosecution

The court should take into account sections 73 and 74 of the Serious Organised Crime and Police Act 2005 (assistance by defendants: reduction or review of sentence) and any other rule of law by virtue of which an offender may receive a discounted sentence in consequence of assistance given (or offered) to the prosecutor or investigator.

STEP FOUR

Reduction for guilty pleas

The court should take account of any potential reduction for a guilty plea in accordance with section 144 of the Criminal Justice Act 2003 and the *Guilty Plea* guideline.

STEP FIVE

Dangerousness

The court should consider whether having regard to the criteria contained in Chapter 5 of Part 12 of the Criminal Justice Act 2003 it would be appropriate to award an extended sentence (section 226A).

STEP SIX

Totality principle

If sentencing an offender for more than one offence, or where the offender is already serving a sentence, consider whether the total sentence is just and proportionate to the offending behaviour.

STEP SEVEN

Ancillary orders

The court must consider whether to make any ancillary orders. The court must also consider what other requirements or provisions may *automatically* apply. Further information is included at Annex A on page 424.

STEP EIGHT

Reasons

Section 174 of the Criminal Justice Act 2003 imposes a duty to give reasons for, and explain the effect of, the sentence.

STEP NINE

Consideration for time spent on bail

The court must consider whether to give credit for time spent on bail in accordance with section 240A of the Criminal Justice Act 2003.

Child sex offences committed by children or young persons (sections 9–12) (offender under 18)

Sexual Offences Act 2003 (section 13)

Sexual activity with a child family member (offender under 18)

Sexual Offences Act 2003 (section 25)

Inciting a child family member to engage in sexual activity (offender under 18)

Sexual Offences Act 2003 (section 26)

Triable either way

Maximum: 5 years' custody

These are 'grave crimes' for the purposes of section 91 of the Powers of Criminal Courts (Sentencing) Act 2000.

For convictions on or after 3 December 2012 (irrespective of the date of commission of the offence), these are specified offences for the purposes of section 226B (extended sentence for certain violent or sexual offences: persons under 18) of the Criminal Justice Act 2003.

Definitive guidelines for the sentencing of offenders under 18 years old are **not** included.

When sentencing offenders under 18, a court must in particular:
- follow the definitive guideline **Overarching Principles—Sentencing Youths**;

and have regard to:
- the principal aim of the youth justice system (to prevent offending by children and young people); and
- the welfare of the young offender.

Annex A

Ancillary orders

This summary of the key provisions is correct as at the date of publication but will be subject to subsequent changes in law. If necessary, seek legal advice.

Ancillary order	Statutory reference
Compensation The court must consider making a compensation order in any case in which personal injury, loss or damage has resulted from the offence. The court must give reasons if it decides not to make an order in such cases.	Section 130 of the Powers of Criminal Courts (Sentencing) Act 2000
Confiscation A confiscation order may be made by the Crown Court in circumstances in which the offender has obtained a financial benefit as a result of, or in connection with, his criminal conduct.	Section 6 and Schedule 2 of the Proceeds of Crime Act 2002
Deprivation of property The court may order the offender is deprived of property used for the purpose of committing, or facilitating the commission of, any offence, or intended for that purpose.	Section 143 of the Powers of Criminal Courts (Sentencing) Act 2000
Disqualification from working with children From 17 June 2013 courts **no longer** have the power to disqualify offenders from working with children pursuant to the Criminal Justice and Court Services Act 2000.	Schedule 10 of the Safeguarding Vulnerable Groups Act 2006 Safeguarding Vulnerable Groups Act 2006 (Commencement No 8 and Saving) Order 2012 (SI 2012/2231) Protection of Freedoms Act 2012 (Commencement No 6) Order 2013 (SI 2013/1180)
Restraining order Following a conviction *or an acquittal*, a court may make a restraining order for the purpose of protecting the victim or another person from harassment or a fear of violence.	Sections 5 and 5A of the Protection from Harassment Act 1997
Serious crime prevention order (SCPO) An SCPO may be made by the Crown Court in respect of qualifying offenders, if the court is satisfied such an order would protect the public by preventing, restricting or disrupting the involvement of the offender in serious crime.	Section 19 and Schedule 1 of the Serious Crime Act 2007

Sexual offences prevention order (SOPO) A SOPO may be made against qualifying offenders if the court is satisfied such an order is necessary to protect the public or any particular member of the public from serious sexual harm from the offender. The terms of the SOPO must be proportionate to the objective of protecting the public and consistent with the sentence and other ancillary orders, conditions and requirements to which the offender is subject.	Section 104 and Schedules 3 and 5 of the Sexual Offences Act 2003

Automatic orders on conviction

The following requirements or provisions are **not** part of the sentence imposed by the court but apply automatically by operation of law. The role of the court is to inform the offender of the applicable requirements and/or prohibition.

Requirement or provision	Statutory reference
Notification requirements A relevant offender automatically becomes subject to notification requirements, obliging him to notify the police of specified information for a specified period. The court should inform the offender accordingly. *The operation of the notification requirement is not a relevant consideration in determining the sentence for the offence.*	Sections 80 to 88 and Schedule 3 of the Sexual Offences Act 2003
Protection for children and vulnerable adults A statutory scheme pursuant to which offenders *will* or *may* be barred from regulated activity relating to children or vulnerable adults, with or without the right to make representations, depending on the offence. The court should inform the offender accordingly.	Section 2 and Schedule 3 of the Safeguarding Vulnerable Groups Act 2006 Safeguarding Vulnerable Groups Act 2006 (Prescribed Criteria and Miscellaneous Provisions) Regulations 2009 (SI 2009/37) (as amended)

Annex B

Approach to sentencing of historic sexual offences

Details of the principal offences are set out in the table at Annex C on page 426.

When sentencing sexual offences under the Sexual Offences Act 1956, or other legislation pre-dating the 2003 Act, the court should apply the following principles[1]:

1. The offender must be sentenced in accordance with the sentencing regime applicable at the *date of sentence*. Under the Criminal Justice Act 2003[2] the court must have regard to the statutory purposes of sentencing and must base the sentencing exercise on its assessment of the seriousness of the offence.
2. The sentence is limited to the maximum sentence available at the *date of the commission of the offence*. If the maximum sentence has been reduced, the lower maximum will be applicable.
3. The court should have regard to any applicable sentencing guidelines for equivalent offences under the Sexual Offences Act 2003.

[1] *R v H and others* [2011] EWCA Crim 2753.
[2] Section 143.

4. The seriousness of the offence, assessed by the culpability of the offender and the harm caused or intended, is the main consideration for the court. The court should not seek to establish the likely sentence had the offender been convicted shortly after the date of the offence.
5. When assessing the culpability of the offender, the court should have regard to relevant culpability factors set out in any applicable guideline.
6. The court must assess carefully the harm done to the victim based on the facts available to it, having regard to relevant harm factors set out in any applicable guideline. Consideration of the circumstances which brought the offence to light will be of importance.
7. The court must consider the relevance of the passage of time carefully as it has the potential to aggravate or mitigate the seriousness of the offence. It will be an aggravating factor where the offender has continued to commit sexual offences against the victim or others or has continued to prevent the victim reporting the offence.
8. Where there is an absence of further offending over a long period of time, especially if combined with evidence of good character, this may be treated by the court as a mitigating factor. However, as with offences dealt with under the Sexual Offences Act 2003, previous good character/exemplary conduct is different from having no previous convictions. The more serious the offence, the less the weight which should normally be attributed to this factor. Where previous good character/exemplary conduct has been used to facilitate the offence, this mitigation should not normally be allowed and such conduct may constitute an aggravating factor.
9. If the offender was very young and immature at the time of the offence, depending on the circumstances of the offence, this may be regarded as personal mitigation.
10. If the offender made admissions at the time of the offence that were not investigated this is likely to be regarded as personal mitigation. Even greater mitigation is available to the offender who reported himself to the police and/or made early admissions.
11. A reduction for an early guilty plea should be made in the usual manner.

Annex C

Historic offences

Offence (Sexual Offences Act 1956 unless stated otherwise)	Effective dates	Maximum
Rape and assault offences		
Rape (section 1)	1 January 1957–30 April 2004	Life
Buggery with a person or animal (section 12)	1 January 1957–30 April 2004 (from 3 November 1994 non-consensual acts of buggery were defined as rape)	Life
Indecent assault on a woman (section 14)	1 January 1957–30 April 2004	1 January 1957–31 December 1960: 2 years 1 January 1961–15 September 1985: 2 years or 5 years if victim under 13 and age stated on indictment 16 September 1985 onwards: 10 years
Indecent assault upon a man (section 15)	1 January 1957–30 April 2004	10 years

Offences against children		
Sexual intercourse with a girl under 13 (section 5)	1 January 1957–30 April 2004	Life
Incest by a maleperson (section 10)	1 January 1957–30 April 2004	Life if victim under 13; otherwise 7 years
Incest by a femaleperson (section 11)	1 January 1957–30 April 2004	7 years
Gross indecency (section 13)	1 January 1957–30 April 2004	Male offender over 21 with male under age of consent: 5 years Otherwise: 2 years
Indecency with a child (section 1 of the Indecency with Children Act 1960)	1 January 1961–30 April 2004	1 January 1961–30 September 1997: 2 years 1 October 1997 onwards: 10 years *Note: on 11 January 2001 the age definition of a child increased from 14 to 16.*
Incitement of a girl under 16 to commit incest (section 54 of the Criminal Law Act 1977)	8 September 1977–30 April 2004	2 years
Abuse of position of trust (section 3 of the Sexual Offences (Amendment) Act 2000)	8 January 2001–30 April 2004	5 years
Indecent images		
Taking indecent photographs of a child (section 1 of the Protection of Children Act 1978)	20 August 1978– present	20 August 1978–10 January 2001: 3 years 11 January 2001 onwards: 10 years
Possession of indecent photographs of a child (section 160 of the Criminal Justice Act 1988)	11 January 1988–present	11 January 1988–10 January 2001: 6 months 11 January 2001 onwards: 5 years
Exploitation offences		
Procurement of woman by threats (section 2) Procurement by false pretences (section 3) Causing prostitution of women (section 22) Procuration of girl under 21 for unlawful sexual intercourse in any part of the world (section 23) Detention in a brothel (section 24) Permitting a defective to use premises for intercourse (section 27) Causing or encouraging prostitution (etc) of a girl under 16 (section 28) Causing or encouraging prostitution of a defective (section 29)	1 January 1957–30 April 2004	2 years
Living on earnings of prostitution (section 30) Controlling a prostitute (section 31)	1 January 1957–30 April 2004	7 years

Trafficking into/within/out of the UK for sexual exploitation (sections 57–59 of the Sexual Offences Act 2003)	1 May 2005–5 April 2013	14 years
Offences against those with a mental disorder		
Intercourse with a defective (section 7) Procurement of a defective (section 9)	1 January 1957–30 April 2004	2 years
Sexual intercourse with patients (section 128 of the Mental Health Act 1956)	1 November 1960 –30 April 2004	2 years
Other offences		
Administering drugs to obtain or facilitate intercourse (section 4)	1 January 1957–30 April 2004	2 years
Burglary with intent to commit rape (section 9 of the Theft Act 1968)	1 January 1969–30 April 2004	14 years if dwelling; otherwise 10 years

With thanks to Sweet & Maxwell, HHJ Rook QC and Robert Ward CBE for their kind permission to reproduce parts of *Sexual Offences Law & Practice*.

Annex D

Fine bands and community orders

FINE BANDS

In this guideline, fines are expressed as one of three fine bands (A, B or C).

Fine Band	Starting point (applicable to all offenders)	Category range (applicable to all offenders)
Band A	50% of relevant weekly income	25–75% of relevant weekly income
Band B	100% of relevant weekly income	75–125% of relevant weekly income
Band C	150% of relevant weekly income	125–175% of relevant weekly income

COMMUNITY ORDERS

In this guideline, community orders are expressed as one of three levels (low, medium and high).

An illustrative description of examples of requirements that might be appropriate for each level is provided below. Where two or more requirements are ordered, they must be compatible with each other.

LOW	MEDIUM	HIGH
In general, only one requirement will be appropriate and the length may be curtailed if additional requirements are necessary	More intensive sentences which combine two or more requirements may be appropriate	

Suitable requirements might include: • 40–80 hours unpaid work; • curfew requirement within the lowest range (for example, up to 12 hours per day for a few weeks); • exclusion requirement, without electronic monitoring, for a few months; • prohibited activity requirement; • attendance centre requirement (where available).	Suitable requirements might include: • appropriate treatment programme; • greater number of hours of unpaid work (for example, 80–150 hours); • an activity requirement in the middle range (20 to 30 days); • curfew requirement within the middle range (for example, up to 12 hours for two to three months); • exclusion requirement, lasting in the region of six months; • prohibited activity requirement.	Suitable requirements might include: • appropriate treatment programme; • 150–300 hours unpaid work; • activity requirement up to the maximum of 60 days; • curfew requirement up to 12 hours per day for four to six months; • exclusion order lasting in the region of 12 months.

The Magistrates' Court Sentencing Guidelines includes further guidance on fines and community orders.

APPENDIX D

PD-5 CPD I General matters 3: VULNERABLE PEOPLE IN THE COURTS

3D.1 In respect of eligibility for special measures, 'vulnerable' and 'intimidated' witnesses are defined in sections 16 and 17 of the Youth Justice and Criminal Evidence Act 1999 (as amended by the Coroners and Justice Act 2009); 'vulnerable' includes those under 18 years of age and people with a mental disorder or learning disability; a physical disorder or disability; or who are likely to suffer fear or distress in giving evidence because of their own circumstances or those relating to the case.

3D.2 However, many other people giving evidence in a criminal case, whether as a witness or defendant, may require assistance: the court is required to take 'every reasonable step' to encourage and facilitate the attendance of witnesses and to facilitate the participation of any person, including the defendant (Rule 8(4)(a) and (b)). This includes enabling a witness or defendant to give their best evidence, and enabling a defendant to comprehend the proceedings and engage fully with his or her defence. The pre-trial and trial process should, so far as necessary, be adapted to meet those ends. Regard should be had to the welfare of a young defendant as required by section 44 of the Children and Young Persons Act 1933, and generally to Parts 1 and 3 of the Criminal Procedure Rules (the overriding objective and the court's powers of case management).

3D.3 Under Part 3 of the Rules, the court must identify the needs of witnesses at an early stage (Rule 3.2(2)(b)) and may require the parties to identify arrangements to facilitate the giving of evidence and participation in the trial (Rule 3.10(c)(iv) and (v)). There are various statutory special measures that the court may utilise to assist a witness in giving evidence. Part 29 of the Rules gives the procedures to be followed. Courts should note the 'primary rule' which requires the court to give a direction for a special measure to assist a child witness or qualifying witness and that in such cases an application to the court is not required (rule 29.9).

3D.4 Court of Appeal decisions on this subject include a judgment from the Lord Chief Justice, Lord Judge in *R v Cox* [2012] EWCA Crim 549, [2012] 2 Cr App R 6; *R v Wills* [2011] EWCA Crim 1938, [2012] 1 Cr App R 2; and *R v E* [2011] EWCA Crim 3028, [2012] Crim LR 563.

3D.5 In *R v Wills*, the Court endorsed the approach taken by the report of the Advocacy Training Council (ATC) 'Raising the Bar: the Handling of Vulnerable Witnesses, Victims and Defendants in Court' (2011). The report includes and recommends the use of 'toolkits' to assist advocates as they prepare to question vulnerable people at court: <http://www.advocacytrainingcouncil.org/vulnerable-witnesses/raising-the-bar>.

3D.6 Further toolkits are available through the Advocate's Gateway which is managed by the ATC's Management Committee: <http://www.theadvocatesgateway.org/>.

These toolkits represent best practice. Advocates should consult and follow the relevant guidance whenever they prepare to question a young or otherwise vulnerable witness or defendant. Judges may find it helpful to refer advocates to this material and to use the toolkits in case management. **3D.7**

'Achieving Best Evidence in Criminal Proceedings' (Ministry of Justice 2011) describes best practice in preparation for the investigative interview and trial: < http://www.justice.gov.uk/downloads/victims-and-witnesses/vulnerable-witnesses/achieving-best-evidence-criminal-proceedings.pdf>. **3D.8**

PD-6 CPD I General matters 3: GROUND RULES HEARINGS TO PLAN THE QUESTIONING OF A VULNERABLE WITNESS OR DEFENDANT

The judiciary is responsible for controlling questioning. Over-rigorous or repetitive cross-examination of a child or vulnerable witness should be stopped. Intervention by the judge, magistrates or intermediary (if any) is minimised if questioning, taking account of the individual's communication needs, is discussed in advance and ground rules are agreed and adhered to. **3E.1**

Discussion of ground rules is required in all intermediary trials where they must be discussed between the judge or magistrates, advocates and intermediary before the witness gives evidence. The intermediary must be present but is not required to take the oath (the intermediary's declaration is made just before the witness gives evidence). **3E.2**

Discussion of ground rules is good practice, even if no intermediary is used, in all young witness cases and in other cases where a witness or defendant has communication needs. Discussion before the day of trial is preferable to give advocates time to adapt their questions to the witness' needs. It may be helpful for a trial practice note of boundaries to be created at the end of the discussion. The judge may use such a document in ensuring that the agreed ground rules are complied with. **3E.3**

All witnesses, including the defendant and defence witnesses, should be enabled to give the best evidence they can. In relation to young and/or vulnerable people, this may mean departing radically from traditional cross-examination. The form and extent of appropriate cross-examination will vary from case to case. For adult non vulnerable witnesses an advocate will usually put his case so that the witness will have the opportunity of commenting upon it and/or answering it. When the witness is young or otherwise vulnerable, the court may dispense with the normal practice and impose restrictions on the advocate 'putting his case' where there is a risk of a young or otherwise vulnerable witness failing to understand, becoming distressed or acquiescing to leading questions. Where limitations on questioning are necessary and appropriate, they must be clearly defined. The judge has a duty to ensure that they are complied with and should explain them to the jury and the reasons for them. If the advocate fails to comply with the limitations, the judge should give relevant directions to the jury when that occurs and prevent further questioning that does not comply with the ground rules settled upon in advance. Instead of commenting on inconsistencies during cross-examination, following discussion between the judge and the advocates, the advocate or judge may point out important inconsistencies after (instead of during) the witness's evidence. The judge should also remind the jury of these during summing up. The judge should be alert to alleged inconsistencies that are not in fact inconsistent, or are trivial. **3E.4**

If there is more than one defendant, the judge should not permit each advocate to repeat the questioning of a vulnerable witness. In advance of the trial, the advocates should divide the topics between them, with the advocate for the first defendant leading the questioning, and the advocate(s) for the other defendant(s) asking only ancillary questions relevant to their client's case, without repeating the questioning that has already taken place on behalf of the other defendant(s). **3E.5**

In particular in a trial of a sexual offence, 'body maps' should be provided for the witness' use. If the witness needs to indicate a part of the body, the advocate should ask the witness to point to the relevant part on the body map. In sex cases, judges should not permit advocates to ask the witness to point to a part of the witness' own body. Similarly, photographs of the witness' body should not be shown around the court while the witness is giving evidence. **3E.6**

PD-7 CPD I General matters 3: INTERMEDIARIES

3F.1 Intermediaries are communication specialists (not supporters or expert witnesses) whose role is to facilitate communication between the witness and the court, including the advocates. Intermediaries are independent of the parties and owe their duty to the court (see Registered Intermediaries Procedural Guidance Manual, Ministry of Justice, 2012): <http://www.cps.gov.uk/publications/docs/RI_ProceduralGuidanceManual_2012.pdf>.

3F.2 Intermediaries for witnesses, with the exception of defendants, are one of the special measures available under the Youth Justice and Criminal Evidence Act 1999 and Part 29 of the Criminal Procedure Rules.

3F.3 There is currently no statutory provision in force for intermediaries for defendants. Section 104 of the Coroners and Justice Act 2009 (not yet implemented) creates a new section 33BA of the Youth Justice and Criminal Evidence Act 1999. This will provide an intermediary to an eligible defendant only while giving evidence. A court may use its inherent powers to appoint an intermediary to assist the defendant's communication at trial (either solely when giving evidence or throughout the trial) and, where necessary, in preparation for trial: *R (AS) v Great Yarmouth Youth Court* [2011] EWHC 2059 (Admin), [2012] Crim LR 478; *R v H* [2003] EWCA Crim 1208, *The Times*, 15 April 2003; *R (C) v Sevenoaks Youth Court* [2009] EWHC 3088 (Admin), [2010] 1 All ER 735; *R (D) v Camberwell Green Youth Court* [2005] UKHL 4, [2005] 1 WLR 393, [2005] 2 Cr App R 1; *R (TP) v West London Youth Court* [2005] EWHC 2583 (Admin), [2006] 1 WLR 1219, [2006] 1 Cr App R 25.

3F.4 Ministry of Justice regulation only applies to Registered Intermediaries appointed for prosecution and defence witnesses through its Witness Intermediary Scheme. All defendant intermediaries—professionally qualified or otherwise—are 'non-registered' in this context, even though they may be a Registered Intermediary in respect of witnesses. Even where a judge concludes he has a common law power to direct the provision of an intermediary, the direction will be ineffective if no intermediary can be identified for whom funding would be available.

3F.5 Assessment should be considered if a child or young person under 18 seems unlikely to be able to recognise a problematic question or, even if able to do so, may be reluctant to say so to a questioner in a position of authority. Studies suggest that the majority of young witnesses, across all age groups, fall into one or other of these categories. For children aged 11 years and under in particular, there should be a presumption that an intermediary assessment is appropriate. Once the child's individual requirements are known and discussed at the ground rules hearing, the intermediary may agree that his or her presence is not needed for the trial.

3F.6 In the absence of an intermediary for the defendant, trials should not be stayed where an asserted unfairness can be met by the trial judge adapting the trial process with appropriate and necessary caution (*R v Cox* [2012] EWCA Crim 549, [2012] 2 Cr App R 6). This includes setting ground rules for all witness testimony to help the defendant follow proceedings; for example, directing that all witness evidence be adduced by simple questions, with witnesses asked to answer in short sentences; and short periods of evidence, followed by breaks to enable the defendant to relax and for counsel to summarise the evidence for him and to take further instructions.

Photographs of Court Facilities

3F.7 Resident Judges in the Crown Court or the Chief Clerk or other responsible person in the magistrates' courts should, in consultation with HMCTS managers responsible for court security matters, develop a policy to govern under what circumstances photographs or other visual recordings may be made of court facilities, such as a live link room, to assist vulnerable or child witnesses to familiarise themselves with the setting, so as to be enabled to give their best evidence. For example, a photograph may provide a helpful reminder to a witness whose court visit has taken place sometime earlier. Resident Judges should tend to permit photographs to be taken for this purpose by intermediaries or supporters, subject to whatever restrictions the Resident Judge or responsible person considers to be appropriate, having regard to the security requirements of the court.

PD-8 CPD I General matters 3: VULNERABLE DEFENDANTS

Before the trial, sentencing, or appeal

If a vulnerable defendant, especially one who is young, is to be tried jointly with one who is not, the court should consider at the plea and case management hearing, or at a case management hearing in a magistrates' court, whether the vulnerable defendant should be tried on his own, but should only so order if satisfied that a fair trial cannot be achieved by use of appropriate special measures or other support for the defendant. If a vulnerable defendant is tried jointly with one who is not, the court should consider whether any of the modifications set out in this direction should apply in the circumstances of the joint trial and, so far as practicable, make orders to give effect to any such modifications. **3G.1**

It may be appropriate to arrange that a vulnerable defendant should visit, out of court hours and before the trial, sentencing or appeal hearing, the courtroom in which that hearing is to take place so that he or she can familiarise himself or herself with it. **3G.2**

Where an intermediary is being used to help the defendant to communicate at court, the intermediary should accompany the defendant on his or her pre-trial visit. The visit will enable the defendant to familiarise him or herself with the layout of the court, and may include matters such as: where the defendant will sit, either in the dock or otherwise; court officials (what their roles are and where they sit); who else might be in the court, for example those in the public gallery and press box; the location of the witness box; basic court procedure; and the facilities available in the court. **3G.3**

If the defendant's use of the live link is being considered, he or she should have an opportunity to have a practice session. **3G.4**

If any case against a vulnerable defendant has attracted or may attract widespread public or media interest, the assistance of the police should be enlisted to try and ensure that the defendant is not, when attending the court, exposed to intimidation, vilification, or abuse. Section 41 of the Criminal Justice Act 1925 prohibits the taking of photographs of defendants and witnesses (among others) in the court building or in its precincts, or when entering or leaving those precincts. A direction reminding media representatives of the prohibition may be appropriate. The court should also be ready at this stage, if it has not already done so, where relevant to make a reporting restriction under section 39 of the Children and Young Persons Act 1933 or, on an appeal to the Crown Court from a youth court, to remind media representatives of the application of section 49 of that Act. **3G.5**

The provisions of the Practice Direction accompanying Part 16 should be followed. **3G.6**

The trial, sentencing or appeal hearing

Subject to the need for appropriate security arrangements, the proceedings should, if practicable, be held in a courtroom in which all the participants are on the same or almost the same level. **3G.7**

Subject again to the need for appropriate security arrangements, a vulnerable defendant, especially if he is young, should normally, if he wishes, be free to sit with members of his family or others in a like relationship, and with some other suitable supporting adult such as a social worker, and in a place which permits easy, informal communication with his legal representatives. The court should ensure that a suitable supporting adult is available throughout the course of the proceedings. **3G.8**

3G.9 It is essential that at the beginning of the proceedings, the court should ensure that what is to take place has been explained to a vulnerable defendant in terms he or she can understand and, at trial in the Crown Court, it should ensure in particular that the role of the jury has been explained. It should remind those representing the vulnerable defendant and the supporting adult of their responsibility to explain each step as it takes place and, at trial, explain the possible consequences of a guilty verdict and credit for a guilty plea. The court should also remind any intermediary of their responsibility to ensure that the vulnerable defendant has understood the explanations given to him/her. Throughout the trial the court should continue to ensure, by any appropriate means, that the defendant understands what is happening and what has been said by those on the bench, the advocates and witnesses.

3G.10 A trial should be conducted according to a timetable which takes full account of a vulnerable defendant's ability to concentrate. Frequent and regular breaks will often be appropriate. The court should ensure, so far as practicable, that the whole trial is conducted in clear language that the defendant can understand and that evidence in chief and cross-examination are conducted using questions that are short and clear. The conclusions of the 'ground rules' hearing should be followed, and advocates should use and follow the 'toolkits' as discussed above.

3G.11 A vulnerable defendant who wishes to give evidence by live link, in accordance with section 33A of the Youth Justice and Criminal Evidence Act 1999, may apply for a direction to that effect; the procedure in Section 4 of Part 29 of the Rules should be followed. Before making such a direction, the court must be satisfied that it is in the interests of justice to do so and that the use of a live link would enable the defendant to participate more effectively as a witness in the proceedings. The direction will need to deal with the practical arrangements to be made, including the identity of the person or persons who will accompany him or her.

3G.12 In the Crown Court, the judge should consider whether robes and wigs should be worn, and should take account of the wishes of both a vulnerable defendant and any vulnerable witness. It is generally desirable that those responsible for the security of a vulnerable defendant who is in custody, especially if he or she is young, should not be in uniform, and that there should be no recognizable police presence in the courtroom save for good reason.

3G.13 The court should be prepared to restrict attendance by members of the public in the court room to a small number, perhaps limited to those with an immediate and direct interest in the outcome. The court should rule on any challenged claim to attend. However, facilities for reporting the proceedings (subject to any restrictions under section 39 or 49 of the Children and Young Persons Act 1933) must be provided. The court may restrict the number of reporters attending in the courtroom to such number as is judged practicable and desirable. In ruling on any challenged claim to attend in the court room for the purpose of reporting, the court should be mindful of the public's general right to be informed about the administration of justice.

3G.14 Where it has been decided to limit access to the courtroom, whether by reporters or generally, arrangements should be made for the proceedings to be relayed, audibly and if possible visually, to another room in the same court complex to which the media and the public have access if it appears that there will be a need for such additional facilities. Those making use of such a facility should be reminded that it is to be treated as an extension of the court room and that they are required to conduct themselves accordingly.

INDEX